Iceland

The Westfjords
p184

North Iceland
p207

East
Iceland
p258

West
Iceland
p160

The Highlands
p307

Reykjavík
p52

Southwest Iceland
& the Golden Circle
p95

Southeast
Iceland
p282

CHRISTIAN KOBER/GETTY IMAGES ©

HALLGRÍMSKIRKJA P59

GRANT FAINT/GETTY IMAGES ©

PUFFINS P40

Contents

Welcome to Iceland

The energy is palpable on this magical island, where astonishing natural phenomena inspire the welcoming, creative locals and draw an increasing number of visitors in search of splendour.

A Symphony of Elements

An underpopulated island marooned near the top of the globe, Iceland is literally a country in the making. It's a vast volcanic laboratory where mighty forces shape the earth: geysers gush, mudpots gloop, ice-covered volcanoes rumble and glaciers grind great pathways through the mountains. Its supercharged splendour seems designed to remind visitors of their utter insignificance in the greater scheme of things. And it works a treat: some crisp clean air, an eyeful of the cinematic landscapes and everyone is transfixed.

The Power of Nature

The power of Icelandic nature turns the prosaic into the extraordinary. A dip in the pool becomes a soak in a geothermal lagoon, a casual stroll can transform into a trek across a glittering glacier, and a quiet night of camping may mean front-row seats to the aurora borealis' curtains of fire or the soft, pinkish hue of the midnight sun. Iceland has a transformative effect on people, too – its sagas turned brutes into poets; its stories of *huldufólk* (hidden people) may make believers out of sceptics. It may just have the world's highest concentration of dreamers, authors, artists and musicians, all fuelled by their surrounds.

A Personal Experience

A visit is as much about the people as it is about the landscapes. The warmth of Icelanders is disarming, as is their industriousness – they're working hard to recover from financial upheaval and to transform Iceland into a destination that, thanks to its popularity with visitors, can host triple its population each year. Pause and consider a medium-sized city in your country – then give it far-flung universities, airports and hospitals to administer, 30-odd active volcanoes to monitor and hundreds of hotels to run. How might they cope? Could they manage as well as the Icelanders – and still have time left over to create spine-tingling music and natty knitwear?

Nordic Nirvana

Don't for a moment think it's only about the great outdoors. The counterpoint to so much natural beauty is found in Iceland's cultural life, which celebrates a literary legacy that stretches from medieval sagas to contemporary thrillers by way of Nobel Prize winners. Live music is everywhere, as are visual art, handicrafts and locavore cuisine. The world's most northerly capital is home to the kind of egalitarianism, green thinking and effortlessly stylish locals that its Nordic brethren are famous for – all wrapped in Iceland's assured individuality.

Why I Love Iceland

By Carolyn Bain, Author

It's hard to answer this without either gushing embarrassingly or resorting to clichés. (OK, I'll admit it, Iceland makes me want to grow up to become a birdwatching vulcanologist who plays in a band.) Like everyone, on my first visit I was awestruck by the landscapes. On subsequent visits, the beauty of those same landscapes can still reduce me to tears – but the locals are what affirm my love for Iceland. Their resourcefulness, quirkiness, interconnectedness and warmth are unparalleled; on this research trip, every day presented human stories and interactions that rivalled Icelandic nature for beauty.

For more about our authors, see page 384

Above: Gígjökull glacier (p147), overlooking the south coast

Iceland

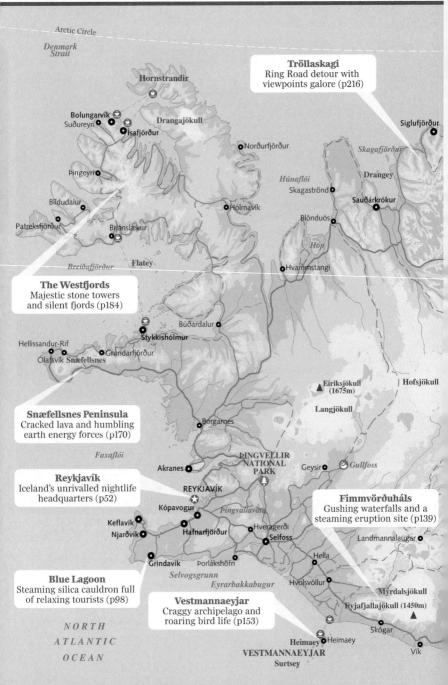

Arctic Circle

Denmark Strait

Hornstrandir

Tröllaskagi
Ring Road detour with
viewpoints galore (p216)

Bolungarvík
Suðureyri
Ísafjörður

Drangajökull

Siglufjörður

Norðurfjörður

Skagafjörður

Þingeyri

Húnaflói
Skagaströnd

Drangey

Bíldudalur

Hólmavík

Sauðárkrókur

Patreksfjörður
Brjánslækur

Blönduós

Hóp

Breiðafjörður Flatey

Hvammstangi

The Westfjords
Majestic stone towers
and silent fjords (p184)

Búðardalur

Hellissandur-Rif
Stykkishólmur

Ólafsvík Snæfellsnes
Grundarfjörður

Eiríksjökull
(1675m)

Hofsjökull

Langjökull

Snæfellsnes Peninsula
Cracked lava and humbling
earth energy forces (p170)

Borgarnes

Faxaflói

Reykjavík
Iceland's unrivalled nightlife
headquarters (p52)

Akranes

ÞINGVELLIR
NATIONAL
PARK

Geysir Gullfoss

REYKJAVÍK

Kópavogur *Þingvallavatn*

Fimmvörðuháls
Gushing waterfalls and a
steaming eruption site (p139)

Keflavík
Njarðvík

Hafnarfjörður

Hveragerði
Selfoss

Landmannalaugar

Grindavík Þorlákshöfn

Hella

Blue Lagoon
Steaming silica cauldron full
of relaxing tourists (p98)

Selvogsgrunn

Eyrarbakkabugur

Hvolsvöllur

Mýrdalsjökull

Vestmannaeyjar
Craggy archipelago and
roaring bird life (p153)

Eyjafjallajökull (1450m)

Skógar

*NORTH
ATLANTIC
OCEAN*

Heimaey Heimaey

Vík

VESTMANNAEYJAR
Surtsey

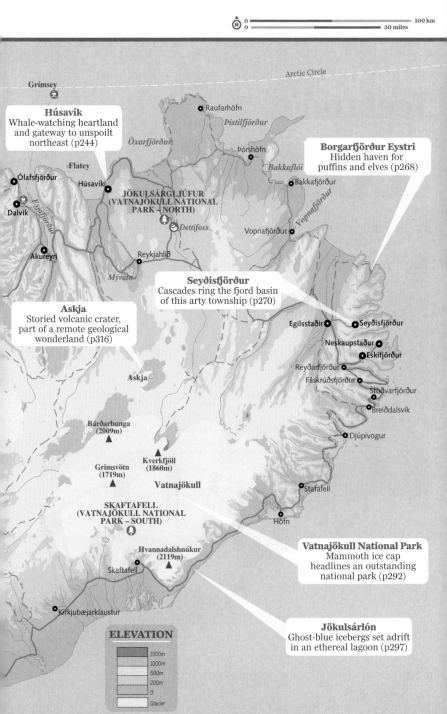

N 0 _____ 100 km
  0 _____ 50 miles

Arctic Circle

Grímsey

Húsavík
Whale-watching heartland
and gateway to unspoilt
northeast (p244)

Raufarhöfn

Pistilfjörður

Öxarfjörður

Þórshöfn

Borgarfjörður Eystri
Hidden haven for
puffins and elves (p268)

Flatey

Bakkaflói

Bakkafjörður

Ólafsfjörður

Húsavík

JÖKULSÁRGLJÚFUR
(VATNAJÖKULL NATIONAL
PARK – NORTH)

Dalvík

Eyjafjörður

Vopnafjörður

Akureyri

Dettifoss

Vopnafjörður

Reykjahlíð

Seyðisfjörður
Cascades ring the fjord basin
of this arty township (p270)

Mývatn

Askja
Storied volcanic crater,
part of a remote geological
wonderland (p316)

Egilsstaðir

Seyðisfjörður

Neskaupstaður

Eskifjörður

Askja

Reyðarfjörður

Fáskrúðsfjörður

Stöðvarfjörður

Breiðdalsvík

Bárðarbunga
(2009m)

Djúpivogur

Grímsvötn
(1719m)

Kverkfjöll
(1860m)

Vatnajökull

Stafafell

SKAFTAFELL
(VATNAJÖKULL NATIONAL
PARK – SOUTH)

Höfn

Vatnajökull National Park
Mammoth ice cap
headlines an outstanding
national park (p292)

Hvannadalshnúkur
(2119m)

Skaftafell

Kirkjubæjarklaustur

ELEVATION

1500m
1000m
500m
200m
0
Glacier

Jökulsárlón
Ghost-blue icebergs set adrift
in an ethereal lagoon (p297)

Iceland's
Top 14

1

Getting into Hot Water

1 Iceland's unofficial pastime is splashing around its surplus of geothermal water. There are 'hot pots' everywhere – from downtown Reykjavík to the isolated peninsular tips of the Westfjords – and not only are they incredibly relaxing, they're the perfect antidote to a hangover and a great way to meet the locals (this is their social hub, the Icelanders' equivalent of the local pub or town square). Everyone knows that the Blue Lagoon (p98) is the big cheese: its steaming lagoon full of silica deposits sits conveniently close to Keflavík airport, making it the perfect send-off before flying home. Below left: Blue Lagoon

Westfjords

2 Iceland's sweeping spectrum of superlative nature comes to a dramatic climax in the Westfjords (p184) – the island's off-the-beaten-path adventure par excellence. Broad, multihued beaches flank the southern coast, roaring bird colonies abound, fjordheads tower above and then plunge into the deep, and a network of ruddy roads twists throughout, adding an extra sense of adventure. The region's uppermost peninsula, Hornstrandir (p200), is the final frontier; the sea cliffs are perilous, the Arctic foxes are foxier and hiking trails amble through pristine patches of wilderness that practically kiss the Arctic Circle. Below right: Hornstrandir

SEAN RANDALL/GETTY IMAGES ©

JOHANN S. KARLSSON/GETTY IMAGES ©

Jökulsárlón

3 A ghostly procession of luminous-blue icebergs drifts serenely through the 25-sq-km Jökulsárlón lagoon (p297) before floating out to sea. This surreal scene (handily, right next to the Ring Road) is a natural filmset: in fact, you might have seen it in *Batman Begins* and the James Bond film *Die Another Day*. The ice calves from Breiðamerkurjökull glacier, an offshoot of the mighty Vatnajökull ice cap. Boat trips among the 'bergs are popular, or you can simply wander the lakeshore, scout for seals and exhaust your camera's memory card.

Northern Lights

4 Everyone longs to glimpse the Northern Lights (p44), the celestial kaleidoscope known for transforming long winter nights into natural lava lamps. The lights, also known as aurora borealis, form when solar flares are drawn by the earth's magnetic field towards the North Pole. What results are ethereal veils of green, white, violet or red light, shimmering and dancing in a display not unlike silent fireworks. Peak aurora sightings occur in the depths of winter, but look for the lights in clear, dark skies anytime between October (maybe September) and April. Right: Northern Lights, seen from Snæfellsnes Peninsula

JACOB MOISAN/GETTY IMAGES ©

ARCTIC-IMAGES/GETTY IMAGES ©

FRANCISCO JAVIER FERNANDEZ BORDONADA/ALAMY ©

JONATHAN BARSOOK/GETTY IMAGES ©

Driving the Ring Road

5 There's no better way to explore Iceland than to hire a set of wheels and roadtrip Route 1, affectionately known as the Ring Road (p36). This 1330km tarmacked trail loops around the island, passing through verdant dales decked with waterfalls, glacier tongues dripping from ice caps like frosting from a cake, desert-like plains of grey outwash sands and velvety, moss-covered lava fields. It's supremely spectacular – but don't forget to take some of the detours. Use the Ring Road as your main artery and follow the veins as they splinter off into the wilderness.

Vatnajökull National Park

6 Europe's largest national park (p292) covers nearly 14% of Iceland and safeguards mighty Vatnajökull, the largest ice cap outside the poles (three times the size of Luxembourg). Scores of outlet glaciers flow down from its frosty bulk, while underneath it are active volcanoes and mountain peaks. Yes, this is ground zero for those 'fire and ice' clichés. You'll be spellbound by the diversity of landscapes, walking trails and activities inside this supersized park. Given its dimensions, access points are numerous – start at Skaftafell in the south or Ásbyrgi in the north. Bottom left: Svínafellsjökull (p295), near Skaftafell

Borgarfjörður Eystri & Seyðisfjörður

7 A tale of two east-side fjords. Stunning, art-fuelled Seyðisfjörður (p270) garners most of the attention – it's only 27 (sealed) kilometres from the Ring Road and welcomes the weekly ferry from Europe into its mountain-lined embrace. Beautiful Borgarfjörður Eystri (p268), on the other hand, is 70km from the Ring Road, many of them bumpy and unsealed. Its selling points are understated: puffins, hidden elves, rugged rhyolite peaks. They both have natural splendour (and bumper hiking trails) in spades. We can't help but love 'em both. Above: Waterfall behind Seyðisfjörður

HALLDORE/SHUTTERSTOCK ©

Fimmvörðuháls

8 If you haven't the time to complete one of Iceland's multiday treks, the 23km, day-long Fimmvörðuháls trek (p139) will quench any wanderer's thirst. Start at the shimmering cascades of Skógafoss (p138), hike up into the hinterland to discover a veritable parade of waterfalls, then gingerly tiptoe over the steaming remnants of the Eyjafjallajökull eruption before hiking along the stone terraces of a flower-filled kingdom that ends in silent Þórsmörk (p146), a haven for campers, hemmed by a crown of glacial ridges. Above: Hikers near Þórsmörk

Reykjavík's Cafe Culture & Bar Scene

9 Despite Iceland's capital being rather petite by international standards, it has all the treats you'd expect of a major European city, and the city's ratio of coffeehouses to citizens is nothing short of staggering. In fact, the local social culture is built around these low-key hangouts (p83) that crank up the intensity after hours, when tea is swapped for tipples and dance moves break out. Caffeine hits and designer microbrews are prepared with the utmost seriousness for accidental hipsters sporting well-worn *lopapeysur* (Icelandic woollen sweaters). Top right: Prikið (p85)

Tröllaskagi

10 Touring Tröllaskagi (p216) is a joy, especially now that road tunnels link the spectacularly sited townships of Siglufjörður and Ólafsfjörður. The peninsula's dramatic scenery is more reminiscent of the Westfjords than the gentle hills that roll through most of northern Iceland. As well as glorious panoramas and quality hiking, worthy pit stops include Hofsós' fjordside swimming pool, Lónkot's local-produce shops and Siglufjörður's outstanding herring museum, plus ski fields, a microbrewery, whale-watching tours, and ferries to offshore islands Grímsey and Hrísey. Below right: Siglufjörður (p217)

9

10

Snæfellsnes Peninsula

11 With its cache of wild beaches and lava fields, the Snæfellsnes Peninsula (p170) is one of Iceland's best escapes – either as a day trip from the capital or as a relaxing long weekend. Jules Verne was definitely onto something when he used the area as his magical doorway to the centre of the earth. New Age types have flocked to the region to harness its mystical energy, and even if you don't believe in 'earth chakras', you'll undoubtedly find greater natural forces at play along the stunning shores. Below: Snæfellsnes coastline at Arnarstapi (p180)

Heimaey & Vestmannaeyjar

12 An offshore archipelago of craggy peaks, Vestmannaeyjar (p153) is a mere 30-minute ferry ride from the mainland but feels miles and miles away in sentiment. A boat tour of the scattered islets unveils seabirds, towering cliffs and postcard-worthy vistas of lonely hunting cabins perched atop patches of floating rocks. The islands' 4000-plus population is focused on Heimaey (p154), a small town of windswept bungalows with a curl of lava that flows straight through its centre – a poignant reminder of Iceland's volatile landscape. Near right: Landlyst (p154), Heimaey

11

MARTIN MOOS/GETTY IMAGES ©

STEVE OLDHAM/GETTY IMAGES ©

PATRICK DIEUDONNE/GETTY IMAGES ©

Askja & Surrounds

13 Accessible for only a few months each year, storied Askja (p314) is a mammoth caldera ringed by mountains and enclosing a sapphire-blue lake. To access this glorious, otherworldly place, you'll need a robust 4WD, a few days of hiking or passage on a super-Jeep tour. Highlands excursions generally incorporate river crossings, impossibly vast lava fields, regal mountain vistas and outlaw hideouts – and quite possibly a naked soak in geothermal waters. If the whims of nature (and especially the Bárðarbunga volcano system) are kind, in future they may survey an eruption-in-progress, or Iceland's freshest lava. Top right: Viti crater (p243), near Askja

Puffins & Whales

14 Iceland's two biggest wildlife drawcards are its most charismatic creatures (p121): the twee puffin, which flits around like an anxious bumblebee, and the mighty whale – a number of species (including the immense blue whale) glide through the frigid blue ringing Iceland's coast. Opportunities to see both abound on land and sea. The whale-watching heartland is Húsavík, but other northern towns also offer cruises (as does Reykjavík). Colonies of puffins are poised and ready for their close-up at numerous coastal cliffs and offshore isles, including Heimaey, Grímsey, Drangey, Látrabjarg and Borgarfjörður Eystri.

Need to Know

For more information, see Survival Guide (p353)

Currency
Icelandic króna (Ikr)

Language
Icelandic
English widely spoken

Money
Credit cards reign supreme, even in the most rural reaches of the country (PIN required for purchases). ATMs available in all towns.

Visas
Generally not required for stays of up to 90 days.

Mobile Phones
Mobile coverage widespread. Visitors with GSM phones can make roaming calls; purchase a local SIM card if you're staying a while.

Time
Western European Time Zone (GMT/UTC; same as London), except daylight-savings time is not observed.

When to Go?

 Mild summers, cold winters

Ísafjörður
GO Jun–Aug

Akureyri
GO year-round

Egilsstaðir
GO Jun–Aug

Reykjavík
GO year-round

Þórsmörk
GO May–Sep

High Season
(Jun–Aug)

➡ Visitors descend en masse – especially to Reykjavík and the south. Prices peak, accommodation bookings are essential.

➡ Endless daylight, plentiful festivals, busy activities.

➡ Interior mountain roads open (to 4WDs), hikers welcome.

Shoulder
(May & Sep)

➡ Breezier weather and occasional snows in the interior.

➡ Optimal visiting conditions for those who prefer smaller crowds and lower prices to cloudless days.

Low Season
(Oct–Apr)

➡ Many minor roads shut due to weather conditions.

➡ Growing number of winter activities on offer, including skiing, snowshoeing, visiting ice caves.

➡ Brief spurts of daylight, long nights with possible Northern Lights viewings.

Useful Websites

Visit Iceland (www.visiticeland.com) Official tourism portal.

Visit Reykjavík (www.visitreykjavik.is) Official site for the capital.

Icelandic Met Office (http://en.vedur.is) Weather forecasts.

Icelandic Road Administration (www.vegagerdin.is) Details road openings and current conditions.

Reykjavík Grapevine (www.grapevine.is) Great English-language newspaper and website.

Lonely Planet (www.lonelyplanet.com/iceland) Destination information, traveller forum and more.

Important Numbers

To dial outside Iceland, dial your international access code, Iceland's country code (☏354) then the seven-digit number (there are no area codes in Iceland).

Emergency services, and search and rescue	☏112
Directory enquiries	☏118
Iceland country code (dialling in)	☏354
International code (dialling out)	☏00
Weather	☏902 0600 (press 1)
Road condition information	☏1777

Exchange Rates

Australia	A$1	Ikr106
Canada	C$1	Ikr108
Europe	€1	Ikr154
Japan	¥100	Ikr110
NZ	NZ$1	Ikr101
UK	UK£1	Ikr197
US	US$1	Ikr130

For current exchange rates see www.xe.com.

Daily Costs

Budget: less than Ikr15,000

➡ Camping: Ikr1000–1400

➡ Dorm: Ikr4000–6000

➡ Hostel breakfast: Ikr1500–2000

➡ Grill-bar grub or soup lunch: Ikr1200–1800

➡ One-way bus ticket Reykjavík to Akureyri: Ikr7000–8000

Midrange: Ikr15,000–30,000

➡ Guesthouse double room: Ikr14,000–20,000

➡ Cafe meal: Ikr2000–3000

➡ Museum entry: Ikr1000

➡ Small vehicle rental (per day): Ikr14,000

Top end: more than Ikr30,000

➡ Boutique double room: Ikr30,000–40,000

➡ Main dish in top-end restaurant: Ikr4000–7000

➡ Daily 4WD rental: Ikr30,000

Opening Hours

Opening hours vary throughout the year and in general are far longer from June to August, and shorter from September to May. Standard opening hours:

Banks 9am-4pm weekdays

Cafe-bars 10am-1am Sunday to Thursday, 10am to between 3am and 6am Friday and Saturday

Cafes 10am-6pm

Petrol stations 8am-10pm or 11pm

Restaurants 11.30am-2.30pm and 6-9pm or 10pm

Shops 10am-6pm Monday to Friday, 10am-4pm Saturday; some Sunday opening in Reykjavík malls and major shopping strips

Supermarkets 9am-8pm (later in Reykjavík)

Vínbúðin (government-run alcohol stores) Variable; many outside Reykjavík only open for a couple of hours per day

Arriving in Iceland

Keflavík International Airport (KEF; p90)

➡ Iceland's primary international airport is 48km west of Reykjavík. Flybus, Airport Express and discount operator K-Express have buses connecting the airport with Reykjavík. Flybus offers pick-up/drop-off at many accommodations (Ikr1950 to Reykjavík, Ikr2500 to hotel).

➡ Cars can be rented from the airport – prebooking highly recommended.

➡ Taxis link KEF with Reykjavík but are rarely utilised due to the high cost (about Ikr15,000), and the ease of bus connections.

Getting Around

Car The most common way for visitors to get around. They're pricey to hire but provide great freedom. A 2WD vehicle will get you almost everywhere in summer (note: not into the highlands, or on F roads, which are only suitable for 4WDs). Summer-only 4WD buses can get you into the highlands, or you'll need a 4WD.

Bus There's a decent bus network operating from around mid-May to mid-September to get you between major destinations (and into the highlands). Outside these months, services are less frequent (or even nonexistent).

Flights If you're short on time, domestic flights can help you maximise your time.

For much more on **getting around**, see p366

What's New

Everything is changing

In Iceland, almost *everything* is undergoing change. The country is now one of the world's hottest travel destinations (it's seen a 20% growth in visitor numbers each year since 2010). The result: new sights and activities, increased tour operators, new and/or expanding accommodation, fun festivals, improved roads and tunnels, new bus routes, more airlines servicing Iceland. And increased demand has seen increased prices (websites are the best source of up-to-date rates).

Winter appeal

Although most visitors come in summer, winter arrivals are also surging – and this means more accommodation providers are staying open year-round, and more winter tours and activities are springing up (p45).

Nature gets in on the act

While locals are changing the nature of travel and the facilities available to visitors, nature itself is changing the landscape: Bárðarbunga volcano (p317) has been rumbling since August 2014, and a fissure eruption has occurred nearby, at Holuhraun.

Impetus for nature protection

With so many visitors, Iceland's unspoilt nature is facing increased traffic (p337), and moves are afoot to make travellers pay a fee to ensure it is protected. Stay tuned for the introduction of some type of nature pass.

New roads, better access

There's a new tunnel being built east of Akureyri, and a new tunnel in the Eastfjords linking Eskifjörður to Neskaupstaður. There are plans to seal the road from Ásbyrgi to Dettifoss; the south coast of the Westfjords has improved, sealed roads.

Hotels booming

Every small town seems to have a handful of new guesthouses, many farms are adding cottages and/or rooms. Far beyond the fast-changing capital, the hotel chains have big plans: Fosshotel has shiny new options in the Eastfjords (in Fáskrúðsfjörður) and Westfjords (Patreksfjörður), with more on the drawing board. Stracta is a newbie chain, with plans to expand beyond its flagship hotel in Hella. There are large new hotels in Mývatn, Siglufjörður, Skógar, Neskaupstaður, Vík and near Þingvellir. And yet, it's still tough to find a room in July!

New sights, new activities

There are ambitious plans for the Langjökull Ice Cave (p169), due to open in 2015. There's a wonderful new volcano museum (p154) in Vestmannaeyjar, a new whale museum (p59) in Reykjavík, a new rock'n'roll museum (p100) in Keflavík. A 'secret lagoon' (p113) has opened in Flúðir, while boat tours on an iceberg lagoon (p297) now operate from Fjallsárlón, west of the more-famous Jökulsárlón. New trails are granting access to outlet glaciers between Jökulsárlón and Höfn (p301).

Wait, there's more

You get the idea? We haven't even touched on the burgeoning food scene, or the handful of new festivals... There is *loads* of new stuff – and this boom shows few signs of abating. And yes, a tiny population of 325,000 is accomplishing all this. Impressive, no?

For more recommendations and reviews, see lonelyplanet.com/iceland

If You Like...

Wildlife

Vestmannaeyjar's puffins
The largest puffin colony in the world lives in this eye-catching archipelago. (p153)

Húsavík's whales View underwater marvels on a boat expedition from Iceland's whale-watching heartland. (p244)

Hornstrandir's Arctic foxes
Iceland's only native mammal thrives in the faraway kingdom of towering cliffs and mossy stones. (p200)

Lake Mývatn's birds Twitchers adore the marshy surrounds of the lake, a magnet for migrating geese and all kinds of waterfowl. (p235)

Vatnsnes Peninsula's seals
Take a seal-spotting cruise from Hvammstangi or drive the peninsula scouting for sunbaking pinnipeds. (p210)

Stunning Scenery

You do realise that choosing between incomparable vistas is like trying to pick a favourite child? This list could be near-endless...

Þingeyri to Bíldudalur The drive between these two townships may be jaw-clenchingly rutty, but the zipper-like fjordheads resemble fleets of earthen ships engaged in a celestial battle. (p191)

Breiðafjörður Thousands of islets dot the sweeping bay as rainbows soar overhead during the occasional summertime sun shower. (p170)

Skaftafell to Höfn Glittering glaciers, brooding mountains and an iceberg-filled lagoon line the 130km stretch along the Ring Road's southeast coast. (p290)

Eastfjords Supermodel Seyðisfjörður steals the limelight, but her fine fjord neighbours are just as photogenic. (p267)

Þórsmörk A magnificent forested kingdom nestled under harsh volcanic peaks, wild stretches of desert and looming glaciers. (p146)

Askja A remote, sapphire-blue lake at the heart of an immense caldera is the destination as you journey across vast, barren lava fields. (p314)

Tröllaskagi The road hugs steep mountainsides, then emerges from tunnels to capture magical vistas of glistening waters. (p216)

Hiking

Landmannalaugar & Þórsmörk Accessible only by 4WD, Iceland's favourite hiking centres are realms offering endless foot fodder, and the hike between them – Laugavegurinn – is the original flavour of wilderness walking. (p143)

Hornstrandir Pristine nature as far as the eye can see in this hiking paradise orbiting the Arctic Circle. (p200)

Skaftafell Follow trails through twisting birch woods or don crampons to tackle offshoots of the mammoth Vatnajökull ice cap. (p290)

Jökulsárgljúfur A veritable smorgasbord of geological wonders, including thundering waterfalls and Iceland's 'Grand Canyon'. (p250)

Kerlingarfjöll A remote highland massif with a growing reputation among the hiking community. (p311)

Borgarfjörður Eystri The base for a superb series of trails – don't miss the giant boulders and green ponds of Stórurð. (p268)

Lagoons & Swimming Pools

Blue Lagoon As touristy as it may be, it's hard not to adore a soak in the steaming silica soup surrounded by dramatic flourishes of frozen lava. (p98)

Mývatn Nature Baths Ease aching muscles at the north's equally scenic answer to the Blue Lagoon. (p242)

Krossneslaug A geothermal Valhalla at the edge of the world where the lapping Arctic waters mingle with a toasty geothermal source. (p206)

Lýsuholslaug Swimming in this pool, filled with mineral-rich waters, is like soaking in a warm gin fizz with a twist of algae. (p181)

Sundlaugin á Hofsós This perfectly sited fjordside swimming pool puts the sleepy northern town of Hofsós on the map. (p217)

Gamla Laugin Mist rises from the 'Secret Lagoon' in Flúðir, surrounded by wildflower-filled meadows. (p113)

History

Reykjavík 871±2 Brilliantly curated exhibit constructed around an excavation site of an ancient Viking hall. (p54)

Settlement Centre Offers excellent insight into Iceland's settlement and one of the more famous sagas (Egil's Saga) through beautiful wooden sculptures. (p161)

Herring Era Museum Herring fishing once brought frenzied activity and untold riches to Siglufjörður; today an outstanding museum re-creates the heyday. (p218)

Víkingaheimar A fresh-faced museum whose centrepiece is a perfect reconstruction of the oldest known Viking-age ship. (p100)

Lakagígar Attempt to comprehend one of the most catastrophic volcanic events in human history. (p288)

Eldheimar A new 'Pompeii of the North' museum gives insight into the devastating 1973 eruption on Heimaey. (p154)

Fáskrúðsfjörður The French flavour of this fjord is celebrated with a new hotel and museum development. (p278)

Top: Seljalandsfoss (p136)

Bottom: Traditional turf house Lindarbakki (p268), Borgarfjörður Eystri (Bakkagerði)

Local Food

Fish soup Any restaurant worth its salt has fish soup on the menu – head to the Snæfellsnes Peninsula and try Narfeyrarstofa (p173) or Gamla Rif (p177).

Lamb Iceland's headliner meat is a locavore's dream, and it falls off the bone at myriad restaurants – one of our favourites is the highlands gateway Fjallakaffi (p244).

Hákarl A pungent tribute to Iceland's unpalatable past – try a piece of this spongy-soggy oddity at Bjarnarhöfn (p175), then check out the shed of fetid meat out the back.

Langoustine The Höfn fishing fleet pulls countless crustaceans from the icy local waters; Höfn's restaurants simply grill and add butter. (p303)

Skyr A delicious yoghurt-y snack available at any supermarket in Iceland. (p349)

Hverabrauð Around Mývatn, sample this cake-like rye bread, baked underground using geothermal heat. (p238)

Waterfalls

Dettifoss Stand back! With the greatest volume of any waterfall in Europe, thundering Dettifoss demonstrates nature at its most awesome. (p253)

Goðafoss The 'Waterfall of the Gods' is loaded with spiritual symbolism and looks like it's been ripped straight from a shampoo commercial. (p235)

Skógafoss Camp within spitting distance of this gorgeous gusher – easily spotted from Rte 1 – then hike up into the highlands to discover 20 more waterfalls just beyond. (p138)

Dynjandi Veins of arctic water cascade outward over terraces of stone that look like the side of a Bundt cake – turn around and you'll be afforded some of the most gorgeous fjord views in all the land. (p191)

Seljalandsfoss A (slippery) path in the rockface gives behind-the-scenes access to this postcard-perfect chute. (p136)

Hengifoss Hike to Iceland's second-highest falls, plummeting into a photogenic, brown-and-red-striped gorge. (p266)

Unique Sleeps

Hótel Egilsen A rundown merchant's house has been transformed into a gorgeous harbour inn with boutique-chic fixtures. (p173)

Hótel Djúpavík Set on the site of an abandoned herring factory, this legendary bolthole will fulfill all your fjord fantasies; Sigur Rós shot part of their documentary here. (p206)

Dalvík HI Hostel Dalvík's charming, vintage-inspired hostel is like no other we've encountered. Budget prices happily belie the boutique decor. (p221)

Silfurberg Soak in a glass-dome-enclosed hot-pot at this luxurious boutique guesthouse in the broad, view-blessed Breiðdalur valley. (p280)

Ion Luxury Adventure Hotel Swim in geothermal waters and dine on organic, local fare, before sleeping in lake-view rooms at this new design hotel. (p109)

Skálanes This remote fjordside farm and nature reserve will gladden the heart of retreat-seeking ecologists and birdwatchers. (p274)

Álftavatn The halfway point on the Laugavegurinn hike, this lakeside base is a sight for sore eyes after a long day of trekking – the remoteness is palpable and there's a great backpacker vibe. (p143)

Architecture & Design

Churches Some of Iceland's most intriguing architectural flourishes are – strangely – its churches; check them out in Stykkishólmur (p170), Akureyri (p222) and, of course, Reykjavík (p59).

Iceland Design Centre An organisation charged with promoting Iceland's designers and architects, and the brains behind the annual DesignMarch event. (p65)

Harpa Reykjavík's dazzling concert hall and cultural centre glows like the switchboard of an alien ship after dark. (p59)

Turf houses A paradigm of pre-modern Iceland, these hobbit houses are wonderfully whimsical and offer an interesting insight into Iceland's past. (p214)

Reykjavík design boutiques The vibrant design culture of the capital makes for great shopping, from sleek, fish-skin purses to knitted *lopapeysur* (Icelandic woollen sweater) and nature-inspired jewellery. (p87)

Þórbergssetur This museum in the southeast honours a beloved local writer and its inspired exterior (resembling a giant bookshelf) is a traffic-stopper. (p299)

Month by Month

January

After December's cheer, the festive hangover hits. The first few weeks of the year can feel like an anticlimax – not helped by the long dark nights and inclement weather.

✖ Þorrablót

This Viking midwinter feast (late January to mid/late February) is marked nationwide with stomach-churning treats such as *hákarl* (fermented shark), *svið* (singed sheep's head) and *hrútspungar* (rams' testicles). All accompanied by shots of *brennivín* (a potent schnapps nicknamed 'black death'). Hungry?

February

The coldest month in many parts of Iceland, though everyday life in the capital can seem untouched. The countryside may be scenic under snow, but mostly dark – there's only seven to eight hours of daylight per day.

✯ Winter Lights Festival

Mid-month, Reykjavík sparkles with this winter-warmer encompassing Museum Night and Pool Night (late-opening museums and swimming pools), illuminated landmarks, light installations, concerts, and celebrations to mark International Children's Day. See www.vetrarhatid.is.

✖ Food & Fun

International chefs team up with local restaurants and vie for awards at this capital feast. Teams are given the finest Icelandic ingredients (lamb and seafood, natch) to create their masterpieces. See www.foodandfun.is.

March

Winter is officially over, but it's not quite time to start celebrating. The country wakes from its slumber; winter activities such as skiing are popular as daylight hours increase.

♟ Beer Day

Hard to imagine, but beer was illegal in Iceland for 75 years. On 1 March, Icelanders celebrate the day in 1989 when the prohibition was overturned. They need little prompting, but pubs, restaurants and clubs around Reykjavík are especially beer-lovin' on this night.

🏃 Iceland Winter Games

Snowy activities take centre stage in Akureryri, Iceland's winter-sports capital – including an international freeski and slopestyle competition, timed to coincide with the Éljagangur (Blizzard) festival. See www.icelandwintergames.com.

✯ DesignMarch

The local design scene is celebrated in Reykjavík at this four-day feast of all things aesthetically pleasing: from fashion to furniture, architecture to food design. It's organised by the Iceland Design Centre; see www.designmarch.is.

April

Easter is celebrated in a traditional fashion (Easter-egg hunts, roast lamb), and spring is in the air. Days lengthen and the mercury climbs, meaning lots of greenery after the snow melts, plus the arrival of thousands of migrating birds.

✨ Sumardagurinn Fyrsti

Rather ambitiously, Icelanders celebrate the first day of summer (the first Thursday after 18 April) with celebrations and street parades. A case of winter-induced madness? No, it's a nod to the Old Norse calendar, which divided the year into only two seasons: winter and summer.

◉ Puffins on Parade

To the delight of twitchers and photographers, in April the divinely comedic puffin arrives in huge numbers (an estimated 10 million birds) for the breeding season, departing for warmer climes by mid-August. There are puffin colonies all around the country.

May

May is shoulder season, and it's not a bad month to visit, just before the tourist season cranks up in earnest. Enjoy prices before they escalate, plus lengthening days, spring wildflowers and first-rate birdwatching.

✨ Reykjavík Arts Festival

Culture vultures flock to Iceland's premier cultural festival, which showcases two weeks of local and international theatre performances, film, dance, music and visual art. See www.listahatid.is for the program.

June

Hello summer! The short, sharp, three-month-long tourist season begins. Pros: the best weather, near-endless daylight, the pick of tours and excursions, the best choice of accommodation. Cons: big crowds, peak prices, the need to book all lodging.

✨ Seafarers' Day

Fishing is integral to Icelandic life, and Seafarers' Day (Sjómannadagurinn) is party time in fishing villages. On the first weekend in June, every ship in Iceland is in harbour and all sailors have a day off. Salty-dog celebrations on the Sunday include drinking, rowing and swimming contests, tugs-of-war and mock sea rescues.

✨ Hafnarfjörður Viking Festival

The peace is shattered as Viking hordes invade this seaside town near Reykjavík for a five-day festival in mid-June. Expect little by way of raiding and pillaging – more like staged fights, storytelling, archery and music. See www.vikingvillage.is.

◉ Whale Watching

Some 11 species of whale are regularly sighted in the waters around Iceland. Sightings happen year-round; the best time is from June to August. Whale-spotting boat tours leave from the Reykjavík area, and from near Akureyri, but Húsavík is the country's whale-watching HQ.

✨ National Day

The country's biggest holiday commemorates the founding of the Republic of Iceland on 17 June 1944 with parades and general patriotic merriness. Tradition has it that the sun isn't supposed to shine. And it usually doesn't!

🏃 Opening of Mountain Roads

The highland regions of Iceland are generally blanketed in snow well into the warmer months. The opening of 4WD-only mountain roads is weather dependent, but generally occurs around mid-June; roads are closed again by late September. The website www.vegagerdin.is keeps you updated.

◉ Midnight Sun

Except for the island of Grímsey, Iceland lies just south of the Arctic Circle. Still, around the summer solstice (21 June) it's possible to view the midnight sun (when the setting sun doesn't fully dip below the horizon), especially in the country's north.

☆ Secret Solstice

Another music festival? Yep, new in 2014 (with headliners Massive Attack) – and this one coincides with the solstice, so there's 24-hour daylight too. It's held at Laugardalur in Reykjavík; more info is at www.secret solstice.is.

✨ Midsummer

The longest day of the year is celebrated with solstice parties and bonfires (staged anytime between 21 and 24 June), although the Icelandic midsummer isn't as major an event as in the rest of the Nordic countries.

🍴 Humar Festival

The tasty *humar* (often translated as lobster, but technically it's langoustine) is pulled fresh from Icelandic waters and served a delectable number of ways in the fishing town of Höfn. The town honours the *humar* each year at Humarhátíð in late June/early July.

July

Iceland's festival pace quickens alongside a (hopefully) rising temperature gauge and a distinct swelling of tourist numbers. Expect busy roads, crowded trails, packed campgrounds, no-vacancy guesthouses etc, and book ahead.

✯ Landsmót Hestamanna

Horse lovers: the week-long national Icelandic horse competition is held in even-numbered years (the host town is rotated). It's a beloved spectator event and excuse for a country festival. See www.landsmot.is.

☆ Folk Music Festival

The tiny but perfect five-day folk music festival in Siglufjörður welcomes Icelandic and foreign musicians. As well as traditional tunes, enjoy courses on Icelandic music, dance and handicrafts. It's in early July; see www.folkmusik.is/en.

☆ ATP Iceland

All Tomorrow's Parties promotes intimate 'boutique'

festivals around the world. After hosting successful events (and headliners Portishead and Nick Cave) in Iceland in 2013 and 2014, it's back in 2015. Concerts are held at Ásbrú, part of the old military base near Keflavík. See www.atpfestival.com.

☆ Skálholt Summer Concerts

The cathedral at the historic religious centre of Skálholt hosts around 40 public concerts, lectures and workshops over a five-week period from July to August. The focus is on contemporary religious music and early music. See www.sumartonleikar.is.

☆ Eistnaflug

The remote Eastfjords town of Neskaupstaður goes *off* in the second week of July, when the population doubles to celebrate the heavy-metal festival Eistnaflug. Metal, hardcore, punk, rock and indie bands share the stage. See www.eistnaflug.is.

☆ Bræðslan

The beloved Bræðslan pop/rock festival has earned a reputation for great music and an intimate atmosphere. Some big local names (and a few international ones) come to play in tiny, out-of-the-way Borgarfjörður Eystri on the third weekend in July. Check out www.braedslan.com.

August

The tourist season continues apace, with southern Europeans flying north for vacation. It's still very busy. By mid-month

the puffins have departed (and some whales, too); by late August the local kids are back at school, and the nights are lengthening.

✯ Verslunarmannahelgi

A public-holiday long weekend (the first weekend in August) when Icelanders flock to rural festivals, family barbecues, rock concerts and wild campground parties.

✯ Þjóðhátíð

This earth-shaking event occurs in Heimaey, Vestmannaeyjar, on the August long weekend, commemorating the day in 1874 when foul weather prevented the islanders from partying when Iceland's constitution was established. More than 11,000 people descend to watch bands and fireworks, and drink gallons of alcohol. See www.dalurinn.is.

✯ Herring Festival

Also on the August long weekend, Siglufjörður celebrates its heady herring-induced heyday with dancing, feasting, drinking and fishy-flavoured activities.

✯ Reykjavík Culture Night

On Culture Night (Menningarnótt), held mid-month, Reykjavíkers turn out in force for a day and night of art, music, dance and fireworks. Many galleries, ateliers, shops, cafes and churches stay open until late. See www.menningarnott.is for a full program.

🏃 Reykjavík Marathon

Your chance to get sporty and sophisticated on the

same day: this event is held on the same date as Culture Night. There are full- and half-marathons, as well as fun runs; more than 15,600 people got sweaty in the 2014 event. See www.marathon.is.

Reykjavík Jazz Festival

From mid-August, Reykjavík toe-taps its way through a week dedicated to jazz, man. Local and international musicians blow their own trumpets at events staged at Harpa. Check out www.reykjavik jazz.is.

Reykjavík Pride

Out and proud since 1999, this festival brings Carnival-like colour to the capital on the second weekend of August. About 90,000 people (over one-quarter of the country's population) attended 2014's Pride march and celebrations. See www.reykjavikpride.com.

September

Tourist arrivals decrease significantly and prices drop, making this a good time to visit. The weather can still be agreeable, but summer-only hotels, attractions and services are closed. Highland roads are closed by month's end.

Réttir

An autumn highlight, the *réttir* is the farmers' round-up of sheep and horses that have grazed wild over summer. The round-up is often done on horseback and the

animals are herded into a corral where the sorting takes place (participants and spectators welcome). Naturally, it's all accompanied by much rural merrymaking.

Reykjavík International Film Festival

This intimate 11-day event from late September features quirky programming that highlights independent film-making, both home-grown and international. There are also panels and masterclasses. Check the program at www.riff.is.

October

October marks the official onset of winter, with cooler temperatures, longer nights and the appearance of the Northern Lights.

Northern Lights

Also called aurora borealis, these colourful, dancing lights are caused by charged particles from solar flares colliding with the earth's atmosphere. They're only viewed in the darkness of night with no cloud cover. The best months for viewing are October to April (September if you're lucky), with peak visibility from December to February.

November

Summer is a distant memory. November sees nights lengthening (sunsets around 4pm) and weather cooling, but Reykjavík parties hard,

with big crowds gathering for its flagship music festival.

Iceland Airwaves

You'd be forgiven for thinking Iceland is just one giant music-producing machine. Since the first edition of Iceland Airwaves was held in 1999, this fab festival has become one of the world's premier annual showcases for new music (Icelandic and otherwise). Check out www.icelandairwaves.is.

Days of Darkness

East Iceland (Egilsstaðir and the fjords) perversely celebrates the onset of winter over 10 days in early/mid-November, with dark dances, ghost stories, magic shows and torch-lit processions during its unusual Days of Darkness (Dagar Myrkurs) festival.

December

A festive atmosphere brings cheer to the darkest time of the year. Christmas markets, concerts and parties keep things bright and cosy, followed by New Year's Eve celebrations. Note that some hotels are closed between Christmas and New Year.

New Year's Eve

Festivities aplenty on 31 December, with dinners, bonfires, fireworks (*lots* of fireworks – these are sold as a fundraiser for the beloved national search and rescue organisation), parties and clubbing till the early hours of New Year's Day.

Plan Your Trip
Itineraries

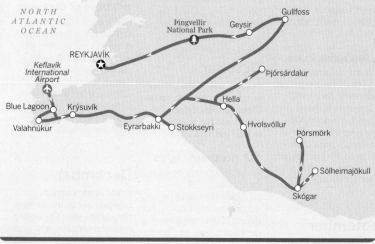

3–4 DAYS Reykjavík Minibreak

If you're on a lengthy layover or enjoying a long weekend away, don't miss the chance to get out into the countryside and take in some of the natural wonders located within a stone's throw of the capital. It's simple to string together top sights, including the Golden Circle, with more off-the-beaten path diversions, and still have a bit of time left to lap up Reykjavík's unique charm.

After landing in **Keflavík International Airport** make a beeline for the **Blue Lagoon** to soak away the jet lag in surreal waters and silica mud. Wander the Reykjanes Peninsula's steaming earths near **Valahnúkur** or **Krýsuvík** before barrelling down the coastal highway for fresh seafood in **Eyrarbakki** or **Stokkseyri**. Choose a base near **Hella** or **Hvolsvöllur** to get out in the open air on horseback: the lush waterfall-rimmed Fljótshlíð valley is a key candidate. Or try to spot the Northern Lights (in the colder months). Active bodies will enjoy the stunning Fimmvörðuháls hike from **Skógar** up through the ridge

Great Geysir (p110), Geysir

between two brooding ice caps (and the site of the Eyjafjallajökull eruption in 2010) then down into **Þórsmörk**, a forested valley dotted with wild Arctic flowers. Or you can take a super-Jeep tour or amphibious bus to Þórsmörk, and then do day hikes around the valley. Those who are tighter on time can trek along the glacial tongue of **Sólheimajökull** instead.

On your way back west, roam the **Þjórsárdalur**, a broad volcanic river valley with a handful of disparate sights, including a Settlement Era farmstead, hidden waterfalls, and the foothills of Hekla volcano. Or, swing up to the gushing cascades at **Gullfoss**, the spurting **Geysir** from which all others got their name, and the rift valley and ancient parliament site **Þingvellir National Park** – the classic Golden Circle route. Wrap up your mini-break with a night in **Reykjavík**. Iceland's capital bustles with an all-star assortment of trendy boutiques, interesting museums and galleries, scrumptious restaurants and lively bars, plus there's easy access to whale-watching trips from the Old Harbour.

Flatey

Stykkishólmur

Grundarfjörður

Öndverðarnes

Arnarstapi

Hellnar   *Breiðavík*

Borgarnes

Upper
Borgarfjörður

Kaldidalur
Corridor

Gullfoss

Geysir

Þingvellir
National Park

REYKJAVÍK

NORTH
ATLANTIC
OCEAN

Best of the West

1 WEEK

With one week to spend, you'll be able to roam further than the popular Golden Circle, and the busy southwest. We like heading northwest from Reykjavík to lesser-travelled West Iceland, which is chock-a-block with history and boasts landscapes ranging from lava fields to broad fjords and ice caps, while giving a greater sense of the wonderful solitude that Iceland offers.

Start in **Reykjavík**, enjoying the city's museums, cafes and bars while getting acclimatised. Then complete the day-long Golden Circle with stops at glittering **Gullfoss**, surging **Geysir**, and historic **Þingvellir National Park**, where you'll witness the tearing apart of the continental plates. If you're feeling adventurous, go inland and bump along the rutted **Kaldidalur Corridor** for stunning vistas through the pinnacles of several ice caps, such as Langjökull with its new ice tunnel. You'll emerge at **Upper Borgarfjörður**, where you can sleep in the quiet countryside and explore enormous lava tubes. If you're not up for the back-country aspects of the Kaldidalur Corridor, head to **Borgarnes** along the coastal route instead, and learn about the sagas at its excellent Settlement Centre.

Next up, explore the wonderful Snæfellsnes Peninsula. Start by horse riding around **Breiðavík** or creeping into the bizarre gorge, Rauðfeldsgjá. Then head west to **Arnarstapi**, where you can hike the coastal trail to **Hellnar** or pick up a Snæfellsjökull glacier tour, exploring Jules Vernes' fabled centre of the earth. The area is part of Snæfellsjökull National Park and offers a multitude of hikes taking in bird cliffs, volcanic craters, lava tubes and protected native flower terrain.

On the tip of the peninsula near **Öndverðarnes** look for pods of orca whales, or catch a whale-watching or puffin-viewing tour near **Grundarfjörður**. Then alight in charming **Stykkishólmur**, where you can take in interesting museums and sup on tasty mussels. If time permits, hop aboard the *Baldur* ferry for a day trip to quaint **Flatey** island, to really disconnect from the world before returning to the capital.

Top: Pub scene, Reykjavík (p83)
Bottom: Harbour, Stykkishólmur (p170)

10 DAYS · Classic Ring Road

For such a wild, wonderful land, much of Iceland is surprisingly compact, and the classic Ring Road trip loops you near the most popular sights. With extra time, you can add myriad other adventures along the way. The Ring Road works as a cycling itinerary as well (though it'll take more than 10 days!).

Start in **Reykjavík**, enjoying the lively city's creature comforts, before heading out in a clockwise fashion. Stop in **Borgarnes** for its fascinating Settlement Centre, historical sights and tasty restaurants. Then zip up to **Stykkishólmur**, an adorable village overlooking a bay studded by islets. With extra time you'd tour the Snæfellsnes Peninsula. But either way, rejoin the Ring Road, breaking free of it once more to explore the quaint townships and coastal vistas of **Tröllaskagi** before gliding through **Akureyri**, Iceland's unofficial northern capital. Head to the geological treasure chest of the **Mývatn** region next, with a stop at **Dettifoss** to experience nature's awesome power first hand. Push eastwards, detouring to **Borgarfjörður Eystri** for summer puffins galore. Take a break in **Seyðisfjörður**, then tackle the long journey through the rest of the east as the road curls along magical fjords.

Pause in **Höfn** for langoustine, then jump on a snowmobile to discover the vast ice cap at **Vatnajökull**. Don't miss the glacial lagoon at **Jökulsárlón**, or neighbouring Fjallsárlón, where giant bergs break off of glaciers and float out to sea. You can warm up your hiking legs in **Skaftafell**, then head south across mossy lava fields and enormous river deltas to **Vík** with its fantastical basalt-columned beach and puffin cliffs. Still feeling spry? Tackle the awesome trek from **Skógar** to **Þórsmörk**, a verdant interior valley. Or continue west along the Ring Road passing enormous waterfalls at **Skógafoss** and **Seljalandsfoss**, then veer away one last time to check out the Golden Circle: **Gullfoss**, **Geysir** and the yawning continental divide and ancient governmental seat at **Þingvellir National Park**. Roll back into **Reykjavík** to spend the remainder of your holiday gossiping with the locals, whether in the city's geothermal pools or during late-night pub crawls.

Top: Jökulsárlón (p297)
Bottom: Puffin, Borgarfjörður Eystri (p268)

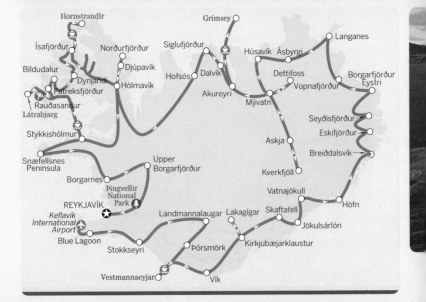

4 WEEKS · The Grand Tour

The more remote and fantastical swathes of Iceland open to you with an extended stay. In addition to seeing major sights, venture further from the Ring Road, into the gorgeous, isolated Westfjords, or four-wheel-drive the Highlands.

From **Keflavík**, rent wheels and head to the **Blue Lagoon** to unwind. Follow the coastal road to arty **Stokkseyri**, then ditch the car to hike from **Landmannalaugar** to verdant **Þórsmörk**. Next, catch the boat to **Vestmannaeyjar**, where puffins flip-flap over fresh lava. Then sojourn near **Vík**, with its black basalt beach.

At **Kirkjubæjarklaustur** venture up to **Lakagígar** to learn about the devastating effects of Laki's eruptions. **Skaftafell** offers hiking and glacier walking. Don't miss a boat ride with icebergs at **Jökulsárlón** and a snowmobile safari on **Vatnajökull**, Europe's largest ice cap. Pause in **Höfn** for legendary langoustine, then relax in hushed **Breiðdalsvík** before negotiating hairpin fjord roads to peaceful **Eskifjörður** and inspiring **Seyðisfjörður**. Follow the rhyolite cliffs down to **Borgarfjörður Eystri** to photograph puffins, then climb through **Vopnafjörður** to the grassy plains of **Langanes**. The quiet northeastern circuit rolls through **Ásbyrgi** to charming **Húsavík**, perfect for whale watching. Scenic **Mývatn** makes a great base for exploring the pounding waterfall, **Dettifoss**, and Iceland's Highland treasures such as the mammoth caldera at **Askja** and silent ice caves at **Kverkfjöll**. Stop for a slice of civilisation in **Akureyri** before touching the Arctic Circle in **Grímsey**. Wander up through **Dalvík**, check out **Siglufjörður**, then treat yourself to a relaxing swim in **Hofsós**.

Next, head to the Westfjords to learn about ancient witchcraft in **Hólmavík**, sleep fjordside in **Djúpavík** and bathe in the **Norðurfjörður** geothermal spring. Use spunky **Ísafjörður** as a launch pad to **Hornstrandir**, Iceland's majestic hiking reserve. Enter the incredible heart of the Westfjords, to find the gushing waters of **Dynjandi**, and use **Bíldudalur** or Þingeyri as a base for exploring jaw-dropping fjords. Head down to **Patreksfjörður** for a square meal and to visit the bird cliffs at **Látrabjarg** and the mindblowing pink-red beach at **Rauðasandur**.

Ferry over to charming **Stykkishólmur** and discover the treasures of the **Snæfellsnes Peninsula**, from golden beaches to craggy lava fields and glistening ice caps. **Borgarnes** and **Upper Borgarfjörður** blend saga sites and hidden caves. Finish the history lesson at **Þingvellir National Park**. Then end the epic journey in **Reykjavík**, the ebullient capital.

Top: Hikers, Landmannalaugar (p140)
Bottom: Öskjuvatn (p316), Askja

Plan Your Trip
Ring Road Planner

Unless you've visited Iceland before, you'll likely struggle to name an Icelandic town besides Reykjavík. You may worry that it might be tricky to plan a visit when so much of the country is vast and unknown. Fear not, the path is clear: the Ring Road.

Best Ring Road Detours

Snæfellsnes Peninsula
A veritable ring road unto itself that takes in lava fields, wild coastline and an infamous ice cap; 200km detour.

Tröllaskagi
Follow Rte 76/Rte 82 as it climbs up towards the Arctic – hair-raising road tunnels and scenic panoramas await; 90km detour.

Borgarfjörður Eystri
Take Rte 94 through rhyolite cliffs and down into this quiet hamlet of visiting puffins and superb hiking trails; 150km detour.

Vestmannaeyjar
Hop on the ferry at Landeyjahöfn to discover a rugged archipelago of islets; 30km detour plus a 30-minute boat ride each way.

Þórsmörk
Park at Seljalandsfoss and take the bus into the forested kingdom rife with scenic walks; 50km detour along a rutty road accessible only by certified vehicles; hiking also an option.

The 'Diamond Circle'
Dreamed up by marketers, the Diamond Circle barrels north from Mývatn to take in the whale-filled bay of Húsavík, the grand canyon and trails of Ásbyrgi, and the roaring falls at Dettifoss; 180km detour.

Route 1

Route 1 (Þjóðvegur 1), known as the Ring Road, is the country's main thoroughfare, comprising 1330 super-scenic kilometres (830 miles) of mostly paved highway. It's rarely more than one lane in either direction. Countless gems line its path, while secondary roads lead off it to further-flung adventures.

When to Go

The Ring Road is generally accessible year-round (there may be exceptions during winter storms); many of the secondary roads are closed during the colder months. Check out www.vegagerdin.is for details of road closures, and www.vedur.is for weather forecasts.

Clockwise or Anticlockwise?

It doesn't matter which way you tackle the Ring Road – the landscape reveals itself in a cinematic fashion from both directions.

If you're travelling during the latter part of summer (August into September), we recommend driving the loop in a clockwise manner – check off your northern must-sees first as warmer weather sticks around a tad longer in the south.

How Long Do I Need?

If you were to drive the Ring Road without stopping (or breaking the speed limit), it would take approximately 16 hours. Thus, a week-long trip in the countryside means an average of about 2½ hours of driving per day. While this might seem a bit full-on for some, remember that the drive is extraordinarily scenic and rarely feels like a haul. In summer, there's plenty of daylight.

We recommend a minimum of 10 days to do justice to the Ring Road (see p32). For travellers planning an itinerary that's under a week, we suggest committing to one or two regions in detail (eg, Reykjavík and the south or west; a week in the north), rather than trying to hoof it around the island.

By Car

Discovering Iceland by private vehicle is by far the most convenient means. It is, as expected, the most expensive method as well.

Renting a Car

It's best to start early when searching for low rates. The internet is your best resource, but take care to ensure that the name of your rental service appears on your booking, and to double-check that all fees are included in the quoted price.

Book early for summer hires – companies do sometimes run out of vehicles.

2WD or 4WD?

A 2WD vehicle is fine if you're planning to drive just the Ring Road and major secondary roads. If you want to explore the interior (driving on 'F' mountain roads), you'll need a robust 4WD – alternatively, hire a 2WD and pay for bus trips or super-Jeep tours to less-accessible areas.

In winter, a small 2WD isn't recommended (rental prices are considerably lower than in summer – consider a 4WD for safety). Snow tyres are fitted to winter rentals.

Breaking Up the Journey

The most important thing to remember about travelling the Ring Road is to use it as a conduit to explore memorable detours. We recommend choosing five mini-bases along the journey to break up the drive – to

---

RING ROAD ADVICE

➡ Don't confuse the Ring Road, which loops the country, with the Golden Circle (a tourist route in the country's southwest; see p106).

---

make things simple, try selecting one stop in each region in which the Ring Road passes through: the west, north, east, southeast and southwest. Depending on the length of your trip, you can spend several nights at each base, engaging in the area's best activities and detours before moving to the next one.

By Bus

Far less convenient than car rental, Iceland's limited bus service is the most cost-effective option for solo travellers, but you should budget double the time of a private vehicle to loop around, lest you spend the majority of the trip staring at the countryside through a window. For comparison, a bus pass that rings two travellers around the island roughly equals the price (without petrol) of a small rental car for a week.

By Bicycle

We don't want to dash your dreams, but cyclists will have a tougher time than expected travelling the Ring Road. The changeable weather makes for tough going, and although the path is mostly paved, there is hardly any room on the road's shoulder to provide a comfortable distance from vehicular traffic. Cycling can be a great way to explore more-rural regions.

By Hitching & Ridesharing

The most cost-effective way to venture around the Ring Road is to stick out your thumb. In summer it's quite easy to hitch all the way around the Ring Road but be aware of the potential risks involved.

Many hostels have rideshare posterboards in their lobbies. A great resource is www.samferda.is, an online rideshare messageboard.

Hiker on Kerlingarfjöll (p311)

Outdoor Adventures

Iceland's spectacular natural beauty encompasses Europe's largest national park and the mightiest ice cap outside the poles, plus a sea full of whales and the world's biggest puffin colonies. There are soaring mountains, hidden valleys, dark canyons, pristine lakes, roaring waterfalls, twisting rivers and fjord-riven coastlines. Getting among it is easy, and utterly exhilarating.

DIRK BLEYER/ROBERT HARDING ©

Best Time to Go...

For Multiday Hiking Wait for spring thaw; trekking is at its best July to mid-September.

For Highlands Exploration Mountain roads open sometime from June to early July, and close again by late September.

For Midnight Sun Around the summer solstice (21 June), the daylight is endless (especially in the north).

For Northern Lights You'll need dark, clear nights; winter is best, but viewings can occur anytime between September and April.

For Skiing The season runs December to April, with best conditions (and increasing daylight) in February and March.

For Whale Watching Tours operate year-round, with peak viewing June to August.

For Puffin Viewing Peak puffin time is mid-May to early/mid-August (maybe slightly earlier; some arrive in April).

For Icy Endeavours Glacier hikes and snowmobile trips can generally be done year-round (conditions permitting). Boat trips are scheduled on Jökulsárlón April to October. Mid-November to March is best for ice caves.

For Horse Riding Multiday treks are great in the shoulder season (May and September to early October) when the weather is cool but mild, and tourist numbers are lower.

Activities

Hiking

The opportunities for hiking in Iceland are endless, from leisurely hour-long strolls to multiday wilderness treks – setting off on foot will open up vast reaches of unspoilt nature. However, the unpredictable weather is always a consideration, and rain, fog and mist can turn an uplifting hike into a miserable trudge. Always be prepared.

Useful Resources

➡ **Ferðafélag Íslands** (www.fi.is) Runs huts, campgrounds and hiking trips throughout the country. Offers solid advice on hikes – especially Laugavegurinn.

Top Short Walks

➡ **Skaftafell** (p290) Everyone's favourite part of Vatnajökull National Park offers a slew of short walks around glinting glaciers and brooding waterfalls.

➡ **Þórsmörk** (p146) An emerald kingdom tucked between the unforgiving hills of the interior; moderate to difficult walks abound.

➡ **Skógar** (p138) Hike up into the interior for a parade of waterfalls; continue on to Fimmvörðuháls and down into Þórsmörk for one of Iceland's most rewarding day-long hikes.

➡ **Snæfellsnes Peninsula** (p170) Half-day hikes galore through crunchy lava fields; don't miss the coastal walk from Hellnar to Arnarstapi.

➡ **Mývatn** (p235) Flat and easy, the marshy Mývatn lakeshore hosts a variety of geological wonders as well as prolific birdlife.

➡ **Borgarfjörður Eystri** (p268) Superb trails among the rhyolite cliffs, or hiking up to the fjordhead for views.

Best Multiday Treks

➡ **Laugavegurinn** (p143) Iceland's classic rite of passage takes you through caramel-coloured dunes, smoking earth and devastating desert. Duration: two to five days

➡ **Ásbyrgi to Dettifoss** (p252) A sampler of Iceland's geological phenomena starts at the northern end of Jökulsárgljúfur (in Vatnajökull National Park) and works its way down the gorge, ending with Europe's most powerful waterfall. Duration: two days

➡ **Royal Horn** (p202) Words can't do justice to Hornstrandir's fan-favourite route and the views of lonely fjords, emerald-green bluffs and swooping gulls. Duration: four to five days

➡ **Fimmvörðuháls** (p139) A parade of waterfalls turns into a blustery desert as you pass between glaciers. Then, the steaming stones from the 2010 eruption appear before the path leads down into flower-filled Þórsmörk. Duration: one to two days

➡ **Hringbrautin** (p311) Largely untouched, this remote interior circuit unveils postcard-worthy vistas that rival those of well-trodden Laugavegurinn. Duration: three days

Wildlife Watching

Iceland's range of wildlife is small but bewitchingly beautiful.

Arctic Foxes

Loveable like a dog but skittish like a rodent, the Arctic fox is Iceland's only native

HIKING CHECKLIST

The specifics of gear required in Iceland will obviously vary, depending on your activity, the time of year, the remoteness of the trail, and how long you'll be exploring (day hike versus multiday trek; staying in a hut versus camping). One constant: the changeability of the weather, and the risks it poses.Some of the following may be obvious to experienced hikers, but there are many newbies who may feel inspired by the wondrous Icelandic landscapes and want to get out onto trails:

☐ Proper navigation tools (topo map and GPS) are vital.

☐ It's essential to dress in layers. First base layer: thermal underwear (wool or synthetic). Second layer: light wool or fleece top; quick-drying trousers. Third layer: waterproof and windproof jacket (ie Gore-Tex). You'll need a breathable rain shell, including waterproof overtrousers. Your daypack should be waterproof.

☐ Avoid cotton clothes such as jeans, T-shirts and socks – these lose insulation properties when wet and take hours to dry. Polypropylene, which is quick-drying (but can be flammable), or merino wool, which warms even when wet (but dries slowly), is recommended.

☐ Take gloves, hat, sunglasses and sunscreen. Woollen or synthetic socks and waterproof, broken-in hiking boots or shoes are recommended (the ankle support afforded by boots is a good idea, but it's a personal choice).

On Longer Trips

☐ Your pack needs a waterproof cover or a plastic liner to keep things dry. A dry set of clothes is essential.

☐ Always carry a first-aid kit, a headlamp/torch, and a survival kit (survival blanket, whistle etc).

☐ You'll need a sleeping bag capable of handling negative Celsius temperatures. Campers will need a tent (wind- and weatherproof), stove and cooking utensils (hut users may or may not need the latter).

☐ Consider packing a swimsuit (for hot springs), lightweight sandals (for river crossings, to keep your boots dry), and hiking poles for steep descents and river crossings.

☐ Plastic bags are handy for separating wet and dry gear, and for carrying out rubbish.

Buying Or Hiring Gear

☐ You can buy hiking and camping gear in larger towns – Reykjavík is best for this; Akureyri also has options. Note that prices in Iceland aren't cheap – consider bringing what you need from home, and/or hiring gear.

☐ A few car-rental places offer camping equipment for rent (this is particularly true of campervan-hire companies). Otherwise, two good rental places in Reykjavík are **Iceland Camping Equipment** (www.iceland-camping-equipment.com) and **Reykjavík Backpackers** (www.reykjavikbackpackers.is/rentalservices/rentcampingequipment).

---

mammal. A sighting is rare, but these are the best spots to try your luck:

➡ **Hornstrandir** (p200) The fox's main domain – join the team of researchers who set up camp here each summer.

➡ **Suðavík** Home of the Arctic Fox Center (p199) – there are often orphaned foxes living in a small habitat onsite.

➡ **Breiðamerkursandur** (p297) One of the main breeding grounds for skuas, the area has drawn a rising number of Arctic foxes hungry for a snack.

Puffins & Seabirds

On coastal cliffs right around the country you can see huge numbers of seabirds, often in massive colonies. The best time for birdwatching is between June and mid-August, when puffins, gannets, guillemots, razorbills, kittiwakes and fulmars get twitchers excited.

The best bird cliffs and colonies:

➡ **Vestmannaeyjar** (p153) Puffins swarm like frantic bees as you sail into the harbour at

Fjallsárlón (p297)

Heimaey. Birds nest on virtually every turret of stone emerging from the southern sea.

➡ **Hornstrandir** (p200) This preserve offers an endless wall of stone that shoots down from the verdant bluffs straight into the waves – countless birds have built temporary homes within.

➡ **Borgarfjörður Eystri** (p268) This hamlet offers one of the best places in Iceland to spot puffins, who build their intricate homes just metres from the viewing platform.

➡ **Látrabjarg** (p188) Famous in the Westfjords for the eponymous bird cliffs.

➡ **Mývatn** (p235) A different ecosystem than towering coastal bird cliffs, Mývatn's swampy landscape is a haven for migratory avians.

➡ **Langanes** (p255) Remote windswept cliffs are home to prolific birdlife; there's a new viewing platform above a colony of northern gannets.

➡ **Ingólfshöfði** (p296) Take a tractor ride to this dramatic promontory, where skuas swoop and puffins pose.

Seals

Seals aren't as ubiquitous as Iceland's birds, but they're fun to spot.

➡ **Hvammstangi & Vatnsnes Peninsula** (p210) A seal museum, boat tours and a peninsula studded with basking pinnipeds.

➡ **Ísafjarðardjúp** (p199) Curling coastline and rock-strewn beaches offer good seal-spotting.

➡ **Jökulsárlón** (p297) As if the ice lagoon wasn't photogenic enough – look out for seals swimming among the 'bergs.

Whales

Iceland is one of the best places in the world to see whales and dolphins. The most common sightings are of minke whales and humpback, but you can also spot fin, sei and blue whales, among others.

Iceland's best spots for whale watching:

➡ **Húsavík** (p244) Iceland's classic whale-watching destination, complete with excellent whale museum; has a 99% success rate during summer.

➡ **Eyjafjörður** (p220) Whale-watching cruises ply the scenic waters of Iceland's longest fjord from Dalvík, Hauganes and now Akureyri.

➡ **Reykjavík** (p68) Easy viewing for visitors to the capital; boats depart from the old harbour right downtown.

Horse Riding

Horses are an integral part of Icelandic life; you'll see them all over the country. Many farms around the country offer short rides – there are a handful of stables within a stone's throw of Reykjavík. Figure from around Ikr6000/9000 for a one-/two-hour ride.

Best Horse-Riding Regions

➡ **Southern Snæfellsnes** (p179) The wild beaches under the shadow of a glinting glacier are perfect places for a ride. Several award-winning stables are located here.

➡ **Hella** (p131) The flatlands around Hella that roll under brooding Hekla host a constellation of horse ranches offering multiday rides and short sessions.

➡ **Skagafjörður** (p212) The only county in Iceland where horses outnumber people has a proud tradition of breeding and training.

Swimming & Spas

Thanks to Iceland's abundance of geothermal heat, swimming is a national institution, and nearly every town has at least one *sundlaug* (heated swimming pool – generally outdoors). Most pools also offer *heitir pottar* (hot-pots; small heated pools for soaking, with the water around 40°C), saunas and Jacuzzis. Admission is usually around Ikr600 (half-price for children).

The clean, chemical-free swimming pools and natural hot springs have a strict hygiene regimen, which involves a thorough *shower without swimsuit* before you enter the swimming area. Instructions are posted in a number of languages. Not following them is a sure-fire way to offend the locals.

Best Resources

➡ **Swimming in Iceland** (www.swimmingin iceland.com)

➡ *Thermal Pools in Iceland* by Jón G Snæland and Þóra Sigurbjörnsdóttir Comprehensive guide to Iceland's naturally occurring springs; sold in most bookstores.

➡ **Blue Lagoon** (www.bluelagoon.com) Iceland's favourite soaking venue and undisputed top attraction.

➡ **Visit Reykjavík** (www.visitreykjavik.is) Click through to 'What to Do' for pools in the capital region.

Glacier Walks & Snowmobiling

Trekking across an icy white expanse can be one of the most ethereal experiences of your Iceland visit. The island has several options that offer a taste of winter even on the warmest of days.

Common-sense safety rules apply: don't get too close to glaciers or walk on them without the proper equipment and guiding.

Best Glaciers & Ice Caps to Explore

➡ **Vatnajökull** (p292) Europe's biggest ice cap, is perfect for snowmobile rides; it also has dozens of offshoot glaciers primed for guided hikes and ice climbs – arrange these from Skaftafell.

➡ **Eyjafjallajökull** (p137) The site of the volcanic eruption in 2010; take a super-Jeep to discover the icy surface then wander over to Magni, nearby, to see the still-steaming earth.

➡ **Snæfellsjökull** (p178) Jules Verne's *Journey to the Centre of the Earth* starts here; try the snowcat tour from Arnarstapi.

➡ **Langjökull** (p169) Close to Reykjavík. Perfect for dog sledding, and with an ambitious ice tunnel in the works, set to open in 2015.

➡ **Sólheimajökull** (p148) An icy tongue unfurling from Mýrdalsjökull ice cap. Ideal for an afternoon trek – strap on the crampons!

Boating, Kayaking & Rafting

A new perspective on Iceland's natural treasures is offered from the water.

Best Boating Hot Spots

➡ **Heimaey** (p154) Zip across the Vestmannaeyjar archipelago taking in the craggy cliffs and swooping birds.

➡ **Stykkishólmur** (p170) Wind through the islands of silent Breiðafjörður.

➡ **Húsavík** (p244) Traditional wooden ships or high-speed zodiacs sail through whale-filled waters to neighbouring islets (and to Grímsey).

Best Kayaking

➡ **Hornstrandir** (p200), **Ísafjörður** (p194) **& Ísafjarðardjúp** (p199) Sea kayaking at its finest; try multiday tours or a one-day adventure to Vigur, an offshore islet.

➡ **Seyðisfjörður** (p270) The charismatic tour guide will leave you wondering what's more charming – the fjord or him.

Best River Trips

➡ **Varmahlíð** (p212) Northern Iceland's white-water rafting base, with two glacial rivers to choose from (family-friendly rapids or full throttle).

➡ **Reykholt** (p112) White-water rafting thrills on the Hvítá, or get your adrenalin pumping on Iceland's only jetboat rides.

Top: Horse riders, Snæfellsnes Peninsula (p170)

Bottom: Pollurinn geothermal pools (p190), Tálknafjörður

SEEING THE NORTHERN LIGHTS

The Inuit thought they were the souls of the dead; Scandinavian folklore described them as the spirits of unmarried women; and the Japanese believed that a child conceived under the dancing rays would be fortunate in life. Modern science, however, has a different take on the aurora borealis.

The magical curtains of colour that streak across the northern night sky are the result of solar wind – a stream of particles from the sun that collides with oxygen, nitrogen and hydrogen in the upper atmosphere. These collisions produce the haunting greens and magentas as the earth's magnetic field draws the wind towards the polar regions.

Catching your own glimpse of the Northern Lights requires nothing more than a dark, partly clear night (ie, few clouds) and a pinch of luck. It's as simple as that.

In recent years many tour companies have been offering pricey 'Northern Lights safaris' – they are essentially taking you to an area with little or no light pollution to increase your viewing odds. You can easily do this yourself, by booking a few nights at a rural inn and waiting for the light show in the evening. Many hotels offer viewing wake-up calls should the lights appear in the middle of the night while you're asleep.

Recent winters have been excellent for Northern Lights, with viewings beginning in September. And you don't always need to be outside a city to enjoy a show – in October 2013, with a strong aurora forecast and to maximise the visibility, Reykjavík city authorities shut down all street lights in a few neighbourhoods for a few hours!

Predicting the likelihood of an aurora is close to impossible, but there are various tools and apps that report factors like solar activity and therefore the likelihood of seeing one in the short term. The comprehensive website of the Icelandic Met Office details aurora activity, cloud cover, sunlight and moonlight, in order to provide an aurora forecast (generally for the week ahead). Check it out at http://en.vedur.is/weather/forecasts/aurora/.

Cycling

Short cycling excursions can be a fun, fit way to explore. In Reykjavík you'll find a couple of biking outlets – some offering day trips to nearby attractions such as the Golden Circle. Bike hire is possible in many other towns around the country.

Travelling around Iceland by bicycle can be more of a challenge than it might seem – shifting weather patterns mean that you'll often encounter heavy winds, and you'll be forced to ride closely alongside traffic on the Ring Road (there are no hard shoulders to the roads).

Scuba Diving & Snorkelling

Little-known but incredibly rewarding, diving in Iceland is becoming increasingly popular. The clear water (100m visibility!), great wildlife, spectacular lava ravines, wrecks and thermal chimneys make it a dive destination like no other. The best dive sites are Silfra (p108) at Þingvellir and the geothermal chimneys (p230) in Eyjafjörður.

A PADI Dry Suit Diver certificate is recommended – you can obtain this in Iceland through a handful of diving companies. The unique PADI Tectonic Plate Awareness course (designed by Dive.is) gives you an understanding of plate tectonics and what it means to dive between them.

Tours

Although joining a bunch of other travellers on an organised tour may not be your idea of an independent holiday, Iceland's rugged terrain and high costs can make it an appealing option. Tours can save you time and money and can get you into some stunning but isolated locations where your hire car will never go. Many tours are by bus, others by 4WD or super-Jeep, and some by snowmobile, quad bikes or light aircraft. Most tours give you the option of tacking on adventure activities such as white-water rafting, horse riding and glacier hikes.

If you're planning to base yourself in Reykjavík and use day-long tours to explore the countryside, it's vital to note that you will spend (dare we say waste) a significant amount of time being transported from the capital out to the island's natural treasures. If a series of short tours is what you're after, you are better off choosing a base in the countryside closer to the attractions that pique your interest.

Diver at Silfra (p108), Þingvellir

There are hundreds of tour operators in Iceland, from small-scale to large. The following represent some of the largest tour operators around Iceland; check their websites to get a sense of what is on offer.

➡ **Air Iceland** (www.airiceland.is) Iceland's largest domestic airline runs a range of combination air, bus, hiking and 4WD day tours around Iceland from Reykjavík and Akureyri. Also runs tours to Greenland from Reykjavík.

➡ **Arctic Adventures** (www.adventures.is) Specialises in action-filled tours – from straight-up sightseeing to mountain biking, sea kayaking and even surfing.

➡ **Iceland Excursions** (www.grayline.is) A bus-tour operator with comprehensive day trips plus and plentiful activities, plus self-drive packages.

➡ **Icelandic Mountain Guides** (www. mountainguides.is) Offers an incredibly diverse range of hiking and mountain- or ice-climbing tours. It also provides equipment rental and private guiding for more serious climbers.

➡ **Reykjavík Excursions** (www.re.is) Reykjavík's most popular day-tour agency, with a comprehensive range of year-round tours.

➡ **Saga Travel** (www.sagatravel.is) Akureyri-based company offering diverse, innovative year-round program throughout the north.

WINTER WONDERLAND
....

Winter travel to Iceland is growing in popularity, and the appeal is clear: Northern Lights, nature at its most raw, and the chance to experience crazy diurnal rhythms. It's a great option if summer crowds (and prices) don't appeal.

It's true that daylight hours are limited (in early January, Reykjavik has around 4½ hours of daylight; by early February that's increased to seven hours). But city life goes on as normal, and opportunities for outdoor adventure are great: frozen waterfalls, snow-covered mountains, ice caves, and activities like skating, skiing, snowmobiling and snowshoeing. You'll probably need help to travel safely and to access the best of the outdoors during this time – day tours are perfect for this, and locals know the best winter secrets. See p67 for more on Reykjavík in winter.

Outdoor Activities

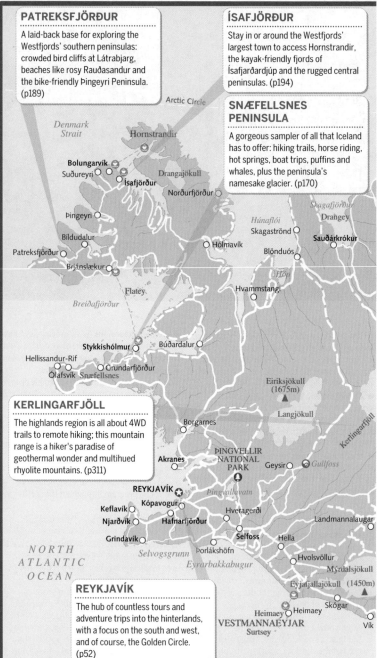

PATREKSFJÖRÐUR

A laid-back base for exploring the Westfjords' southern peninsulas: crowded bird cliffs at Látrabjarg, beaches like rosy Rauðasandur and the bike-friendly Þingeyri Peninsula. (p189)

ÍSAFJÖRÐUR

Stay in or around the Westfjords' largest town to access Hornstrandir, the kayak-friendly fjords of Ísafjarðardjúp and the rugged central peninsulas. (p194)

SNÆFELLSNES PENINSULA

A gorgeous sampler of all that Iceland has to offer: hiking trails, horse riding, hot springs, boat trips, puffins and whales, plus the peninsula's namesake glacier. (p170)

KERLINGARFJÖLL

The highlands region is all about 4WD trails to remote hiking; this mountain range is a hiker's paradise of geothermal wonder and multihued rhyolite mountains. (p311)

REYKJAVÍK

The hub of countless tours and adventure trips into the hinterlands, with a focus on the south and west, and of course, the Golden Circle. (p52)

Arctic Circle

Denmark Strait

Hornstrandir

Bolungarvík
Suðureyri
Ísafjörður
Drangajökull

Norðurfjörður

Þingeyri

Bildudalur

Patreksfjörður

Brjánslækur

Flatey

Breiðafjörður

Stykkishólmur   Búðardalur

Hellissandur-Rif
Ólafsvík   Grundarfjörður
Snæfellsnes

Borgarnes

Akranes

ÞINGVELLIR NATIONAL PARK

Geysir   Gullfoss

REYKJAVÍK
Kópavogur
Keflavík
Njarðvík   Hafnarfjörður

Grindavík

Hvetagerði

Selfoss   Hella

Þingvallavatn

NORTH ATLANTIC OCEAN

Selvogsgrunn   Þorlákshöfn

Eyrarbakkabugur

Hvolsvöllur

Landmannalaugar

Mýrdalsjökull

Eyjafjallajökull (1450m)

Skógar

Heimaey   Heimaey

VESTMANNAEYJAR
Surtsey

Vík

Skagafjörður

Drangey

Húnaflói
Skagaströnd

Sauðárkrókur

Hólmavík   Blönduós

Hóp

Hvammstangi

Eiríksjökull (1675m)

Langjökull

Kerlingarfjöll

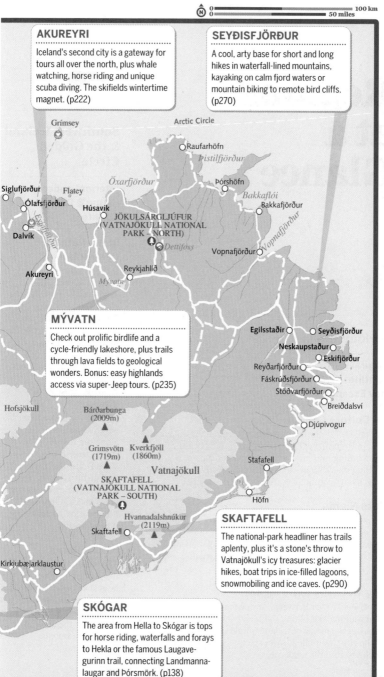

N 0 — 100 km
0 — 50 miles

AKUREYRI

Iceland's second city is a gateway for tours all over the north, plus whale watching, horse riding and unique scuba diving. The skifields wintertime magnet. (p222)

SEYÐISFJÖRÐUR

A cool, arty base for short and long hikes in waterfall-lined mountains, kayaking on calm fjord waters or mountain biking to remote bird cliffs. (p270)

Grímsey

Arctic Circle

Raufarhöfn

Þistilfjörður

Öxarfjörður

Þórshöfn

Siglufjörður Flatey

Bakkaflói

Ólafsfjörður Húsavík

Bakkafjörður

Dalvík

JÖKULSÁRGLJÚFUR
(VATNAJÖKULL NATIONAL
PARK – NORTH)

Dettifoss

Vopnafjörður

Vopnafjörður

Akureyri

Reykjahlíð

Mývatn

MÝVATN

Check out prolific birdlife and a cycle-friendly lakeshore, plus trails through lava fields to geological wonders. Bonus: easy highlands access via super-Jeep tours. (p235)

Egilsstaðir Seyðisfjörður

Neskaupstaður

Eskifjörður

Reyðarfjörður

Fáskrúðsfjörður

Stöðvarfjörður

Breiðdalsví

Hofsjökull Bárðarbunga
(2009m)

Djúpivogur

Grimsvötn Kverkfjöll
(1719m) (1860m)

Vatnajökull

Stafafell

SKAFTAFELL
(VATNAJÖKULL NATIONAL
PARK – SOUTH)

Höfn

Hvannadalshnúkur
(2119m)

Skaftafell

SKAFTAFELL

The national-park headliner has trails aplenty, plus it's a stone's throw to Vatnajökull's icy treasures: glacier hikes, boat trips in ice-filled lagoons, snowmobiling and ice caves. (p290)

Kirkjubæjarklaustur

SKÓGAR

The area from Hella to Skógar is tops for horse riding, waterfalls and forays to Hekla or the famous Laugave-gurinn trail, connecting Landmanna-laugar and Þórsmörk. (p138)

Regions at a Glance

Reykjavík

Cultural Hub
Nightlife
Easy Escapes

The Culture Capital

With miles of nothing but nature all around, Reykjavík is Iceland's confirmed repository of all things cultural, from winning museums and sleek gallery spaces to a sparkling music scene, a fat year-round festival calendar and a colourful guild of craftsfolk and designers.

White Nights

Reykjavík is notorious for its small but fierce nightlife. The best nights out start with coffee at one of the dozens of cafes, 'pre-gaming' drinks at a friend's apartment, an unholy pilgrimage between several beer bars, and a 4am sticky-floored romp to Top 40 beats.

Long Weekend Extravaganza

The perfect layover between Europe and North America: urban walking and biking tours take in the capital's top sights, but the magic of Iceland unfolds just beyond – and the city's well-oiled travel machine can instantly launch you into the wilderness.

p52

Southwest Iceland & the Golden Circle

Interior Landscapes
Hiking & Biking
Birdlife

In the Path of Destruction

If the southwest printed bumper stickers, they would say 'the further you go, the better it gets' – wander into the interior and you'll find vistas of mythic proportions sitting under the watchful glare of several grumbling volcanoes.

Hiking, Biking & Vikings

High in the hills a hiker's paradise awaits, while along the shores of the south coast and the Reykjanes Peninsula bikers will find plenty of trails. Toss in a smattering of Saga-era relics and you have endless itinerary fodder for every type of tourist.

For the Birds

The stunning Vestmannaeyjar archipelago has the largest colony of puffins in the world, and they offer a spirited welcome as they shoot over the arriving ferries like wobbly firecrackers.

p95

West Iceland

Technicolour
Landscapes
Sagas & History
Horse Riding

Infinite Islets

The Snæfellsnes Peninsula is a technicolour realm composed of exotic splashes of sere lava, green waterfall-cut meadows, Arctic-blue water, and a dazzling ice cap. One its most impressive vistas is Breiðafjörður – a bay reflecting cloud-filled skies and speckled with thousands of isles.

Sand, Stone & Sagas

The Snæfellsnes' long peninsular arm offers endless options for active souls – long coastal walks, hikes through lava fields, and rides on its infamous ice cap. History buffs can take a trip back in time: the west is often dubbed Sagaland for its rich Viking history.

Off Course by Horse

The southern shores of the Snæfellsnes Peninsula are among the best places to ride the small, tough Icelandic horse – follow the crests of sand or trot into the hills to find hidden geothermal sources.

p160

The Westfjords

Fjord Landscapes
Hornstrandir Hiking
Arctic Foxes

The End of the Line

On maps, the undulating coastline of the Westfjords makes the region resemble giant lobster claws snipping away at the Arctic Circle. The landscapes of this dramatic enclave of sea and stone inspire fables of magical, faraway lands.

Explore the Arctic

Sitting at the edge of the Arctic, its jagged peninsulas stretching north, Iceland's final frontier is the perfect setting for rugged mountain biking, sea kayaking, sailing and springtime skiing. Hornstrandir hiking reserve is the jewel in the crown.

Foxy Friends

Wild-maned horses rove throughout, but the main draws are the impressive bird cliffs dotting the region, and the fleet Arctic foxes scurrying between grassy hillocks. With pre-planning, you can volunteer to monitor Iceland's only native mammal.

p184

North Iceland

Changing Landscapes
Bumper Activities
Whale Watching

One With the Works

What landscapes *doesn't* north Iceland offer? There are offshore islands, lonely peninsulas, icy peaks, pastoral horse farms, belching mudpots, sleepy fishing villages, epic waterfalls, shattered lava fields, breaching whales...

The Active North

Horse riding is best in the northwest. Birdwatching around Lake Mývatn is world-class, but remote Langanes and Arctic Grímsey hold their own. Hike the northern reaches of Vatnajökull National Park, or ski Tröllaskagi.

Whale Wonderland

Seals inhabit Vatnsnes Peninsula; puffins and seabirds nest all over. Waterbirds take to Mývatn like ducks to water. The biggest draw lurks beneath: Húsavík is the whale-watching master; towns along western Eyjafjörður, including Akureyri, are its apprentice.

p207

East Iceland

Watery Landscapes
Activities
Wildlife

Fan-fjord-tastic

The Eastfjords' scenery is particularly dramatic around the northern fjord villages, backed by sheer-sided mountains etched with waterfalls. Inland, the scenic lake Lagarfljót (and the forest on its eastern shore) is ripe for exploration, as is the 1833m mountain Snæfell, part of Vatnajökull National Park.

On Land & Water

Kayaking the waters of Seyðisfjörður is a breathtaking highlight; mountain biking here is good for landlubbers. Birdwatching and horse riding at Húsey are first-rate. Trails in and around the fjords offer peak panoramas and hiking delights.

Puffins, Monsters, Reindeer

Wild reindeer roam the mountains, and Iceland's version of the Loch Ness monster calls Lagarfljót home. Birdlife is prolific, at the remote farms of Húsey and Skálanes, or the puffin-viewing platform at Borgarfjörður Eystri.

p258

Southeast Iceland

Ice Cap Landscapes
Glacier-top Activities
Birdlife

Glacial Glory

Containing glittering glaciers, toppling waterfalls, the iceberg-filled Jökulsárlón lagoon and Iceland's favourite walking area (Skaftafell), it's little wonder the southeast is among Iceland's most-visited regions. Contrasting this beauty is the stark grey sands of the eerie sandar.

Ice-Cap Endeavours

Various places offer ice climbing, glacier walks, snowmobiling, quad biking and hiking. Boat trips among the glacial lagoon 'bergs are in demand, you can do a little mountain biking in Skaftafell, or there's the underrated activity of cracking langoustine claws in Höfn.

Bountiful Birds, Scene-Stealing Seals

Seals are a photogenic addition to the camera-friendly waters of Jökulsárlón, while great skuas make their homes in the sandar and harass visiting humans and birds. Ingólfshöfði is over-run with nesting puffins and other seabirds.

p282

The Highlands

Lunar Landscapes
Isolation
Remote Hiking

Lunar Landscapes

This region is practically uninhabited – there are no towns or villages, only summertime huts and accommodation. NASA astronauts once trained here, and recent Holuhraun eruptions are adding a whole new dimension to ancient lava fields.

Barren Beauty

Touring the highlands will give you a new understanding of the word 'desolation'. The solitude is exhilarating, the views are vast. Some travellers are disappointed by the interior's ultrableakness and endless grey-sand desert, others are humbled by the sight of nature in its rawest form.

Hard-Core Hiking

It's immensely tough but equally rewarding to hike or bike interior routes. Kerlingarfjöll and the Askja region have first-class hiking; Hveravellir has hot springs. Many visitors may be happiest touring the sights from the comfort of a super-Jeep tour!

p307

On the Road

The Westfjords
p184

North Iceland
p207

West Iceland
p160

The Highlands
p307

East Iceland
p258

Reykjavík
p52

Southwest Iceland & the Golden Circle
p95

Southeast Iceland
p282

Reykjavík

POP 204,775

Best Places to Eat

➡ Dill (p82)

➡ Þrír Frakkar (p82)

➡ Snaps (p81)

➡ Sægreifinn (p80)

➡ Gló (p81)

Best Places to Stay

➡ Hótel Borg (p73)

➡ Reykjavík Residence (p77)

➡ Icelandair Hotel Reykjavík Marina (p74)

➡ KEX Hostel (p75)

➡ Room With A View (p75)

Why Go?

The world's most northerly capital combines colourful buildings, quirky, creative people, eye-popping design, wild nightlife and a capricious soul to devastating effect.

In many ways Reykjavík is strikingly cosmopolitan for its size. After all, it's merely a town by international standards, and yet it's loaded with excellent museums, captivating art, rich culinary choices, and funky cafes and bars. When you slip behind the shiny tourist-centric veneer (it *is* a great base for tours to the countryside) you'll find a place and a populace that mix aesthetic-minded ingenuity with an almost quaint, know-your-neighbours sense of community.

Add a backdrop of snow-topped mountains, churning seas and crystal-clear air, and you, like many visitors, may fall helplessly in love, returning home already saving to come back.

Road Distances (km)

	Reykjavík	Borgarnes	Ísafjörður	Akureyri	Egilsstaðir	Höfn
Borgarnes	74					
Ísafjörður	457	384				
Akureyri	389	315	567			
Egilsstaðir	698	580	832	265		
Höfn	459	519	902	512	247	
Vík	187	246	630	561	511	273

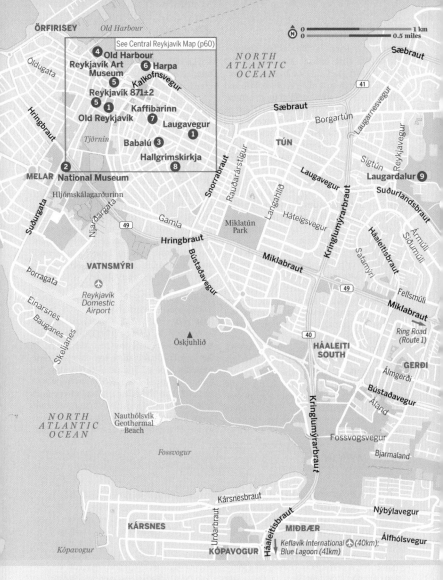

Reykjavík Highlights

1 Explore lovely **Old Reykjavík** (p54) and shop **Laugavegur** (p87)

2 Peruse the fascinating **National Museum** (p65)

3 Join the cool cats sipping coffee at quirky cafes such as **Babalú** (p80)

4 Hit the museums or take a whale-watching tour at the **Old Harbour** (p58)

5 Immerse yourself in art or archaeology at the **Reykjavík Art Museum** (p55) or **Reykjavík 871±2** (p54)

6 Enjoy a performance or simply explore **Harpa** (p59), the capital's twinkling concert hall

7 Join the *djammið* (p86), a wild pub crawl through tiny nightspots such as **Kaffibarinn** (p84)

8 Survey the city from the heights of the modernist steeple of **Hallgrímskirkja** (p59)

9 Enjoy a soak in the **Laugardalur** (p65) geothermal pool

History

Ingólfur Arnarson, a Norwegian fugitive, became the first official Icelander in AD 871. The story goes that he tossed his *öndvegissúlur* (high-seat pillars) overboard, and settled where the gods washed them ashore. This was at Reykjavík (Smoky Bay), which he named after steam rising from geothermal vents. According to 12th-century sources, Ingólfur built his farm near modern-day Aðalstræti (where excavations have unearthed a Viking longhouse).

Reykjavík remained just a simple collection of farm buildings for centuries. In 1225 an important Augustinian monastery was founded on the offshore island of Viðey, although this was destroyed during the 16th-century Reformation.

In the early 17th century the Danish king imposed a crippling trade monopoly on Iceland, leaving the country starving and destitute. In a bid to bypass the embargo, local sheriff Skúli Magnússon, the 'Father of Reykjavík', created weaving, tanning and wool-dyeing factories – the foundations of the city – in the 1750s.

Reykjavík really boomed during WWII, when it serviced British and US troops stationed at Keflavík. The capital grew at a frenetic pace until it took a slamming in the credit crisis of 2008. Today, with continuously rising visitor numbers and endlessly innovative locals, central Reykjavík has exploded with renewed growth.

☉ Sights

The compact city centre contains most of Reykjavík's attractions, which range from interesting walking and shopping streets to excellent museums and picturesque lakeside or seaside promenades. Around the outskirts you find the places that Reykavikers go to relax.

◉ Old Reykjavík & North of Tjörnin

★**Old Reykjavík**　　　　　　NEIGHBOURHOOD
(Map p60) With a series of sights and interesting historic buildings, the area dubbed Old Reykjavík is the heart of the capital, and the focal point of many historic walking tours. The area is anchored by Tjörnin, the city-centre lake, and sitting between it and Austurvöllur park to the north are the Raðhús (city hall) and Alþingi (parliament).

★**Reykjavík 871±: The Settlement Exhibition**　　　　　MUSEUM
(Map p60; ☑411 6370; www.reykjavikmuseum. is; Aðalstræti 16; adult/child Ikr1300/free; ☉9am-8pm, English-language tour 11am Mon, Wed & Fri Jun-Aug) This fascinating archeological ruin/museum is based around a 10th-century Viking longhouse unearthed here from 2001 to 2002, and the other settlement-era finds from central Reykjavík. It imaginatively combines technological wizardry and archaeology to give a glimpse into early Icelandic life.

REYKJAVÍK IN...

One Day

Start with a walk around the Old Reykjavík (p54) quarter near Tjörnin then peruse the city's best museums, such as the impressive National Museum (p65), Reykjavík Art Museum (p55) or Reykjavík 871±2 (p54). In the afternoon, wander up arty Skólavörðustígur to the immense Hallgrímskirkja (p59). For a perfect view, take an elevator up the tower, then circle down to stroll Laugavegur, the main shopping drag.

Sit for people-watching and drinks at Bravó (p84) or Tíú Droppar (p84) then head to dinner. Many of the more lively restaurants – including Vegamót (p82) and Kex (p84) – turn into party hangouts at night. On weekends, join Reykjavík's notorious pub crawl (p86). Start at perennial favourite Kaffibarinn (p84) or beer-lovers' Kaldi (p84), then tag along with locals to the latest drinking holes.

Two Days

After a late night out, enjoy brunch at Bergsson Mathús (p78), Grái Kötturinn (p81) or Laundromat Café (p78). Then head down to the Old Harbour (p58) for a wander, museums or a whale-watching tour (p68). For hot springs, gardens, beautiful Cafe Flóra and cool art, head to Laugardalur (p65) in the afternoon.

Book ahead if you'd like a swanky evening at one of Reykjavík's top Icelandic restaurants, such as Dill (p82) or Þrír Frakkar (p82), then hit Loftið (p84), one of the new breed of cocktail bars. Alternatively, catch a show at Harpa (p59) or a movie at Bíó Paradís (p86).

The museum's name comes from the estimated date of the tephra layer beneath the longhouse, but don't miss the fragment of **boundary wall**, at the back of the museum that is older still (and the oldest man-made structure in Reykjavík).

Among the captivating hi-tech displays are interactive multimedia tables explaining the area's excavations, a wrap-around panorama showing how things would have looked at the time of the longhouse, and a space-age-feeling panel that allows you to steer through different layers of the longhouse construction. Artefacts range from great awk bones to fish oil lamps and an iron axe. The latest finds from ancient workshops near the current Alþingi include a spindle whorl inscribed with runes.

The museum is a joint ticket with open-air Árbæjarsafn (p66), 4km east of the centre.

★ Reykjavík Art Museum — ART MUSEUM

(Listasafn Reykjavíkur; www.artmuseum.is; adult/child Ikr1300/free) The excellent Reykjavík Art Museum is split over three well-done sites: the large, modern downtown Hafnarhús (p55) focusing on contemporary art; Kjarvalsstaðir (p63), in a park just east of Snorrabraut, and displaying rotating exhibits of modern art; and Ásmundarsafn (p66), a peaceful haven near Laugardalur for viewing sculptures by Ásmundur Sveinsson.

One ticket is valid at all three sites, and if you buy after 3pm you get a 50% discount should you want a ticket the next day.

➡ ★ Reykjavík Art Museum – Hafnarhús — ART MUSEUM

(Map p60; ☑590 1200; www.artmuseum.is; Tryggvagata 17; ⊙10am-5pm Fri-Wed, to 8pm Thu) Reykjavík Art Museum's Hafnarhús is a marvellously restored warehouse converted into a soaring steel-and-concrete exhibition space. Though the well-curated exhibitions of cutting-edge contemporary Icelandic art change frequently (think installations, videos, paintings and sculpture), you can always count on an area with the comic-book-style paintings of Erró (Guðmundur Guðmundsson), a political artist who has donated several thousand works to the museum. The **cafe** has great harbour views.

★ Tjörnin — LAKE

(Map p60) This placid lake at the centre of the city is sometimes locally called the Pond. It echoes with the honks and squawks of more than 40 species of visiting birds, including swans, geese and Arctic terns; feeding

---

> ### ➊ THREE FOR THE PRICE OF ONE
>
> ➡ The Reykjavík Art Museum ticket covers all three of its sites.
>
> ➡ The National Gallery ticket also covers nearby Ásgrímur Jónsson Collection and further-afield Sigurjón Ólafsson Museum.

---

the ducks is a popular pastime for the under-fives. Pretty sculpture-dotted parks such as **Hljómskálagarður** (Map p56) line the southern shores, and their paths are much used by cyclists and joggers. In winter, hardy souls strap on ice skates and turn the lake into an **outdoor rink**.

Austurvöllur — PARK

(Map p60) Grassy Austurvöllur was once part of first-settler Ingólfur Arnarson's hay fields. Today it's a favourite spot for cafe lounging or lunchtime picnics and summer sunbathing next to the Alþingi, and is sometimes used for open-air concerts and political demonstrations. The **statue** in the centre is of Jón Sigurðsson, who led the campaign for Icelandic independence.

Alþingi — HISTORIC BUILDING

(Parliament; Map p60; www.althingi.is; Kirkjustraeti) **FREE** Iceland's first parliament, the Alþingi, was created at Þingvellir in AD 930. After losing its independence in the 13th century, the country gradually won back its autonomy, and the modern Alþingi moved into this current basalt building in 1881; a stylish glass-and-stone annexe was completed in 2002. Visitors can attend **sessions** (four times weekly October to May; see website for details) when parliament is sitting.

Raðhús — NOTABLE BUILDING

(Map p60; Vonarstræti; ⊙8am-7pm Mon-Fri, noon-6pm Sat & Sun) **FREE** Reykjavík's waterside Raðhús is a beautifully positioned postmodern construction of concrete stilts, tinted windows and mossy walls rising from Tjörnin. Inside there's one of the city's top cafe-restaurants, Við Tjörnina (p79), and an interesting 3D map of Iceland.

Reykjavík Museum of Photography — MUSEUM

(Ljósmyndasafn Reykjavíkur; Map p60; ☑411 6390; www.photomuseum.is; Tryggvagata 15, 6th fl, Grófarhús; ⊙noon-7pm Mon-Thu, to 6pm

Reykjavík

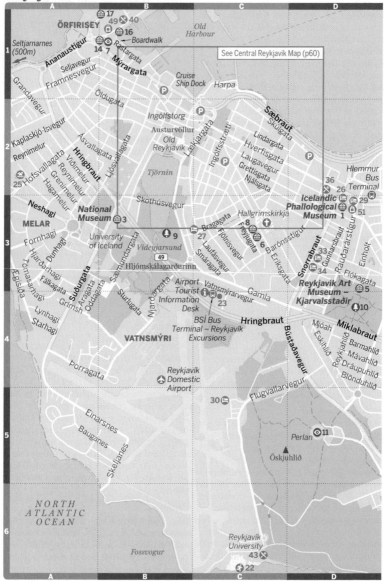

Fri, 1-5pm Sat & Sun) FREE This gallery room above Reykjavík City Library is worth a visit for its top-notch exhibitions of regional photographers. If you take the lift up, descend by the stairs, which are lined with vintage black-and-white photos.

Volcano House MUSEUM
(Map p60; ☎555 1900; www.volcanohouse.is; Tryggvagata 11; adult/child Ikr1990/500; ☺hourly 10am-9pm) This modern theatre with a lava exhibit in the foyer screens a 55-minute pair of films about the Vestmannaeyjar (West-

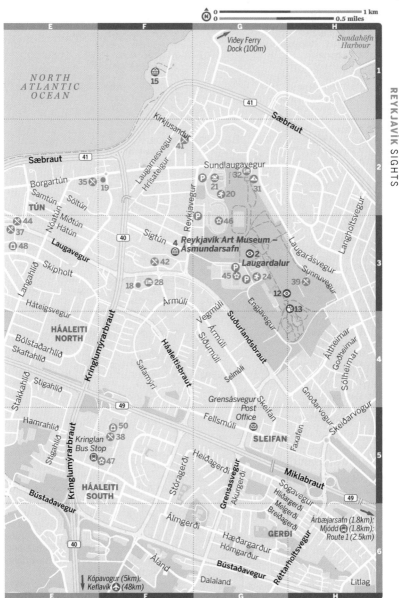

man Islands) volcanoes and Eyjafjallajökull. They show in German once daily in summer.

Dómkirkja   CHURCH
(Map p60; www.domkirkjan.is; Kirkjustræti; ☺10am-4.30pm Mon-Fri, mass 11am Sun) Iceland's main

cathedral, Dómkirkja is a modest affair, but it played a vital role in the country's conversion to Lutheranism. The current building (built in the 18th century and enlarged in 1848) is small and perfectly proportioned, with a plain wooden interior animated by glints of gold.

Reykjavík

◎ Old Harbour

★**Old Harbour**   NEIGHBOURHOOD
(Map p60; Geirsgata) Largely a service harbour until recently, the Old Harbour has blossomed into a hot spot for tourists, with several museums, volcano and Northern Lights films and worthwhile restaurants. Whale-watching and puffin-viewing trips depart from the pier. Photo ops abound with views of fishing boats, Harpa concert hall and snowcapped mountains beyond. At the time of writing there was also a freestyle summertime children's **play area** with giant spindles and ropes, along Mýrargata.

Víkin Maritime Museum   MUSEUM
(Víkin Sjóminjasafnið; Map p56; ☎517 9400; www.sjominjasafn.is; Grandagarður 8; adult/child Ikr1200/free; ☉10am-5pm Jun–mid-Sep, 11am-5pm Tue-Sun mid-Sep–May) Based appropriate-

ly in a former fish-freezing plant, this small museum celebrates the country's seafaring heritage, focusing on the trawlers that transformed Iceland's economy. Your ticket also allows you aboard coastguard ship *Óðinn* by guided tour (11am, 1pm, 2pm and 3pm, reduced hours during winter, closed January and February). The boat is a veteran of the 1970s Cod Wars, when British and Icelandic fishermen came to blows over fishing rights in the North Atlantic.

The on-site **cafe** (Grandagarður 8; snacks Ikr800-1890) offers relaxing views of the boat-filled harbour, and has a great sunny-weather terrace. The museum is planning a facelift by 2016, at which point it may close for renovations.

Saga Museum   MUSEUM
(Map p56; ☎511 1517; www.sagamuseum.is; Grandagarður 2; adult/child Ikr2000/800; ☉9am-

6pm) The endearingly bloodthirsty Saga Museum is where Icelandic history is brought to life by eerie silicon models and a multilanguage soundtrack with thudding axes and hair-raising screams. Don't be surprised if you see some of the characters wandering around town, as moulds were taken from Reykjavík residents (the owner's daughters are the Irish princess and the little slave gnawing a fish!).

There's also a room for posing in Viking dress, a documentary about the making of the museum (look for *Icelandic Idol*–winner Kalli Bjarni in the audience) and cafe Kol og Salt.

Whales of Iceland MUSEUM
(Map p56; ☑571 0077; www.whalesoficeland.com; Fiskislóð 23-25; adult/child Ikr2800/1550; ☺10am-7pm May-Sep, to 6pm Oct-Apr) Ever stroll beneath a blue whale? This brand-new museum houses full-sized models of the 23 whales found off Iceland's coast. The largest museum of this type in Europe, it also displays models of whale skeletons and has a cafe and gift shop.

Aurora Reykjavík EXHIBITION
(Northern Lights Centre; Map p56; ☑780 4500; www.aurorareykjavik.is; Grandagarður 2; adult/child Ikr1600/1000; ☺9am-9pm) Learn about the classical tales explaining the Northern Lights, and the scientific explanation, then watch a 35-minute surround-sound panoramic HD re-creation of Icelandic auroras.

Cinema at Old Harbour Village No 2 FILM
(Map p60; ☑899 7953; www.thecinema.is; Geirsgata 7b; adult/child Ikr1500/750) A tiny theatre perches at the top of one of the rehabbed Old Harbour warehouses. Nature films include volcanoes (Hekla, Eyjafjallajökull, Westmann Islands), the creation of Iceland, Þingvellir and the Northern Lights, and are mostly shown in English with occasional German screenings. See schedule online.

☉ Laugavegur & East of Tjörnin

★Hallgrímskirkja CHURCH
(Map p60; ☑510 1000; www.hallgrimskirkja.is; Skólavörðustígur; tower adult/child Ikr700/100; ☺9am-9pm Jul & Aug, to 5pm Sep-Jun) Reykjavík's immense white-concrete church (1945–86), star of a thousand postcards, dominates the skyline, and is visible from up to 20km away. Get an unmissable view of the city by taking an elevator trip up the 74.5m-high tower. In contrast to the high

drama outside, the Lutheran church's interior is quite plain. The most eye-catching feature is the vast 5275-pipe organ installed in 1992. The church's size and radical design caused controversy, and its architect, Guðjón Samúelsson (1887–1950), never saw its completion.

The columns on either side of the tower represent volcanic basalt, part of Samúelsson's desire to create a national architectural style. Out front, gazing proudly into the distance is a statue (Map p60) of the Viking Leifur Eiríksson, the first European to discover America. Designed by Alexander Stirling Calder (1870–1945), it was a present from the USA on the 1000th anniversary of the Alþing (National Assembly) in 1930.

Hallgrímskirkja (pronounced *hatl*-krims-*kirk*-ya) was named after poet Reverend Hallgrímur Pétursson (1614–1674), who wrote Iceland's most popular hymn book: *Passíusálmar* (Passion Hymns).

From mid-June to mid-August, hear choir concerts (admission Ikr2000) at noon on Wednesday, and organ recitals at noon on Saturday and some Thursdays (admission Ikr1700), and on Sunday at 5pm (admission Ikr2500). Services are held Sunday at 11am, with a small service Wednesday at 8am. There is an English service the last Sunday of the month at 2pm.

★Harpa CULTURAL BUILDING
(Map p60; ☑box office 528 5050; www.harpa.is; Austurbakki 2; ☺box office 9am-6pm Mon-Fri, 10am-6pm Sat & Sun) With its ever-changing facets glistening on the water's edge, Reykjavík's sparkling Harpa concert hall and cultural centre is a beauty to behold. In addition to

---

ⓘ REYKJAVÍK CITY CARD

Reykjavík City Card (24/48/72hr Ikr2900/3900/4900) Offers free admission to Reykjavík's municipal swimming/thermal pools and to most of the main galleries and museums, plus discounts on some tours, shops and entertainment. Also gives free travel on the city's Strætó buses and on the ferry to Viðey. The card is available at the tourist office, some travel agencies, 10-11 supermarkets, HI hostels and some hotels.

Kids enter free at many museums, but there is a reduced-priced Children's City Card (Ikr1000/2000/3000 for 24/48/72 hours) covering other services.

Central Reykjavík

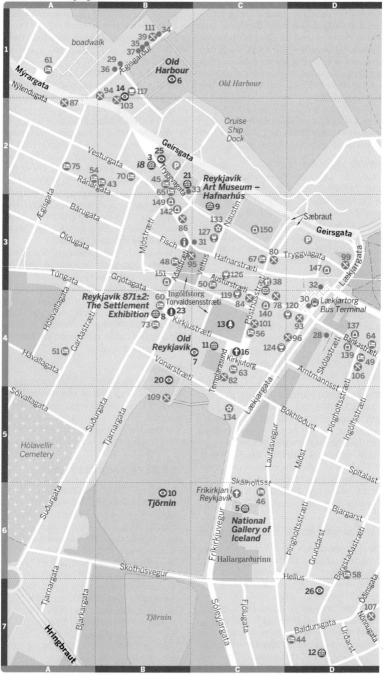

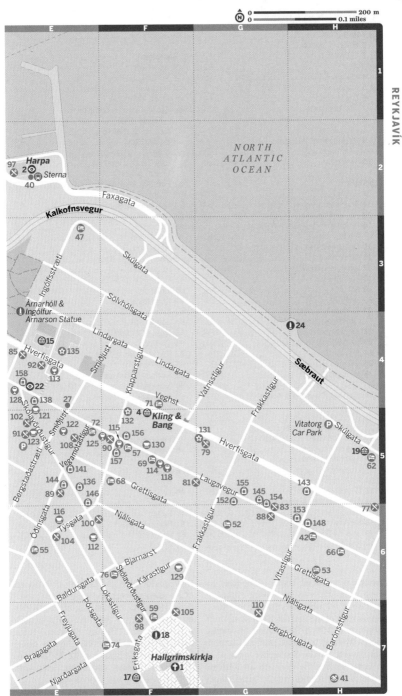

0 — 200 m
0 — 0.1 miles

NORTH
ATLANTIC
OCEAN

Harpa
97
2
40 Sterna

Faxagata

Kalkofnsvegur

47

Skúlgata

Ingólfsstræti

Sölvhólsgata

Árnarhóll &
Ingólfur
Arnarson Statue

15
135

85 Hverfisgata
92
158 113
22
128 138 27
102 121
91 123 108 125 90
144 136 146
89
116
Tysgata 100
104 112
55

Smiðjust

Lindargata

Lindargata

Klapparstígur

Veghst
71
132 4 **Kling &
Bang**
122 72 115 156
131
130
157 57 79
69 114 118
81
68 Grettisgata
141

Njálsgata

Bjarnarst

Óðinsgata

Tysgata

Skólavörðustígur
Bergstaðastræti

Vegamótastígur

Vatnsstígur

Frakkastígur

24

Sæbraut

Vitatorg
Car Park

Skúlgata
19
62

Hverfisgata

Laugavegur
155
152 145 154
88 83
52
143
153 148
42
66
77

Bjarnarst

76 Kárastígur
129

Skólavörðustígur
Lokastígur

Baldursgata

Þórsgata

Bragagata

Freyjugata

59
98 105

18
Hallgrímskirkja

74
17
Eiriksgata

Njarðargata

Frakkastígur

Grettisgata

110

Njálsgata

Vitastígur

Bergþórugata

Barónsstígur

53

41

1

Central Reykjavík

a season of top-notch shows (some free), it's worth stopping by to explore the shimmering interior with harbor vistas, or take a 45-minute **tour** of the hall (Ikr1500; 9am, 11am, 1.30pm and 3.30pm daily June to August, 3.30pm Monday to Friday, 11am and 3.30pm Saturday and Sunday September to May).

Harpa dazzles the eye with an intricate lattice of convex and concave glass panels that sparkle at night like the switchboard of an alien spaceship. Designed by Danish firm Henning Larsen Architects, Icelandic firm Batteríið Architects, and Danish-Icelandic artist Olafur Eliasson, Harpa opened in 2011. The lobby houses design boutiques and a branch of **12 Tónar** music store, and gourmet restaurant Kolabrautin (p82) perches on the upper level.

★ Reykjavík Art Museum –
Kjarvalsstaðir   ART MUSEUM
(Map p56; ☎517 1290; www.artmuseum.is; Flókagata, Miklatún Park; adult/child Ikr1300/free;
⊙10am-5pm) The angular glass-and-wood
Kjarvalsstaðir, which looks out onto Miklatún
Park (Map p56), is named for Jóhannes Kjarval (1885–1972) one of Iceland's most popular
classical artists. He was a fisherman until his

crew paid for him to study at the Academy of
Fine Arts in Copenhagen, and his wonderfully
evocative landscapes share space alongside
changing installations of mostly Icelandic
20th-century paintings.

★ Icelandic
Phallological Museum   MUSEUM
(Hið Íslenzka Reðasafn; Map p56; ☎561 6663; www.
phallus.is; Laugavegur 116; adult/child Ikr1250/free;

⊙10am-6pm) Oh, the jokes are endless here, but though this unique museum houses a huge collection of penises, it's actually very well done. From pickled pickles to petrified wood, there are 283 different members on display, representing all Icelandic mammals and beyond. Featured items include contributions from sperm whales and a polar bear, miniscule mouse bits, silver castings of each member of the Icelandic handball team and a single human sample – from deceased mountaineer Páll Arason.

The acquisition of Arason's 'specimen' was the subject of odd-ball documentary, *The Final Member* (2012). Five other donors-in-waiting have already promised to bequeath their manhood (signed contracts are mounted on the wall). Quirky sidenote: all displays are translated into Esperanto. No credit cards.

★ **National Gallery of Iceland** MUSEUM
(Listasafn Íslands; Map p60; www.listasafn.is; Fríkirkjuvegur 7; adult/child Ikr1000/free; ⊙10am-5pm Tue-Sun Jun-Aug, 11am-5pm Sep-May) This pretty stack of marble atriums and spacious galleries overlooking Tjörnin offers ever-changing exhibits drawn from the 10,000-piece collection. The museum can only exhibit a small sample at any time; shows range from 19th- and 20th-century paintings by Iceland's favourite sons and daughters (including Jóhannes Kjarval and Nína Sæmundsson) to sculptures by Sigurjón Ólafsson and others. The museum ticket also covers entry to the Ásgrímur Jónsson Collection (p64) and Sigurjón Ólafsson Museum (p66).

Ásgrímur Jónsson Collection ART MUSEUM
(Map p60; ☑515 9625; www.listasafn.is; Bergstaðastræti 74; adult/child Ikr1000/free; ⊙2-5pm Tue, Thu & Sun mid-May–mid-Sep, 2-5pm Sun mid-Sep–Nov & Feb–mid-May) Iceland's first professional painter, Ásgrímur Jónsson (1876–1958), was the son of a farmer. He lived and worked here, and you can visit his former atelier to see his work incorporating folk tales and Icelandic nature.

Einar Jónsson Museum ART MUSEUM
(Map p60; ☑561 3797; www.lej.is; Eiriksgata; adult/child Ikr1000/free; ⊙1-5pm Tue-Sun Jun–mid-Sep, 1-5pm Sat & Sun mid-Sep–Nov & Feb-May) Einar Jónsson (1874–1954) is one of Iceland's foremost sculptors, famous for intense symbolist works. Chiselled representations of Hope, Earth and Death burst from basalt cliffs, weep over naked women and slay dragons. Jónsson designed the building, which was built between 1916 and 1923, when this empty hill was the outskirts of town. It also contains his austere penthouse flat and studio, with views over the city.

The **sculpture garden** (Map p56; Freyjugata) FREE behind the museum contains 26 bronzes, in the shadow of Hallgrímskirkja.

Culture House ART MUSEUM
(Þjóðmenningarhúsið; Map p60; www.thjodminjasafn.is; Hverfisgata 15; adult/child Ikr1000/free; ⊙11am-5pm) At the time of writing this museum was being reimagined as a collaboration between the National Museum, National Gallery and four other organisations as a study of the artistic heritage of Iceland from Settlement to today. Slated to open by early 2015.

REYKJAVÍK'S ART GALLERIES

Reykjavík has many small contemporary art galleries, and local designers often open shops.

Kling & Bang (Map p60; ☑696 2209; www.this.is/klingogbang; Hverfisgata 42; ⊙2-6pm Thu-Sun) Perennially cutting-edge young artists' exhibition space is a favourite with locals.

i8 (Map p60; ☑551 3666; www.i8.is; Tryggvagata 16; ⊙11am-5pm Tue-Fri, 1-5pm Sat) This gallery represents some of the country's top modern artists, many of whom show overseas as well.

Gallerí Fold (Map p56; ☑551 0400; www.myndlist.is; Rauðarárstígur 14-16; ⊙10am-5pm Mon, to 6pm Tue-Fri, 11am-5pm Sat, noon-5pm Sun) Large Icelandic art dealer and auction house.

ASÍ Art Museum (Map p56; ☑511 5353; www.listasafnasi.is; Freyjugata 41; ⊙1-5pm Tue-Sun) Owned by the Icelandic Confederation of Labour, and showing 20th-century Icelandic art from its collection as well as rotating contemporary art.

NÝLO (Nýlistasafnið – The Living Art Museum; Map p60; ☑551 4350; www.nylo.is; Skúlgata 28; ⊙by appointment noon-5pm Tue-Fri) Emerging and established contemporary artists. Also holds occasional live music or theatre.

Volcano Show   FILM
(Red Cross Cinema; Map p60; ☑ 845 9548; Hellusund 6a; admission Ikr1500; ⊙ twice daily) Eccentric eruption-chaser Villi Knudsen is the cinematographer and presenter of this film show in a little theatre in an outbuilding on a residential street (not to be confused with Volcano House; p56). Some are captivated by Villi and his films about 50 years of Icelandic volcanoes (eg images of the town Heimaey being crushed by molten lava), although some footage is a bit old and wobbly, so it's not for everyone.

Sun-Craft   MONUMENT
(Map p60; Sæbraut) Reykjavík is littered with fascinating sculptures, but it's Jón Gunnar Árnason's ship-like *Sun-Craft* sculpture that seems to catch visitors' imaginations. Scooping in a skeletal arc along the seaside, it offers a photo shoot with snowcapped mountains in the distance.

◉ South of the Centre

★ National Museum   MUSEUM
(Þjóðminjasafn Íslands; Map p56; ☑ 530 2200; www.nationalmuseum.is; Suðurgata 41; adult/child Ikr1500/free, audioguide Ikr300; ⊙ 10am-5pm May–mid-Sep, 11am-5pm Tue-Sun mid-Sep–Apr; ꘗ 1, 3, 6, 12 or 14) This superb museum displays artefacts from Settlement to the modern age. Exhibits give an excellent overview of Iceland's history and culture, and the audioguide adds loads of detail. The strongest section describes the Settlement Era – including how the chieftains ruled and the introduction of Christianity – and features swords, drinking horns, silver hoards and a powerful little bronze figure of Thor. The priceless 13th-century **Valþjófsstaðir church door** is carved with the story of a knight, his faithful lion and a passel of dragons.

Upstairs, collections span from 1600 to today and give a clear sense of how Iceland struggled under foreign rule and finally gained independence. Simple, homely objects utilise every scrap; check out the gaming pieces made from cod ear bones, and the wooden doll that doubled as a kitchen utensil.

Free English tours run at 11am on Wednesdays, Saturdays and Sundays from mid-May to September.

Perlan   NOTABLE BUILDING
(Map p56; www.perlan.is; ⊙ 10am-10pm, cafe to 9pm; ꘗ 18) **FREE** The mirrored dome of Perlan covers huge geothermal-water tanks

on Öskjuhlíð hill, about 2km from the city centre. The wrap-around viewing deck offers a tremendous 360-degree panorama of Reykjavík and the mountains. There's a cafe (often busy with tour groups), so in a downpour you can admire the same views over coffee. The top of the dome contains the high-end Perlan dinner restaurant.

Two **artificial geysers** keep small children enthralled. Numerous **walking and cycling trails** criss-cross the hillside; one path leads down to Nauthólsvík beach (p67).

◉ Laugardalur

★ Laugardalur   NEIGHBOURHOOD, PARK
(Map p56; ꘗ 2, 14, 15, 17 or 19) Laugardalur encompasses a verdant stretch of land 4km east of the centre. It was once the main source of Reykjavík's hot-water supply: it translates as 'Hot-Springs Valley', and in the park's centre you'll find relics from the old wash house. The park is a favourite with locals for its huge swimming complex (p67), fed by the geothermal spring, alongside a spa, cafe (p83), skating rink, botanical gardens, sporting and concert arenas and a kids' zoo/entertainment park.

In the surrounding residential streets you'll find Frú Lauga farmers market (p83), Reykjavík Art Museum – Ásmundarsafn (p66) and waterfront Sigurjón Ólafsson Museum (p66).

⭐**Reykjavík Art Museum –**
Ásmundarsafn   ART MUSEUM
(Ásmundur Sveinsson Museum; Map p56; ☑553
2155; www.artmuseum.is; Sigtún; adult/child
Ikr1300/free; ⊙10am-5pm May-Sep, 1-5pm Oct-
Apr; ☐2, 14, 15, 17 or 19) There's something
immensely playful about Ásmundur Sveinsson's (1893–1982) vast collection of sculptures housed in the studio and museum he
designed: the rounded, white Ásmundarsafn. Monumental concrete creations fill the
garden outside, while the peaceful haven of
the interlocking cupolas showcases works in
wood, clay and metals, some of them mobile,
exploring themes as diverse as folklore and
physics. Soaring skylights and white marble
give way to a fun dome, where the acoustics
create the museum's strict 'must-sing policy'.

Getting into the spirit of things, the council later added an igloo-shaped bus stop in
front.

Reykjavík Botanic Gardens   GARDENS
(Grasagarður; Map p56; www.grasagardur.is; Laugardalur; ⊙10am-10pm May-Sep, to 5pm Oct-Apr) `FREE`
These gardens contain more than 5000 varieties of subarctic plant species, colourful seasonal flowers, the wonderful in-season Café
Flóra (p83), and lots of bird life (particularly
grey geese and their fluffy little goslings).

Reykjavík Zoo & Family Park   ZOO
(Fjölskyldu og Húsdýragarðurinn; Map p56;
☑575 7800; www.mu.is; Laugardalur; adult/
child Ikr750/550, 1-/10-/20-ride ticket Ikr270/
2300/4300; ⊙10am-6pm Jun–mid-Aug, to 5pm
mid-Aug–May; ⊕) This childrens' park in
Laugardalur gets packed with happy local
families on sunny days. Don't expect lions
and tigers; think seals, foxes and farm animals in simple enclosures, and tanks of
cold-water fish. The family park section is
jolly, with a miniracetrack, child-size bull-
dozers, a giant trampoline, boats and kids'
fairground rides.

Sigurjón Ólafsson Museum   ART MUSEUM
(Listasafn Sigurjóns Ólafssonar; Map p56; ☑553
2906; www.lso.is; Laugarnestangi 70; adult/
child Ikr500/free; ⊙2-5pm Tue-Sun Jun–mid-
Sep, 2-5pm Sat & Sun mid-Sep–Nov & Feb-May)
Sculptor Sigurjón Ólafsson (1908–82) used
this peaceful seafront building as a studio.
Now it showcases his varied, powerful work:
portrait busts, driftwood totem poles and
abstract pillars. A salty ocean breeze blows
through the modern rooms, and the area is
interlaced with waterfront paths with clear

views back to Reykjavík. There are **classical
concerts** (Ikr2000) on Tuesdays in July at
8.30pm. The museum is a branch of the National Gallery; the same ticket covers both.
Buses 5 and 12 pass nearby.

👁 **Outskirts**

Seltjarnarnes   NEIGHBOURHOOD
(www.seltjarnarnes.is; ☐11) Seltjarnarnes, 5km
west of Reykjavík centre, is a coastal area
that feels a world away. With 106 visiting
species recorded, the offshore island of
Grótta is a haven for birdwatching and
boasts a red-and-white lighthouse. It is accessible at low tide, but is closed May to July
to protect nests. Get here along the pretty
coastal path, popular with walkers, joggers
and cyclists.

Waves rush in to the lava-strewn
beach, the air has that salt-sea tang, fish-
drying racks sit by the shore and Arctic terns
scream overhead. There are also super views
across the fjord to Esja (909m).

Árbæjarsafn   MUSEUM
(www.reykjavikmuseum.is; Kistuhylur 4, Ártúnsholt;
adult/child Ikr1300/free; ⊙10am-5pm Jun-Aug,
by tour only 1pm Mon-Fri Sep–May; ⊕; ☐12, 19
or 24) About 20 quaint old buildings have
been transported from their original sites
to open-air Árbæjarsafn, 4km east of the
city centre beyond Laugardalur. Alongside 19th-century homes are a turf-roofed
church and various stables, smithies, barns
and boathouses – all very picturesque. There
are summer arts-and-crafts demonstrations
and domestic animals, and it's a great place
for kids to let off steam. Tickets also provide
entry to Reykjavík 871±2 (p54).

🏃 **Activities**

You can rent bikes (p68) to zoom along lake
or seaside trails, or pop into hot-pots all over
town. Reykjavík is also the main hub for activity tours to a range of destinations beyond
the city limits.

Reykjavík's naturally hot water is the
heart of the city's social life (as in many Icelandic towns); children play, teenagers flirt,
business deals are made and everyone catch-
es up on the latest gossip at the baths. Volcanic heat keeps the temperature at a mellow 29°C, and most baths have *heitir pottar*
(hot-pots): Jacuzzi-like pools kept a toasty
37°C to 42°C. Admission at the public baths
costs Ikr600 for adults (Ikr130 for children);
bring towels and bathing suits – or rent

REYKJAVÍK IN WINTER

It's bitterly cold and the sun barely rises, but there are advantages to wintery Iceland. The major joy is watching the glory of the Northern Lights. Many bus tours continue to operate in winter, taking you to frozen white Gullfoss, caves full of icicles, and snow-covered mountains. There're also snowmobiling, back-country skiing and heli-skiing tours.

The **Reykjavík Skating Hall** (Skautahöllin; Map p56; ☑ 588 9705; www.skautaholl.is; Múlavegur 1, Laugardalur; adult/child Ikr850/600, skate hire Ikr400; ☺ noon-3pm Mon-Wed, noon-3pm & 5-7.30pm Thu, 1-7.30pm Fri, 1-6pm Sat & Sun Sep-Apr) in Laugardalur throws open its doors September to April. Some people also skate on Tjörnin when it freezes.

Skiing

The downhill ski season runs November to April, depending on snowfall. The three ski areas close to Reykjavík (Bláfjöll, Hengill and Skálafell) are managed by **Skíðasvæði** (Map p60; ☑ 530 3000; www.skidasvaedi.is; Pósthússtræti 3-5).

Bláfjöll (☑ 561 8400; day pass adult/teen/child Ikr3100/1200/800; ☺ 2-9pm Mon-Fri, 10am-5pm Sat & Sun) Iceland's premier ski slopes at 84-sq-km Bláfjöll have 14 lifts, and downhill, cross-country and snowboarding facilities. You can hire gear at reasonable rates. Bláfjöll is about 25km southeast of Reykjavík on Rte 417, just off Rte 1. A shuttle bus (Ikr1500 return) leaves from the Mjódd bus station once daily in season – check with **Skíðasvæði** (www.skidasvaedi.is) for departure times.

them on-site. For further information and more locations, see www.spacity.is.

Reykjavíkers get very upset by dirty tourists in their clean, chemical-free pools. To avoid causing huge offence, you must wash thoroughly without a swimsuit before hopping in.

★**Laugardalslaug**   GEOTHERMAL POOL, HOT-POT
(Map p56; Sundlaugavegur 30a, Laugardalur; adult/child Ikr600/130, suit/towel rental Ikr800/550; ☺ 6.30am-10pm Mon-Fri, 8am-10pm Sat & Sun; ♿) One of the largest pools in Iceland, with the best facilities: Olympic-sized indoor pool and outdoor pools, seven hot-pots, a saltwater tub, steam bath and a curling 86m water slide.

★**Laugar Spa**   SPA, GYM
(Map p56; ☑ 553 0000; www.laugarspa.is; Sundlaugavegur 30a, Laugardalur; day pass Ikr4990; ☺ 6am-10.30pm Mon-Fri, 8am-10pm Sat, to 8pm Sun) Super-duper Laugar Spa, next door to the Laugardalslaug geothermal pool, offers myriad ways to pamper yourself. There are six themed saunas and steam rooms, a sea-water tub, a vast and well-equipped gym, fitness classes, and beauty and massage clinics with detox wraps, facials and hot-stone therapies. The spa is 18+ and entry includes access to Laugardalslaug.

The spa's **cafe** serves smoothies (Ikr750) and a healthy daily special (Ikr1690). There is Icelandic-language childcare.

Árbæjarlaug   GEOTHERMAL POOL, HOT-POT
(☑ 411 5200; Fylkisvegur 9, Elliðaárdalur; ☺ 6.30am-10pm Mon-Thu, to 8pm Fri, 9am-8pm Sat & Sun; ♿; ☐ 19) About 10km southeast of the centre, slickly designed Árbæjarlaug is known as the best family pool: it's half inside and half outside, and lots of watery amusements (slides, waterfalls and massage jets) keep kids entertained.

Sundhöllin   GEOTHERMAL POOL, HOT-POT
(Map p60; ☑ 411 5350; Barónsstígur 16; ☺ 6.30am-10pm Mon-Thu, to 8pm Fri, 8am-4pm Sat, 10am-6pm Sun; ♿) Reykjavík's oldest swimming pool (1937), designed in art-deco-style by architect Guðjón Samúelsson, is smack in the centre and offers the only indoor pool within the city, plus Hallgrímskirkja views from the decks.

Nauthólsvík Geothermal Beach   BEACH
(Map p56; ☑ 511 6630; www.nautholsvik.is; admission summer/winter free/Ikr500, valuables storage summer/winter Ikr200/free, towel or swimsuit rental Ikr300; ☺ 10am-7pm mid-May–mid-Aug, reduced hours mid-Aug–mid-May; ♿; ☐ 19) The small sandy arc of Nauthólsvík Geothermal Beach, on the edge of the Atlantic, gets packed on sunny summer days. During opening hours in summer only, geothermal water is routed in to keep the lagoon between 15°C and 19°C. There is also a busy hot-pot (38°C year-round), a snack bar and changing rooms.

Vesturbæjarlaug   GEOTHERMAL POOL, HOT-POT
(Map p56; ☑411 5150; Hofsvallagata; ☉6.30am-10pm Mon-Thu, to 8pm Fri, 9am-8pm Sat & Sun; ☑; ☑11, 13 or 15) Within walking distance of the centre, Vesturbæjarlaug has a 25m pool, steam, sauna and four hot-pots.

🕮 Courses

★ Creative Iceland   CRAFT COURSE
(www.creativeiceland.is) Get involved with graphic design, cooking, arts, crafts, music... you name it! This service hooks you up with local creative people offering workshops in their art or craft.

Icelandic Culture and Craft Workshops   CRAFT COURSE
(☑566 8822; www.cultureandcraft.com; courses from Isk11,900) Half-day knitting workshops using Icelandic wool.

🕼 Tours

Walking, bike and bus tours are the main way to take in the city. Whale-watching, puffin-spotting and sea-angling trips allow a jaunt off-shore.

As lovely as the capital's sights are, though, Reykjavík is also the main hub for tours to amazing landscapes and activities around Iceland. Those without wheels, time or the desire to travel the countryside independently can use Reykjavík as a cosmopolitan base for all forms of tours from super-Jeeps and buses to horse riding, snowmobiling and heli-tours. If you have time, though, head out on your own.

City Tours

The tourist office has loads of free maps and self-guided walking tour brochures, from *Literary Reykjavík* to *The Neighbourhood of the Gods*, and info on guided walking tours. The hardcore can buy the more in-depth *Reykjavík Walks* (2014) by Guðjón Friðriksson at local bookshops.

There are several downloadable free smartphone apps, including two by **Locatify** (www.locatify.com).

★ Literary Reykjavík   WALKING TOUR
(Map p60; www.bokmenntaborgin.is; Tryggvagata 15; ☉3pm Thu Jun-Aug) **FREE** Part of the Unesco City of Literature initiative, literary walking tours of the centre start at the main library and include the Dark Deeds tour focusing on crime fiction. There is also a downloadable *Literary Reykjavík* app.

Free Walking Tour Reykjavik   WALKING TOUR
(Map p60; www.freewalkingtour.is; ☉noon & 2pm Jun-Aug, reduced in winter) **FREE** One-hour, 1.5km walking tour of the centre, starting at the little clock tower on Lækjartorg Sq.

Haunted Iceland   WALKING TOUR
(Map p60; www.hauntedwalk.is; adult/child Ikr2500/free; ☉8pm Sat-Thu Jun–mid-Sep) Ninety-minute tour including folklore and ghost-spotting, departing from the main tourist office.

City Sightseeing Reykjavík   BUS TOUR
(☑580 5400; www.city-sightseeing.com; adult/child Ikr3500/1750; ☉hourly 10am-6pm Jun–mid-Sep) Hop-on-hop-off bus taking in all the major sights around town; starts at Harpa.

Cycling Tours

Reykjavík Bike Tours   CYCLING TOUR
(Map p60; ☑694 8956; www.icelandbike.com; Ægisgarður 7, Old Harbour; bike rental per 4hr from Ikr3500, tours from Ikr5500; ☉9am-5pm Jun-Aug, reduced hours Sep-May) Outfitter rents bikes and offers tours of Reykjavík and the countryside. For example: Classic Reykjavík (2½ hours, 7km); Coast of Reykjavík (2½ hours, 18km); and Golden Circle and Bike (eight hours, 25km of cycling in 1½ hours). It also offers Reykjavík segway (Ikr10,000) and walking (from Ikr20,000) tours.

Bike Company   BICYCLE RENTAL, CYCLING TOUR
(Map p60; ☑590 8550; www.bikecompany.is; Bankastræti 2; bike rental per 5hr Ikr3500; ☉9am-5pm Mon-Fri) Bicycle tours and hire, with other outlets at Icelandic Travel Market and Trip travel agencies.

Whale-Watching, Fishing & Boat Tours

Although the northern waters near Akureyri and Húsavík are known for whale watching, Reykjavík is still a great option.

Prices start around Ikr8500 for a two- to three-hour trip, Ikr4250 for kids. Tours generally run all year with more departures in the warmer months, which is also prime viewing season. If you don't spot whales many outfits offer vouchers to come back and try again.

Several companies also offer **sea-angling** (adult/child from Ikr11,500/5750) and **puffin-viewing** trips (adult/child from Ikr5000/2500), though you'll often see puffins on small islets while whale watching.

Elding Adventures at Sea   WHALE WATCHING
(Map p60; ☑519 5000; www.whalewatching. is; Ægisgarður 5; ☉harbour kiosk 8am-9pm) 🖋

The city's most established and ecofriendly outfit, with an included whale exhibition and refreshments sold onboard. Elding also offers angling and puffin-watching trips, combo tours, and runs the ferry to Viðey.

Special Tours BIRDWATCHING, WHALE WATCHING
(Map p60; ☑560 8800; www.specialtours.is; Ægisgarður 13; ☉harbour kiosk 8am-8pm) The smallest, fastest boat in the fleet of operators, used for sea angling and whale watching (20 minutes to reach the prime viewing spot). It uses a smaller vessel for puffin tours, and offers multiple combo tours.

Fish Partner FISHING TOUR
(☑571 4545; www.fishpartner.com; day tours from Ikr23,900) Offers fishing day tours and a huge array of custom and multiday possibilities:

sea angling, trout fishing, volcano fishing, heli-fishing.

Reykjavík By Boat BOAT TOUR
(Map p60; ☑841 2030; www.reykjavikbyboat.is; Ægisgarður 11; adult/child Ikr4000/1600) Offers a 1½-hour trip on a small wooden boat from the Old Harbour, around Engey islet (with a puffin colony), to Viðey and back.

Reykjavík Sea Adventures BIRDWATCHING, FISHING TOUR
(Map p60; ☑775 5777; www.seaadventures.is; Ægisgarður 3) Sea-angling (mid-April to September) and puffin tours (mid-May to August).

Sea Safari BIRDWATCHING, WHALE WATCHING
(Map p60; ☑861 3840; www.seasafari.is; Ægisgarður 9) One- to 1½-hour whale watching (Ikr15,000) or puffin tour in a Zodiac.

REYKJAVÍK TOURS

CHOOSING YOUR DAY TRIP

If you have more than a day in Reykjavík, get out into Iceland's incredible natural beauty. Popular day-tour destinations get swamped in high season, but if you have the luxury of a rental car you can visit at off hours or head to lesser-stomped grounds. You can also use the Straetó, Sterna, Reykjavík Excursions and Trex buses (p90) for transport, instead of tours.

Golden Circle With three beloved attractions – **Þingvellir** (p106) (beautiful site of the original outdoor parliament and the continental rift), **Geysir** (huge eponymous geyser area; p110) and **Gullfoss** (enormous waterfalls; p111) – the Golden Circle is the ultimate and much-marketed taste of Icelandic countryside. You can combine a Golden Circle tour with virtually any activity from quad-biking to caving and rafting. Full-day trips generally depart around 8.30am returning around 6pm; shorter trips leave around noon, returning at 7pm. In summer there are evening trips (7pm to midnight). In your own car it takes about four hours.

Blue Lagoon (p98) Hugely popular, with crowds to match. Many day trips from Reykjavík tie in a visit to the lagoon. It's also seamless to visit on your journey to/from Keflavík International Airport. In high season it's best at night.

Snæfellsnes Peninsula (p170) Less-travelled, gorgeous portion of the country that you can add to the popular Golden Circle loop or visit on its own. Expect short hikes along crunchy lava fields, snowmobiling on the glacier, seaside villages and whale-watching or boat tours to offshore puffin-inhabited islets.

South Coast (p114) A wild assortment of geological wonders including active volcanoes, glorious hikes and shivery ice caps. Tours run year-round from Reykjavík and regional hubs.

Þórsmörk (p146) Though beautiful back-country volcanic valley Þórsmörk has loads of hiking routes that take more time, you should be able to squeeze in one short walk on a super-Jeep tour. In summer you can also go by bus arriving around midday and returning in the early afternoon.

Landmannalaugar (p140) For day trippers, a (very short) visit to the geothermal Landmannalaugar region can only be done on a super-Jeep tour or bus, and you'll spend most of the day on the road. Jeep stops along the way, though, often include Hekla. Beware: Landmannalaugar is packed in summer.

Jökulsárlón (p297) This incredible glacial lagoon is quite far from the capital, making it one of the longest day trips. You'll arrive when the lagoon is at its most crowded. If possible, it'd be better to overnight on the south coast and go to the lagoon in the off hours.

Iceland Angling Travel FISHING TOUR
(☑ 867 5200; www.icelandangling.com) Day trips and custom holidays for fishing of all sorts around Iceland.

Bus & Activity Tours

A day-long bus tour from Reykjavík is one of the most cost-effective, efficient ways to see spectacular natural wonders if you're on a short holiday. They're also good if you want to combine sightseeing with activities such as snowmobiling, horse riding, rafting or scuba diving. And keep in mind that many Icelandic buses are outfitted for the back country, with high suspensions and rugged tyres.

Tours need to be booked in advance and may be cancelled if there are insufficient numbers or if the weather turns bad. Expect to pay from Ikr9000 for a basic Golden Circle or Reykjanes Peninsula tour, Ikr11,600 for a South Shore tour, Ikr39,900 for diving near Þingvellir and Ikr31,900 for a 16-hour trip to Vatnajökull National Park and Jökulsárlón glacial lagoon. Young children generally travel free or at discounted rates.

There seem to be zillions of operators these days, offering even more itineraries and combinations than ever. We list just a sample; check online for their full slate of offerings.

Reykjavík Excursions BUS TOUR
(Kynnisferðir; Map p56; ☑ 580 5400; www.re.is; Vatnsmýrarvegur 10, BSÍ Bus Terminal) The most popular bus-tour operator (with large groups) has an enormous booklet full of

---

① TOUR TIPS
....

➡ Many companies offer all sorts of tours: whale watching, bus tours, super-Jeep tours, city walks and/or combo-tours that include many of the activities listed here. We just break out a few options: check online with each company for their full menus.

➡ All tour times, descriptions and prices are as of the time of writing. Things are changing fast in Iceland. Check online.

➡ Many operators offer hotel pickup/drop-off.

➡ If you want to head far afield, plan some nights outside of Reykjavík so you don't spend loads of back-and-forth time on buses.

➡ Bring binoculars and a telephoto lense for whale watching or puffin-spotting.

---

summer and winter programs. Extras include horse riding, snowmobiling and themed tours tying in with festivals. Also offers 'Iceland on Your Own' bus tickets and passports for transport.

Iceland Excursions BUS TOUR
(Gray Line Iceland; Map p60; ☑ 540 1313; www.grayline.is; Hafnarstræti 20) Bus-tour operator with comprehensive day trips that often combine destinations and activities such as white-water rafting and horse riding. Book online for the best prices; expect large groups.

Sterna BUS TOUR
(Map p60; ☑ 551 1166; www.sterna.is; Harpa Concert Hall; ☉ 7am-6.30pm) Straight-up bus tours around Iceland, with various transport passports for independent travellers.

Arctic Adventures ADVENTURE TOUR
(Map p60; ☑ 562 7000; www.adventures.is; Laugavegur 11; ☉ 8am-10pm) With young and enthusiastic staff, this company specialises in action-filled tours: kayaking, rafting, horse riding, quad-biking, glacier walking and so on. It has a booking office with gear shop Fjallakofinn (p89) in central Reykjavík.

Icelandic Mountain Guides ADVENTURE TOUR
(☑ 587 9999; www.mountainguides.is; Stórhöfði 33) This full-action outfit specialises in mountaineering, trekking, ice climbing and the like. It also markets itself as 'Iceland Rovers' for its super-Jeep tours.

Gateway to Iceland BUS TOUR
(☑ 534 4446; www.gatewaytoiceland.is) Gets great reviews from independent travellers because its minibus tours are smaller than the mass market ones, and for its interesting guides.

Bustravel BUS TOUR
(☑ 511 2600; www.bustravel.is) Very popular among the hostelling crowd for informative driver-guides. Groups are large, prices low.

Go Green BUS TOUR
(☑ 694 9890; www.gogreen.is) 🍃 Small, high-end operator that uses methane-powered vehicles and follows environmentally conscious practices.

Icelandic Knitter CULTURAL TOUR
(☑ 661 6230; www.icelandicknitter.com) Designer Hélène Magnússon offers knitting tours that take in spinning, wool work, design, folklore and hiking/sightseeing, in partnership with Icelandic Mountain Guides.

Extreme Iceland ADVENTURE TOUR
(☑588 1300; www.extremeiceland.is) Host of bus, super-Jeep, caving, quad-bike, Northern Lights and snowmobiling tours.

Iceland Horizons BUS TOUR
(☑866 7237; www.icelandhorizon.is) Smaller minibus operator with only 14 seats; readers have rated its three tours highly.

Guðmundur Jónasson Travel BUS TOUR
(Map p56; ☑511 1515; www.gjtravel.is; Borgartún 34) Tried-and-true day excursions along the Ring Road and into the highlands.

Green Energy Travel BUS TOUR
(☑453 6000; www.get.is) New small-group operator; hopes to switch to methane gas or biodiesel fuels once more established.

Season Tours TOUR
(☑863 4592; www.seasontours.is) Huge range of guided tours (including city excursions) that explore the landscape, history, Viking settlement etc.

Super-Jeep & Supertruck Tours

Super-Jeep tours offer small groups (four to six people) a more customised experience. You'll reach your destinations a lot faster, and you can get out further into wild terrain. Prices are correspondingly higher than bus trips (eg Þórsmörk for Ikr36,900, Eyjafjallajökull for Ikr39,900).

Icelandic Mountain Guides (p70) also offers super-Jeep trips. The tourist office has brochures for loads more.

Mountaineers of Iceland ADVENTURE TOUR
(☑580 9900; www.mountaineers.is) Excellent, knowledgeable guides, many with experience on the national rescue team. Lots of super-Jeep, super-truck and snowmobiling tours, including heli-snowmobiling.

Superjeep.is JEEP TOUR
(☑660 1499; www.superjeep.is) Full range of super-Jeep trips with all the add-ons (snowmobiling, quad-biking etc).

Into the Wild JEEP TOUR
(☑866 3301; www.intothewild.is) Full roster of super-Jeep excursions, from the Golden Circle to Eyjafjallajökull and Landmannalaugar.

Caving & Lava Tunnel Tours

Exploring the wild underground world of Iceland's volcanic terrain is a wonderful way to experience the geology of the island. Many lava tubes and caverns are seen by tour only. Main sites from Reykjavík include Reyk-

janes Peninsula and upper Borgarfjörður. **Arctic Adventures, Icelandic Mountain Guides** and many bus and super-Jeep tour operators lead caving expeditions. Figure around Ikr15,900 for a three-hour excursion.

Inside the Volcano ADVENTURE TOUR
(☑863 6640; www.insidethevolcano.com; admission Ikr37,000; ☉mid-May–Sep) This one-of-a-kind experience takes adventure-seekers into a perfectly intact 4000-year-old magma chamber. Hike 50 minutes to the crater and a mining cart lowers groups of four 120m into the bottom of a vase-shaped chasm that once gurgled with hot lava. Lights are dim and time inside is limited. Participants must be over 12 years old.

Horse-Riding Tours

Trotting through lava fields on an Icelandic horse under the midnight sun is an unforgettable experience. Horse farms around Reykjavík and the south offer tours for all ages and experiences, and can collect you from your hotel. Most operate year-round.

Stables offer everything from 90-minute outings to multiday tours, and you can combine riding with other activities, such as visiting the Golden Circle or Blue Lagoon. Some offer guesthouse accommodation. Plan on Ikr9000 to Ikr12,000 for a 90-minute ride.

Eldhestar HORSE RIDING
(☑480 4800; www.eldhestar.is; Vellir, Hveragerði) Located near Hveragerði, Eldhestar is one of the most established riding outfits in Iceland. Trots take place on the surrounding grasslands.

Íshestar HORSE RIDING
(☑555 7000; www.ishestar.is; Sörlaskeið 26, Hafnarfjörður) One of the largest, oldest stables in the country with well-organised trots through crumbling lava fields.

Laxnes HORSE RIDING
(☑566 6179; www.laxnes.is; Mosfellsbær) Small, family-owned Laxnes is run by an older couple whose nephews take newbies out for relaxed trots. On the way out to Þingvellir. Also offers combo tours.

Íslenski Hesturinn HORSE RIDING
(☑434 7979; www.theicelandichorse.is; Surtlugata 3) With experienced local guides, this outfit near the capital takes special care to match you with a horse that suits your capabilities; small groups.

DAY TRIP TO GREENLAND

You can grab a day tour to Greenland from Reykjavík since it takes just under two hours to fly there. In summer, **Air Iceland** (www.airiceland.is) offers regular tours to Kulusuk in east Greenland (from Ikr104,000). Hidden in a tapestry of icy whites and cool blues, on a mountainous island, Kulusuk has only 250 inhabitants. The village of brightly coloured wood-box houses and its icy bay reveal themselves to day trippers during the stunning walk over from the airport. Although the traditional Greenlandic drum dance demo is a tad kitsch, the rest of the experience is like one giant dream sequence.

Greenland Travel (☑ +45 7873 5069; www.greenland-travel.com) offers multiday tours.

Viking Horses   HORSE RIDING
(☑ 660 9590; www.vikinghorses.is; Almannadalsgata 19) Run by a family, this stable is popular for its higher-end (Ikr14,900) small-group rides around Hólmsheiði hill and surrounding lakes.

Reykjavík Riding Center   HORSE RIDING
(☑ 477 2222; www.reykjavikridingcenter.is; Brekknaás 9) Located near Reykjavík's main equestrian centre, this outift takes small groups (no more than 10) of all levels around the Rauðholar (Red Hills), and offers a midnight sun tour.

Glacier Walks & Ice-Climbing Tours

Crunching across a rugged glacier is a thrill. Tours take visitors to Sólheimajökull (p148), the most accessible glacial tongue of massive Mýrdalsjökull. Glacier walks run year-round; ice climbing runs September to April. For ice climbing you have to be able to pull your own weight (literally, up). Figure on Ikr20,900 for a short glacier walk and Ikr29,900 for ice climbing. Prices are significantly lower if you base yourself near the glacier and go with local guides.

Reykjavík-based operators are Arctic Adventures (p70) and Icelandic Mountain Guides (p70).

Quad-Biking Tours

Quad-biking tours explore the lava fields of Reykjanes Peninsula. Many of the main bus/activity tour operators (eg Arctic Adventures, Reykjavík Excursions) offer quad-bike options. Plan for an hour to cost around Ikr10,900 per person travelling as a duo, Ikr14,400 if you are solo and Ikr42,000 for a six-hour safari.

ATV Adventures   QUAD-BIKE TOUR
(☑ 857 3001; www.atv4x4.is; Tangasund 1, Grindavík; per person from Ikr9900) Huge array of quad-bike and buggy tours and combinations, all around Reykjanes Peninsula, with pickup from Keflavík or Reykjavík. Driving licence required. Tour leaders can also drive the ATV.

Quad Safari   QUAD-BIKE TOUR
(☑ 414 1533; www.quad.is; Mosfellsbær) Pricey ATV outings in the hills near Mosfellsbær. Evening rides give sunset and city-light views.

Rafting & Speedboating Tours

The Hvítá river, located along the Golden Circle, is the top spot for white-water rafting and speedboating near Reykjavík. Fun for the family, these trips run from Reykholt (p112), but offer Reykjavík pickups.

Scuba Diving & Snorkelling Tours

Iceland has some of the most unique snorkelling and scuba diving in the world. The following operators offer dives at Silfra, a fissure filled with crystalline water near Þingvellir on the Golden Circle. Advance booking is essential; outfitters can pick you up in town or meet you on-site. In June and July it's possible to do a midnight dive.

Plan for about Ikr19,990 for a snorkel session and Ikr34,990 for two scuba dives. PADI certification is required for scuba.

Some of the bigger activity-tour companies also offer dive options.

Dive.is   DIVING
(☑ 578 6200; www.dive.is; 2 dives at Þingvellir Ikr34,990) The oldest and most established operator in Iceland, with snorkeling, diving and combo tours.

Scuba Iceland   DIVING
(☑ 892 1923; www.scuba.is; 2 dives at Þingvellir Ikr34,990) Good reputation for small groups, and offers dives at Silfra, Strýtan (stalagmites and geothermal chimneys) and a wreck in Eyjafjörður (two-day tour Ikr60,000).

Snowmobiling Tours

Though most opportunities to jump on a snowmobile lie far beyond the capital, there are several operators that go to nearby

Langjökull. (There are no day trips to Mýrdalsjökull proper, and day trips to Vatnajökull are done by air.) One hour with two riders, costs about Ikr19,000 per rider; for solo riders it's Ikr24,000. The best operators in Reykjavík are Mountaineers of Iceland (p71) and Arctic Adventures (p70).

Northern Lights Tours

During winter, most bus and activity companies offer Northern Lights trips taking onlookers into the countryside to escape urban light interference when viewing the aurora borealis. Trips last around four hours – usually from 10pm to 2am. Since there's no guarantee when you'll see these magnificent curtains of light, or where they'll be, we recommend spending a night or two in the countryside to maximise viewing possibilities.

If you're not in Iceland during aurora season, you can have a multimedia immersion at Aurora Reykjavík (p59).

Air Tours

Larger budgets offer the possibility of day trips and tours by air to far-flung or remote destinations such as Lake Mývatn, the Westfjords, the steaming earth of the south coast and highlands, Vestmannaeyjar, and even Greenland.

Eagle Air Iceland FLIGHT TOUR
(Map p56; ☑ 562 4200; www.eagleair.is; Reykjavík Domestic Airport) Eagle Air Iceland offers sightseeing flights over volcanoes and glaciers. Also five set routes from Reykjavík: Vestmannaeyjar (Westman Islands); Höfn; Húsavík; and in the Westfjords, Bíldudalur and Gjögur.

Air Iceland FLIGHT TOUR
(☑ 570 3030; www.airiceland.is; Reykjavík Domestic Airport) Iceland's largest domestic airline runs a wide range of combination air, bus, hiking, rafting, horse-riding, whale-watching and glacier day tours around Iceland from Reykjavík and Akureyri. It also runs day tours to Greenland and the Faroe Islands from Reykjavík.

Atlantsflug FLIGHT TOUR
(☑ 854 4105; www.flightseeing.is; Reykjavík Domestic Airport) Offers flightseeing tours from Reykjavík, Bakki Airport and Skaftafell. From Reykjavík Domestic Airport you can overfly Eyjafjallajökull crater or Reykjanes Peninsula, or take a day-trip with tours around Skaftafell and Jökulsárlón glacial lagoon.

Reykjavík Helicopters FLIGHT TOUR
(☑ 589 100; www.rehe.is; Reykjavík Domestic Airport; tours from Ikr69,000) Helicopter trips all over: including Glymur (Iceland's tallest waterfall) and volcanoes such as Eyjafjallajökull and Hekla.

Norðurflug FLIGHT TOUR
(☑ 562 2500; www.helicopter.is) Helicopters fly over Reykjavík, or zip to craters, waterfalls, glaciers and beyond. Their multitude of trips go as far as the Westfjords, Mývatn and Askja.

★ Festivals & Events

Reykjavíkers celebrate a host of festivals with gleeful enthusiasm. For a month-by-month list, see p24.

🛏 Sleeping

Reykjavík has loads of accommodation choices, with hostels, midrange *gistiheimili* (guesthouses) and simple business-class hotels galore, but top-end boutique hotels and apartments seem to be opening daily. June through August accommodation books out entirely; reservations are essential. Everything is priced like any major European capital: high. Plan for hostels and camping if you're looking to save. Short-term apartment rentals are often the best value. Most places open year-round and many offer discounts or variable pricing online, especially from October to April.

Most guesthouses are in converted houses, so rooms often share bathrooms, kitchens and TV lounges. Some offer sleeping-bag accommodation.

🏛 Old Reykjavík & North of Tjörnin

Salvation Army Guesthouse HOSTEL **€**
(Map p60; ☑ 561 3203; www.guesthouse.is; Kirkjustræti 2; dm/s/d from Ikr3500/9500/13,900; ☺ Jun-Aug; ☞) Simple, clean rooms come in loads of sizes. Step outside and the whole of Reykjavík is at your feet. Linen Ikr900.

★ Hótel Borg LUXURY HOTEL **€€€**
(Map p60; ☑ 551 1440; www.hotelborg.is; Pósthússtræti 9-11; d from Ikr43,600; @☞) This historic hotel dates from 1930 and is now tricked out with super-smart beige, black and cream decor, parquet floors, leather headboards and flatscreen Bang & Olufsen TVs. The tower suite is two stories of opulence with panoramic views. At the time of

writing, a huge renovation-expansion had shuttered gourmet Borg restaurant, slated to reopen early 2015 under chef Völundur Völundarson; his bistro **Nora Magasin** is next door.

Kvosin Downtown Hotel   APARTMENT €€€
(Map p60; ☑ 571 4460; www.kvosinhotel.is; Kirkjutorg 4; apt incl breakfast Ikr43,200-65,000; ☜) Firmly a part of the luxury apartment wave, these superbly located mod pads range from 'tiny' to 'larger than life' and come with a dollop of humour. Nespresso machines and all the mod cons are standard; breakfast is included at nearby Bergsson Mathús (p78).

Hótel Reykjavík Centrum   HOTEL €€€
(Map p60; ☑ 514 6000; www.hotelcentrum.is; Aðalstræti 16; d & apt Ikr25,600-69,400; ☜) Mezzanines and a glass roof unite two historic central buildings, giving this hotel a spry, light feel. Its 89 neatly proportioned rooms and apartments all have mini-refrigerators, satellite TVs and coffee-making gear. Prices vary wildly online depending on date.

City Center Hotel   HOTEL €€€
(Map p60; ☑ 571 1400; www.citycenterhotel.is; Austurstræti 6; d from Ikr30,800; @☜) Modern and easy on the eyes, this makes a straightforward shack-up in the town centre, with Micro Bar (p84) downstairs for all your beer-drinking needs. Fifth-floor rooms have balconies, all have TVs and mini-fridges.

CenterHótel Plaza   HOTEL €€€
(Map p60; ☑ 595 8550; www.plaza.is; Aðalstræti 4; d incl breakfast from Ikr34,000; @☜) A full service hotel in an enviably quaint and central spot in the Old Reykjavík quarter, this fresh-faced member of the CenterHótel chain has business-oriented rooms with polished wooden floors, and great views from the higher levels.

Radisson Blu 1919 Hotel   HOTEL €€€
(Map p60; ☑ 599 1000; www.radissonblu.com; Pósthússtræti 2; d from Ikr40,400; @☜) Although part of a large chain, this is a boutique place with plenty of style. Attractive rooms sport large beds and flatscreen TVs, and up the carved iron stairwells lie large, comfy suites.

🛏 Old Harbour

★**Reykjavík Downtown Hostel**   HOSTEL €
(Map p60; ☑ 553 8120; www.hostel.is; Vesturgata 17; 4-/10-bed dm Ikr7900/5700, d with/without

bathroom Ikr23,800/20,700; @) Squeaky clean and well run, this effortlessly charming hostel gets such good reviews that it regularly lures large groups and the non-backpacker set. Enjoy friendly service, guest kitchen and excellent rooms. Discount Ikr700 for HI members.

Guesthouse Butterfly   GUESTHOUSE €€
(Map p60; ☑ 894 1864; www.butterfly.is; Ránargata 8a; d with/without bathroom Ikr22,500/17,850; ☉mid-May–Aug; ☜) On a quiet, central residential street, you can't miss Butterfly's flamboyant mural. Neat, simply furnished rooms, a guest kitchen, and friendly Icelandic-Norwegian owners make you feel right at home. The top floor has two self-contained apartments with kitchen and balcony (Ikr26,960).

Álfhóll Guesthouse   GUESTHOUSE €€
(Map p60; ☑ 898 1838; www.alfholl.is; Ránargata 8; s/d/tr without bath Ikr13,500/18,500/23,000, d Ikr23,000, apt Ikr27,000-34,000; ☉mid-May–Aug; ☜) This tidy guesthouse, with a name that translates to Elf House, has clean, modern rooms with washbasins and crisp, colourful bedspreads.

Three Sisters   APARTMENT €€
(Þrjár Systur; Map p60; ☑ 565 2181; www.threesisters.is; Ránargata 16; apt from Ikr24,500; ☉mid-May–Aug; @☜) A twinkly-eyed former fisherman runs the Three Sisters, a corner townhouse in old Reykjavík, now divided into eight studio apartments. Comfy beds are flanked by old-fashioned chairs and state-of-the-art flatscreen TVs. Each room has a kitchen.

★**Icelandair Hotel
Reykjavík Marina**   BOUTIQUE HOTEL €€€
(Map p60; ☑ 560 8000; www.icelandairhotels.is; Mýrargata 2; d Ikr27,800-35,800; @☜) This large design hotel on the Old Harbour is adding a whole new wing. Captivating art, cool nautical-chic design elements, up-to-the-second mod cons and clever ways to conserve space make small rooms winners overall. Attic rooms on the harbour side have excellent sea views. The lively lobby sports a live satellite feed to sights all over Iceland, and the happening Slippbarinn (p85).

Ocean Comfort Apartments   APARTMENT €€€
(Map p60; ☑ 571 7555; www.oceancomfort.is; Tryggvagata 18b; apt Ikr31,000-54,000; ☜) Part of a new building complex a block back from the waterfront, and smack in the centre of

town, these apartments embody their name: ocean views and comfortable family living. Each has a balcony and laundry, plus all the mod cons; the ocean view apartments start at Ikr37,000.

Black Pearl   APARTMENT €€€
(Map p60; ☑ 527 9600; www.blackpearlreykjavik. com; Tryggvagata 18 & 18c; apt Ikr61,200-155,400; P@⊙) One of the newest entries on Reykjavík's high-end scene, these fully kitted-out apartments fill several black towers just back from the waterfront. Full-service reception provides personal attention (valet, laundry, childcare), but spacious, cleanly decorated apartments that sleep two to six offer independence. Think king-sized beds, design furniture and balconies, some with water views.

🛏 Laugavegur & East of Tjörnin

★KEX Hostel   HOSTEL €
(Map p60; ☑ 561 6060; www.kexhostel.is; Skúlagata 28; 4-/16-bed dm Ikr6900/3900, d with/without bathroom Ikr28,500/19,700; @⊙) An unofficial headquarters of backpackerdom and popular local gathering place, KEX is a megahostel with heaps of style (think retro Vaudeville meets rodeo) and sociability. Overall it's not as prim as the other hostels – and bathrooms are shared by many – but KEX is a perennial favourite for its friendly vibe and booming restaurant-bar with water views and interior courtyard.

Hlemmur Square   HOSTEL, HOTEL €
(Map p56; ☑ 415 1600; www.hlemmursquare. com; Laugavegur 105; dm/d from Ikr5000/38,000; @⊙) Pick your poison at this new hostel and hotel: big dorm rooms come with crisp linens and in various configurations; totally deluxe, spacious doubles, come with king-sized beds, some have balconies and sea views. Bathrooms are modern, the vibe is upbeat and there's a spacious downstairs lobby-cafe.

Loft Hostel   HOSTEL €
(Map p60; ☑ 553 8140; www.lofthostel.is; Bankastræti 7; dm/d from Ikr6650/23,800; @⊙) Perched high above the action on bustling Bankastræti, this modern hostel attracts a decidedly younger crowd, including locals who come for its trendy bar and cafe terrace. This sociable spot comes with prim dorms, linen included and ensuite bathrooms in each. HI members discount dorm/double Ikr700/2800.

ℹ SHORT-TERM RENTALS

Reykjavík's sky-high summertime accommodation prices have led enterprising locals in the capital's prized neighbourhoods to rent their apartments (or rooms) to short-stay visitors. Prices often beat commercial rates, though of course there's no maid, concierge etc. Try **Airbnb** (www.airbnb.com) and **Couchsurfing** (www.couchsurfing.org) and aim for Reykjavík 101 to be centrally located.

Reykjavík Hostel Village   HOSTEL €
(Map p56; ☑ 552 1155; www.hostelvillage.is; Flókagata 1; dm/d/q without bathroom from Ikr6200/15,250/23,000; ⊙) Pick between dorms, singles, doubles or quads with refrigerators and kettles in any one of five area houses. A few apartments, too. Linen for dorms costs Ikr1500.

Reykjavík Backpackers   HOSTEL €
(Map p60; ☑ 578 3700; www.reykjavikbackpackers. com; Laugavegur 28; dm/d from Ikr4990/17,490; ⊙) Though the Bunk Bar looks attractive on the street level, the dorms at this very centrally located place are a bit rumpled. A back building holds newer doubles. Guest kitchen.

★Room With A View   APARTMENT €€
(Map p60; ☑ 552 7262; www.roomwithaview.is; Laugavegur 18; apt Ikr24,400-67,940; ⊙) This ridiculously central apartment hotel offers swank studios and one- to four-bedroom apartments (that sleep 10!), decorated in luxe-Scandinavian style including kitchenettes, CD players, TVs and washing machines. They have those eponymous sea or city views, plus access to a sundeck and Jacuzzi. Each apartment varies: check online for details. The only downside is Friday and Saturday nightlife noise.

★Grettisborg Apartments   APARTMENT €€
(Map p60; ☑ 694 7020; www.grettisborg.is; Grettisgata 53b; apt from Ikr25,500; ⊙) Like sleeping in a magazine for Scandinavian home design, these thoroughly modern studios and apartments come in 50 shades of grey (no, not like that), sporting fine furnishings and sleek built-ins.

OK Hotel   BOUTIQUE HOTEL €€
(Map p60; ☑ 578 9850; booking@apartmentk. is; Laugavegur 74; studio from Ikr25,000-93,000; ⊙) A creatively funky vibe pervades rooms

kitted out in individual style, like the Mona Lisa room with cool mismatched furniture and La Giaconda art on the walls. Two- to six-person studios have kitchenettes, everything feels light, spacious and fun, and the downstairs K-Bar (p82) is a hit. They get dinged by guests occasionally for unattentive service.

REY Apartments
APARTMENT €€

(Map p60; ☎771 4600; www.rey.is; Grettisgata 2a; apt Ikr26,500-54,300; ☎) For those leaning towards private digs rather than hotel stays, REY is a very handy choice with a huge cache of modern apartments scattered across several Escher-like stairwells.

Galtafell Guesthouse
GUESTHOUSE €€

(Map p56; ☎551 4344; www.galtafell.com; Laufásvegur 46; d/apt incl breakfast from Ikr18,500/29,300; ☎) In a quiet, lakeside neighbourhood within easy walking distance of the centre, the four one-bedroom apartments in this converted historic mansion contain fully equipped kitchens and cosy seating areas. Three doubles share a guest kitchen. The garden and entry spaces feel suitably lovely.

Forsæla Apartmenthouse
GUESTHOUSE, APARTMENT €€

(Map p60; ☎551 6046; www.apartmenthouse.is; Grettisgata 33b; d without bathroom incl breakfast Ikr12,200, apt/house from Ikr36,000/78,000) This lovely option in Reykjavík's centre stars a 100-year-old wood-and-tin house for four to eight people, which comes with all the old beams and tasteful mod-cons you could want. Three apartments have small, cosy bedrooms and sitting rooms, kitchens and washing machines. Plus there's B&B lodging with shared bathrooms. Minimum three-night stay in apartments and the house.

Castle House & Embassy Apartments
APARTMENT €€

(Map p60; ☎511 2166; www.hotelsiceland.net; Skálholtsstígur 2a; apt from Ikr20,800; ☎) Pleasant self-contained apartments are satisfyingly central and commendably quiet. More personal than a hotel, they still come with room service: fresh towels appear daily and washing-up seems to magically clean itself. Of the two locations, Embassy Apartments (Map p60; Garðastræti 40) is on the northwest side of Tjörnin, Castle House on the east.

Villa
GUESTHOUSE €€

(Map p60; ☎823 1268; www.villa.is; Skólavörðustígur 30; d Ikr20,200-24,800; ☎) Famous Icelandic

architect Guðjón Samúelsson designed this mansion located on the fun shopping street leading to another of his creations: Hallgrímskirkja. The recently renovated rooms offers white furnishings with splashes of colour, and an unbeatable address.

Guesthouse Óðinn
GUESTHOUSE €€

(Map p60; ☎561 3400; www.odinnreykjavik.com; Óðinsgata 9; s/d without bathroom incl breakfast Ikr14,500/18,900, d/apt 23,800/39,600; ☺Jun-Aug; ☎) This family-run guesthouse has simple white rooms with bright, fun artwork. Their buffet breakfast is served in a handsome room with sea views. Also has one- and two-bedroom apartments.

Sunna Guesthouse
GUESTHOUSE €€

(Map p60; ☎511 5570; www.sunna.is; Þórsgata 26; d/apt incl breakfast from Ikr24,800/29,200; ☎@☎) All the various room and apartment configurations are simple and sunny with honey-coloured parquet floors. Several at the front have good views of Hallgrímskirkja. Families can choose between studios or spacious apartments with room for eight.

Hótel Leifur Eiríksson
HOTEL €€

(Map p60; ☎562 0800; www.hotelleifur.is; Skólavörðustígur 45; d incl breakfast from Ikr26,000) This hotel glories in one of the best locations in Reykjavík: arty Skólavörðustígur just in front of Hallgrímskirkja, and more than half of the 47 rooms have excellent church views. Rooms are fairly small and basic, but you're paying for the hotel's coordinates rather than its interior design.

Hótel Frón
HOTEL €€

(Map p60; ☎511 4666; www.hotelfron.is; Laugavegur 22a; d/studio incl breakfast from Ikr27,000/28,000; @☎) This basic blue hotel is excellently located overlooking Laugavegur (although rooms at the front can be noisy at weekends). The newer wing has good doubles, large studios with kitchenettes, and a family apartment; older rooms are less inspiring.

4th Floor Hotel
GUESTHOUSE €€

(Map p56; ☎511 3030; www.4thfloorhotel.is; Laugavegur 101; d with/without bathroom incl breakfast from Ikr21,600/18,500, apt from Ikr38,500; @☎) At the Hlemmur bus station end of Laugavegur, this centrally located property offers accommodation ranging from tiny economy rooms with shared bathrooms to larger, en-suite rooms (four with sea views and two with balconies), to smart studio apartments that are worth every króna.

Snorri's Guesthouse
GUESTHOUSE €€

(Map p56; ☑552 0598; www.guesthousereyk javik.com; Snorrabraut 61; d with/without bathroom Ikr22,600/16,400; ☎) On the corner of large Snorrabraut, this pebble-dashed building has impeccably maintained rooms in muted shades. The more expensive 'family' rooms and friendly owner make it a good base.

Baldursbrá Guesthouse
GUESTHOUSE €€

(Map p60; ☑552 6646; http://notendur.centrum. is/~heijfis; Laufásvegur 41; d incl breakfast from Ikr18,000; ☎) This little guesthouse, on a quiet street near Tjörnin, is popular for decent-sized, comfy rooms with washbasins. Additional facilities include a sitting room– TV lounge, garden with hot-pot and barbecue. Some laud the kindness of its owners, others say the opposite.

★ Reykjavík Residence
APARTMENT €€€

(Map p60; ☑561 1200; www.rrhotel.is; Hverfisgata 45; apt from Ikr29,300; @☎) Plush city-centre living feels just right in these two converted historic mansions. Linens are crisp, service attentive and the light a glowing gold. They come in loads of configurations from suites and studios with kitchenettes to two- and three-bedroom apartments. Recently established with all-modern fittings.

CenterHótel Arnarhvoll
HOTEL €€€

(Map p60; ☑595 8540; www.centerhotels.com; Ingólfsstræti 1; d from Ikr34,700; @☎) A glossy hotel on the waterfront, Arnarhvoll offers unimpeded views of the bay and Mt Esja. Cool, Scandinavian-designed rooms with clean lines and large windows let in all that lovely Nordic light; it's definitely worth paying for a sea view. Rooms are a bit small, but extremely comfortable beds compensate. The small sauna and steam room, and the Ský bar, add flair.

CenterHótel Þingholt
BOUTIQUE HOTEL €€€

(Map p60; ☑595 8530; www.centerhotels.com; Þingholtsstræti 3-5; d from Ikr40,000, ste from Ikr61,700; @☎) Full of character, Þingholt was designed by architect Gulla Jónsdóttir, who used natural materials to create one of Reykjavík's most distinctive boutique hotels. Compact rooms feel cosy with atmospheric lighting, stylish dark-grey flooring and black-leather headboards and furniture. Some have sleek tubs in the bedrooms.

Alda Hotel
BOUTIQUE HOTEL €€€

(Map p60; ☑553 9366; www.aldahotel.is; Laugavegur 66-68; d Ikr34,900-59,600; ☎) This smart, new addition to Reykjavík's city centre hotel scene offers sleek rooms with all the mod cons, including a spa and fitness centre and a spacious lounge. All of the deluxe 4th-floor rooms have balconies, suites often have two bathrooms, and some rooms have ocean views.

Hótel Holt
LUXURY HOTEL €€€

(Map p60; ☑552 5700; www.holt.is; Bergstaðastræti 37; d from Ikr39,500; @☎) Expect a totally cool blast to the luxurious past. Built in the '60s as one of Reykjavík's first hotels, Holt is decked out with original paintings, drawings and sculptures (it boasts the largest private art collection in Iceland), set off by warm-toned decor. Downstairs a handsome amber-hued library bar with a huge selection of single-malt whiskeys, abuts top-notch Gallery Restaurant (p82).

Hótel Óðinsvé
HOTEL €€€

(Map p60; ☑511 6200; www.hotelodinsve.is; Þórsgata 1; d from Ikr33,600; @) A solid hotel with personality, Oðinsvé contains 43 sunny rooms with wooden floors, original artworks and classic furnishings. They're all very different – some are split-level, some have balconies and many sport bathtubs.

🛏 South of the Centre

Icelandair Hotel Natura
HOTEL €€

(Map p56; ☑444 4503; www.icelandairhotels. com; Nauthólsvegur 52; d Ikr26,800-35,800; P@☎) A bit out of the way, Natura is best for those using the domestic airport. Large, with modern rooms, local art and Sóley organic bath products.

🛏 Laugardalur

Reykjavík City Hostel
HOSTEL €

(Map p56; ☑553 8110; www.hostel.is; Sundlaugavegur 34; dm/d from Ikr4150/17,900; P@☎) 🖉 Reykjavík's original hostel is a large, eco-friendly complex with a fun backpacker vibe. Two kilometres east of the centre in Laugardalur, it abuts the campground and swimming pool, and is served by the Fly-bus and many tour operators. It boasts bike rental, three guest kitchens and a spacious deck. HI members discount is Ikr700; for kids aged four to 12, the discount is Ikr1500.

Reykjavík Campsite
CAMPGROUND €

(Map p56; ☑ 568 6944; www.reykjavikcampsite.is; Sundlaugavegur 32; sites per adult/child Ikr1500/free; ☺ mid-May–mid-Sep; P @ 🛜) Reykjavík's only campground (2km east of the centre in Laugardalur, next to the swimming pool and City Hostel) is popular in summer with campers come to town. There's space for 650 people in three fields, so you're likely to find a spot. Extensive, modern facilities include free showers, bike hire (five hours Ikr3500), kitchens and barbecue areas.

Hilton Reykjavík Nordica
HOTEL €€

(Map p56; ☑ 444 5000; www.hilton.com; Suðurlandsbraut 2; d from Ikr26,465; @🛜) Spacious, easy-going Scandinavian chic makes this Hilton an effortless stay: amenities include 24-hour room service, gym, spa and gourmet restaurant Vox (p83). Light-filled rooms in subtle shades of cream and mocha have enormous beds; those on the upper floors have super sea views. It's about 2km from the centre, near Laugardalur, but free bus passes are included.

✖ Eating

From take away hot dogs to gourmet platters on white-clothed tables, little Reykjavík has an astonishing assortment of eateries. Loads of seafood and Icelandic or 'new Nordic' restaurants serve tried-and-true variations on local fish and lamb, but the capital is also the main spot for finding international eats.

Reykjavík also has an amazing coffee culture and cafe scene. Cool, cosy cafes encourage lingering, and though they're tops for morning coffee and light lunches, as evening comes along, many undergo a Jekyll-and-Hyde transformation – coffee becomes beer, DJs materialise in dark corners, and suddenly you're in a kick-ass bar. Some restaurants morph into late-night bars, too, with their kitchens closing around 10pm and the party rocking into the wee hours.

Kolaportið Flea Market (p88) also has a section with traditional Icelandic foods.

✖ Old Reykjavík & North of Tjörnin

Bergsson Mathús
CAFE €

(Map p60; ☑ 571 1822; www.bergsson.is; Templarasund 3; mains Ikr1300-2200; ☺ 7am-7pm Mon-Fri, to 5pm Sat & Sun; ☑) This popular, no-nonsense cafe features homemade breads, fresh produce and filling lunch specials. Stop by on weekends when locals flip through magazines, gossip and devour scrumptious brunch plates.

Bæjarins Beztu
HOT DOGS €

(Map p60; www.bbp.is; Tryggvagata; hot dogs Ikr380; ☺ 10am-2am Sun-Thu, to 4.30am Fri & Sat; 🖰) Icelanders swear the city's best hot dogs are at this truck near the harbour (patronised by Bill Clinton and late-night bar hoppers). Use the vital sentence *Eina með öllu* ('One with everything') to get the quintessential favourite with sweet mustard, ketchup and crunchy onions.

Lobster Hut
SEAFOOD €

(Map p60; cnr Lækergata & Tryggvagata; mains Ikr990-1890; ☺ 11am-8pm) What's it gonna be? Lobster soup? Lobster salad? Sandwich? This little food truck dishes it all out for fine diners on the run. If you can't see the truck on Tryggvagata, check down on the corner of Hverfisgata.

Jómfrúin
SANDWICH SHOP €

(Map p60; ☑ 551 0100; www.jomfruin.is; Lækjargata 4; sandwiches from Ikr1690; ☺ 11am-6pm) Wayward Danes seek out this no-frills joint specialising in *smørrebrød*: traditonal Danish open-face sandwiches with any number of Nordic topppings.

Hlölla Bátar
FAST FOOD €

(Map p60; www.hlollabatar.com; Ingólfstorg; subs Ikr900-1600; ☺ 11am-2am Sun-Thu, 10am-7am Fri & Sat) Keep it local with a greasy sub sandwich in Ingólfstorg Sq.

★ Nora Magasin
BISTRO €€

(Map p60; ☑ 578 2010; Pósthússtræti 9; mains Ikr1900-2500; ☺ 11.30am-1am Sun-Thu, to 3am Fri & Sat) Hip and open-plan, this buzzy bistro-bar serves up a tasty run of burgers, salads and fresh fish mains creatively conceived by popular chef Völundur Völundarson. Coffee and cocktails run all night, but the kitchen closes at 10pm or 11pm.

Laundromat Café
INTERNATIONAL €€

(Map p60; www.thelaundromatcafe.com; Austurstræti 9; mains Ikr1000-2700; ☺ 8am-midnight Mon-Wed & Sun, to 1am Thu & Fri, 10am-1am Sat; 🛜🖰) This popular Danish import attracts both locals and travellers who devour heaps of hearty mains in a cheery environment surrounded by tattered paperbacks. Go for the 'Dirty Brunch' (Ikr2690) on weekends, to sop up the previous night's booze. Oh, and yes, there are (busy) washers and dryers in the basement (per wash/15-minute dry Ikr500/100).

Við Tjörnina
ICELANDIC €€

(Map p60; ☑551 8666; www.vidtjornina.is; Vonarstræti, Raðhús; Ikr3600-4600; ☺noon-5pm & 6-10pm) Freshly relocated to the city hall, with wrap-around windows and lake views, people are loyal to this well-regarded restaurant for its beautifully presented Icelandic seafood and other regional dishes such as lamb fillet with barley. By day it's a relaxing cafe.

Icelandic Fish & Chips
ORGANIC, SEAFOOD €€

(Map p60; ☑511 1118; www.fishandchips.is; Tryggvagata 11; fish Ikr1450; ☺11.30am-9pm) 🌿 Pick your fish, and voilà, spelt-batter fried it becomes. Pair it with local beer, organic salads (Ikr750 to Ikr950) and 'Skyronnaises' – *skyr*-based sauces (eg rosemary or green apple; Ikr280) that add a zing to this most traditional of dishes.

Café Paris
INTERNATIONAL €€

(Map p60; ☑551 1020; www.cafeparis.is; Austurstræti 14; mains Ikr2300-5300; ☺8am-1am Sun-Thu, to 2am Fri & Sat; 🛜) This is one of the city's prime people-watching spots, particularly in summer, when outdoor seating spills onto Austurvöllur Sq, and at night, when the leather-upholstered interior fills with tunes and tinkling wine glasses. The mediocre selection of sandwiches, salads and burgers is secondary to the scene.

★ Grillmarkaðurinn
FUSION €€€

(Grill Market; Map p60; ☑571 7777; www.grillmarkadurinn.is; Lækargata 2a; mains Ikr4200-7200) Tippety-top dining is the order of the day here, from the moment you enter the glass atrium with the golden-globe lights to your first snazzy cocktail, and on through the meal. Service is impeccable, and locals and visitors alike rave about the food: locally sourced Icelandic ingredients prepared with culinary imagination by master chefs.

The tasting menu (Ikr9400) is an extravaganza of their best dishes.

Fiskfélagið
INTERNATIONAL €€€

(Map p60; www.fishcompany.is; Vesturgata 2a; mains lunch Ikr1600-2800, dinner Ikr3800-5400; ☺11.30am-2pm & 6-11.30pm) The 'Fish Company' takes Icelandic seafood recipes and spins them through a variety of far-flung inspirations from Fiji coconut to Spanish chorizo. Dine in an intimate-feeling stone-and-timber room with copper light fittings and quirky furnishings.

Self-Catering

10-11
SUPERMARKET

(Map p60; Austurstræti 17; ☺24hr) Ever-present 10-11 are similar to 7-Elevens in other countries. Open all night, with inflated prices. Other locations include **Barónsstígur** (Map p60; Barónsstígur 4; ☺24hr), **Borgartún** (Map

---

EATING THE LOCALS: WHALE, SHARK & PUFFIN

Many restaurants and tour operators in Iceland tout their more unusual delicacies: whale (*hvál/hvalur*), shark (fermented and called *hákarl*) and puffin (*lundi*). Before you dig in, consider that what may have been sustainable with 325,000 Icelanders becomes taxing on species and delicate ecosystems when 1,000,000 tourists annually get involved. Be aware:

➡ 35% to 40% of Icelandic whale meat consumption is by tourists.

➡ 75% of Icelanders do not buy whale meat.

➡ 80% of the minke whale is thrown away after killing.

➡ Fin whales are classified as endangered.

➡ Iceland's Ministry of Industries and Innovation maintains the whale catch is sustainable, at less than 1% of local stock, despite international protest.

➡ The Greenland shark, which is used for *hákarl,* has a conservation status of 'near threatened'.

➡ In 2003 there were an estimated 8 million puffins in Iceland, in 2014 there were about 5 million – a 37% drop.

➡ At the time of writing, Icelandic puffins were experiencing an enormous breeding failure in their largest colonies, in Vestmannaeyjar (Westman Islands).

While we do not exclude restaurants that serve these meats from our listings, you can opt not to order the meat, or easily find whale-free spots at www.icewhale.is/whale-friendly-restaurants.

REYKJAVÍK'S COFFEE CULTURE

Reykjavíkers take their coffee seriously, and there are many sweet corners in which to dwell and sip your joe, or grab it on the go.

Babalú (Map p60; ☑ 555 8845; Skólavörðustígur 22a; ⊗8am-9pm; 🐾) This mellow cafe feels like the den of one of your eccentric friends. Books and board games abound and the baked goods, terraces and comfy couches are the main draw. Paninis are just okay, so fill up instead on homemade chocolate cake and apple crumble.

Reykjavík Roasters (Map p60; www.reykjavikroasters.is; Kárastígur 1; ⊗8am-6pm Mon-Fri, 9am-7pm Sat & Sun) These folks take their coffee seriously. This tiny hipster joint is easily spotted on warm days with its smattering of wooden tables and potato sacks dropped throughout the paved square. Swig a perfect latte with a flaky croissant.

Kaffi Mokka (Map p60; ☑ 552 1174; www.mokka.is; Skólavörðustígur 3a; ⊗9am-6.30pm) The decor at Reykjavík's oldest coffee shop has changed little since the 1950s, and its original mosaic pillars and copper lights either look retro-cool or dead tatty, depending on your mood. The mixed clientele – from older folks to tourists to trendy artists – dig the selection of sandwiches, cakes and waffles.

Café Haiti (Map p60; ☑ 588 8484; www.cafehaiti.is; Geirsgata 7c; ⊗8am-10pm Mon-Thu, to 11pm Fri, 9am-11pm Sat, to 10pm Sun) If you're a coffee afficionado, this tiny cafe in the Old Harbour is the place for you. Owner Elda buys her beans from her home country Haiti, and roasts and grinds them on-site, producing what regulars swear are the best cups of coffee in the country.

C is for Cookie (Map p60; Týsgata 8; ⊗7.30am-6pm Mon-Fri, 11am-5pm Sat, noon-5pm Sun) Named in honour of *Sesame Street*'s Cookie Monster, this cheerful spot has super coffee, plus great homemade cakes, salad, soup and grilled sandwiches.

Kaffifélagið (Map p60; Skólavörðustígur 10; ⊗7.30am-6pm Mon-Fri, 10am-4pm Sat) A popular hole-in-the-wall for a quick cuppa on the run with a couple of outdoor tables, too.

---

p56; Borgartún 26; ⊗24hr) and **Laugalækur** (Map p56; Laugalækur 9; ⊗24hr).

✗ Old Harbour

★ Sægreifinn　　　　　　　SEAFOOD €
(Seabaron; Map p60; ☑ 553 1500; www.saegreifinn. is; Geirsgata 8; mains Ikr1350-1900; ⊗11.30am-11pm) Sidle into this green harbour-side shack for the most famous lobster soup (Ikr1300) in the capital, or to choose from a fridge full of fresh fish skewers to be grilled on the spot. Though the original sea baron sold the restaurant a few years ago, the place retains a homey, laid-back feel.

Walk the Plank　　　　　　SEAFOOD €
(Map p60; Ægisgarður; mains Ikr1500-1900; ⊗10am-8pm) On decent-weather days and around whale-watching departures, this tiny food truck opens its window and dishes up yummy crab-cake sliders on the quay.

Hamborgara Búllan　　　　FAST FOOD €
(Hamborgarabúlla Tómasar; Map p60; ☑ 511 1888; www.bullan.is; Geirsgata 1; mains Ikr730-1400; ⊗11.30am-9pm; 🖟) The Old Harbour's outpost of burgerdom and Americana proffers savoury patties that are perennial local favourites. Russell Crowe was spotted here while filming in 2012.

★ Valdi's　　　　　　　　ICE CREAM €
(Map p56; ☑ 586 8088; www.valdis.is; Grandagarður 21; scoop Ikr425; ⊗11.30am-11pm May-Aug; 🖟) Throughout summer, happy families flock here, take a number and join the crush waiting for a scoop chosen from the huge array of homemade ice creams. Totally casual, totally fun.

Coocoo's Nest　　　　　　CAFE €€
(Map p56; Grandagarður 23; mains Ikr1500-2700; ⊗11am-7pm Tue-Fri, to 10pm Sat, to 4pm Sun; 🐾) Pop into this cool eatery tucked behind the old harbour for popular weekend brunches (11am to 4pm) paired with decadent cocktails (Ikr1800). Casual, small and groovy, with mozaic plywood tables; the menu changes, but it's always scrumptious.

Forréttabarinn　　　　　　TAPAS €€
(Starter Bar; Map p60; ☑ 517 1800; www.forrettabarinn.is; Nýlendugata 14, entrance from Mýrar-

gata; plates Ikr1480-2250; ⊘11.30am-10pm Sun-Wed, to midnight Thu-Sat) Tapas restaurants are popular in the capital, and this hip joint near the harbour is a favourite for its new menu of creative plates such as cod and pork belly with celery root puree. There is also an airy and relaxed bar area, with weathered wood tables and broad couches.

✕ Laugavegur & East of Tjörnin

★Gló
ORGANIC, VEGETARIAN €

(Map p60; ☑553 1111; www.glo.is; Laugavegur 20b; mains Ikr1700-2500; ⊘11am-9pm; 🎧🍴) Join the cool cats in this upstairs, airy restaurant serving fresh, large daily specials loaded with Asian-influenced herbs and spices. Though not exclusively vegetarian, it's a wonderland of raw and organic foods with your choice from a broad bar of elaborate salads, from root veggies to Greek. It also has branches in **Laugardalur** (Map p56; ☑553 1111; Engjateigur 19; mains Ikr1700-2500; ⊘11am-9pm Mon-Fri, to 5pm Sat) and Hafnarfjörður (p92).

★Bakarí Sandholt
BAKERY €

(Map p60; ☑551 3524; www.sandholt.is; Laugavegur 36; mains Ikr250-980; ⊘6.30am-9pm) Reykjavík's favourite bakery is usually crammed with folks hoovering up the generous assortment of fresh baguettes, croissants, pastries and sandwiches. The soup of the day (Ikr1300) comes with delicious sourdough bread.

★Ostabúðin
SEAFOOD, DELI €

(Cheese Shop; Map p60; ☑562 2772; Skólavörðustígur 8; mains Ikr1040-1540; ⊘10am-6pm Mon-Thu, to 6.30pm Fri, 11am-4pm Sat) It doesn't get more local than this. Head to this gourmet cheese shop and deli Monday to Friday from 11.30am to 1.30pm (only those hours!) and you can sit in the back room for the friendly owner's catch of the day, cooked up in either a large portion or a huge portion, accompanied by their homemade bread.

You can also pick up other local goods, like terrines and duck confit, on the way out.

★Grái Kötturinn
CAFE €

(Map p60; ☑551 1544; Hverfisgata 16a; mains Ikr1000-2500; ⊘7.15am-3pm Mon-Fri, 8am-3pm Sat & Sun) Blink and you'll miss this tiny six-table cafe (a favourite of Björk's). It looks like a cross between an eccentric bookshop and an art gallery, and dishes up delicious breakfasts of toast, bagels, pancakes, or bacon and eggs served on thick, buttery slabs of freshly baked bread.

Grænn Kostur
VEGETARIAN €

(Map p60; ☑552 2028; www.graennkostur.is; Skólavörðustígur 8b; mains Ikr1200-1900; ⊘11.30am-9pm Mon-Sat, 1-9pm Sun; 🍴) Tucked away in a small shopping arcade behind Skólavörðustígur, this friendly little cafe serves great-tasting veggie daily specials and raw desserts.

Soup Car
SOUP €

(Map p60; Frakkastígur; soup Ikr690-1000; ⊘11.15am-7pm Jun-Sep) This friendly food truck at the foot of Hallgrímskirkja keeps it simple: delicious spicy lamb stew or 'vegan power soup' with fresh bread. Cheerfully painted tables dot the sidewalk for those who want to stick around while they sup. Hours are weather dependent.

Vitabar
FAST FOOD €

(Map p60; Bergþórugata 21; mains Ikr900-1600; ⊘11.30am-11pm, bar to 1am or 2am Fri & Sat) Sidle up to the bar to order your short-order burger with all the fixings. They've got BBQ burgers and some of the best handcut fries you'll find. This is a tile-and-formica kind of joint, with American rock on the stereo and locals quaffing pints of cold Einstök and Viking.

Noodle Station
ASIAN €

(Map p60; ☑5513199; Skólavörðustígur 21a; mains Ikr1190; ⊘11am-10pm Mon-Fri, noon-10pm Sat & Sun) No-frills noodle soups of ambiguous Asian origin are dished out by the bowlful at this trusty popular establishment.

The Deli
PIZZERIA €

(Map p60; www.deli.is; Bankastræti 14; slices Ikr400; ⊘10am-10pm Mon-Wed, to 2am Thu, to 7am Fri & Sat) Reykjavík's best pizza by the slice is homemade, well-dressed and open late.

★Snaps
FRENCH €€

(Map p60; ☑511 6677; www2.snaps.is; Þórsgata 1; dinner mains Ikr3000-4000; ⊘11.30am-11pm Sun-Thu, to midnight Fri & Sat) Reserve ahead for this French bistro that's a mega-hit with locals. Snaps' secret is simple: serve scrumptious seafood and classic bistro mains (think steak or *moules frites*) at surprisingly decent prices. Lunch specials (11.30am to 2pm; Ikr1890) and scrummy brunches (11.30am to 4pm Saturday and Sunday; Ikr900 to Ikr3300) are a big draw, too. Seats fill a lively glassed-in porch and have views of the open kitchen.

★ **K-Bar**   FUSION €€
(Map p60; ✆ 571 6666; Laugavegur 74; mains lunch Ikr1600-1800, dinner Ikr2000-3000; ◷ 7.30am-10pm Sun-Thu, to 11.30pm Fri & Sat) Leather banquettes and hammered copper tables at this cool bar-restaurant fill up with lively locals thrilled to dig into creative California-Korean style cuisine from tempura cod sliders to BBQ beef. Cocktails are delish, too, as are local tap beers (Ikr950 to Ikr1400). Brunchy foods like eggs benedict (Ikr1890) are served until 4pm.

★ **Þrír Frakkar**   ICELANDIC, SEAFOOD €€
(Map p60; ✆ 552 3939; www.3frakkar.com; Baldursgata 14; mains Ikr3200-5300; ◷ 11.30am-2.30pm & 6-11.30pm Mon-Fri, 6-11.30pm Sat & Sun) Owner-chef Úlfar Eysteinsson has built up a consistently excellent reputation at this snug little restaurant – apparently a favourite of Jamie Oliver. Specialities range throughout the aquatic world from salt cod and halibut to *plokkfiskur* (fish stew) with black bread. Non-fish items run toward guillemot, horse, lamb and whale.

Kolabrautin   ITALIAN €€
(Map p60; ✆ 519 9700; www.kolabrautin.is; Austurbakki 2, Harpa; mains Ikr3400-5900; ◷ 11.30am-2pm & 5.30-10.30pm Mon-Fri, 5.30-10.30pm Sat & Sun) Kolabrautin uses Icelandic ingredients with Mediterranean techniques high up on the top of the Harpa concert hall. Start with a splashy cocktail before digging in to spaghetti with local langoustine, or wood-roasted catfish with parmesan and chilli.

Vegamót   INTERNATIONAL €€
(Map p60; ✆ 511 3040; www.vegamot.is; Vegamótastígur 4; mains Ikr2400-4000; ◷ 11.30am-1am Mon-Thu, 11am-4am Fri & Sat, noon-1am Sun; 🤝) A long-running bistro-bar-club, with a name that means 'crossroads,' this is still a trendy place to eat, drink, see and be seen at night (it's favoured by families during the day). The 'global' menu ranges all over: from Mexican salad to Louisiana chicken. Weekend brunches (Ikr2000 to Ikr2500) are a hit, too.

Ban Thai   ASIAN €€
(Map p56; www.banthai.is; Laugavegur 130; mains Ikr1890-2500; ◷ 6-10pm Sun-Thu, to 11.30pm Fri & Sat) Ban Thai is by far the local favourite for Thai food. Find it just east of the Hlemmur bus terminal; it also has a cheaper takeaway outlet, **Yummi Yummi** (Map p56; ✆ 588 2121; Hverfisgata 123; mains Ikr1190; ◷ 11.30am-9pm Mon-Fri, 5-9pm Sat & Sun) across the street.

Hverfisgata 12   PIZZERIA €€
(Map p60; ✆ 437 0203; Hverfisgata 12; pizzas Ikr2100-2800; ◷ 11.30am-11pm; 🚶) There's no sign, but those in the know come to this cream-coloured converted corner house for some of the city's best pizzas with fabulous family-style ambience. Cheerful staff work behind the copper bar, and round tables fill bay windows. The bar stays open to 1am most days.

Austur Indíafélagið   INDIAN €€
(East India Company; Map p60; ✆ 552 1630; www.austurindia.is; Hverfisgata 56; mains Ikr3700-5000; ◷ 6-10pm Sun-Thu, to 11pm Fri & Sat) The northernmost Indian restaurant in the world is an upmarket experience, with a choice of sublime dishes (a favourite: tandoori salmon). One of its finest features, though, is its lack of pretension – the atmosphere is relaxed and the service warm.

★ **Dill**   SCANDINAVIAN €€€
(Map p60; ✆ 552 1522; www.dillrestaurant.is; Hverfisgata 12; 3-course meal from Ikr8100; ◷ 7-10pm Wed-Sat) Top 'New Nordic' cuisine is the major drawcard at this elegant yet simple bistro. The focus is very much on the food – locally sourced produce served as a parade of courses. The owners are friends with the famous Noma clan, and have drawn much inspiration from the celebrated Copenhagen restaurant. Popular with locals and visitors alike, a reservation is a must.

Friðrik V   ICELANDIC €€€
(Map p60; www.fridrikv.is; Laugavegur 60; lunch mains/3-course dinner Ikr1750/7500; ◷ 11.30am-1.30pm Tue-Fri & 5.30-10pm Tue-Sat) One of the top spots to splash out on a gourmet Icelandic meal, Friðrik's eponymous master chef is known throughout the country for championing the 'slow food' movement. Each dish is a carefully prepared combination of locally sourced items presented in a forward-thinking manner.

Gallery Restaurant   INTERNATIONAL €€€
(Map p60; ✆ 552 5700; www.holt.is; Bergstaðastræti 37, Hotel Holt; mains Ikr 4350-7000) One of the capital's top restaurants, the Gallery lives up to its name, with original artwork lining the walls, making it feel like a smart friend's drawing room. A combination of Icelandic and French, expect to eat lavishly. The daytime brasserie menu (mains Ikr2000 to Ikr3000) is a tad simpler.

Sushisamba FUSION €€€
(Map p60; ☑ 568 6600; www.sushisamba.is; Þing-holtsstræti 5; mains Ikr1900-6000, multicourse menus Ikr7000-9000; ⊙ 5-11pm Sun-Thu, to midnight Fri & Sat) The reported location of Tom-Kat's last dinner as a married couple (you can apparently request to sit at their table if you book ahead), Sushisamba puts an international spin on straight-up sushi, alongside meat and seafood mains.

Argentína STEAKHOUSE €€€
(Map p56; ☑ 551 9555; www.argentina.is; Baróns-stígur 11a; mains Ikr4000-7200; ⊙ 6-10pm Sun-Thu, 5.30-11pm Fri & Sat) This dark steakhouse prides itself on its succulent locally raised beef and fresh grilled fish, with a wine list to match. The bar is open to midnight or 1am.

Self-Catering

Frú Lauga – City Centre MARKET
(Map p60; ☑ 534 7185; www.frulauga.is; Óðinsgata 1; ⊙ 11am-6pm Mon-Fri, to 4pm Sat; ☑) ✔ The city centre location of Frú Lauga, Reykjavík's most reliable farmers market, sources an excellent range of farm-fresh dairy, meat, veggies, herbs and spices, and various locally made balms and unguents.

Bónus SUPERMARKET €
(Map p60; Laugavegur 59; ⊙ 11am-6.30pm Mon-Thu, 10am-7.30pm Fri, noon-6pm Sat) The best value supermarket in the centre. Also at **Kringlan shopping centre** (Map p56; Kringlan Shopping Centre; ⊙ noon-6.30pm Mon-Thu, 10am-7.30pm Fri, to 6pm Sat, noon-6pm Sun).

Krambúð SUPERMARKET
(Map p60; Skólavörðustígur 42; ⊙ 8am-11.30pm Mon-Fri, 10am-11.30pm Sat & Sun) Pricey but central and open late.

South of the Centre

Nauthóll ICELANDIC €€€
(Map p56; ☑ 599 6660; www.nautholl.is; Nauthólsvegur 106; mains Ikr2290-7000; ⊙ 11am-10pm Mon-Sat, to 5pm Sun) Out of the city centre beside Nauthólsvík Geothermal Beach, this reliable option for Icelandic faves sits in a delicate glass box with views out to the waterway. It's casual by day.

Laugardalur

★ **Café Flóra** CAFE €
(Flóran; Map p56; ☑ 553 8872; www.floran.is; Botanic Gardens; cakes Ikr850, mains Ikr950-2500; ⊙ 10am-10pm Jun-Aug; ☑) ✔ Sun-dappled

tables fill a greenhouse in the Botanic Gardens and spill onto a flower-lined terrace at this lovely cafe that specialises in wholesome local ingredients – some grown in the gardens themselves! Soups come with fantastic sourdough bread, and the snacks range from cheese platters with nuts and honey to pulled-pork sandwiches. Coffee and homemade cakes round it all out.

Frú Lauga MARKET
(Map p56; ☑ 534 7165; www.frulauga.is; Laugalækur 6; ⊙ 11am-6pm Mon-Fri, to 4pm Sat; ☑) ✔ Reykjavík's trailblazing farmers market sources its ingredients from all over the countryside, featuring treats like *skyr* desserts from Erpsstaðir (p183), organic vegetables, rhubarb conserves, meats, honey and a range of carefully curated international pastas, chocolates, wine and the like. There's also a city centre branch (p83).

Vox ICELANDIC €€€
(Map p56; ☑ 444 5050; www.vox.is; Suðurlandsbraut 2; mains Ikr4100-6200; ⊙ 11.30am-10.30pm) The Hilton's five-star restaurant recently underwent a mod facelift and continues to pack 'em in for New Nordic cuisine and a famous Sunday brunch.

🍸 Drinking & Nightlife

Sometimes it's hard to distinguish between cafes, restaurants and bars in Reykjavík, because when night rolls around (be it light or dark out) many of the city's coffee shops and bistros turn the lights down and the volume up, and swap cappuccinos for cocktails. A new breed of higher-end cocktail bars is emerging to flesh out the beery bar scene, and some of the hotels and hostels have trendy bars, too.

The best prices (otherwise quite high) are at happy hours. Download the smartphone app *Reykjavík Appy Hour*. Reykjavík is known for its pub crawl scene.

ⓘ BUYING BOOZE

➡ Alcohol is pricey in bars and restaurants, with happy hours bringing the best deals.

➡ The only shops licensed to sell alcohol are government-owned liquor stores called **Vínbúðin** (www.vinbudin.is), with five branches around central Reykjavík.

➡ Buy when you arrive at Keflavík International Airport's duty-free store for the deepest discounts.

★**Kaffibarinn** BAR

(Map p60; www.kaffibarinn.is; Bergstaðastræti 1; ☺2pm-1am Sun-Thu, to 4.30am Fri & Sat) This old house with the London Underground symbol over the door contains one of Reykjavík's coolest bars; it even had a starring role in the cult movie *101 Reykjavík* (2000). At weekends you'll feel like you need a famous face or a battering ram to get in. At other times it's a place for artistic types to chill with their Macs.

★**KEX Bar** BAR

(Map p60; www.kexhostel.is; Skúlagata 28; ☺noon-11pm; 🛜) Believe it or not, locals flock to this hostel bar-restaurant (mains Ikr1700 to Ikr2500) in an old cookie factory (*kex* means cookie) with broad windows facing the sea, an inner courtyard and loads of happy hipsters. The vibe is 1920s Vegas, with saloon doors, an old-school barber station, scuffed floors and happy chatter.

★**Micro Bar** BAR

(Map p60; Austurstræti 6; ☺2pm-midnight Jun-Sep, 4pm-midnight Oct-May) Boutique brews is the name of the game at this low-key spot near Austurvöllur. Bottles of beer represent a slew of brands and countries, but more importantly you'll discover 10 local draughts on tap from the island's top microbreweries: the best selection in Reykjavík. Its five-beer minisampler costs Ikr2500; happy hour (5pm to 7pm) offers Ikr600 beers.

★**Loftið** COCKTAIL BAR

(Map p60; 🖉551 9400; www.loftidbar.is; Austurstræti 9, 2nd fl; ☺2pm-1am Sun-Thu, 4pm-4am Fri & Sat) Loftið is all about high-end cocktails and good living. Dress up to join the fray at this airy upstairs lounge with a zinc-bar,

retro tailor-shop-inspired decor, vintage tiles and a swank crowd. The well booze here is the top-shelf liquor elsewhere, and they bring in jazzy bands on Thursday nights.

★**Kaldi** BAR

(Map p60; www.kaldibar.is; Laugavegur 20b; ☺noon-1am Sun-Thu, to 3am Fri & Sat) Effortlessly cool with mismatched seats and teal banquettes, plus a popular smoking courtyard, Kaldi is awesome for its full range of Kaldi microbrews, not available elsewhere. Happy hour (4pm to 7pm) gets you one for Ikr650. Anyone can play the inhouse piano.

Tiú Droppar CAFE

(Ten Drops; Map p60; 🖉551 9380; Laugavegur 27; ☺9am-1am Mon-Thu, 10am-1am Sat & Sun; 🛜) Tucked into a cosy teapot-lined basement, Tiú Droppar is one of those quintessential Reykjavík cafes that serves waffles, brunches (Ikr640 to Ikr990) and sandwiches, then in the evenings morphs into a wine bar with occasional live music. It's said that the Sunday night pianist can play anything by ear.

Kiki GAY

(Map p60; www.kiki.is; Laugavegur 22; ☺11pm-4.30am Fri & Sat) Ostensibly a queer bar, Kiki is also *the* place to get your dance on (with pop and electronica the mainstays), since much of Reyjavík's nightlife centres around the booze, not the groove.

Bravó BAR

(Map p60; Laugavegur 22; ☺6.30pm-1am Mon-Thu, to 4.30am Fri & Sat; 🛜) Friendly, knowledgeable bartenders, a laid-back corner-bar vibe with great people-watching, cool tunes on the sound system and happy hour (5pm to 9pm) draught local beers for Ikr500 – what's not to love?

GAY & LESBIAN REYKJAVÍK

Reykjavík is very gay friendly; the annual **Reykjavík Pride parade** (www.reykjavikpride.com) is one of Iceland's most-attended events, with a quarter of the *country's* population parading in 2014. Visit **Gayice** (www.gayice.is) for LGBT travel tips.

Literary Reykjavík (p68) has an app with a Queer Literature feature, and for a queer night out, head to Kiki dance club.

Samtökin '78 (Map p60; 🖉552 7878; www.samtokin78.is; Laugavegur 3, 4th fl; ☺office 1-5pm Mon-Fri, Queer Centre 8-11pm Thu) The LGBT organisation Samtökin '78 provides information during office hours and operates a community centre on Thursday nights.

Pink Iceland (🖉562 1919; www.pinkiceland.is; Laugavegur 3; ☺9am-5pm Mon-Fri) Iceland's first gay-and-lesbian owned-and-focused travel agency. It arranges all manner of travel, events and weddings and offer tours, including a two-hour walking tour of Reykjavík (Ikr5500).

ICELANDIC BOOZE

Icelanders have a lot of time in winter to perfect their crafts. It's no wonder then that a slew of good local distilleries and breweries have sprung up. Here's a quick cheat sheet for your next bar-room order:

Brennivín Caraway-flavoured 'black death' schnapps, nicely neon-green (80 proof).

Opal Flavoured vodka in several menthol and licorice varieties (52 proof).

Flóki Icelandic single-malt whisky.

64° Reykjavík Microdistillery producing Katla vodka, aquavit, herbal liqueurs and schnapps (think juniper or blueberry).

Reyka Iceland's first distillery, in Borgarnes, with crystalline vodka.

Beer!

Egils, Gull, Thule and Viking are the most common beers (typically lagers) in Iceland. But craft breweries are taking the scene by storm and you can ask for them in most Reykjavík and larger city bars.

Borg Brugghús (www.borgbrugghus.is) Award-winning craft brewery with scrumptious beers from Brió pilsner to Úlfur IPA and Garún stout, all whimsically named. Its sheep-dung-smoked IPA Fenrir is an acquired taste.

Einstök Brewing Company (www.einstokbeer.com) Akureyri-based craft brewery with a fab Viking label and equally distinctive Icelandic Pale Ale, among other ales and porters.

Kaldi (www.bruggsmidjan.is) Produced using Czech techniques, Kaldi's popular micro-brews are widely available, and its cool Kaldi (p84) bar offers seasonal draught beers on offer nowhere else.

Steðji Brugghús (www.stedji.com) This little, family-run Borgarnes brewhouse crafts several beers each year, from strawberry beer to lager.

Ölvisholt Brugghús (www.brugghus.is) Solid range of microbrews from south Iceland, includes eye-catching Lava beer.

Slippbarinn COCKTAIL BAR
(Map p60; ✆ 560 8080; www.slippbarinn.is; Mýrargata 2; ◷ 11.30am-midnight Sun-Thu, to 1am Fri & Sat) Jetsetters unite at this buzzy hotel, restaurant and bar at the Old Harbour. It's bedecked with vintage record players and chatting locals sipping some of the best cocktails in town.

Prikið PUB
(Map p60; ✆ 551 2866; www.prikid.is; Bankastræti 12; ◷ 8am-1am Mon-Thu, to 4.30am Fri, 11am-4.30am Sat, 11am-1am Sun) Being one of Reykjavík's oldest joints, the feel at Prikið falls somewhere between diner and saloon: great if you're up for greasy eats (mains Ikr1700 to Ikr3500) and socialising. Things get dance-y in the wee hours, and if you survive the night, it's popular for its next-day 'hangover killer' breakfast (Ikr2590).

Boston BAR
(Map p60; ✆ 577 3200; Laugavegur 28b; ◷ 4pm-1am Sun-Thu, to 3am Fri & Sat) Boston is cool, arty and found up through a doorway on Laugavegur that leads to its laid-back lounge where DJs spin from time to time.

Dillon BAR, LIVE MUSIC
(Map p60; ✆ 578 2424; Laugavegur 30; ◷ 2pm-1am Sun-Thu, to 3am Fri & Sat) Beer, beards and the odd flying bottle...atmospheric Dillon is a RRRRROCK pub with a great beer garden. Frequent concerts hit its tiny corner stage.

Paloma CLUB
(Map p60; Naustin 1-3; ◷ club 10pm-4.30am Fri & Sat, basement bar nightly from 8pm) One of Reykjavík's best late-night dance clubs, with DJs upstairs laying down electronica and pop, and a pool table in the basement. Find it in the same building as the Dubliner.

Lebowski Bar BAR
(Map p60; Laugavegur 20a; ◷ 11.30am-1am Sun-Thu, to 4am Fri & Sat) Named after the eponymous 'Dude' of moviedom, the grungy Lebowski Bar is smack in the middle of the action with Americana smothering the

walls, and loads of white Russians (from Ikr1500) – a favourite from the film.

Hressingarskálinn PUB
(Map p60; www.hresso.is; Austurstræti 20; ⊙9am-1am Sun-Thu, 10am-4.30am Fri & Sat; ⊛) Known as Hressó, this large cafe-bar serves a diverse menu until 10pm (from porridge to *plok-kfiskur;* mains Ikr1700 to Ikr4500), then at weekends it loses its civilised veneer and concentrates on drinks and dancing. DJs offer pop and rock Thursday through Saturday.

Bast BAR
(Map p60; ☑519 7579; www.bast.is; Hverfisgata 20; ⊙11am-midnight Mon-Wed, to 1am Thu-Sat, to 8pm Sun) A young, happy post-work crowd fills this warehouse-like space hosting good DJs.

Lavabarinn CLUB
(Map p60; Lækjargata 6; ⊙5pm-1am Thu, to 4.30am Fri & Sat) DJs get this former illegal gentlemen's club pumping with house, R&B, electronica and pop.

English Pub PUB
(Enski Barinn; Map p60; www.enskibarinn.is; Austerstræti 12a; ⊙noon-1am Sun-Thu, to 4.30am Fri & Sat) Reliable pub for catching football matches.

☆ Entertainment

The vibrant Reykjavík live-music scene is ever-changing. There are often performances at bars and cafes, and local theatres and Harpa concert hall (p59) bring in all of the performing arts.

To catch up on the latest in Icelandic music and performing arts, and to see who's playing, consult free English-language newspaper *Grapevine* (www.grapevine.is), Visit Reykjavík (www.visitreykjavik.is), What's On in Reykjavík (www.whatson.is/magazine), Musik.is (www.musik.is) or city music shops.

Some ticket sales are online at Midi (www.midi.is) or Dash Tickets (www.dashtickets.is).

★Bíó Paradís CINEMA
(Map p60; www.bioparadis.is; Hverfisgata 54; adult Ikr1600; ⊛) This totally cool cinema, decked out in movie posters and vintage officeware, screens specially curated Icelandic films with English subtitles. It's a chance to see movies that you may not find elsewhere. Plus there's a happy hour from 5pm to 7.30pm.

Café Rosenberg LIVE MUSIC
(Map p60; ☑551 2442; Klapparstígur 25-27; ⊙3pm-1am Mon-Thu, 4pm-2am Fri & Sat) This big, booklined storefront is dotted with

---

DJAMMIÐ: HOW TO PARTY IN REYKJAVÍK

Reykjavík is renowned for its weekend party scene that goes strong into the wee hours, and even spills over onto some of the weekdays (especially in summer). *Djammið* in the capital means going out on the town, or you could say *pöbbarölt* for a 'pub stroll'. (This should not be confused with the infamous countryside *rúntur,* which involves Icelandic youth driving around their town in one big automotive party.)

Much of Reykjavík's partying happens in cafes and bistros that transform into raucous beer-soaked bars at the weekend, and at the many dedicated pubs and clubs. But it's not the quantity of drinking dens that makes Reykjavík's nightlife special – it's the upbeat energy that pours from them.

Thanks to the high price of alcohol, things generally don't get going until late. Icelanders brave the melee at the government alcohol store Vínbúðin (www.vinbudin.is), then toddle home for a prepub party. Once they're merry, people hit town around midnight, party until 5am, queue for a hot dog, then topple into bed or the gutter, whichever is more convenient. Considering the quantity of booze swilling, the scene is pretty good-natured.

Rather than settling into one venue for the evening, Icelanders like to cruise from bar to bar, getting progressively louder and less inhibited as the evening goes on. 'In' clubs may have long queues, but they tend to move quickly with the constant circulation of revellers.

Most of the action is concentrated near Laugavegur and Austurstræti. Places usually stay open until 1am Sunday to Thursday and 4am or 5am on Friday and Saturday. You'll pay around Ikr800 to Ikr1200 per pint of beer, and cocktails hit the Ikr1800 to Ikr2600 mark. Some venues have cover charges (around Ikr1000) after midnight, and many have early-in-the-evening happy hours that cut costs to between Ikr500 or Ikr700 per beer; download smartphone app *Reykjavík Appy Hour.*

Things change fast – check *Grapevine* for the latest listings. You should dress up to fit in, although there are some more relaxed pub-style joints. The legal drinking age is 20.

couches and cocktail tables, and hosts all manner of live acts, from local singer-songwriters to jazz groups, with broad-paned windows looking onto the street.

Húrra LIVE MUSIC
(Map p60; Tryggvagata 22; ⊘5pm-1am Sun-Thu, to 4.30am Fri & Sat; 🐾) Dark and raw, this large bar opens up its back room to make a concert venue, with live music or DJs most nights. Run by the same folks as Bravó, they've got six beers on tap and happy hour runs until 10pm (beer/wine Ikr500/700).

National Theatre THEATRE
(Þjóðleikhúsið; Map p60; 🖉551 1200; www.leikhusid.is; Hverfisgata 19; ⊘closed Jul) The National Theatre has three separate stages and puts on plays, musicals and operas, from modern Icelandic works to Shakespeare.

Reykjavík City Theatre THEATRE, DANCE
(Borgarleikhúsið; Map p56; 🖉568 8000; www.borgarleikhus.is; Listabraut 3, Kringlan; ⊘closed Jul & Aug) Stages plays and musicals, and is home to the **Icelandic Dance Company** (Map p56; 🖉588 0900; www.id.is).

Iðnó Theatre THEATRE
(Map p60; 🖉551 9181; www.idno.is; Vonarstræti 3) Icelandic theatre, tending toward the comedic.

Laugardalshöllin CONCERT VENUE
(Map p56; Engjavegur 8, Laugardalur) Huge venue for major international acts.

Laugardalsvöllur National Stadium STADIUM
(Map p56; 🖉510 2914) Iceland's football (soccer) passion is huge. Cup and international matches are played at this national stadium in Laugardalur. See the sports sections of Reykjavík's newspapers or **Football Association of Iceland** (Knattspyrnusamband Íslands - KSÍ; 🖉510 2900; www.ksi.is), and buy tickets directly from the stadium.

🛍 Shopping

Reykjavík's vibrant design culture makes for great shopping: from sleek, fish-skin purses and knitted *lopapeysur* (Icelandic woollen sweaters) to unique music or lip-smacking Icelandic schnapps *brennivín*. Laugavegur is the most dense shopping street. You'll find interesting shops all over town, but fashion concentrates near the Frakkastígur and Vitastígur end of Laugavegur. Skólavörðustígur is strong for arts and jewellery. Bankastræti and Austurstræti have many touristy shops.

SÓLEY ORGANICS: ICELANDIC BATH PRODUCTS

Sóley Organics (www.soleyorganics.com) doesn't have its own boutique, but look out for its wonderful, locally made bath and beauty products at all **Heilsuhúsið** (Map p60; 🖉552 2966; www.heilsuhusid.is; Laugavegur 20; ⊘10am-6pm Mon-Fri, 11am-4pm Sat) health stores and Lyfja pharmacies in Iceland. You can also find them at Hagkaup in the Kringlan or Smáralind shopping centres and at Keflavík Airport Duty Free, as well as used in many upscale spas.

Don't forget – all visitors are eligible for a 15% tax refund on their shopping, under certain conditions (see p361).

★**Kirsuberjatréð** ARTS & CRAFTS
(Cherry Tree; Map p60; 🖉562 8990; www.kirs.is; Vesturgata 4; ⊘10am-7pm Mon-Fri, to 5pm Sat, to 4pm Sun) This women's art-and-design collective in an interesting 1882 former bookstore sells weird and wonderful fish-skin handbags, music boxes made from string, and, our favourite, beautiful coloured bowls made from radish slices. It's been around for 20 years and now has 12 designers.

★**Kraum** ARTS & CRAFTS
(Map p60; www.kraum.is; Aðalstræti 10; ⊘9am-6pm Mon-Fri, noon-5pm Sat & Sun) The brainchild of a band of local artists, Kraum literally means 'simmering', like the island's quaking earth and the inventive minds of its citizens. Expect a fascinating assortment of unique designer wares, such as fish-skin apparel and driftwood furniture, on display in Reykjavík's oldest house.

★**Kiosk** CLOTHING
(Map p60; 🖉445 3269; Laugavegur 65; ⊘10am-6pm Mon-Fri, 11am-5pm Sat, 1-4pm Sun Jun-Aug, reduced hours Sep-May) This wonderful designers' cooperative is lined with creative women's fashion in a glass-fronted boutique. Designers take turns (wo)manning the store.

★**KronKron** CLOTHING, SHOES
(Map p60; 🖉562 8388; www.kronkron.com; Laugavegur 63b; ⊘10am-6pm Mon-Fri, to 5pm Sat) This is where Reykjavík goes high fashion, with the likes of Marc Jacobs and Vivienne Westwood. But we really enjoy its Scandinavian designers (including Kron by KronKron) offering silk dresses, knit capes,

scarves and even wool underwear. Their handmade shoes are off the charts (also sold down the street at Kron).

★Kron   SHOES
(Map p60; ☑551 8388; www.kron.is; Laugavegur 48; ⊙10am-6pm Mon-Fri, to 5pm Sat) Kron sells its own outlandishly wonderful handmade shoes with all the flair you'd expect of an Icelandic label. Colours are bright, textures are cool, and they're even wearable (those practical Icelanders!).

★Mál og Menning   BOOKS
(Map p60; ☑580 5000; Laugavegur 18; ⊙9am-10pm Mon-Fri, 10am-10pm Sat) Friendly, popular and well-stocked independent bookstore carries great English-language books for getting under the skin of Iceland. Check out *Thermal Pools in Iceland* by Jón G Snæland and Þóra Sigurbjörnsdóttir; you can browse it in the lively cafe. Also sells CDs, games and newspapers.

★Kolaportið Flea Market   MARKET
(Map p60; www.kolaportid.is; Tryggvagata 19; ⊙11am-5pm Sat & Sun) Held in a huge industrial building by the harbour, this weekend market is a Reykjavík institution. Don't expect much from the selection of secondhand clothes and old toys, just enjoy the experience. There's also a food section that sells traditional eats such as *rúgbrauð* (geothermally baked rye bread), *brauðterta* ('sandwich cake', a layering of bread with mayonnaise-based fillings) and *hákarl* (fermented shark).

Lucky Records   MUSIC
(Map p56; ☑551 1195; www.luckyrecords.is; Rauðarárstígur 10; ⊙9am-10pm Mon-Fri, 11am-

10pm Sat & Sun) This deep den of musical goodness holds loads of modern Icelandic music, but plenty of vintage vinyl, too. The huge collection spans hip hop to jazz and electronica. Occasional live music.

12 Tónar   MUSIC
(Map p60; www.12tonar.is; Skolavörðustígur 15; ⊙10am-8pm) A very cool place to hang out, 12 Tónar is responsible for launching some of Iceland's favourite bands. In the three-floor shop you can listen to CDs, drink coffee and sometimes catch a live performance. There's a new branch in the Harpa concert hall, too.

Eymundsson   BOOKS
(Map p60; www.eymundsson.is; Austurstræti 18; ⊙9am-10pm Mon-Fri, 10am-10pm Sat & Sun) This big central bookshop has a superb choice of English-language books, newspapers, magazines and maps, along with a great cafe. A second branch can be found on **Skólavörðustígur** (Map p60; Skólavörðustígur 11; ⊙9am-10pm Mon-Fri, 10am-10pm Sat & Sun).

Leynibuðin   CLOTHING
(Map p60; www.leynibudin.is; Laugavegur 55; ⊙11am-6pm Mon-Fri) A consortium of young designers, Leynibuðin is a veritable minimarket of locally crafted apparel. Items border on hipster and grunge – it's a great introduction to the city's made-at-home trend.

Skúma Skot   ARTS & CRAFTS
(Map p60; ☑663 1013; Laugavegur 23; ⊙10am-6pm Tue-Fri, to 4pm Sat & Sun) Nine designers create these unique handmade porcelain items, women's and kids' clothing, paintings and cards. It's in a tiny house behind the Booking Lounge travel agency.

WOOLLY JUMPERS: LOPAPEYSUR

Lopapeysur are the ubiquitous Icelandic woolly jumpers you will see worn by locals and visitors alike. Made from naturally water-repellant Icelandic wool, they are thick and cosy, with simple geometric patterns or regional motifs. They are no longer the bargain they were in the '60s, so when shopping, be sure to make the distinction: do you want hand-knit or machine made? You'll notice the price difference (some cost well over €200), but either way these beautiful but practical items are exceptionally wearable souvenirs.

Handknitting Association of Iceland (Handprjónasamband Íslands; Map p60; ☑552 1890; www.handknit.is; Skólavörðustígur 19; ⊙9am-9pm Mon-Fri, to 6pm Sat, 10am-6pm Sun) Traditional handmade hats, socks and sweaters are sold at this knitting collective, or you can buy yarn, needles and knitting patterns and do it yourself. The association's smaller branch (Map p60; ☑562 1890; Laugavegur 53b; ⊙9am-7pm Mon-Fri, 10am-5pm Sat) sells made-up items only.

Álafoss (Map p60; ☑562 6303; www.alafoss.is; Laugavegur 8; ⊙9am-10pm) Loads of hand- or machine-made *lopapeysur* and other wool products. Their outlet store (☑566 6303; www.ala-foss.is; Álafossvegur 23, Mosfellsbær; ⊙9am-6pm Mon-Fri, to 4pm Sat) also sells yarn and needles.

Spark
ARTS & CRAFTS

(Map p60; ☑552 2656; www.sparkdesignspace.com; Klapparstígur 33; ⊙10am-6pm Mon-Fri, noon-4pm Sat) This gallery and shop has a rotating selection of unique local designers. Expect art and knitwear, and look out for the fish-bone model-making kit.

Gangleri Outfitters
CAMPING EQUIPMENT

(Map p60; ☑583 2222; www.outfitters.is; Hverfisgata 82; ⊙10am-7pm Mon-Fri, 11am-5pm Sat & Sun) Full-service camping gear sales and rentals: tents, sleeping bags, stoves, backpacks, hiking boots, climbing gear etc.

Fjallakofinn
CAMPING EQUIPMENT

(Map p60; ☑510 9505; www.fjallakofinn.is; Laugavegur 11; ⊙9am-7pm Mon-Fri, 10am-4pm Sat, noon-5pm Sun) In the same building with Arctic Adventures, this shop offers loads of brand-name camping and climbing gear, GoPros and more. But expect to pay a premium. It offers **gear rental**, and has a branch at Kringlan.

66° North
CLOTHING

(Map p60; ☑535 6680; www.66north.is; Bankastræti 5; ⊙9am-10pm) Iceland's premier outdoor-clothing company began by making all-weather wear for Arctic fishermen. This metamorphosed into costly, fashionable streetwear: jackets, fleeces, hats and gloves. The kids' branch is a block away, and there are boutiques in Kringlan Shopping Centre.

Geysir
CLOTHING

(Map p60; ☑519 6000; www.geysir.com; Skólavörðustígur 16; ⊙10am-10pm) For traditional Icelandic clothing, Geysir boasts an elegant selection of sweaters, blankets, and men's and women's clothes, shoes and bags.

Gaga
CLOTHING

(Map p60; ☑551 2306; www.gaga.is; Vesturgata 4; ⊙10am-6pm Mon-Fri, to 4pm Sat) Whacky knitted and felt gear from designer Gaga Skorrdal.

Aurum
JEWELLERY

(Map p60; ☑551 2770; Bankastræti 4; ⊙10am-6pm Mon-Fri, 11am-5pm Sat) Guðbjörg at Aurum is one of Reykjavík's more interesting designers; her whisper-thin silver jewellery is sophisticated stuff, its shapes often inspired by leaves and flowers.

Iceland Giftstore
SOUVENIRS

(Rammagerðin; Map p60; ☑535 6690; www.icelandgiftstore.com; Hafnarstræti 19; ⊙9am-10pm Mon-Fri, 10am-10pm Sat & Sun) If you can see your way past the stuffed puffin in the window, you'll find one of the city's better souvenir shops, with loads of woollens, crafts and collectibles. It also has a Keflavík International Airport location.

Viking
SOUVENIRS

(Map p60; www.theviking.is; Laugavegur 1; ⊙9am-10pm) You can't miss this crammed souvenir shop with giant trolls out front and tourists thronging through the trinket-filled store. It also has a branch at Hafnarstræti 1.

Kría
BICYCLE

(Map p56; www.kriacycles.com; Grandagarður 7, Old Harbour; ⊙10am-6pm Mon-Fri, 11am-3pm Sat) Full-service bike sales and repair.

Reykjavík Foto
ELECTRONICS

(Map p60; ☑577 5900; www.reykjavikfoto.is; Laugavegur 51; ⊙10am-6pm Mon-Fri, 11am-4pm Sat) Loads of cameras, tripods and water-resistant bags, with helpful service.

Kringlan
SHOPPING CENTRE

(Map p56; www.kringlan.is; ☐S1-4, S6, 13 or 14) Reykjavík's main shopping centre, 1km from town, has 150 shops. Even bigger Smáralind (p94) is in Kópavogur.

ℹ Orientation

The city is spread out along a small peninsula, with Reykjavík Domestic Airport and long-distance bus terminals BSÍ and Mjódd in the south, and the picturesque city centre and harbour occupying the north. The international airport is 48km away at Keflavík.

The city centre's social and commercial main street is Laugavegur. At its eastern end is Hlemmur bus terminal, one of the two main city bus stations. Moving westwards, this narrow, one-way lane blossoms with Reykjavík's shops and bars. It changes its name to Bankastræti, then to Austurstræti as it runs across the centre. Running uphill off Bankastræti at a jaunty diagonal, artists' street Skólavörðustígur ends at spectacular modern church, Hallgrímskirkja.

Busy boulevard Lækjargata cuts straight across Bankastræti/Austurstræti. To its west is Old Reykjavík. To the northwest lies Reykjavík's harbour and to the southwest Tjörnin lake.

ℹ Information

EMERGENCY

Emergency (☑112) Ambulance, fire brigade or police.

Landspítali University Hospital (☑543 1000; www.landspitali.is; Fossvogur) Casualty department open 24/7.

INTERNET ACCESS

Almost all accommodations and many cafes have wi-fi. You can use terminals (Ikr250 per hour) at the main tourist information office and libraries.

Aðalbókasafn (Reykjavík City Library; www. borgarbokasafn.is; Tryggvagata 15; ⊙10am-7pm Mon-Thu, 11am-7pm Fri, 1-5pm Sat & Sun) Excellent main library.

LAUNDRY

Laundry is a perennial (pricey) problem in Iceland if you don't have lodging that offers it. In Reykjavík, you can head to Laundromat Café (p78) for its downstairs machines.

Úðafoss (⊉551 2301; Vitastígur 13; per 5kg Ikr3380; ⊙8am-6pm Mon-Fri) One of Reykjavík's only central laundries; same-day service available.

MEDICAL SERVICES

Health Centre (⊉585 2600; Vesturgata 7) Book in advance.

Læknavaktin (⊉1770; ⊙5pm-8am Mon-Fri, 24hr Sat & Sun) Non-emergency medical advice.

MONEY

Credit cards are accepted everywhere (except municipal buses); ATMs are ubiquitous. Currency exchange fees at hotels or private bureaus can be obscenely high.

POST

Main Post Office (Map p60; www.postur.is; Pósthússtræti 5; ⊙9am-6pm Mon-Fri) Has poste restante.

TELEPHONE

Public phones are rare in mobile-crazy Reykjavík. Try the tourist office, post office, by the southwestern corner of Austurvöllur, on Lækjargata, or at Kringlan Shopping Centre.

TOURIST INFORMATION

Reykjavík has an excellent main tourist office, and loads of travel agencies that specialise in booking tours.

Main Tourist Office (Upplýsingamiðstöð Ferðamanna; Map p60; ⊉590 1550; www. visitreykjavik.is; Aðalstræti 2; ⊙8.30am-7pm Jun–mid-Sep, 9am-6pm Mon-Fri, to 4pm Sat, to 2pm Sun mid-Sep–May) Friendly staff and mountains of free brochures, plus maps and Strætó city bus tickets for sale. Book accommodation, tours and activities. Also one site for getting your duty-free refund.

TRAVEL AGENCIES

Icelandic Travel Market (⊉552 4979; www. icelandictravelmarket.is; Bankastræti 2; ⊙8am-9pm May-Aug, to 7pm Sep-Apr) Information, tour bookings and bike rental (Ikr3500 per five hours).

Trip (⊉433 8747; www.trip.is; Laugavegur 54; ⊙9am-9pm) Books tours, and rents cars and bicycles.

ⓘ Getting There & Away

AIR

Keflavík International Airport (KEF; ⊉425 6000; www.kefairport.is; ☎) International flights (excluding Greenland and the Faroe Islands); 48km west of Reykjavík. Has tourist information (Map p56; ⊉425 0330, booking service 570 7799; ⊙6am-8pm Mon-Fri, noon-5pm Sat & Sun), money changers, 10-11 grocery and cafes.

Reykjavík Domestic Airport (Reykjavíkurflugvöllur; Map p56; www.reykjavikairport.is; Innanlandsflug) Two kilometres south of Tjörnin. Domestic flights as well as flights to Greenland and the Faroe Islands. Air Iceland (⊉570 3030; www.airiceland.is) has an airport desk, but save money booking online. Eagle Air (⊉562 4200; www.eagleair.is) operates flights and sightseeing services here.

BUS

You can travel from Reykjavík by day tour (p69; many of which offer hotel pickup), or use Strætó and several of the tour companies for transport, getting on and off its scheduled buses. It also offers various bus transport passes (see p367). The free *Public Transport in Iceland* map has a good overview of routes.

Bus service is reduced or cut in winter, but things are changing rapidly in Iceland. For destinations on the northern and eastern sides of Iceland (eg Egilsstaðir, Mývatn and Húsavík), you usually change in Höfn or Akureyri; for the West change in Borgarnes.

In 2015 the Westfjords starts new service from Reykjavík via Holmavík to Ísafjörður (year-round); and via Stykkishólmur and the ferry to Brjánslækur and Ísafjörður (summer only) or Patreksfjörður (year-round). Check www.westfjords.is for the latest information.

Strætó (⊉540 2700; www.straeto.is/english) Operates Reykjavík long-distance buses from Mjódd Bus Terminal (p92), 8km southeast of the centre, which is served by local buses 3, 4, 11, 12, 17, 21, 24 and 28. Strætó also operates city buses and offers a smartphone app. For long distance buses *only* you can use cash, credit/debit card with PIN or (wads of) bus tickets.

BSÍ Bus Terminal – Reykjavík Excursions (Map p56; ⊉562 1011; www.bsi.is; Vatnsmýrarvegur 10; ☎) Reykjavík Excursions (and their Flybus) uses the BSÍ terminal (pronounced *bee-ess-ee*), south of the centre. There's a ticketing desk, tourist brochures, lockers, luggage storage (Ikr500 per bag per day), Budget car hire, and a cafeteria with wi-fi. The terminal is served by Reykjavík buses 1, 3, 6, 14, 15 and 19. Reykjavík Excursions offers pre-booked hotel pickup to bring you to the terminal.

Sterna (Map p60; ☑ 551 1166; www.sterna. is; ☎) Sales and departures from the Harpa concert hall. Buses everywhere except the west and Westfjords.

Trex (☑ 587 6000; www.trex.is; ☎) Departs from the Main Tourist Office or Harpa concert hall and Reykjavík Campsite. Buses to Þórsmörk and Landmannalaugar in the South.

❶ Getting Around

TO/FROM THE AIRPORT

The journey from Keflavík International Airport to Reykjavík takes about 50 minutes. Taxis cost around Ikr15,000. Three easy bus services con-nect Reykjavík and the airport and are by far the best bet; kids get discounted fares.

From the Reykjavík Domestic Airport it's a 1km walk into town, there's a taxi rank, or bus 15 stops near the Air Iceland terminal and bus 19 stops near the Eagle Air terminal. Both go to the centre and Hlemmur bus station.

Flybus (☑ 580 5400; www.re.is; ☎) Operated by Reykjavík Excursions, Flybus meets all international flights. One-way tickets cost Ikr1950. Pay Ikr2500 for hotel pickup/drop-off (which shuttles you from/to the Flybus at the BSÍ terminal); you must book this a day ahead. A separate service runs to the Blue Lagoon (from where you can continue to the centre or the airport; Ikr3600). Tickets online, at many hotels, or at the airport booth.

The Flybus will also drop-off/pickup in Garðabær and Hafnarfjörður, just south of Reykjavík.

BUS SERVICES FROM REYKJAVÍK

Below are sample routes and fares; check bus companies for current rates. Strætó usually offers the lowest fares. Private companies such as Reykjavík Excursions (RE) and Sterna also ply these routes, and may offer pickup, but usually cost more unless you buy a bus passport.

DESTINATION	COMPANY & LINE	PRICE (IKR)	DURATION	FREQUENCY	YEAR-ROUND
Akureyri	Strætó 57	7700	6½hr	daily	Yes
Blue Lagoon	Sterna/RE	2000	45min	daily	Yes
Borgarnes	Strætó 57	1400	1¼hr	daily	Yes
Geysir/Gullfoss	RE	5000	2½hr	daily	mid-Jun–mid-Sep
Höfn	Strætó 51	10,150	8½hr	daily	Yes
Hólmavík	Strætó 59	5250	3½hr	daily	Yes
Keflavík	REX/Flybus	1500	40min	several daily	Yes
Kirkjubæjarklaustur	Strætó 51	8100	5hr	daily	Yes
Landmannalaugar	Trex/RE	8400/9000	5½hr	daily	mid-Jun–Aug
Mývatn	RE	20,500	12hr	3 weekly	Jul–Aug
Selfoss	Strætó 51/52	1400	1hr	many daily	Yes
Skaftafell	Sterna	7200	6½hr	daily	Yes
Skógar	Strætó 51/Sterna	200/3600	3¼hr	daily	Jun–mid-Sep
Stykkishólmur	Strætó 57 to 58	3150	3hr	2 daily	Yes
Landeyjarhöfn port for Vestmannaeyjar Islands	Strætó 52	3500	2¼hr	daily	Yes
Vík í Mýrdal	Strætó 51	4900	4hr	2 daily	Yes
Þingvellir	RE	2500	45min	daily	mid-Jun–mid-Sep
Þórsmörk	Trex/RE	800/7500	3½hr	2 daily	Jun–mid-Sep

K-Express (☑ 823 0099; www.kexpress.is)
At the time of writing K-Express offered three
daily buses between Keflavík International
Airport and Keflavík Town, Reykjavík Campsite,
Hallgrímskirkja and the Harpa concert hall for
Ikr1300. They depart (and have a desk) about
500m from the terminal, at the building with
the Sixt rental car agency. Get tickets from the
bus driver or online.

Airport Express (☑ 540 1313; www.airport-
express.is; ☎) Operated by Gray Line Tours
between Keflavík International Airport and
Lækjartorg Sq in central Reykjavík (Ikr1900),
or via hotel pickup/drop-off (Ikr2400). See
website for schedule.

BICYCLE

Reykjavík has a steadily improving network of
cycle lanes – ask the tourist office for a map. You
are allowed to cycle on pavements as long as
you don't cause pedestrians problems. For bike
rentals, see p68.

BUS

Strætó (www.straeto.is/english) operates
regular, easy buses around Reykjavík and its
suburbs (Seltjarnarnes, Kópavogur, Garðabær,
Hafnarfjörður and Mosfellsbær); it also operates long distance buses. They have online
schedules, a smartphone app and a route book

for sale at Hlemmur bus station (Ikr0.50). Many
free maps like *Welcome to Reykjavík City Map*
also include bus-route maps.

Buses run from 7am until 11pm or midnight
daily (from 10am on Sunday). Services depart
at 20-minute or 30-minute intervals. A limited
night-bus service runs until 2am on Friday and
Saturday. Buses only stop at designated bus
stops, marked with a yellow letter 'S'.

Tickets & Fares

The fare is Ikr350; you can buy tickets at the bus
station or pay on board, though no change is giv-
en. Buy one-/three-day passes (Ikr900/2200)
at the two bus stations, the tourist office, many
hotels, Kringlan and Smáralind shopping malls
and bigger swimming pools. If you need to take
two buses to reach your destination, get a *skipti-
miði* (transfer ticket, good for 75 minutes) from
the driver.

The Reykjavík City Card also acts as a Strætó
bus pass.

Bus Stations & Lines

The two central terminals are **Hlemmur** (Map
p56; ☑ 540 2701; ⊙ office 8am-8pm Mon-
Fri, noon-8pm Sat & Sun), at the eastern end of
Laugavegur, and **Lækjartorg Sq** (Map p60),
in the centre of town, and more of a bus stop
than a terminal. **Mjódd** (☑ 557 7854), southeast

HAFNARFJÖRÐUR'S HIDDEN WORLDS

Many Icelanders believe that their country is populated by hidden races – *jarðvergar*
(gnomes), *álfar* (elves), *ljósálfar* (fairies), *dvergar* (dwarves), *ljúflingar* (lovelings), *tívar*
(mountain spirits), *englar* (angels) and *huldufólk* (hidden people). Although some are
embarrassed to say they believe, most refuse to say hand-on-heart that they *don't* believe. You'll see many Icelandic gardens feature small wooden *álfhól* (elf houses).

Hafnarfjörður (population 27,400), 12km south of Reykjavik, is believed to lie at the
confluence of several strong ley lines (mystical lines of energy) and rests on a 7000-year-
old flow that, according to locals, hides a parallel elfin universe. Visitors walk through
Hellisgerði (www.elfgarden.is; ⊙1-5pm Tue-Sun), a peaceful park filled with lava grottoes
and apparently one of the favourite places of the hidden people. A 90-minute pricey
Hidden Worlds tour (☑ 694 2785; www.alfar.is; per person Ikr3900; ⊙2.30pm Tue & Fri
Jun-Aug) leaves from the **tourist office** (☑ 585 5500; www.visithafnarfjordur.is; Strandgata
6; ⊙8am-4pm Mon-Fri), which also sells elf maps. On weekends get info at Pakkhúsið.

Hafnarfjörður Museum (☑ 585 5780) FREE, the town's other main attraction, is
divided over several old tin-clad houses near the harbour, exploring local history. Start
at **Pakkhúsið** (Vesturgata 8; ⊙11am-5pm Jun-Aug, Sat & Sun Sep-May), the primary site.
There are hot springs and mud pools and vibrant mineral lakes south of town, in Krýsuvík
(p105).

In a pinch, overnight at **Lava Hostel & Campsite** (☑ 565 0900, 895 0906; www.haf-
narfjordurguesthouse.is; Hjallabraut 51; campsites per adult Ikr1200, dm from Ikr4500, d without
bathroom Ikr13,000; ⊙mid-May–mid-Sep; ☎). Find good eats at popular café **Súfistinn**
(☑ 565 3740; www.sufistinn.is; Strandgata 9; mains Ikr1200-1600; ⊙8.15am-11.30pm Mon-Fri,
10am-11.30pm Sat, 11am-11.30pm Sun), or delicious, creative vegetarian food at **Gló** (☑ 553
1111; www.glo.is; Strandgata 34; mains Ikr1700-2500; ⊙11am-9pm Mon-Fri, to 5pm Sat & Sun).

Get here on bus 1 (30 minutes from Reykjavík). The **Flybus** (www.re.is) to Keflavík
International Airport will stop in Hafnarfjörður if pre-arranged.

of the centre is for long distance buses. Many buses make a loop around Tjörnin lake and serve the centre, the National Museum and BSÍ bus terminal before heading onwards. Some examples:

1 Hlemmur bus station, Lækjartorg bus station, National Museum, BSÍ bus terminal, hospital, Hamraborg bus station (Kópavogur), Fjörður bus station (Hafnarfjörður)

14 Old Harbour, Lækjartorg bus station, National Museum, BSÍ bus terminal, hospital, Hlemmur bus station, Laugardalur (for swimming pool, City Hostel and campsite)

15 Domestic airport, BSÍ bus terminal, hospital, Hlemmur bus station, Laugardalur, Háholt bus station (Mosfellsbær).

CAR & MOTORCYCLE

A car is unnecessary in Reykjavík as it's so easy to explore on foot and by bus. Car and camper hire for the countryside are available at both airports, the BSÍ bus terminal, and some city locations.

Parking

Street parking in the centre is limited and costs Ikr120 per hour (coins and ATM or credit cards with PIN only); it's free between 6pm and 10am from Monday to Saturday and all day Sunday. Parking outside the centre is free.

Vitatorg Car Park (1st hour Ikr80, subsequent hours Ikr50; ☺7am-midnight) Covered parking lot.

TAXI

Taxi prices are high. Flagfall starts at around Ikr660. Tipping is not required. From the BSÍ to the Reykjavík Downtown Hostel costs about Ikr2000.

There are usually taxis outside bus stations, airports, and bars on weekend nights (huge queues for the latter), plus on Bankastræti near Lækjargata.

BSR (☑561 0000; www.taxireykjavik.is)
Hreyfill (☑588 5522; www.hreyfill.is)

GREATER REYKJAVÍK

Viðey

On fine-weather days, the tiny uninhabited island of Viðey makes a wonderful day trip. Just 1km north of Reykjavík's Sundahöfn Harbour, it feels a world away. Surprising modern artworks, an abandoned village and great birdwatching add to its remote spell. The only sounds are the wind, the waves and the golden bumblebees buzzing among the tufted vetch and hawkweed.

Little Viðey was settled around 900 and was farmed until the 1950s. It was home to a powerful monastery from 1225, but in 1539 it was wiped out by Danish soldiers during the Reformation.

⊙ Sights & Activities

Just above the harbour, you'll find one of Iceland's oldest stone houses, **Viðeyarstofa** – which houses a **cafe** (mains Ikr800-2900; ☺11.30am-6pm Wed-Mon, to 8pm Tue mid-May–Sep, 1.30-4pm Sat & Sun Oct–mid-May) – as well as an 18th-century wooden **church** with some original decor, and a small **monument** to Skúli Magnússon. Excavations of the old **monastery foundations** unearthed 15th-century wax tablets and a runic love letter, now in the National Museum; other finds are displayed in the Viðeyarstofa.

Higher above the harbour is Ólafur Eliasson's interesting panelled art installation, the **Blind Pavilion** (2003). Nearby is Yoko Ono's **Imagine Peace Tower** (2007), a 'wishing well' that blasts a dazzling column of light into the sky every night between 9 October (John Lennon's birthday) and 8 December (the anniversary of his death). See Viðey's website for Peace Tower tours from Reykjavík. Further along, **Viðeyjarnaust cabin** has a barbecue, if you bring all your own supplies.

In summer there are Tuesday evening **cultural tours** with varying themes. Check online at www.videy.com/en.

Island Paths   WALKING, BIKING

The whole island is crisscrossed with walking paths. Some you can bicycle, others are more precarious. A good map at the harbour shows which are which. You can hire a **bike** (2/5hr rental Ikr2500/3500; ☺Jun-Aug), bring your own or come with a Bike Company (p68) tour. The island is great for **birdwatching** (30 species breed here) and **botany** (over one-third of all Icelandic plants grow on the island). In late August, some Reykjavikers come to pick wild caraway, which was originally planted here by Skúli Magnússon.

From the harbour, trails to the southeast lead past the natural sheep fold **Réttin**, the tiny grotto **Paradíshellir** (Paradise Cave), and then to the **abandoned fishing village** at Sundbakki. Most of the south coast is a protected area for birds and is closed to visitors from May to June.

Trails leading to the northwest take you past low ponds, monuments to several

FAROE FORAY

Flights and ferries give Arctic adventurers three or four days to explore the truly magical Faroe Islands. A half-week is just enough time to see the following highlights:

Tórshavn The first thing you'll notice are striking turf roofs adorning almost every bright-coloured building in the marina. Although light on sights, Tórshavn makes a great base if you're planning a series of day trips.

Gjógv Gjógv ('jaykf') may be hard to pronounce, but it's oh-so-easy to love. Tiny turf-roofed cottages cluster around a harbour that looks as though a lightning bolt ripped straight through the terrain. There's good hiking and an inn.

Mykines Marking the western limits of the island chain, Mykines (*mee*-chi-ness) offers innumerable bird colonies (puffins!), haunting basalt sea-stacks and solitary cliffs. Considered remote by Faroese standards (11 inhabitants), it is connected to Vágar by helicopter and ferry.

Hestir Hestir, just south of Streymoy, is best known for hollow grottoes carved into the cliffs by pounding waves.

shipwrecks, and the low cliffs of Eiðisbjarg, to Vesturey at the northern tip of the island. Richard Serra's Áfangar (Milestones; 1990) sculptures, made from huge pairs of basalt pillars, dot this part of the island.

ⓘ Getting There & Away

Viðey Ferry (☑ 533 5055; www.videy.com; return adult/child Ikr1100/550; ☺ hourly 10.15am-5.15pm mid-May–Sep, reduced services Oct–mid-May) Viðey ferry takes five minutes from Skarfabakki, 4.5km east of the centre. During summer, two boats a day start from Elding at the Old Harbour and the Harpa concert hall. Bus 5 stops closest to Skarfabakki, and it's a point on the Reykjavík hop-on-hop-off tour bus.

Kópavogur

POP 32,300

Kópavogur, the first suburb south of Reykjavík, is just a short bus ride away but feels far from the tourist trail. There are a few sights in the cultural complex Menningarmiðstöð Kópavogs (next door to the distinctive arched church) and a huge shopping mall.

◎ Sights

Natural History Museum of Kópavogur   MUSEUM
(Náttúrufræðistofa Kópavogs; ☑ 570 0430; www.natkop.is; Hamraborg 6a; ☺ 10am-7pm Mon-Thu, 11am-5pm Fri, 1-5pm Sat) **FREE** This museum explores Iceland's unique geology and wildlife. There's an orca skeleton, a good collection of taxidermied animals, geological

specimens and some of Mývatn lake's unusual *marimo* balls.

Salurinn   CULTURAL BUILDING
(☑ 570 0400; www.salurinn.is; Hamraborg 6) Iceland's first specially designed concert hall is built entirely from local materials (driftwood, spruce and crushed stone) and has fantastic acoustics. See the website for its (mostly classical) concert program.

Gerðarsafn Art Museum   ART MUSEUM
(☑ 570 0440; www.gerdarsafn.is; Hamraborg 4; adult/child Ikr500/free; ☺ 11am-5pm Tue-Sun) Next door to Kópavogur's concert hall, this beautifully designed museum dedicated to Icelandic stained glass artist and sculptor Gerður Helgadóttir hosts excellent rotating modern-art exhibitions, and has a notable permanent collection of 20th-century Icelandic art. Its small cafe has mountain views.

🛍 Shopping

Smáralind   SHOPPING CENTRE
(☑ 528 8000; www.smaralind.is; Hagasmári 1, Kópavogur; ☺ 11am-7pm Mon-Wed & Fri, to 9pm Thu, to 6pm Sat, 1-6pm Sun) Iceland's largest mall. Take bus 1, 2 or 28, or their free shuttle May through August, which leaves from Reykjavík Tourist Office and stops off at Kópavogur museums (see schedule online).

ⓘ Getting There & Away

Buses 1 and 2 leave from Hlemmur or Lækjartorg in central Reykjavík, stopping at the Hamraborg stop in Kópavogur (look for the church). It takes about 15 minutes.

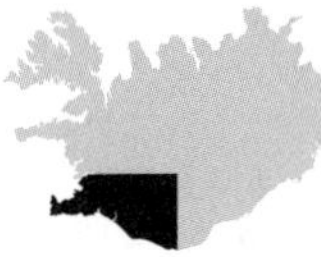

Southwest Iceland & the Golden Circle

Why Go?

Black beaches stretch along the Atlantic, geysers spout from geothermal fields, and waterfalls glide across escarpments while brooding volcanoes and glittering ice caps score the inland horizon. The beautiful southwest has many of Iceland's most legendary natural wonders, so it's a relatively crowded and increasingly developed area. The Golden Circle (a tourist route comprising three famous sights: Þingvellir, Geysir and Gullfoss) draws by far the largest crowds outside of Reykjavík, but visit during off-hours or venture further afield and you'll find awe-inspiring splendour.

The further you go the better it gets. Tourist faves like the silica-filled Blue Lagoon and the earth-rending parliament at Þingvellir are just beyond the capital. Churning seas lead to the Vestmannaeyjar archipelago offshore. At the region's far reaches lie the powerful Hekla and Eyjafjallajökull volcanoes, hopping Skógar and Vík, and the hidden valleys of Þórsmörk and Landmannalaugar.

Best Places to Eat

➜ Lindin (p110)
➜ Slippurinn (p158)
➜ Við Fjöruborðið (p126)
➜ Vitinn (p104)
➜ Suður-Vík (p152)

Best Places to Stay

➜ Ion Luxury Adventure Hotel (p109)
➜ Fljótsdalur HI Hostel (p136)
➜ Efstidalur II (p110)
➜ Héraðsskólinn (p109)
➜ Garðar (p150)

Road Distances (km)

	Keflavík	Selfoss	Gullfoss	Landmannalaugar	Vík
Selfoss	100				
Gullfoss	156	71			
Landmannalaugar	230	130	147		
Vík	226	130	177	218	
Reykjavík	51	57	113	185	186

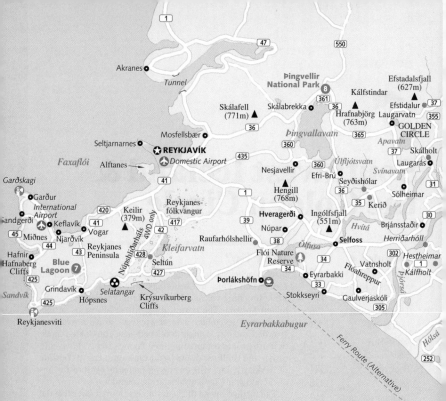

Southwest Iceland & the Golden Circle Highlights

1 Marvel at black basalt columns, sea stacks and rocky buttes on **Reynisfjara** (p149), near buzzy Vík

2 Set sail for **Vestmannaeyjar** (p153),

with its zippy puffins and small town tucked between lava flows

3 Camp in **Þórsmörk** (p146), a lush kingdom surrounded by brooding glaciers

4 Explore the **Þjórsárdalur** (p129), a valley of raw terrain and Saga settlements carved by the powerful Þjórsá river

5 Traverse caramel-coloured peaks at **Landmannalaugar**

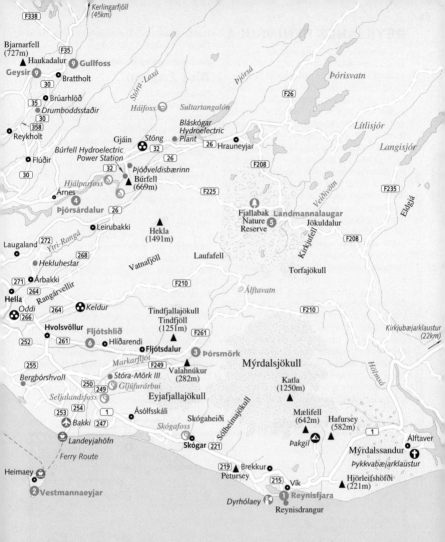

(p140), then set off on
Iceland's most famous hike,
the Laugavegurinn

6 Ride horses beneath
waterfalls at **Fljótshlíð** (p135)

7 Wash away your cares at

the **Blue Lagoon** (p98),
the Vegas version of Icelandic
hot-potting

8 See the continental plates
part at historic **Þingvellir
National Park** (p106)

9 Wait for water to shoot
skywards at **Geysir** (p110),
or watching it tumble down at
Gullfoss (p111)

REYKJANES PENINSULA

The Reykjanes Peninsula expands in drama as you move away from the highway between Keflavík International Airport and Reykjavík. You'll find not only the Blue Lagoon, Iceland's most famous attraction, filling a part of the vast lava fields, but other gorgeous and interesting sights all around – many of them based around active volcanoes. The busiest towns are no-frills Keflavík and nearby Njarðvík, but the sweet, windswept fishing hamlets Garður and Sandgerði are just minutes to the west of the airport on a small northwestern spur, and are great for whale watching. The rest of the Reykjanes, from dramatic Reykjanestá in the southwest, to the Reykjanesfólkvangur wilderness reserve in the southeast, is an untamed landscape of multi-hued volcanic craters, mineral lakes, bubbling hotsprings, and rugged, quad-bike-ready mountains and coastal lava fields.

The Reykjanes Peninsula has formed a Geopark Project (http://reykjanesgeopark.tumblr.com), to protect, research and celebrate the region's unusual geology (pillow lava! oceanic ridge! meeting of tectonic plates! four volcanic systems!) and local culture.

Public transport to Keflavík and the Blue Lagoon is fast and frequent from Reykjavík, and while there is limited public bus service to other villages, you'll do best with private transport to reach the more remote parts of the peninsula.

Blue Lagoon

Blue Lagoon GEOTHERMAL POOL
(Bláa Lónið; ☑ 420 8800; www.bluelagoon.com; Jun-Aug admission adult/14 & 15 yr/under 14 from €40/20/free, visitor pass (no lagoon entry) €10; ⊙ 9am-9pm Jun & 11-31 Aug, to 11pm Jul-10 Aug, 10am-8pm Sep-May) As the Eiffel Tower is to Paris, so the Blue Lagoon is to Iceland...with all the positive and negative connotations implied. Those who say it's too expensive, too commercial, too crowded aren't wrong, but you'll be missing something special if you don't go.

In a magnificent black-lava field, the milky-teal spa is fed water from the futuristic Svartsengi geothermal plant; with its silver towers, the roiling clouds of steam, and people daubed in white silica mud, it's an otherworldy place.

The superheated water (70% sea water, 30% fresh water, at a perfect 38°C) is rich in blue-green algae, mineral salts and fine silica mud, which condition and exfoliate the skin – sounds like advertising speak, but you really do come out as soft as a baby's bum. The water is hottest near the vents where it emerges, and the surface is several degrees warmer than the bottom.

Reykjanes Peninsula

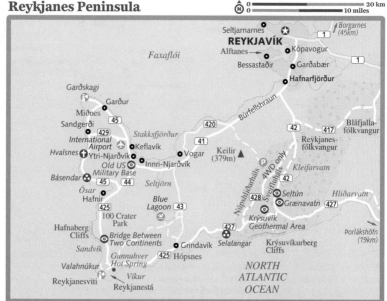

ⓘ TOP TIPS FOR THE BLUE LAGOON

➡ Cut long lines with e-tickets (www.bluelagoon.com) or vouchers from tour companies (Air Iceland, Reykjavík Excursions).

➡ Look online for ticket packages, special promotions and winter rates.

➡ Avoid summertime mayhem (worst from 10am to 2pm); go in off hours: first thing or after 7pm.

➡ Lagoon water can corrode silver and gold; leave watches and jewellery in your locker.

➡ You must practise standard Iceland pool etiquette: thorough naked pre-pool showering.

➡ Entry to the lagoon includes shampoo and conditioner (you'll need lots of conditioner afterwards as briny water plays havoc with hair).

➡ Your entry wristband is used to scan entry to lockers and to pay for drinks in the in-lagoon bar.

➡ You can stay in the pool for a half hour after closing, and in the changing rooms for one hour after closing.

➡ Going to the lagoon on a tour or in transit to the airport can sometimes save time and money. By bus, Reykjavík Excursions (p100) connects Keflavík International Airport, the Blue Lagoon, and Reykjavík.

➡ At the car park you'll find luggage check (Ikr300 per day, per bag); perfect if you're going to the lagoon on your way from/to the airport.

The lagoon has been developed for visitors with an enormous, modern complex of changing rooms (with 700 lockers!), restaurants, rooftop viewpoint, and gift shop (less shocking than it sounds), and landscaped with hot-pots, steam rooms, sauna, bar and a piping-hot waterfall that delivers a powerful hydraulic massage – like being pummelled by a troll. A VIP section has its own interior wading space, lounge and viewing platform.

For extra relaxation, you can lie on a floating mattress and have a masseuse knead your knots (30/60 minutes €60/95). You must book spa treatments well in advance. Towel or bathing-suit hire is €5.

The complex is just off the road between Keflavík and Grindavík.

👉 Tours

In addition to the myriad spa opportunities at the Blue Lagoon, you can combine your visit with package tours, or hook up with nearby ATV Adventures (p104) for quad-bike or cycling tours (Ikr9,900 from Blue Lagoon through the lava fields) or bicycle rental. They can pick up and drop off at the Blue Lagoon.

🛏 Sleeping & Eating

The Blue Lagoon has a good restaurant, cafe, lagoon bar, hotel, and gift shop selling all sorts of curative soaps and gels.

Blue Lagoon – Clinic Hotel HOTEL €€€
(☑ 420 8806; www.bluelagoon.com; s/d incl breakfast Ikr38,500/46,200; @ 🛜) The modern Blue Lagoon clinic hotel is a 600m walk across the lava field from Iceland's most famous attraction. Rooms are soothing and sleek, with heated-floor bathrooms, and each has a small porch for viewing the surrounding moonscape. The hotel has its own pool of Blue Lagoon water. Rates include entry to Blue Lagoon.

Northern Light Inn HOTEL €€€
(☑ 426 8650; www.northernlightinn.is; s/d incl breakfast Ikr26,500/34,500; @ 🛜) Spacious, stylish rooms line the lava field at this bungalow hotel. There's a sunny sitting room, and free (from 5am to 11pm) transfers to Keflavík airport and the lagoon (the lagoon is only 1km away). On-site **Max's Restaurant** (mains Ikr3400-5000; ⏱ noon-10pm) boasts a smattering of Nordic fare, and floor-to-ceiling windows look out over lava and the steam-spewing geothermal plant.

Blue Café CAFE €
(snacks Ikr780-1950; ⏱ 9am-10pm Jun-Aug, to 9pm Sep-May) Simple, cafeteria-style eating at the Blue Lagoon, with smoothies, sandwiches and prefab sushi.

LAVA Restaurant ICELANDIC €€€
(www.bluelagoon.com; lunch/dinner mains Ikr3950/5900; ⏱ noon-10pm, Jul-10 Aug, to

---

ⓘ SOUTHWEST RESOURCES

South Iceland Tourist Information (www.south.is) Has a thorough print booklet and excellent free detailed maps for each sub-region. Get them at local tourist offices.

Visit Reykjanes Website (www.visit reykjanes.is)

8.30pm or 9pm rest of year) The Blue Lagoon's cavernous dining room is the domain of chef Viktor Örn Andrésson. Though the room can feel like a function hall, views to the lagoon are serene, the waitstaff excellent and the menu features Iceland's favourite dishes prepared with well-conceived recipes.

ⓘ Getting There & Away

The lagoon is 47km southwest of Reykjavík and 23km southeast of Keflavík International Airport. Bus services run year-round, as do tours (which sometimes offer better deals than a bus ticket plus lagoon admission). You must book in advance.

Blue Lagoon partners with **Reykjavík Excursions** (☑ 580 5400; www.re.is), which runs buses to the lagoon from/to Reyjavík and from/to the airport. The most frequent operator (11 to 13 daily June to August; see www.bluelagoon. com for details), you can do a round trip from either Reykjavík or the airport, or stop off at the lagoon on your way between the two.

Reykjavík Excursions runs Reyjavík or airport transfers to/from Blue Lagoon (round trip/round trip including lagoon admission Ikr3600/Ikr9800).

Reykjanes Express (www.reykjanesexpress. is) services include Bus GRI, which travels between Reykjavík's BSÍ Terminal, the Blue Lagoon, and Grindavík (three daily).

Bustravel (☑ 511 2600; www.bustravel.is) services include airport–Reykjavík transfers (Ikr3200).

Keflavík & Njarðvík (Reykjanesbær)

The twin towns of Keflavík and Njarðvík, on the coast about 47km southwest of Reykjavík, are a rather ungainly expanse of suburban boxes and fast-food outlets. Together they're known as 'Reykjanesbær'. Don't stay here unless you have an early flight; it's worth the 40-minute ride into Reykjavík.

⊙ Sights

⊙ Keflavík

The waterfront strip in Keflavík has most hotels, restaurants and the museum Duushús. To the east on the seashore is an impressive Ásmundur Sveinsson sculpture, used as a climbing frame by the local kids. Just beyond, on the edge of the little harbour, find a black cave where a larger-than-life Giantess (Skessa; Gróf small boat harbour; ⊙ 1-5pm Sat & Sun) FREE, a character from Herdís Egilsdóttir's children's books, sits in a rocking chair.

★ **Duushús** MUSEUM
(☑ 421 3796; Grófin; ⊙ noon-5pm Mon-Fri, 1-5pm Sat & Sun) FREE In a long red warehouse by the harbour, Duushús is Keflavík's historic cultural centre. There's a permanent exhibition of around 60 of Grímur Karlsson's many hundreds of miniature ships, made over a lifetime; a gallery with international art exhibitions; and a changing local-history display.

Icelandic Museum of Rock 'n' Roll MUSEUM
(Rokksafn Íslands; ☑ 420 1030; www.rokksafn. is; Hjallavegur 2; admission Ikr1500; ⊙ noon-5pm Mon-Sat) This new museum delves into the history of the awesome Icelandic music scene: from Björk to Sigur Rós and Of Monsters and Men. Admission includes an audio guide with music. There's also the Music Hall of Fame, instruments for you to jam on, a cafe, and a shop where you can stock up on local music.

⊙ Njarðvík

★ **Víkingaheimar** EXHIBITION CENTRE
(Viking World; ☑ 422 2000; www.vikingaheimar.is; Víkingabraut 1; adult/child Ikr1200/free; ⊙ 11am-6pm May-Aug, noon-5pm Sep-Apr) At the eastern end of Njarðvík's waterfront, the spectacular Víkingaheimar is a Norse exhibition centre built in one beautiful, sweeping architectural gesture. The centrepiece is 23m-long *Íslendingur*, an exact reconstruction of the Viking Age *Gokstad* longship. It was built almost single-handedly by Gunnar Marel Eggertsson, who then sailed it from Iceland to New York in 2000 to commemorate the 1000th anniversary of Leif's journey to America.

Additional rooms display ancient relics, most likely from the Celtic settlement, and upstairs there's an exhibit about the Norse gods geared towards children.

Keflavík

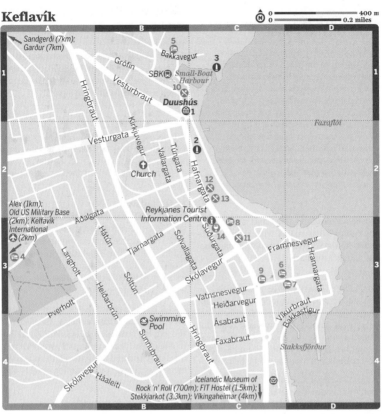

Stekkjarkot   HISTORIC BUILDING
(⊙ 1-5pm Tue-Sun Jun-Aug, winter by appointment)
FREE On the point near Víkingaheimar, tiny
folk museum Stekkjarkot is a restored turf
house, abandoned in 1924 with parts dating
to the 19th-century.

🏃 Tours

Viking Guide   TOURS
(✆ 841 1448; www.facebook.com/VikingGuide;
Keflavík) Pinched for time? A local guide will
take you on tours of Reykjanes Peninsula,
Reykjavík or the Golden Circle.

🛏 Sleeping

Most hotels in the area provide free airport
transfer.

Alex   HOTEL €
(✆ 421 2800; www.alex.is; Aðalgata 60; d without bath incl breakfast Ikr14,900, cottage d incl
breakfast Ikr15,900; @ 🖥) On the main road

GOODBYE TO THE MILITARY BASE

Keflavík owed a great deal of its former prosperity to the nearby American military base, Naval Air Station Keflavík, which navy airplanes used for antisubmarine patrols. The base closed in September 2006, ending 55 years of occupation (but still sees occasional visits by the US military: try to spot its planes when you fly in). The former barracks have been turned into accommodation for students at Keilir (www.keilir.net), which has a pilot's program, and the general public.

between Keflavík (1.5km) and the airport, this complex has rooms with shared bathrooms in a no-frills main building and cool tiny cottages out back.

FIT Hostel
HOSTEL €

(☑ 421 8889; www.fithostel.is; Fitjabraut 6a; dm from Ikr4000; @ 🛜) In an industrial estate towards Njarðvík, on busy Rte 41, this hostel feels rough around the edges and is not for everyone, but it's the cheapest option near the airport. Buses to Reykjavík and Keflavík pass in front, but a car would be helpful.

Icelandair Hotel Keflavík
HOTEL €€

(☑ 421 5222; www.icehotel.is; Hafnargata 57; d from Ikr25,000; @ 🛜) The highest end option within the airport's orbit, these two multistorey wings with a retro 'Flughotel' sign are thoughtfully decorated and thoroughly modern. On-site restaurant.

Hótel Berg
B&B €€

(☑ 422 7922; www.hotelberg.is; Bakkavegur 17; s/d incl breakfast Ikr23,100/26,200; @ 🛜) This homey guesthouse overlooking a little inlet harbour has common spaces with charming touches, and modern rooms with flatscreen TVs and original photography on the walls. It's located at the northern (and most charming) end of Keflavík, and is a wonderfully welcoming place to stay.

Airport Hotel Smári
HOTEL €€

(☑ 595 1900; www.hotelsmari.is; Blikavöllur 2, Keflavík International Airport; s/d/tr incl breakfast Ikr28,500/28,500/32,000; P @ 🛜) The only hotel actually at the airport, Smári is about 100m from the terminal and offers a tower of solid business-style rooms with flat-

screen TVs. Superior rooms are bigger, with two double beds.

Hótel Keilir
HOTEL €€

(☑ 420 9800; www.hotelkeilir.is; Hafnargata 37; d/q incl breakfast from Ikr23,000/29,300; 🛜) Basic rooms, some with water views, in the centre of Keflavík's seafront main street.

A10 Deluxe
B&B €€

(☑ 568 0210; www.a10deluxe.com; Aðalgata 10; d/tr incl breakfast Ikr23,400/26,200, s without bathroom incl breakfast Ikr10,900) Sleek, clean and simple is the order of the day at this residential-area B&B on the main drag out of town.

Hótel Keflavík
HOTEL €€

(☑ 420 7000; www.hotelkeflavik.is; Vatnsnesvegur 12-14; d/f incl breakfast Ikr31,000/64,000; @ 🛜) Serviceable, central rooms; rates vary wildly online. The hotel also runs a small mural-painted guesthouse (s/d without bathroom Ikr14,700/18,500) across the street, which is a bit dark inside.

Bed & Breakfast Keflavík Airport
HOTEL €€

(☑ 426 5000; www.bbkeflavik.com; Valhallarbraut 761; d/q incl breakfast Ikr20,000/26,200; @ 🛜) In one of the former military base buildings, this large, spruced-up hotel offers an assortment of simple accommodation, close to the airport.

🍴 Eating & Drinking

There are enough greasy grills in Keflavík to give you an instant burger-induced coronary. Several good places line the main street, plus Icelandair Hotel Keflavík has an excellent restaurant.

Thai Keflavík
THAI €

(☑ 421 8666; www.thaikeflavik.is; Hafnargata 39; mains Ikr1690-2400; ⏱ 11.30am-10pm Mon-Fri, 4-10pm Sat & Sun; 🛜) With authentic Thai dishes, this restaurant is a great choice if you're up to your eyeballs in fish and lamb. There's outdoor seating during warm weather.

Olsen Olsen
FAST FOOD €

(☑ 421 4457; Hafnargata 17; snacks Ikr950-2100; ⏱ 11am-10pm) During the 1950s, thanks to American-introduced rock 'n' roll, Keflavík was the coolest place in Iceland. This US-style diner transports locals back to the glory days, with shiny silver tables, red plastic seats and pictures of Elvis.

Kaffi Duus SEAFOOD, INDIAN €€
(☑ 421 7080; www.duus.is; Duusgata 10, Duushús;
mains Ikr2650-4500; ☺11am-11pm) This friendly nautical-themed cafe-restaurant-bar is
decorated with walrus tusks and overlooks
the small-boat harbour. It serves generous
platefuls of fresh fish, plus pasta, salads,
burgers and, incongruously, Indian food. It's
a popular evening hang-out.

Ráin ICELANDIC €€
(☑ 421 4601; www.rain.is; Hafnargata 19a; mains
Ikr1700-5300; ☺11am-10pm Mon-Fri, 4-10pm Sat &
Sun) Decorated like the interior of a wooden
cruise ship from the '70s, Ráin offers Icelandic favourites with great sea views.

Paddy's BAR
(☑ 421 8900; Hafnargata 38) A hole-in-the-wall
that can get raucous at weekends and has
occasional live music.

ℹ Information

Reykjanes Tourist Information Centre (☑ 421
5660; www.visitreykjanes.is; Hafnargata 36;
☺9am-5pm Mon-Fri, 10am-2pm Sat) Reykjanes
Peninsula information, maps and brochures.
Also has an airport branch.

ℹ Getting There & Around

Bicycle rental (Ikr1000 per hour) is available
through Thai Keflavík (p102).

TO/FROM THE AIRPORT

Most of Reykjanesbær's lodgings offer free
transfers to/from Keflavík International Airport
for guests. A taxi costs about Ikr5000 – call
Airport Taxi (☑ 420 1212; www.airporttaxi.
is) or **Hreyfill-Bæjarleiðir** (☑ 588 5522; www.
hreyfill.is).

AIR

Apart from flights to Greenland and the Faroe
Islands, all of Iceland's international flights use
Keflavík International Airport (www.kef
airport.is).

BUS

SBK (☑ 420 6000; www.sbk.is; Grófin 2-4,
Keflavík) runs local buses. **Reykjanes Express**
(www.reykjanesexpress.is) runs the following
services:

➡ Bus REX goes to the BSÍ bus terminal in
Reykjavík (adult/child Ikr1600/800, eight daily
Monday to Friday, three daily Saturday and
Sunday).

➡ Bus 4 goes to Garður and Sandgerði (both
services Ikr570, six daily).

Airport buses can also drop you near the town
limits.

Northwestern Reykjanes

The western edge of the Reykjanes Peninsula is rugged and exposed – perfect if you love
wild rain-lashed cliffs and beaches. There
are several fishing villages and some sights
among the lava fields.

Garður

POP 1409

From Keflavík, if you follow Rte 41 for 9km,
through the village of Garður (www.sand
gerdi.is), you'll reach the beautiful wind-
battered **Garðskagi headland**, one of the
best places in Iceland for **bird spotting** – it's
a big breeding ground for sea birds, and it's
often the place where migratory species first
touch down. It's also possible to see seals,
and maybe **whales**, from here.

Two splendid **lighthouses**, one tall
and one tiny, add drama, and you can get
near-360-degree sea views from the tall
one. There's also a small **folk museum**
(☑ 422 7220; www.svgardur.is; adult/child Ikr500/
free; ☺1-5pm Apr-Oct), filled with a pleasing
mishmash of fishing boats, birds' eggs and
sewing machines. Upstairs, balconied **2
Lighthouses Restaurant** (Tveir Vitar; ☑ 422
7214; Garðurbraut 100; mains Ikr1950-5000;
☺8am-noon Mon, to 10pm Tue-Thu, to 11pm Fri,
10am-11pm Sat, 10am-10pm Sun Apr-Oct) has superb views over the ocean to Snæfellsjökull.

There's a tranquil, free **camping** area by
the lighthouse, with toilets and fresh water;
and a guesthouse in town.

Garður is served by **Reykjanes Express**
(www.reykjanesexpress.is) bus 4 (Ikr570, 15 minutes, six daily) to Sandgerði and Keflavík.

Sandgerði & Around

Five kilometres south of Garður, Sandgerði
(population 1571) is an industrious fishing
village.

Sudurnes Science & Learning Center
(☑ 423 7551; http://thekkingarsetur.is/english/
exhibitions; Gerðavegur 1; adult/child Ikr600/300;
☺10am-4pm Mon-Fri, 1-5pm Sat & Sun May-Sep,
10am-2pm Mon-Fri Oct-Apr) has a fascinating exhibit about Polar explorer Jean-
Batiste Charcot, whose ship *Pourquois Pas?*
wrecked near here in 1936 (all but one per-
ished). There are original artefacts from the
wreck and memorabilia. Other displays include stuffed and jarred Icelandic creatures
(look out for the walrus and the freaky *Gor-
gonocephalus*) and a small aquarium.

SOUTHWEST ICELAND & THE GOLDEN CIRCLE NORTHWESTERN REYKJANES

Vitinn (☑ 423 7755; www.vifinn.is; Vitatorg 7; mains Ikr4100-6850; ☺ 11.30am-9pm May-Sep, reduced hours Oct-Apr), across the street, is not to be missed. A friendly husband-and-wife team serves heaps of seafood (stored in tanks out back in the courtyard) in marine-chic surrounds. The crab bisque is delicious, and they are putting in a greenhouse to grow their own herbs and veg.

There are pleasant **beaches** on the coast south of Sandgerði, and the surrounding marshes are frequented by more than 190 species of **birds**. About 5km south you'll find a lonely church at **Hvalsnes** featured in a famous Icelandic hymn by Hallgrímur Pétursson (1616–74), written at the death of his young daughter who was buried here.

Two kilometres south, you can walk to the ruins of Saga Age fishing village **Básendar**, which was destroyed by a tidal wave in 1799.

Sandgerði is served by **Reykjanes Express** (www.reykjanesexpress.is) bus 4 (Ikr570, 15 minutes, six daily) to Sandgerði and Keflavík.

Southwestern Reykjanes

If you turn off Rte 41 onto Rte 44 just outside Keflavík, you'll first pass the deserted **US military base** before reaching the fading fishing village of **Hafnir**. There's nothing much to see here – just humps and bumps in a field, thought to be a 9th-century longhouse belonging to Ingólfur Arnarson's foster brother, and the anchor of the 'ghost ship' *Jamestown*, which drifted ashore mysteriously in 1870 with a full cargo of timber but no crew.

There are **bird cliffs** at Hafnaberg, south of which you'll reach the **Bridge Between Two Continents** where a teeny footbridge spans a sand-filled gulf between the North American and European plates.

In the far southwest of the peninsula the landscape alternates between lava fields and wild volcanic crags and craters, thus it's been named **100 Crater Park**. Several power plants here exploit geothermal heat to produce salt from sea water and to provide electricity for the national grid. **Power Plant Earth** (Orkuverið Jörð; ☑ 436 1000; www.powerplantearth.is; admission Ikr1000; ☺ 12.30-4.30pm Sat & Sun Jun-Sep) is an interactive exhibition about energy. You also get a glimpse into the vast, spotless turbine hall, and there are scaled representations of the planets positioned around the peninsula.

One of the most wild and wonderful spots on the peninsula is **Valahnúkur**, where a windy road leads off Rte 425 through 13th-century lava fields. Turn right at the T-intersection and go 900m on an unpaved road to dramatic, climb-able **cliffs** and **Reykjanes-viti lighthouse**, the oldest (1878) in Iceland.

From Valahnúkur and the nearby coast you can see the flat-topped rocky islet **Eldey**, 14km offshore, home to the world's largest gannet colony. Some claim the last great auk was killed there, though Faroese dispute this, insisting that the event occurred at Stóra Dímun. Today Eldey is a protected bird reserve.

If you take the left branch of the above T-intersection, in 500m you reach a steaming multicoloured **geothermal area**. This includes the hot spring **Gunnuhver**, named after the witch-ghost Gunna, who was trapped by magic and lured into the boiling water to her death.

Grindavík

Grindavík, the only settlement on the south coast of Reykjanes, is one of Iceland's most important fishing centres. Here, all flimflam is rejected in favour of working jetties, cranes and warehouses.

The town's only tourist attraction is **Kvíkan** (Magma; ☑ 420 1190; www.visitgrindavik.is; Hafnargata 12a; adult/child Ikr1200/free; ☺ 10am-5pm), a museum with two exhibits: a well-curated one on the fish-salting industry, and one and about the earth's energy.

☞ Tours

ATV Adventures   QUAD-BIKE, CYCLING TOURS
(☑ 857 3001; www.atv4x4.is) The major provider for quad-bike rides around the peninsula: explore lava fields, see shipwrecks, from Ikr9900 per seat with a driver, or from Ikr15,000 per person for a two-person self-drive buggy (need driver's licence). Also runs cycling tours from Blue Lagoon (Ikr9900) and has bicycle rental (four/eight hours Ikr2900/3900; Ikr4900 for eight hours with Blue Lagoon delivery).

Salty Tours   TOURS
(☑ 820 5750; www.saltytours.com; Borgarhraun 1, Grindavík) Day tours of Reykjanes (Ikr13,000) and beyond.

Arctic Horses   HORSE RIDING
(☑ 848 0143; www.arctichorses.is; Hópsheiði 16, Grindavík) Small, family-run outfit with horse

rides along the peninsula. Popular lighthouse tour (adult/child Ikr8000/5000) lasts one to 1½ hours.

🍴 Sleeping & Eating

Campsite   CAMPGROUND €

(☑ 660 7323; www.visitgrindavik.is; Austurvegur 26; camp sites per person Ikr900; ☺ mid-May–mid-Sep) Grindavík's fresh-faced campsite near the harbour is a patch of green with good amenities, including barbecues and playground, tourist office and two-for-one Kvíkan museum admission.

Guesthouse Borg   GUESTHOUSE €

(☑ 895 8686; www.guesthouseborg.com; Borgarhraun 2; s/d without bathroom incl breakfast Ikr9000/14,000; @ 🛜) Borg is an older home in the centre of town with the cosiness of 'grandma's place'. Kitchen and laundry access.

★ Bryggjan   CAFE €

(Harbour; snacks Ikr600-1400; ☺ 8am-11pm Mon-Fri, 10am-11pm Sat & Sun; 🛜) Facing the harbourfront, in a block of warehouses, this adorable cafe serves up light meals amid framed photos, old fishing buoys, and relaxing locals.

Salthúsið   SEAFOOD €€

(☑ 426 9700; www.salthusid.is; Stamphólsvegur 2; mains Ikr1400-3900; ☺ noon-10pm mid-May–mid-Sep) The classy wooden Salthúsið specialises in local *saltfiskur* (saltfish), which is prepared in different ways, plus there's salmon, lobster, chicken and lamb.

ℹ Information

Tourist Information Centre (☑ 420 1190; www.visitgrindavik.is; ☺ 10am-5pm mid-May–mid-Sep) Two branches: in Kvíkan museum and the campground. There's an internet terminal.

ℹ Getting There & Away

Reykjanes Express (www.reykjanesexpress.is) bus GRI travels between Reykjavík's BSÍ Terminal, the Blue Lagoon, and Grindavík (Ikr1600, one hour, three daily).

Reykjanesfólkvangur

For a taste of Iceland's raw countryside, visit this 300-sq-km wilderness reserve, a mere 40km from Reykjavík. Established in 1975, the reserve protects the elaborate lava formations created by the dramatic Reykjanes ridge volcanoes. Its three showpieces are

Kleifarvatn, a deep mineral lake with submerged hot springs and black-sand beaches; the spitting, bubbling Krýsuvík geothermal zone at Seltún; and the southwest's largest bird cliffs, the epic Krýsuvíkurberg. The whole area is criss-crossed by walking trails. Get good maps at Keflavík, Grindavík or Hafnarfjörður tourist offices. You'll see parking turnouts at the head of the most popular walks: the loop around Kleifarvatn, and the tracks along the craggy Sveifluháls and Núpshlíðarháls ridges.

Kleifarvatn

This deep, brooding lake sits in a volcanic fissure, surrounded by wind-warped lava cliffs and black-sand shores. Legend has it that a wormlike monster the size of a whale lurks below the surface – but the poor creature is running out of room, as the lake has been shrinking ever since two major earthquakes shook the area in 2000. For a macabre fictional book on this event, seek out Arnaldur Indriðason's thriller *The Draining Lake* (2004). A walking trail runs around the edge, offering dramatic views and the crunch of volcanic cinders underfoot.

Krýsuvík & Seltún

The volatile **geothermal field Austurengjar**, about 2km south of Kleifarvatn, is often called Krýsuvík after the nearby abandoned farm. Even by Icelandic standards, this area is prone to geological tantrums. The temperature below the surface is 200°C and the water is boiling as it emerges from the ground. A borehole was sunk here to provide energy for Hafnarfjörður during the 1990s, but it exploded without warning in 1999 and the project was abandoned.

At Seltún, boardwalks meander round a cluster of **hot springs**. The mudpots and steaming sulfuric *solfataras* (volcanic vents) shimmer with rainbow colours from the minerals in the earth.

Nearby is the lake **Grænavatn**, an old explosion crater filled with interesting teal water – caused by a combination of minerals and warmth-loving algae.

Krýsuvíkurberg Cliffs

About 3km south of Seltún across the Krýsuvíkurhraun lava fields, a dirt track leads down to the coast at Krýsuvíkurberg (marked on the main road as Krýsuvíkurbjarg).

These sweeping black cliffs stretch for 4km and are packed with 57,000 seabird breeding pairs in summer, from guillemots to occasional puffins. A walking path runs their length.

THE GOLDEN CIRCLE

The Golden Circle takes in three popular attractions all within 100km of the capital: Þingvellir, Geysir and Gullfoss. It is an artificial tourist circuit (ie no valley, natural topography, etc marks its extent) loved (and marketed) by thousands, and not to be confused with the Ring Road, which wraps around the entire country (and takes a week or more to properly complete). The Golden Circle offers the opportunity to see a meeting point of the continental plates and site of the ancient Icelandic parliament (Þingvellir), a spouting hot spring (Geysir) and a roaring waterfall (Gullfoss), all in one doable-in-a-day loop. Visiting under your own steam allows you to visit at off-hours and explore exciting attractions further afield. Almost every tour company in the Reykjavík area offers a Golden Circle excursion (from bus to bike to super-Jeep), often combinable with other sights as well.

If you're planning to spend the night in the relatively small region, the Laugarvatn area is a good base, or choose from accommodation scattered along Rte 35.

Þingvellir

Þingvellir National Park (www.thingvellir.is), 23km east of Reykjavík, is Iceland's most important historical site and a place of vivid beauty. The Vikings established the world's first democratic parliament, the Alþingi

DIY GOLDEN CIRCLE

It's very easy to tour the Golden Circle on your own (by bike or car) – plus, it's fun to tack on additional elements that suit your interests. In the Golden Circle area signs are well marked, roads well paved, and the distances relatively short (it takes about four hours to drive the loop without any add-on stops). You can also cobble some of it together by bus (and buses do go into highlands not accessible by 2WD). The excellent *Uppsveitir Árnessýslu* map details the region.

The primary points of the Golden Circle are Þingvellir (a meeting-point of the continental plates and site of the ancient Icelandic parliament), Geysir (an erupting geyser), and Gullfoss (a pounding waterfall carving through a canyon). DIYers can add the following elements to their tour:

Laugarvatn (p109) Located between Þingvellir and Geysir, this small lakeside town has two must-tries: Lindin, an excellent restaurant, and Fontana, a swanky geothermal spa.

Þjórsárdalur (p129) Largely untouristed, the quiet valley along the Þjórsá river is dotted with ancient Viking ruins and mysterious natural wonders like Gjáin. Ultimately it leads up into the highlands (a main route to Landmannalaugar, the starting point of the famous Laugavegurinn hike).

Reykholt & Flúðir (p112 & p113) On your way south from Gullfoss, you can go river-rafting on the Hvítá river from Reykholt or swing through the geothermal Flúðir area, to its new natural spa and to pick up fresh veggies for your evening meal.

Eyrarbakki & Stokkseyri (p117) South of Selfoss, these two seaside townships are strikingly different than others nearby. Feast on seafood and check out local galleries that informally set up shop each year.

Kaldidalur Corridor (p169) Not all rentals are allowed to drive this bumpy dirt track (Rte 550), but if you have a sanctioned vehicle, you can explore this isolated road that curves around hulking glaciers. It starts near Þingvellir and ends near Húsafell, so if you have time, do the traditional Golden Circle in reverse, then head westward, where many more adventures await.

Kerlingarfjöll (p311) You'll need a 4WD (or to go by bus) to travel beyond Gullfoss, but if you have one, it's worth continuing on to this highland reserve, a rising hiker haven, about two hours beyond the falls.

(pronounced *ál-thingk-ee,* also called *Alþing*), here in AD 930. The meetings were conducted outdoors, and as with many saga sites, there are only the stone foundations of ancient encampments. The site has a superb natural setting, in an immense, fissured rift valley caused by the meeting of the North American and Eurasian tectonic plates, with rivers and waterfalls. The country's first national park, it was made a Unesco World Heritage Site in 2004.

History

Many of Iceland's first settlers had run-ins with royalty back in mainland Scandinavia. These chancers and outlaws decided that they could live happily without kings in the new country, and instead created district *þings* (assemblies) where justice could be served by and among local chieftains (*goðar*).

Eventually, a nationwide *þing* became necessary. Bláskógur – now Þingvellir (Parliament Fields) – lay at a crossroads by a huge fish-filled lake. It had plenty of firewood and a setting that would make even the most tedious orator dramatic, so it fitted the bill perfectly. Every important decision affecting Iceland was argued out on this plain – new laws were passed, marriage contracts were made, and even the country's religion was decided here. The annual parliament was also a great social occasion, thronging with traders and entertainers.

Over the following centuries, escalating violence between Iceland's most powerful groups led to the breakdown of law and order. Governance was surrendered to the Norwegian crown and the Alþing was stripped of its legislative powers in 1271. It functioned solely as a courtroom until 1798, before being dissolved entirely. When it regained its powers in 1843, members voted to move the meeting place to Reykjavík.

⊙ Sights

From the Park Service Centre on Rte 36, follow Rte 361 down to the only standing structures in the great rift. What follows is a natural progression of sites, starting from the car park.

★ The Tectonic Plates   CANYONS, WATERFALLS
The Þingvellir plain is situated on a tectonic plate boundary where North America and Europe are tearing away from each other at a rate of 1mm to 18mm per year. As a result,

HALLDÓR LAXNESS HOUSE

Gljúfrasteinn Laxness Museum
(☑586 8066; www.gljufrasteinn.is; Mosfellsbær; adult/child Ikr800/free; ⊙9am-5pm Jun-Aug, 10am-5pm Tue-Sun Sep-May, also closed Sat & Sun Jan-Feb & Nov) Nobel Prize–winning author Halldór Laxness (1902–98) lived in Mosfellsbær all his life. His riverside home is now the Gljúfrasteinn Laxness Museum, easy to visit on the road from Reykjavík to Þingvellir (Rte 36). The author built this upper-class 1950s house and it remains intact with original furniture, writing room, and Laxness' fine-art collection (needlework, sweetly, by his wife Auður). An audio-tour leads you round. Look for his beloved Jaguar parked out front.

the plain is scarred by dramatic fissures, ponds and rivers, including the great rift **Almannagjá**. A path runs along the fault between the cliff-top visitors centre and the Alþingi site.

The river **Öxará** cuts the western plate, tumbling off its edge in a series of pretty cascades. The most impressive is **Öxarárfoss**, on the northern edge of the Alþingi site. The pool **Drekkingarhylur** was used to drown women found guilty of infanticide, adultery or other serious crimes.

There are other smaller fissures on the eastern edge of the site. During the 17th century nine men accused of witchcraft were burnt at the stake in **Brennugjá** (Burning Chasm). Nearby are the fissures of **Flosagjá** (named after a slave who jumped his way to freedom) and **Nikulásargjá** (after a drunken sheriff discovered dead in the water). The southern end of Nikulásargjá is known as **Peningagjá** (Chasm of Coins) for the thousands of coins tossed into it by visitors.

Þingvallabær   HISTORIC BUILDINGS
The little farmhouse in the bottom of the rift, Þingvallabær was built for the 1000th anniversary of the Alþing in 1930 by state architect Guðjón Samúelsson. It's now used as the park warden's office and prime minister's summer house.

Þingvallakirkja   CHURCH
(⊙9am-7.30pm mid-May–Aug) Behind the Þingvallabær farmhouse, Þingvallakirkja is

one of Iceland's first churches. The original was consecrated in the 11th century, but the current wooden building only dates from 1859. Inside are several bells from earlier churches, a 17th-century wooden pulpit, and a painted altarpiece from 1834. The Independence-era poets Jónas Hallgrímsson and Einar Benediktsson are interred in the small cemetery behind the church.

Búðir
RUINS

Straddling both sides of the Öxará river, you'll find the ruins of various temporary camps called *búðir* (literally booths). These stone foundations were covered during sessions and were where parliament-goers camped. They also acted like stalls at today's music festivals, selling beer, food and vellum to assembled crowds. Most of the remains date from the 17th and 18th centuries; the largest, and one of the oldest, is **Biskup-abúð**, which belonged to the bishops of Iceland and is located north of the church.

★ The Alþingi
LANDMARK

Near the dramatic Almannagjá fault and fronted by a boardwalk is the **Lögberg** (Law Rock), where the Alþing convened annually. This was where the *lögsögumaður* (law speaker) recited the existing laws to the assembled parliament (one third each year). After Iceland's conversion to Christianity, the site shifted to the very foot of the Almannagjá cliffs, which acted as a natural amplifier, broadcasting the voices of the speakers across the assembled crowds. That site is marked by the Icelandic flag.

Decisions were reached by the Lögrétta (Law Council), made up of 146 men (48 voting members, 96 advisers and two bishops), who are thought to have assembled at **Neðrivellir** (Low Fields), the flat area in front of the cliffs.

Þingvellir Visitors Centre
VISITORS CENTRE

(Gestastofa; ⊙9am-5pm) **FREE** At the top of the Almannagjá rift is a simple visitors ventre with a video on the area's nature and history, and a shop. The small adjacent boardwalk offers great valley views. At the time of research an expansion was underway. Toilets cost Ikr200. You can park here and walk down, or walk up from the Alþingi site.

Þingvallavatn
LAKE

Filling much of the rift plain, Þingvalla-vatn is Iceland's largest lake, at 84 sq km. Pure glacial water from Langjökull filters through bedrock for 40km before emerging

here. It's joined by the hot spring Vellankat-la, which spouts from beneath the lava field on the northeastern shore. Þingvallavatn is an important refuelling stop for **migrating birds** (including the great northern diver, barrow's golden-eye and harlequin duck).

Weirdly, its waters are full of *bleikja* (Arctic char) that have been isolated for so long that they've evolved into four subspecies.

🏃 Activities

One of the most other-worldly activities in Iceland is strapping on a scuba mask (or snorkel) and wetsuit and exploring the crystalline **Silfra fissure**, one of the cracks in the rift valley. You must book ahead with a Reykjavík dive operator (p72). People with their own equipment must have licences, dive in groups of at least two, and buy the permit (Ikr1000) from the visitors centre.

You can also check in with park centres for **lake fishing** rules (some areas are off-limits), and get a permit (Ikr2000 per pole per day; 20 April to 15 September).

In the valley on the Rte 36 approach from Reykjavík, you can go horse riding with Laxnes (p71).

👉 Tours

Free one-hour guided tours set off from the church at 10am from June to August.

🛏 Sleeping & Eating

There is some basic accommodation to the south of the lake near Bruarholt such as **Hótel Borealis** (📞561 3661; www.hotelbor ealis.is; Bruarholt; d with/without bathroom incl breakfast Ikr27,700/17,800) and scout camp **Útilífsmiðstöð Skáta Úlfljótsvatni** (📞482 2674; www.ulfljotsvatn.is; Úlfljótsvatn; camp site/ dm per person Ikr1200/3400).

Þingvellir Campsites
CAMPGROUND €

(camp sites per adult/tent Ikr1300/100; ⊙Jun-Aug) Overseen by the park information centre, the best two areas are at Leirar, near the cafe: Syðri-Leirar is the biggest and Nyrðri-Leirar has laundry facilities. Fagrabrekka and Hvan-nabrekka are for campers only (no cars). Vatnskot, is down by the lake, and has toilets and cold water (no electricity).

Cottages @ Lake Thingvellir
COTTAGES €€

(Skálabrekka; 📞892 7110; www.lakethingvellir. is; cottage Ikr16,200, plus per person per night Ikr2300) Four pine cottages with views to the lake near the national park entrance along Rte 36.

★ Ion Luxury
Adventure Hotel
BOUTIQUE HOTEL €€€

(☑482 3415; www.ioniceland.is; Nesjavellir vid Þingvallavatn; s/d Ikr44,000/51,000; P @ ⚲ ⚹) ⚐ A leader in a new breed of deluxe countryside hotels, Ion is all about local food, sustainable practices and hip, modern rooms. Its **restaurant** (www.ioniceland.is; Nesjavellir vid, Þingvallavatn; dinner mains Ikr4400-6200; ☺11.30am-10pm) with slow-food local ingredients, bar with floor-to-ceilng plate glass windows, geothermal pool and organic spa are sumptuous. Rooms are a tad smallish, but kitted out impeccably, with fun touches like horse portraits on a wall.

Find it in a quiet geothermal valley (near the local power station) on the south side of Þingvallavatn.

National Park Cafe
CAFE €

(National Park Information Centre; soup Ikr950; ☺9am-10pm Apr-Oct) This very basic cafeteria in the information centre sells hot dogs and soup of the day with bread.

ℹ Information

Þingvellir Information Centre (Leirar Þjónustumiðstöð; ☑482 2660; www.thingvellir. is; ☺9am-5pm May-Sep) On Rte 36, on the north side of the lake, the information centre has details about the national park, as well as a cafe (p109). Þingvellir Visitors Centre (p108) also has information.

ℹ Getting There & Away

The easiest way to get here is on a Golden Circle tour or in a hire car.

Reykajvík Excursions (☑580 5400; www. re.is) services:
➡ Bus 6/6A Reykjavík–Gullfoss (Ikr2,500 BSÍ Bus Station to/from Þingvellir, one daily mid-June to mid-September, stopping at various points around Þingvellir for 75 minutes, then continuing to Laugarvatn, Geysir, Gullfoss and back).

Sterna (☑551 1166; www.sterna.is) services:
➡ Bus F35/F35A Reykjavík–Akureyri (Ikr1800 Harpa to/from Þingvellir, one daily late-June to early September; stops for 45 minutes at the park information centre and continues to Laugarvatn, Geysir, Gullfoss, Kjölur Highlands and Kerlingarfjöll to Akureyri).

Laugarvatn

Laugarvatn (Hot Springs Lake) is fed not only by streams running from the misty fells behind it, but by the hot spring Vígðalaug,

famous since medieval times. A village, also called Laugarvatn, sits on the lake's western shore, and it is one of the better places to base yourself in the Golden Circle area.

🏃 Activities

★ Fontana
GEOTHERMAL POOL

(☑486 1400; www.fontana.is; adult/child/under 12yr Ikr3200/1600/free; ☺10am-11pm Jun-Sep, 1-9pm Mon-Fri, 11am-9pm Sat & Sun Oct-May) This swanky lakeside soaking spot boasts three mod wading pools, and a cedar-lined steam room that's fed by a naturally occurring vent below. The cool cafe (snacks Ikr500 to Ikr1200) has lake views. You can rent towels or swimsuits (Ikr800) if you left yours at home.

Laugarvatn Swimming Pool
GEOTHERMAL POOL

(☑486 1251; adult/child Ikr500/250; ☺10am-10pm Mon-Fri, to 6pm Sat & Sun) If you want skip the Fontana hot-pot hoopla, there's a regular geothermal swimming pool next door that costs a fraction of the price with none of the glitz.

🧭 Tours

Laugarvatn Adventures
ROCK CLIMBING, CAVING

(☑862 5614; www.caving.is) Runs two- to three-hour caving and rock-climbing trips in the hills around town.

🛏 Sleeping & Eating

★ Héraðsskólinn
HOSTEL, GUESTHOUSE €

(☑537 8060; www.heradsskolinn.is; dm/s/d/q without bathroom from Ikr4200/12,900/13,900/25,900; ⚹) This brand new hostel and guesthouse fills an enormous renovated historical landmark school, built in 1928 by Guðjón Samúelsson. The beautiful, lakeside building with peaked roofs offers both private rooms with shared bathrooms (some sleep up to six) and dorms, plus a spacious library/living room and a cafe (open 7am to 10pm).

Laugarvatn HI Hostel
HOSTEL €

(☑486 1215; www.laugarvatnhostel.is; dm/s/d without bathroom Ikr4100/6300/9500, s/d Ikr13,400/16,650; @ ⚹) This large hostel, spread over several buildings along the village's main street, is professional and comfortable. There's a three-storey building with plenty of kitchen space (great lake views while washing up). Some buildings are much smaller and house-like. HI members discount Ikr700.

SOUTHWEST ICELAND & THE GOLDEN CIRCLE LAUGARVATN

Laugarvatn Campsite CAMPGROUND €
(☑486 1155; camp sites per person Ikr1000;
☉May-Sep) By the highway just outside the
village, it becomes a noisy Icelandic party
venue on summer weekends.

★**Efstidalur II** GUESTHOUSE €€
(☑486 1186; www.efstidalur.is; Efstidalur 2; s/d/
tr incl breakfast from Ikr19,240/23,800/28,500,
mains Ikr1200-5000; 🛜) Located 12km northeast of Laugarvatn on a working dairy farm,
Efstidalur offers wonderfully welcoming
digs, tasty meals and amazing ice cream.
Adorable semi-detached cottages have brilliant views of hulking Hekla and the restaurant serves beef from the farm and trout
from the lake. The fun ice-cream bar scoops
farm ice cream, and has windows looking
into the dairy barn.

Hótel Edda HOTEL €€
(☑444 4000; www.hoteledda.is; ☉Jun–mid-Aug;
@🛜) Laugarvatn's two big schools become
Edda hotels in summer. The 98-room ML
Laugarvatn has serviceable college-like
rooms (double with shared bathroom
Ikr15,400). ÍKÍ Laugarvatn is ritzier by far:
its 29 rooms (double Ikr22,300) all have
private bathrooms, half with beautiful panoramic lake views. Its in-house restaurant has
great Hekla views as well.

★**Lindin** ICELANDIC €€
(☑486 1262; www.laugarvatn.is; Lindarbraut 2; restaurant mains Ikr3600-5500, bistro mains Ikr1800-
4000; ☉noon-10pm May-Sep, reduced hours
Oct-Apr) Owned by Baldur, an affable, celebrated chef, Lindin is the best restaurant for
miles. In a sweet little silver house, the restaurant faces the lake and is purely gourmet,
with high-concept Icelandic fare featuring
local or wild-caught ingredients. The casual,
modern bistro serves a more informal menu
from soups to an amazing reindeer burger.
Book ahead for dinner in high-season.

🛍 Shopping

Gallerí Laugarvatn ARTS & CRAFTS
(☑847 0805; www.gallerilaugarvatn.is; Háholt 1;
☉1-6pm) Local handicrafts, from ironwork
to ceramics and woolens. Also operates a
small B&B.

ℹ Getting There & Away

Strætó (☑540 2700; www.bus.is) services:
➡ Bus 73 Selfoss–Flúðir–Reykholt–Laugarvatn–Selfoss (Ikr1400 from Selfoss, 1¼ hours,
one daily).

Reykjavík Excursions (☑580 5400; ww.re.is)
services:
➡ Bus 6/6A Reykjavík–Gullfoss (one daily mid-
June to mid-September, 2¼ hours, continues to
Geysir, Gullfoss and back).
➡ Bus 610/610A Reykjavík–Akureyri (one daily
mid-June to early September, 1½ hours, con-
tinues to Geysir, Gullfoss, Kjölur Highlands and
Kerlingarfjöll to Akureyri).

Sterna (☑551 1166; www.sterna.is) services:
➡ Bus F35/F35A Reykjavík–Akureyri (Ikr3400
Harpa to/from Laugarvatn, 2¼ hours, one daily
late Jun to early September, continues to Geysir, Gullfoss, Kjölur Highlands and Kerlingarfjöll
to Akureyri).

Geysir

One of Iceland's most famous tourist attractions, Geysir (*gay*-zeer, which literally
means gusher) is the original hot-water
spout after which all other geysers are
named. Discovered in the **Haukadalur
geothermal region**, The Great Geysir has
been active for perhaps 800 years, and once
gushed water up to 80m into the air. But
the geyser goes through periods of lessened
activity, which seems to have been the case
since 1916. Earthquakes can stimulate activity, though eruptions are rare. Luckily for
visitors, the very reliable geyser, **Strokkur**,
sits alongside. You rarely have to wait more
than five to 10 minutes for the hot spring
to shoot an impressive 15m to 30m plume
before vanishing down its enormous hole.
Stand downwind only if you want a shower.

The undulating, hissing geothermal area
containing Strokkur and Geysir were free to
enter at the time of research, though there is
discussion of instituting a fee.

The large **Geysir Center** (☑480 6800;
www.geysircenter.com; ☉10am-10pm Jun-Aug, to
6pm Sep-May) has been erected to corral the
masses across the street. Here you'll find
three options for eating, a souvenir shop of
mall-like proportions with Icelandic name
brands and an N1 petrol station. **Geysir-
stofa** (☑480 6800; ☉10am-5pm May-Aug, noon-
4pm Sep-Apr) FREE, inside the centre, is an
audiovisual exhibition about geysers, volcanoes and earthquakes.

🏃 Activities

Geysir Golf Course GOLF
(Haukadalsvöllur, ☑893 8733; www.geysirgolf.is; 9
holes Ikr3000) Nine well-groomed holes look
out on Geysir.

Tours

Geysir Hestar HORSE RIDING
(☑ 847 1046; www.geysirhestar.com; Kjóastaðir 2)
Go 4km east of Geysir to Kjóastaðir horse
farm to find Geysir Hestar, which offers
horse riding in the area as well as along
Hvítará Canyon to Gullfoss, with trips for all
skill levels.

Iceland Safari SUPER-JEEP TOUR
(☑ 544 5454; www.icelandsafari.com; Geysir)
Super-Jeep tours around the southwest,
with a base 1km south of Geysir.

Sleeping & Eating

The Geysir Center has three eating options:
a massive restaurant (mains Ikr1490 to
Ikr2450), a cafe (mains Ikr1480 to Ikr2000)
and a fast food joint (Ikr990 to Ikr1690).

Skjól Camping HOSTEL, CAMPGROUND €
(☑ 899 4541; www.skjolcamping.com; camp sites
per person Ikr1200, 2-/8-bed dm Ikr8000/5000;
☺ mid-May–mid-Sep; ☎) Simple dorms and
field camping with a summertime bar, 3.5km
northeast of Geysir, next to Kjóastaðir Horse
Farm. There's also sleeping-bag accommodation (Ikr4000), and musical instruments for
jamming.

Hótel Geysir HOTEL, CAMPGROUND €€
(☑ 480 6800; www.geysircenter.is; Geysir; s/d
from Ikr22,000/25,000, campsites per person
Ikr1500, buffet lunch Ikr3500, dinner mains Ikr2700-
5700; ☺ Feb-Dec, campsite May-Sep; @☎) This
alpine-style hotel across the street from Geysir is constantly busy because of its locale.
There's a geothermal pool and two hot-pots,
and during summer, the good restaurant
can be completely overrun with tour buses
at the buffet lunch. The hotel has a nearby
campsite.

Getting There & Away

Reykajvík Excursions (☑ 580 5400; www.re.is)
services:
➙ Bus 6/6A Reykjavík–Þingvellir–Gullfoss
(Ikr4250 BSÍ Terminal to Geysir, three hours,
one daily mid-June to mid-September, stops for
1½ hours then continues to Gullfoss and back).
➙ Bus 610/610A Reykjavík–Akureyri (Ikr4250,
two hours, one daily mid-June to early September, continues to Gullfoss, Kjölur Highlands and
Kerlingarfjöll to Akureyri).

Sterna (☑ 551 1166; www.sterna.is) services:
➙ Bus F35/F35A Reykjavík–Þingvellir–Akureyri
(Ikr400 Harpa to/from Geysir, 2½ hours, one
daily late June to early September, stops for

35 minutes, then continues to Gullfoss, Kjölur
Highlands and Kerlingarfjöll to Akureyri).

Gullfoss

Iceland's most famous waterfall, Gullfoss
(Golden Falls) is a spectacular double cascade. It drops 32m, kicking up tiered walls
of spray before thundering away down a
narrow ravine. On sunny days the mist
creates shimmering rainbows, and it's also
magical in winter when the falls glitter with
ice. On grey, drizzly days, mist can envelop
the second drop, making Gullfoss slightly
underwhelming.

Visited since 1875, the falls came within
a hair's breadth of destruction during the
1920s, when a team of foreign investors
wanted to dam the Hvítá river for a hydroelectric project. The landowner, Tómas
Tómasson, refused to sell to them, but the
developers went behind his back and obtained permission directly from the government. Tómasson's daughter, Sigríður,
walked (barefoot!) to Reykjavík to protest,
even threatening to throw herself into the
waterfall if the development went ahead.
Thankfully, the investors failed to pay the
lease, the agreement was nullified and the
falls escaped destruction. Gullfoss was donated to the nation in 1975 and has been a
nature reserve ever since.

Above Gullfoss is a small **tourist information centre, shop and cafe** (www.gullfoss.
is; mains Ikr750-1890; ☺ 9am-9.30pm Jun-Aug,
9am-6pm Sep-May; ☎), which is famous for
its organic lamb soup made from locally
sourced ingredients. A tarmac path suitable
for wheelchairs leads to a lookout over the
falls, and a set of steps continues down to
the edge.

There's accommodation a few kilometres before the falls at **Hótel Gullfoss**
(☑ 486 8979; www.hotelgullfoss.is; d incl breakfast
Ikr24,700; ☎), a modern bungalow hotel. Its
clean en suite rooms overlook the moors
(get one facing the valley) and there are two
hot-pots and a restaurant (mains Ikr2100 to
Ikr5000) with sweeping views.

Getting There & Away

Gullfoss is the final attraction on the traditional
Golden Circle tour. You can continue along Rte
F35 beyond the falls (the Kjölur Route; p310)
for 14.8km while it's paved, after which you need
to have 4WD as it heads deep into the highlands.

Reykjavík Excursions (☑580 5400; www.re.is) services:

➳ Bus 610/610A (Reykjavík–Akureyri, Reykjavík–Gullfoss Ikr5000, one daily mid-June to early September; stops at the falls for an hour, as well as Kerlingarfjöll).

➳ Bus 6/6A (Reykjavík–Þingvellir–Geysir– Gullfoss, Ikr5000, five hours, one daily mid-June to mid-September; stops at the falls for an hour).

Sterna (☑551 1166; www.sterna.is) services:

➳ Bus F35/F35A (Reykjavík–Þingvellir– Akureyri, Reykjavík–Gullfoss Ikr4900, one daily late June to early September; stops at the falls for 25 minutes, as well as at Kerlingarfjöll).

Gullfoss to Selfoss (Route 35)

If you're completing the Golden Circle in the traditional direction, then the route from Gullfoss back to the Ring Road at Selfoss will be the final stage of your trip. Along the way you'll find plenty to lure you to stop. Most people follow surfaced Rte 35, which passes through Reykholt with its river rafting. You can also detour slightly to Fluðir with its geothermal greenhouses and hot spring, and Skálholt, once Iceland's religious powerhouse.

If you'd like to continue east rather than return to Reykjavík, the western Þjórsárdalur area (p129) is the next valley of interesting sights.

Reykholt

The rural township of Reykholt – one of several Reykholts around the country – is centred on the hot spring Reykjahver and has a geothermal pool, but for visitors, the main attraction is that the nearby **Hvítá** river is south Iceland's centre for white-water rafting.

👉 Tours

Arctic Rafting　　　　　　　RAFTING
(☑571 2200; www.arcticrafting.com; ☉mid-Apr–Sep) Full range of Hvítá river rafting and combination (horse riding, quad-bike, snowmobile) tours. Three- to four-hour trips start at Ikr11,990 per person; with Reykjavík transport Ikr16,990 to Ikr18,490. The company's base is near Reykholt at Drumboddsstaðir, and its Reykjavík office is at Arctic Adventures (p70). There's a restaurant at the base camp and accommodation nearby.

Iceland Riverjet　　　　　　JETBOAT
(☑863 4506; www.icelandriverjet.com; Skólabraut 4; ☉Apr–mid-Oct) Forty-minute jetboat rides (adult/child Ikr13,900/8000) zip along the Hvítá. Based in the same complex as Café Mika, the company also offers pick-up and combo tours with the Golden Circle.

🛏 Sleeping & Eating

Húsið　　　　　　　　　　B&B €
(☑486 8680; Bjarkarbraut 26; d without bathroom incl breakfast Ikr12,300; ☜) Friendly Húsið is a small guesthouse on a quiet residential cul-de-sac. There's a hot tub, barbecue and kitchen.

★**Fagrilundur Guesthouse**　　GUESTHOUSE €€
(www.fagrilundur.is; Skólabraut 1; d with/without bathroom incl breakfast Ikr23,000/17,000; ☜) A flower-pot-lined walk through the forest leads to a fairy-tale wooden cottage. Cosy rooms have patterned quilts and there's a shared porch. The attentive owners offer a warm welcome, celebrated breakfasts and loads of local advice.

Café Mika　　　　　　INTERNATIONAL €€
(☑896 6450; Skólabraut 4; mains Ikr1000-3900; ☉10am-9pm; ☜) Café Mika has an outdoor pizza oven, sandwiches and Icelandic mains, and sells handcrafted chocolate.

ℹ Getting There & Away

Strætó (☑540 2700; www.bus.is) services:

➳ Bus 73 Selfoss–Flúðir–Reykholt–Laugarvatn–Selfoss (Ikr1750 from Selfoss, 45 minutes, one daily).

➳ Bus 72 Selfoss–Flúðir–Reykholt–Laugarás–Selfoss (Ikr1750 from Selfoss, 45 minutes, two daily).

Skálholt & Laugarás

Skálholt is a very important religious centre; it was one of two bishoprics (the other was Hólar in the north) that ruled Iceland's souls from the 11th to the 18th centuries. It rose to prominence under Gissur the White, the driving force behind the Christianisation of Iceland. The Catholic bishopric lasted until the Reformation in 1550, when Bishop Jón Arason and his two sons were executed by order of the Danish king. Skalhólt continued as a Lutheran centre until 1797, when the bishopric shifted to Reykjavík.

Unfortunately, the great cathedral that once stood here was destroyed by a major earthquake in the 18th century. Today there's a modern Protestant **theological centre** with a **visitor centre** (☑486 8870; www.skalholt.is; lkr500; ☺9am-6pm), a **turfhouse** re-creation of Þorlagsbúð, and a prim **church** with a **museum** in the basement containing the stone sarcophagus of Bishop Páll Jónsson (bishop from 1196 to 1211). According to *Páls Saga,* the earth was wracked by storms and earthquakes when he died. Spookily, a huge storm broke at the exact moment that his coffin was reopened in 1956. The centre also has peaceful accommodation, a restaurant and summertime concerts.

The neighbouring village of Laugarás is essentially a community of farms, some of which sell their produce on-site. Visit **Engi** (☑486 8913; www.engi.is; Laugarás; ☺noon-6pm), which sells greenhouse-grown fruit and vegetables and cute souvenirs. It's marked at the entrance to Laugarás when arriving from Skálholt.

Laugarás is served by Strætó buses 72 and 73 from Selfoss (lkr1750, 40 minutes, two daily) and Sterna bus 35A returns from Akureyri to Reykjavík via Laugarás.

Kerið

Around 15.5km north of Selfoss on Rte 35, **Kerið** (adult/child lkr350/free; ☺9am-9pm Jun-Aug) is a 6500-year-old explosion crater with vivid red and sienna earth and an ethereal green lake. Björk once performed a concert from a floating raft in the middle. At the time of research, local property owners had (controversially) started charging for entrance to Kerið; this may change.

Five kilometres up nearby Rte 36, **Hótel Grimsborgir** (☑555 7878; www.grimsborgir. com; d incl breakfast lkr38,500, 2-bedroom apt lkr60,000; ☎) offers fully kitted-out luxury hotel suites and apartments.

Flúðir

As you approach the local hub, little agrarian Flúðir, interesting rock buttes crop up from the rolling green plains. Flúðir is known throughout Iceland for its geothermal greenhouses that grow the majority of the country's mushrooms and it's also a popular weekend getaway for Reykjavikers with private cottages. More recently it's a super stop not only for good food, but also its recently refurbished hot springs.

⭷ Activities

★**Gamla Laugin**   GEOTHERMAL POOL
(Secret Lagoon; ☑555 3351; www.secretlagoon. is; adult/child lkr2500/free; ☺1-10pm) Get here before the real crowds come! Opened in 2014, this lovely hot spring is a refurbished version of the one the town used informally for years. It's a broad, calm geothermal pool, mist rising, surrounded by natural rocks and with a gravelly bottom. The walking trail along its edge passes the local river and a series of sizzling vents and geysers. Meadows around fill with wildflowers in summer. During off-hours you might have it totally to yourself.

Find it signposted (there's also a sign for Hvammar) down a rutted track on the northern bank of the river Litla-Laxá in Flúðir.

☕ Sleeping & Eating

The local camp site along the Litla-Laxá river is usually crammed, especially on weekends. There's a **farm stand** at Melar on the western edge of town, on Rte 311 and a **Samkaup-Strax** (☺9am-10pm Mon-Fri, 10am-10pm Sat & Sun) supermarket.

Icelandair Hótel Flúðir   HOTEL €€
(☑486 6630; www.hotelfludir.is; Vesturbrún 1; d lkr23,000; @☎) These two silver motel-style strands of rooms are comfortable, with parquet floors, en suite bathrooms and a restaurant.

Grund   GUESTHOUSE €€
(Gistiheimilið Flúðum; ☑565 9196; www.gistingfludir.is; s/d without bathroom incl breakfast lkr13,000/21,000, mains lkr1750-4900; ☎) Run by kindly Dagný, this adorable guesthouse has a handful of homey rooms filled with antiques. The popular restaurant prides itself in offering fresh local food.

Efra Sel Farmers Market   MARKET
(☑820 7590; ☺11am-6pm Jun-Aug, Sat & Sun May) The farmers market, about 3km northwest of town, near the golf course on Rte 359, offers the best produce of the region: veggies, meat, strawberries, rhubarb pie and bread, plus has picnic tables out front.

★**Minilik Ethiopian Restaurant**   ETHIOPIAN €€
(☑846 9798; www.minilik.is; mains lkr1850-3000; ☺noon-8pm Jun–6 Sep; ☑) Sweet-faced Azeb cooks up traditional Ethiopian specialties in this welcoming, unpretentious spot. There are loads of vegetarian options, but

also lamb such as *awaze tibs* or chicken *(doro kitfo)*. As far as we know, this is the only Ethiopian restaurant in Iceland, and it should beckon all lovers of spice.

❶ Getting There & Away

Strætó (☑ 540 2700; www.bus.is) buses 72 and 73 from Selfoss (Ikr1750, 40 to 60 minutes, two to three daily) serve Flúðir.

THE SOUTH

As you work your way east from Reykjavík, Rte 1 (the Ring Road) emerges into austere volcanic foothills punctuated by surreal steam vents, around Hveragerði, then swoops through a flat, wide coastal plain, full of verdant horse farms and greenhouses, before the landscape suddenly begins to grow wonderfully jagged, after Hella and Hvolsvöllur. Mountains thrust upwards on the inland side, some of them volcanoes wreathed by mist (Eyjafjallajökull, site of the 2010 eruption), and the first of the awesome glaciers appears, as enormous rivers like the Þjórsá cut their way to the black-sand beaches rimming the Atlantic.

Throughout, roads pierce deep inland, to realms of lush waterfall-doused valleys such as Þjórsárdalur and Fljótshlíð, and awe-inspiring volcanoes such as Hekla. Two of the most renowned inland spots are Landmannalaugar, where vibrantly coloured rhyolite peaks meet bubbling hot springs; and Þórsmörk, a forested valley tucked safely away from the brutal northern elements under a series of wind-foiling ice caps. They are linked by the famous Laugavegurinn hike, Iceland's most popular trek. Though these areas lie inland on roads that are sometimes impassable by standard vehicles, most visitors access them on tours or amphibious buses from the southern Ring Road. Þórsmörk, one of Iceland's most popular hiking destinations, can be done as a day trip.

Public transport (and traffic) is solid along the Ring Road, which is studded with interesting settlements: Hveragerði, famous for its geothermal fields and hot springs; Skógar, the leaping-off point for Þórsmörk; and Vík, surrounded by glaciers, vertiginous cliffs and black beaches. South of the Ring Road the tiny fishing villages of Stokkseyri and Eyrarbakki are refreshingly local feeling. The south coast is also filled with family farms, some rich with saga heritage, offering lovely rural guesthouses.

The popular southwest area (www.south.is) is developing quickly and infrastructure keeps improving. Nevertheless, it gets very busy in high season, so advanced accommodation booking is essential.

Hveragerði & Around

The grid of boxy buildings that is Hveragerði emerge from otherworldly lava fields and hills pierced, surreally, by natural steaming vents. You're not here for the architecture, you're here for Hveragerði's highly active geothermal field, which heats hundreds of greenhouses. Nationally, the town is famous for its horticultural college and naturopathic clinic. There are also some fantastic hikes in the area.

Pick up the handy *Hveragerði, The Capital of Hot Springs and Flowers* map, which details all of the sights, activities and dining options in the area.

◎ Sights & Activities

★ Hverasvæðið   GEOTHERMAL POOL
(☑ 483 4601; Hveramörk 13; adult/child Ikr200/free; ◷ 9am-6pm Mon-Sat, 10am-4pm Sun) The geothermal park Hverasvæðið, in the centre of town, has mudpots and steaming pools where visitors can dip their feet (but no more). You can book ahead for a guided walk to learn about the area's unique geology and greenhouse power. Or they'll give you an egg and apparatus (Ikr100) for boiling it in the steaming vents. There's a small cafe with geothermally baked bread.

★ Reykjadalur   GEOTHERMAL POOL
(Hot River Valley) Reykjadalur is a delightful geothermal valley where there's a bathable hot river – bring your swimsuit. There are maps at the tourist office to find the trail; from the trailhead car park, it's a 3km hike through fields of sulphur-belching plains. Stick to marked paths, lest you melt your shoes, and leave no trash. In recent years the area has taken a beating due to thoughtless visitors.

★ Listasafn Árnesinga   ART MUSEUM
(☑ 483 1727; www.listasafnarnesinga.is; Austurmörk 21; ◷ noon-6pm May-Sep, noon-6pm Thu-Sun Oct-Apr) **FREE** This airy modern art gallery puts on great contemporary-art exhibitions, and has a fine cafe too.

Hverageröi

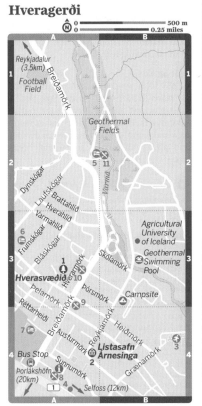

N 0 — 500 m
0 — 0.25 miles

HNLFÍ Health Clinic & Spa   SPA
(Heilsustofnun Náttúrulækningafélags Íslands; ☑ 483 0300; www.hnlfi.is; Grænumörk 10) Iceland's most famous clinic treats both prescription-bearing patients and visitors seeking relaxing massages (Ikr7500 to Ikr12,000), deep-heat mud baths (Ikr6400) and more. HNLFÍ has excellent facilities, including indoor and outdoor pools, hot-pots, a sauna, a steam bath and modest accommodation (double with/without bathroom including breakfast Ikr24,000/16,500).

☞ Tours

Iceland Activities   ADVENTURE TOUR
(☑ 777 6263; www.icelandactivities.is; Mánamörk 3-5; ⊙ 8am-5pm Mon-Fri, 9am-4pm Sat) This family-run adventure company specialises in biking, surfing and hiking tours (from Ikr11,900) in the southwest.

Sólhestar   HORSE RIDING
(☑ 892 3066; www.solhestar.is; Borgargerði, Ölfus) Various half-day and full-day riding tours through the volcanic wilds or down on the beach (three-hour tours from Ikr9000). It's 8km south of Hverageröi on the Ring Road; go 500m north on Rte 374.

🛏 Sleeping

★ **Hjarðarból Guesthouse**   GUESTHOUSE €
(☑ 567 0045; www.hjardarbol.is; s/d/q Ikr12,500/15,420/22,400; 🛜) This buttercup-yellow set of cottages and guesthouse buildings is pastoral and welcoming, with friendly hosts, and is located in the rolling fields 8km southeast of Hverageröi, just off the Ring Road. There's also an historic house to rent.

Raufarhólshellir   LAVA TUBE
This 11th-century lava tube is 1360m long (Iceland's third largest), and contains wonderful lava columns. You'll need a torch (flashlight) and sturdy boots, but even so the going is treacherous from earlier cave-ins. In winter, cold air is funnelled down and trapped inside, producing amazing ice formations. You'll find the tube southwest of Hverageröi off Rte 39, which passes right over it – park on the south side. Local operators offer tours.

Orkusýn   EXHIBITION
(Hellisheiði Geothermal Power Plant; ☑ 412 5800; www.orkusyn.is; adult/child Ikr900/free; ⊙ 9am-5pm) Seventeen kilometres west of Hverageröi, just north of the Ring Road, you'll see the sleek shell of Hellisheiði Geothermal Power Plant, one of the few that provide 25% of Iceland's electricity. Orkusýn, a multimedia exhibition, lays out the details of harnessing the earth's hot-water power.

ℹ️ SOUTH ICELAND VISITOR INFORMATION

Tourist Information Centre (Upplýsingamiðstöð Suðurlands; ☑ 483 4601; www.southiceland.is; Sunnumörk 2-4; ⊙ 8.30am-6pm Mon-Fri, 9am-3pm Sat, 9am-1pm Sun Jun-Aug, reduced hours rest of year) Hveragerði has the regional tourist office for the entire south: this is THE spot to stock up on free subregional maps and brochures. It shares space with the post office and a small exhibit about the earthquake that ripped through in 2008; there's a freaky earthquake simulator (Ikr200).

Gistiheimilið Frumskógar GUESTHOUSE €
(☑ 896 2780; www.frumskogar.is; Frumskógar 3; s/d/apt without bathroom incl breakfast from Ikr9400/15,000/20,000; 🛜) This cosy guesthouse apartment-style accommodation also boasts a hot-pot and steam bath.

★ Frost & Fire Hotel BOUTIQUE HOTEL €€
(Frost og Funi; ☑ 483 4959; www.frostandfire.is; Hverhamar; s/d incl breakfast Ikr20,500/27,000; 🅿 @ 🛜) This lovely little hotel sits along a bubbling stream and beneath fizzing geothermal spouts. The comfortable rooms with subtle Scandi-sleek details and original artwork stretch along the river ravine. The heat-pressured sauna and simmering hot-pots are fed by the hotel's private borehole.

Hótel Örk HOTEL €€
(☑ 483 4700; www.hotel-ork.is; Breiðamörk 1c; d incl breakfast Ikr22,500-30,500; @ 🛜) This hulking hotel favoured by tour groups has rather dated rooms, but offers some family-friendly amenities: sauna, nine-hole golf course, billiards, and an excellent swimming pool with a slide and hot tubs. The in-house restaurant is decidedly up-scale.

🍴 Eating

The town has several busy bakeries, like **Hverabakarí** (☑ 483 4879; Breiðamörk 10; ⊙ 8.30am-6pm) and **Almar** (Sunnumörk 2; soup Ikr820; ⊙ 7am-6pm Mon-Fri, 8am-5pm Sat, 9am-5pm Sun; 🛜), fast-food joints and supermarkets. Several restaurants offer bread cooked using geothermal heat.

Varma ICELANDIC €€
(lunch mains Ikr1670-3700, dinner mains Ikr3750-5000; ⊙ 8am-10pm) At the Frost & Fire hotel, this wonderfully scenic restaurant boasts floor-to-ceiling windows over the stream and gorge. Dishes are Icelandic, using fresh, local ingredients and herbs and often geothermal cooking techniques.

Kjöt og Kúnst INTERNATIONAL €€
(☑ 483 5010; www.kjotogkunst.com; Breiðamörk 21; mains Ikr2000-4400; ⊙ noon-9pm Mon-Sat Jun-Aug, reduced hours Sep-May) On the touristy side, but there are Icelandic dishes (soup, fish and lamb) in among the sandwiches and pizzas. Cakes and geothermal bread, too.

ℹ️ Getting There & Away

The bus stop is at the petrol stations on the main road into town (check whether your stop is the Shell or N1).

Strætó (☑ 540 2700; www.straeto.is) services include:
➡ Buses 51 & 52 Reykjavík–Vík/Höfn & Reykjavík–Landeyjahöfn (Ikr1050 to/from Reykjavík, 35 minutes, 11 daily Monday to Friday, eight daily Saturday and Sunday).

Sterna (☑ 551 1166; www.sterna.is) services:
➡ Bus F35A, returning from Akureyri to Reykjavík can stop with pre-booking.

Reykjavík Excursions (☑ 580 5400; www.re.is) services:
➡ Buses 9/9A Reykjavík–Þórsmörk, 11/11A Reykjavík–Landmannalaugar, 17/17A Reykjavík–Mývatn, 18 Reykjavík–Álftavatn–Emstrur, 20/20A Reykjavík–Skaftafell, 21/21A Reykjavík–Skógar, 610/610A Reykjavík–Kjölur–Akureyri all stop in Hveragerði.

Trex (☑ 587 6000; www.trex.is) services:
➡ Buses T21/T22 & T23/T24 Reykjavík–Landmannalaugar and T11/T12 Reykjavík–Þórsmörk can stop with pre-booking.

Þorlákshöfn

In the past, most people came to the fishing town of Þorlákshöfn, 20km south of Hveragerði, to catch the ferry to the Vestmannaeyjar. Now the ferry departs from Landeyjahöfn on the southwest coast near Hvolsvöllur. When it's stormy and the new port fills with sand, the ferry does leave from here. There's little other reason to come. It is served by **Strætó** (☑ 540 2700; www.bus.is) bus 53 from Reykjavík's Mjódd station (Ikr1050, 45 minutes, two daily Monday to Friday) and bus 74 from Selfoss (Ikr700, 45 minutes, three daily Monday to Friday).

Eyrarbakki

It's hard to believe, but tiny Eyrarbakki was Iceland's main port and a thriving trading town well into the 20th century. Farmers from all over the south once rode here to barter for supplies at the general store – crowds were so huge it could take three days to get served! Another of Eyrarbakki's claims to fame is that it's the birthplace of Bjarní Herjólfsson, who made a great sea voyage in AD 985 and was probably the first European to see America. Unfortunately, Bjarní turned back and sold his boat to Leifur Eiríksson, who went on to discover Vinland and ended up with all the glory. Today the town is known for its prison – the largest in Iceland.

Sights

Húsið á Eyrarbakka   MUSEUM
(House at Eyrarbakki; ☑ 483 1504; www.husid. com; Hafnarbrú 3; adult/child incl Sjöminjasafnið á Eyrarbakka Ikr800/free; ☉ 11am-6pm May-Sep) One of Iceland's oldest houses, built by Danish traders in 1765, Húsið á Eyrarbakka has glass display cabinets explaining the town's history, rooms restored with original furniture, and a stuffed bird collection. Keep an eye out for Ólöf Sveinsdóttir's shawl, hat and cuffs, knitted from her own hair.

Sjöminjasafnið á Eyrarbakka   MUSEUM
(☑ 483 1082; Túngata 59; adult/child incl Húsið á Eyrarbakka Ikr800/free; ☉ 11am-6pm May-Sep) Just behind Húsið á Eyrarbakka, this small maritime museum has displays on the local fishing community. Its main exhibit is the beautiful 12-oared fishing boat, *Farsæll*.

★ Flói Nature Reserve   NATURE RESERVE
Birdwatchers should head 3km northwest of Eyrarbakki to Flói Nature Reserve, an important estuary and marshland on the eastern bank of the Ölfusá. It's visited by many wetland birds – common species include red-throated divers and various kinds of ducks and geese – most present during nesting season (May to July). There's a 2km circular hiking trail through the marshes. For more information, contact the **Icelandic Society for the Protection of Birds** (☑ 562 0477; www.fuglavernd.is).

Sleeping & Eating

Rein   GUESTHOUSE €€
(☑ 777 5677; www.rein-guesthouse.is; Þykkvaflöt 4; d incl breakfast Ikr21,500) This quiet guesthouse

has three rooms in its wooden-walled attic. Although creaking timbers and shabby-chic furniture give the house a cute, historic feel, it was actually built in 1997.

Sea Side Cottages   COTTAGES €€€
(☑ 898 1197; www.seasidecottages.is; Eyrargata 37a; cottage from Ikr60,000) Living up to their name, these two quaint cottages are just metres away from the pounding Atlantic. Each is tricked out in fine fashion, with thoughtful antiques, flat-screen TVs, fully equipped kitchens and outdoor seating.

★ Rauða Húsið   SEAFOOD €€
(☑ 486 8701; www.raudahusid.is; Búðarstígur 4; mains Ikr1900-3500; ☉ 11.30am-9pm Mon-Thu, to 10pm Fri-Sun; 🔊) This elegant white-linen restaurant fills a red house (hence the name), and has cheery staff and great fresh seafood, though the menu is broad, with plenty to choose from.

★ Hafið Blaá   SEAFOOD €€
(☑ 483 1000; www.hafidblaa.is; Óseyri; mains Ikr2000-4000; ☉ noon-9pm Mon-Thu, noon-10pm Fri-Sun Jun-Aug) Three kilometres west of Eyrarbakki on Rte 34, this seafood restaurant sits on the water's edge in an ovoid building, with a beautiful arcing-wood interior. Even if you don't get a table overlooking the ocean, the sweeping estuary views on the opposite side are equally impressive.

Getting There & Away

Strætó (☑ 540 2700; www.bus.is) services:
➡ Bus 74 Selfoss–Stokkseyri–Eyrarbakki–Þorlákshöfn (Ikr350, 30 minutes, three daily Monday to Friday).
➡ Bus 75 Selfoss–Eyrarbakki (Ikr350, 30 minutes, eight daily Monday to Friday).

Stokkseyri

Stokkseyri can seem like Eyrarbakki's twin to the east, but it's not. Although it, too, is a small fishing village, it has a fun dose of quirky sites and summer art galleries, that make it an entertaining high-season stop.

Sights & Activities

The summer art galleries all cluster around the central square and restored warehouse, on the south side of Rte 33 (called Hásteinsvegur/Eyrarbraut in town).

(Continued on page 126)

1. Ice cave, Vatnajökull 2. Geothermal area near Hekla
3. Snæfellsnes Peninsula 4. Eruption under Eyjafjallajökull

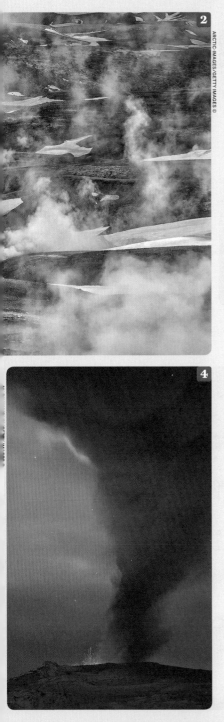

ARCTIC-IMAGES/GETTY IMAGES ©

Fire & Ice

'Land of fire and ice' might be an overused marketing slogan, but it's not hyperbole. Serene, majestic scenery belies Iceland's fiery heart – there are some 30 active volcanoes, and many of them lie under thick ice. When their fire-breathing fury is unleashed, the world often has no choice but to take notice (remember Eyjafjallajökull?).

Vatnajökull

The island's ice queen (p292) is Europe's largest ice cap and the namesake for its largest national park. Don't miss the chance to explore this endless kingdom of white aboard a snowmobile.

Eyjafjallajökull

We've all heard the name (or at least heard people try to pronounce the name) of the treacherous eruption (p137) that spewed impenetrable tufts of ash over Europe in 2010, causing the cancellation of thousands of flights.

Hekla & Katla

Like wicked stepsisters from some Icelandic fairytale, Hekla (p131) and Katla (p153) are volatile beasts that dominate many of the southern vistas, threatening to belch forth steam, smoke and oozing lava that melts the nearby glaciers and floods the southern plains.

Snæfellsjökull

Jules Verne's famous journey to the centre of the earth starts here – the Snæfellsnes Peninsula's prominent glacial fist (p178) that can be easily glimpsed from Reykjavík on clear days.

Magni & Móði

Iceland's newest mountains (p139) were formed during the eruptions of 2010. Bring a pack of *pýlsur* (hot dogs) with you as you mount Magni – the still-steaming earth will cook them in no time flat.

1. Icelandic horses 2. Seal pup 3. Arctic fox
4. Puffin

PÉTUR WAZMUR JÓNSSON/GETTY IMAGES ©

Wildlife Watching

Iceland's magical natural realm is the playground for some headlining acts, including breaching whales, basking seals, elusive Arctic foxes and bumper birdlife (the scene stealer: cute, clownish puffins, of course). The support cast of wandering sheep and wild-maned horses are still impossibly photogenic against a cinematic, mountainous backdrop.

The bird life in Iceland is abundant, especially during the warmest months when migrating species arrive to nest. On coastal cliffs and islands around the country, you can see a mind-boggling array of seabirds. Posted coastal hikes offer access to some of the most populous bird cliffs in the world – don't miss a chance to cavort with puffins (see p40 for info on how to find them).

Whale watching has become one of Iceland's most cherished pastimes – boats depart throughout the year (limited service in the colder months) to catch a glimpse of these lurking beasts as they wave their fins and spray the air. The northern waters around Húsavík and Akureyri are a haven for feeding creatures (usually minke and fin species); travellers who are short on time can hop on a boat that departs directly from downtown Reykjavík (see p68). In winter, it's possible to see orcas crash through the frigid waters – the best point of departure is the Snæfellsnes Peninsula (see p170).

BEST WILDLIFE-WATCHING SPOTS

Vestmannaeyjar (p153) Zoom between islets as you snap photos of a Peterson Field Guide's worth of bird life.

Borgarfjörður Eystri (p268) It's like you've died and gone to puffin heaven, where encounters with these clumsy birds are up close and personal.

Húsavík (p244) Sample Iceland's original flavour of whale watching at this charming fishing village. There are tours aplenty, especially in summer.

Krossneslaug

Hofsós

Selárdalslaug

Pollurinn

Drangsnes

Mývatn
Nature Baths

Egilsstaðir

Lýsuhólslaug

Laugarvatn

REYKJAVÍK

Flúðir

Hveragerði

Landmannalaugar

Blue
Lagoon

2 WEEKS The Hot-Pot Hop

Slap on those swim trunks and enjoy Iceland's favourite pastime: wading in warm, mineral-rich hot springs that soothe the mind and soul. Hop across this geothermic kingdom, dipping your toes in each source.

➡ Start in **Reykjavík** (p52) and do as the locals – bring your backstroke and some gossip to share at the public pools.

➡ Next, try **Blue Lagoon** (p98), the Disney-land of swimming spots, and spread gobs of rich silica on your face.

➡ Pause in **Hveragerði** (p114), one of Iceland's most geothermally active areas – bubbling water abounds.

➡ Head to **Landmannalaugar** (p140), where a steaming stream is the perfect cure-all after some serious hiking.

➡ Cruise by **Flúðir** (p113) and see just who else is in on the secret of the locals' natural, meadow-surrounded lagoon

➡ Swing through mod Fontana, in **Laugarvatn** (p109), with its naturally occurring geyser-sauna (you'll see!).

➡ Soak in **Lýsuhólslaug** (p181) and emerge from the algae soup with baby-soft skin.

➡ Scout out **Pollurinn** (p190), just outside of Tálknafjörður – a favourite local hang-out.

➡ Blink and you'll miss the roadside hot-pots in **Drangsnes** (p205), built into a sea wall.

➡ Bask in the otherworldly beauty at **Krossneslaug** (p206), set along the wild, pebble-strewn shore.

➡ Check out **Hofsós** (p217) – from within the pool it feels as though you're swimming in the sea.

➡ The north's mellower version of Blue Lagoon is found at **Mývatn Nature Baths** (p242).

➡ Finish up at Selárdalslaug (p256), tucked between two hillocks near Vopnafjörður, then fly back to Reykjavík from **Egilsstaðir** (p259).

Top: Blue Lagoon
Bottom: Reykjadalur (p114), Hveragerði

Icelandic Culture

Weather not conducive for hiking? Never fear – let Iceland's rich culture and creativity take you places. There's a storytelling heritage forged by sagas; music and design that channel nature in inspiring ways; and a celebration of both tradition and experimentation. Above all, it's a willingness to wear your Icelandic identity on your sleeve (or in your knitwear).

1. Reykjavík Culture Night
Reykjavíkers gather each year in mid-August to celebrate Culture Night (Menningarnótt; p26).

2. Lopapeysur
Locals and visitors alike can be seen wearing these traditional jumpers (p88) made from Icelandic wool.

3. Harpa
Reykjavík's sparkling concert hall (p59) was designed by Henning Larsen Architects, Batteríið Architects and artist Olafur Eliasson.

4. Skyr
This rich and creamy yoghurt-like Icelandic staple (p349) is a must-try.

Veiðisafnið
MUSEUM

(☑ 483 1558; www.hunting.is; Eyrarbraut 49; adult/child Ikr1500/750; ☺ 11am-6pm Apr-Sep, 11am-6pm Sat & Sun Feb-Mar & Oct-Nov) You may be snagged by the roadside sign: 'Have you seen a giraffe today?' Here a local hunter displays his collection of prey from all around the world. It's very professionally done, with dozens of well-lit taxidermied animals accompanied by info on where they were bagged and how. We're talking zebras, boars, two full-sized lions, among many others (yes, a giraffe). A chat with the friendly owner brings fascinating stories, but anti-hunting folks won't like it here.

Draugasetrið
EXHIBITION

(Ghost Centre; www.draugasetrid.is; Hafnargata 9; adult/child Ikr2000/1000, incl Icelandic Wonders Ikr3500/1500; ☺ 1-6pm Jun-Aug) Draugasetrið, on the top floor of a huge maroon-and-black warehouse in the centre, is a veritable haunted house run by a gaggle of blood-thirsty teens. A 50-minute iPod-guide (in many languages) recites 24 spooky stories in a series of dry-ice-filled stations. Not recommended for small fry. There's a waterview cafe, too. On the other side of the building, the accompanying Icelandic Wonders (☑ 483 1202; adult/child Ikr1500/990; ☺ 11am-6pm Jun-Aug) involves trolls, elves and Northern Lights (so is a better bet for young children).

Orgelsmiðjan
ORGAN WORKSHOP

(☑ 566 8130; www.orgel.is; Hafnargata 9; adult/child Ikr700/free; ☺ 10am-6pm Mon-Fri, by appointment Sat & Sun) Iceland's only organ builder, Björgvin Tómasson allows visitors to his workshop, with exhibits and occasional concerts. Find it on the seashore-side of Draugasetrið's warehouse.

Rjómabúið á Baugsstöðum
HISTORIC BUILDING

(Baugsstaðir Creamery; ☑ 483 1082; www.husid.com; admission Ikr500; ☺ 1-6pm Sat & Sun Jul & Aug, or by appointment) About 6km east of Stokkseyri, this old 1905 creamery dairy still has its original machinery. Interestingly, most of its products were sold to England – so some readers' grandparents may have eaten Stokkseyri butter!

Sundlaug Stokkseyrar
SWIMMING POOL, HOT-POT

(☑ 480 3260; adult/child Ikr600/free; ☺ 1-9pm Mon-Fri, 10am-5pm Sat & Sun Jun–mid-Aug, reduced hours rest of year) The town's popular swimming pool and hot-pots.

☞ Tours

Kajakferðir Stokkseyri
KAYAKING

(☑ 868 9046; www.kajak.is; Heiðarbrún 24; ☺ Apr-Oct) Explore the nearby lagoon by kayak or get out on the ocean (tours Ikr4950 to Ikr7850). Based at the town pool, Sundlaug Stokkseyrar.

🍽 Sleeping & Eating

For cheap meals, there's a grill at the Shell petrol station.

Art Hostel
HOSTEL €

(☑ 854 4510; Hafnargata 9; d with/without bathroom Ikr14,000/12,400; ☺ cafe 1-5pm Jun-Aug) On the 2nd floor of the central culture complex and warehouse, above mosaic, painting and photography galleries, you'll find recently done-up rooms from small twins to larger studios with microwaves and bathrooms. There's a cafe-bar too. Book via www.booking.com.

Kvöldstjarnan
GUESTHOUSE €

(Evening Star; ☑ 483 1800; www.kvoldstjarnan.is; Stjörnusteinum 7; d without bathroom incl breakfast Ikr14,500, 3-bedroom apt Ikr34,700; ☎) The five bright, white rooms here come with washbasins and fluffy feathery duvets. There's a small lounge area, barbecue and sparkling kitchen. The owner's father created impressive flowerbeds, in spite of salty ocean breezes. Also has an apartment.

★ Við Fjöruborðið
SEAFOOD €€

(☑ 483 1550; www.fjorubordid.is; Eyrarbraut 3a; mains Ikr2600-5550; ☺ noon-9pm Jun-Aug, from 5pm Sep-May; ☎) This large seafood restaurant sits on the shore, just behind the ocean berm, and is known for making some of the best lobster bisque in Iceland. Slurp your bisque amid chatting locals, glass fishing buoys and marine memorabilia. Reserve for dinner.

🛈 Getting There & Away

Strætó (☑ 540 2700; www.bus.is) services:

➡ Bus 74 Selfoss–Stokkseyri–Eyrarbakki–Þorlákshöfn (Ikr350, 20 minutes, three daily Monday to Friday).

➡ Bus 75 Selfoss–Eyrarbakki (Ikr350, 20 minutes, eight daily Monday to Friday).

Flóahreppur

For being so close to the most travelled portion of the Ring Road, it's a wonder you can feel like you've fallen into a rural region of rolling pastures leading to the ocean. Bordered by the Ring Road in the north, Rte 34 in the west, the Þjórsá river in the east, and the Atlantic Ocean in the south, this small agricultural area has a few laidback farms with accommodation.

Sleeping & Eating

Gaulverjaskóli HI Hostel
HOSTEL €

(☑551 0654; www.south-hostel.is; Gaulverjaskóli; camp sites per adult Ikr1000, dm/d Ikr4500/13,500; ☻Feb–mid-Nov; ☎) Friendly owners have poured their hearts into renovating this former school; today it's a clean, quiet hostel and campground with a welcoming common space in the attic, and a spacious kitchen. It's based in a tiny hamlet marooned in a vast expanse of flat agricultural land, 9km from Stokkseyri along the coastal road leading back towards Selfoss.

Breakfast and a lamb-stew dinner can be ordered in advance. HI members discount Ikr600.

Vatnsholt
GUESTHOUSE €€

(☑899 7748; www.stayiniceland.is; Vatnsholt 1-2; d with/without bath Ikr23,000/19,000, f from Ikr33,000; ☻mid-Feb–mid-Dec; @☎) A wonderful place if you have the kids in tow, Vatnsholt is located about 16km southeast of Selfoss, just 8km off the Ring Road. Here you'll find over 30 sun-filled bedrooms scattered throughout a sweeping farmstead with views to Eyjafjallajökull, Hekla, Vestmannaeyjar and the steaming earths at Hveragerði.

Bike rentals, a restaurant, a menagerie of animals (including Elvis the dancing goat) and an elaborate playground could have you staying longer than you expect.

Selfoss

Selfoss is the largest town in southern Iceland, an important trade centre, and witlessly ugly. Iceland's Ring Road is its main street – the only reason to stop is to transfer buses or load up on groceries. If you find yourself with time on your hands between buses, Selfoss has a fine **geothermal pool** (☑480 1960; Bankavegur; adult/child Ikr600/free; ☻6.30am-9.30pm Mon-Fri, 9am-7pm Sat & Sun) with hot-pots and water slides.

Tours

Iceland South Coast Travel
TOUR

(☑777 0705; www.isct.is) Bundle of tours include the south coast (from Ikr19,900), Gold-

en Circle, Vestmannaeyjar or Jökulsárlón. Based in Selfoss but can do Reykjavík and various south coast pickups.

Sleeping

★Geirakot
GUESTHOUSE €

(☑482 1020; geirakot@simnet.is; Geirakot farm; s/d without bathroom incl breakfast Ikr9500/15,000; ☎) Sweet Geirakot is a nice alternative to Selfoss town if you need to stop in the vicinity. A friendly family on a dairy farm has renovated the grandparents' small farmhouse into a homey guesthouse. Breakfast is lovely, local and served on china. Sleeping-bag space is Ikr4800. Book through Icelandic Farm Holidays (www.farmholidays.is).

Gesthús
CAMPGROUND, GUESTHOUSE €

(☑482 3585; www.gesthus.is; Engjavegur 56; camp sites per person Ikr1000, d without bathroom Ikr14,600; ☎) At this friendly place by the park, you choose between camping, doubles in two-room cabins with shared kitchen and bathroom, or a full summer house with desks, kitchenettes and TVs. Hot-pots cost Ikr250 for campers, but are free for other guests.

Selfoss HI Hostel
HOSTEL €

(B&B Hostel; ☑482 1600; www.hostel.is; Austurvegur 28; dm/d without bathroom Ikr5000/12,000; ☎) There's plenty of common space and comfortable lounge chairs, but the vibe is sleep-and-go not stay-and-chill. HI members discount Ikr700.

Hótel Selfoss
HOTEL €€€

(☑480 2500; www.hotelselfoss.is; Eyravegur 2; s/d from Ikr31,90000/37,500; @☎) This 99-room behemoth near the bridge looks horrendous from the outside, but it has a calm interior with snappy business-style rooms, great facilities, including a large spa and an excellent in-house restaurant (mains Ikr3600 to Ikr5900). Get a room overlooking the lovely river, not the dire car park.

Eating

Selfoss is the best place in the south to stock up on groceries before setting off for remote areas. It has most major supermarkets, including **Bónus** (☑481 3710; Larsenstræti 5; ☻11am-6.30pm Mon-Thu, 10am-7.30pm Fri, 10am-6pm Sat, 11am-6pm Sun) and **Krónan** (☑585 7195; Austurvegur 3-5; ☻10am-8pm Mon-Fri, to 7pm Sat & Sun), loads of fast food and a **Vínbúðin** (☑482 2011; Vallholt 19; ☻11am-6pm Mon-Thu, to 7pm Fri, to 4pm Sat) liquor store.

Selfoss

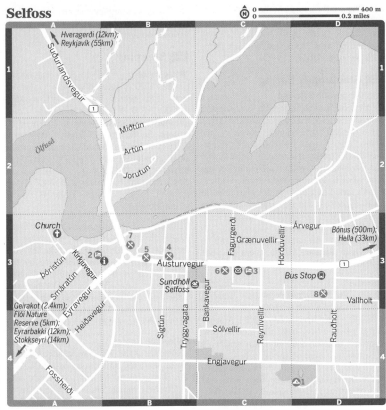

Selfoss

Sleeping
1 Gesthús D4
2 Hótel Selfoss A3
3 Selfoss HI Hostel C3

Eating
4 Kaffi Krús B3
5 Krónan B3
6 Sunnlenska Bókakaffið C3
7 Tryggvaskála B3
8 Vínbúðin D3

Sunnlenska Bókakaffið　　CAFE €
(☑ 482 3079; http://bokakaffid.blog.is; Austurvegur 22; ⊙ noon-6pm Mon-Sat; ☎) This independent bookshop (with both new and secondhand books) also offers coffee and cake.

★ **Tryggvaskála**　　ICELANDIC €€
(☑ 482 1390; www.tryggvaskala.is; Austurvegur 1; mains Ikr2460-5000; ⊙ 11.30am-10pm) Trygg-vaskála's actually worth stopping for. This new restaurant (the brainchild of the Kaffi Krús guys) fills Selfoss' first house (built for bridge workers in 1890). Lovingly renovated and on the riverfront with a romantic mood, the intimate dining rooms are filled with antique touches, and the fine-dining Icelandic menu sources local produce.

Kaffi Krús　　INTERNATIONAL €€
(☑ 482 1266; www.kaffikrus.is; Austurvegur 7; mains Ikr890-3000; ⊙ 9.30am-11pm Jun-Aug, reduced hours rest of year) The 'coffee mug' is a popular cafe in a charming old house along the main road. There's outdoor space and a large selection of Icelandic and international dishes from nachos to pasta.

ℹ Information

Tourist Information Centre (☑ 480 1990; http://tourinfo.arborg.is; Eyravegur 2; ⊙ 10am-7pm Mon, 9am-7pm Tue-Fri, 10am-4pm Sat

May-Aug) In the same building as Hótel Selfoss; the tourist office in Hveragerði is better.

❶ Getting There & Away

Most buses between Reykjavík and Höfn, Skaftafell, Fjallabak, Þórsmörk, Flúðir, Gullfoss, Laugarvatn and Vík stop at the N1 station in Selfoss.

Strætó (☑ 540 2700; www.straeto.is) services include:
➡ Buses 51 & 52 Reykjavík–Vík/Höfn & Reykjavík–Landeyjahöfn (Ikr1400, 50 minutes, 11 daily Monday to Friday, eight daily Saturday and Sunday).
➡ Buses 72 & 73 Selfoss–Flúðir (Ikr1750, 40 to 60 minutes, two to three daily).
➡ Bus 74 Selfoss–Stokkseyri–Eyrarbakki–Þorlákshöfn (Ikr350 to Ikr700, three daily Monday to Friday).
➡ Bus 75 Selfoss–Eyrarbakki (Ikr350, 20 minutes, eight daily Monday to Friday).

Sterna (☑ 551 1166; www.sterna.is) services:
➡ Bus 12/12A Reykjavík–Vík–Höfn, (Ikr1400 to/from Reykjavík, 55 minutes, one daily June to mid-September).

Reykjavík Excursions (☑ 580 5400; www.re.is) services:
➡ Buses 9/9A Reykjavík–Þórsmörk, 11/11A Reykjavík–Landmannalaugar, 17/17A Reykjavík–Mývatn, 18 Reykjavík–Álftavatn–Emstrur, 20/20A Reykjavík–Skaftafell, 21/21A Reykjavík–Skógar, 610/610A Reykjavík–Kjölur–Akureyri all stop in Selfoss.

Trex (☑ 587 6000; www.trex.is) services:
➡ Buses T21/T22 and T23/T24 Reykjavík–Landmannalaugar (Selfoss–Landmannalaugar Ikr6800, three hours, two daily mid-June to mid-September).
➡ Buses T11/T12 Reykjavík–Þórsmörk (Selfoss–Þórsmörk Ikr5800, 2¾ hours, one daily mid-June to mid-September).

Western Þjórsárdalur

The powerful Þjórsá is Iceland's longest river, a fast-flowing, churning mass of milky glacial water that courses 230km from Vatnajökull down to the Atlantic. Including its tributaries, it accounts for almost one-third of Iceland's hydroelectric power. Rte 32 follows the western side of the river, and as it moves upstream and into the highlands you traverse broad plains split by the enormous river which lead to volcanic fields and finally the foothills of the mountains beyond. It is a relatively un-touristed area with Viking ruins, hidden waterfalls and prehistoric-feeling river landscapes.

This is one of the preferred routes to reach Landmannalaugar (the starting point for the famous Laugavegurinn Hike) by vehicle (via 4WD-only Rte F26). It's also possible (if you don't have a 4WD) to make a day's loop up this side of the valley, cross over the river after the Búrfell Hydroelectric Plant and return down the other side of the valley to Hella on Rte 26. There is no public transport.

Árnes & Around

Stop in the tiny settlement of Árnes, near the junction of Rtes 30 and 32, where a large white building houses the informative **Þjórsárstofa** (Þjórsá Visitor Centre; ☑ 486 6115; www.thjorsarstofa.is; ⏰ 10am-6pm Jun-Aug) **FREE**. It has an excellent free 10-minute surround-sound-style film about the river valley and what you will see further along, as well as multimedia displays and a good restaurant.

🛏 Sleeping & Eating

Árnes HI Hostel — HOSTEL, CAMPGROUND €
(☑ 486 6048; www.hostel.is; camp sites per adult Ikr1000, dm Ikr3900; 🛜) This hostel isn't the cosiest place on earth, but it has serviceable twin rooms and dorm space, a guest kitchen, and a small pool nearby (Ikr500; open June to August).

Hótel Hekla — HOTEL €€
(☑ 486 5540; www.hotelhekla.is; Brjánsstaðir; d/q Ikr30,000/46,200; @🛜) As you head up the Þjórsá valley, this hotel complex sits just off Rte 30, 17km before Árnes. Large, modern doubles have flat-screen TVs, excellent family rooms are bigger still. The lounge feels like a warm library, and the restaurant serves up good Icelandic staples using local produce. A hot-pot and sauna add to the fun.

Þjórsárstofa Restaurant — ICELANDIC €€
(Matstofan; mains Ikr950-3200; ⏰ 9am-9pm Jun-Aug; 🛜) The Þjórsárstofa has a good restaurant with an ever-changing menu of regional cuisine and local beers.

❶ Getting There & Away

From the junction of Rtes 30 and 32, **Strætó** (☑ 540 2700; www.straeto.is) bus 76 (two daily Monday to Friday) runs with buses 72 and 73 to Árnes. (Buses to Landmannalaugar follow a route further east.)

Stöng, Búrfell & Around

As the Þjórsá's valley gets more remote inland, the drama and unusual sights increase. There is no accommodation.

☉ Sights

The following sights are arranged in the order you'll encounter them driving northeast on Rte 32.

Hjálparfoss   WATERFALL

Heading further along Rte 32 from Árnes towards Stöng and Þjóðveldisbær, take a short (1km) detour along a signposted track to the delightful waterfall Hjálparfoss, which tumbles in two chutes over twisted basalt columns and into a blue pool.

★ Stöng   RUIN

FREE Buried by white volcanic ash in 1104 during one of Hekla's eruptions, this ancient farm once belonged to Gaukur Trandilsson, a 10th-century Viking who lived a tempestuous life. Excavated in 1939 (Iceland's first proper archaeological dig), it's an important site, used to help date Viking houses elsewhere. The ruins are covered by a large wooden shelter at the end of a very rough dirt road that branches off Rte 32 about 20km beyond Árnes (best with 4WD, especially after rain).

Brief mentions in some 12th-century graffiti in Orkney, in Njál's Saga and in a scurrilous medieval rhyme hint that Trandilsson had a fling with the housewife at the nearby farm Steinastöðum and was killed over the affair in an axe duel. Contemplate this as you explore the site, where you'll find stone-lined fire pits and door lintels made from octagonal basalt columns and an impressively desolate lava landscape.

★ Gjáin   CANYON

A walking path behind Stöng farm takes you a couple of kilometres to a strange and lovely lush little valley, Gjáin, full of twisting lava, otherworldy caves and spectacular waterfalls. Gjáin simply means rift, and it was a filming location in *Game of Thrones*.

Háifoss   WATERFALL

From Stöng you can walk 10km northeast along a 4WD track to Iceland's second-highest waterfall, Háifoss, which plunges 122m off the edge of a plateau. You can also get most of the way there by 4WD.

Þjóðveldisbærinn   NOTABLE BUILDING

(☑ 488 7713; www.thjodveldisbaer.is; adult/child Ikr700/free; ☉ 10am-6pm Jun-Aug) Þjóðveldisbærinn is a reconstruction of Stöng, exactly reproducing its layout and its neighbouring church. Find it near the entrance to the Búrfell Power Station.

★ Búrfell Hydroelectric
Power Station   EXHIBITION

(www.landsvirkjun.com; ☉ 10am-5pm Jun-Aug) **FREE** On Rte 32, before it crosses the Þjórsá, the high-tech and hands-on Búrfell hydroelectric plant, decorated by one of Sigurjón Ólafsson's largest sculptures, allows visitors to its really engrossing multimedia centre, complete with games for generating hydroelectric power and exhibits on osmosis, tidal, wind and solar power. The whole place thunders with its turbines churning, which you can visit, along with a firetruck for the kids. It's really bizarre when contrasted with the wild landscape outside.

Eastern Þjórsárdalur

Between the township of Hella in the south and Landmannalaugar in the north, you'll find the sweeping seaside floodplains of the river Þjórsá merging into increasingly mind-blowing volcanic formations and lava fields til you reach Hekla – one of Iceland's most ominous volcanoes.

Route 26 (to Hekla & Landmannalaugar)

The road to Hekla – Rte 26 – winds its way beyond a cluster of horse farms offering a variety of riding trips, and connects with Rte 32 which can take you down the equally dramatic western side of the river valley.

Most buses to Landmannalaugar (p140) go via Rte 26 and Leirubakki.

☉ Sights & Activities

Heklusetrið   EXHIBITION

(Hekla Center; ☑ 487 8700; www.leirubakki.is; Leirubakki; adult/child Ikr800/400; ☉ 9am-10pm Jun-Aug) The Hekla Center is part of the Leirubakki compound (camping, hotel, restaurant, petrol). It details the explosive history of Hekla in a deliberately dark building with flashing lights and multimedia exhibits. You'll learn that the volcano is long overdue to erupt. The centre also has regional information, and offers **horse riding**, and **local walks**.

⬅ Tours

The many horse farms around eastern Þjórsárdalur offer rides, and most have accommodation. Expect to pay Ikr6500 to Ikr9000 for a one-hour ride to Ikr13,000 for a three-hour ride, though prices can drop for groups.

Hekluhestar   HORSE RIDING
(✑ 487 6598; www.hekluhestar.is; Austvaðsholt) Hidden along Rtes 271 and 272, 9km northeast of Hella, a friendly French-Icelandic family specialises in six- to eight-day Highland rides. Sleeping-bag accommodation is available (Ikr4000, linen Ikr2000).

Herríðarhóll   HORSE RIDING
(✑ 487 5252; www.herridarholl.is; Herríðarhóli) Multiday horse tours and short rides, plus a warm welcome to those who simply want a farmstay (double with shared bathroom Ikr16,900). West of Hella, then 6km north of the Ring Road on Rte 284.

Hestheimar   HORSE RIDING
(✑ 487 6666; www.hestheimar.is) Take family-run riding trips, rent horses, or bunk in a variety of comfortable accommodation at this horse farm above a bubbling stream. On Rte 281, 7km northwest of Hella.

Kálfholt   HORSE RIDING
(✑ 487 5176; www.kalfholt.is; Kálfholt 2, Ásahreppi) This family-run farm offers one of the best ranges of hourly rides, day trips and two- to eight-day treks for every skill level. On Rte 288, 17km west of Hella and south of the Ring Road. Comfy lodging is in two little cabins (per person including breakfast Ikr7500).

HEKLA

The name of Iceland's most famous and active volcano means Hooded One, as its 1491m-high summit is almost always shrouded in ominous-looking clouds. Hekla has vented its fury numerous times throughout history, and during the Middle Ages it was commonly believed to be the gateway to hell.

Viking-era settlers built farms on the rich volcanic soils around Hekla, only to be wiped out by the eruption of 1104, which buried everything within a radius of 50km. Since then there have been 15 major eruptions – the 1300 eruption covered more than 83,000 sq km in ash.

In recent years, hellish Hekla has been belching out ash in steady 10-year intervals. This ash has a high fluorine content and has poisoned thousands of sheep. The most recent eruption (in 2000) produced a small pyroclastic flow (a high-speed and highly destructive torrent of rock particles and gas, which typically travels at over 130km per hour and can reach temperatures of 800°C). As you travel the region, look for grey pumice...it's probably from Hekla.

Locals live with the knowledge that the mighty mound could erupt at any time; it is long overdue.

For more on Hekla, check out the exhibition at Leirubakki (p130).

Climbing Hekla

You can climb Hekla, but there's never much warning before eruptions, usually indicated by multiple small earthquakes 30 to 80 minutes before it blows. Stick to days when the summit is free of heavy clouds, and carry plenty of water – the area's ash makes you thirsty. Most climbs are done June to September.

There's a small car park where mountain road F225 branches off Rte 26 (about 45km northeast of Hella). Most hire cars aren't allowed on F roads and need to be parked here, but it's a long and dusty walk (16km) to the foot of the volcano (or try your luck at hitching).

With a large 4WD you can continue along F225 to the trailhead at the bottom of Hekla (about 14.7km); the largest vehicles can continue a few kilometres further, but most have to park here. From this lower trailhead, a well-marked path climbs steadily up to the ridge on the northeastern flank of the mountain, then onto the summit crater; expect snow walking at altitude. Although the peak is often covered in snow, the floor of the crater is still hot. The trip to the summit takes about 3½ hours.

Alternatively, you can organise bespoke super-Jeep tours from anywhere in the region.

🛏 Sleeping & Eating

Most of the horse farms (p131) in the plains around Hella have accommodation for their riders and welcome other travellers as well. Campers can pitch a tent at **Laugaland** (☑895-6543; www.tjalda.is/en/laugaland; camp sites per adult Ikr900) or Hótel Leirubakki.

Rjúpnavellir   COTTAGE, CAMPGROUND €
(☑892 0409; www.rjupnavellir.is; Landsveit; camp site per person Ikr900; 🕾) Just where the paved road ends, and the closest accommodation to Rte 26–F225 junction, you'll find these two large cabins with sleeping-bag space (Ikr3800) and cooking facilities, and a six-person cottage (Ikr18,000). Showers cost Ikr300, linen Ikr1750.

Hótel Leirubakki   HOTEL €€
(☑487 8700; www.leirubakki.is; Leirubakki; camp sites per adult Ikr1000, d with/without bathroom incl breakfast Ikr29,900/22,600, mains Ikr1890-5690; @🕾) This large farmstead is one of the last outposts before you hit volcanoes and highlands. The well-run house and more modern hotel block are a good base for Hekla climbers. The restaurant serves Icelandic faves such as lamb and trout (from a nearby stream). There's a great hot-pot in the lava field, an N1 petrol pump, and sleeping-bag accommodation (Ikr5900).

❶ Getting There & Away

Landmannalaugar buses stop in Leirubakki.

Trex (☑587 6000; www.trex.is) services:
➡ Buses T21/T22 & T23/T24 Reykjavík–Landmannalaugar (Leirubakki–Landmannalaugar Ikr4200, 1¾ hours, two daily mid-June to mid-September).

Reykjavík Excursions (☑580 5400; www.re.is) services:
➡ Bus 11/11A Reykjavík–Landmannalaugar (Reykjavík–Leirubakki Ikr5500, two hours, one daily mid-June to mid-September).
➡ Bus 17/17A Reykjavík–Mývatn (Leirubakki–Mývatn Ikr14,500, 9¼ hours, three weekly late-June to August).

Hella & Around

This small agricultural community sits on the banks of the pretty Ytri-Rangá river in an important horse-breeding area. The nearest town to shadow-wreathed volcano Hekla, 35km north, and a crossroads for lots of interesting spots, it's becoming an increasingly popular stopover.

◉ Sights & Activities

The town of Hella itself has little of interest to tourists, who use it as a base camp for horse riding or adventures beyond. The handicrafts cooperative **Hekla Handverkshús** (☑864 5531; Þrúðvangur 35; ◷1-5pm May-

---

THE EDDAS

The medieval monastery at **Oddi**, in Rangárvellir about 8km south of Hella on Rte 266, was the source of the Norse Eddas, the most important surviving books of Viking poetry. The *Prose Edda* was written by the poet and historian Snorri Sturluson around 1222. It was intended to be a textbook for poets, with detailed descriptions of the language and meters used by the Norse *skalds* (court poets). It also includes the epic poem 'Gylfaginning', which describes the visit of Gylfi, the king of Sweden, to Ásgard, the citadel of the gods. In the process, the poem reveals Norse creation myths, stories about the gods, and the fate in store for men at Ragnarök, when this world ends.

The *Poetic Edda* was written later in the 13th century by Sæmundur Sigfússon. It's a compilation of works by unknown Viking poets, some predating the settlement of Iceland. The first poem, 'Voluspá' (Sibyl's Prophecy), is like a Norse version of Genesis and Revelations: it covers the beginning and end of the world. Later poems deal with the story of how Óðinn discovered the power of runes, and the legend of Siegfried and the Nibelungs, recounted in Wagner's *Ring Cycle*. The most popular poem is probably 'Þrymskviða', about the giant Thrym, who stole Þór's hammer and demanded the goddess Freyja in marriage in exchange for its return. To get his hammer back, Þór disguised himself as the bride-to-be and went to the wedding in her place. Much of the poem is devoted to his appalling table manners at the wedding feast, during which he consumes an entire ox, eight salmon and three skins of mead.

Today Oddi is simply a church and farmsteads.

Sep, Sat & Sun Oct-Apr) doubles as an informal tourist information desk.

Sundlaugin Hellu   GEOTHERMAL POOL, HOT-POT
(☑487 5334; Útskálum 4; adult/child Ikr600/250; ☺6.30am-9pm Mon-Fri, noon-6pm Sat & Sun Jun-mid-Aug, reduced hours rest of year) Hella's top attraction might be its fantastic geothermal swimming pool, with hot-pots, sauna and a cool water slide (April to October) to keep the kids happy.

☞ Tours
Mud Shark   FISHING, SUPER-JEEP
(☑691 1849; www.mudshark.is) Beach-fishing trips (Ikr60,000) or super-Jeep tour to the Þykkvibær black-sand beach (Ikr15,000); lower prices for more people.

🛏 Sleeping & Eating
Lodging and eating options in Hella are efficient but without rural splendour. There's a Kjarval supermarket (☑585 7585; Suður-landsvegur 1) with a small bakery next door.

Árhús   CAMPGROUND €
(South Door; ☑487 5577; www.arhus.is; Rangár-bakkar 6; camp sites per tent Ikr2500, cottage with/without bathroom from Ikr16,500/12,400, mains Ikr2000-5000; ☎) Set along the river, just south of the Ring Road, Árhús has a cluster of cottages (from a simple room to a complete cabin with kitchenette and bathroom), ample camping space, a guest kitchen, and a top town restaurant (open noon to 10pm).

Stracta Hótel   HOTEL €€
(☑531 8010; www.stractahotels.is; Rangárflatir 4; d with/without bathroom incl breakfast from Ikr26,500/17,000, 3-/6-person studio incl breakfast from Ikr33,000/43,200, dinner Ikr5500; ☎) Brand-new Stracta is first in a series of higher-end tourist hotels started by Icelandic footballer Hermann Hreiðarsson. Rooms range from modern, comfortable doubles to studios with microwaves and refrigerators, on up to two-bedroom, family-friendly apartments. The upstairs restaurant has sweeping views of Vestmannaeyjar and volcanoes, while the bistro (open10am to 1am) overlooks the spa and courtyard.

Guesthouse Nonni   GUESTHOUSE €€
(☑894 9953; www.bbiceland.com; Arnarsan-dur 3; s/d without bathroom incl breakfast Ikr16,200/17,700; ☎) Run by friendly Nonni, who loves cooking a large breakfast for his guests (fresh bread and flower-shaped waffles), this small guesthouse on a residential street has five wooden-walled rooms tucked up a cork stairwell.

Guesthouse Brenna   HOUSE €€
(☑487 5532; http://guesthousebrenna.wordpress.com; Þrúðvangur 37; house Ikr25,000) This adorable riverside house sleeps eight and has a little kitchen, washing machine, and a comfy sitting room. Linen costs Ikr1000. Prices drop with additional nights. No individual rooms rented.

Hótel Rangá   HOTEL €€€
(☑487 5700; www.hotelranga.is; Suðurlandsvegur; d/ste incl breakfast from Ikr48,400/89,400, lunch mains Ikr2600-3700, dinner mains Ikr4400-9900; @☎) Just south of the Ring Road 8km east of Hella, Hótel Rangá looks like a log cabin but caters to Iceland's high-end travellers. Service is top-notch, and wood-panelled rooms and luxurious common areas cosy. The restaurant has broad windows across open pastures. To splash out, go for a 'World Pavilion' suite.

Understated 'Asia' – which looks like a Japanese ryokan – is apparently Charlize Theron's pick.

Hellubió   INTERNATIONAL €€
(☑853 7777; Þrúðvangur 32; mains Ikr2000-5000) This large silver roadhouse with bright potted flowers out front stands out for its simple menu of local food from lobster soup to burgers, plus draught beer, friendly staff, and excellent chocolate cake.

❶ Getting There & Away
Buses stop at the Olís petrol station.

Strætó (☑540 2700; www.straeto.is) services include:
➡ Buses 51 & 52 Reykjavík–Vík–Höfn and Reykjavík–Landeyjahöfn (Reykjavík–Hella Ikr2450, 1½ hours, five daily).

Sterna (☑551 1166; www.sterna.is) services:
➡ Bus 12/12A Reykjavík–Vík–Höfn (Reykjavík–Hella Ikr2200, 1½ hours, one daily June to mid-September).

Reykjavík Excursions (☑580 5400; www.re.is) services:
➡ Buses 9/9A Reykjavík–Þórsmörk, 11/11A Reykjavík–Landmannalaugar, 17/17A Reykjavík–
➡ Mývatn, 18 Reykjavík–Álftavatn–Emstrur, 20/20A Reykjavík–Skaftafell, 21/21A Reykjavík–Skógar; all stop in Hella (Ikr2500).

Trex (☑551 1166; www.trex.is) services:
➡ Buses T21/T22 and T23/T24 Reykjavík–Landmannalaugar (Hella–Landmannalaugar Ikr5500, 2¼ hours, two daily mid-June to mid-September).

» Buses T11/T12 Reykjavík–Þórsmörk (Hella–Þórsmörk Ikr4200, two hours, one daily mid-June to mid-September).

Hvolsvöllur & Around

The farms around Hvolsvöllur were the setting for the bloody events of *Njál's Saga*, one of Iceland's favourites; today, though, the saga sites exist mainly as place names, peaceful grassed-over ruins or modern agricultural buildings. Hvolsvöllur itself is not much more than a pit stop, with a couple of petrol stations and a cluster of houses.

◉ Sights & Activities

★ **Sögusetrið**   MUSEUM
(Saga Centre; ☑ 487 8781; www.njala.is; Hlíðarvegur 14; adult/child Ikr900/free; ⊙ 9am-6pm mid-May–mid-Sep, 10am-5pm Sat & Sun mid-Sep–mid-May) Hvolsvöllur's Saga Centre is devoted to the dramatic events of *Njál's Saga*, which took place in the surrounding hills. Interactive displays explain the many highlights of the story. In 2013 an intricate 90m embroidery called **Njál's Saga Tapestry** (www.njalurefill.is; ⊙ 10am-6pm Tue-Sat Jun-Aug, reduced hours Sep-May) was begun; visitors can pay to add stitches (Ikr1000) to the enormous collaborative project, or just observe. There's also a longhouse **cafe** and **tourist information** (brochures, maps and helpful staff).

Keldur   RUIN
(☑ 530 2200; www.thjodminjasafn.is; admission Ikr700; ⊙ 10am-5pm mid-Jun–mid-Aug) About 5km west of Hvolsvöllur, unsurfaced Rte 264 winds about 8km north along the Rangárvellir valley to the medieval turf-roofed farm at Keldur. This historic settlement once belonged to Ingjaldur Höskuldsson, a character in *Njál's Saga*. The structure is managed by the National Museum Historic Buildings Collection.

⌁ Tours

★ **South Iceland Adventures**   HIKING, ADVENTURE
(☑ 770 2030; www.siadv.is) One of South Iceland's best bespoke adventure operators. Founder, Siggi Bjarni, knows the area well and is a great bet for guided hikes along Fimmvörðuháls or Laugavegurinn. Loads of day tours with pick-up include super-Jeep trips (Eyjafjallajökull Ikr31,900; Landmannalaugar Ikr37,900), canyoning and ice climbing. Winter trips too.

⌂ Sleeping & Eating

Sleeping and eating options in town aren't brilliant; stay in the countryside. Both petrol stations have grills; the **farmers market** (Sveitamarkaðurinn Hvolsvelli; ⊙ 9am-6pm Jun-Aug) doesn't have much food, but there's a Kjarval supermarket.

Vestri-Garðsauki   GUESTHOUSE €
(☑ 487 8078; www.gardsauki.is; d without bathroom Ikr12,000; 🅿) Located just off Rte 1, this friendly Icelandic-German farming family tends to four tidy rooms that – while located in the basement – receive good summer sunlight. The owners offer informal walking or car-based trips in the area, and can arrange flightseeing.

Bergþórshvoll   GUESTHOUSE €
(☑ 487 7715; www.bergthorshvoll.is; d/q without bathroom Ikr12,000/16,000) This slightly 1970s-feeling guesthouse is on Bergþórsvoll, Njál's former farm, now a sheep farm. Rooms are comfortable in a shared house with kitchen, laundry and a large living room with volcano views. Find it 21km south of Hvolsvöllur by the coast; Rte 255 and then 252 lead there.

Hótel Hvolsvöllur   HOTEL €€
(☑ 487 8050; www.hotelhvolsvollur.is; Hlíðarvegur 7; s/d incl breakfast Ikr23,500/28,300; @🅿) This large bland-looking hotel is better than it appears. The 64 rooms are constantly being updated (newest have wood floors and sparkling bathrooms) and staff are friendly.

Gallerí Pizza   FAST FOOD €€
(☑ 487 8440; Hvolsvegur 29; mains Ikr1600-2950; ⊙ 12.30-10pm Sun-Thu, noon-10pm Fri & Sat) The town pizzeria, one street back from the main road, is a busy, no-frills place with vinyl booths and munching locals. The Bearnaise burger is a favourite.

Eldstó Art Café   CAFE €€
(www.eldsto.is; Austurvegur 2; mains Ikr1390-2700; ⊙ 8am-10pm Jun-Aug; 🅿) Eldstó offers fresh-brewed coffee, homemade daily specials (like coconut curry soup), and a couple of outdoor Ring Roadside tables. Owners are ceramicists, and also offer accommodation upstairs.

❶ Getting There & Away

Buses to Þórsmörk stop in Hvolsvöllur. **Strætó** (☑ 540 2700; www.straeto.is) services:

NJÁL'S SAGA

One of Iceland's best-loved (and longest) sagas is also one of the most complicated. The story involves two friends and neighbours, Gunnar Hámundarson and Njál Þorgeirsson. A petty squabble between their wives is a prelude to the feuds and battles that ultimately leave almost every character dead. Written in the 13th century, it recounts 10th-century events that took place in the hills around Hvolsvöllur.

Doomed hero Gunnar of Hlíðarendi (near Fljótsdalur) falls for and marries the beautiful, hot-tempered Hallgerður, who has long legs but – ominously – a 'thief's eyes'. Hallgerður has a falling-out with Bergþóra, wife of Njál. Things become increasingly strained between Gunnar and Njál as Hallgerður and Bergþóra begin murdering each other's servants.

In one important episode, Hallgerður sends a servant to burgle food from a man named Otkell. When Gunnar comes home and sees Hallgerður's stolen feast, his temper snaps. 'It's bad news indeed if I've become a thief's accomplice', he says, and slaps his wife – an act that later comes back to haunt him. (Spoiler alert: each of Hallgerður's two previous husbands was killed as an outcome of slapping her.)

Through more unfortunate circumstances, Gunnar ends up killing Otkell and is sentenced to exile. As he rides away from home, his horse stumbles. Fatally, he takes one last glance back at his beloved farm Hlíðarendi and is unable to leave the valley after all. His enemies gather their forces and lay siege to the farm, but Gunnar manages to hold off the attackers until his bowstring breaks. When he asks Hallgerður for a lock of her hair to repair it, she refuses, reminding him of the slap she received (years earlier) – and Gunnar is killed.

The feud continues as Gunnar and Njál's clan members try to avenge their slaughtered kin. Njál himself acts as a peace broker, forming treaties between the two families, but in the end, the complicated peacemaking is all for naught. Njál and his wife are besieged in their farm. Tucking themselves in bed with their little grandson between them, the couple allow themselves to be burnt alive.

The only survivor of the fire is Njál's son-in-law Kári, who launches a legal case against the arsonists, commits a bit of extrajudicial killing himself and is finally reconciled with his arch-enemy, Flosi, who ordered the burning of the Njál family.

➡ Buses 51 & 52 Reykjavík–Vík–Höfn & Reykjavík–Landeyjahöfn (Reykjavík–Hvolsvöllur Ikr2800, 1½ hours, five daily).

Sterna (✆ 551 1166; www.sterna.is) services:
➡ Bus 12/12A Reykjavík–Vík–Höfn (Reykjavík–Hvolsvöllur Ikr2500, 1¾ hours, one daily June to mid-September).

Reykjavík Excursions (✆ 580 5400; www.re.is) services:
➡ Buses 9/9A Reykjavík–Þórsmörk, 18 Álftavatn–Reykjavík, 20/20A Reykjavík–Skaftafell, 21/21A Reykjavík–Skógar (Reykjavík–Hvolsvöllur Ikr3000, all stop in Hella).

Trex (✆ 587 6000; www.trex.is) services:
➡ Buses T11/T12 Reykjavík–Þórsmörk (Hvolsvöllur–Þórsmörk Ikr4200, 1½ hours, one daily mid-June to mid-September).

Hvolsvöllur to Skógar

After Hvolsvöllur, the Ring Road loops east towards Skógar with three important sideroads. The first is Fljótshlíð (Rte 261), just at the eastern end of Hvolsvöllur; the second is Rte 254, which shoots south 12km to Landeyjahöfn (p159) where the ferry leaves for Vestmannaeyjar; and the third is Rte 249 north to Þórsmörk. Staying on the Ring Road, will bring you along the base of hulking Eyjafjallajökull, made famous with its ashy 2010 explosion.

Fljótshlíð

Rte 261 follows the mossy green edge of the lush Fljótshlíð hills, offering great views of their waterfalls, such as **Gluggafoss**, on one side, and the Markarfljót river delta and Eyjafjallajökull on the other.

The surfaced section of the road ends soon after the farm and church at **Hlíðarendi**, once the home of Gunnar Hámundarson from *Njál's Saga*. With a 4WD you can continue along road F261 towards Landmannalaugar and **Tindfjöll** – a hiker's paradise. Though it

ℹ BOOK AHEAD

Moving west from Hvolsvöllur all the way to Vík, many local farms have pretty, rural guesthouses. It's a beautiful, but incredibly popular place to stay, so they get booked solid in summer. Reservations are essential. Look on Icelandic Farm Holidays (www.farmholidays.is) and booking.com for more choices; we offer but a top sample.

The excellent, free regional map *Rangárþing Mýrdalur* shows everything (available at tourist offices).

seems tantalisingly close, Þórsmörk can only be reached via Rte F249.

☞ Tours

South Iceland Adventures (p134) runs hiking and canyoning tours in Tindfjöll and the region.

Óbyggðaferðir   QUAD-BIKE
(☑ 661 2503; www.atvtravel.is; Lambalæk) Quad-bike tours around Eyjafjallajökull, Þórsmörk and beyond. A three to four-hour trip per single/double rider costs Ikr18,000/25,000; day trips per single/double rider cost Ikr46,000/58,000.

🛏 Sleeping & Eating

★ Fljótsdalur HI Hostel   HOSTEL €
(☑ 487 8498; www.hostel.is; Fljótshlíð; dm Ikr4100; ☺ mid-Mar–Oct) It's very basic and not for everyone, but if you're looking for a peaceful, remote base for highland walks, with a beautiful garden, homey kitchen, cosy sitting room, and mountain views that make your knees tremble, then you'll find it here. There are only seven bare mattresses in the attic and two four-bed rooms on the main floor. Book ahead. HI Members discount Ikr700.

Find it 27km east of Hvolsvöllur. The road gets rough toward the end; bring all supplies.

★ Hótel Fljótshlíð   HOTEL €€
(Guesthouse Smáratún; ☑ 487 1416; www.smaratun. is; Smáratún; camp sites per person Ikr1300, d with/without bathroom Ikr23,000/12,400, cottage from Ikr23,700; 🐾) This attractive white farm with a blue-tin roof has four- to six-person summerhouses, smart hotel-style rooms, cheaper guesthouse rooms (with shared facilities),

sleeping-bag places (Ikr4400), and spots for tents. The husband runs the restaurant's kitchen, and the affable wife takes guests on evening strolls through the flood plains while telling stories about the 2010 eruption. It's 12.5km east of Hvolsvöllur.

Route 249/F249 (To Þórsmörk)

The road to Þórsmörk (Rte 249/F249) begins just east of the Markarfljót river leading north off the Ring Road. Although it quickly turns into a spectacular 4WD-only road, some interesting sights at the start of the road can be reached by car.

Seljalandsfoss is a pick-up point for Þórsmörk-bound buses (it is impossible to reach by private vehicle due to big rivers).

◎ Sights & Activities

★ Seljalandsfoss & Gljúfurárbui   WATERFALLS
From the Ring Road you'll see the beautiful high falls at Seljalandsfoss, which tumble over a rocky scarp into a deep, green pool. A (slippery) path runs around the back of the waterfall. A few hundred metres further down the Þórsmörk road, Gljúfurárbui gushes into a hidden canyon. Sterna and Reykjavík Excursions buses from Reykjavík to Skógar and beyond stop at Seljalandsfoss.

☞ Tours

★ Southcoast Adventure   ADVENTURE TOUR
(☑ 867 3535; www.southadventure.is) South Coast Adventure is a small tour operator run by enthusiastic locals with loads of regional knowledge, SAR experience, and excellent reputations. Book tailormade super-Jeep tours (two-/five-hour tours from Ikt14,900/29,900) from Þórsmörk to Landmannaulagar and longer hikes like Fimmvörðuháls or Laugavegurinn. Also offers snowmobiling, volcano tours and glacier walks and winter trips. Info desk is at Hamragarðar (p136) on 2WD-friendly Rte 249.

🛏 Sleeping & Eating

Hamragarðar   CAMPGROUND €
(☑ 867 3535; camp sites per person Ikr1200) Camp right next to the hidden waterfall at Gljúfurárbui at the start of Rte 249. The small cafe (9am to 11pm June to August) sells cake and coffee, has laundry and a shared kitchen, and there's an info area for South Coast Adventure.

★ **Stóra-Mörk III**   GUESTHOUSE, COTTAGES €€

(☑ 487 8903; www.storamork.com; sleeping-bag accommodation Ikr3900, d with/without bathroom Ikr16,300/11,500) About 5km beyond the cluster of traffic at the falls (Rte 249), a dirt track leads to historic Stóra-Mörk III farmhouse (mentioned, of course, in *Njál's Saga*), which offers large, homey rooms with shared facilities. The main house has some rooms with private bathrooms, a large kitchen and dining room with excellent mountain-to-sea views. Two new cottages, too.

Rte 1 (Under Eyjafjallajökull)

The Ring Road (Rte 1) goes directly through the flood zone that was inundated with muddy ash during the infamous Eyjafjallajökull (*ay*-ya-*fiat*-la-yo-gootl) eruption in 2010. There's a loose string of guesthouses and farmsteads.

○ Sights

Eyjafjallajökull Visitor Centre   EXHIBITION

(Þorvaldseyri Visitor Center – Iceland Erupts; ☑ 487 8815; www.icelanderupts.is; Þorvaldseyri; adult/child Ikr750/free; ⊙ 9am-6pm Jun-Aug, 10am-4pm May & Sep, 11am-4pm Oct-Apr) This centre, about 7km before Skógar, is on a farm on the southern flanks of Eyjafjallajökull which was impacted by the 2010 eruption. A 20-minute film (usually in English) tells the family's story, from the ominous warnings to the devastating aftermath of the flooding ash. Movie snippets include tender family moments and highlights from the team of local rescuers that dug the farm out.

Seljavallalaug   GEOTHERMAL POOL

FREE Seljavallalaug, a peaceful 1923 pool, is filled by a natural hot spring. From Edinborg (7km west of Skógar) follow Rte 242 and signs to Seljavellir; park by the farm, and walk up the beautiful river valley for about 10 minutes.

☞ Tours

Skálakot   HORSE RIDING

(☑ 487 8953; www.skalakot.com) Horse farm Skálakot (15km west of Skógar on Rte 246) offers an array of shorter rides (one hour Ikr6000) and longer treks (five-hour glacier-and-beach ride Ikr27,000). It also offers a range of accommodation.

🍴 Sleeping & Eating

Skálakot   GUESTHOUSE, FARMSTAY €

(☑ 487 8953; www.skalakot.com; dm Ikr3500, d without bathroom Ikr12,000, farmstay with full board Ikr17,000) The newly built facilities at the Skálakot horse farm offer accommodation in dorms, guesthouse rooms with shared bathroom, plus full farmstay experiences. It's 15km west of Skógar on Rte 246.

Country Hotel Anna   COUNTRY HOTEL €€

(☑ 487 8950; www.hotelanna.is; Moldnúpur; s/d incl breakfast Ikr19,800/26,900, mains Ikr4200-5100; 🕸) ⏀ This inn's namesake, Anna, wrote books about her world-wide voyages – and her descendants' country hotel upholds her passion for travel with seven sweetly old-fashioned rooms furnished with antiques and embroidered bedspreads. The hotel and its little restaurant (open 6pm to 8pm May to mid-September) sit at the foot of the volcano on Rte 246.

Guesthouse Edinborg   GUESTHOUSE €€

(☑ 566 7979; www.greatsouth.is; Lambafell; d incl breakfast Ikr21,500; @🕸) Formerly named Hótel Edinborg (and still signposted that way on the main road), this tall, tin-clad farmhouse has inviting wood-floored rooms with comfy beds and private bathrooms, and an attic seating area with glacier views. It feels out in the remote countryside despite being just off the Ring Road. It also operates nearby **Hótel Lambafell** (☑ 487 1212; www.lambafell.is; Lambafell; d/q incl breakfast from Ikr20,000/35,200; 🕸).

Drangshlíð   HOTEL €€

(☑ 487 8868; Ring Road; s/d incl breakfast Ikr17,000/24,600, mains Ikr3600-4900; @🕸) The 200-year-old farm at Drangshlíð, 3km west of Skógar, has had a spate of building of late. The best of the comfortable, if

SOUTHWEST ICELAND & THE GOLDEN CIRCLE HVOLSVÖLLUR TO SKÓGAR

FLIGHTSEEING THE VOLCANOES

Atlantsflug (☑ 854 4105; www.flightseeing.is) From Bakki Airport, on the coast 5km northwest of Landeyjahöfn, Atlantsflug offers 30-minute to 75-minute overflights (Ikr22,300 to Ikr44,000) of Eyjafjallajökull, glaciers and highlands. Flights also run to Heimaey, Vestmannaeyjar (Westman Islands; one-way Ikr8000) and also depart from Skaftafell and Reykjavík.

somewhat utilitarian, rooms are in the back building where rooms are larger, some with pasture views. The restaurant (open 6pm to 9pm), was also expanded, accommodating the tour-bus crowd. Book on Icelandic Farm Holidays (www.farmholidays.is).

★ **Gamla Fjósið** ICELANDIC €€
(Old Cowhouse; ☑ 487 7788; www.gamlafjosid. is; Hvassafell; mains Ikr1100-6500; ☺ 11am-9pm Jun-Aug, reduced hours Sep-May; ☎) Built in a former cowshed that was in use until 1999, this charming eatery's focus is on farm-fresh and grass-fed meaty mains – from burgers to Volcano Soup, a spicy meat stew. The hardwood floor and low beams are cheered with polished dining tables, large wooden hutches and cheerful staff.

Skógar

Skógar nestles under the Eyjafjallajökull ice cap just off the Ring Road. This little tourist settlement is the start (or occasionally end) of the hike over the Fimmvörðuháls Pass to Þórsmörk, and is one of the activities centres in the southwest. At its western edge, you'll see the dizzyingly high waterfall, Skógafoss, and on the eastern side you'll find a fantastic folk museum.

◉ Sights

★ **Skógar Folk Museum** MUSEUM
(Skógasafn; ☑ 487 8845; www.skogasafn.is; adult/child Ikr1750/free, outside structures only Ikr800; ☺ museum 9am-6pm Jun-Aug, 10am-5pm May & Sep, 11am-4pm Oct-Apr) The highlight of little Skógar is the wonderful Skógar Folk Museum, which covers all aspects of Icelandic life. The vast collection was put together by 91-year-old Þórður Tómasson over more than 75 years. There are also restored buildings (church, turf-roofed farmhouse, cowsheds etc), and a huge, modern building houses an interesting transport and communication museum, cafe Skógakaffi (open 10am to 5pm), and shop.

★ **Skógafoss** WATERFALL
The 62m-high waterfall, Skógafoss, topples over a rocky cliff at the western edge of Skógar in dramatic style. Climb the steep staircase alongside for giddy views, or walk to the foot of the falls, shrouded in sheets of mist and rainbows. Legend has it that a settler named Þrasi hid a chest of gold behind Skógafoss...

☞ Tours

Several major operators have their base in or around Skógar and offer tours to natural wonders from glaciers to volcanoes and beyond. Excellent operators near Skógar are Southcoast Adventure (p136), which offers guided hikes of Fimmvörðuháls, among many other adventure tours, and South Iceland Adventures (p134) in Hvolsvöllur, again tops for treks, super-Jeeps, ice climbing etc. Both can pick up from Skógar.

Icelandic Mountain Guides ADVENTURE
(☑ 587 9999, Skógar office 894 2956; www.mountainguide.is) One of the largest and best operators in Iceland, Icelandic Mountain Guides has a downtown Reykjavík office and Skógar branch. Locally, it runs glacier-walks and ice climbs on Sólheimajökull (Ikr8900 to Ikr25,900), guided Fimmvörðuháls hikes (Ikr26,900), plus many more tours further afield. The office is also an information centre and booking operation (tours, horse riding, accommodation). Offers Reykjavík pickup.

Arcanum ADVENTURE
(☑ 487 1500; www.arcanum.is) This popular tour operator offers daily Sólheimajökull glacier walks (Ikr7000), ice climbing (Ikr14,000), super-Jeep, quad-bike and other tours geared towards all ages. It has a small booking table at Fossbúð (p140), but is based on Ytri-Sólheimar I farm 11km east of Skógar. Offers Reykjavík pick up and local accommodation.

☷ Sleeping & Eating

Although Skógar is set up for tourists with various places to stay, it's essential to book well ahead in high season.

★ **Skógar Campsite** CAMPGROUND €
(camp sites per person Ikr1200; ☺ Jun-Aug) Great location, right by Skógafoss; the sound of falling water makes a soothing lullaby. There's a small toilet block with fresh water; pay at the hostel nearby.

Hótel Edda Skógar HOTEL €
(☑ 444 4000; www.hoteledda.is; d without bathroom Ikr15,200; ☺ early Jun-late Aug; ☎) Perfectly serviceable with a few less scratches than the other Edda hotels, this summer inn close to the museum is split over two buildings. All rooms have shared bathrooms.

Skógar HI Hostel HOSTEL €
(☑ 487 8801; www.hostel.is; dm/d Ikr4100/11,200; ☺ late May–mid-Sep; ☎) A solid link in the HI

chain, this spot is located a stone's throw from Skógafoss in an old school with utilitarian rooms. There's a guest kitchen and a laundry (Ikr800).

★ **Skógar Guesthouse**   GUESTHOUSE €€
(☑ 894 5464; www.skogarguesthouse.is; s/d without bathroom incl breakfast Ikr17,000/23,100; ☎)
This charming white farmhouse is tucked

FIMMVÖRÐUHÁLS TREK

Fimmvörðuháls – named for a pass between two brooding glaciers – dazzles the eye with a parade of wild inland vistas. Linking Skógar and Þórsmörk, the awesome hike is 23.4km long, and can be divided into three distinct sections of somewhat equal length. Figure around 10 hours to complete the trek, which includes stops to rest, and to check out the steaming remnants of the Eyjafjallajökull eruption. It's best to tackle the hike from July to mid-September. Pack wisely; you can experience all four seasons over the course of this hike. If in doubt, go with a guide, as there are two treacherous passes, and tours here are great.

➡ **Part 1: Waterfall Way** From Skógafoss to the 'bridge'. Starting on the right side of splashy Skógafoss, the path zooms up and over the falls quickly, revealing a series of waterfalls just behind. Stay close to the tumbling water as you climb over small stones and twisting trees – there are 22 chutes in all, each one magnificent. The path flattens out as the trees turn to windswept shrubs. Then, set your sights on the 'bridge', which is a crude walkway over the gushing river below. It's imperative that you make the crossing on the walkway otherwise you won't make it over and down into Þórsmörk later on.

➡ **Part 2: The Ashtray** From the 'bridge' to the eruption site. After crossing the crude bridge onto the left side of the moving water you start to enter the gloomy heart of the pass between two glaciers: Eyjafjallajökull and Mýrdalsjökull. The weather can be quite variable here – it could be raining in the pass when there is sunshine in Skógar. Expect to bundle up at this point as you move through icy rifts in the earlier parts of summer; from August on the region feels like some kind of giant ashtray. If you want to break up the hike over two days, there's a 20-person hut positioned 600m away from the main trail about halfway through this section of the walk (not to be confused with the easily noticeable Baldvinsskáli emergency hut). It's called **Fimmvörðuskáli** (☑ 893 4910; www.utivist.is; N 63°37.320', W 19°27.093'; per person Ikr4200), and it's run by Útivist (who often fill it with their clients; book ahead). Unfortunately, in bad weather it can be difficult to find. There's no campsite. Continuing on, the initial eruption site from the Eyjafjallajökull eruption reveals itself; here you'll find steaming earth and the world's newest mountains – Magni and Móði. Climb up to the top of Magni and roast some wieners over one of the sizzling vents.

➡ **Part 3: Goðaland** From the eruption site down into Þórsmörk. After climbing down from Magni, the last part of the hike begins. The barren ashiness continues for a while, then an otherworldly kingdom reveals itself – a place ripped straight from the pages of a fairy tale. Here in Goðaland – the aptly named 'Land of the Gods' – wild Arctic flowers bloom as stone cathedrals emerge in the distance. Vistas of green continue as you descend into Þórsmörk to complete the journey.

Although the hike is relatively short compared to some of Iceland's famous multiday treks, it's important to bring a GPS along – especially for the second portion of the hike when the way isn't always obvious. The following nine GPS markers can keep DIYers on track:

1. N 63°31.765, W 19°30.756 (start)
2. N 63°32.693, W 19°30.015
3. N 63°33.741, W 19°29.223
4. N 63°34.623, W 19°26.794 (the 'bridge')
5. N 63°36.105, W 19°26.095
6. N 63°38.208, W 19°26.616 (beginning of eruption site)
7. N 63°39.118, W 19°25.747
8. N 63°40.561, W 19°27.631
9. N 63°40.721, W 19°28.323 (terminus at Básar)

back inside the trees, beyond the Hótel Edda, almost to the cliff face. A friendly family offers impeccably maintained quaint rooms with crisp linens and cosy quilts, a large immaculate kitchen and bathrooms, and a hot tub on a wood deck beneath the maples. It feels well out of the tourist fray despite being in central Skógar.

Hótel Skógafoss   HOTEL €€

(☑ 487 8780; www.hotelskogafoss.is; d with/without waterfall view Ikr20,000/14,900, mains Ikr1200-2300) This brand-new hotel opened in 2014 and offers simple, modern rooms (half of which have views of Skógafoss) with top bathrooms. The bistro-bar (open 11am to 9.30pm June to September) is one of the best eating and drinking spots in town, with plate glass windows looking onto the falls and local beer on tap.

Hótel Skógar   HOTEL €€€

(☑ 487 4880; www.hotelskogar.is; s/d incl breakfast Ikr30,300/34,400, mains Ikr3000-4900; 🛜) This architecturally interesting hotel has small, eclectic rooms with quirky antiques, some with hill views. The upstairs 'deluxe' room has a king-size bed and waterfall views. A hot tub and a sauna in the garden and an elegant, good restaurant (open noon to 3pm and 6pm to 10pm) round it all out.

Also has a nearby house for rent.

Fossbúð   FAST FOOD €€

(☑ 487 4880; mains Ikr1200-3000; ⊙ 7am-9pm Jun-Aug; 🛜) Advertised as a restaurant, Fossbúð is really a convenience store and place for quick snacks: soup, hamburgers, sandwiches, bagged chips and chocolate bars. Arcanum (p138) has a small tour table here.

❶ Getting There & Away

Strætó (☑ 540 2700; www.bus.is) services:
➡ Bus 51 Reykjavík–Vík–Höfn (Reykjavík–Skógar Ikr4200, 2½ hours, two daily).

Sterna (☑ 551 1166; www.sterna.is) services:
➡ Bus 12/12A Reykjavík–Vík–Höfn (Reykjavík–Skógar Ik3600, 2¼ hours, one daily June to mid-September).

Reykjavík Excursions (☑ 580 5400; www.re.is) services:
➡ Bus 20/20A Reykjavík–Skaftafell (Reykjavík–Skógar Ik6000, 3¼ hours, one daily mid-June to early September).
➡ Bus 21/21A Reykjavík–Skógar (Reykjavík–Skógar Ik6000, three hours, two daily mid-June to August).

Landmannalaugar

Mind-blowing multicoloured mountains, soothing hot springs, rambling lava flows and clear blue lakes make Landmannalaugar one of Iceland's most unique destinations, and a must for explorers of the interior. It's a favourite with Icelanders and visitors alike... as long as the weather cooperates.

Part of the Fjallabak Nature Reserve, Landmannalaugar (600m above sea level) includes the largest geothermal field in Iceland outside the Grímsvötn caldera in Vatnajökull. Its multihued peaks are made of rhyolite – a mineral-filled lava that cooled unusually slowly, causing those amazing colours.

The area is the official starting point for the famous Laugavegurinn hike (p143), and there's some excellent day hiking amid the caramel hills as well.

🏃 Activities

There's plenty to do in and around Landmannalaugar, though many hikers skip the area's wonders in favour of setting off right away for their multiday hike to Þórsmörk. If you plan to stick around you'll be happy to know that the crowds dwindle in the evenings, and despite the base's chaotic appearance, you'll find peace in the hills above.

Hot Springs

Follow the wooden boardwalk just 200m from the Landmannalaugar hut, to find a steaming river filled with bathers. Both hot and cold water flow out from beneath Laugahraun and combine in a natural pool to form an ideal hot bath. Landmannalaugar could be translated as the People's Pools... and here they are.

Horse Riding

Landmannalaugar has on-site **horse-riding tours** (☑ 868 5577; www.hnakkur.com) from July to mid-August. A one-hour tour costs Ikr7500 per person, the whole day Ikr23,000. The horse farms in the plains around Hella also offer riding (usually longer trips) in and around the Landmannalaugar area.

Hiking

If you're planning on doing day hiking in the Landmannalaugar area, stop by the warden's house to purchase the useful day-trip map (Ikr300), which details all of the best hikes in the region.

On cloudier days try the day-hike to the ill-named **Ljótipollur** (Ugly Puddle), an incredible red crater filled with bright-blue water, and brown trout. The intense, fiery red comes from iron-ore deposits. Oddly enough, although it was formed by a volcanic explosion, the lake is rich in trout. The walk to the Puddle offers plenty of eye candy, from tephra desert and lava flow to marsh and braided glacial valleys. To get there you can climb over the 786m-high peak **Norðurnámur** or just traverse its western base to emerge on the Ljótipollur road (a 10km to 13.3km return trip, depending on the route).

When the weather is clear, try a walk that takes in the region's spectacular views. Climb to the summit of rainbow-streaked **Brennisteinsalda** – covered in steaming vents and sulphur deposits – for a good view across the rugged and variegated landscape (it's a 6.5km round-trip from Landmannalaugar). From Brennisteinsalda it's another 90 minutes along the Þórsmörk route to the impressive **Stórihver** geothermal field.

The blue lake **Frostastaðavatn** lies behind the rhyolite ridge immediately north of the Landmannalaugar hut. Walk over the ridge and you'll be rewarded with far-ranging views as well as close-ups of the interesting rock formations and moss-covered lava flows flanking the lake. If you walk at least one way on the road and spend some time exploring around the lake, the return trip takes two to three hours.

Guided hikes (through operators from Hvolsvöllur to Skógar areas) can also be a great way to explore the area.

🛏 Sleeping & Eating

Landmannalaugar has a large base with camping and hut facilities that, in the middle of summer, can look like surprisingly raggle-taggle, with hundreds of tents, several structures inundated with hikers, and drying laundry dangling throughout. The base – simply known as **Landmannalaugar** (✍ 860 3335; N 63°59.600', W 19°03.660'; hut per person Ikr6500) is operated by Ferðafélag Íslands (Icelandic Touring Association), like the huts on the Laugavegurinn hike, and its website is loaded with information. The base accommodates 75 people in closed (and close) quarters. There's a kitchen area, showers (Ikr500 for five minutes of hot water), and several wardens on-site. Campers can pitch a tent in the designated areas (Ikr1200

per person) – they have access to the toilet and shower facilities as well. Wild camping is strictly prohibited, as the entire area is in the protected Fjallabak Nature Reserve.

The complex opens for the season depending on when the roads are clear: any time from late May to sometime in June. It closes for sure by mid-October, but it can be earlier if there's loads of snow or the water has to be turned off.

At the time of research there was a proposal to limit or close camping and lodging in Landmannalaugar, but it seems unlikely or far-off still.

Also on the Landmannalaugar grounds is the **Mountain Mall** (www.landmannalaugar. info), set up inside two buses, selling basic supplies from hats, hot tea and maps, fishing licenses and fresh fish from nearby mountain lakes.

ℹ Information

The Landmannalaugar hut wardens can answer questions, including directions and advice on hiking routes. They also sell a map of day hikes (Ikr300) and the Laugavegurinn hike (Ikr1700), as well as a booklet in English and Icelandic on the hike (Ikr1900). Note that wardens do not know if it will rain (yes, this is the most frequently asked question here). At the time of research there was no wi-fi, but there was mobile-phone reception.

The start of the Laugavegurinn hike is behind the Landmannalaugar hut, marked in red.

ℹ Getting There & Away

BUS

Landmannalaugar can be reached by rugged, semi-amphibious bus from three different directions:

From Reykjavík Buses travel along the western part of the Fjallabak Rte, which first follows Rte 26 east of the Þjórsá to F225.

From Skaftafell Buses follow the Fjallabak Rte (F208).

From Mývatn Buses cut across the highlands via Nýidalur on the Sprengisandur Rte (F26; p312).

It's possible to travel from Reykjavík and be in Landmannalaugar for two to six hours before returning to Reykjavík, or three hours before going on to Skaftafell. That's about enough time to take a dip in the springs and/or a short walk. Schedules change, but morning buses usually reach Landmannalaugar by midday. At the time of research, Trex had the last bus (T24) of the day returning to Reykjavík at 6pm in July and August only. You can also overnight in

Landmannalaugar and catch a bus out whenever you're done exploring.

Trex (☑ 587 6000; www.trex.is) services:

➤ Bus T21/T22 Reykjavík–Landmannalaugar (Ikr8400, 3¼ hours, one daily mid-June to early September).

➤ Bus T23/T24 Reykjavík–Landmannalaugar (one daily July and August).

Reykjavík Excursions (☑ 580 5400; www.re.is) services:

➤ Bus 10/10A Skaftafell–Landmannalaugar (Ikr9000, four hours, one daily late June to early September).

➤ Bus 11/11A Reykjavík–Landmannalaugar (Ikr9000, 4¼ hours, one to two daily mid-June to mid-September).

➤ Bus 14/14A Mývatn–Landmannalaugar (Ikr16,500, 10 hours, three weekly late June to late August).

CAR

There are three routes to Landmannalaugar from the Ring Road. If you have a small 4WD, you will have to leave your vehicle about 1km before Landmannalaugar as the river crossing here is just too perilous for little cars. Two-wheel-drive rentals are not allowed to drive on F roads, but we've seen a few private vehicles (we're going to assume that they're not rental cars) parked at the edge of the gushing river crossing as well.

Note: just because you see buses on a remote road doesn't mean your car is equipped for the rivers and terrain. The buses are specially out-fitted with high, sturdy suspensions and rugged tires for rutted terrain and river crossings.

You can also take a super-Jeep tour with local tour-operators, which will take you out to Landmannalaugar from Reykjavík, or anywhere in the south.

There's no petrol at Landmannalaugar. The nearest petrol pumps are 40km north at Hrauneyjar (www.hrauneyjar.is), close to the beginning of the F208 and also in the Fjallabak Reserve; and 90km southeast at Kirkjubæjarklaustur, but to be on the safe side you should fill up along the Ring Road if approaching from the west or the north.

F208 Northwest You can follow the west side of the Þjórsá (Rte 32), passing Árnes, then take Rte F208 down into Landmannalaugar from the north. This is the easiest path to follow for small 4WDs. After passing the power plant, the road from Hrauneyjar becomes horribly bumpy and swerves between power lines all the way to Ljótipollur (the 'Ugly Puddle').

F225 On the east side of the Þjórsá, follow Rte 26 inland through the low plains behind Hella, loop around Hekla, then take Rte F225 west until you reach the base. This route is harder to tackle (rougher roads).

F208 Southeast The hardest route comes from the Ring Road between Vík and Kirkjubæjarklaustur. This is the Skaftafell–Landmannalaugar bus route.

FJALLABAK ROUTE

In summer, the Fjallabak (pronounced *fiat*-la-back) Rte (F208) makes a spectacular alternative to the coast road between Hella, in southwest Iceland, and Kirkjubæjarklaustur, if you have a large 4WD. Its name translates as 'Behind the Mountains', and that's exactly where it goes.

Leave the Ring Road from Hella on Rte 26 (the east side of the Þjórsá), then take Rte F208 from near the Sigölduvirkjun power plant until you reach Landmannalaugar. From there, F208 continues east past the **Kirkjufell** marshes and beyond **Jökuldalur**, before coursing through the icy veins of a riverbed for 10km, climbing up to the **Hörðubreið lookout**, then descending down into **Eldgjá**. The 40km stretch from Eldgjá to **Búland** is in reasonable shape, but there are some rivers to ford before the road turns into Rte 208 and emerges back along the Ring Road southwest of Kirkjubæjarklaustur.

A 2WD vehicle wouldn't have a hope of completing even a small portion of the route and car-hire companies prohibit taking 2WD vehicles on F roads.

You can follow the entire route by bus by leaving Reykjavík at 8am and switching to Skaftafell-bound Reykjavík Excursions bus 10A in Landmannalaugar. The journey takes about 12 hours. You can break it up by spending nights at the Landmannalaugar base and exploring the area before taking the second leg of the bus journey.

Since much of the Fjallabak Rte is along rivers (or rather, in rivers!), it's not ideally suited to mountain bikes either. People attempt it, but it's not casual cycling by any stretch.

Well-established trekking company **Fjallabak** (www.fjallabak.is) leads multiday guided treks and assisted backpacking (from Ikr155,000) throughout the southern back-country, with a specialty in the Fjallabak Nature Reserve area, which the Fjallabak Rte passes through.

From Mývatn It takes all day to make the journey between Landmannalaugar and Mývatn along the **Sprengisandur Rte** (4WD only).

Laugavegurinn Hike: Landmannalaugar to Þórsmörk

The hike from Landmannalaugar to Þórsmörk – commonly known as Laugavegurinn – is where backpackers earn their stripes in Iceland. It means 'Hot Spring Road', and it's easy to understand why. The harsh, otherworldly beauty of the landscape morphs in myriad ways as you traipse straight through the island's interior, with much of the earth steaming and bubbling from the intense activity below its surface. Expect wildly coloured mountainsides, glacial rivers and the glaciers themselves, and then you'll finally emerge at a verdant nature reserve in Þórsmörk. It is the most popular hike in Iceland and infrastructure is sound, with carefully positioned huts along the zigzagging 55km route. But it is essential that you book months in advance if you intend to use them. Campers do not need to reserve.

🛏 Sleeping & Eating

As the Laugavegurinn trail is very well travelled, you'll find a constellation of carefully positioned huts along the way – all owned and maintained by **Ferðafélag Íslands** (☑ 568 2533; www.fi.is). These huts sleep dozens of people but must be booked (and prepaid) months in advance – the wardens recommend booking in early spring. We cannot stress enough that these beds go quickly. Also note that bunk beds at most huts sleep four people each – two (side by side) on each level. If you are alone, expect to be paired with a stranger.

Huts usually have a solar panel for wardens to charge their communications equipment and perhaps lights for the hut, but there is no electricity for hikers. There is a strict quiet rule from midnight to 7am in all huts.

You can camp in designated areas around the huts, though these spaces are often exposed to the elements – streamline your tent with the wind, then pin it down with extra boulders. All camping costs Ikr1200 per person, and does not need to be reserved. Campers do not have access to hut kitchens but they can use toilets and running water.

Huts are usually open late June to early September, but that is weather dependent; check ahead. Huts are locked in winter. Wild camping is strictly forbidden along the whole trail, as these are protected nature reserves.

There is no food for sale along the trail.

A number of huts accept credit cards. Huts are listed here in hiking order from north to south.

Hrafntinnusker   HUT, CAMPGROUND €
(Höskuldsskáli; N 63°93.326; W 19°16.808'; hut per person Ikr6500) This hut holds 52 people (around 22 of whom sleep on mattresses on the floor in a converted attic space). It is at 1027m elevation – be prepared for particularly inhospitable conditions if you are camping, and it's the barest-bones of the huts. There's an outhouse and geothermal heating, but no refuse facilities and no showers – you must carry your rubbish to Álftavatn.

Some campers cook their food on the natural steam vents nearby – ask the warden (July and August only) to point you in the right direction. When there is no warden, water must be sourced from a stream or snow.

Álftavatn   HUT, CAMPGROUND €
(N 63°51.470; W 19°13.640'; hut per person Ikr6500) Opening coincides with the opening of local F roads (anywhere from early to late June depending on weather), and it closes in mid-September. Two huts here hold 72 people in total; both have drinking water and mattresses. Kitchen facilities have gas stoves. Showers cost Ikr500.

Hvanngil   HUT, CAMPGROUND €
(N 64°50.026; W 19°12.507'; hut per person Ikr6500) This hut is on an alternative path, 5km south of Álftavatn. It holds 60 people, and has a kitchen and shower (Ikr500). It's a good choice for people tackling Laugavegurinn in two days. It tends to be much less busy than Álftavatn.

Emstrur   HUT, CAMPGROUND €
(Botnar; N 63°45.980; W 19°22.450'; hut per person Ikr6500) Emstrur has 60 beds divided into three huts. There are two showers (Ikr500 for five minutes of hot water), toilets and a gas stove. There are no garbage facilities or power outlets. Although it's located under the glacier, the other huts have a more striking position along the trail. Note that mobile-phone reception is particularly spotty here.

Laugavegurinn Hike

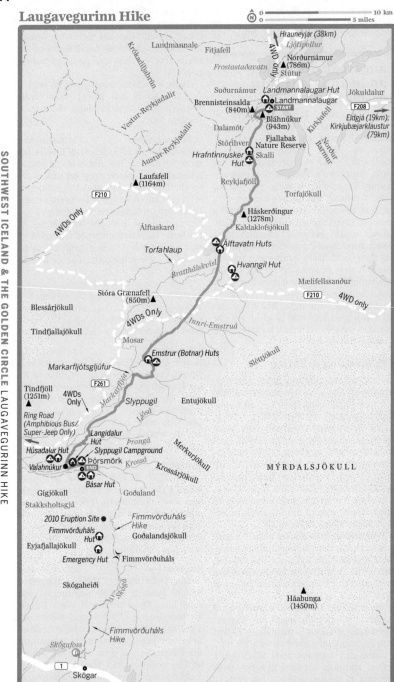

HIKING LAUGAVEGURINN

Laugavegurinn in Four Days

Touring organisation Ferðafélag Íslands (p146) breaks Laugavegurinn into four sections (see its website for a detailed description), and many hikers opt to tackle one section each day for four days, as carefully positioned sleeping huts (and adjoining campsites) punctuate the start and end point of each leg.

Part 1: Landmannalaugar to Hrafntinnusker (12km; three to five hours) A relatively easy start to your adventure, the walk to the first hut passes the boiling earth at Stórihver and sweeping fields of glittering obsidian. If you want to extend the walk, start at Landmannalaugar and hike to Hrafntinnusker via Skalli – the warden's office in Landmannalaugar has a handout that details this quieter route. You'll need to fill up on fresh water before you depart as there's no source until you reach the first hut. About 2km before Hrafntinnusker there's a memorial to a solo Israeli hiker who died on the trail in 2005 after ignoring a warden's warning – a reminder to properly prepare for your hike and always keep your ear to the ground.

Part 2: Hrafntinnusker to Álftavatn (12km; four to five hours) At Hrafntinnusker you can try a couple of short local hikes without your pack before setting off – there are views at Söðull (20 minutes return) and Reykjafjöll (one hour return), and a hidden geothermal area behind the ice caves (three hours return) – ask the warden for walking tips. Views aplenty are found on the walk to Álftavatn as well – hike across the northern spur of the Kaldaklofsfjöll ice cap for vistas from the summit. Walking into Álftavatn you'll see looming Tindfjallajökull, Mýrdalsjökull and the infamous Eyjafjallajökull before reaching the serenely beautiful lake where you'll spend the night.

Part 3: Álftavatn to Emstrur (16km; six to seven hours) To reach Emstrur you'll need to ford at least one large stream – you can take your shoes off and get wet or wait at the edge of the river for a 4WD to give you a lift over. Not to be missed is the detour to Markarfljótsgljúfur – a gaping green canyon. It's well marked from Emstrur, and takes about an hour to reach (you come back the same way).

Part 4: Emstrur to Þórsmörk (15km; six to seven hours) Barrenness turns to lush Arctic flowers and brilliantly verdant lands. If you're not planning on staying in Þórsmörk, you need to arrive before the last bus leaves.

Laugavegurinn in Three Days

If you're fit, it's within your reach to complete the hike in three days instead of four. Cover Part 1 and Part 2 in one day, arriving at Álftavatn after a full eight to 10 hours of hiking. Hike to Emstrur on your second day, and arrive in Þórsmörk on the evening of your third.

Laugavegurinn in Two Days

If you're a fleet, avid hiker, you can complete all 55km of the hike in two long days. On your first day hike all the way to Álftavatn, or better yet, continue the additional 5km to reach Hvanngil. It's possible to combine Part 3 and Part 4 on your second day, as these 30km are relatively flat. There's an overall 100m decline.

Laugavegurinn in Five Hours

Wanna get nuts? Join the endurance race **Laugavegur Ultra Marathon** (www.marathon.is; ⊗ Jul) when Iceland's toughest runners complete the entire hike in under five hours. The latest record: Þorbergur Ingi Jónsson at 4:07:47.

Laugavegurinn Extended

If weather conditions are favourable, there's no reason to rush. You can use the huts as hiking bases, and explore paths that veer away from the main Laugavegurinn trail. You can also spend time based in Landmannalaugar before setting off, though we prefer Þórsmörk.

❶ Information

Ferðafélag Íslands (Iceland Touring Association; ☑ 568 2533; www.fi.is) runs the facilities in the area and its website is loaded with information, including details on the hike. They publish (and sell at Landmannalaugar) a small booklet about the hike in English and Icelandic offering detailed information about the landscape, sights and path (Ikr1900), and also sell a map (Ikr1700).

Most adventure operators throughout south Iceland offer Laugavegurinn guiding. In addition to the traditional hike, some can do longer variations off the beaten track (literally), to hiker-free mountain passes that run parallel to the main trail.

Most hikers walk from north to south to take advantage of the net altitude loss and the facilities at Þórsmörk. From Þórsmörk you can catch a bus or continue hiking to Skógar on the Fimmvörðuháls hike (p139), which takes an extra day or two (about an additional 22km).

WEATHER & GEAR

We highly recommend bringing along a map and GPS if you plan on tackling the walk without a guide.

The track is almost always passable for hiking from early July through to mid-September. Early in the season (late June to early July) there can be icy patches that are difficult to manoeuvre – projected hut openings offer a good gauge of conditions. Huts are locked out of season, so hiking the trail out of season is decidedly discouraged (and dangerous).

At any time of year the Landmannalaugar to Þórsmörk hike is not to be undertaken lightly. It is imperative that you pack appropriate hardcore waterproof and warm clothing and gear, as weather conditions change dramatically in an instant. You will be fording rivers, and fog and rain can come up at any time. That means no jeans or cotton clothes next to your skin at all. If you are not a seasoned hiker and don't know what to bring, do your research first. Wardens have reported a huge uptick in unprepared hikers needing intervention. Don't be one of them.

You'll also need to carry sufficient food and water.

LUGGAGE TRANSPORT

You don't have to schlep all your bags along the Laugavegurinn hike. Going with a tour company, they usually transport your extra bags from the start to the end of the trail, and even, sometimes, between huts.

If you buy a bus ticket to Landmannalaugar, Trex (p142) will transport luggage and parcels to Þórsmörk for free. Otherwise, you can pay them by the piece: 1/2/3 pieces costs Ikr1700/2700/3400.

ALTERNATIVE ACCESS POINTS

Improbable though it may seem, Reykjavík Excursions bus 18 goes from Reykjavík to Álftavatn, Hvanngil and Emstrur daily from late June through August (Reykjavík–Álftavatn Ikr9000, four hours) with short stops to get out and walk around.

Þórsmörk

The confluence of several larger river-carved valleys, the hidden valley of Þórsmörk (*thors*-mork, literally Thor's forest) sits at the beginning of the ever deepening Icelandic interior. A nature reserve, Þórsmörk is a verdant realm of forest and flower-filled lees that looks onto curling gorges, icy rivers, and three looming glaciers (Tindfjallajökull, Eyjafjallajökull and Mýrdalsjökull). The glaciers protect the quiet spot from some of the harsher weather; it is often warmer or drier in Þórsmörk than nearby. Be warned, though: Þórsmörk's lovely setting and proximity to Reykjavík (130km) make it a popular spot in summer.

Þórsmörk may seem relatively close to the Ring Road on a map, but you'll need to take a bus or go by high-clearance 4WD (super-Jeep tour!) to ford the rivers on the way to the reserve. As you get close, coming from the south, you must cross the dangerous Krossá river. Regular 4WDs cannot make it. You'll see that they are parked where people have hitched rides with buses or super-Jeeps.

Or hike in from Skógar or Landmannalaugar.

The higher, northeastern reaches of the area are known as **Goðaland** (Land of the Gods), which is – as the name suggests – divine. Rock formations twist skyward like the stone arches of an ancient cathedral. Fluorescent Arctic flowers burst forth from spongy moss bringing brilliant slashes of colour. At its higher altitudes, Goðaland often has rougher weather than Þórsmörk.

Goðaland is the endpoint for the glorious Fimmvörðuháls hike (p139), which starts in Skógar. The main camping area in Goðaland is Básar (p148); to go between it and Þórsmörk by car you must make the dangerous Krossá river crossing mentioned above. Walkers use footbridges.

Húsadalur (Volcano Huts Thorsmork) is open year-round, but buses tend to run May to mid-October. The rest of the year you'll need private transport to reach Þórsmörk.

🏃 Activities

Although Þórsmörk is the terminus for the uber-popular Laugavegurinn hike, many tired trekkers catch a bus out of the reserve immediately, missing spectacular day hiking (sans backpack). Some continue along the Fimmvörðuháls trail (p139) into Skógar, a truly incredible walk, but better approached in the opposite direction (depart from Skógar).

Coming by guided super-Jeep tour can be a lovely treat, revealing more than what you'll find on your own.

It's also possible to volunteer to help with trail maintenance at Þórsmörk Trail Volunteers (www.trailteam.is), an Iceland Forest Service initiative.

★ Stakksholtsgjá   HIKING

Stakksholtsgjá is a wonderful alternately rocky and mossy gorge with a hidden waterfall. Walk along the river bed, hop across the river, and when it splits in two veer left down a narrower canyon. Scamper over boulders and you'll spot a crashing waterfall (or dramatic icicles in winter). The walk takes around 90 minutes. Reykjavík Excursions buses also stop here.

★ Valahnúkur Circle   HIKING

A 2½-hour loop takes you up to the brilliant viewpoint at Valahnúkur, which takes in canyons, glaciers and sightlines all the way to the ocean. From Húsadalur, follow the trail up to the viewpoint then down into Langidalur. From there pass along the ridge between the valleys back to your starting point. Or, do it in reverse.

You can hike one way and connect with buses on either side, as well.

Tindfjöll Circle   HIKING

The longest of the most popular 'short hikes' in the area takes around 4½ hours from Langidalur and around six hours from Húsadalur. It will take you along the Tindfjöll gorge and ridge. Húsadalur (Volcano Huts Thorsmork) sells maps.

Wander through the Slyppugil Valley (or follow the like-named ridge), then hike across moraine along the side of a second ridge. You'll then pass through Tröllakirkja – the trolls' church – with its sweeping stone arches. A lush green field appears next before revealing a postcard-worthy viewpoint to the Þórsmörk valley. Follow the top of the sandstone ridge until you find yourself at the coursing Krossá river, which leads you back to Langidalur, or Húsadalur further on.

Yoga & Massage   YOGA, MASSAGE

(www.volcanohuts.com) At the time of research, friendly Emil, a certified masseuse and yoga instructor was offering two yoga sessions daily (Ikr2500), deep-tissue massage by appointment (10 minutes/one hour Ikr2000/10,900), and sweat-lodge ceremonies (Ikr10,000) at Volcano Huts Thorsmork.

👉 Tours

Guides throughout the south, such as Southcoast Adventure (p136), South Iceland Adventures (p134) and Icelandic Mountain Guides (p138) are a great value-add as not only do they get you to the region, but they can take you to hidden valleys, waterfalls and glacier approaches that the buses do not reach, while sharing local geological and cultural insights. For example, Gígjökull glacial tongue with its formerly enormous morraine was one of the main sites of flooding when Eyjafjallajökull erupted; you can get close enough to lick it.

🛏 Sleeping & Eating

There are three lodging areas in the Þórsmörk area: Langidalur (sometimes referred to as Þórsmörk) with huts as well as at nearby Slyppugil, Básar (technically in Goðaland) and Húsadalur (also called Volcano Huts Thorsmork). All have huts and campsites, cooking facilities and running water. They get rammed during summer months, so it's crucial to book space in the huts in advance. We recommend bringing a sleeping bag and your own food. Note that wild camping is forbidden in the area, as it is a nature preserve.

Húsadalur   HUT, CAMPGROUND €

(Volcano Huts Thorsmork; ☑ 552 8300; www.volcanohuts.com; camp sites per person Ikr1600, dm/s/d & tr/cottage without bathroom Ikr6500/15,000/19,000/25,000; 🛜) Thriving Volcano Huts Thorsmork fills the Húsadalur area with dorm-style huts, private rooms, four- to five-person cottages (with basic kitchenettes), campground and a restaurant (breakfast/lunch/dinner costs Ikr2000/Ikr2500/Ikr4500). Lunch tends to be soup and fresh bread with coffee and cake, dinner a simple buffet. There's a guest kitchen, hot-pot and sauna, a masseuse/yoga instructor and lots of action. Linen costs Ikr3000.

Sells trail maps. Showers included.

Langidalur
HUT, CAMPGROUND €

(Þórsmörk; Skagfjörðsskáli; ☑ 893 1191; www.fi.is; N 63°40.960', W 19°30.890'; camp site per person Ikr1200, hut per person Ikr6500; ☺ mid-May–Sep) Langidalur – also referred to simply as Þórsmörk, or Skagfjörðsskáli – is the most rustic option of the four in Þórsmörk, but is well-maintained. It sleeps 75, and there's well-tended camping space, a dining hut, large shower block and guest kitchens. Operated by Ferðafélag Íslands, which manages the Laugavegurinn huts.

A small shop offers hot coffee and tea, plus basic provisions: camping gas, wool socks (Ikr2500), soup (Ikr500), jam, light beer etc and is open variable hours from May to September.

Slyppugil
CAMPGROUND €

(☑ 575 6700; www.hostel.is; camp site per person Ikr1000; ☺ mid-Jun–mid-Aug) This new campground run by Hostelling International sits within sight (about 500m) from Langidalur and has showers, toilets and barbecues. The warden can help with information on day hikes.

Básar
HUT, CAMPGROUND €

(☑ 562 1000; www.utivist.is; Goðaland, N 63°40,559', W 19°29,014'; camp site per person Ikr1200, hut per person Ikr4200) Básar is the choice base for Icelanders, largely due to its beautiful position in the trees. Space is very cramped, but there's hut accommodation for 83 people, which can be booked through Útivist. Grass and wooden planks lead around the private camping space, which gets extremely crowded on summer weekends. Showers cost Ikr400.

🛈 Getting There & Away

BUS

Reykjavík buses to/from Þórsmörk stop in Hveragerði, Selfoss, Hella, Hvolsvöllur and Seljalandsfoss en route. The Reykjavík Excursions schedule is paticularly helpful in hopping around the sites within Þórsmörk. Note: buses are special amphibiously equipped rigs for fording rivers.

Reykjavík Excursions (☑ 580 5400; www.re.is) services:
➤ Buses 9/9A Reykjavík–Þórsmörk (Ikr7500, 3¼ to four hours, one daily May–mid-October stopping at Húsadalur, Stakksholtsgjá Canyon, Básar, Langidalur; plus two additional services mid-June to August). Returning 9A buses have a slightly simplified route heading back towards Reykjavík; if you want the bus to stop at Básar or Langidalur, you must request it the night before with the hut supervisor. Other sample

prices: Hella or Hvolsvöllur Ikr5000, Seljalandsfoss Ikr4000, from the impassable Krossá river crossroads Ikr2000. You can also transfer between buses to get to Skógar (buses 9 and 20; Ikr5000) or Landmannalaugar (buses 9 and 11; Ikr11,000).

Trex (☑ 587 6000; www.trex.is) services:
➤ Buses T11/T12 Reykjavík–Þórsmörk (Ikr6800, four hours, one daily mid-June to early September; stops at Gígjökull, Básar and Langidalur). Other sample prices: Hveragerði or Selfoss Ikr5800; Hella, Hvolsvöllur or Seljalandsfoss Ikr4200.

CAR

You cannot drive all the way into Þórsmörk with your private vehicle. End of story. If you have your own 4WD with excellent clearance, you can plough down Rtes 249 and F249 until you reach the crossroads for Húsadalur and Básar at the Krossá river. It's there that you must leave your car – you will not be able to ford the gushing river unless you're driving a super-Jeep and know what you're doing. The buses that serve Þórsmörk are special amphibious vehicles outfitted to pass the deep river and boulder-littered ravines. If you park at the crossroads, you can hitch with the bus (Ikr2000 per person) or a super-Jeep.

HIKING

Þórsmörk is usually the terminus of the popular Laugavegurinn hike (p143), with the beginning at Landmannalaugar. It's also popular to reach Þórsmörk from Skógar on the beautiful Fimmvörðuháls hike (p139). If you are planning to reach Þórsmörk by foot we recommend one of these; walking along Rtes 249 and F249 from Seljalandsfoss is far less scenic.

It takes around 30 minutes to walk between Langidalur and Húsadalur on the shortest path.

Skógar to Vík

As the Ring Road arcs east from Skógar to Vík the haunches of the foothills rise to the glaciers, mountaintops and volcanoes inland, while rivers descend from mysterious gorges, and coarse across the broad sweep of pastures to black-sand beaches and the crashing ocean. This rural area may be dotted with farmhouses (many of which have guesthouses), but considering the volume of summertime visitors, it still feels alternately dramatic and pastoral.

⊙ Sights

★ **Sólheimajökull**
GLACIER

One of the easiest glacial tongues to reach is Sólheimajökull. This icy tongue unfurls from the main Mýrdalsjökull ice cap and is a favourite spot for glacial walks and ice climbing. A 4.2km rutted dirt track (Rte 221) leads off the Ring Road to a small car park and **Cafe Solheimajökull** (852 2052; snacks Ikr820-1500; 10am-6pm May-Sep, reduced hours Oct-Apr), from where you can walk the 800m to the ice along a wide track edging the glacial lagoon. Don't attempt to climb onto the glacier unguided.

Crevasses form often, so to walk on the glacier, you should go with any of the area tour operators (p138); tours depart from the cafe.

Mýrdalsjökull ICE CAP

This gorgeous glacier is Iceland's fourth-largest ice cap, covering 700 sq km and reaching a thickness of almost 750m in places. The volcano Katla snoozes beneath, periodically blasting up through the ice to drown the coastal plain in a deluge of meltwater, sand and tephra. Local operators run tours along the glacial crown as part of longer trips. Don't explore the area on your own; the ice is unstable and the track to the caldera can be impossible to navigate.

Sólheimasandur BEACH, LANDMARK

On November 21, 1973, a US Navy airplane was forced to crash land at Sólheimasandur. The crew all survived, but the wreckage of the militarised Douglas DC-3 remains on the black-sand beach, a lean shell whipped by the wind. To get here, you'll need a 4WD and a local guide (or a GPS: 63.459523, -19.364618). It's east of the Sólheimajökull/Rte 221 turnoff and south down a farm lane to the beach. Try to preserve the environment.

★ Dyrhólaey LANDMARK, WILDLIFE RESERVE

One of the south coast's most recognisable natural formations is the rocky plateau and huge stone sea arch at Dyrhólaey (deer-lay), which rises dramatically from the surrounding plain 10km west of Vík, at the end of Rte 218. The promontory is a nature reserve that's rich in bird life, including puffins. It's closed during nesting season (15 May to 25 June), but at other times you can visit its crashing black beaches and get awesome views from atop the archway.

The archway itself, is best seen from Reynisfjara.

According to *Njál's Saga*, Kári – the only survivor of the fire that wiped out Njál's clan – had his farm here. Another Viking Age connection is the cave **Loftsalahellir**,

ℹ️ RESPECT

Tantalising as the glaciers may be, glinting just off the roadside, it is paramount to realise that no one goes on them without experienced, local guidance. Crevasses can form suddenly and are often invisible (beneath snow), gasses can be emitted by volcanic activity, and flooding (sometimes invisible from above) can destabilise the ice even further. With the growing popularity of tourism in Iceland, the numbskull-ish behaviour of inexperienced visitors occasionally makes the news (one man drove his family onto the glacier in a rental car). Don't be one of them.

reached by a track just before the causeway to Dyrhólaey, which was used for council meetings in Saga times.

★ Reynisfjara LANDMARK, BEACH

On the west side of **Reynisfjall**, the high ridge above Vík, Rte 215 leads 5km down to the black-sand beach at Reynisfjara. The raw beach is backed by an incredible stack of **basalt columns** that look like a magical church organ and there are outstanding views west to Dyrhólaey. The surrounding cliffs are pocked with caves formed from twisted basalt, and puffins bellyflop from here into the crashing sea during the summer. Immediately offshore are the towering sea stacks Reynisdrangur (p151).

You may recognise the scene from Bon Iver's 2011 music video, *Holocene,* practically an ode to Iceland.

🚩 Tours

Arcanum (p138) is based on the Ytri-Sólheimar I farm 11km east of Skógar and offers many regional adventure tours (treks, snowmobiling, ice climbing, glacier walking, super-Jeep tours etc), as do all of the tour operators from Hvolsvöllur to Vík. Many also offer Reykjavík pick-up.

Mountain Excursions ADVENTURE

(897 7737; www.volcanohotel.is) A small outfit run by two brothers offering two-hour Sólheimajökull glacier hikes (Ikr9000) and super-Jeep tours that vaguely follow a portion of the Fimmvörðuháls route (from Ikr22,000). Based at Volcano Hotel (p150).

🛏 Sleeping & Eating

Camping is prohibited on Dyrhólaey.

⭐ Garðar
GUESTHOUSE €

(✆ 487 1260; http://reynisfjara-guesthouses.com; Reynisfjara; cottages Ikr12,000-17,000) Garðar, at the end of Rte 215, is a magical and view-blessed place. Friendly farmer Ragnar rents out self-contained beachside huts: one snug stone cottage sleeps two (in a bunk bed), two roomier timber cottages sleep up to four. Linen costs Ikr1000 per person.

Gistiheimliliið Reynir
GUESTHOUSE €

(✆ 894 9788; www.reyni.is; Reynisfjara; d without bathroom Ikr14,000) This family-owned silver strip of mini-cottages looks out over the ocean at Dyrhólaey, and each has its own toilet. Guests share showers and a good kitchen. A newer building has twin bedrooms and six-person family rooms (Ikr27,000) with shared bathrooms.

Mið-Hvoll Cottages
COTTAGES €

(✆ 863 3238; www.hvoll.com; cottages Ikr19,000) This stand of four new cosy wooden cottages sits within sight of Dyrhólaey in a pastoral area south of the Ring Road, with mountains and ocean views. Each kitchen-equipped cottage sleeps five; linen and towel cost Ikr1500 per person. The owners also offer horse riding on nearby beaches and pastures (from Ikr5000) for all ages and skill levels.

Find them about 12km west of Vík down tiny Rte 216, just west of the turnoff for Dyrhólaey (Rte 218).

⭐ Vellir
GUESTHOUSE €€

(Ferðaþjónustan Vellir; ✆ 849 9204; http://f-vellir.123.is; d with/without bath incl breakfast Ikr24,700/20,300, cottage from Ikr25,000; 🛜) Located 1.5km down dirt Rte 219, the friendly farmstay at Vellir sits near Pétursey, a massive earthen mound that was once an island eons ago. Rooms are modern and some have sea views. There are also two cottages for rent. You can see both the ice on Mýrdalsjökull and the Atlantic Ocean on a clear day. Homecooked dinner is available by pre-order (Ikr5900).

Giljur Gistihús
GUESTHOUSE €€

(✆ 866 0176; s/d without bathroom incl breakfast Ikr11,700/18,400, d/tr incl breakfast Ikr23,100/34,600; ⊘ Jun–mid-Sep) Just 7km west of Vík and tucked back off the Ring Road at the foot of lush cliffs creased by a waterfall and dotted with grazing horses, this small farm guesthouse offers rooms with shared or private bathroom and a hearty breakfast. Book on Icelandic Farm Holidays (www.farmholidays.is).

Guesthouse Steig
GUESTHOUSE €€

(✆ 487 1324; www.guesthousesteig.is; d with/without bathroom Ikr28,800/20,100; @ 🛜) Sixteen kilometres west of Vík and 1.5km north of the Ring Road on dirt track, sweet Guesthouse Steig is a simple farm building filled with surprisingly spacious, modern and bright rooms. Staff are friendly, and it feels like a real, relaxing rural homestay.

Volcano Hotel
HOTEL €€

(✆ 486 1200; www.volcanohotel.is; s/d incl breakfast from Ikr26,400/28,900; 🛜) This seven-room hotel, 11.5km west of Vík, plays with a volcano motif in its decor: floors are made from a mosaic of pebbles, and candles glow throughout. Mountain Excursions, a small tour operator, is based here.

Hótel Dyrhólaey
HOTEL €€

(✆ 487 1333; www.dyrholaey.is; d Ikr28,400; @ 🛜) On a bluff 10km west of Vík, this 88-room hotel is popular with tour groups. Large rooms with basic mod cons sprout off three wings with wide, carpeted hallways. The restaurant is open from 11am to 9pm from May to October.

Svarta Fjaran
CAFE €€

(Black Beach; ✆ 859 7141; Reynisfjara; snacks Ikr 990, dinner mains Ikr2400-5200; ⊘ 11am-9pm) Spectacularly set black volcanic cubes, meant to mimic the nearby black beach Reynisfjara with its famous basalt columns, house this new cafe that serves homemade cakes and snacks during the day and offers a full dinner menu at night. Plate glass windows give views to the ocean and Dyrhólaey beyond.

Vík (Vík í Mýrdal)

The welcoming little community of Vík has become a booming hub for a very beautiful portion of the south coast. Iceland's southernmost town, it's also the rainiest, but that doesn't stop the madhouse atmosphere in summer when every room within 100km is booked solid. For the beautiful basalt beach Reynisfjara (p149) and its puffin cliffs, and the rocky plateau Dyrhólaey (p149), both just to the west, to the volcanoes running from Skógar to Jökulsárlón glacier lagoon and beyond, all topped by ice caps, Vík is a convenient base with loads of services. White waves wash up on black sands and the cliffs glow green from all that rain. Put simply, it's beautiful.

◉ Sights

Reynisdrangur   LANDMARK, BEACH

Vík's most iconic cluster of sea stacks is known as Reynisdrangur, which rise from the ocean like ebony towers at the western end of Vík's black-sand beach. They're traditionally believed to be trolls that got caught out in the sun. The nearby cliffs are good for puffin watching. A bracing walk up from Vík's western end takes you to the top of **Reynisfjall** ridge (340m), offering superb views. (On the other side of the point is Reynisfjara; p149.)

Brydebúð   MUSEUM

(⌂ 487 1395; http://brydebud.vik.is; Víkurbraut 28; museum adult/child Ikr500/free; ⊙ 11am-8pm Jun-Aug) In town, the tin-clad house Brydebúð was built in Vestmannaeyjar in 1831 and moved to Vík in 1895. Today it houses the tourist office, Halldórskaffi and a small museum with displays on local fishing, and explanations of what it's like to live under the volcano Katla.

Víkurkirkja   CHURCH

(Hátún) High above town, Vík's 1930s church has stained-glass windows in spiky geometrical shapes, but we like it more for its village views.

☞ Tours

Skógar (33km west of Vík) is the hub for activity tours on the south coast; also see Hvolsvöllur. In Vík, you can check with the hostel for tours to Mýrdalsjökull.

Katla Track   SUPER-JEEP

(⌂ 849 4404; www.katlatrack.is) Katla Track runs three- to six-hour 'Under the Volcano' tours (Ikr24,900 to 29,900) that take in local landmarks and explore Mýrdalsjökull.

⌂ Sleeping

Check Icelandic Farm Holidays (www.farmholidays.is) and booking.com for nearby farm guesthouses beyond those in our Skógar to Vík listings. Also consider guesthouses en route to Kirkjubæjarklaustur (p287).

Vík HI Hostel   HOSTEL €

(Norður-Vík Hostel; ⌂ 487 1106; www.hostel. is; Suðurvíkurvegur 5; dm/d without bathroom Ikr4100/11,200; @ 🖥) Vík's small, homey, year-round hostel is in the beige house on the hill behind the village centre. Good facilities include guest kitchen and bike hire (per half/full day Ikr2000/Ikr3000). Staff also arrange 2½-hour glacier tours to Mýrdalsjökull. HI member discount Ikr700.

Vík Campsite   CAMPGROUND €

(Tjaldsvæðið Vík, ⌂ 487 1345; Austurvegur; camp sites per adult Ikr1300; ⊙ Jun-Aug or early-Sep) The campsite sits under a grassy ridge at the eastern end of town, just beyond the Hótel Edda. An octagonal building houses cooking facilities, washing machine, toilets and free showers. There's two little cottages (Ikr10,000), too.

★ Icelandair Hótel Vík   HOTEL €€

(⌂ 487 1480, booking 444 4000; www.icelandair-hotels.com; Klettsvegur 1-5; d from Ikr24,500; 🖥) This sleek, black, window-fronted new hotel is improbably tucked just behind the Hótel Edda, on the eastern edge of town, near the campground. The hotels share a lobby (and have the same friendly owners), but that's where the resemblance ends. The Icelandair hotel has suitably swanky rooms, some with views to the rear cliffs or the sea. The light, natural decor is inspired by the local environment.

Heimagisting Erika   B&B €€

(⌂ 487 1117; www.erika.is; Sigtún 5; B&B per person without bathroom Ikr9900; 🖥) German Erika is a warm hostess with a lovely panorama-filled house and a couple of guest rooms. Her highly praised breakfasts feature homemade jams, syrups and herbal teas (many for sale). Bookings essential; cash only.

Hótel Edda Vík   HOTEL €€

(⌂ 444 4840; www.hoteledda.is; d with/without bathroom Ikr24,500/21,700; ⊙ May-Sep; @ 🖥) With a lengthier opening season than most Edda hotels, this modern place on a busy spot near the Icelandair Hotel and the N1 petrol station has unmemorable but decent rooms, 31 of which have phone, TV and bathroom, and 10 cottages with en suite bathrooms.

Puffin Hostel   HOSTEL €€

(⌂ 487 1212; www.vikhotel.is; Víkurbraut 24a; d/q without bathroom Ikr21,600/29,200) It's pricey for what you get, and probably best only as a last-ditch place to stay, but this century-old hostel operated by Welcome Hotel is very central. Walls are thin, everything's small and cleanliness spotty. Guest kitchen. Towel and linen included, but blanket costs Ikr800.

Welcome Hotel Vík
HOTEL €€€

(☑ 487 1212; www.vikhotel.is; Víkurbraut 24-26; d/q incl breakfast Ikr32,300/44,500; @ 🛜) This busy complex of basic, pebble-floored rooms is packed in high season, often by tour groups. Prices are a bit stiff for what you get, but all rooms have tea/coffee-making gear. Occasional deals on booking.com. Its Restaurant Lundi (p152) is popular among visitors.

🍴 Eating

Víkurskáli
INTERNATIONAL, FAST FOOD €

(☑ 487 1230; Austurvegur 18; mains Ikr1120-2990; ☺ 11am-9pm) Grab a booth and a burger at the old-school grill inside the N1 with a view of Reynisdrangur. Daily specials from casserole to lamb stew.

★ Suður-Vík
ICELANDIC, ASIAN €€

(☑ 487 1515; Suðurvíkurvegur 1; mains Ikr1750-4950; ☺ noon-10pm) The friendly ambience, from hardwood floors and interesting artwork to smiling staff, helps elevate this new restaurant beyond the competition. Food is Icelandic hearty, from heaping steak sandwiches with bacon and bearnaise sauce, to Asian (think Thai satay with rice). In a warmly lit silver building atop town. Book ahead in summer.

Halldórskaffi
INTERNATIONAL €€

(☑ 487 1202; www.halldorskaffi.is; Víkurbraut 28; mains Ikr3000-5500; ☺ 11am-9pm Jun-Aug, reduced hours Sep-May) Inside Brydebúð museum, this lively timber-lined all-rounder is very popular in high season for its crowd-pleasing menu ranging from burgers and pizza to lamb fillet. The coffee (Lavazza) is a decent brew. Book ahead or prepare to wait in summer. And weekend nights it stays open later as a bar.

Ströndin Bistro
INTERNATIONAL €€

(☑ 487 1230; www.strondin.is; Austurvegur 18; mains Ikr1950-4200; ☺ 6-10pm) Behind the N1 petrol station is this semi-smart wood-panelled option enjoying sea-stack vistas. Go local with lamb soup or fish stew, or global with pizzas and burgers.

Restaurant Lundi
ICELANDIC €€

(dinner mains Ikr2400-3100; ☺ 11am-9pm) The inhouse restaurant at Welcome Hotel Vík is popular with visitors for Icelandic staples from meatballs to lamb.

Self-Catering

Kjarval
SUPERMARKET

(☑ 487 1325; Víkurbraut 4; ☺ 10am-6pm Mon-Fri, 10am-2pm Sat) Groceries.

Vínbúðin
LIQUOR STORE

(Ránarbraut 1; ☺ 5-6pm Mon-Thu, 2-6pm Fri) National liquor chain with limited hours.

🛍 Shopping

Víkurprjón
SOUVENIRS

(Austurvegur 20; ☺ 24hr) The big 24hr souvenir and knitwear shop next to the N1 station is a coach-tour hit. Swing in to watch woolly jumpers being made on site.

ℹ Information

Tourist Information Centre (☑ 487 1395; www.visitvik.is; Víkurbraut 28; ☺ 11am-8pm Mon-Fri, 1-8pm Sat & Sun Jun-Aug, reduced hours May & Sep; 🛜) Inside Brydebúð; free wi-fi.

ℹ Getting There & Away

Vík is a major stop for all Reykjavík–Höfn bus routes; buses stop at the N1 petrol station.

Strætó (☑ 540 2700; www.straeto.is) services include:
➜ Bus 51 Reykjavík–Vík–Höfn (Reykjavík–Vík Ikr4900, 2¾ hours, two daily) If you take the early bus you can stop in Vík then continue on to Höfn on the later bus; however, from September to May service is reduced and you can't count on that connection.

Sterna (☑ 551 1166; www.sterna.is) services:
➜ Bus 12/12A Reykjavík–Vík–Höfn (Reykjavík–Vík Ikr4300, four hours, one daily June to mid-September).

Reykjavík Excursions (☑ 580 5400; www.re.is) services:
➜ Bus 20/20A Reykjavík–Skaftafell (Reykjavík–Skógar Ikr7500, four hours, one daily mid-June to early September).
➜ Bus 21/21A Reykjavík–Skógar (Reykjavík–Skógar Ikr6000, 3½ hours, one daily mid-June to August) At the time of research, one of the two services to Skógar goes as far as Vík each day.

East of Vík

Mælifell

On the edge of the Mýrdalsjökull glacier, the 642m-high Mælifell ridge and the countryside around it are spectacular. The simple, idyllic campsite at Þakgil (☑ 893 4889;

www.thakgil.is; Höfðarbrekkuafrétti; camp site per person Ikr1500, cabins Ikr20,000; ☉ Jun-Aug), a green bowl among stark mountains, makes a convenient base for explorations, and has showers and cottages with bathrooms and kitchenettes. You can walk up Mælifell, or even get onto the glacier – a path leads to the nunatak (hill or mountain completely surrounded by a glacier) Huldufjöll. You can drive to Þakgil, 14km along a rough dirt road (Rte 214) that branches off Rte 1 about 5km east of Vík, or there is a hiking trail from Vík.

At the start of Rte 214, 5.5km east of Vík, **Hótel Katla-Höfðabrekka** (☑487 1208; www. hofdabrekka.is; Höfðabrekka; d incl breakfast from Ikr20,000; ☉Mar-Oct; @☏) is a large country hotel with 72 comfy wood-panelled rooms in annexes of varying vintage, plus four hotpots, and a restaurant.

Mýrdalssandur

The vast black-lava sand flats of Mýrdalssandur, east of Vík, are formed from material washed out from underneath Mýrdalsjökull during Katla eruptions. This 700-sq-km desert is bleak and desolate (some say haunted), but rather awe-inspiring. It looks lifeless, but Arctic foxes and seabirds are common sights.

South of Rte 1, the small peak of **Hjörleifshöfði** (221m) rises above the sands and offers good views towards Vestmannaeyjar. On the other side of Rte 1, the green hill of **Hafursey** (582m) is another option for walks from Vík.

VESTMANNAEYJAR

Jagged and black, the Vestmannaeyjar (sometimes called the Westman Islands) form 15 eye-catching silhouettes off the southern shore. The islands were formed by submarine volcanoes around 11,000 years ago, except for Surtsey, the archipelago's newest addition, which rose from the waves in 1963. Surtsey was made a Unesco World Heritage Site in 2008, but its unique scientific status means that it is not possible to land there except for scientific study.

Heimaey is the only inhabited island. Its little town and sheltered harbour lie between dramatic *klettur* (escarpments) and two ominous volcanoes – blood-red Eldfell and conical Helgafell. These days Heimaey is famous for its puffins (around 10 million

KATLA GEOPARK

In 2011 Iceland formed its first 'geopark' to protect a region of great geological importance, promote local culture and sustainable development, and educate visitors. The **Katla Geopark** (☑560 2043; www.katlageopark.is) extends from Hvolsvöllur northeast to the great Vatnajökull and down to the volcanic black-sand beaches. It includes its namesake Katla volcano, the infamous Eyjafjallajökull and the tortured earth at Lakagígar. All told, that's about 9% of Iceland.

Of all the volcanoes in Iceland, it is thought that Katla may cause the most trouble to Icelanders over the next few years. This highly active 30km-long volcano, buried deep under the Mýrdalsjökull glacier, has erupted roughly twice per century in the past. Since the last eruption was in 1918, it's now several decades overdue.

It's expected that when Katla does blow, days of ashfall, tephra clouds and lightning strikes will follow the initial explosion, with flash floods caused by the sudden melting of glacial ice. The geological record shows that past eruptions have created tidal waves, which have boomeranged off the Vestmannaeyjar and deluged the area where the town of Vík stands today.

Local residents receive regular evacuation training for the day when Katla erupts. In the event of an eruption, all mobile phones within range of a tower (including yours) will receive a warning. After the alert, farmers must hang a notice on their front doors to show that they have evacuated, before unplugging their electric fences, opening cattle sheds so that their animals can flee to higher ground, and heading for one of the evacuation centres in Hella, Hvolsvöllur or Skógar.

There is no park office, but the geopark website offers information, and national TV station RÚV has a webcam near Vík, set up to film the floods when Katla erupts (see www.ruv.is/katla).

birds come here to breed); Þjóðhátíð, Iceland's biggest outdoor festival, held in August; and its new volcano museum.

Heimaey

The small town of Heimaey (*hey*-my) is encased in a fortress of jagged lava; its port sits at the end of a contorted waterway that carves a path between towering cliffs dotted with bird nests. Although only a few kilometres from the mainland, Heimaey feels light years away, lost amid the frigid waters of the North Atlantic.

Over the centuries the island was a marauders' favourite. The English raided Heimaey throughout the 15th century, building the stone fort Skansinn as their HQ. In 1627 Heimaey suffered its most violent attack at the hands of Algerian pirates, who went on a killing spree, murdering 36 islanders and kidnapping 242 more (almost three-quarters of the population). The rest managed to escape by abseiling down cliffs or hiding in caves along the west coast. Those who were kidnapped were taken as slaves to north Africa; years later, 27 islanders had their freedom bought for them...and had a long journey home.

The volcanoes that formed Heimaey have come close to destroying the island on several occasions. The most famous eruption in modern times began unexpectedly at 1.45am on 23 January 1973, when a vast fissure burst open, gradually mutating into the volcano Eldfell, and prompting the island's evacuation.

◉ Sights & Activities

The island's sights cluster in the main village, on the point around Skalinn and then in the fascinating fresh lava field and volcano, plus puffin viewing cliffs.

Pick up a copy of *Hiking High in Vermannaeyjar* or ask at the tourist office for a detailed walking and cycling map of Heimaey. Walks through the lava fields, along puffin nesting areas and on the island's western shores are particularly ethereal. The tourist office has bicycle rental (two hours Ikr2700).

There's a saltwater **swimming pool** (Sundlaug Vestmannaeyja; ☑ 488 2400; Brimhólabraut; adult/child Ikr500/180; ☺ 6.15am-9pm Mon-Fri, 10am-7pm Sat & Sun), with hot-pots, a water slide and a gym.

◉ Town Centre

★ **Eldheimar** MUSEUM
(Pompeii of the North; ☑ 488 2000; www.eldheimar.is; Gerðisbraut 10; adult/10-18yr/child Ikr1900/1000/free; ☺ 11am-6pm Jun–mid-Sep, reduced hours rest of year) More than 400 buildings lie buried under lava from the 1973 eruption, and on the edge of the flow 'Pompei of the North' is a new musuem revolving around one house excavated from 50m of pumice, along what was formerly Suðurvegur. The modern volcanic-stone building allows a glimpse into the home with its crumbling walls and intact but toppled knick-knacks, and is filled with multimedia exhibits on the eruption and its aftermath, from compelling footage and eyewitness accounts to the homeowners' story.

An audioguide leads you through it all, and upstairs, there's a catwalk over the wreckage, a space dedicated to all things Surtsey (p159), and a cafe with broad views across town.

★ **Skansinn** FORT, HISTORICAL QUARTER
This lovely green area by the sea has several unique historical sights. The oldest structure on the island was Skansinn, a 15th-century fort built to defend the harbour (not too successfully – when Algerian pirates arrived in 1627, they simply landed on the other side of the island). Its walls were swallowed up by the 1973 lava, but some have been rebuilt. Above them, you can see the remains of the town's **old water tanks**, also crushed by molten rock.

➡ **Landlyst** MUSEUM
(☺ 11am-5pm mid-May–mid-Sep) FREE A shocking 80% of Heimaey's babies once died at birth, until in the 1840s an island woman, Sólveig, was sent abroad to be trained as a midwife. The tiny wooden house Landlyst was Sólveig's maternity hospital (and is the second oldest building on the island). Today it contains a small display of her bloodletting equipment and other 19th-century medical paraphernalia.

➡ **Stafkirkjan** CHURCH
(☺ 11am-5pm mid-May–mid-Sep) The bitumen-coated Stafkirkjan is a reconstruction of a medieval wooden stave church. It was presented by the Norwegian government in 2000 to celebrate 1000 years of Christianity.

★ **Sæheimar** AQUARIUM, MUSEUM
(☑ 481 1997; www.saeheimar.is; Heiðarvegur 12; adult/child Ikr1000/free; ☺ 11am-5pm mid-

Heimaey

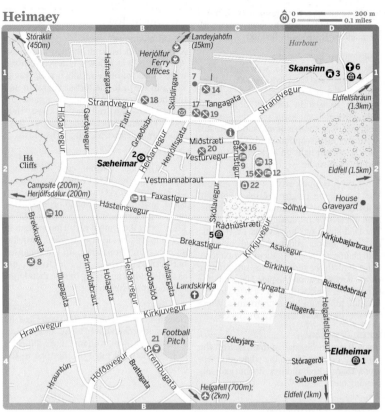

Heimaey

May–mid-Sep, 1-4pm Sat mid-Sep–mid-May) The Aquarium and Natural History Museum has an interesting collection of stuffed birds and animals, videos on puffins and catfish, and fish tanks of Icelandic fish. It's great fun for the family, and there's often a teenage puffin wobbling about – the museum is an informal bird hospital as well. Joint ticket with Sagnheimar Byggðasafn Ikr1500.

Sagnheimar Byggðasafn MUSEUM

(Folk Museum; ☑488 2045; www.sagnheimar.is; Raðhústræti; adult/child Ikr1000/600; ☺11am-5pm mid-May–mid-Sep, 1-4pm Sat mid-Sep–mid-May) Housed in the city library, this interactive folk museum tells the story of Heimaey from the era of marauding pirates up to the 1979 eruptions and beyond. Displays also shed light on local sports heroes and native bird life.

Stóraklif & Heimaklettur VIEWPOINT

The top of the craggy precipice Stóraklif is a treacherous 30-minute climb from behind the N1 petrol station at the harbour. The trail starts on the obvious 4WD track; as it gets steeper you're 'assisted' by ropes and chains (don't trust them completely), but it's worth the terror for the outstanding views. Further out on the pier, Heimaklettur is more perilous, with wild rickety ladders. Both are top puffin-breeding grounds. When it's rainy or slick, neither is a good idea.

House Graveyard LANDMARK

If you traverse the edge of town nearest the 1973 lava flow you'll see the edges of where more than 400 buildings lie buried, bits peeking out.

⊙ Out of Town

★ Eldfellshraun LAVA FIELD

Known as Eldfellshraun, the new land created by the 1973 lava flow is now criss-crossed with a maze of otherworldly hiking tracks that run down to the fort at Skansinn and the house graveyard, and all around the bulge of the raw, red eastern coast. Here you'll find small black-stone beaches, Gaujulundur lava garden and a lighthouse.

★ Eldfell VOLCANO

The 221m-high volcanic cone Eldfell appeared from nowhere in the early hours of 23 January 1973. Once the fireworks finished, heat from the volcano provided Heimaey with geothermal energy from 1976 to 1985. Today the ground is still hot enough in places to bake bread or char wood. Eldfell is an easy climb from town, up the collapsed northern wall of the crater; stick to the path, as the islanders are trying to save their latest volcano from erosion.

Helgafell VOLCANO

Helgafell (226m) erupted 5000 years ago. Its cinders are grassed over today, and you can scramble up here without much difficulty from the football pitch on the road to the airport.

THE 1973 ERUPTION

Without warning, at 1.45am on 23 January 1973 a mighty explosion blasted through the winter's night as a 1.5km-long volcanic fissure split the eastern side of the island. The eruption area gradually became concentrated into a growing crater cone, which fountained lava and ash into the sky.

Normally the island's fishing boats would have been out at sea, but a force-12 gale had prevented them from sailing the previous afternoon. Now calm weather and a harbourful of boats allowed all but 200 to 3000 of the island's 5273 inhabitants to be evacuated to the mainland. Incredibly, there was just a single fatality (from toxic gases).

Over the next five months more than 30 million tonnes of lava poured over Heimaey, destroying 360 houses and creating a brand-new mountain, the red cinder cone Eldfell. One-third of the town was buried beneath the lava flow, and the island increased in size by 2.5 sq km.

As the eruption continued, advancing lava threatened to close the harbour and make the evacuation permanent – without a fishing industry, there would have been little way to survive on the island. In an attempt to slow down the inexorable flow of molten rock, firefighters hosed the lava with over six million tonnes of cold sea water. The lava halted just 175m short of the harbour mouth – actually improving the harbour by creating extra shelter.

The islanders were billeted with friends and family on the mainland, watching the fireworks and waiting to see if they could ever go home. Finally, the eruption finished, five months after it started, at the end of June. Two-thirds of the islanders returned to face a mighty clean-up operation.

The fantastic new Eldheimar (p154) museum gives a view into it all.

Herjólfsdalur
LANDMARK

FREE Sheltered by an extinct volcano, green and grassy Herjólfsdalur was the home of Vestmannaeyjar's first settler, Herjólfur Barðursson. Excavations have revealed remains of a Norse house where a replica now stands. The island's campsite is also here.

On the cliffs west of the golf course, there's a little **monument** to the 200 people who converted to Mormonism and departed for Utah in the 19th century.

Westman Islands Golf Course
GOLF

(✑481 2363; www.gvgolf.is) Golfers can hire clubs at the wild, wonderful 18-hole seaside golf course in Herjólfsdalur. Green fees are Ikr7000.

West Coast
HIKING, BIRD WATCHING

Several perilous tracks climb the steep slopes around Herjólfsdalur, running along the top of Norðklettur to **Stafnsnes**, one of the prime puffin-breeding areas. The ascent is exhilarating, but there are some sheer drops. A gentler walk runs south along the western coast of the island, passing above numerous lava caves where local people hid from the pirates in 1627. At **Ofanleitishamar**, hundreds of puffins nest in the cliffs.

Stórhöfði
HIKING, BIRD WATCHING

A windy **meteorological station** has been built on Stórhöfði (122m), the rocky peninsula at Heimaey's southern end. It's linked to the main island by a narrow isthmus (created by lava from Helgafell's eruption 5000 years ago), and there are good views from the summit. There's also a small **bird-watching hut** for puffin viewing about halfway up the hill; go from the first turnout on the right to the end of a trail across sheep pasture, marked with a hiking sign.

It's possible to scramble down to the isthmus' boulder beach at **Brimurð** and continue north along the cliffs on the east coast, returning by a road just before the airport. From June to August **Kervíkurfjall** and **Stakkabót** are good places for puffin viewing.

🧭 Tours

Ribsafari
BOAT, HIKING TOUR

(✑661 1810, 846 2798; www.ribsafari.is; Harbour; 1hr tour per adult/child Ikr8000/4500, Surtsey tour Ikr16,500/9500; ☺mid-Apr–mid-Oct) One-hour tours run daily (11am, 2pm or by appointment) in a rubber zodiac that jets through the archipelago. The small boat allows the captain to navigate through little caves and

between rocky outcrops for up-close views of bird colonies. Charter trips to Surtsey (note: you cannot get off the boat) require a minimum of 10 people.

Circumnavigate the entire cluster of islands for Ikr11,500/6500 (100 minutes).

Viking Tours
BOAT, BUS

(✑488 4884; www.vikingtours.is; Harbour; ☺mid-May–mid-Sep) Stop by Café Kró (p158) to sign up for boat (adult/child Ikr5900/4900) or bus trips (adult/child Ikr4900/3900) with the friendly folks at Viking Tours. Boats zip around the island, slowing for the big bird-nesting sites on the south coast, and sailing into the sea cave Klettshellir. Trips coincide with ferry departures, making it convenient for day-trippers.

Lyngfell
HORSE RIDING

(✑898 1809; www.lyngfell.123.is) Lyngfell, on the road to Stórhöfði, offers horse riding (one hour Ikr6000).

Lukku
HORSE RIDING

(✑481 1478; lukkan@hestaleigave.com) Horse riding along the coast and lava fields.

Segway Tours
SEGWAY TOUR

(✑891 6818; www.segwaytours.is) Zip around town.

✦ Festivals

★ Þjóðhátíð
MUSIC

(National Festival; www.dalurinn.is; admission Ikr18,900) Three-day Þjóðhátíð is the country's biggest outdoor festival. Held at Herjólfsdalur festival ground over the last weekend in July or the first weekend in August, it involves music, dancing, fireworks, a big bonfire, gallons of alcohol and, as the night progresses, lots of drunken sex (it's something of a teen rite of passage), with upwards of 17,000 people attending. A song is written for each festival.

Extra flights are laid on from Reykjavík, but you must book transport and accommodation months in advance.

Historically, the festival was first celebrated when bad weather prevented Vestmannaeyjar people from joining the mainland celebrations of Iceland's first constitution (1 July 1874). The islanders held their own festival a month later, and it's been an annual tradition ever since.

🛏 Sleeping

The 30-minute ferry ride from the mainland means many people visit Vestmannaeyjar as a day trip, though we highly recommend spending the night. Out of festival season it's usually not hard to find lodging. Visit www.vestmannaeyjar.is for a full list of accommodation.

Gistiheimilið Hreiðrið
GUESTHOUSE €

(☑481 1045; http://tourist.eyjar.is; Faxastígur 33; s/d/q without bathroom Ikr7500/12,000/18,000; ☞) Run by helpful Ruth, this winning guesthouse has a family feel. Features include a well-stocked kitchen, a cosy TV lounge and it also runs walking tours in summer. Sleeping-bag accommodation costs Ikr4200.

Aska Hostel
HOSTEL €

(☑662 7266; Bárustigur 11; dm/d/q without bathroom Ikr4400/13,900/21,300; ☞) This cheery yellow historic building is home to a new hostel in the village centre.

Gistiheimilið Árný
GUESTHOUSE €

(☑899 2582; www.arny.is; Illugagata 7; d without bathroom Ikr12,500; ☞) A charming couple runs this neat suburban house, which also offers guests a kitchen and washing machine. Upstairs rooms have epic views, and the sunroom dining area is fun.

Sunnuhöll HI Hostel
HOSTEL €

(☑481 2900; www.hotelvestmannaeyjar.is; Vestmannabraut 28; dm Ikr4500; ☞) We have a soft spot for homey Sunnuhöll hostel, with its handful of prim rooms. The recent surge in day-trippers means that dorms are rarely full, and there's generally a quiet and laidback vibe. Reception is at Hótel Vestmannaeyjar. HI members discount Ikr700.

Campsite
CAMPGROUND €

(Tjaldsvæði; camp site per person Ikr1300; ☺Jun-Aug) Cupped in the bowl of an extinct volcano, the Herjólfsdalur campsite has hot showers, a laundry room and cooking facilities. You can also pitch a tent inland and across the street next to the football field at Þórsheimili, which is less windy.

Hótel Vestmannaeyjar
HOTEL €€

(☑481 2900; www.hotelvestmannaeyjar. is; Vestmannabraut 28; d/q incl breakfast Ikr24,700/30,500; @☞) Iceland's first cinema is now a pleasant hotel, with modern rooms (some with good town and harbour views), friendly staff and top restaurant Einsi Kaldi downstairs.

✗ Eating & Drinking

Heimaey has a surprisingly robust food scene for such a remote-feeling isle. In addition to the listings below, there is a nice selection of cafes and eateries on and around Bárustigur. Several petrol-station snack bars also serve fast food.

Café Kró
CAFE €

(Harbour; snacks Ikr200-1200; ☺10am-6pm mid-May–mid-Sep; ☞) Touristy Café Kró is run by Viking Tours and serves coffee, tea, cakes and soups.

★ Slippurinn
ICELANDIC €€

(☑481 1515; www.slippurinn.com; Strandvegur 76; mains Ikr2000-3900; ☺5.30-11pm Sun-Thu, to 1am Fri & Sat; ☞) Lively Slippurinn fills the upper storey of a beautifully remodeled old machine workshop that once serviced the ships in the harbour and now has great views to it. The tool shelves are still in their original positions, with tables made from old boat scraps beneath them. The food is delicious Icelandic with a few bright flavours from the Med.

★ Gott
ORGANIC €€

(☑431 3060; Bárustigur 11; mains Ikr1290-2650; ☞) Fresh fusion food is done with care, using organic, healthy ingredients in this jolly corner dining room. Think cod fillet with cauliflower puree or spelt-wrapped grilled chicken. Plus veggie options.

★ Einsi Kaldi
SEAFOOD €€€

(☑481 1415; www.einsikaldi.is; Vestmannabraut 28; mains Ikr2700-6000; ☺11.30am-3.30pm & 5-10pm mid-May–mid-Aug, 5-10pm mid-Aug–mid-May) On the ground floor of Hótel Vestmannaeyjar, Einsi Kaldi is Heimaey's highest-end dining experience, with well-crafted seafood recipes and mod mood lighting.

Höllin
BAR

(☑896 6818; Strembugata 13) The town's theatre has an upstairs bar called Háaloftð (open Friday and Saturday noon to late and some Thursdays), where locals hang out and bands occasionally play. Check their Facebook page (Háaloftið Vestmannaeyjum) for lineups.

Self-Catering

Vöruval
SUPERMARKET

(Vesturvegur 18; ☺9am-7pm) Groceries in a geodesic dome.

SURTSEY

In November 1963 the crew on the fishing boat *Ísleifi II* noticed something odd – the sea south of Heimaey appeared to be on fire. Rather than flee, the boat drew up for a closer look – and its crew were the first to set eyes on the world's newest island.

The incredible subsea eruption lasted for 4½ years, throwing up cinders and ash to form a 2.7 sq km piece of real estate (since eroded to 1.4 sq km). What else could it be called but Surtsey (Surtur's Island), after the Norse fire giant who will burn the world to ashes at Ragnarök.

It was decided that the sterile island would make a perfect laboratory, giving a unique insight into how plants and animals colonise new territory. **Surtsey** (www.surtsey.is) is therefore totally off-limits to visitors (unless you're a scientist specialising in biocolonisation). Just so you know: in the race for the new land, the blue-green algae *Anabaena variabilis* got there first. Another discovery? Fossils were carried up by lava during the eruption and are now part of the island.

You can get a vicarious view of Surtsey's thunderous birth by visiting the display at the Eldheimar Museum (p154). Both Ribsafari and Viking Tours will run boat trips around the island if there's enough interest.

Krónan   SUPERMARKET
(Strandvegur 48; ⏰11am-7pm Mon-Fri, to 6pm Sat & Sun) For self-catering, there's the Krónan.

Vínbúðin   LIQUOR STORE
(☑481 1301; Strandvegur 50; ⏰11am-6pm Mon-Thu, to 7pm Fri, to 4pm Sat) Local government liquor store.

🛍 Shopping

Útgerðin   CLOTHING, ARTS & CRAFTS
(☑481 1062; Vestmannabraut 37; ⏰10am-7pm) This large, modern shop is a good bet for Icelandic crafts and design.

ℹ Information

Tourist Information Centre (www.vestmannaeyjar.is; Strandvegur; ⏰9am-6pm Mon-Fri, 10am-5pm Sat, 1-5pm Sun Jun-Aug; 🐾) The summer tourist office is staffed by local teens at a cafe-bookstore. Pick up pamphlets and trail maps.

ℹ Getting There & Around

AIR

Vestmannaeyjar Airport (Vestmannaeyjaflugvöllur; VEY) is about 3km from central Heimaey; a **taxi** (☑897 1190) costs about Ikr2500, or you can walk. At the time of research there were no scheduled flights from Bakki (near the ferry port at Landeyjahöfn); however, a flightseeing tour with Atlantsflug (p137) could be taken one way (ie you get out in Heimaey).

There are two daily flights between Reykjavík's domestic airport and Vestmannaeyjar on **Eagle Air** (☑562 4200; www.eagleair.is) for approximately Ikr20,000 one way.

BOAT

Eimskip's ferry **Herjólfur** (☑481 2800; www.eimskip.is; adult/child/car/bicycle Ikr1260/630/2030/630) sails from Landeyjahöfn (about 12km off the Ring Road between Hvolsvöllur and Skógar) to Heimaey year-round. The journey takes about 30 minutes. You must always reserve ahead for cars, and passengers should book ahead in high season, especially at peak daytripper hours: the morning to Vestmannaeyjar and the afternoon back. You must arrive by 30 minutes before departure. Landeyjahöfn ferry terminal has vending machines, bathrooms and water, but no other services.

From 15 May to 14 September boats depart Vestmannaeyjar daily at 8.30am, 11.30am, 2.30pm, 5.30pm and 8.30pm (on Tuesdays there's no 2.30pm boat); from Landeyjahöfn the boats depart at 10am, 1pm, 4pm, 7pm and 10pm (again, no 4pm boat on Tuesdays). Low-season boats leave Vestmannaeyjar on a reduced schedule.

In really foul weather (summer or winter), the port at Landeyjahöfn can fill with sand, in which case the ferry sails to/from Þorlákshöfn instead on a reduced schedule of two per day. The sail takes 2¾ hours, and the fare is substantially more. Changes are posted on the website and Facebook page, and you need to check on your rebooking. It takes roughly two hours to drive from Landeyjahöfn west to Þorlákshöfn.

Getting to or from Landeyjahöfn, **Strætó** (☑540 2700; www.bus.is) bus 52 runs from Reykjavík (Mjódd terminal)–Hveragerði–Selfoss–Hella–Hvolsvöllur–Landeyjahöfn (Ikr3500, 2¼ hours, three daily in summer); plus there's a Landeyjahöfn **taxi** (☑862 1864).

West Iceland

Best Places to Eat

➡ Narfeyrarstofa (p173)

➡ Settlement Centre Restaurant (p166)

➡ Fjöruhúsið (p180)

➡ Plássið (p174)

➡ Gamla Rif (p177)

Best Places to Stay

➡ Hótel Egilsen (p173)

➡ Hótel Flatey (p174)

➡ Fljótstunga (p169)

➡ Lýsuhóll (p182)

➡ Bænir og Brauð (p173)

Why Go?

Geographically close to Reykjavík yet far, far away in sentiment, West Iceland (known as Vesturland; www.west.is) is a splendid microcosm of what Iceland has to offer. Yet most tourists have missed the memo, and you're likely to have much of this wonderful region to yourself.

The long arm of Snæfellsnes Peninsula is a favourite for its glacier, Snæfellsjökull, and the area around its national park is tops for birding, whale watching, lava field hikes and horse riding. Inland beyond Reykholt you'll encounter lava tubes and remote highland glaciers, including enormous Langjökull with its new ice cave. Icelanders honour West Iceland for its local sagas: two of the best known, *Laxdæla Saga* and *Egil's Saga*, took place along the region's brooding waters, marked today by haunting cairns and an exceptional museum in lively Borgarnes. West Iceland offers everything from windswept beaches to historic villages and awe-inspiring terrain in one neat, little package.

Road Distances (km)

	Borgarnes	Húsafell	Stykkishólmur	Hellnar	Búðardalur
Húsafell	65				
Stykkishólmur	99	158			
Hellnar	122	179	90		
Búðardalur	79	103	86	145	
Reykjavík	74	129	173	194	152

HVALFJÖRÐUR

Hvalfjörður and the surrounding area feels suddenly pastoral despite being a mere 30-minute drive from the capital. Although lacking the majesty of the Snæfellsnes Peninsula, the fjord offers quick day-trip fodder. Those in a hurry to get to Borgarnes and beyond should instead head straight through the 5.7km-long tunnel (Ikr1000) beneath the fjord. Cyclists aren't permitted in the tunnel.

Interestingly, during WWII the fjord contained a submarine station; more than 20,000 American and British soldiers passed through.

On the southern side of Hvalfjörður you'll find dramatic mount Esja (914m), a great spot for wilderness hiking. The trail to the summit begins at Esjuberg, just north of Mosfellsbær, and ascends via Krehólakambur (850m) and Kistufell (830m).

At the head of the fjord, Glymur, Iceland's highest waterfall (198m), can be reached by following the turn-off to Botnsdalur. From the end of the road, it'll take a couple of hours to reach the cascade. Try to visit after heavy rains or snowmelt for full effect.

The church at Saurbær farmstead has beautiful stained glass by Gerður Helgadóttir. The church is named for Reverend Hallgrímur Pétursson, who served here from 1651 to 1669, and composed Iceland's most popular religious work, *Passion Hymns*.

Hvalfjörður has several places to stay, including Hótel Glymur (⌕430 3100; www.hotel glymur.is; d from Ikr44,300; @ 🛜), where contemporary amenities abound: from two-storey 'executive doubles' to villas with private plunge pools; there's also a good restaurant.

Akranes

POP 6744

Set under striking Akrafjall (572m), the town of Akranes lies at the tip of the peninsula separating Hvalfjörður from Borgarfjörður. Largely an administrative and factory town, it's worth a stop for its sprawling Museum Centre (⌕431 5566; www.museum.is; adult/child Ikr500/free; ☺10am-5pm Jun-Aug, 1-5pm Sep-May), with a folk museum, restored boathouse, drying shed, church and fishing boats.

BORGARBYGGÐ

Buzzy Borgarnes and its broad Borgarfjörður were the landing zone for several famous Icelandic settlers. Inland, up the river-twined valley, you'll find fecund farms leading to powerful stone-strewn lava tubes and highlands, the gateway to ice caps beyond.

Borgarnes

POP 1824

Unassuming Borgarnes has got it going on. For such a tiny place, it bubbles with local life. One of the original settlement areas for the first Icelanders, it's loaded with history, and sits on a scenic promontory along the broad waters of Borgarfjörður. Zip past the busy petrol stations and go into the old quarter to encounter the fun small-town vibe and one of Iceland's best museums.

◉ Sights

★ Settlement Centre   MUSEUM
(Landnámssetur Íslands; ⌕437 1600; settlementcentre.is; Brákarbraut 13-15; 1 exhibition adult/child Ikr1900/1500, 2 exhibitions adult/child Ikr2500/1900; ☺10am-9pm Jun-Sep, 11am-5pm Oct-May; 🛜) Housed in an imaginatively restored warehouse by the harbour, the must-see Settlement Centre offers fascinating insights into the history of Icelandic settlement and the Saga era. The museum is divided into two exhibitions, each take about 30 minutes to visit. The Settlement Exhibition covers the discovery and settlement of Iceland. Egil's Saga Exhibition recounts the amazing adventures of Egil Skallagrímsson (the man behind *Egil's Saga*) and his family. A detailed multilingual audio guide is included.

This is not your run-of-the-mill Icelandic folk museum: the Settlement Centre offers deep background into Iceland's history and flora and fauna, and a firm context in which to place your Icelandic visit. And *Egil's Saga* is one of the most nuanced and action packed of the sagas. The centre has placed cairns (p166) throughout town marking key sites from *Egil's Saga*. It also has a top-notch restaurant.

BORGARNES' LOCAL LIQUORS

Steðji Brugghús (⌕896 5001; www. stedji.com; tours Ikr1500; ☺tours by appointment) This little family-run brewhouse 25km north of Borgarnes off Rte 50 has a small range, from strawberry beer to lager and seasonal beers. Tours by appointment, with tastings.

Reyka Vodka (www.reyka.com) Iceland's first distillery, in Borgarnes, offers crystalline vodka.

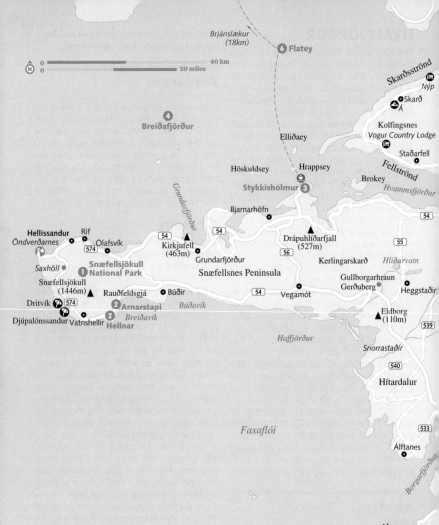

West Iceland Highlights

1 Tramp through crunchy lava fields, along windswept coastlines, and over Snæfellsjökull, the icy heart of the magical **Snæfellsjökull National Park** (p178)

2 Follow seabirds along the carpet of velvety moss through trail-side crags between **Hellnar** (p179) and **Arnarstapi** (p180)

3 Wander past charming chocolate-box houses in the harbour town **Stykkishólmur** (p170)

4 Sail past swooping puffins and search for whales

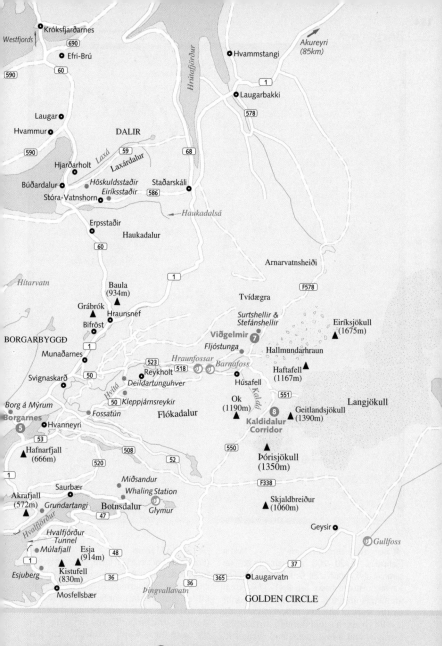

on a boat ride on beautiful
Breiðafjörður (p170)

⑤ Step back into Saga times
at the impressive Settlement
Centre in fun-loving
Borgarnes (p161)

⑥ Cast away all of your cares
and spend a night (or six) on
the island of **Flatey** (p174)

⑦ Explore the fascinating
subterranean remains of a

violent volcanic eruption at
Viðgelmir (p169)

⑧ Trace the raw edges of
Langjökull glacier on the
Kaldidalur Corridor (p169)

Borgarnes

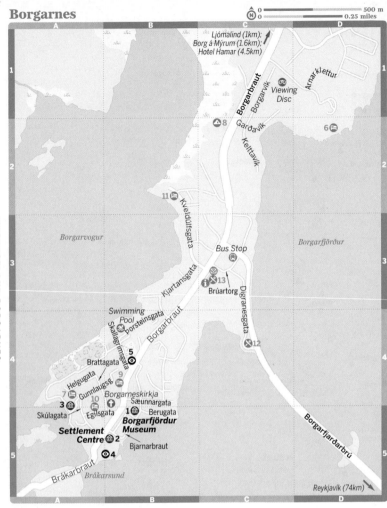

Ljómalind (1km);
Borg á Mýrum (1.6km);
Hotel Hamar (4.5km)

Viewing Disc

Borgarbraut

Borgarvík

Arnarklettur

Garðavík

Kelittavík

Kveldúlfsgata

Borgarvogur

Borgarfjörður

Bus Stop

Kjartansgata

Brúartorg

Digranesgata

Swimming Pool

Þorsteinsgata

Skallagrímsg.

Borgarbraut

Brattagata

Helgugata

Gunnlaugsg.

Borgarneskirkja

Sæunnargata

Skúlagata

Egilsgata

Berugata

Borgarfjörður Museum

Bjarnarbraut

Settlement Centre

Brákarbraut

Brákarsund

Borgarfjarðarbrú

Reykjavík (74km)

★ **Borgarfjörður Museum**   MUSEUM

(Safnahús; ☎ 430 7200; www.safnahus.is; Bjarnarbraut 4-6; adult/child Ikr900/600; ⏰1-5pm Jun-Aug, reduced hours Sep-May) This small municipal museum has an engaging exhibit on the story of children in Iceland over the last 100 years. It's told through myriad photographs and found items, and though it's accompanied by English translations, don't be shy about having museum staff show you through. The story behind each photograph is captivating; you'll be thinking about this exhibit long after you've left.

★ **Borg á Mýrum**   LANDMARK

(Rock in the Marshes) The farm, Borg á Mýrum, just northwest of Borgarnes on Rte 54, is the site where Skallagrímur Kveldúlfsson, Egil's father, made his farm at Settlement. Named for the large **rock** (borg) behind the farmstead (private property), you can walk up to the **cairn** for views all around. You can also visit the small **cemetery** which includes an ancient gravestone marked by runes.

The large abstract sculpture by Ásmundur Sveinsson represents a part of *Egil's Saga*, when he mourned the death of his sons and was rejuvenated by composing a poem.

Borgarnes

Brákin
LANDMARK

Þorgerður Brák was Egil's nursemaid, thought to be a Celtic slave. In one of the more dramatic moments in *Egil's Saga*, she heroically saves Egil's life (from an attempted crime of passion, by his own father, Skallagrímur Kveldúlfsson), and jumps into the sea to escape the enraged Skallagrímur. Today a sculpture marks a spot near where she leapt, ultimately to her death: Skallagrímur hit her with a stone, and she never emerged from the water again.

The strait she swam, between Borgarnes and the islet offshore, is named Brákarsund for her. The town celebrates an annual festival, Brákarhátíð, in her honour.

Art Gallery Complex
GALLERY

(Skúlagata 17; ☺ 4-6pm Tue, Thu & Fri, 1-4pm Sat) This quaint new complex on the old town waterfront has an upper storey filled with local artists' studio-galleries: Gallerý Júlí, Gló and Sóla. Browse crafts made from lava and bones, glassware, jewellery, paintings and more. The complex is also home to Edduveröld (p166).

✦ Festivals

Brákarhátíð
CULTURAL

(www.brakarhatid.is; ☺ late Jun) A festival in honour of Þorgerður Brák, a heroine from Egil's Saga. Expect town decorations, parades, a concert and a lively, offshore, mud-football match.

🛏 Sleeping

★ Bjarg
GUESTHOUSE €

(📞 437 1925; bjarg@simnet.is; d without bathroom incl breakfast Ikr14,500; 🛜) One of the most beautifully situated places to stay in the area, this attractive series of linked cottages 1.5km north of the centre overlooks the fjord with the mountains across the way. It has warm, cosy rooms with tasteful wood panelling and crisp white linens. There are shared guest kitchens, a good buffet breakfast, a barbecue, spotless bathrooms and a turf-roofed cottage that sleeps four.

Borgarnes HI Hostel
HOSTEL €

(📞 695 3366; www.hostel.is; Borgarbraut 11-13; dm Ikr4100, d with/without bathroom Ikr15,500/11,200; @🛜) This no-frills sleeping spot gets the job done. Despite the murals and African masks on the cinder-block walls, it still feels a bit like a high-school dorm. HI members discount Ikr700.

Borgarnes Campsite
CAMPGROUND €

(Borgarbraut; campsites per person/tent Ikr750/ 100) There's a fjord-side campground on the main road running up the peninsula. A ranger comes by at 9am and 9pm to collect fees.

Kría Guesthouse
GUESTHOUSE €€

(📞 845 4126; www.kriaguesthouse.is; Kveldúlfsgata 27; s/d without bathroom incl breakfast Ikr12,000/16,000; 🛜) Kría offers two rooms with great water views in a private home on a quiet residential street. There's a pleasant shared kitchen and a large wheelchair-accessible bathroom, plus outdoor seating with views and a hot-pot.

Borgarnes B&B
B&B €€

(📞 842 5866; www.borgarnesbb.is; Skúlagata 21; s/d without bathroom incl breakfast Ikr11,300/16,000, d with bathroom incl breakfast Ikr18,600; @🛜) Go for one of the two rooms on the ground floor with antique wooden doors and modern fixtures (the rest are in the basement); they have fab views of the bay. Great buffet breakfast.

Icelandair Hotel Hamar
HOTEL, GUESTHOUSE €€

(📞 433 6600; www.icehotels.is; Golfvöllurinn; hotel d Ikr28,400, guesthouse d without bathroom Ikr10,500; @🛜) Hotel Hamar sits on a popular golf course 4km north of town. We found the silver prefab exterior to be slightly off-putting, but surprisingly sleek decor and a cache of mod cons hide within. Better still are rustic guesthouse rooms, up the hill in the clubhouse, with views of the mountains and fjord. On-site restaurants.

Hótel Borgarnes HOTEL €€
(☎437 1119; www.hotelborgarnes.is; Egilsgata 12-14; s/d incl breakfast Ikr21,00/24,700; ⏱Apr-Nov; @📶) Large and relatively characterless, Hótel Borgarnes has boring business-style rooms that are largely the domain of package tourists.

Eating

Borgarnes has great eats. For the usual array of burgers and pizza, try the grill at the N1 petrol station.

Bónus SUPERMARKET €
(Digranesgata 6; ⏱11am-6.30pm Mon-Thu, 10am-7.30pm Fri, 10am-6pm Sat, noon-6pm Sun) The Bónus sits at the edge of the fjord bridge coming into town.

Vínbúðin LIQUOR STORE €
(Borgarbraut 58-60, Hyrnu Torg centre; ⏱11am-6pm Mon-Thu, to 7pm Fri, to 4pm Sat Jun-Aug, reduced rest of year) National liquor store chain.

★**Settlement Centre Restaurant** INTERNATIONAL €€
(☎437 1600; Brákarbraut 13; mains Ikr2400-5600; ⏱10am-9pm; 📶) The Settlement Centre's restaurant, in a light-filled room built into the rock face, is airy, upbeat, and one of the region's best bets for food. Choose from traditional Icelandic and international eats (lamb, fish stew etc). The lunch buffet (noon to 3pm; Ikr2100) is very popular. Book ahead for dinner.

While you wait, flip to the back of the menu and read up on the history of the town's oldest buildings (including the one you're sitting in!).

★**Edduveröld** CAFE €€
(☎437 1455; www.edduverold.is; Skúlgata 17; mains Ikr700-4200; ⏱10am-9pm Sat-Thu, to 1am Fri; 📶🖋) Casual and friendly, with a wonderful waterfront deck, Edduveröld is the newest entry in town for delicious homemade dishes, from super cakes to full meals of roast lamb or fresh fish.

Shopping

★**Ljómalind** MARKET
(Farmers' Market; ☎437 1400; www.ljomalind.is; Sólbakka 2; ⏱11am-6pm Jun-Aug, reduced hours rest of year) 🌿 A recent collaboration between local producers, this packed farmers market sits at the edge of town near the roundabout. It stocks everything from fresh dairy from Erpsstaðir (p183) and organic meat, to locally made bath products, handmade wool sweaters, jewellery and all manner of imaginative collectables.

Information

Tourist Information Centre (☎437 2214; www.west.is; Borgarbraut 58-60; ⏱9am-6pm Mon-Fri, 10am-4pm Sat, noon-4pm Sun Jun-Aug, 9am-5pm Mon-Fri Sep-May; 📶) West Iceland's main tourist information centre; in the big shopping centre.

Getting There & Away

Borgarnes is the major transfer point between Reykjavík and Akureyri, Snæfellsnes and the Westfjords. The **bus stop** (Borgarbraut) is at the cluster of petrol stations (N1, Orkan).

Strætó (☎540 2700; www.bus.is) services:

- Bus 57 to Reykjavík (Ikr1400, 1½ hours, two daily)

EGIL'S SAGA

Egil's Saga starts by recounting the tale of Kveldúlfur, grandfather of the warrior-poet Egil Skallagrímsson, who fled to Iceland during the 9th century after a falling out with the king of Norway. Kveldúlfur grew gravely ill on the journey, and instructed his son, Skallagrímur Kveldúlfsson, to throw his coffin overboard after he died and build the family farm wherever it washed ashore – this happened to be at Borg á Mýrum (p164). Egil Skallagrímsson grew up to be a fierce and creative individual who killed his first adversary at the age of seven, went on to carry out numerous raids on Ireland, England and Denmark, and saved his skin many a time by composing eloquent poetry. Learn about him at Borgarnes' excellent Settlement Centre (p161).

For those who'd like to go deep into how the saga ties to the landscape around Borgarnes, download the detailed **Locatify SmartGuide** (www.locatify.com; included in Settlement Centre admission, otherwise €15) smartphone or iPad app, which tells the stories of local landmarks from the tale. The Settlement Centre has marked eight of the sites with **cairns**, including Brákin (p165), Borg á Mýrum, and **Skallagrímsgarður**, the burial mound of the father and son of saga hero Egil Skallagrímsson.

➺ Bus 57 to Akureyri (Ikr6650, 5 hours, two daily)

➺ Bus 58 to Stykkishólmur (Ikr1750, 1½ hours, two daily, can change to 82 at the Vatnaleið crossroads for buses to Hellissandur and Arnarstapi)

➺ Bus 59 to Holmavík (Ikr3850, 2¼ hours, one daily Monday, Wednesday, and Friday to Sunday)

➺ Bus 81 to Reykholt (Ikr700, 1 hour and 20 minutes, one daily Monday to Friday).

Sterna (☑ 551 1166; www.sterna.is) services:

➺ Bus 60a to Reykjavík (Ikr1400, 1 hour, one daily Monday to Friday mid-June to August)

➺ Bus 60 to Akureyri (Ikr5700, 4 hours, one daily Monday to Friday mid-June to August).

Around Borgarnes

There is lots of great-value accommodation around Borgarnes; the Borgarnes tourist information centre can supply more, as can Icelandic Farm Holidays (www.farmholidays.is).

🛏 Sleeping

⭐**Fossatún** HOTEL, CAMPGROUND €
(☑ 433 5800; www.fossatun.is; Rte 50; campsites per person Ikr1200, guesthouse/cottage d Ikr13,900/20,500; ☺ camping mid-May–mid-Sep, guesthouse year round; @ 🛜 🛗) This family-friendly spot has a guesthouse, cottages and a campground next to a beautiful roaring waterfall. The spacious on-site restaurant (mains Ikr2000 to Ikr2900; noon to 2pm and 6pm to 8.30pm) overlooks the falls and themed walking paths. Located on the southern branch of Rte 50, about 23km east of Borgarnes and 18km southwest of Reykholt.

The friendly owner is a well-known children's book author (minigolf and a playground keep things kid-focussed) and former record producer (there's an amazing 3000-record collection; you can play 'em).

Ensku Húsin GUESTHOUSE €€
(☑ 437 1826; www.enskuhusin.is; Rte 54; d with/without bathroom Ikr22,000/17,900; 🛜) Located 8km northwest of central Borgarnes on Rte 54, this former fishing lodge with a dramatic riverside setting has been refitted with generous coats of old-school charm. Upstairs rooms retain much of the long-ago feel, while a newer motel block is '70s-retro. The friendly owners also offer accommodation in a restored farmhouse 2km away.

🛍 Shopping

⭐**Ullarselið** CLOTHING, ARTS & CRAFTS
(☑ 437 0077; www.ull.is; Hvanneyri; ☺ noon-6pm Jun-Aug, 1-5pm Thu-Sat Sep-May) Find your

way to off-the-beaten path village Hvanneyri, 12km east of Borgarnes, and in among fjord-side homes you'll find this fantastic wool centre. Handmade sweaters, scarves, hats and blankets share space with skeins of beautiful handspun yarn, and interesting bone and shell buttons. Plus there are needles and patterns to get you started. Look out for local Borgafjörður designs, featuring geese, ptarmigan or salmon. They also custom knit!

Upper Borgarfjörður

Reykholt

Incredibly unassuming, Reykholt (www.reykholt.is) is a sleepy outpost (just a few farmsteads really) that on first glance offers few clues to its past as a major medieval settlement. It was home to one of the most important medieval chieftains and scholars, Snorri Sturluson (also killed here), and today the main sights revolve around him.

◉ Sights

Snorrastofa MUSEUM
(☑ 433 8000; www.snorrastofa.is; admission Ikr1200; ☺ 10am-6pm May-Aug, to 5pm Mon-Fri Sep-Apr) The interesting medieval study centre Snorrastofa is devoted to celebrated medieval poet, historian and statesman Snorri Sturluson, and is built on his old farm, where he was brutally slain. The centre houses displays explaining Snorri's life and accomplishments, including a 1599 edition of his *Heimskringla* (sagas of the Norse kings). There's also material on the laws, literature and society of medieval Iceland, and on the excavations of the site. You can ask to see the modern church and reading room upstairs.

Snorralaug SPRING
FREE The most important relic of Snorri's farm is Snorralaug (Snorri's Pool), a circular, stone-lined pool fed by a hot spring. The stones at the base of the pool are original (10th century), and it is believed that this is where Snorri bathed. A wood-panelled tunnel beside the spring (closed to the public) leads to the old farmhouse – the site of Snorri's gruesome murder. The pool may be the oldest handmade structure in Iceland.

Church CHURCH
Among the more modern buildings found on Snorri's ancient farm is a quaint church dating from 1896, which is open to the

public. A 1040–1260 cistern for a smithy was found beneath it in 2001; look for the viewing glass in the floor.

Deildartunguhver
SPRING

(Rte 518) Find Europe's biggest hot spring, Deildartunguhver, about 5km west of Reykholt, just off Rte 518. Look for billowing clouds of steam, which rise from scalding water bubbling from the ground (180L per second and 100°C!). A take-and-pay tomato stall is usually set up in the parking lot – the tomatoes are grown in a nearby greenhouse which harnesses the spring's energy.

Icelandic Goat Centre
FARM

(☑ 435 1448; www.geitur.is; Rte 523, Háafell; tour per person Ikr1000; ⊙ 1-6pm Jun-Aug) Farm workers walk you through pretty fields with endangered Icelandic goats; coffee or tea included. The farm's most famous resident is Casanova, a bright-eyed goat who had a starring turn in *Game of Thrones* (running from a dragon). Call ahead; at time of research the fate of the centre was undecided. Find it on dirt-road Rte 523, northeast of Reykholt.

🛏 Sleeping & Eating

Steindórsstaðir
GUESTHOUSE €

(☑ 435 1227; www.steindorsstadir.is; Rte 517, Reykholtsdalur; d without bathroom Ikr13,600; 🐾) Set on a farm in the rolling fields about 2km from Reykholt proper, this sweet guesthouse offers cosy clean rooms with countryside views. There's a shared kitchen, a hot tub (with views, too!) and friendly owners. Some sleeping bag accommodation.

Fosshótel Reykholt
HOTEL €€

(☑ 435 1260, 562 4000; www.fosshotel.is; d incl breakfast from Ikr24,600; @ 🐾) The only accommodation in Reykholt proper, the Fosshótel is a modern block with basic motel-style rooms, a couple of hot-pots and a restaurant.

Hverinn Restaurant
INTERNATIONAL €

(☑ 571 4433; www.hverinn.is; Kleppjámsreykir; mains Ikr1350-2500; ⊙ 10.30am-8pm May–mid-Sep) Simple eats from daily soups to burgers are on offer at this large roadside restaurant with friendly staff. Also has basic groceries. Find it about 5km west of Reykholt near the junction of Rtes 518 and 50.

ℹ Getting There & Away

Strætó (☑ 540 2700; www.bus.is) services:
➾ Bus 81 to Borgarnes (Ikr700, 1 hour 20 minutes, one daily Monday to Friday).

Húsafell

Tucked into an emerald, river-crossed valley, with the river Kaldá on one side and a dramatic lava field on the other, Húsafell's encampment of summer cottages is a popular outdoor retreat for Reykjavík residents, and an access-point for nearby Langjökull glacier. There's no public transport to Húsafell.

ⓒ Tours

Ice Explorer
ADVENTURE TOUR

(☑ 588 5555; www.adventure.is; tours from Húsafell Ikr15,000) Monster truck tours (8x8) on Langjökull glacier; Reykjavík pick up possible. Other tours, including the Golden Circle, available.

SNORRI STURLUSON

The chieftain and historian Snorri Sturluson (1179–1241) is one of the most important figures in medieval Icelandic history, and in fact, he was one of the main chroniclers of Norse sagas and histories. Snorri was born at Hvammur near Búðardalur (further north); was raised and educated at the theological centre of Oddi near Hella; and later married the heir to the (historic) farm Borg á Mýrum (p164) near Borgarnes. He eventually left Borg and retreated to the wealthy church estate at Reykholt. At the time, Reykholt was home to 60,000 to 80,000 people and was an important trade centre at the crossroads of major routes across the country. Snorri composed many of his most famous works at Reykholt, including *Prose Edda* (a textbook of medieval Norse poetry) and *Heimskringla* (a history of the kings of Norway). Snorri is also widely believed to be the hand behind *Egil's Saga,* a family history of Viking *skald* (court poet) Egil Skallagrímsson.

At the age of 36 Snorri was appointed *lögsögumaður* (law speaker) of the Alþing (Icelandic parliament), and endured heavy pressure from the Norwegian king to promote the king's private interests. Instead, Snorri busied himself with his writing and the unhappy Norwegian king Hákon issued a warrant for his capture – dead or alive. Snorri's political rival and former son-in-law Gissur Þorvaldsson saw his chance to impress the king and possibly snag the position of governor of Iceland in return. He arrived in Reykholt with 70 armed men on the night of 23 September 1241 and hacked the historian to death in the basement of his farmhouse.

Dog Sledding
ADVENTURE TOUR

(☑ 863 6733; www.dogsledding.is; tours with Húsafell pick up from Ikr22,900) Runs dog-sledding tours on nearby Langjökull; visitors sit on the rig but do not drive the team. Reykjavík or Húsafell pick up or meet at the glacier. Other sites available in winter.

🛏 Sleeping

Húsafell
CAMPGROUND €

(Ferðaþjónustan Húsafelli; ☑ 435 1550, campground 435 1551; www.husafell.is; campsites/huts per person Ikr1300/3500, restaurant mains Ikr1790-2490; ☺ restaurant 11.30am-8pm) The Húsafell vacation resort is a one-stop shop, with campsites, huts and summer houses, plus a **minimarket, restaurant** and outdoor **geothermal swimming pool** (adult/child Ikr700/400, open 10am to 8pm daily June to September, reduced in low season).

Gamli Bær
GUESTHOUSE €

(☑ 895 1342; sveitasetrid@simnet.is; Rte 518; d with/without bathroom incl breakfast from Ikr14,000/11,000) Renovated 1908 farmhouse with shared or private bathrooms; just east up the valley from Húsafell, on Rte 518.

Hallmundarhraun

East of Húsafell, along Rte 518, the vast, barren lava flows of Hallmundarhraun make up a wonderful eerie landscape dotted with gigantic lava tubes. These long, tunnel-like caves are formed by flows of molten lava beneath a solid lava crust, and it's possible to visit several of them.

If you've got a 4WD, it's also possible to continue into the interior along Rte F578 beyond Surtshellir, through the lakes at **Arnarvatnsheiði**, and on to **Hvammstangi**. Note that Rte F578 is usually only open seven weeks a year; see www.vegagerdin.is.

⊙ Sights

★ Viðgelmir
LAVA TUBE

(☑ 435 1198; www.fljotstunga.is; tours Ikr3000; ☺ May-Sep) The easiest lava tube to visit, and the largest in Iceland, 1100-year-old, 1.5km-long Viðgelmir is located on private property near the farmstead Fljótstunga. It sparkles with ever-changing ice formations. You can't visit on your own, but the friendly family at Fljótstunga offers 90-minute tours at 10am, noon, 3pm and 5pm May to August, and by reservation in September to April. Helmet and torch included.

Surtshellir
LAVA TUBE

Just a bit to the southeast of Fljótstunga on Rte 518, a bright yellow sign marks the turn-off to **Arnarvatnsheiði** along Rte F578 (rental cars not allowed). Follow the bumpy track for 7km to reach Surtshellir, a dramatic, 2km-long lava tube connected to **Stefánshellir**, a second tunnel about half the size. You can explore Surtshellir on your own, if you have caving gear.

🛏 Sleeping

★ Fljótstunga
COTTAGES €

(☑ 435 1198; www.fljotstunga.is; sites per person Ikr1000, cottages from Ikr8000; 🔊) 🍴 This beautifully situated farm offers a series of lovely little cabins with views down the valley. They are exceptional value considering the wild location and rustic charm. Deep discounts for sleeping bag accommodation. Camping is also allowed and has shower access. Artist residencies.

Langjökull & Kaldidalur Corridor

Southeast of Húsafell, the absolutely incredible Kaldidalur valley skirts the edge of a series of glaciers, offering incredible views of the Langjökull ice cap and, in clear weather, Eiríksjökull, Okjökull and Þórisjökull. The Kaldidalur Corridor, also simply known as unsurfaced Rte 550, is slow but dramatic going (mountain ice, barren rock), and often fogged in in summer. It links south to the Golden Circle, offering the option to create an extended loop from Reykjavík. Access to Rte 550 is limited to sanctioned vehicles – ask your rental outfit before setting off.

The primary way to see the Kaldidalur Corridor is with your own wheels, but tours are available on Langjökull and of its new ice cave, departing from Reykjavík or Húsafell. Do not attempt to drive up onto the glacier yourself.

Langjökull Ice Cave
CAVE

(www.icecave.is; ☺ Mar-Oct) At the time of research, work was underway on digging an enormous 300m long tunnel and series of caves, at 1260m above sea level, into Langjökull glacier. Slated to open mid–2015, the tunnel and caves will contain exhibitions, a cafe and a small chapel, yes, for those who want to tie the knot inside a glacier. Tours can be had (March to October) from Húsafell or the glacier edge (Ikr17,900), or from Reykjavík (Ikr29,900) with the possibility of looping in the Golden Circle.

A maximum of 80 visitors at a time will travel up the glacier by monster truck, then have about 45 minutes touring the glacier – which will continue to creep down the mountain in the years to come.

SNÆFELLSNES PENINSULA

Sparkling fjords, dramatic volcanic peaks, sheer sea cliffs, sweeping golden beaches and crunchy lava flows make up the diverse and fascinating landscape of the 100km-long Snæfellsnes Peninsula. The area is crowned by the glistening ice cap Snæfellsjökull, immortalised in Jules Verne's *Journey to the Centre of the Earth*. Good roads and regular buses mean that it's an easy trip from Reykjavík, offering a cross section of the best Iceland has to offer in a very compact region.

Stykkishólmur, on the populated northern coast, is the region's largest town and a logical base. Moving west along the northern coast, you'll pass smaller townships. On the western part of the peninsula, Snæfellsjökull National Park encompasses not only its glacier but bird sanctuaries and lava fields. The quiet southern coast has several good horse farms beneath towering crags.

Stykkishólmur

POP 1091

The charming town of Stykkishólmur, the largest on the Snæfellsnes Peninsula, is built up around a natural harbour tipped by a basalt islet. It's a picturesque place with a laid-back attitude and a sprinkling of brightly coloured buildings from the late 19th century. With a comparatively good choice of accommodation and restaurants, and handy transport links, Stykkishólmur makes an excellent base for exploring the region.

It featured in Ben Stiller's *The Secret Life of Walter Mitty* (2013).

◉ Sights & Activities

★ **Breiðafjörður**   FJORD

Stykkishólmur's jagged peninsula pushes north into stunning Breiðafjörður, a broad waterway separating the Snæfellsnes from the looming cliffs of the distant Westfjords. According to local legend, there are only two things in the world that cannot be counted: the stars in the night sky and the craggy islets in the bay. You *can* count on epic vistas and a menagerie of wild birds (puffins, eagles, guillemots etc). Take **boat trips**, including whale watching and puffin viewing, from Stykkishólmur, Grundarfjörður and Ólafsvík.

★ **Norska Húsið**   MUSEUM

(Norwegian House; ☑433 8114; www.norska husid.is; Hafnargata 5; admission Ikr800; ◔noon-5pm Jun-Aug; ☏) Stykkishólmur's quaint maritime charm comes from the cluster of wooden warehouses, shops and homes orbiting the town's harbour. Most date back about 150 years. One of the most interesting (and oldest) is the Norska Húsið, now the regional museum. Built by trader and amateur astronomer Árni Thorlacius in 1832, the house has been skilfully restored and displays a wonderfully eclectic selection of local antiquities. On the 2nd floor you visit Árni's home, an upper-class 19th-century residence, decked out in his original wares. The museum hosts occasional **art exhibitions**.

★ **Súgandisey**   LIGHTHOUSE

The basalt island Súgandisey, features a scenic **lighthouse** and grand views across Breiðafjörður. Reach it via the stone causeway from Stykkishólmur harbour.

Volcano Museum   MUSEUM

(Eldfjallasafn; ☑433 8154; www.eldfjallasafn.is; Aðalgata 8; adult/child Ikr800/free; ◔11am-5pm May-Sep) The Volcano Museum, housed in the town's old cinema, is the brainchild of vulcanologist Haraldur Sigurðsson, and features art depicting volcanoes, plus a small collection of interesting lava ('magma bombs'!) and artefacts from eruptions. A film screens upstairs. You can book a full-day geology tour (Ikr17,000) around the Snæfellsnes Peninsula with Haraldur.

Library of Water   ART MUSEUM

(Vatnasafn; ☑857 1221; www.libraryofwater. is; Bókhlöðustígur 17; adult/child Ikr500/free; ◔1-6pm Jun-Aug, by appointment Sep-May) For relaxing views of town and bay, head up the hill to the Library of Water. This window-lined space showcases an installation by American artist Roni Horn (b 1955). Light reflects and refracts through 24 glass pillars filled with Icelandic glacier water. There's also a chess set, if you feel like lingering.

Stykkishólmskirkja   CHURCH

(☑438 1288; www.stykkisholmskirkja.is; ◔10am-5pm) Stykkishólmur's futuristic church,

Snæfellsnes Peninsula

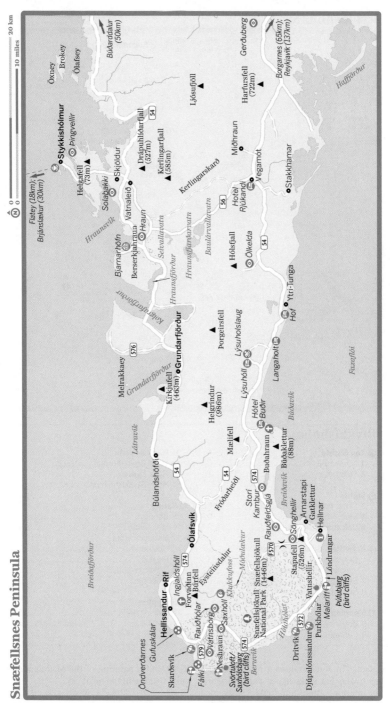

0 20 km
0 10 miles

Breiðafjörður

Öxney
Brokey
Ólafsey
Búðardalur (50km)

Gerðuberg
Borgarnes (65km); Reykjavík (137km)
Harfursfell (722m)
Hafnarfjörður

Flatey (18km);
Brjánslækur (30km)

Stykkishólmur
Þingvellir
Helgafell (73m)
Skjöldur
Drápuhlíðarfjall (527m)
Ljósufjöll
54

Sólabakki
Vatnaleið
Kerlingarfjall (585m)
Miðhraun

Hraunsvík
Bjarnarhöfn
Hraun
Hraunsvík
Berserkjahraun
Kerlingarskarð
Vegamót
Stakkhamar

Selvallavatn
Hotel Rjúkandi
56

Kolgrafarfjörður
Hraunsfjörður
Baulárvallavatn
Hólsfjall
Ölkelda
54

Hraunsfjörður
Ytri-Tunga

Melrakkaey
576
Þorgeirsfell
Hóf
Faxaflói

Grundarfjörður
Grundarfjörður
Lýsuhólslaug
Langaholt

Látravík
Kirkjufell (463m)
Lýsuhóll

Helgrindur (986m)
Hótel Búðir
Búðavík

Búlandshöfði
Mælifell
Búðahraun
Búðaklettur (88m)
54

54
Fróðarheiði
Stóri Kambur
Breiðavík
Arnarstapi
GatKlettur

Ólafsvík
574
Rauðfeldsgjá
Hellnar

Rif
Ingjaldshóll
574
F570
Söng
Stapafell (526m)

Hellissandur
Forvaðinn Búrfell
Eysteinsdalur
Klukkufoss
Móðulækur
Snæfellsjökull (1446m)
Snæfellsjökull National Park

Öndverðarnes
Gufuskálar
Skarðsvík
Rauðhólar
Saxhóll
Holahólar
Vatnshellir
Malarrif
Lóndrangar

Falki
579
Vatnsborg
Neshraun
Dritvík
572
Purkhólar
Þúfubjarg (bird cliffs)

Svörtuloft/
Saxhólsbjarg (bird cliffs)
Djúpalónssandur

Bervík

Stykkishólmur

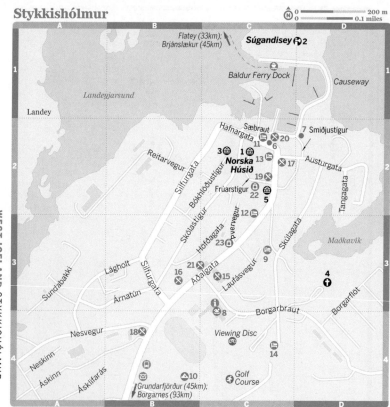

Stykkishólmur

designed by Jón Haraldsson, has a sweeping bell tower that looks like a whale vertebra. The interior features hundreds of suspended lights and a painting of the Madonna and child floating in the night sky.

Sundlaug

Stykkishóms GEOTHERMAL POOL, HOT-POT

(⏱433 8150; Borgarbraut 4; adult/child
Ikr600/200; ☉7.05am-10pm Mon-Thu, to 7pm Fri,
& 10am-6pm Sat & Sun Jun-Aug, reduced hours Sep-
May) Water slides and hot-pots are the highlights at the town's geothermal swimming
pool, in the municipal sports complex.

🌿 Tours

Seatours BOAT TOUR

(Sæferðir; ⏱433 2254; www.seatours.is; Smið-
justígur 3; ☉8am-8pm mid-May–mid-Sep, 9am-
5pm mid-Sep–mid-May) Various boat tours,
including much-touted 'Viking Sushi', a
1½-hour/2¼-hour boat ride (Ikr5250/7090)
taking in islands, bird colonies (puffins until
August), and basalt formations. A net brings
up shellfish to devour raw. Also offers dinner
cruises, and runs the Baldur Ferry to Flatey.
Partners with Reykjavík Excursions for Reykjavík pick up. On-site shop and cafe.

Iceland Ocean

Tours BOAT TOUR, BIRDWATCHING TOUR

(⏱517 5555; www.icelandoceantours.is; Hafnargata 4; tours from Ikr5200, bicycle hire per day
Ikr3000; ☉Apr-Sep) Cruise in a Zodiac RIB
(rigid inflatable boat) around the beautiful
bay; it's possible to get quite close to islets for
viewing colonies of birds (puffins!) and seals.
Also midnight sun and Flatey Island tours.

Gordon WALKING TOUR, ADVENTURE TOUR

(⏱517 5555; www.gordon.is; Hafnargata 4) Offshoot of Iceland Ocean Tours, with walking
tours of Stykkishólmur (Ikr1200) and super-
Jeep tours of Snæfellsnes Peninsula and glacier (Ikr29,000), with pick up available.

🛏 Sleeping

Online booking engines, the tourist office
and the locally available *Stykkishólmur:
Town of a Thousand Islands* brochure list
more accommodations (such as a homestay
at Langey guesthouse).

Harbour Hostel HOSTEL €

(⏱517 5353; www.harbourhostel.is; Hafnargata
4; dm/d without bathroom from Ikr3400/12,900;
☎📶) Part of the Iceland Ocean Tours outfit, this new harbour-side hostel offers some
of the town's best cheap lodging, with dorm
rooms, doubles and family rooms.

Campground CAMPGROUND €

(mostri@stykk.is; Aðalgata 27; campsites per person Ikr1000; ☉mid-May–Aug; ☎) Basic; managed by the golf course nearby.

★ Hótel Egilsen BOUTIQUE HOTEL €€

(⏱554 7700; www.egilsen.is; Aðalgata 2; s/d
Ikr22,000/28,500; @☎) One of our favourite
little inns in Iceland, this boutique hotel fills
a lovingly restored timber house that creeks
in the most charming way when winds howl
off the fjord. The friendly owner has outfitted
cosy (tiny!) rooms with traditional wool blankets, original artwork and organic Coco-Mat
mattresses. Complimentary iPads and a
home-made breakfast sweeten the deal.

Bænir og Brauð GUESTHOUSE €€

(⏱820 5408; www.baenirogbraud.is; Laufásvegur 1;
d Ikr15,900-17,900; ☎) A fine example of Stykkishólmur's quality guesthouse scene, this
snug, immaculate house sits along the fjord,
and some rooms have lovely views of the
bay. Greta, the kindly owner, also owns Hótel Egilsen down the road.

Hótel Stykkishólmur HOTEL €€

(⏱430 2100; www.hringhotels.is; Borgarbraut 8;
s/d incl breakfast Ikr23,000/26,300; ☉Apr-Sep;
@☎) The best rooms in this jarring silver
box up on a hill have super bay and island
views. Rooms are modern and comfortable.
There's an on-site restaurant (mains Ikr2800
to Ikr4800).

Hótel Breiðafjörður HOTEL €€

(⏱433 2200; www.hotelbreidafjordur.is; Aðalgata 8; guesthouse dm/d without bathroom
Ikr3500/9800, hotel d incl breakfast Ikr21,700;
☉May-Sep; @☎) Lacking character, but
rooms are clean with faux-wood finishes.
The hotel also manages a nearby bare-bones
guesthouse with dorm rooms, doubles with
shared baths and a common kitchen.

🍴 Eating

Nesbrauð BAKERY €

(⏱438 1830; Nesvegur 1; snacks Ikr355-1200;
☉8am-5pm) On the way out of town, this
bakery is a good choice for a quick breakfast or lunch. Stock up on sugary confections
such as *kleinur* (traditional twisty doughnuts) or *ástar pungur* (literally 'love balls';
fried balls of dough and raisins).

Meistarinn FAST FOOD €

(Aðalgata; hot dogs Ikr490, sub sandwiches Ikr750-
1490; ☉noon-8pm Jun-Aug) This friendly *pýl-
suvagninn* (wiener wagon) has the best hot
dogs in town. Each menu item is named after someone from Stykkishólmur.

★ Narfeyrarstofa ICELANDIC €€

(⏱438 1119; www.narfeyrarstofa.is; Aðalgata 3;
mains Ikr3600-5100; ☉noon-10pm Apr–mid-Oct,

6-10pm Sat & Sun mid-Oct–Mar; 🍴) This charming restaurant run by an award-winning chef (known for his superlative desserts) is the Snæfellsnes' darling fine-dining destination. Book a table on the 2nd floor to dine under gentle eaves and the romantic lighting of antique lamps. Ask your waiter about the portraits on the wall – the building has an interesting history.

⭐ Plássið   ICELANDIC, BISTRO €€

(📞 436 1600; www.plassid.is; Frúarstígur 1; mains Ikr1400-4200; ⊙ 11.30am-3pm & 6-10pm; 🍴 👶)
The newest creation of the owners of Narfeyrarstofa, this bistro-style old-town building is a perfect family-friendly spot, with elegant touches (wine glasses, mod furnishings) and friendly service. Using local ingredients, it serves up a full run of regional specials, and the catch of the day is usually delicious, paired with salad or barley risotto. Local beers, too.

Sjávarpakkhúsið   ICELANDIC €€

(📞 438 1800; Hafnargata 2; mains Ikr2750-5000; ⊙ noon-10pm Sun-Thu, to 3am Fri & Sat Jun-Aug, reduced hours Sep-May; 📶) This old fish-packing house has been transformed into a wood-lined cafe-bar with harbourfront outdoor seating. The speciality is blue-shell mussels straight from the bay, but it's also a great daytime hang-out. On weekend evenings it turns into a popular bar where locals come to jam.

Self-Catering

Bónus   SUPERMARKET €

(Borgarbraut 1; ⊙ 11am-6.30pm Mon-Thu, 10am-7.30pm Fri, 10am-6pm Sat, noon-6pm Sun) Near the swimming pool.

Vínbúðin   LIQUOR STORE €

(Aðalgata 24; ⊙ 2-6pm Mon-Thu, 1-7pm Fri, 11am-2pm Sat Jun-Aug, reduced rest of year) Across the main road from Bónus.

🛍 Shopping

Several artists have small galleries along harbour-side streets.

Leir 7   ARTS & CRAFTS

(www.leir7.is; Aðalgata 20; ⊙ 2-5pm) Artist Sigríður Erla produces tableware from the fjord's dark clay at this pottery studio in the heart of town.

FLATEY

Of Breiðafjörður's innumerable islands, little Flatey (literally 'flat island') is the only one with year-round inhabitants. In the 11th century Flatey was home to a monastery, and today the appealing island is a popular stopover for travellers heading to (or from) the Westfjords. Push the slo-mo button on life, and enjoy a windswept afternoon amid brightly coloured houses and swooping Arctic terns.

Sleeping

Hótel Flatey (📞 555 7788; www.hotelflatey.is; s/d incl breakfast Ikr21,500/24,500; ⊙ Jun–late Aug) Hótel Flatey has some of the most charming, nooklike rooms in Iceland, and the on-site **restaurant** (lunch mains Ikr1900 to Ikr3200, dinner three-course menu Ikr8100 to Ikr8500; open noon to 9pm) is fantastic as well. On weekends, slip down into the basement for live evening jam sessions with some of the locals.

Krákuvör (📞 438 1451; campsites per person Ikr1000; ⊙ Jun-Aug) One of the island's farms, about 300m from the pier, Krákuvör offers modest accommodation and camping.

Læknishús (📞 438 1476; d without bathroom Ikr11,000; ⊙ Jun-Aug) Læknishús is about 400m from the pier and offers simple farm accommodation in summer.

Getting There & Away

To cross Breiðafjörður aboard the Baldur Ferry (p175) and stop off in Flatey, you must take the first ferry of the day, disembark, and board the second daily ferry across, or one the next day (boats only pause on the island for around five minutes as they cross the fjord). No cars are allowed on Flatey, so for those taking a car to the Westfjords, it is possible to send it on across (no additional charge) while staying behind in Flatey.

To visit Flatey as a day trip from Stykkishólmur, take either boat during summer, disembark at Flatey and catch the ferry as it returns to Stykkishólmur. Note that the twice-per-day ferry service only runs in summer. You can also visit with local tour companies.

Gallerí Lundi   ARTS & CRAFTS
(Aðalgata 4a; ☺ 12.30-6pm May-Sep) Local hand-icrafts sold by friendly villagers. Also offers coffee.

❶ Information

Tourist Information Centre (📋 433 8120; www.west.is; Borgarbraut 4; ☺ 9am-5pm Mon-Fri Jun-Aug; 🛜) In the recreational complex wih the swimming pool. Friendly sports-centre staff offer tips when the information centre is closed.

❶ Getting There & Away

BOAT

Baldur Ferry (📋 433 2254; www.seatours. is) Car ferry between Stykkishólmur and Brjánslækur in the Westfjords (2½ hours), via Flatey (1½ hours). From early June to late August there are daily departures from Styk-kishólmur at 9am and 3.45pm, returning from Brjánslækur at 12.15pm and 7pm. During the rest of the year there is only one ferry per day, leaving Stykkishólmur at 3pm (no boats on Saturdays), returning at 6pm.

Adult fares to Brjánslækur are Ikr5250. Reserve ahead for vehicles (additional Ikr5250). Round trip from Stykkishólmur to Flatey costs Ikr7160. Check online for concession and winter fares.

BUS

You can get to Reykjavík (2½ hours) by changing in Borgarnes. All service is greatly reduced in winter, and bus 82 is sometimes by appointment.

Strætó (📋 540 2700; www.bus.is) services:
➡ Bus 58 to Borgarnes (Ikr1750, 1½ hours, two daily)

➡ Bus 82 to Arnarstapi via Ólafsvík and Hellis-sandur (Ikr1750, 1¼ hours, two daily).

Stykkishólmur to Grundarfjörður

The scenic stretch between Stykkishólmur and Grundarfjörður is filled with myth and mystique, from spiritual mountains to saga-storied lava fields, with the bright water just offshore.

Helgafell   MOUNTAIN
About 5km south of Stykkishólmur, the holy mountain Helgafell (73m) was once venerated by worshippers of the god Þór. Although quite small, the mountain was so sacred in Saga times that elderly Icelanders would seek it out near the time of their death. To-day, locals believe that wishes are granted to those who climb the mount.

In the late 10th century, Snorri Goði, a prominent Þor worshipper, converted to

Christianity and built a church at the top of the hill; its ruins still remain. The nearby farm of the same name was where the con-niving Guðrun Ósvífursdóttir of *Laxdæla Saga* lived out her later years in isolation. Her grave marks the base of the mount.

Berserkjahraun   LAVA FIELD
About 15km west of the intersection of Rte 54 and Rte 56 lies the dramatic, spiky lava field at Berserkjahraun. Crowned by looming moun-tains, this lunar landscape gets its name from *Eyrbyggja Saga* (see p176).

Bjarnarhöfn Shark Museum   MUSEUM
(📋 438 1581; www.bjarnarhofn.is; admission Ikr1000; ☺ 9am-8pm Jun-Aug, reduced hours Sep-May) The farmstead at Bjarnarhöfn is the re-gion's leading producer of *hákarl* (fermented shark meat), a traditional Icelandic dish. The museum has exhibits on the history of this culinary curiosity, along with the family's fishing boats and processing tools. A video explains the butchering and fermenting pro-cedure: Greenland shark, which is used to make *hákarl*, is poisonous if eaten fresh. Fer-mentation neutralises the toxin. NB: Green-land shark is classified near-threatened.

Find the museum off Rte 54 on the fjord-side, northeastern edge of Berserkjahraun.

Each visit to the museum comes with a bracing nibble of *hákarl*, accompanied by *brennivín*, 'black death' schnapps. Ask about the drying house out back. You might find hundreds of dangling shark slices dry-ing; the last step in the process.

Grundarfjörður

POP 826

Spectacularly set on a dramatic bay, little Grundarfjörður is backed by waterfalls and surrounded by ice-capped peaks often shroud-ed in cottony fog. More prefab than wooden, the town feels like a typical Icelandic fishing community, but the tourist facilities are good and the surrounding landscape can't be beat.

◎ Sights

★ **Kirkjufell**   MOUNTAIN
Kirkjufell (463m), guardian of Grunda-rfjörður's northern vista, is said to be one of the most photographed spots in Iceland. You'll see Ben Stiller skateboarding past in *The Secret Life of Walter Mitty* (2013). Ask the Saga Centre if you want to climb it (around €40 for a guide). Two spots involv-ing a rope climb make it dangerous to scale when wet or without local knowledge.

GONE BERSERK

According to *Eyrbyggja Saga*, long ago a farmer from Hraun grew weary of having to walk around the jagged lava flows to visit his brother at the farm in Bjarnarhöfn. Returning from a voyage to Norway, he brought back two berserkers – insanely violent fighters who were employed as hired thugs in Viking times – to work on his farm, but to his dismay one of the berserkers took a liking to his daughter. He turned to the local chieftain, Snorri Goði, for advice, but Snorri had his eye on the farmer's daughter as well and he recommended setting the berserker an impossible task. The farmer decided to promise the amorous berserker his daughter's hand in marriage if he was able to clear a passage through the troublesome lava field – surely impossible.

To the shock and horror of both Snorri and the farmer, the two berserkers quickly set to work and managed to rip a passage straight through the treacherous moonscape. Rather than honouring his promise, the farmer trapped the berserkers in a sauna and murdered them, allowing Snorri to marry his daughter. Today, a path through the Berserkjahraun (p175) can still be seen, and a grave was discovered containing the remains of two large men.

Kirkjufell is backed by the roaring waterfalls, **Kirkjufellsfoss**; more camera fodder.

Saga Centre   MUSEUM
(Eyrbyggja Heritage Centre; ☑ 438 1881; www.grundarfjordur.is; Grundargata 35; ⊙ 9am-5pm mid-May–mid-Sep; @ ☎) The Saga Centre is a tourist information centre, cafe (Emil's Cafe), library, internet point and small museum rolled into one. The museum displays an old fishing boat and gear, plus a children's toy collection. Wi-fi costs Ikr500 per device per hour. It sells national park maps.

☞ Tours

★Láki Tours   WHALE WATCHING, WILDLIFE
(☑ 546 6808; www.lakitours.com) Láki Tours has excellent fishing, puffin-spotting and whale-watching trips from Grundarfjörður or Ólafsvík. The Puffin Tour (Ikr5000) from Grundarfjörður goes to wonderful basalt island, **Melrakkaey**, with colonies of puffins, kittiwakes and other sea birds, and super views of Kirkjufell. Whale-watching tours (Ikr7900 to Ikr8900) depend on the season, but cover the best whale terrain in the region; orcas, fin, sperm, blue, minke and humpback whales are all possibilities. Check online for tours and departure points. Also has shop and cafe.

Snæfellsnes Excursions   BUS TOUR
(☑ 616 9090; www.sfn.is; tours from Ikr10,000) Day trips around the major sites of Snæfellsnes Peninsula, from Stykkishólmur, Grundarfjörður and Ólafsvík.

🛏 Sleeping

Refer to **Icelandic Farm Holidays** (www.farmholidays.is) for accommodation on nearby headlands.

Grundarfjörður HI Hostel   HOSTEL €
(☑ 562 6533; www.hostel.is; Hlíðarvegur 15; dm from Ikr4100, d with/without bathroom from Ikr15,500/11,200; @ ☎) This outfit features everything from prim dorm rooms to smart, apartment-style lodging. Reception is in the red house (at the listed address), while accommodation is spread across several buildings in town. Members discount Ikr700.

Hótel Framnes   HOTEL €€
(☑ 438 6893; www.hotelframnes.is; Nesvegur 8; d/q incl breakfast Ikr23,220/34,110; @ ☎ 🐾) This comfy dock-side inn has a spacious lobby, and rooms and apartments with either sea or mountain views. The in-house **restaurant** (mains Ikr4000 to Ikr5000; open 6.30pm to 9.30pm) opens every evening to serve the daily catch.

🍴 Eating

Emil's Cafe   CAFE €
(Grundargata 35, Saga Centre; mains Ikr1190-1690; ⊙ 9am-10pm; ☎) In the Saga Centre, this cheery cafe is tops for cappuccinos, hot soup and sandwiches.

Meistarinn   FAST FOOD €
(hot dogs Ikr490-540, sandwiches Ikr650-1490; ⊙ Jun-Sep) The Meistarinn hot dog wagon has menu items named after members of the Danish royal family.

Supermarket   SUPERMARKET €
(Grundargata 38; ⊙ 9am-10pm Jun-Aug, reduced hours Sep-May) A small supermarket and N1 petrol station with a grill are within sight of the Saga Centre.

RúBen   INTERNATIONAL €€
(☑ 438 6446; Grundargata 59; mains Ikr2100-4900; ⊙ 10am-11pm Sun-Thu, to 1am Fri & Sat

Jun-Aug, reduced hours Sep-May) This joint is popular with locals for its friendly staff, no-nonsense diner-style menu, and broad menu: from pasta to soup, burgers, fish and chips or lamb. Big breakfasts (Ikr1200 to Ikr2500) are served until 2pm.

ⓘ Getting There & Away

Strætó (☑ 540 2700; www.bus.is) services:
➻ Bus 82 Stykkishólmur–Arnarstapi (Ikr700 to Stykkishólmur, two daily in Jun-Aug, three weekly in Sep-May; runs via Ólafsvík and Hellissandur; stops at the N1 station in Grundarfjörður).

Ólafsvík

POP 981

Quiet, workaday Ólafsvík won't win any hearts with its pungent fish smell (from the fish-processing plant). Although it's the oldest trading town in the country (it was granted a trading licence in 1687), few of the original buildings survive. For visitors it's best as a jumping-off point for whale watching or a quick stop at Hraun for a meal.

⊙ Sights

Pakkhúsið   MUSEUM
(Packhouse; ☑ 433 6930; Ólafsbraut; adult/child Ikr500/free; ⊙ noon-5pm Jun-Aug) A mildly interesting folk museum telling the story of the town's development as a trading centre.

Ólafsvíkurkirkja   CHURCH
(http://kirkjanokkar.is; ⊙ 8am-6pm Jun-Aug) Ólafsvík's modern church is made entirely of triangular pieces.

☞ Tours

Some Láki Tours (p176) whale-watching trips depart from here: the waters offshore and west to the tip of the peninsula are the region's best for whale sightings.

🛏 Sleeping & Eating

Campground   CAMPGROUND €
(Dalbraut; campsites per person/tent/camper van Ikr500/500/1000; ⊙ Jun-Aug) You can pitch a tent at the local campground, though we prefer the one in nearby Hellissandur.

Hringhótel Ólafsvík   HOTEL €€
(☑ 436 1650; www.hringhotels.is; Ólafsbraut 20; d & studio Ikr19,300; @ 🛜) This large hotel has merely functional rooms in its main building, but the annexe across the street has good studios with kitchenettes, some with sea views. Popular with tour groups.

Hraun   INTERNATIONAL €€
(☑ 431 1030; Grundarbraut 2; mains Ikr2000-5000; ⊙ noon-midnight daily Jun-Aug, noon-2pm Mon-Thu, noon-midnight Fri-Sun Sep-May; 🛜) This new establishment on the main road cheerfully fills a blonde-wood building with a broad front deck. The only gig in town besides fast food, it does excellent fresh mussels, burgers and fish, and has beer on tap.

ⓘ Information

Tourist Information Centre (☑ 433 6929; Kirkjutún 2; ⊙ 9am-noon & 12.30-5pm Mon-Fri, 10am-4pm Sat & Sun Jun-Aug, reduced hours Sep-May) Snæfellsbær region's tourist information centre; in a white building behind the Packhouse.

ⓘ Getting There & Away

Strætó (☑ 540 2700; www.bus.is) services – call to book in winter:
➻ Bus 82 Stykkishólmur–Arnarstapi (Ikr1050 to Stykkishólmur, two daily in high season, three weekly in low season; stops at the petrol station).
➻ To get to Reykjavík (Ikr3850, 3½ hours) you must change for bus 58 at the Vatnaleið crossroads, and then again in Borgarnes.

Rif

POP 161

Blink-and-you'll-miss-it Rif is a harbour village that makes Ólafsvík look like the big city. Dramatic waterfall **Svödufoss**, with its barrelling cascades and dramatic hexagonal basalt, can be seen in the distance.

Between Rif and Hellissandur, spot the lonely **church** (built 1903) at **Ingjaldshóll**, the setting of *Víglundar Saga*. If the church doors are open, you can see a **painting** depicting Christopher Columbus' possible visit to Iceland in 1477; it's thought he came with the merchant marine and inquired about Viking trips to Vinland.

🛏 Sleeping & Eating

Frystiklefinn   HOSTEL €
(☑ 865 9432; www.frystiklefinn.is; Hafnargata 16; dm Ikr4600) This quirky new joint combines austere six-bed dorms with a cool theatre and live music venue. In summer there's an active program of plays, storytelling and music. Check online for the schedule, and for winter opening.

★ **Gamla Rif**   CAFE €
(☑ 436 1001; Háarifi 3; cakes from Ikr850, fish soup Ikr1900; ⊙ noon-8pm Jun-Aug) Gamla Rif is run

by two fishermen's wives who have perfected a variety of traditional snacks. They dispense local travel tips with a smile, and serve tasty coffee and cakes. They also make a mean fish soup (from their husbands' daily catch) with fresh bread, if you're feeling peckish.

Hellissandur

POP 396

Hellissandur is the original fishing village in the area. There's not much to it any more, except great views of the glacier and fjord.

◉ Sights

Sjómannagarður MUSEUM
(Maritime Museum; ☑ 436 6619; Útnesvegur; adult/child Ikr500/free; ☺ 9.30am-noon & 1-6pm Tue-Fri, 1-6pm Sat & Sun Jun–mid-Aug, 1-6pm Tue-Sun mid-Aug–mid-Sep) This small maritime museum houses *Bliki*, the oldest fishing boat in Iceland, and a cool replica of a fisher's turf house, plus loads of old photos and memorabilia. Look for the set of lifting stones once used to test the strength of prospective fishermen.

🛏 Sleeping & Eating

Campground CAMPGROUND €
(campsites per person/tent Ikr500/500) This full-service campground is one of our favourites, set right in the middle of a spiky lava field.

★Hótel Hellissandur HOTEL €€
(☑ 430 8600; www.hotelhellissandur.is; Klettsbuð 7; d incl breakfast Ikr16,250; 🐾) This solid hotel may be plain from the outside, but it's got good, clean rooms with modern bathrooms, and some top-floor rooms have views to the glacier. For the price, the cheerful staff and abundant mod cons make it well worth a stop. There's also a surprisingly yummy **restaurant** (mains Ikr1790 to Ikr4900), with Icelandic staples, plus burgers and the like.

❶ Getting There & Away

Strætó (☑ 540 2700; www.bus.is) services:
➽ Bus 82 Stykkishólmur–Arnarstapi (Ikr1400 to Stykkishólmur, stops at the N1 petrol station).

Snæfellsjökull National Park

Snæfellsjökull National Park (☑ 436 6860; www.snaefellsjokull.is) encompasses much of the western tip of Snæfellsnes Peninsula, and wraps around the rugged slopes of the glacier Snæfellsjökull, the icy fist at the end of the long Snæfellsnes arm. Around its flanks lie lava tubes, protected lava fields which are home to native Icelandic fauna, and prime coastal bird- and whale-watching spots.

When the fog swirling around the glacier lifts, you'll see the mammoth ice cap, which was made famous when Jules Verne used it as the setting for *Journey to the Centre of the Earth*. In his book, a German geologist and his nephew embark on an epic journey into the crater of Snæfells, guided by a 16th-century Icelandic text with the following advice:

> *Descend into the crater of Yocul of Sneffels, which the shade of Scartaris caresses, before the kalends of July, audacious traveller, and you will reach the centre of the earth. I did it.*
> *Arne Saknussemm*

Today, the park is criss-crossed with hiking trails, and during proper weather it is possible to visit the glacier with a tour or guide. Hellnar is home to the National Park Visitor Centre (p180), and area tourist offices sell maps and give advice, too. The park's online map is also excellent. Rangers have an active summer program of free park guided tours; check online or email.

Snæfellsjökull

It's easy to see why Jules Verne selected Snæfell for his adventure: the peak was torn apart when the volcano beneath it exploded and then collapsed back into its own magma chamber, forming a huge caldera. Among certain New Age groups, Snæfellsjökull is considered one of the world's great 'power centres'.

Today the crater is filled with the ice cap (highest point 1446m) and is a popular summer destination. The best way to reach the glacial summit is to link up with a tour in Hellnar or Arnarstapi. They approach the peak from the south, on Rte F570; Rte F570's northern approach (near Ólafsvík) is frustratingly rutty (4WD needed) and frequently closed due to weather-inflicted damage. Even the well trained and outfitted are not allowed to ascend the glacier without a local guide; contact the National Park Visitor Centre in Hellnar for more information, or take a tour (p180).

Öndverðarnes

At the westernmost tip of Snæfellsnes, Rte 574 cuts south, while Rte 579, a tiny gravel and occasionally surfaced track, heads further west across an ancient lava flow to the tip of the Öndverðarnes peninsula, which is great for whale watching.

As the road winds through charcoal lava cliffs you'll pass Skarðsvík, a golden beach with basalt cubes alongside. A Viking grave was discovered here in the 1960s and it's easy to understand why this stunning spot would have been a favoured final resting place.

After Skarðsvík the track gets much bumpier (still manageable for a 2WD). Park at the turn-off (left side) to walk through craggy lava flows to the imposing volcanic crater Vatnsborg, or continue driving straight on until you reach a T-intersection. To the left lie the dramatic Svörtuloft bird cliffs (Saxhólsbjarg) and a tall, orange lighthouse. To the right, the bumpy track runs parallel to the sea to a squat, orange lighthouse. From its parking area, you can walk to the very tip of the peninsula, for whale watching, or walk 200m northeast to Fálki, an ancient stone well which was thought to have three waters: fresh, holy and ale!

Saxhöll Crater

Southwest of the Öndverðarnes area, on Rte 574, follow the marked turn-off to the roadside scoria crater Saxhöll, which was responsible for some of the lava in the area. There's a drivable track leading to the base, from where it's an uneven 300m climb for views over the enormous Neshraun lava flows.

Djúpalón Beach & Dritvík

On the southwest coast, Rte 572 leads off of Rte 574 to the wild black-sand beach Djúpalónssandur. It's a dramatic place to walk with rock formations (an elf church and kerling, a troll woman), two brackish pools (for which the beach was named), and the rock-arch Gatklettur. An asphalt car park and public toilets allow tour bus access, and crowds.

Down on the beach you can still see four lifting stones where fishing-boat crews would test the strength of aspiring fishermen. The smallest stone is Amlóði (Bungler) at 23kg, followed by Hálfdrættingur (Weak) at 54kg, Hálfsterkur (Half-Strong) at 100kg, and the largest, Fullsterker (Fully Strong), at 154kg. Hálfdrættingur marked the frontier of wimphood, and any man who couldn't heft it was deemed unsuitable for a life at sea. Alongside, the black sands are covered in pieces of rusted metal from the English trawler *Eding*, which was shipwrecked here in 1948.

A series of rocky sea stacks, some of which are thought to be a troll church, emerge from the ocean up the coast, as you tramp north over the craggy headland to reach the black-sand beach at Dritvík. From the 16th to the 19th century Dritvík was the largest fishing station in Iceland, with up to 60 fishing boats, but now there are only ruins near the edge of the lava field.

Vatnshellir

This 8000-year old lava tube with multiple caverns lies 32m below the earth's surface, 1km north of Malariff. The pull-out is visible from Rte 574, and the tube can only be visited by guided tour.

Cave Vatnshellir LAVA TUBE TOUR, GUIDED TOUR (☑665 2818; www.vatnshellir.is; tours adult/child Ikr2500/1000) Offers much-loved 45-minute tours of the Vatnshellir lava tube. Guides shed light on the fascinating geological phenomena and region's troll-filled lore. Helmet and torch included. Dress warmly, wear hiking boots, and preferably gloves too. Tours depart on the hour from 10am to 6pm, mid-May to September. Cave Vatnshellir also offers glacier tours.

Malariff & Lóndrangar

About 2km south of Djúpalónssandur, a paved road leads down to the rocket-shaped lighthouse at Malariff, from where you can walk 1km east along the cliffs to the rock pillars at Lóndrangar, which surge up into the air in surprising pinnacles. Locals say that elves use the lava formations as a church. A bit further to the east lie the Þúfubjarg bird cliffs, also accessible from Rte 574.

Southern Snæfellsnes

To the east of the national park, coastal Rte 574 passes the hamlets of Hellnar and Arnarstapi, with their glacier tour companies and interesting sea-sculpted rock formations. It continues east along the broad southern coastal plain, hugging huge sandy bays such as Breiðavík on one side, and towering peaks with waterfalls on the other. This stretch has some super horse riding.

Strætó bus 82 runs from Stykkishólmur in the northeast, around the peninsula's western tip, and then back east as far as Arnarstapi. There is no public transport going further east along the peninsula's southern side; private wheels are best.

Hellnar

POP 8

Bárður, the subject of *Bárðar saga Snæfellsáss* was part giant, part troll and part human. He chose an area near Hellnar, a picturesque spot overlooking a rocky bay, as his home (called **Laugarbrekka**). Towards the end of his intense saga, he became the guardian spirit of Snæfell. Today Hellnar is a tiny fishing village (once huge) where the shriek of seabirds fills the air and whales are regularly sighted.

◎ Sights

Bárðarlaug, up near the main road, was supposedly Bárður's bathing pool, though the pond is no longer hot. Down on the shore, the cave **Baðstofa** is chock-a-block with nesting birds. Nearby is the head of the **trail to Arnarstapi**. Ancient, velvety moss-cloaked lava flows tumble east through the **Hellnahraun**.

★ **Hellnar Visitor Centre –**
Gestastofa PARK, MUSEUM
(Snæfellsjökull National Park Visitor Centre; ☑591 2000, 436 6888; www.snaefellsjokull.is; ☺10am-5pm 20 May–10 Sep, reduced hours rest of year; ☏) **FREE** This is the spot for information on Snæfellsjökull National Park: it's an information office with maps (Ikr2000) and brochures (Ikr300), as well as a museum featuring displays on local geology, history, flora, fauna and customs. Rangers have an active summer program of **free park guided tours**; check online or email. Primus Café is on-site. NB: the park office in Hellissandur is administrative only and not open to the public.

⊨ Sleeping & Eating

★ **Hótel Hellnar** HOTEL €€
(☑435 6820; www.hellnar.is; s/d incl breakfast from Ikr22,800/26,200; ☺May-Sep; ☏) ◈ Hótel Hellnar, with its sun-filled, comfortable rooms, is the area's choice sleeping option (and thus often booked). Even if you're not overnighting, we highly recommend having dinner at the **restaurant** (dinner mains Ikr3450-4950; ☺6-9.30pm May-Sep) which sources local organic produce for its Icelandic menu, plus offers heavenly *skyr* cake for dessert. Reserve ahead.

HIKING THE COAST

Local maps detail myriad hiking trails connecting the sights of the Snæfellsnes Peninsula. One of the most popular (and scenic!) is the 2.5km coastal walk (around 40 minutes) between Hellnar and Arnarstapi. This slender trail follows the jagged coastline through a nature reserve, passing lava flows and eroded stone caves.

Primus Café CAFE €
(☑865 6740; Hellnar Visitor Centre; mains Ikr 1390-1980; ☺10am-9pm) Welcoming spot for cakes, soups and simple meals.

★ **Fjöruhúsið** SEAFOOD, CAFE €€
(☑435 6844; mains Ikr2300-2800, cake Ikr950; ☺10am-10pm Jun-Aug, reduced hours Apr-May & Sep-Oct) It's well worth following the stone path down to the ocean's edge for the renowned fish soup at quaint Fjöruhúsið. Located by the bird cliffs at the trailhead of the scenic Hellnar–Arnarstapi path, it also serves coffee in sweet, old-fashioned china.

Arnarstapi

Linked to Hellnar by both the main road and a wonderful coastal hike, this hamlet of summer cottages is nestled between the churning Arctic waters and the gnarled pillars of two neighbouring lava fields. A **monument** pays tribute to Jules Verne and a comical signpost measures distances to major cities via the earth's core. A second, enormous troll-like **monument** stands as a tribute to Bárður, the region's guardian spirit, and the leading character in a local saga.

Arnarstapi is the best place to organise an ascent to the Snæfellsjökull glacial crown, though some tour companies come in from Reykjavík (such as Arctic Adventures, p70).

⫷ Tours

Cave Vatnshellir (p179) and Gordon (p173) offer tours of the Snæfellsjökull glacier.

★ **Go West!** ADVENTURE TOUR, CYCLING TOUR
(☑695 9995; www.gowest.is) ◈ Friendly couple Jon Joel and Maggy run ecofriendly biking, hiking, boating, cycling, hot spring and glacier tours. Snæfellsjökull glacier tours (Ikr9000 to Ikr22,000) are hikes, with crampons, ice axe etc included. Also runs tours in Southern Iceland, or with Reykjavík pick up.

Snæfellsjökull Glacier Tours SNOWMOBILE TOUR
(☑663 3371; www.theglacier.is; snowcat/snowmobile tours Ikr11,000/25,000; ☺Mar-Jul) March to July six daily 1½-hour snowcat (truck with chain wheels) tours ascend the glacier to about 1410m. Up to mid-June there are also snowmobile tours.

⊨ Sleeping

Snjófell GUESTHOUSE, CAMPGROUND €
(☑435 6783; www.snjofell.is; campsites per tent Ikr1500, d/q Ikr14,500/19,100; ☺May-Sep; ☝)

Snjófell has basic accommodation and dining. Travellers pitch tents on grass outside (no showers), or bed down in the guesthouse. The turf-roofed restaurant (mains Ikr2000 to Ikr4500) focuses on local fish.

ℹ️ Getting There & Away

There is no public transport going east. To get to Reykjavík, you can take bus 82 to the Vatnaleið crossroads (at Rtes 56 and 55) and change for bus 58 to Borgarnes, where you change once more.

Strætó (📱 540 2700; www.bus.is) services:
→ Bus 82 Stykkishólmur–Anarstapi (two daily in summer, three weekly in winter).

Rauðfeldsgjá

Just north of Arnarstapi and Stapafell, on Rte 574, a small track branches off to the stunning Rauðfeldsgjá, a steep, narrow cleft that disappears into the cliff wall. Birds wheel overhead, a stream runs along the bottom of the gorge, and you can slink between the sheer walls for quite a distance. The gorge figures in a dramatic part of the local saga of Bárður, described on a sign at the parking area.

Breiðavík

East of Rauðfeldsgjá, Rte 574 skirts the edges of an enormous sandy bay at Breiðavík. The windswept coast, with its yellow expanse of sand, is wonderfully peaceful, though tricky to access. The pasture-filled region running along the coastal mountains from here east to Vegamót is considered one of the best places in Iceland for horse riding, and there are several stables of international repute.

On the eastern edge of Breiðavík, look for the placard telling the grisly tale of Axlar-Björn, Iceland's notorious 16th-century serial killer, who made his living in lean times by murdering travellers here.

🐴 Tours

Stóri Kambur HORSE RIDING
(📱 852 7028; www.storikambur.is) Family-run operation offering 1½- to three-hour rides on the beach, with glacier views when it's clear.

Búðir & Búðahraun

Búðir has a lonely church and a hotel, but there is no sign of its former fishing village along its craggy, mossy inlets. A walking trail leads across the elf-infested nature preserve, Búðahraun lava field. The ancient lava field is protected; if you look down into its

hollows and cracks you'll find flourishing flowers and ferns, many of them themselves protected native Icelandic species. The path also leads to the crater **Búðaklettur**. According to local legend, a lava tube beneath Búðahraun, paved with gold and precious stones, leads all the way to Surtshellir in upper Borgarfjörður. It takes about three hours to walk to the crater and back.

🛏️ Sleeping

Hótel Búðir HOTEL €€€
(📱 435 6700; www.hotelbudir.is; Búðir; d incl breakfast Ikr34,900-49,900; @ 🛜) Windswept and on gorgeous, remote coastline, Hótel Búðir tries to be stylish, though it's beseiged by tour groups. No 28 has the best views (and a teeny balcony). The restaurant (mains Ikr4700 to Ikr5700) is sometimes closed to those not in prebooked tour groups.

Lýsuhóll to Gerðuberg

Horse ranches dot this area (several offering accommodation). Grassy fields and sandy beaches with lava fields and mountain backdrops, making for great riding country.

⊙ Sights & Activities

Gerðuberg LANDMARK
Just where Rte 54 curves between the Snæfellsnes Peninsula and the mainland, you'll find the dramatic basalt towers of Gerðuberg rising from the plain.

Ytri-Tunga WILDLIFE
The deserted farmstead at Ytri-Tunga, just east of Hof, occasionally has a colony of seals offshore.

★ Lýsuhólslaug GEOTHERMAL POOL
(admission Ikr550; ⊙1-8pm Jun–mid-Aug) The geothermal source for Lýsuhólslaug pumps

DETOUR: RTE 590

The dramatic coastline of the oft-forgotten peninsula between the Snæfellsnes and Westfjords is traced by this 100km track (okay for 2WD; along Rte 60 look for the turn-off at Fellströnd). Windswept farmsteads lie frozen in time, and boulder-strewn hills, crowned with flattened granite, roll skyward.

Near the beginning of the track, the farm at **Hvammur** produced a whole line of prominent Icelanders, including Snorri Sturluson of *Prose Edda* fame. It was settled in around 895 by Auður the Deep-Minded, the wife of the Irish king Olaf Godfraidh, who has a bit part in *Laxdæla Saga*. Árni Magnússon, who rescued most of the Icelandic sagas from a fire in Copenhagen in 1728, was also raised at Hvammur.

You can spend the night at recently renovated **Vogur Country Lodge** (☑894 4396; www.vogur.org; s/d/q Ikr19,200/22,800/28,500; 🛜🅿) or remote, lovely **Nýp** (☑896 1930; www.nyp.is; Skarðsströnd; d incl breakfast Ikr15,500; 🛜) 🏖. There's also a campground, Á, just before **Skarð** – a farm that has remained in the hands of the same family for over 1000 years.

carbonated, mineral-filled waters in at a perfect 37°C to 39°C. Don't be alarmed that the pool is a murky green: the iron-rich water attracts some serious algae. Find it just beyond the horse ranch at Lýsuhóll.

🧭 Tours

★ Lýsuhóll
HORSE RIDING

(☑435 6716; www.lysuholl.is; d/q incl breakfast Ikr18,500/30,000, cottage Ikr20,000; 🛜) Equine enthusiasts should look no further than this friendly horse farm. The affable owner proudly displays her awards at the breakfast table. Even if you're not riding, the farm and its cottages are fun places to stay. Guides will show you around the stables, and there are both short excursions (one hour Ikr5000) and multiday tours.

🛏 Sleeping

Gistiheimilið Hof
APARTMENTS, COTTAGES €

(☑435 6802; www.gistihof.is; d with/without bathroom Ikr15,600/12,480, 2-bedroom houses Ikr26,000; 🛜🅿) Friendly Hof has a varied selection of basic apartment-style accommodation, each with their own hot tub, as well as freestanding cabins with private bathrooms, and their own shared kitchen cabin. There is also sleeping bag accommodation, whole houses to stay in, and beautiful views.

Gistihúsið Langaholt
GUESTHOUSE €€

(☑435 6789; www.langaholt.is; Görðum; sites per person Ikr1000, d Ikr24,000; ☺restaurant 8am-9pm; 🛜) Langaholt is a golfing haven, guesthouse, campground and gastronomic pit stop, run by an affable father and two sons. Modern, simple rooms often have great views, and the restaurant serves up tasty seafood (Ikr1900 to Ikr3900). Nine holes of golf costs Ikr2500 (clubs available for rent).

Hotel Rjúkandi
HOTEL €€

(☑435 6690; www.rjukandi.com; Vegamót; d from Ikr19,300, snacks Ikr350-890; ☺cafe 10am-9pm; 🛜) Vegamót means crossroads, and that's exactly where you'll find this hotel, cafe and restaurant. You'll probably spot its cafe, Rjúkandi Kaffi, first. It's next to the N1 station, and is loaded with home-made cakes, daily soups and happy locals. If you'd like to stay overnight, you can get a simple, clean room, built in 2013, with private bath.

It recently opened a **restaurant**, which serves beautifully presented Icelandic fare.

DALIR

The scenic corridor of rolling fields and craggy river-carved buttes between west Iceland and the Westfjords served as the setting for the *Laxdæla Saga*, the most popular of the Icelandic sagas. The story revolves around a love triangle between Guðrun Ósvífursdóttir, said to be the most beautiful woman in Iceland, and the foster brothers Kjartan Ólafsson and Bolli Þorleiksson. In typical saga fashion, Guðrun had both men wrapped around her little finger and schemed and connived until both were dead – Kjartan at the hands of Bolli, and Bolli at the hands of Kjartan's brothers. Most Icelanders know the stories and characters by heart and hold the area in which the story took place in great historic esteem.

Eiríksstaðir

Eiríksstaðir Reconstruction
LANDMARK

(☑434 1118; www.leif.is; adult/child Ikr1250/free; ☺9am-6pm Mon-Fri Jun-Aug) The farm Eiríksstaðir was home to Eiríkur Rauðe (Erik the Red), father of Leifur Eiríksson, the first

European to visit America. Although only a faint outline of the original farm remains, a reconstruction turf house was built using only the tools and materials available at the time. Period-dressed guides show visitors around and tell the story of Erik the Red, who went on to found the first European settlement in Greenland. Find Eiríksstaðir 8km inland on gravel and paved Rte 586, east of Stóra-Vatnshorn's church, on Haukadalsá river.

Búðardalur

POP 171

◎ Sights

Leifsbúð   MUSEUM
(☑434 1441; www.dalir.is; ◎10.30am-6pm Mon-Fri, 11am-4pm Sat & Sun Jun-Aug; 🛜) There's a folk museum, tourist information centre and cafe all rolled into one at Leifsbúð down by the harbour. Look out for the Viking exhibit featuring Leifur Eiríksson and Erik the Red.

🛏 Sleeping

Dalakot   GUESTHOUSE €€
(☑434 1644; www.dalakot.is; Dalbraut 2; s/d/tr without bathroom Ikr11,900/15,900/20,900, d/tr with bathroom Ikr18,900/23,900; ◎restaurant noon-10pm; 🛜) Guesthouse Dalakot has sparkling, simple rooms and restaurant with a broad menu, plus daily Icelandic specials (mains Ikr1500 to Ikr2800).

🛍 Shopping

Bolli Craft   ARTS & CRAFTS
(☑434 1410; www.facebook.com/bollicraft; Vesterbraut 12) Cool local arts and crafts include handmade sweaters and charming elves.

❶ Getting There & Away

Strætó (☑540 2700; www.bus.is) services:
➡ Bus 59 Borgarnes–Holmavík (one daily Monday, Wednesday, and Friday to Sunday; stops in Búðardalur at the N1 petrol station).

Hjarðarholt & Around

Although the Dalir is central to several of the best-loved Icelandic sagas, little remains of the original farms. For example no trace remains of Hjarðarholt, the one-time home of Kjartan Ólafsson and his father, Ólaf the Peacock. Their farmstead was said to be one of the wonders of the Norse world, with scenes from the sagas carved into the walls, and a huge dining hall that could seat 1100. You will find a beautiful **church** on the site with great views over

ERPSSTAÐIR DAIRY FARM
. . . .
Erpsstaðir (☑843 0357; www.erpsstadir.is; admission to cowshed adult/child Ikr600/free; ◎1-5pm Jun–mid-Sep; 🅿) is the perfect place to stretch your legs. This dairy farm on the gorgeous Rte 60 (between Búðardalur and the Ring Road) specialises in delicious home-made ice cream (Ikr400). You can tour the farm, greet the buxom bovines, chickens, rabbits and even guinea pigs, then gorge on a scoop. The farm also sells *skyr* and cheese; try the rocket-shaped *skyr-konfekt*, a delicious dessert made from a hard white chocolate shell encasing thick *skyr*. It'll blow you away. Erpsstaðir also offers accommodation (from Ikr13,000) if you're contemplating ice cream for breakfast...

the valley. Nearby, and also on the Laxá river, **Höskuldsstaðir** was the birthplace of Hallgerður Longlegs (also called Longtresses), wife of Gunnar of Hlíðarendi, who starred in *Njál's Saga*. Other important residents of the farm include Bolli and his foster brother Kjartan from *Laxdæla Saga*.

Laugar & Around

Just north of the spot where Rte 590 heads west off of Rte 60 you'll find the encampment at **Laugar**, the birthplace of *Laxdæla Saga* beauty Guðrun Ósvífursdóttir. Historians believe they've found **Guðrun's bathing pool**: the hot pool is well marked above the entrance to Hótel Edda, and has a small changing kiosk. **Tungustapi**, in the distance, is a large elf cathedral.

Friendly **Hótel Edda** (☑444 4930; www.hoteledda.is; Sælingsdalur; sites per person Ikr1000, d with/without bathroom Ikr22,000/11,000; ◎6 Jun–late Aug; @🛜☀) has a newer wing with modern rooms, an older dormitory-style annexe with shared bathrooms, and sleeping-bag space. The **restaurant** (mains Ikr2600-4100; ◎6-9pm 6 Jun–late Aug) gets good reviews for its local angelica-fed lamb.

Don't miss the neat **Dalir Heritage Museum** (☑434 1328; ◎1-6pm Jun-Aug) **FREE** in the hotel basement. The curator is a wonderful character who knows a great deal about Dalir's brilliant history, and if you make your way through the inumerable artefacts, there's an unexpected reconstruction of a traditional *baðstofa* (living/sleeping room).

The Westfjords

Why Go?

The Westfjords is where Iceland's dramatic landscapes come to a riveting climax and where mass tourism disappears – only about 14% of Iceland's visitors ever see the region. Jagged bird cliffs and broad multihued dream beaches flank the south. Rutted dirt roads snake north along jaw-dropping coastal fjords and over immense central mountains, revealing tiny fishing villages embracing traditional ways of life. In the far north, the Hornstrandir hiking reserve crowns the quiet region, and is home to cairn-marked walking paths revealing birdlife, Arctic foxes and ocean vistas. The Strandir Coast is less visited still, with an end-of-the-line, mystical feel, geothermal springs and minuscule oceanside hamlets.

Leave plenty of time for a trip to the Westfjords. Unpaved roads weave in and out of fjords and over pothole-pitted mountain passes. The going is slow, but the scenery is never short of breathtaking, the local life always compelling. You may not want to leave.

Best Places to Eat

➡ Heimsendi Bistro (p190)
➡ Simbahöllin (p192)
➡ Húsið (p197)
➡ Tjöruhúsið (p197)
➡ Stúkuhúsið (p190)

Best Places to Stay

➡ Hótel Djúpavík (p206)
➡ Hótel Laugarhóll (p205)
➡ Bíldudalur HI Hostel (p191)
➡ Einarshúsið (p198)
➡ Camping in Hornstrandir Reserve (p203)

Road Distances (km)

	Patreksfjörður	Þingeyri	Ísafjörður	Hólmavík	Norðurfjörður
Þingeyri	129				
Ísafjörður	175	47			
Hólmavík	234	265	221		
Norðurfjörður	333	348	303	105	
Reykjavík	397	405	450	230	334

SOUTH COAST

The sparsely populated south coast of the Westfjords is a tiny version of what's to come on the wild and wonderful peninsulas further north. Remote fjords (in a smaller version here) twist along the coast, and though there's a new road being built to cut across their desolate isolation, its still a bare and dramatic place. It's the primary breeding area for the endangered white-tailed eagle.

The ferry to Stykkishólmur on the Snæfellsnes Peninsula arrives here, or you can enter by car from the historic Dalir region in west Iceland, taking you through deserted rolling hills and agricultural fields, then along salt-encrusted rocky bays.

Reykhólar & Around

Reykhólar sits on the southern edge of the Reykjanes Peninsula, a minor geothermal area and gateway to the southernmost section of the Westfjords. Gilsfjörður is an eagle breeding ground, and west along the coast, the key inlets for eagle spotting are: Þorskafjörður, Djúpifjörður, and Vatnsfjörður. There is no bus service to the area.

◎ Sights & Activities

White-Tailed Eagle Centre EXHIBITION
(☑894 1011; www.visitreykholahreppur.is; Króksifjarðarnes; ☉mid-Jun–mid-Aug) FREE The White-Tailed Eagle Centre highlights the attempts to increase the population of the struggling species, which peaked in 2011 at 66 nests. It also has a handicraft and flea market. The centre is just west of the causeway on Rte 60 that crosses Gilsfjörður.

Norður Salt LANDMARK
(www.nordursalt.com) Norður Salt, on the point in Reykhólar, processes sea salt from the local salt bays. You can peek in their windows.

Reykhólar Tourist Office Museum MUSEUM
(admission Ikr750; @☎) The well-managed tourist office (www.visitreykholahreppur.is; cafe snacks Ikr400-1000; ☉11am-5pm Jun-Aug) has a little museum with antique boats, stuffed birds and a movie of local life in the 1950s and '60s. There's a small onsite cafe with wi-fi and an internet terminal, plus lots of Westfjords information.

Reykhólar Sea Baths HOT-POT
(Sjávarsmiðjan; ☑577 4800; www.sjavarsmidjan.is; adult/child Ikr2900/1000; ☉1-5pm Thu-Sun Jun-Aug) In windswept Reykhólar, the seaweed baths give you soft skin and a view of the coastal plane, rimmed by salt bays.

🛏 Sleeping

Gistiheimilið Álftaland GUESTHOUSE €
(☑434 7878; www.alftaland.is; s/d Ikr11,500/15,500; ☎) Gistiheimilið Álftaland offers no-frills rooms, two soothing hot-pots out back, and a guest kitchen. Sleeping bag accommodation costs Ikr6000.

Hótel Bjarkalundur HOTEL €€
(☑434 7762; www.bjarkalundur.is; d with/without bathroom incl breakfast Ikr24,900/18,500; ☉May-Oct) On Rte 60, just north of the turn-off to Reykhólar, Hótel Bjarkalundur is a solid summer hotel in a large farmhouse, with a petrol station and a restaurant serving Icelandic grub (mains Ikr1700 to Ikr4500). Vaðalfjöll, the largest elf palace in the Westfjords (or so says the hotel owner), sits just north.

Djúpidalur to Vatnsfjörður

The 128km of stunningly desolate fjords between Þorskafjörður and Vatnsfjörður offer remote Iceland at its best. Look for eagles and relish the solitude. At the time of research, the finishing touches were just going in on paving the road from Kollafjörður to Vatnsfjörður, including a couple of causeways that bridge the fjords. The unpaved road from Þorskafjörður to Kollafjörður will remain rough (but open to 2WDs).

The Djúpidalur geothermal field lies 20km west of Bjarkalundur, on remote Djúpifjörður. Amazingly, the welcoming Guesthouse Djúpidalur (☑434 7853; djupidal@simnet.is; dm Ikr6000; ☉year-round), on a sheep farm, has the fjord to itself, and offers an indoor geothermal swimming pool (adult/child Ikr400/100; ☉8am-11pm) that's open to the public, plus good accommodation. Sleeping bag accommodation costs Ikr4000.

Flókalundur

Flókalundur, the junction between the road up to Arnarfjörður and Ísafjörður, and the bumpy Rte 62 to the southwestern peninsulas, sits at the head of Vatnsfjörður. The two-house encampment at Flókalundur was named after the Viking explorer Hrafna-Flóki Vilgerðarson, who gave Iceland its name in AD 860.

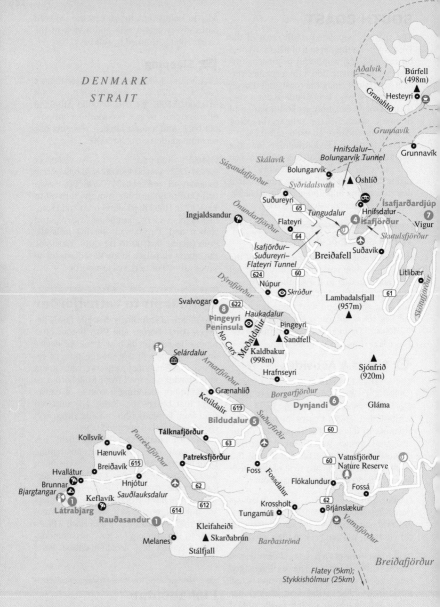

The Westfjords Highlights

❶ Watch tilting puffins swoop around crowded bird cliffs at **Látrabjarg** (p189), then explore the neighbouring rosy beach **Rauðasandur** (p188)

❷ Rove saw-toothed cliffs while spying on Arctic foxes in the **Hornstrandir Nature Reserve** (p200)

❸ Take in the wild serenity of the **Strandir Coast** (p203), stopping at charmingly

seductive Djúpavík before soaking in the waters at Krossneslaug

❹ Kayak the fjords, then tip back a local draught beer in **Ísafjörður** (p194), the

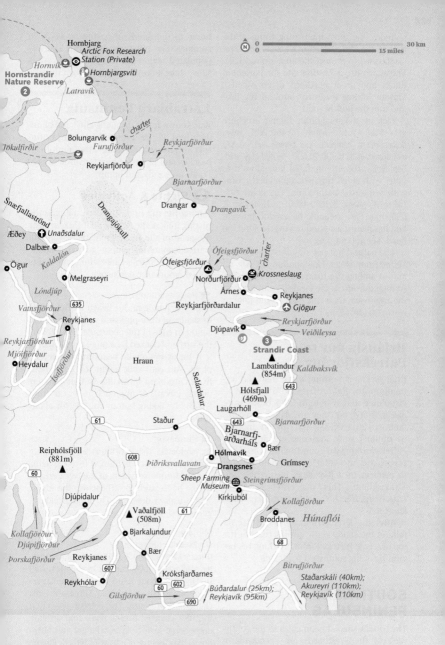

Hornbjarg
Arctic Fox Research
Station (Private)
Hornvík
Hornbjargsviti
Hornstrandir
Nature Reserve
2
Latravík

Jökulfirðir
Bolungarvík
Furufjörður
Reykjarfjörður
charter
Reykjarfjörður

Snæfjallaströnd
Drangajökull
Drangar
Drangavík
Æðey
Unaðsdalur
Kaldalón
Dalbær
Öfeigsfjörður
Ögur
Öfeigsfjörður
Melgraseyri
Norðurfjörður
Krossneslaug
Lóndjúp
Árnes
Reykjanes
Vatnsfjörður
635
Reykjarfjörðardalur
Gjögur
Reykjanes
Reykjarfjörður
Mjóifjörður
Djúpavík
Veiðileysa
Heydalur
Ísafjörður
Strandir Coast
3
Hraun
Lambatindur
(854m)
Kaldbaksvík
Selárdalur
Hólsfjall
(469m)
643
Staður
Laugarhóll
643
61
Bjarnarfj-
arðarháls
Bjarnarfjörður
Reiphólsfjöll
(881m)
Hólmavík
Bær
608
Þiðriksvallavatn
Drangsnes
Grímsey
60
Sheep Farming
Museum
Steingrímsfjörður
Djúpidalur
Vaðalfjöll
(508m)
61
Kirkjuból
Kollafjörður
Kollafjörður
Djúpifjörður
Bjarkalundur
Broddanes
Húnaflói
Þorskafjörður
Bær
68
Reykjanes
607
Króksfjarðarnes
Bitrufjörður
Reykhólar
60
602
Staðarskáli (40km);
Akureyri (110km);
Reykjavík (110km)
Gilsfjörður
690
Búðardalur (25km);
Reykjavík (95km)

0 ——————— 30 km
0 ——————— 15 miles

Westfjords' cosmopolitan
capital
5 Spook yourself with sea-
monster lore before heading
out to the tip of breathtaking
Arnarfjörður at **Bíldudalur**
(p191)

6 Let the mists of **Dynjandi**
(p191) pound down around
you as you climb its dizzying
cascades

7 Duel with Arctic terns on
Vigur island, learn about Arctic

foxes, or kayak by seals on vast
Ísafjarðardjúp (p199)

8 Bike the remote,
windswept track on **Þingeyri
Peninsula** (p193)

Today, the most interesting thing in the area is the **Vatnsfjörður Nature Reserve**, established to protect the area around Lake Vatnsdalsvatn, a nesting site for harlequin ducks and great northern divers (loons). Various **hiking trails** run around the lake and into the hills beyond.

Pick up a Vatnsfjörður hiking brochure at **Hótel Flókalundur** (☑ 456 2011; www.flokalundur.is; campsites per person Ikr1200, s/d incl breakfast Ikr16,700/21,600; ☺ mid-May–mid-Sep; ☎), a recently updated bungalow-style hotel with small tidy wood-panelled rooms with renovated bathrooms. The solid **restaurant** (mains Ikr1690-4800; ☺ 11am-2pm & 6-10pm) serves Icelandic basics and burgers and has plate glass windows overlooking the fjord. There's camping too.

The natural hot-pot **Hellulaug** lies about 500m from Hótel Flókalundur, off Rte 62 and in among the rocks near the seashore. At high tide, do as the locals do and jump in the frigid sea, then run back to the pool to warm up (38°C).

Brjánslækur to Patreksfjörður

Brjánslækur is nothing more than the terminus for the *Baldur* ferry (p175) from Stykkishólmur and Flatey. In 2014 buses were discontinued, but they are slated to recommence in 2015. One should run to Ísafjörður in summer only, and one should run to Patreksfjörður year-round (with a need for prebooking in winter). You should be able to connect to a Reykjavík bus service via Stykkishólmur. There may also be service to Látrabjarg. Check www.westfjords.is for the latest news.

After the ferry terminal, rugged Rte 62 follows the sandy coast until it reaches the top of scenic Patreksfjörður, marking the beginning of the southwest peninsulas.

SOUTHWEST PENINSULAS

The trident-shaped peninsulas in the southwest of the Westfjords are spectacularly scenic. It's a truly wild-feeling area, where white, black, red and pink beaches meet shimmering blue water, and towering cliffs and stunning mountains cleave the fjords. The region's most popular destination is Látrabjarg, a 12km stretch of cliffs that is

home to thousands of nesting seabirds in summer. The pitted roads in this sparsely populated region are rough and driving is slow – take a deep breath, you'll get there!

Látrabjarg Peninsula

Best known for its dramatic cliffs and abundant bird life, the remote Látrabjarg Peninsula also has wonderful deserted multihued beaches and plenty of long, leisurely walks. Roads are sandy and bumpy.

◉ Sights & Activities

Joining Rte 612 from Rte 62, you'll pass the rusting hulk of the fishing boat *Garðar* near the head of the fjord. From there you will start encountering empty, golden beaches, the airstrip at Sauðlauksdalur, and sights dotted around the peninsula.

★ **Rauðasandur**   BEACH
Stunning Rauðasandur beach stretches out in shades of deep pink and red sands on the southern edge of the peninsula. Pounded by the surf and backed by a huge azure lagoon, it is an exceptionally beautiful and serene place. You can walk along the coast path from Látrabjarg bird cliffs to Rauðasandur (about 20km), or approach it by car from Rte 612 by taking bumpy Rte 614 for about 10km.

★ **Breiðavík**   BEACH
At Breiðavík, the enormous and stunning golden-sand beach is framed by rocky cliffs and the turquoise waters of the bay. Certainly one of Iceland's best beaches, the idyllic spot is usually deserted. The large Breiðavík guesthouse is here.

Minjasafn Egils Ólafssonar Museum   MUSEUM
(Hnjótur Museum; ☑ 456 1511; www.hnjotur.is; Hnjótur; adult/child Ikr1000/free; ☺ 10am-6pm May-Aug)
In Hnjótur, about 10km west of Sauðlauksdalur, it's worth stopping at Minjasafn Egils Ólafssonar Museum. The eclectic collection includes salvaged fishing boats and displays on regional history from whaling and farming to 1947 footage of a trawler wreck. There's a basic cafe (snacks from Ikr450).

Hvallátur   BEACH
About 8km west of Breiðavík, the tiny hamlet of Hvallátur has a gorgeous white-sand beach, but no services.

★**Látrabjarg Bird Cliffs**   BIRDWATCHING

At the tip of the peninsula, the **Bjargtangar lighthouse**, Europe's westernmost point (if you don't count the Azores), comes into view and just up the slope you'll find the renowned Látrabjarg bird cliffs. Extending for 12km along the coast and ranging from 40m to 400m, the dramatic cliffs are mobbed by nesting seabirds in early summer and it's a fascinating place even for the most reluctant of twitchers. Unbelievable numbers of puffins, razorbills, guillemots, cormorants, fulmars, gulls and kittiwakes nest here from June to mid-August.

On calm days, seals are often seen basking on the skerries around the lighthouse. It's best bird viewing in the evening when birds return to their nests. Beware: there are no railings along the cliffs, so when winds are high, use caution.

Tours

Patreksfjörður tour operators offer guided birdwatching and hiking and can meet you on the peninsula.

Festivals

Rauðasandur Festival   MUSIC

(www.raudasandurfestival.is) Popular three-day early-July music festival with camping on the beach at Melanes.

Sleeping & Eating

Brunnar Camping   CAMPGROUND €

You can camp at Brunnar, about 2km before (northeast of) Látrabjarg bird cliffs. There are pit toilets but no reliable running water. Camping at the cliffs is prohibited.

Melanes Camping   CAMPGROUND €

(565 1041; campsites per person Ikr800; ☉ Jun–mid-Sep) A simple campground at Melanes sits back on the grass behind the Rauðasandur cove, 4km from the turn-off from Rte 614 to Rauðasandur. It offers running water and two flush toilets. It hosts the annual Rauðasandur festival (p189).

Breiðavík   GUESTHOUSE €€

(456 1575; www.breidavik.is; campsites per person Ikr1900, d with/without bathroom incl breakfast Ikr27,000/18,500; ☉ mid-May–mid-Sep; 🛜) Breiðavík guesthouse, located behind the incredible cream-coloured beach of the same name, has a bit of a lock on the accommodation market. Prices are stiff for what is offered: basic rooms, sleeping-bag accommodation (Ikr10,000) and camping. But the setting is sublime, and it sure is nice

to overnight on the peninsula. It also has facilities such as a laundry, a restaurant, a guest kitchen and a barbecue.

Hótel Látrabjarg   HOTEL €€

(456 1500; www.latrabjarg.com; Örlygshöfn; d with/without bathroom from Ikr27,00/21,500; ☉ mid-May–mid-Sep) This former boarding school has been converted into a comfortable hotel with plain, tasteful rooms and a restaurant. To get to the hotel, turn right onto Rte 615 just after the museum at Hnjótur and go about 3km.

Kirkjuhvammur   CAFE

(866 8129; Rauðasandur; snacks Ikr1000-2500; ☉ 1-6pm mid-Jun–Aug) There's a small cafe on a the farm called Kirkjuhvammur, just back from Rauðasandur. At low tide you can walk right down to the reef.

🛈 Getting There & Away

In 2014 buses were discontinued, but in 2015 they may begin running between Brjánslækur and Látrabjarg, and perhaps Rauðasandur. Check www.westfjords.is for the latest information. Otherwise, come by private car or tour.

Patreksfjörður

POP 662

The largest village in this part of the Westfjords, zippy little Patreksfjörður is a great jumping-off point for visits to the Látrabjarg Peninsula. The no-frills town has dramatic views to the bluffs and good services for those preparing to head out to more remote fjords.

🛈 PETROL & DRIVING

It's important to gas up when you have the chance throughout the Westfjords, because petrol stations can be few and far between.

➡ The Westfjords official tourist map shows the N1 petrol stations.

➡ Many of the stations have unmanned pumps; using these requires a credit card with a PIN.

➡ You can also buy N1 cards stocked with credit when you do find someone manning a full-service station. We recommend it, just in case your own credit card does not work in a pinch.

➡ Expect lots of unpaved, often rugged, but universally beautiful roads; most are accessible with a 2WD.

The town was named after St Patrick of Ireland, who was the spiritual guide of Örlygur Hrappson, the first settler in the area.

ⓖ Tours

★ Westfjords Adventures
HIKING TOUR, JEEP TOUR

(🖉 456 5006; www.westfjordsadventures.is; Aðalstræti 62) The area's top tour provider offers everything from birdwatching and hikes on the Látrabjarg Peninsula (from Ikr12,900 for eight hours) to day-long Jeep tours around the fjords (from Ikr19,900) or along the remote Kjaran's Avenue, a rough gravel track hewn into the fjord (Ikr28,900). It offers a menu of boat, whale-watching, and fishing tours (from Ikr6000) on Patreksfjörður, tours further afield, and rents bikes (two hours/per day Ikr2500/6000).

It also sells maps, gives advice, and books accommodation.

Umfar
HIKING TOUR

(🖉 892 9227; www.umfar.is) A hiking specialist, Umfar works with Westfjords Adventures on Látrabjarg Peninsula walks.

🛏 Sleeping

Patreksfjörður Camping
CAMPGROUND €

(Aðalstræti 107; campsites per person Ikr1300; ☉ Jun–mid-Sep) Municipal campground in a grassy field along the main fjord-side drag. Has showers and a kitchen.

Fox Hostel
HOTEL €

(🖉 892 3414; www.foxhostel.is; Aðalstræti 62; s/d Ikr11,600/15,600; 🖥) Opened in 2014, this hotel has bright, sunny rooms, some with fjord views, and private bathrooms, in a renovated co-op building.

Fosshótel Westfjords
HOTEL €€

(Fosshótel Vestfirðir; 🖉 456 2004; www.foss-hotel.is; Aðalstræti 100; s/d incl breakfast from Ikr26,200/29,400; 🖥) One of the town's historic buildings has been well-renovated into this hotel with modern rooms offering private baths, flat-screen TVs, and views to either the fjord or the mountain. There's a restaurant, too.

✕ Eating

Patreksfjörður is the best place to stock up on groceries or eat out before heading to more remote fjords.

★ Stúkuhúsið
CAFE €€

(🖉 456 1404; www.stukuhusid.is; Aðalstræti 50; mains Ikr1630-4690; ☉ 11am-11pm Jun-Aug, noon-4pm Wed-Sat Sep-May; 🖥🖉) This cool spot in an adorable, sunny little house with fjord views perches on the street running parallel to and above the water. It cooks up daily specials, soups, sandwiches and decadent pastries, and makes a mean cappuccino.

★ Heimsendi Bistro
INTERNATIONAL €€

(🖉 456 5150; Eyrargata 5; mains Ikr1590-4900; ☉ 4-9pm Sun-Wed, to 1am Thu & Fri, to 3am Sat Jun–mid-Sep; 🖥🖉) This brand new eatery in a mod, refurbished red-sided building down by the docks, whips up creative Icelandic dishes incorporating unexpected spices and techniques. The mood is fresh and open, with pallets for stairs and other found objects for decorations; the food is exceptional. It can get lively on summer nights, and decks fill when the sun is warm.

Vínbúðin
LIQUOR STORE €

(🖉 456 2244; Þórsgata 10; ☉ 2-6pm Mon-Thu, to 7pm Fri, 11am-2pm Sat Jun-Aug, reduced hours Sep-May) National liquor store chain.

ⓘ Getting There & Away

In 2014 buses were discontinued, but in 2015 they are expected to run from Patreksfjörður to Brjánslækur (1¼ hours) year-round, with connections to Reykjavík via Stykkishólmur. A 'Flybus' runs by request from Patreksfjörður to meet flights into Bíldudalur. Check www.westfjords.is for the latest information.

Westfjords Adventures is also a Europcar rental outlet.

Tálknafjörður

POP 278

Set amid rolling green hills, rocky peaks and a wide fjord, sleepy Tálknafjörður is a bit bland, but surrounded by magnificent scenery.

🏃 Activities

★ Pollurinn
GEOTHERMAL POOL

The cement-lined natural hot-pots (46°C) at Pollurinn (literally, The Puddle), 3.8km beyond the Tálknafjörður Swimming Pool along Rte 617, are signposted with a tiny white sign with black lettering. Backed by the mountains, the shallow pools look out on the broad sweep of the fjord.

Tálknafjörður Swimming Pool
GEOTHERMAL POOL, HOT-POT

(🖉 456 2639; www.talknafjordur.is; adult/child Ikr370/250; ☉ 10am-9pm Jun-Aug, 4-8pm Mon-Fri, 1-3pm Sat & Sun Sep-May) Fed by one of the few geothermal fields in the area, the Tálknafjörður Swimming Pool is the town's main hang-out. In summer, pool staffers provide tourist information. Ask here for the detailed hiking map, *Vestfirðir & Dalir 4* (and try the gorgeous 10km cairn-marked hike to Bíldudalur). Staff here also administer the local campground.

🛏 Sleeping

Tálknafjörður Campground CAMPGROUND €
(campsites per person Ikr1000; ⊘ Jun-Aug) This campground beside the swimming pool has laundry, cooking facilities and showers.

Guesthouse Bjarmaland GUESTHOUSE €
(☑ 891 8038; www.guesthousebjarmaland.is; Bugatún 8; d with/without bathroom Ikr15,600/13,000; 🖘) Spotless accommodation awaits at Guesthouse Bjarmaland, where sleeping-bag space costs Ikr3700.

✕ Eating

Hópið INTERNATIONAL €
(☑ 456 2777; Hrafnardalsvegur; mains Ikr1200-1400; ⊘ 11am-11pm Mon-Fri, to 1am Sat Jun-Aug, reduced hours Sep-May) Hópið is a low-key joint with a pool table. It serves burgers and basic Icelandic mains.

ℹ Getting There & Away

The Patreksfjörður–Bíldudalur 'Flybus' stops in Tálknafjörður; ask at the town's swimming pool for details. It only runs in conjunction with flights.

Bíldudalur

POP 171

Set on a gloriously calm bay surrounded by towering peaks, the attractive fishing village Bíldudalur (www.bildudalur.is) has one of the finest fjord-side positions in the country. Arriving by road from either direction, you're treated to spectacular views. Bíldudalur was founded in the 16th century and today is a major supplier of prawns.

The **Skrímslasetur Icelandic Sea Monster Museum** (☑ 456 6666; www.skrimsli.is; Strandgata 7; adult/child Ikr1000/free; ⊘ 11am-6pm), across from the church, has moody, fun, impressively elaborate and dramatic multimedia exhibits about local and foreign monster legends. The interactive multimedia table tells 180 stories of sightings around Arnarfjörður. While it's great for larger kids, wee ones might get freaked out (especially by the giant-sized models). It also has a small cafe.

Bíldudalur HI Hostel (Gistiheimilið Kaupfélagið; ☑ 456 2100; www.hostel.is; Hafnarbraut 2; dm/s/d with shared bathroom

NATURAL SPRINGS

At the head of tiny Reykjarfjörður, 23km southeast of Bíldudalur (in the direction of Rte 60), plan to stop at the glorious geothermal pools of **Reykjarfjarðarlaug**. Up front you have a concrete pool (32°C), in the back there's a natural, stone one (45°C), and all around are soaring seabirds, mountains and fjord views.

Ikr4100/6900/12,140), which was a harbour-front supermarket during the 1950s, provides super, immaculate accommodation. The inviting little spot has basic but squeaky-clean rooms and a nice kitchen. HI members discount Ikr700.

There's a small grocery and snack stand at the petrol station.

Eagle Air (☑ 562 4200; www.ernir.is) runs flights to/from Reykjavík (approximately Ikr25,800, 45 minutes, one daily) and **Bíldudalur Airport** (BIU), 8km south of town. **Flybuses** (☑ 893 2636) run on request to/from Patreksfjörður via Tálknafjörður to connect with flights. The closest car rentals are in Patreksfjörður and Ísafjörður.

CENTRAL PENINSULAS

Dynjandi

★ **Dynjandi** WATERFALL
Tumbling in a broad sweep over a 100m-rocky scarp at the head of Dynjandivogur bay, Dynjandi (Fjallfoss) is the most dramatic waterfall in the Westfjords. The bumpy drive to Dynjandi, from either direction, is famous in Iceland for its incredible views; you'll see how the falls are the catchment area for peaks and inland valleys all around.

In 2015 there is slated to be a bus between Ísafjörður and Brjánslækur, summer only, that should stop at Dynjandi. Check www.westfjords.is for the latest information.

Climbing up from the car park you'll pass many smaller falls until you reach the thundering main chute. You're allowed to approach the massive cascade as it plunges over the mountainside, and views over the broad fjord are spectacular.

The surrounding area is a protected nature reserve, but there's a free (albeit noisy) campground at the falls, with pit toilets and running water.

WORTH A TRIP

ARNARFJÖRÐUR & SELÁRDALUR

The drive out to the tip of Arnarfjörður, along Rte 619 beyond Bíldudalur, is absolutely magnificent. The tiny track rims soaring mountains, lush pastured valleys and untouched beaches, and looks onto the churning fjord and the incredible landscape on its northern side. Towards sunset and on partly cloudy days, the light shifts continually, and rainbows often form.

At the tip of the fjord (24km), local artist Samúel Jónsson lived out his remaining years at a remote farm in Selárdalur, and filled his days by creating a series of 'naive', cartoonlike sculptures. Visitors can peruse the surreal remains of his farm, now called **Samúel Jónsson's Art Museum** (admission by donation Ikr500). There's a flamboyant house, a circle of lions (created from a postcard Samúel saw of the Alhambra), an ornate church and Samúel's home.

Hrafnseyri to Þingeyri

Rutted Rte 60 joins the southern reaches of the Þingeyri Peninsula at farmstead Hrafnseyri, the birthplace (on 17 June 1811) of Jón Sigurðsson, the architect of Iceland's independence. The interesting, modern **Jón Sigurðsson Memorial Museum** (☑ 456 8260; www.hrafnseyri.is; adult/child Ikr800/free; ⊙ 10am-6pm Jun–early Sep) outlines his life and has a reconstruction of his turf house, a 19th-century church and a small cafe. It's on a beautiful point with fjord views.

Rte 60 between Hrafnseyri and Þingeyri is closed for six to eight months in winter. Check www.vegagerdin.is.

Þingeyri

POP 247

This tiny village, on the north side of the peninsula, was the first trading station in the Westfjords, but these days the world seems to have passed Þingeyri by. Although there's little to see here, the town is a good jumping-off point for hiking, biking and horse riding on Þingeyri Peninsula.

◎ Sights

Old Blacksmith's Workshop　　　MUSEUM
(adult/child Ikr800/free; ⊙ 9am-6pm mid-May–mid-Sep) The Old Blacksmith's Workshop in Þingeyri is part of Ísafjörður's Westfjords Heritage Museum (p194); the ticket includes admission to both sights.

☞ Tours

Eagle Fjord Tours　　　GUIDED TOUR
(☑ 894 1684; www.eaglefjord.is; ⊙ Jun-Sep) Small company runs tours around Þingeyri

(Ikr2900), sea-angling excursions (Ikr11,500) and boat outings.

🛏 Sleeping

Þingeyri Campsite　　　CAMPGROUND €
(campsites per tent Ikr1200; ⊙ mid-May–mid-Sep) The Þingeyri campground is behind the swimming pool.

Við Fjörðinn　　　GUESTHOUSE €
(☑ 456 8172; www.vidfjordinn.is; Aðalstræti 26; s/d without bathroom Ikr9,500/13,000) This friendly guesthouse has bright, cheerful rooms with simple decor and plain white linens. The sparkling bathrooms are shared, and there's a good guest kitchen and a TV lounge.

Sandafell　　　HOTEL €€
(☑ 456 1600; http://hotelsandafell.com; Hafnarstræti 7; d with/without bathroom incl breakfast Ikr24,500/16,100; ⊙ late May–early Sep) The straightforward Sandafell hotel and restaurant is down in the village centre.

✗ Eating

★**Simbahöllin**　　　CAFE €
(☑ 899 6659; www.simbahollin.is; Fjarðargata 5; snacks & mains Ikr600-2900; ⊙ 10am-10pm mid-Jun–mid-Aug, noon-6pm early Jun & late Aug) Simbahöllin is an unpretentious cafe with friendly baristas serving tasty Belgian waffles during the day and hearty lamb tagines at night. The welcoming bolthole rents high-quality mountain bikes (Ikr10,000 per day), and arranges horse-riding tours (from Ikr9500 for two hours).

ℹ Information

Þingeyri Tourist Office (☑ 456 8304; www. thingeyri.is; Hafnarstræti 6; ⊙ 10am-6pm Mon-Fri, 11am-6pm Sat & Sun Jun-Aug; @ 🤶) On the main road.

ℹ️ Getting There & Away

Municipal bus (📞 456 5518; www.isafjordur. is) services:
- Flateyri (Ikr350, 30 minutes, three daily Monday to Friday).
- Ísafjörður (Ikr350, 30 minutes, three daily Monday to Friday).

Starting in 2015, a daily bus (June to August) is scheduled to connect Ísafjörður and Brjánslækur (the terminal for the Stykkishólmur ferry), and it will stop in Þingeyri. Check www.westfjords.is for the latest information.

Þingeyri Peninsula

The Þingeyri Peninsula and its dramatic peaks offer spectacular hiking and biking. You can rent mountain bikes at Simbahöllin (p192) in Þingeyri and follow the dirt road that runs northwest along the eastern edge of the peninsula and along Dýrafjörður to the scenic valley at Haukadalur, an important Viking site. If landslides don't block the road, you can continue right around the peninsula, passing cliffs where birds perch and the remote lighthouse at Svalvogar. Do not attempt this track with a 2WD car – you will not make it.

Inland, the Westfjords' highest peak, Kaldbakur (998m), is a good hiking spot. The steep trail to the summit begins from the road about 2km west of Þingeyri town.

Dýrafjörður & Önundarfjörður

A series of gorgeous broad valleys stretch across the northern shore of Dýrafjörður. On bumpy track Rte 624, at the fjord-side edge of the valleys, there's a lovely weatherboard church and one of Iceland's oldest botanic gardens, Skrúður (⏰24hr) FREE, which was established as a teaching garden in 1905 and has arched whalebones at the entrance.

Beyond Skrúður, about 7km from Rte 60 along Rte 624, is Núpur Guesthouse (📞456 8235; www.hotelnupur.is; campsites per tent Ikr2500, d with/without bathroom incl breakfast Ikr23,600/17,000; ⏰mid-May–mid-Sep), where brothers Siggi and Gummi have done their darnedest to turn this former schooling complex into desirable digs. Sleeping-bag accommodation costs Ikr4500, and there's a guest kitchenette. In 2015 a daily bus (June to August) is scheduled to connect Ísafjörður and Brjánslækur, the ferry terminal for Stykkishólmur; it can stop at the Núpur turn-off on request. Check www.westfjords.is for the latest information.

After Núpur Guesthouse, Rte 624 passes an abandoned farmhouse before swerving inland to head over the top of the rugged peninsula. It takes about 20 minutes by car to reach Ingjaldsandur at the mouth of Önundarfjörður. Set in a picturesque valley, this isolated beach is a fantastic spot to watch the midnight sun as it flirts with the sea before rising back up into the sky.

Back on Rte 60, near upper Önundarfjörður, is a marked turn-off for Kirkjuból (📞456 7679; www.kirkjubol.is; d with/without bathroom incl breakfast Ikr20,000/14,300; ⏰Jun-Aug; 🏠). The lovely, remote white-and-green farmstead is squeaky-clean inside, with rooms sporting some antiques, a guest kitchen and a living room.

A second turn-off further north (also marked Kirkjuból!) leads 5km to the popular Korpudalur HI Hostel (Korpudalur Kirkjuból; 📞456 7808; www.korpudalur.is; campsites per tent Ikr1300, dm/d with shared bathroom from Ikr4800/12,400; ⏰mid-May–mid-Sep; 🏠). The stunning location at the fjord-head, homemade breakfast bread, and cottages out back make this 100-year-old farmhouse well worth visiting. HI members discount Ikr700. Pickups are available from Ísafjörður for Ikr1500.

In 2015 a daily bus (June to August) is scheduled to connect Ísafjörður and Brjánslækur, the ferry terminal for Stykkishólmur; it can stop at the Kirkjuból junctions on request. Check www.westfjords.is for the latest information.

Flateyri

POP 204

Once a giant support base for Norwegian whalers, Flateyri is now a dull little place set on a striking gravel spit sticking out into broad Önundarfjörður. There is little of interest to tourists besides the beautiful scenery and the Nonsense Museum (📞894 8836; Hafnarstræti 11; admission Ikr700; ⏰12.30-5pm Jun-Aug), which contains the private collections of several locals. You'll find hundreds of pens, matchboxes and model ships showcased in pathologically organised displays.

Iceland ProFishing (📞456 6667; www.icelandprofishing.com; Hafnarstræti 9; ⏰Apr-Sep) is based here, renting boats for angling trips around the fjords (guides can be hired) and offering multiday trips with lodging in Suðureyri.

Municipal buses (📞456 5518; www.isafjordur.is) travel between Ísafjörður, Flateyri and

Þingeyri (Ikr350, 30 minutes, three daily Monday through Friday). To be picked up in Flateyri, call ahead or the bus may not drive into the village. In 2015 a daily bus (June to August) is scheduled to connect Ísafjörður and Brjánslækur, the ferry terminal for Stykkishólmur; it can stop in Flateyri on request. Check www.westfjords.is for the latest information.

Suðureyri

POP 271

Perched on the tip of 13km-long Súgandafjörður, the fishing community of Suðureyri (www.sudureyri.is) was isolated for years by the forbidding mountains. Now connected with Ísafjörður and Flateyri by a 9km tunnel network (p194), the village is a natural stop for anglers; its waters are the best place in Iceland to catch halibut. The local **hot-pots and pool** (☑450 8490; Túngata 8; adult/child Ikr600/300; ⏰10am-8pm Mon-Fri, to 6pm Sat & Sun Jun-Aug, reduced hours Sep-May) are a popular hang-out.

👉 Tours

Iceland ProFishing (p193) in Flateyri also fishes from Suðureyri.

Fisherman　　　　　　　　　　FISHING TOUR
(☑450 9000; www.fisherman.is) The Fisherman hotel-restaurant complex promotes the life of the fishing village with rod rental, visits to the local fish factory (Ikr1500), the chance to join a working trawler (Ikr22,900) and more.

🛌 Sleeping

Fisherman Hotel　　　　　　　HOTEL €€
(☑450 9000; www.fisherman.is; Aðalgata 14; campsites per person Ikr1500, d with/without bathroom incl breakfast Ikr21,900/16,500; @ 🖝) This friendly hotel has bright rooms, crisp linens, pine furniture and a top seafood restaurant, Talisman (mains Ikr3700-4900; ⏰6-9pm).

🔒 Shopping

Á Milli Fjalla　　　　　　　　HANDICRAFTS
(☑456 6163; Aðalgata; ⏰1-6pm Mon-Fri, 1-4pm Sat & Sun Jul & Aug) An intriguing boutique selling locally crafted knits, ceramics and unique trinkets. Apparently Björk likes to shop here.

ℹ Getting There & Away

Municipal buses (www.isafjordur.is) service:
➡ Suðureyri (Ikr350, 20 minutes, three daily Monday to Friday).

Ísafjörður

POP 2527

Hub of Westfjords adventure tours, and by far the region's largest town, Ísafjörður (www.isafjordur.is) is a pleasant and prosperous place and an excellent base for travellers. The town is set on an arcing spit that extends out into Skutulsfjörður, and is hemmed in on all sides by towering peaks and the dark waters of the fjord.

The centre of Ísafjörður is a charming grid of old timber and tin-clad buildings, many unchanged since the 18th century, when the harbour was full of tall ships and Norwegian whaling crews. Today it is a surprisingly cosmopolitan place, and after some time spent travelling in the Westfjords, it'll feel like a bustling metropolis with its tempting cafes and fine choice of restaurants.

There's hiking in the hills around the town, skiing in winter, and regular summer boats ferry hikers across to the remote Hornstrandir Peninsula.

⦿ Sights & Activities

Ísafjörður's formal attractions are thin on the ground. Of minor interest is the **whalebone arch** made from a whale's jawbone in the central town park, the nearby **seamen's monument** and the modernist **church**. The altarpiece has over 100 doves, each made by a local during a group art project.

★**Westfjords Heritage Museum**　　MUSEUM
(Byggðasafn Vestfjarða; ☑456 3293; www.nedsti.is; Neðstíkaupstaður; adult/child Ikr800/free; ⏰9am-6pm mid-May–mid-Sep) Part of a cluster of historic wooden buildings by the harbour, the Westfjords Heritage Museum is in the **Turnhús** (1784) which was originally a warehouse. It is crammed with fishing and nautical exhibits, tools from the whaling days, fascinating old photos depicting town life over the centuries, and accordions. To the right is the **Tjöruhús** (1781), now a pleasant seafood restaurant. The **Faktorhús** (1765), which housed the manager of the village shop, and the **Krambúd** (1757), originally a storehouse, are now private residences.

The museum ticket is also good for the Old Blacksmith's Workshop (p192) in Þingeyri.

★**Ísafjörður–**
Suðureyri–Flateyri Tunnel　　LANDMARK
(Vestfjarðagöng) ⒻⓇⒺⒺ Completed in 1996, this 9km-long tunnel network beneath the mountains becomes an unusual one-lane tunnel

Ísafjörður

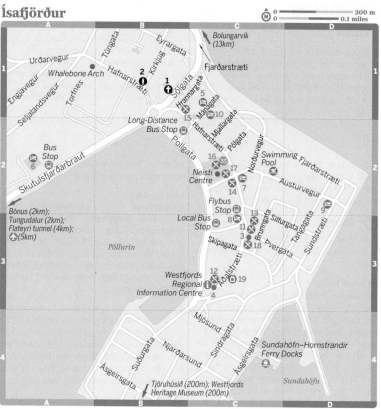

Ísafjörður

in parts of the 6km stretch from Ísafjörður to Flateyri. In the middle of the mountain it branches, and a 3km section of tunnel shoots off to Suðureyri. Worry not, pull-outs throughout allow oncoming traffic to alternate as they ride through the damp chutes.

Path Towards Óshlíð HIKING, CYCLING

A precarious path leads around the point from Ísafjörður toward Bolungarvík and the mountain Óshlíð. The teeny dangerous track, which is prone to rock falls and avalanches, used to be the only route to

WORTH A TRIP

VIGUR

With one farm and scads of puffins, charming Vigur is a popular destination for day trippers from Ísafjörður. The tiny island sits at the mouth of Hestfjörður, offering sweeping fjord views in every direction. There's not much to do on the island besides taking a stroll (grab a stick from the windmill and hold it over your head – the Arctic terns are fierce here!), visiting the eider ducks and savouring cakes at the cafe. Look out for the interesting egg collection inside.

West Tours in Ísafjörður and Ögur Travel (p200) in Ögur run tours and boats to the island.

Bolungarvík. If you use caution, you can walk or cycle along the bit nearest the tunnel to Bolungarvík and see Hornstrandir and Snafjallaströnd in the distance.

☞ Tours

Both West Tours and Borea run regular ferry services to Hornstrandir Nature Reserve (p200).

★ **West Tours**　　　　　ADVENTURE TOUR
(Vesturferðir; ☑ 456 5111; www.vesturferdir.is; Aðalstræti 7; ⊙ 8am-6pm Mon-Fri, 8.30am-4.30pm Sat, 10am-3pm Sun Jun-Aug, 9am-5pm Sep-May) Popular, professional West Tours organises a mind-boggling array of trips throughout the Westfjords. There are tours of Vigur (Ikr8900), hiking in Hornstrandir (Ikr9600 to Ikr37,900) and kayaking trips (Ikr9900 to Ikr25,900). Biking, horse riding, boat and angling tours, birdwatching and cultural excursions are but a few of the other activities on offer.

Housed in the same building as the tourist information centre, it also runs ferries to Hornstrandir and rents scooters (two hours/per day Ikr4000/8000) and bicycles (four hours/per day Ikr3000/5000).

★ **Borea**　　　　KAYAKING TOUR, HIKING TOUR
(☑ 456 3322; www.borea.is; Aðalstræti 22b; ⊙ 8am-10pm) Borea is an adventure outfitter offering fjord kayaking (from Ikr9900) and excellent hiking in Hornstrandir (from Ikr16,900). It also runs ferry services from Bolungarvík to Hornstrandir and operates Kviar, its private cabin in the reserve. Its base is at Bræðraborg cafe.

☷ Sleeping

Litla Guesthouse　　　　　GUESTHOUSE €
(☑ 893 6993; www.guesthouselitla.is; Sundstræti 43; s/d without bathroom Ikr14,000/15,000; ☎) Wooden floors, crisp white linen, fluffy towels and TVs are available in the high-quality rooms of Litla, a cosy guesthouse with tasteful decor. Two rooms share each bathroom, and there's a guest kitchen.

Mánagisting Guesthouse　　　GUESTHOUSE, APARTMENTS €
(Gistiheimilið Mánagisting; ☑ 615 2014; www.simnet.is/managisting; Mánagata 4; d without bathroom Ikr11,200, studio Ikr15,000; ☎) Simple shared rooms line the halls of this no-frills guesthouse with kitchens and sitting rooms. But the studios with bathroom and kitchen are the real deals.

Tungudalur Campground　　　CAMPGROUND €
(☑ 864 8592; www.gih.is; sites per person Ikr1300; ⊙ mid-Jun–mid-Sep; ☎) This campground is almost 5km out of town and very scenic, set by a pretty waterfall, Bunarfoss, in Tungudalur. The last stop on the town bus will take you to within 1km of the site. Coin laundry.

★ **Gamla Gistihúsið**　　　　GUESTHOUSE €€
(☑ 456 4146; www.gistihus.is; Mánagata 5; dm Ikr5100, s/d without bathroom incl breakfast Ikr16,000/20,000; ☎) Bright, cheerful and impeccably kept, this excellent guesthouse has simple but comfortable rooms with plenty of cosy touches. The bathrooms are shared, but each double room has telephone, washbasin and bathrobes. An annexe just down the road has a guest kitchen and more modern rooms.

Hótel Horn　　　　　　　HOTEL €€
(☑ 456 4611; www.hotelhorn.is; Austurvegi 2; s/d/f Ikr20,000/23,000/30,500; ☎ ⊕) This big new hotel in the centre offers basic rooms with private bathrooms. Family rooms sleep five and also have a kitchenette.

Hótel Edda　　　　HOTEL, CAMPGROUND €€
(☑ 444 4960; www.hoteledda.is; Mantaskólinn; d with/without bathroom Ikr21,700/15,200; ⊙ mid-Jun–mid-Aug) No-frills summer accommodation is available at the town's secondary school. Choose from basic sleeping-bag accommodation (Ikr5000) in the classrooms, or rooms with shared or private bathrooms.

Gentle Space APARTMENTS €€
(☑ 892 9282; www.gentlespace.is; apt Ikr21,500-24,900) Rents immaculate, fully equipped apartments in the centre.

Hótel Ísafjörður BUSINESS HOTEL €€€
(☑ 456 4111; www.hotelisafjordur.is; Silfurtorg 2; s/d from Ikr25,000/30,500; @ ⑦) The rooms on the higher floors in this central, classic business hotel have great views over the tin-roofed town and the waters beyond.

✕ Eating & Drinking

Bræðraborg CAFE €
(www.borea.is; Aðalstræti 22b; mains Ikr1190-1590; ⊙9am-7pm Mon-Sat, 10am-5pm Sun Jun-Aug, reduced hours Sep-May; ⑦⌘) Bræðraborg is a comfy travellers' cafe where people munch on healthy snacks and chat with other visitors. The cafe is the headquarters for Borea tours.

★Húsið INTERNATIONAL €€
(☑ 456 5555; Hrannargata 2; mains Ikr1290-2990; ⊙11am-10pm Sun-Thu, to 1am Fri & Sat; ⑦) Sidle up to the varnished, rough-hewn wood tables inside this tin-clad house, or kick back on the sunny terrace for scrumptious, relaxed meals or local beer on tap. Groovy tunes play as hip staff sling soup, sandwiches, burgers, pizza and Icelandic staples such as lamb. It's a fun hang-out regardless of what you're up to, and there are occasional DJs and live music.

★Tjöruhúsið SEAFOOD €€
(☑ 456 4419; Neðstakaupstaður 1; mains Ikr2500-5000; ⊙noon-2pm & 6.30-10pm Jun-Sep, reduced hours Oct-May) The warm and rustic restaurant next to the heritage museum offers some of the best seafood around. Go for the *plokkfiskur* (flaked fish, potatoes and onions) or try the catch of the day, fresh off the boat from the harbour down the street.

Edinborg CAFE €€
(☑ 456 8335; Aðalstræti 7; mains Ikr2000-3500; ⊙11.30am-10pm Jun-Aug, noon-9pm Sep-May; ⑦) In the same building as the tourist office, this relaxed spot attracts travellers who stop by for beer or coffee on the sunny patio. The house bread is made with a special recipe that incorporates beer. The owners also run Núpur Guesthouse (p193), a couple of fjords south.

Thai Koon THAI €€
(Hafnarstræti 9, Neisti Centre; mains Ikr1690-1890; ⊙11.30am-10pm Mon-Fri, noon-10pm Sat, 5-10pm Sun) After a stretch of limited food options in remote Iceland, this small Thai canteen seems decidedly exotic. There's no grand ambience but the curries and noodles are reliably tasty and served up in heaping portions.

Við Pollinn ICELANDIC, SEAFOOD €€
(☑ 456 3360; www.vidpollinn.is; Silfurtorg 2; mains Ikr3300-4900; ⊙7-10am, 11.30am-2pm & 6-9pm or 10.30pm) Although the decor feels a bit bland, Hótel Ísafjörður's restaurant has an excellent selection of local cuisine prepared with flair. The windows offer great views over the fjord – you might even see your next meal getting hauled into the harbour.

Hamraborg FAST FOOD €€
(Hafnarstraeti 7; mains Ikr1000-2790; ⊙9am-11.30pm; ⑦) Voted Iceland's best fast-food joint by national radio polls, this outpost of burgers and pizza attracts locals who gossip over Béarnaise burgers. Sport frequently plays on the TV.

Self-Catering

Ísafjörður is the place to stock up before heading to remote areas.

Gamla Bakaríð BAKERY €
(Aðalstræti 24; ⊙7am-6pm Mon-Fri, to 5pm Sat, 8am-5pm Sun) For breakfast, lunch or a mid-morning sugar fix, there's a clutch of tempting bakeries in town. Gamla Bakaríð offers a full range of sweet treats (biscuits, doughnuts and cakes) as well as fresh bread.

Bónus SUPERMARKET €
(⊙11am-6.30pm Mon-Thu, 10am-7.30pm Fri, 10am-6pm Sat, noon-6pm Sun) Moderately priced Bónus supermarket is on the main road into town.

Samkaup SUPERMARKET €
(Hafnarstræti; ⊙10am-8pm Mon-Sat, noon-8pm Sun) In the Neisti Centre on Hafnarstræti.

Vínbúðin LIQUOR STORE €
(☑ 456 3455; Aðalstræti 20; ⊙11am-6pm Mon-Thu, to 7pm Fri, to 4pm Sat Jun-Aug, reduced hours Sep-May) National liquor chain.

🛍 Shopping

Rammagerð Ísafjarðar ARTS & CRAFTS
(☑ 456 3041; Aðalstræti 16; ⊙1-5pm) Rammagerð Ísafjarðar sells quality knitting and other local crafts.

ℹ Information

Westfjords Regional Information Centre
(☑ 450 8060; www.isafjordur.is; Aðalstræti 7, Edinborgarhús; ⊙8am-6pm Mon-Fri, 8.30am-2pm Sat, 10am-2pm Sun Jun-Aug, reduced

THE WESTFJORDS ÍSAFJÖRÐUR

hours Sep-May; @) By the harbour in the **Edinborgarhús** (1907), helpful staff have loads of info on the Westfjords and Hornstrandir Reserve. Internet terminal with free 10-minute session; luggage storage Ikr200 per day.

❶ Getting There & Away

AIR

Air Iceland (✉ 456 3000; www.airiceland.is) flies between **Ísafjörður Airport** (IFJ; ✉ 570 3000), 5km south on the fjordm and Reykjavik twice daily. It also offers day tours.

A Flybus (see below), timed to meet flights, runs between the airport and Bolungarvík (Ikr1500), and stops near the Hótel Ísafjörður (Ikr1000).

BOAT

In summer, West Tours ferries to Hornstrandir (p203) depart from the Sundahöfn docks on the eastern side of the isthmus. Borea ferries to Hornstrandir (p203) depart from Árbæjarkantur pier in Bolungarvík.

BUS

Ísafjörður is the major bus hub in the Westfjords. The **long-distance bus stop** (www.westfjords.is) is at the N1 petrol station on Hafnarstræti. In 2014 long-distance buses were discontinued, but buses to/from Hólmavík are slated to run year-round in 2015, and summer-only to/from Brjánslækur (Stykkishólmur ferry terminal) via Þingeyri and Dynjandi. Both Hólmavík and Brjánslækur buses should have transfers to Reykjavik. Hólmavík may have a transfer to Akureyri.

Municipal buses (✉ 456 5518; www.isafjordur.is) services all stop along the waterfront.

➡ Ísafjörður, Flateyri and Þingeyri (Ikr350, three daily Monday to Friday).

➡ Suðureyri (Ikr350, 20 minutes, three daily Monday to Friday).

➡ Súðavík (Ikr1000, 20 minutes, Monday to Friday; you must reserve the day before).

➡ Bolungarvík (Ikr1000, 15 minutes, three daily Monday to Friday).

Flybuses (Airport–Ísafjörður Ikr1000; Ísafjörður–Bolungarvík Ikr1000; Airport–Bolungarvík Ikr1500), keyed to Icelandair flights (but anyone can use them), run Bolungarvík–Ísafjörður–Airport–Ísafjörður–Bolungarvík. In Ísafjörður they stop near the Hótel Ísafjörður.

Check with the tourist office or www.westfjords.is on all buses, as the situation is in flux.

CAR

For ridesharing check www.bilfar.is.

Avis (✉ 591 4000; www.avis.is; Ísafjörður Airport)

Europcar (✉ 840 6074; www.holdur.is; Ísafjörður Airport)

Hertz (✉ 522 4490; www.hertz.is; Ísafjörður Airport)

❶ Getting Around

City buses (Ikr350) operate from 7.30am to 6.30pm on weekdays (until 10.30pm in winter) and connect the town centre with Hnífsdalur and Tungudalur; they stop along the waterfront.

West Tours (p196) rents bikes and scooters.

Bolungarvík

POP 933

Despite its stunningly dramatic position at the end of the fjord, Bolungarvík is run-down and uninspiring. It has a couple of cool sights, though, and is a good place from which hikers can launch into the Hornstrandir Reserve. Bolungarvík used to be connected to Ísafjörður by a perilous track (p195) around the mountain Óshlíð, but now there is a 5.4km tunnel, and the other path is unused.

◉ Sights

★**Ósvör Maritime Museum**   MUSEUM
(Ósvör Sjóminjasafn; ✉ 892 5744; www.osvor.is; adult/child Ikr950/free; ⊙9am-5pm Mon-Fri, 10am-5pm Sat & Sun Jun-Aug, by appointment Sep-May) Ósvör Maritime Museum, housed in a series of old turf-and-stone fishing shacks, down a turn-off just after the tunnel into town, is well worth a visit. A guide in a typical lambskin fisherman's outfit shows you round (his English isn't tops), explaining the history of the area and traditional seafaring life from Settlement to the era of plastics. The cramped fishermen's hut is full of interesting relics. A traditional rowing boat is also on display.

Natural History Museum   MUSEUM
(✉ 456 7507; www.nabo.is; Vitastígur 3; adult/child Ikr950/free; ⊙9am-5pm Mon-Fri, 10am-5pm Sat & Sun Jun–mid-Aug, 9am-5pm Mon-Fri mid-Aug–May) In the town's main shopping arcade, the Natural History Museum has a comprehensive collection of minerals (lignite from when Iceland was covered in forests) and taxidermied animals – including a giant blue whalebone more than 100 years old and a polar bear shot by local fishermen while swimming off the Hornstrandir coast.

⊨ Sleeping

★**Einarshúsið**   GUESTHOUSE €€
(✉ 456 7901; www.einarshusid.is; Hafnargata 41; d with shared bathroom incl breakfast Ikr16,900; ⊙May-Sep, restaurant 11am-10pm) Einarshúsið is a turn-of-the-century heritage home on the harbour, and the best place to eat and sleep rolled into one. Super-friendly owners

dote on guests, who gorge on tasty seafood (mains Ikr1500 to Ikr4200) or spend the night in five lovely rooms upstairs, decorated in the house's original style (circa 1902), but with modern bathrooms.

❶ Getting There & Away

BUS

Buses (www.bolungarvik.is) service:
➜ Ísafjörður (Ikr1000, three daily Monday to Friday).

Flybus (Ísafjörður–Bolungarvík Ikr1000; Airport–Bolungarvík Ikr1500) Flybuses to Ísafjörður Airport are keyed to flights.

FERRY

Borea's ferry service (p203) to Hornstrandir departs from Árbæjarkantur pier in Bolungarvík.

Vaxon (☑ 862 2221; www.vaxon.is) Vaxon boat charter can also take you to Hornstrandir or around the fjords.

Ísafjarðardjúp

The largest of the fjords in the region, 75km-long Ísafjarðardjúp takes a massive swathe out of the Westfjords' landmass. Circuitous Rte 61 winds in and out of a series of smaller fjords on the southern side, making the drive from Ísafjörður to Hólmavík like sliding along each tooth of a fine comb.

Súðavík

POP 171

Just east of Ísafjörður, the small fishing community of Súðavík commands an imposing view across the fjord to Snæfjallaströnd peninsula. Although the township is nothing more than a string of bright, box-shaped houses, it is definitely worth stopping to visit the **Arctic Fox Center** (Melrakkasetur; ☑ 456 4922; www.arcticfoxcenter.com; adult/child Ikr900/free; ⊙ 9am-8pm Jun-Aug, 10am-5pm May & Sep, reduced hours Oct-Apr; ☎). The study of the Arctic fox has been under way on nearby Hornstrandir for years, and the locally loved exhibition centre details the life of the local fox and its relationship with humans and its habitat. Don't forget to play with the orphaned fox(es) in the pen outside.

The centre sits inside the renovated farmstead of Eyrardalur – one of the oldest buildings in the area. Even if foxes aren't your bag, the on-site **Fox Cafe** (soup Ikr1400-1800), staffed by volunteers, is a great place to hang out with welcoming locals – try the daily soup, which comes with home-made bread.

In 2015, the Ísafjörður–Hólmavík bus will stop in Súðavík (Ísafjörður–Súðavík Ikr1000, 20 minutes, Monday to Friday); check www.westfjords.is for the latest information.

Skötufjörður

⭐ **Litlibær** CAFE €
(☑ 456 4809; Skötufjörður; waffles & coffee Ikr1000; ⊙ 10am-5pm Jun-Aug) Litlibær is a cafe with interesting memorabilia set up in an historic 19th-century farmstead on Skötufjörður. The owner was born and raised on the land, and these days his family dotes on weary tourists, offering tasty

---

VOLUNTEERING AT THE ARCTIC FOX RESEARCH STATION

Trying to find an excuse to extend your Icelandic vacation? Look no further than the Arctic Fox Research Station, situated on the northern cliffs of the jaw-dropping Hornstrandir Peninsula – a photographer's Eden and naturalist's dream.

The research station at Hornbjarg is quite informal – just a cluster of tents and an outhouse. Each day from June to August, the team of researchers/volunteers sets off for six-hour viewing shifts during which they monitor fox behaviours and changes in location. There's a lot of sitting and looking involved, but we can't think of a more stunning location to take in the views.

There are no requirements for becoming a volunteer, but applications are competitive and preference is given to those studying biology, conservation science or photography. Volunteers are asked to give at least one week of their time. You'll also need to pay for your own transport and have the usual trappings of an outdoor adventure: tent, hiking boots, thermal sleeping bag and clothing appropriate for negative temperatures. The research centre will handle food and cooking equipment.

You can also volunteer at the Arctic Fox Center headquarters in cosy Súðavík, near Ísafjörður. Staff working here must spend a minimum of two weeks, and run the coffee house plus care for any orphaned foxes on site. Volunteers are offered free food and camping, with a common kitchen and bathroom.

heart-shaped waffles, coffee and tips on spotting the seals and Celtic ruins nearby. After filling your belly, scout out the picnic table about 200m north – they've set out a small box with binoculars for viewing the blubbery beasts.

Ögur

Ögur Travel　　　　　　　ADVENTURE TOURS
(☑857 1840; www.ogurtravel.com; ☺May-Sep) Book ahead to join Ögur Travel, run by seven siblings, on kayaking or hiking trips (from Ikr5000) for a few hours or a few days. A popular kayak is the seven-hour tour of Vigur island (Ikr22,000), which takes in the incredible scenery and local bird life. Tours run from their cute, welcoming **cafe** (snacks Ikr800-1900; ☺10am-6pm Jun-Aug) on the point just east of Skötufjörður. If you're coming from Ísafjörður and reach the field of abandoned cars, you've gone too far.

Mjóifjörður

Heydalur　　　　　　　GUESTHOUSE €€
(☑456 4824; www.heydalur.is; Mjóifjörður; sites per person Ikr1200, s/d from Ikr11,050/15,100, cabins from Ikr19,500; ☏) Heydalur is a good place to break up the journey along Rte 61 as it wiggles along the undulating coast. At the head of Mjóifjörður, 11km from the main road, Heydalur is run by affable Stella, who cooks up delicious meals in the **restaurant** (mains Ikr1800 to Ikr4000; 8am to 10pm June to August) in a restored barn.

Say hello to the parrot (he'll say hello back!) while savouring excellent soups, home-made breads, organic veggies and the popular lamb curry. Local activities include guided horse riding (Ikr5250 per hour) and kayaking (Ikr6300 for 2½ hours).

Reykjarfjörður

At the end of tiny Reykjarfjörður **Hótel Reykjanes** (☑456 4844; www.hotelreykjanes. is; campsites per tent Ikr2400, s/d with shared bathroom Ikr9900/13,800; @☏) is housed in a huge white complex that was once the district's school. Best only if you can't drive any further, rooms here are basic (most bathrooms shared), but there's a 50m outdoor **geothermal pool** (adult/child Ikr400/250) fed by a steamy spring. Sleeping bag accommodation costs Ikr4600. Simple meals cost Ikr1100 to Ikr4000. Ask about **Salt-verk Reykjanes** (www.saltverk.com), the salt-

producing atelier 200m away. There's also **Reykjanes' old pool**, built in 1889, a second massive pool hidden on a hill.

Snæfjallaströnd

On the eastern shore of Ísafjarðardjúp, the unsurfaced Rte 635 leads north to **Kaldalón**, where a beautiful green valley runs up to the receding **Drangajökull** ice cap. It's possible to hike up to the snow line, but don't venture any further without a local guide, as dangerous crevasses form in the ice and are often invisible under the snow pack.

Further north, **Snæfjallaströnd** was abandoned in 1995, but adventurous hikers can walk along the 'Postal Road' from the church at Unaðsdalur along the coast to the bunkhouse at **Grunnavík**, from where you can catch boats to Ísafjörður and Hesteyri.

Just before the church at Unaðsdalur, **Dalbær** (☑898 9300; www.snjafjallasetur.is/tourism. html; ☺mid-Jun–Aug) is a great wilderness outpost on the edge of Hornstrandir with sleeping bag accommodation and camping.

HORNSTRANDIR

Craggy mountains, precarious sea cliffs and plunging waterfalls ring the wonderful, barely inhabited Hornstrandir Peninsula, at the northern end of the Westfjords. This is one of Europe's last true wilderness areas, covering some of the most extreme and inhospitable parts of the country. It's a fantastic destination for hiking, with challenging terrain and excellent opportunities for spotting Arctic foxes, seals, whales and teeming bird life.

A handful of hardy farmers lived in Hornstrandir until the 1950s, but since 1975 the 580 sq km of tundra, fjord, glacier and alpine upland have been protected as **Hornstrandir Nature Reserve** (☑591 2000; www. ust.is/hornstrandir) and are a national monument. The area has some of the strictest preservation rules in Iceland, thanks to its incredibly rich, but fragile, vegetation. Descendants of some of the old farmers have recently returned and rebuilt their old houses; much of the land is privately owned (so always ask permission before fishing or camping if a place looks inhabited).

Weather & Gear

There are no services available in Hornstrandir and hikers must be fully prepared to tackle all eventualities. The passes are steep,

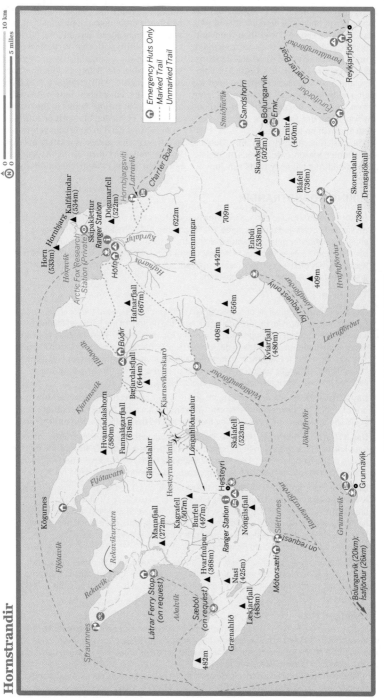

Hornstrandir

heavy rains will make rivers impassable, fog can be dense, and you'll need to carry all your gear, so hiking can be slower than you might expect. In addition, most trails are unmarked, primitive and uneven, so it's essential to carry a good map (try *Vestfirðir & Dalir:* 1), a compass, and a GPS. Rangers stress the need for high-quality, completely weatherproof gear as you will often be hiking in rain, without any way to get dry. Don't force a rescue operation due to ill preparation.

The best time to visit is in July. Outside the summer season (which runs from late June to mid-August; ferry boats run June to August) there are few people around and the weather is even more unpredictable. It is essential to plan ahead and get local advice, as vast snow drifts with near-vertical faces can develop on the mountain passes, rivers can be unfordable, etc. Before 15 June it is mandatory to register with a **ranger** (☑ 591 2000).

There are emergency huts with radios and heaters at various points in the park for use in case of sudden blizzards or storms.

You always need to book your return boat in advance; this serves as a safety measure, in case you don't turn up for it. Ask local operators about current conditions before

HIKING HORNSTRANDIR

How is one supposed to choose from the array of trails that zigzag across Hornstrandir's peninsula? Locals and tourists agree: the Royal Horn (or 'Hornsleið') is, hands down, your best option for getting a taste of all that the reserve has to offer. This four-to-five-day hike from Veiðileysufjörður to Hesteyri can also be easily modified if you run into bad weather. Trails on this route are clearly marked, but there are very few tourists, so it's a great way to experience this remote land.

The Royal Horn

Day 1 Sail from Bolungarvík or Ísafjörður to Veiðileysufjörður, one of the local *jökulfirðir* (glacier fjords). The hike begins on a street near the bottom of the fjord and follows a cairn-marked trail up the slope and through the mountain pass. From the pass you can descend the mountain on either side until you reach the campground at Höfn in Hornvík. The hike from Veiðileysufjörður to Hornvík can take anywhere between four and eight hours. There's a ranger station at the campground here, so feel free to get the latest weather forecast and information about trail conditions.

Day 2 Stay in Hornvík for a second night and use your second day to visit **Hornbjarg**, one of Iceland's most beautiful bird cliffs with diverse flora and fauna. Alternatively, you could spend the second day exploring the area around the lighthouse, **Hornbjargsviti**.

Day 3 Hike from Hornvík to Hlöðuvík. The partly marked trail goes through a mountain pass and is relatively easy to find. Camping in Hlöðuvík is best by the **Hlöðuvíkurós** (the mouth of the Hlöðuvík river). Like Hornvík, Hlöðuvík faces north – it's the perfect place to watch the spectacular midnight sun. Figure around six hours to reach Hlöðuvík.

Day 4 Hike through **Kjarnsvíkurskarð** (a mountain pass) and **Hesteyrarbrúnir** pass to Hesteyri (figure around eight hours). **Hesteyri** is an old village that was abandoned around the middle of the 20th century. There are still several well-kept houses amid the fields of angelica. Ruins of a turn-of-the-century whaling station are found near the village. The coffee shop in Hesteyri is a good place to stop at the end of your hike – you can wait here for the ferry back to Bolungarvík or Ísafjörður.

Day 5 If the ferry isn't running the day you arrive, enjoy a night in Heysteri and spend one more day exploring the area before catching the boat. Pitch your tent at the campground just south of the village, or, if you prebooked, stay at the Doctor's House (p203) in Hesteyri.

Abridged Hike

You can take the ferry to Veiðileysufjörður, hike up to Hornvík, spend a night (or two) there, and walk down to Lónafjörður to link back up with a boat, *but only if you have prebooked it*. The walk from Hornvík to Lónafjörður takes around six to seven hours. Or you could backtrack to Veiðileysufjörður.

Alternatively, just sail in and use Hesteyri as a day-hike base (prebook if you want sleeping bag accommodation).

setting off. Guided trips can also be easily arranged with Ísafjörður operators.

Tours

The two main operators running tours (boating, hiking, kayaking, skiing etc) into Hornstrandir are West Tours (p196) and Borea (p196), both based in Ísafjörður.

Sleeping

Wild-camping in Hornstrandir is free (carry out all rubbish). Camping on private grounds with facilities costs around Ikr1000. Expect to pay upwards of Ikr6500 for sleeping-bag space, which must be reserved well in advance, especially in Hesteyri.

There are three options for sleeping-bag accommodation in the main part of Hornstrandir: Hesteyri, Hornbjargsviti, and Grunnavík (which may close in 2015). Two additional options are in the far-eastern part of the reserve: Reykjarfjörður and Bolungarvík.

Doctor's House in Hesteyri　　HOSTEL €
(☑845 5075, Hesteyri 899 7661; www.hesteyri. net; dm Ikr8000; ⊗mid-Jun–late Aug) By far the most developed lodging in Hornstrandir, Hesteyri has accommodation for 16 in the old doctor's house, with daytime coffee and pancakes available and a guest kitchen. Book well ahead.

Hornbjargsviti　　HOSTEL €
(☑FÍ 568 2533; www.fi.is; campsites per person Ikr1200, dm Ikr6500; ⊗mid-Jun–late Aug) Run by Ferðafélag Íslands (FI), and attached to the lighthouse of the same name on the east coast, this hostel sleeps 50 and has a kitchen and coin-operated showers (Ikr500).

Grunnavík　　HOSTEL €
(☑848 0511, 456 4664; www.grunnavik.is; dm Ikr6000) Grunnavík has space for around 20. At the time of research there was the chance that it would close.

Bolungarvík　　HUT €
(☑893 6926, 456 7192; hut per person Ikr4000) Bolungarvík's basic hut sits on the southeast coast of Hornstrandir and is usually used by hikers walking in or out.

Reykjarfjörður　　HUT, COTTAGE €
(☑896 1715, 456 7215; www.reykjarfjordur.is; campsites per person Ikr1000, dm Ikr4000, cottage from Ikr15,000) Choose from camping, a sleeping-bag bed (no electricity) or a small cottage that sleeps five. There's also a geothermal pool and hot-pot.

🛈 Getting There & Away

BOAT

Take a ferry boat from from Ísafjörður, Bolungarvík or Norðurfjörður (on the Strandir Coast) to Hornstrandir from June to August. One-way rides cost Ikr7200 to Ikr13,500, depending on your destination. It is strongly advised to book your return boat ticket, for safety reasons. You can book all boats direct, or through West Tours (p196).

From Ísafjörður, West Tours (p196) runs **Sjóferðir** (West Tours; ☑ 456 5111; www. sjoferdir.is) boats to the following, among other destinations:

➡ Aðalvík (Ikr8300, two weekly)
➡ Grunnavík (Ikr7400, one weekly)
➡ Hesteyri (Ikr7600, five weekly)
➡ Hornvík (Ikr13,200, one weekly)
➡ Hrafnfjörður (Ikr11,300, one weekly)
➡ Veiðileysufjörður (Ikr9800, two weekly).

From Bolungarvík, Borea (p196) runs **Bjarnarnes** (Borea; ☑ 456 3322; www.boreaadventures.com) boats to:

➡ Aðalvík (Ikr8500, two weekly)
➡ Grunnavík (Ikr7200, four weekly)
➡ Hesteyri (Ikr7500, four weekly)
➡ Hornvík (Ikr13,500, one weekly)
➡ Veiðileysufjörður (Ikr9600, three weekly).

Hrafnfjörður, Lónafjörður and Slétta (Sléttunes) are by request only. Early June and late August there is an eight-person minimum.

Urðartindur Boats (☑ 843 1880; www. urdartindur.is; near Norðurfjörður, Strandir Coast) With advance notice, an Urðartindur boat can be chartered from Norðurfjörður on the Strandir Coast to Drangar, Reykjarfjörður, Þaralátursfjörður/Furufjörður, Bolungarvík (in Hornstrandir, not the town of the same name west of Ísafjörður) and Látravík/Hornbjargsviti.

HIKING

It is possible to hike into the reserve from Norðurfjörður on the Strandir Coast. It'll take three days to reach Reykjarfjörður hut; and Bolungarvík hut is one more day beyond that. On days one and two you can wild-camp at Ófeigsfjörður and Drangar.

There's a trail from Grunnavík as well.

STRANDIR COAST

Sparsely populated, magnificently peaceful and all but deserted by travellers, the Westfjords' eastern spine is one of the most dramatic places in all of Iceland. Indented by a series of bristlelike fjords and lined with towering crags, the drive north of Hólmavík, the region's only sizeable settlement, is rough, wild and incredibly rewarding.

THE WESTFJORDS STRANDIR COAST

The end of the line in Iceland, Strandir was thought to be the home of the island's great, persecuted, sorcerers. South of here, gently rolling hills stretch along the isolated coastline as far as Staðarskáli, where the sudden rush of traffic tells you that you've returned to the Ring Road and the travelling masses.

There are buses as far as Hólmavík, but you'll need your own vehicle and a sense of adventure to get further.

Staðarskáli to Hólmavík

Although lacking the natural drama on show further north, the long drive along Rte 68 from Staðarskáli (formerly Brú) to Hólmavík is pleasantly pastoral, with rolling hills dotted by small farmhouses and lonely churches, alongside the vast fjords.

The small **Sheep Farming Museum** (Sauðfjársetur á Ströndum; ☑ 451 3324; www.strandir.is/saudfjarsetur; adult/child Ikr800/free; ☉ 10am-6pm Jun-Aug), 12km south of Hólmavík, details the region's farming history through photos and artefacts. Chessboards and home-made rhubarb pie at their **cafe** (snacks Ikr700 to Ikr1200) may keep you around longer than expected.

For accommodation, try **Kirkjuból** (☑ 451 3474; www.strandir.is/kirkjubol; s/d with shared bathroom Ikr8300/13,200) with basic guesthouse rooms and a guest kitchen, just south of the museum, or **Broddanes HI Hostel** (☑ 618 1830; www.broddanes.is; dm/d with shared bathroom Ikr4400/13,900; ☉ mid-May–mid-Sep; 🛜), on the point south of Kollafjörður, in a mod building.

Strætó (☑ 540 2700; www.bus.is) services:
➔ Bus 57 Staðarskáli–Reykjavík (Ikr3500, two daily) and Staðarskáli–Akureyri (Ikr3700, two daily).

Hólmavík

POP 373

Fishing town Hólmavík offers sweeping views over the still waters of Steingrímsfjörður and has a quirky witchcraft museum. The no-nonsense village is the best place to stock up on supplies before venturing off into the more rugged territory further north.

⊙ Sights & Activities

★ **Museum of Icelandic Sorcery & Witchcraft**   MUSEUM
(Strandagaldur; ☑ 451 3525; www.galdrasyning.is; Höfðagata 8-10; adult/child Ikr900/free; ☉ 9am-6pm) The award-winning Museum of Icelandic Sorcery & Witchcraft is by the central harbour. Unlike the witches of the infamous Salem trials in New England, almost all of Iceland's convicted witches were men. Most of their occult practices were simply old Viking traditions or superstitions, but hidden *grimoires* (magic books) full of puzzling runic designs were proof enough for the local witch hunters (the area's elite) to burn around 20 souls (mostly peasants) at the stake. Great multilingual descriptions detail their spells, and don't miss the 'necropants'. The tourist information office is also here.

Another part of the museum, a turf-roofed 'sorcerer's cottage' (p205), lies up the coast in Bjarnarfjörður.

Strandahestar   HORSE RIDING
(☑ 451 3262; www.strandahestar.is; Víðidalsá) Horse riding for all levels. Book at the tourist office.

🛏 Sleeping & Eating

There's a small grocery, campground (campsites per person Ikr1000) and cheap eats at the petrol station. NB: petrol requires N1 cards (not available on-site), chip cards, or cards with PINs.

Finna Hótel   HOTEL €
(☑ 451 3136; www.finnahotel.is; Borgarbraut 4; s/d incl breakfast Ikr10,600/15,700; @ 🛜) Friendly Finna sits on the hill, with basic but clean and comfortable rooms, and a good breakfast. Sleeping-bag accommodation costs Ikr5000 to Ikr6800 per person.

Steinhúsið   GUESTHOUSE, APARTMENT €
(☑ 856 1911; www.steinhusid.is; Höfðagata 1; s/d with shared bathroom Ikr9000/12,500, apt 19,000; 🛜) A pleasant option across from the witchcraft museum, Steinhúsið has a small collection of prim rooms with living space and a kitchen, and a basement apartment.

Sorcery Cafe   CAFE €€
(www.galdrasyning.is; Höfðagata 10; mains Ikr1300-2400; ☉ 9am-6pm) The menu changes daily at this friendly museum cafe: look for mussels fresh from the fjord and wild berries for dessert.

Café Riis   INTERNATIONAL €€
(☑ 451 3567; Hafnarbraut 39; mains Ikr1500-3900; ☉ 11.30am-9pm Jun-Aug) The town's popular pub and restaurant is set in a historic wooden building with carved magic symbols on the bar. Roasted chicken breast and trout are the menu's biggest hits.

ⓘ Information

Tourist Information Centre (☑ 451 3111; www.holmavik.is/info; Höfðagata 8-10; ☺9am-6pm; @☎) In the Witchcraft Museum, with internet access, and lots of info including hiking maps (Ikr1300).

ⓘ Getting There & Away

Buses stop at the N1 petrol station.

Strætó (☑ 540 2700; www.bus.is) services:
➠ Bus 59 Hólmavík–Búðardalur–Borgarnes (Ikr3850, five weekly mid-May to mid-September, two weekly mid-September to mid-May) with connections to Reykjavík (Ikr5250, 4½ hours). You must connect in Bifröst for Bus 57 service to Akureyri.

In 2015 year-round buses between Ísafjörður and Hólmavík were slated to begin again. Check www.westfjords.is for the latest information.

Drangsnes

POP 71

Across Steingrímsfjörður from Hólmavík, Drangsnes (pronounced *drowngs*-ness) is a remote little village with views across to north Iceland and the small uninhabited island of **Grímsey** (one of several Grímsey islands in Iceland). On Drangsnes' waterfront, rocky stack **Kerling** is believed to be the remains of a petrified **troll**. **Uxi**, her bull, is the formation out at sea near Grímsey.

A favourite Drangsnes attraction are its free, waterfront **geothermal hot-pots** FREE built into the sea wall along the main road. Eagle eyes will have to spot a small swimming sign and white building with blue trim containing showers and WCs. Remember to do as Icelanders do and shower completely before entering the hot-pots. There are three geometric Jacuzzis are directly across the street. There's also the town's swimming pool, **Drangsnes Sundlaug** (☑ 451 3201; www.drangnes.is; Grundargata 15; adult/child Ikr600/free; ☺11am-6pm Jun-Aug, reduced hours Sep-May), with two sparkling hot-pots – handy when the seaside weather is too tumultuous.

Located next to the Kerling, **Malarhorn** (☑ 451 3238; www.malarhorn.is; Grundargata 17; d with/without bathroom Ikr18,000/12,000, apt from Ikr32,000; ☎🅟) has a variety of accommodation including a peaceful row of crisp pine cabins that feel thoroughly modern yet remarkably cosy, plus apartments. Malarhorn runs three-hour **boat tours** of Grímsey (Ikr7000) with its puffin-breeding ground. Malarhorn's cafe **Malarkaffi** (mains Ikr1600-3800; ☺8am-9pm Jun-Aug, by appointment Sep-May) serves a super array of fish on its 2nd-storey verandah overlooking the fjord.

There's a petrol pump in Drangsnes.

Bjarnarfjörður & Kaldbaksvík

North of Drangsnes, a rough road winds around a series of gorgeous crumbling escarpments and tiny driftwood-filled bays. There are no services on this route, but if you've got your own vehicle, the utter tranquility, incredible views and sheer sense of isolation are truly remarkable. For those interested in the sagas, you'll be keen to know that *Njál's Saga* starts here.

Hótel Laugarhóll (☑ 451 3380; www.laugarholl.is; d with/without bath incl breakfast Ikr20,600/16,000; @☎), at Bjarnarfjörður, is run by friendly former school teachers – in fact they once taught in this very building, which has now been turned into a welcoming hotel. Crisp white duvets lie neatly folded on every bed, some with original artwork hanging just above. There's a yummy **restaurant** serving soups at lunch (Ikr1200) and an elaborate buffet at dinner (Ikr5900; 6.30pm to 8.30pm). Peruse the small **art gallery**, or take a dip in their beautifully situated **geothermal pool** (admission Ikr400; ☺8am-10pm Jun-24hr Sep-May) and hot-pot.

Hótel Laugarhóll's pool is fed by **Gvenderlaug**, a landmark 42°C miracle-producing pool (no bathing!) that was blessed by the bishop Gvendur the Good in the 13th century and is now a national monument; find it signposted behind the hotel.

Also signposted behind the hotel is the turf-roofed **Sorcerer's Cottage** (☺8am-10pm Jun-Aug) FREE, part of the witchcraft museum (p204) in Hólmavík, which shows what living conditions were like for the purported sorcerers.

North of Bjarnarfjörður the scenery becomes more rugged and there are fine views across to the Skagi Peninsula in north Iceland. This road often closes with the first snows in autumn and may not reopen until spring; ask locally for information on conditions.

At **Kaldbaksvík** the steep sides of a broad fjord sweep down to a small fishing lake that serenely reflects the surrounding mountains. Just beyond the lake, a 4km trail runs up to the summit of craggy **Lambatindur** (854m). You'll notice copious amounts of enormous driftwood piled up along the shore on this coast – most of it has arrived from Siberia across the Arctic Ocean.

Reykjarfjörður

Tucked beneath a looming rock wall and an enormous waterfall at Reykjarfjörður, and approached by way of incredible mountain roads and fjord views, is the strangely enchanting factory at Djúpavík. Once a thriving centre for herring processing, the area was all but abandoned when the plant closed in 1950. The deserted factory (which has since been reclaimed) and a beached trawler dominate this hamlet of quaint dorms and houses, and create a magical, memorable mood on this enormous, remote, deep fjord.

🛏 Sleeping

★ **Hótel Djúpavík**   INN €

(☑ 451 4037; www.djupavik.com; d in inn/cottage with shared bathroom Ikr12,500/11,800; 🛜) This charming inn, decorated with antiques and set in the herring factory's former women's dormitory block, is warmly welcoming from the moment you step into its bustling ground floor **restaurant** (mains Ikr1800 to Ikr4000). The understated charm spreads from the main inn to the sprinkling of guesthouse cottages (some with sleeping bag accommodation Ikr3800) with kitchens. It's set on one of the most stunning bays in Iceland. Hotel bookings essential in summer.

It's worth taking a **tour of the abandoned factory** (Ikr1000) with the friendly hotel staff. Part is used by the owner as a workshop, part is marvellously and photogenically defunct, and part has been turned into the summertime **Steypa photography exhibition** (www.claus-in-iceland.com; ☉ Jun-Aug) FREE. Look for the factory in Sigur Rós' 2007 concert video *Heima*.

Norðurfjörður & Around

North of Djúpavík, there are two interesting churches at **Árnes** – one is a traditional wooden structure, and the other (virtually across the street) is dramatically futuristic. The small museum, **Kört** (☑ 451 4025; www.trekyllisvik.is; Árnes 2; adult/child Ikr800/free; ☉ 10am-6pm Jun-Aug), has displays on fishing, and farming, and sells handicrafts.

Kistan (meaning 'the coffin'), an area of craggy rocks, served as the region's main site for witch executions. Iceland's last documented case of witch burning took place here. It's marked on the main road, but is easier to find if you ask for directions.

Clinging to life at the end of the bumpy road up the Strandir Coast is the tiny fishing hamlet **Norðurfjörður**. The township has a cafe, a petrol pump and a few guesthouses, and it's the last place to stock up and indulge in home comforts before heading off to Hornstrandir on foot or by boat charter.

Krossneslaug (adult/child Ikr450/200) is a geothermal (infinity) pool and hot-pot that shouldn't be missed. Up a dirt track about 3km beyond Norðurfjörður, you'll park, then walk down to where it sits at the edge of the universe on a wild black-pebble beach. It's an incredible place to watch the midnight sun flirt with the roaring waves.

🛏 Sleeping & Eating

★ **Urðartindur**   GUESTHOUSE €

(☑ 843 8110; www.urdartindur.is; campsites per person Ikr1100, d Ikr14,000; ☉ May-Sep) These simple, modern guest rooms with private bathrooms and refrigerators are blessed with unobstructed fjord views and a balcony along a black-sand beach. Two cottages (Ikr17,000) each sleep up to four. Ask Arinbjörn, the kindly owner, about a secret hiking path that leads to a hidden lake. Sleeping-bag accommodation costs Ikr5000 per person. Arinbjörn also offers boat charters (p203) to Hornstrandir.

Bergistangi   HOSTEL €

(☑ 451 4003; www.bergistangi.is; d Ikr8600) On the hill overlooking the harbour, this friendly guesthouse has good guest rooms, sleeping-bag accommodation (Ikr3000 per person) and a guest kitchen.

Kaffi Norðurfjörður   INTERNATIONAL €€

(☑ 692 6096; www.nordurfjordur.is; mains Ikr1950-3500; ☉ 11am-9pm late May–late Aug; 🛜) The food is nothing to write home about, but the fjord views are lovely, and you can play old vinyl records in the corner.

ⓘ Getting There & Away

AIR

Eagle Air (☑ 562 4200; www.eagleair.is) flies twice a week between Reykjavík and the airstrip at Gjögur, 16km southeast of Norðurfjörður. The online fare for a one-way ticket is €168 and the trip takes 50 minutes.

BOAT

Arinbjörn at Urðartindur guesthouse offers boat charters (p203) to Hornstrandir Reserve from Norðurfjörður.

North Iceland

Why Go?

Iceland's mammoth and magnificent north is a geologist's heaven. A wonderland of moonlike lava fields, belching mudpots, epic waterfalls, snowcapped peaks and whale-filled bays – this is Iceland at its best. The region's top sights are variations on one theme: a grumbling, volcanically active earth.

There are endless treats to uncover: little Akureyri, with its surprising moments of big-city living; windy fjordside pastures full of stout Viking horses; fishing villages clinging tenaciously to life at the end of unsealed roads.

Prepare to be enticed by offshore islands populated by colonies of seabirds and a few hardy locals; lonely peninsulas stretching out towards the Arctic Circle; white-water rapids ready to deliver an adrenalin kick; national-park walking trails to reach unparalleled views; unhyped and underpopulated ski fields; and underwater marvels that woo divers into frigid depths.

Best Places to Eat

➡ Geitafell (p211)

➡ Hannes Boy (p219)

➡ Vogafjós (p239)

➡ Lónkot (p217)

➡ Kaffihús Bakkabræðra (p221)

Best Places to Stay

➡ Skjaldarvík (p228)

➡ Dalvík HI Hostel (p221)

➡ Kaldbaks-Kot (p248)

➡ Sæluhús (p228)

➡ Gamla Pósthúsið (p214)

Road Distances (km)

	Reykjavík	Akureyri	Siglufjörður	Húsavík	Reykjahlíð (Mývatn)
Akureyri	389				
Siglufjörður	384	76			
Húsavík	476	92	168		
Reykjahlíð (Mývatn)	478	100	176	54	
Þórshöfn	613	235	311	142	172

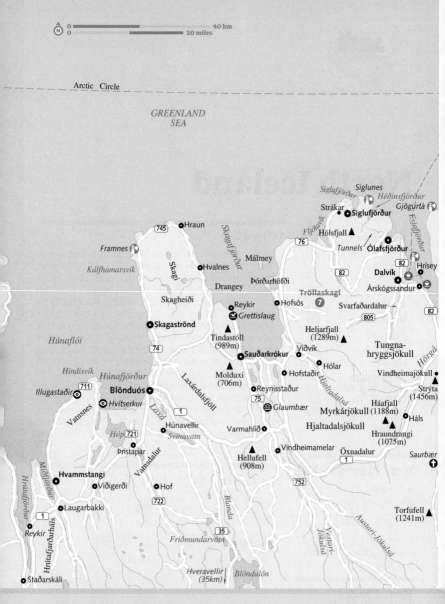

North Iceland Highlights

1 Discover northern Iceland's version of city living in **Akureyri** (p222)

2 Cross Iceland's only true slice of the Arctic Circle – the tern-filled and troll-infested island of **Grímsey** (p226)

3 Wander around lava castles, pseudocraters and hidden fissures at otherworldly **Mývatn** (p235)

4 Hold your breath as gentle giants emerge from the deep on a whale-watching trip from **Húsavík** (p244)

5 Step gingerly through the rust-coloured world at

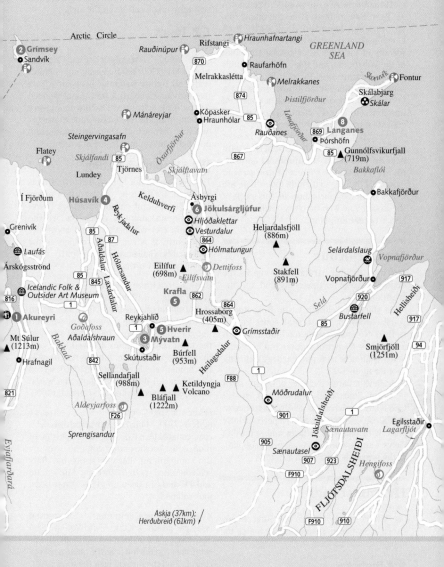

Hverir (p243), then crunch shattered lava underfoot at **Krafla** (p243)

❻ Savour thundering chutes, hypnotic rock forms and a storied canyon at **Jökulsárgljúfur** (p250)

❼ Tour **Tröllaskagi** (p216), eyeballing vast vistas and rugged mountainscapes between perfect pit stops

❽ Get twitchy at the viewing platform over the bird-filled cliffs of **Langanes** (p255)

EASTERN HÚNAFLÓI

Sparsely populated and scattered with only a handful of tiny settlements, the bay of Húnaflói is rich in wildlife. It's known as Bear Bay, named after the many polar bears that have drifted on sea ice from Greenland and come ashore here. The scenery of the area is far gentler than that of the Westfjords, and the low, treeless hills provide nesting sites for rich birdlife. Add some neatly manicured towns, some seals, horse-riding opportunities and a cluster of museums, and there's plenty to keep you occupied en route to Akureyri.

Pick up the *Húnaþing vestra* booklet (online at www.visithunathing.is), with detailed info about Hvammstangi and surrounds. Pick up the *Discover Rural Iceland* (www.farmholidays.is) guide too – there are heaps of homey farmstays in this neck of the woods. The website www.northwest.is is also excellent for planning.

Hrútafjörður

The inlet of little Hrútafjörður marks the divide between northwest Iceland and the Westfjords.

As you follow Route 1 (the Ring Road), you'll encounter Staðarskáli (once known as Brú). No more than a road junction with a big, busy N1 petrol station and cafeteria, Staðarskáli acts as a popular leg-stretching spot for motorists.

At Reykir, barely a cluster of houses 13km north of Staðarskáli, **Sæberg HI Hostel** (☑ 894 5504; www.hostel.is; dm/d without bathroom Ikr3700/9200; ◌ Mar-Oct; ☎) is a peaceful little place with hot-pots, cottages and sprawling views. Campers are welcome; bring supplies, as the nearest shop is 15km away.

Hvammstangi

POP 560

Six kilometres north of the Ring Road, sweet, slow-paced Hvammstangi builds its appeal around its local seal colonies.

◉ Sights

Selasetur Íslands   MUSEUM
(☑ 451 2345; www.selasetur.is; Brekkugat; adult/child Ikr950/free; ◌ 9am-7pm Jun-Aug, shorter hours Sep-May) The town's prime attraction is the harbourfront Icelandic Seal Centre, where you can learn about conservation of seals, historic seal products and traditional folk tales involving seals. There's also a helpful tourist information desk located here, happy to explain where to find the best seal-watching locations in the area.

☞ Tours

Selasigling   BOAT TOUR
(☑ 897 9900; www.sealwatching.is; 1¾hr tour adult/child Ikr7900/3900) Selasigling operates seal- and nature-watching boat trips from the harbour, onboard a traditional wooden fishing boat. Scheduled 1¾-hour tours leave at 10am, 1pm and 4pm daily June to August (weather permitting). There are angling and midnight-sun sailings by arrangement.

🛏 Sleeping & Eating

The harbour is the hub of the town's tourist action. By the time you read this, a new seafood restaurant called Sjávarborg (www.sjavarborg-restaurant.is; check the website for hours etc) will have opened above the Seal Centre. It is run by the owners of the high-quality Gauksmýri lodge (p211) so it should be well worth a look.

Guesthouse Hanna Sigga   GUESTHOUSE €
(☑ 451 2407; www.simnet.is/gistihs; Garðavegur 26; s/d without bathroom Ikr8900/13,500; ☎) An excellent choice, this homey and welcoming guesthouse is on a residential street in the town centre. Rooms are well kept, and there's a guest kitchen, but the real draw is the homemade breakfast (Ikr1600) served in a beautiful nook overlooking the water. Sleeping-bag accommodation costs Ikr4300.

Hvammstangi Cottages   COTTAGES €
(☑ 860 7700; http://hvammstangichalets.webs. com; cottages from Ikr15,000; ☎) A cluster of nine cute, cookie-cutter cottages lives by the campground. Each is petite but fully self-contained with bathroom, kitchenette and TV, and can sleep up to five (three beds, plus sofabed).

Kirkjuhvammur Campsite   CAMPGROUND €
(sites per person Ikr1000; ◌ mid-May–mid-Sep) The large, well-maintained Kirkjuhvammur campsite is up the hill near the photogenic old church. Find the turn-off near the town pool.

Hlaðan Kaffihús   CAFE €
(Brekkugata 2; meals Ikr1500-2700; ◌ 9am-9pm Mon-Sat, 10am-9pm Sun mid-May–mid-Sep; ☎) At the harbour is this sweet cafe, luring customers with the usual suspects: soups, sandwiches and cakes.

VATNSNES PENINSULA

Poking out into Húnaflói, stubby Vatnsnes Peninsula is a starkly beautiful place with a ridge of craggy hills marching down its spine. Rte 711, a rough gravel road, weaves along the coast and makes a splendid detour off the Ring Road (it's about 82km in total, from the Ring Road to Hvammstangi and around the peninsula on Rte 711.)

On the west side there's a simple campsite at **Illugastaðir farm** (sites per person Ikr1000; ☺20 Jun-Aug), with wonderful views of peaks along the Strandir coast in the Westfjords. There are lovely walks through bird-filled fields to a popular site for sunbaking seals; note that the farm is closed from 1 May to 20 June due to eider duck nesting.

This storied farm is the site of the crime leading to the last public execution in Iceland (1830). Agnes Magnúsdóttir and Friðrik Sigurðsson were convicted of the murder of two men at Illugastaðir, and they were executed by beheading at Þrístapar, a site south of Blönduós. Their remains lie in a grave at Tjörn churchyard, further north along the peninsula.

The story of the crime and executions was the basis for a 1995 Icelandic film *Agnes*, and a recent acclaimed novel, *Burial Rites*, by Australian writer Hannah Kent.

Three kilometres past Illugastaðir (roughly 25km from Hvammstangi) is the wonderfully unique **Geitafell** (www.geitafell.is; fish soup Ikr2950; ☺11am-10pm Jun-Aug), a restaurant in a converted barn where fish soup is the star (*skyr*, a yoghurt-like dessert, is another highlight on the short menu). The property owners, Sigrún and Robert, are longtime locals with fascinating stories. Robert's father was a Scottish minister who came to preach (and teach football skills) in Iceland; Robert has a small history exhibition next to the restaurant, in his 'Scottish castle'.

On the peninsula's east coast you'll happen upon a signed path leading to the splendidly photogenic 15m-high sea stack **Hvítserkur**. Legend has it that Hvítserkur was a troll caught by the sunrise while attempting to destroy the monastery at Þingeyrar; we think he looks like a huge stone beast drinking from the water.

Just south of Hvítserkur (or 30km north of the Ring Road) is a trail to a seal-watching spot. Inland is **Ósar HI Hostel** (☎862 2778; www.hostel.is; dm/d without bathroom Ikr4000/11,300; ☺May-Sep; ☎), one of Iceland's nicest hostels (thanks to friendly owner Knútur, good views and the nearby wildlife). The hostel is on a working dairy farm, with rooms, cottages, and a Mongolian yurt where breakfast is served! Bring your own food as there are no shops nearby. Members get a discount of Ikr700 per person; linen hire costs Ikr1500. Ósar is also home to public toilets and a bar (in the reception area) serving beer, coffee and snacks.

🛈 Getting There & Away

The summer Sterna buses (60, 60a) that travel the Ring Road (Rte 1) between Reykjavík and Akureyri only service the Hvammstangi crossroads, 6km from town.

The year-round Strætó bus 57 between Reykjavík and Akureyri also stops at the crossroads. Strætó runs a separate service to/from the crossroads to link up with these services, but it must be prebooked with at least two hours' notice (bus 83; Ikr350).

Strætó (☎540 2700; www.straeto.is) services:
➾ Bus 57 to Reykjavík (Ikr4550, 3½hr, 2 daily)
➾ Bus 57 to Akureyri (Ikr3500, 2hr, 2 daily)

Hvammstangi to Blönduós

Iceland's northwest is real horse territory, and horse-lovers will be in heaven at **Gauksmýri** (☎451 2927; www.gauksmyri.is; d with/without bathroom incl breakfast Ikr21,600/14,800; @☎), a highly regarded horse farm and lodge on the Ring Road 3km east of the turn-off to Hvammstangi. Two-hour horse rides (Ikr10,000) leave four times a day in summer. Gauksmýri's **restaurant** does a full dinner buffet (Ikr5200; open mid-May to mid-September; bookings advised) where the variety of meats may rankle (it includes whale and foal, but also local salmon, lamb and trout). A soup-and-salad buffet is offered at lunchtime, while snacks and coffee are served in the afternoon.

Serious horse riders should book ahead with **Brekkulækur** (☎451 2938; www.abbi-island. is), which offers adventurous and acclaimed multiday trips (€1340 to €3190 for eight to 15 days). The farm (with guesthouse) is 9km south of the Hvammstangi turn-off on Rte 704.

Travelling east past Gauksmýri, take Rte 715 south for 6km to reach the scenic waterfalls at

Kolugljúfur, an enchanting canyon that was once home to a beautiful trolless.

Around 19km before you reach Blönduós, another quick 6km detour (this time along Rte 721) leads you to a precious stone church, Þingeyrar (adult/child Ikr600/free; ⊙10am-5pm), sitting quietly and photogenically on Hóp lagoon. The current structure was erected in the 1860s, but 800 years earlier the site hosted a district þing (assembly) and a Benedictine monastery. There's a small museum here too (free admission).

Blönduós

POP 810

A couple of museums and an unusual modern church – the underwhelming service town Blönduós is about as simple as that. There isn't much to woo you off the road, but it's an OK place to break the journey and refuel. Overnight options are uninspiring.

The churning Blanda river divides the town in half. The N1 station marks the northern entrance (its grill bar is the liveliest place in town).

◉ Sights & Activities

Textile Museum   MUSEUM
(Heimilisiðnaðarsafnið; www.textile.is; Árbraut 29; adult/child Ikr900/free; ⊙10am-5pm Jun-Aug) Set in a head-turning modern building on the north bank of the Blanda River, this small museum displays local handicrafts, painstakingly intricate embroideries and early Icelandic costumes.

Sea Ice Exhibition Centre   MUSEUM
(Hafíssetrið; www.blonduos.is/hafis; Blöndubyggð 2; adult/child Ikr500/free; ⊙11am-5pm Jun-Aug) Housed in a 1733 merchant's house, the centre's small but informative exhibits look at the formation and types of sea ice, weather patterns and early Icelandic settlers. You'll also come face to face with the polar bear that visited the region during the summer of 2008 (as with all infrequent polar-bear arrivals on Icelandic shores, she was shot).

⌂ Sleeping & Eating

Glaðheimar   CAMPGROUND, COTTAGES €
(☑820 1300; www.gladheimar.is; campsites per person Ikr1200, cottages Ikr21,000) In a lovely setting near the river, Glaðheimar has camping and an assortment of self-contained cottages sleeping up to six people (larger cottages have the bonus of a hot tub, a few

also have sauna). Linen costs extra. There are also sleeping-bag beds available (from Ikr6000). The reception building doubles as the town's **tourist information centre**.

Potturinn   INTERNATIONAL €€
(www.pot.is; Nordurlandsvegur 4; mains Ikr1500-4000; ⊙11am-10pm) A surprisingly diverse menu greets diners at this decent place neighbouring the N1. There's soup and salad all day, good burgers and pizza, plus the unexpected (eg tandoori chicken, Mexican tortilla).

Samkaup-Úrval   SUPERMARKET
(Húnabraut 4; ⊙10am-7pm Mon-Fri, 10am-6pm Sat, 1-5pm Sun) Self-catering supplies.

❶ Getting There & Away

Sterna (☑551 1166; www.sterna.is) services:
➠ Bus 60a to Reykjavík (Ikr4500, 3½hr, 1 daily Mon-Fri mid-Jun–Aug)
➠ Bus 60 to Akureyri (Ikr2700, 1¾hr, 1 daily mid-Jun–early Sep)

Strætó (☑540 2700; www.straeto.is) services:
➠ Bus 57 to Reykjavík (Ikr5600, 4hr, 2 daily)
➠ Bus 57 to Akureyri (Ikr2450, 2¼hr, 2 daily)

WESTERN SKAGAFJÖRÐUR

Skagafjörður is renowned for horse breeding and wild landscapes – this, plus its historic remains and adrenalin-infused activities, make it a rewarding destination. Look out for the growing emphasis on culinary tourism, and the red stamps on menus highlighting local produce. For more information, see www.visitskagafjordur.is.

Varmahlíð

POP 120

This Ring Road service centre is slightly more than a road junction and yet not quite a town, and it's a great base for white-water rafting and horse riding.

⌖ Tours

As well as outstanding horse trails, the area around Varmahlíð is home to northern Iceland's best white-water rafting. Trips run from about May to September.

Both companies listed raft on the more placid Vestari-Jökulsá (West Glacial River; Class 2+ rapids), and the Austari-Jökulsá (East Glacial River; Class 4+ rapids).

Note that prices listed in this section are from summer 2014. Check websites for updated prices.

Viking Rafting RAFTING
(☑ 823 8300; www.vikingrafting.com) Options include a family-friendly four-hour trip on the Vestari-Jökulsá (Ikr11,900; minimum age six); a challenging six-hour adventure on the Austari-Jökulsá (Ikr21,990); and the ultimate rafting expedition, a three-day trip (Ikr109,990) which starts from the Sprengisandur highlands.

The company's base camp is at Hafgrímsstaðir, 15km south of Varmahlíð on Rte 752 (sealed). Pick-ups for the longer trips can be arranged from Akureyri.

Bakkaflöt RAFTING
(☑ 453 8245; www.bakkaflot.com) South along Rte 752 (11km from the Ring Road), the farm Bakkaflöt offers three hours on the Vestari-Jökulsá (Ikr10,900), and six hours on the Austari-Jökulsá (Ikr18,900). The centre also has good accommodation.

Hestasport HORSE RIDING
(☑ 453 8383; www.riding.is) One of Iceland's most respected riding outfits, with its helpful office just off the Ring Road on Rte 752. It offers one-/two-hour tours along the Svartá river for Ikr6500/10,000, and full-day rides for Ikr19,000. Longer trips are also available (book well in advance), including eight-day trips through the highlands (Ikr304,000).

Lýtingsstaðir HORSE RIDING
(☑ 453 8064; www.lythorse.com) The lovely farm Lýtingsstaðir, 20km south of Varmahlíð on Rte 752, has a great program of hourly riding or longer multiday trips. It offers a great 'Stop and Ride' package that includes one night in a self-contained cottage and a two-hour ride for Ikr31,000 (two people, including linen). Longer tours (from Ikr170,500 for six days) are also available.

Horse Shows
Horse farms in the area often host hour-long horse shows that showcase the five gaits of the Icelandic horse, and detail the breed's history. Shows are usually scheduled for groups, and individuals can then attend. Ask at the tourist office if you're interested, or contact the farms direct.

Flugumýri (☑ 453 8814; www.flugumyri.is) often stages these shows; we also like the weekly 'Horses & Heritage' evening program from Lýtingsstaðir (p213), encompassing facts, stories and snacks (Ikr2500).

🛏 Sleeping & Eating
There are plenty of rural places to crash in the area; ask at the information centre. If you are doing rafting or riding tours with Bakkaflöt or Lýtingsstaðir, note that they both have excellent sleeping options. These are open to all; see websites for details.

Campsite CAMPGROUND €
(http://tjoldumiskagafirdi.is; campsites per person Ikr1100; ☉ mid-May–mid-Sep) Follow the signs from the hotel to reach this secluded spot.

★ Hestasport Cottages COTTAGES €€
(☑ 453 8383; www.riding.is/cottages; cottages for 2/4/6 Ikr23,100/32,400/38,500; 🛜) Perched on the hill above Varmahlíð (follow the road past the town hotel), this cluster of seven high-quality, self-contained timber cottages has good views, comfy rooms and a very inviting stone hot-pot. There are photos of the interior of each cottage on Hestasport's website; some sleep up to six.

Hótel Varmahlíð HOTEL €€
(☑ 453 8170; www.hotelvarmahlid.is; s/d incl breakfast Ikr20,900/26,800; @ 🛜) Freshly modernised rooms are found at this friendly small hotel. Its excellent **restaurant** (mains Ikr3100 to Ikr4800; open 11.30am to 9pm mid-May to mid-September) is one of the best places to try fine regional produce, including lamb (from the manager's own farm), cod and the local delicacy, foal. There's a more casual cafe menu too.

KS Supermarket SUPERMARKET
(☉ 9am-11.30pm Jun-Aug, shorter hours Sep-May) The supermarket by the N1 is open until late. Be sure to stop by the superb handicrafts store next door too.

ℹ Information
Tourist Information Centre (☑ 455 6161; www.visitskagafjordur.is; ☉ daily year-round) Inside the N1 service station, this efficient centre is a room of brochures and maps, with a staffed info desk. Ask here for directions to the hidden waterfall Reykjafoss.

ℹ Getting There & Away
All buses stop at the N1.

SBA-Norðurleið (☑ 550 0700; www.sba.is) services:
➾ Bus 610a to Reykjavík via the Kjölur route (Ikr11,400, 9hr, 1 daily mid-Jun–mid-Sep)

Sterna (☑ 551 1166; www.sterna.is) services:
➾ Bus 60a to Reykjavík (Ikr5300, 4hr, 1 daily Mon-Fri mid-Jun–Aug)

» Bus 60 to Akureyri (Ikr1800, 1hr, 1 daily mid-Jun–early Sep)

» Bus F35a to Reykjavík via the Kjölur route (Ikr11,000, 12hr, 1 daily mid-Jun–early Sep

Strætó (☏ 540 2700; www.straeto.is) services:

» Bus 57 to Reykjavík (Ikr5950, 5hr, 2 daily)

» Bus 57 to Akureyri (Ikr2100, 1¼hr, 2 daily)

» Bus 57 to Sauðárkrókur (Ikr700, 20min, 2 daily)

Öxnadalur

If you haven't the time to explore scenic Skagafjörður or magnificent Tröllaskagi, never fear: you'll still be treated to some incredible vistas courtesy of Öxnadalur, a narrow, 30km-long valley on the Ring Road between Varmahlíð and Akureyri. Stunning peaks and thin pinnacles of rock flank the mountain pass; the imposing 1075m spire of **Hraundrangi** and the surrounding peaks of **Háafjall** are among the most dramatic in Iceland.

🛏 Sleeping

Engimýri Guesthouse　　　　GUESTHOUSE **€€**
(☏ 462 7518; www.engimyri.is; d with/without bathroom Ikr18,900/15,900; @ 🛜) Engimýri Guesthouse has a plum location in the middle of the Öxnadalur splendour, some 35km west of Akureyri. There's a restaurant, hot-pot, hiking trails, and the chance to take quad-bike tours through the valley (Ikr17,400/29,000 for one/two hours; daily tours at 2pm).

Glaumbær

Following Rte 75 north from Varmahlíð towards Skagafjörður's marshy delta leads to the 18th-century turf-farm museum at **Glaumbær** (www.glaumbaer.is; adult/child Ikr1200/free; ⊙9am-6pm mid-May–mid-Sep). It's the best museum of its type in northern Iceland and well worth the easy 8km detour off the Ring Road.

The traditional Icelandic turf farm was a complex of small separate buildings, connected by a central passageway. At Glaumbær you can see this style of construction, with some building compartments stuffed full of period furniture, equipment and utensils. It gives a fascinating insight into the cramped living conditions of the era.

Also on the site are two 19th-century houses – one is home to **Áskaffi** (cake Ikr390-950; ⊙9am-6pm), an impossibly quaint tearoom with old-world atmosphere and dollhouse dishware. Peruse the brochure explaining the history behind its delicious traditional Icelandic tarts, cakes and pancakes.

Snorri Þorfinnsson, the first European born in North America (in 1004), is buried near the **church** at Glaumbær.

Sauðárkrókur

POP 2570

As the winding Jökulsá river collides with the marshy delta of upper Skagafjörður, you'll find scenic Sauðárkrókur sitting quietly at the edge of the windy waterway.

Economically, Sauðárkrókur is doing quite nicely, thank you, with fishing, tanning and trading keeping the community afloat and the population vibrant. The town has all the services you'll need, plus excellent sleeping and eating options; tourist information is dispensed by the town museum.

⊙ Sights

Minjahúsið　　　　MUSEUM
(Aðalgata 16b; adult/child Ikr900/free; ⊙noon-7pm Jun-Aug) There's a quirky ensemble of exhibits at the excellent 'heritage house', including a series of restored craftsmen's workshops, a pristine A-model Ford from 1930, and a stuffed polar bear caught locally in 2008.

Tannery Visitor Centre　　　　TANNERY
(Gestastofa Sútarans; www.sutarinn.is; Borgamýri 5; ⊙9am-6pm Mon-Fri, 11am-3pm Sat Jun–mid-Sep, 1-4pm Wed & Fri mid-Sep–May) At 10am and 2pm weekdays you can tour Iceland's only tannery (Ikr500), or stop by the visitor centre anytime to admire (and purchase) the products: gorgeous sheepskins, colourful leather goods, and unique products made from fish skin processed at the tannery.

🛏 Sleeping

MicroBar & Bed　　　　GUESTHOUSE **€**
(☏ 467 3133; microbar2@outlook.com; Aðalgata 19) At the great new MicroBar on the main street, the '& Bed' part of the equation is 10 budget beds in five rooms above the bar – it might not be a great option for light sleepers, but it's a great choice for beer lovers. The guesthouse was still in the pipeline when we visited; check MicroBar's Facebook page for updates.

Campsite　　　　CAMPGROUND **€**
(http://tjoldumiskagafirdi.is; sites per person Ikr1100; ⊙mid-May–mid-Sep) The campsite beside the swimming pool is a bit barren and treeless, but has decent facilities.

★ Gamla Posthúsið　　　　APARTMENT **€€**
(☏ 892 3375; www.ausis.is; Kirkjutorg 5; apt from Ikr22,400; 🛜) Australian Vicki moved to

DRANGEY

The tiny rocky islet of Drangey (*drown*-gay), in the middle of Skagafjörður, is a dramatic flat-topped mass of volcanic tuff with 180m-high sheer cliffsides rising abruptly from the water. The cliffs serve as nesting sites for around a million seabirds (lots of puffins), and have been used throughout Iceland's history as 'nature's grocery store'. *Grettir's Saga* recounts that both Grettir and his brother Illugi lived on the island for three years and were slain there. Brave (foolhardy?) saga fans come to the area to re-create Grettir's feat, swimming the 7km between Drangey and Reykir.

Drangeyjarferðir (📞821 0090; www.drangey.net; tours adult/child Ikr9800/5000) offers four-hour boat trips to Drangey, departing from Reykir at 11am daily from June to mid-August; call the day beforehand to book. Sea-angling trips can also be arranged.

town in 2010 and took it upon herself to restore the old post office opposite the church. The two resulting one-bedroom apartments make a superb home away from home. Each boasts a full modern kitchen, a welcome pack of food, oodles of room and Scandi-chic decor. Winter prices are almost halved, making them a bargain.

Guesthouse Mikligarður   GUESTHOUSE €€
(📞453 6880; www.arctichotels.is; Kirkjutorg 3; s/d without bathroom incl breakfast Ikr10,200/17,100; 🛜) This lovely, welcoming spot near the church has comfortable, modern rooms with TV and tasteful decor (most share bathrooms). There's also a spacious guest kitchen and TV lounge.

Hótel Tindastóll   HOTEL €€€
(📞453 5002; www.arctichotels.is; Lindargata 3; r incl breakfast from Ikr27,900; 🛜) Legend has it that Marlene Dietrich once stayed at this charming boutique hotel, which dates from 1884. The individually decorated rooms blend period furniture and modern style. Outside there is an irresistible stone hot-pot, and in the basement there's a cosy bar. There is also a new annexe of modern rooms, but the period rooms have loads more character.

✕ Eating & Drinking

Ólafshús   ICELANDIC €€
(www.olafshus.is; Aðalgata 15; lunch Ikr1590-1890, dinner mains Ikr1500-5000; ⏰11am-10.30pm; 🛜🍴) A bold blue paint job announces this quality year-round option, where you can go radical with pan-fried foal, fancy-pants with lobster tails, or safe with pizza and pasta. The spotlight is shone on local produce – a good excuse to try Gæðingur, the locally microbrewed beer.

Kaffi Krókur   ICELANDIC €€
(www.kaffikrokur.is; Aðalgata 16; mains Ikr1490-2990; ⏰11.30am-11pm Sun-Wed, to 1am Thu,

to 3am Fri & Sat Jun-Aug; 🛜) This cafe has a more understated beige exterior and a crowd-pleasing menu. It's known for its lobster and shrimp sandwich, filled crêpes and warm rhubarb cake. In winter it's the local pub (with live music), open only on Thursday, Friday and Saturday nights.

Skagfirðingabúð   SUPERMARKET
(Ástorg; ⏰9am-7pm Mon-Fri, 10am-4pm Sat) South of town, close to the N1.

MicroBar & Bed   BAR
(📞467 3133; Aðalgata 19) Cool mountain-peak graphics and vintage sofas set the scene at this excellent new addition to Sauðárkrókur's main drag. From the same crowd behind Reykjavík's beloved booze bar comes this convivial spot where local brews are on tap, plus loads more in bottles. Gæðingur is the local draught pick: Indian Pale Ale, wheat beer or stout. Skál!

ℹ Getting There & Away

The bus stop is at the N1 south of the centre.
Strætó (📞540 2700; www.straeto.is) services:

➸ Bus 57 to Reykjavík (Ikr5950, 4½hr, 2 daily)
➸ Bus 57 to Akureyri (Ikr2100, 1½hr, 2 daily)
➸ Bus 57 to Varmahlíð (Ikr700, 20min, 2 daily)
➸ Bus 85 to Hólar and Hofsós (Ikr700 to either destination, 2 daily Wed, Fri & Sun) These services only operate if prebooked. Call Strætó at least two hours before departure.

Around Sauðárkrókur

North of Sauðárkrókur, Skagafjörður's western coast is a stunningly silent place capped by scenic mountains. Guarding the mouth of Skagafjörður are the uninhabited islands of Drangey and Málmey, tranquil havens for nesting seabirds.

Tindastóll (989m) is a prominent Skagafjörður landmark, extending for 18km along the coast. The mountain and its caves are believed to be inhabited by an array of sea monsters, trolls and giants. The summit of Tindastóll affords a spectacular view across all of Skagafjörður. The easiest way to the top is along the marked trail that starts from the high ground along Rte 745 west of the mountain (it's a strenuous hike). There's skiing here in winter.

At Tindastóll's northern end is a geothermal area, Reykir, that was mentioned in *Grettir's Saga*. Grettir supposedly swam ashore from the island of Drangey and soothed his aching bones in an inviting spring. Today, Grettislaug (Grettir's Bath; ☑ 821 0090; www.drangey.net; adult/child Ikr750/350; ☺ morning-midnight) is a popular bathing hole, alongside a second hot-pot.

In the immediate vicinity of Grettislaug are a small cafe, well-equipped campground (campsites per person Ikr1000) and guesthouse (per person Ikr7500) with sleeping-bag beds for Ikr4800. Boats to Drangey leave from here, and there are great walks in the area.

Drivers beware: it's a rough, skiddy 15km on gravel from Sauðárkrókur to Grettislaug.

TRÖLLASKAGI

Tröllaskagi (Troll Peninsula) rests its mountainous bulk between Skagafjörður and Eyjafjörður. Here, the craggy mountains, deep valleys and gushing rivers are more reminiscent of the Westfjords than the gentle hills that roll through most of northern Iceland. In great news for travellers seeking spectacular road trips, tunnels now link the northern Tröllaskagi townships of Siglufjörður and Olafsfjörður, once dead-end towns that saw little tourist traffic.

The journey from Varmahlíð to Akureyri along the Ring Road (Rte 1) measures 95 very scenic kilometres, but if you have some time up your sleeve and a penchant for getting off the beaten track, the 186km journey between those two towns following the Tröllaskagi coastline (Rtes 76 and 82) conjures up some magical scenery, and plenty of excuses to pull over and explore.

Hólar í Hjaltadalur

With its prominent church dwarfed by the looming mountains, tiny Hólar (www.holar.is) makes an interesting historical detour. The bishopric of Hólar was the ecumenical and educational capital of northern Iceland between 1106 and the Reformation, and it continued as a religious centre and the home of the northern bishops until 1798, when the bishop's seat was abolished.

Hólar then became a vicarage until 1861, when the vicarage was shifted west to Viðvík. In 1882 the present agricultural college was established – it's now known as Hólar University College, specialising in equine science, aquaculture and rural tourism. In 1952 the vicarage returned to Hólar.

❂ Sights

A historical-trail brochure (available at the accommodation info desk) guides you round some of the buildings at Hólar. Nýibær is a historical turf farm dating from the mid-19th century and inhabited until 1945. Also worth seeing is Auðunarstofa, a replica of the 14th-century bishop's residence, built using traditional tools and methods.

Cathedral   CHURCH
(☺ 10am-6pm Jun–mid-Sep) Completed in 1763, Hólar's red-sandstone cathedral is the oldest stone church in Iceland and brimming with historical works of art, including a 1674 baptismal font carved from a piece of soapstone that washed in from Greenland on an ice floe.

The extraordinary carved altarpiece was donated by the last Catholic bishop of Hólar, Jón Arason, around 1520. After he and his sons were executed at Skálholt for opposition to the Danish Reformation, his remains were brought to Hólar and entombed in the bell tower. The present church tower was built in 1950 as a memorial.

Icelandic Horse History Centre   MUSEUM
(www.sogusetur.is; adult/child Ikr900/450; ☺ 10am-6pm Tue-Fri, 1-5pm Sat Jun-Aug) The admission price gets you a personalised tour around this comprehensive exhibit on Iceland's unique breed and its role in Iceland's history. It's fittingly located in an old stable at the heart of the Hólar estate.

🛏 Sleeping & Eating

Hólar Tourism Service   GUESTHOUSE, COTTAGES €€
(☑ 455 6333; www.holar.is; d with/without bathroom Ikr19,800/16,700, d apt Ikr21,300; @ 🛜 🖾) The college accommodation block offers summer stays in vacant student rooms and apartments. Alternatively, wooden cottages in the grounds sleep up to six, and are available year-round. There is a restaurant and swimming pool; and a camping area nearby.

Hofsós

POP 180

The sleepy fishing village of Hofsós has been a trading centre since the 1500s, but was recently put on map with its designer swimming pool.

◎ Sights & Activities

Icelandic Emigration Center   MUSEUM
(Vesturfarasetrið; ☑ 453 7935; www.hofsos.is; adult Ikr700-1500, children free; ⊙ 11am-6pm Jun-Aug) Several restored harbourside buildings have been turned into a museum exploring the reasons behind Icelanders' emigration to the North America, their hopes for a new life, and the reality of conditions when they arrived. Incredibly, this small country lost 16,000 emigrants from 1870 to 1914, leaving behind a 1914 population of only 88,000.

The main exhibition, 'New Land, New Life', follows the lives of emigrating Icelanders through carefully curated photographs, letters and displays.

The centre provides an absorbing history lesson, even if you're not of Icelandic descent, and it's a fine place to start if you're tracing roots. Entry price depends on the number of exhibits you wish to visit.

★ Sundlaugin á Hofsós   SWIMMING POOL
(adult/child Ikr550/220; ⊙ 9am-9pm Jun-Aug, 7am-1pm & 5-8pm Mon-Fri, 11am-3pm Sat & Sun Sep-May) The village's magnificent outdoor swimming pool (with adjacent hot-pot) has placed Hofsós firmly in the country's collective conscience. It was opened in 2010 thanks to donations from two local women, and its fjordside design, integrated into the landscape and offering almost-infinity views, is close to perfect.

⌖ Tours

Haf og Land   BOAT TRIPS
(☑ 849 2409; www.hafogland.is; tours adult/child Ikr7500/3500) Newly established operator running boat trips from the small harbour (by the museum), taking in the scenery and birdlife around the tiny island of Málmey and the bizarre promontory Þórðarhöfði (tethered to the mainland by a delicate spit). Tours generally leave at 9.30am and 5pm, but you need to book.

⨳ Sleeping & Eating

The emigration centre can help arrange sleeping-bag space (Ikr4900) at the simple Prestbakki cottage

Sunnuberg   GUESTHOUSE €€
(☑ 893 0220, 861 3474; gisting@hofsos.is; Suður-braut 8; s/d Ikr10,000/14,500) Cosy rooms with bathroom are available at homey Sunnuberg, 200m past the pool, opposite the petrol pump and grocery store (note: no kitchen at Sunnuberg).

Sólvík   ICELANDIC €€
(mains Ikr980-3300; ⊙ 10am-9pm Jun-Aug) Down at the small harbour among the museum buildings, Sólvík is a sweet country-style restaurant with a short, simple menu of local classics (cod, lamb, burgers).

Hofsós to Siglufjörður

Wonderfully blustery, **Lónkot** (☑ 453 7432; www.lonkot.com; d with/without bathroom incl breakfast Ikr25,900/20,900; ⊙ Jun-Aug; 🛜) is a gourmet pit stop along the rugged coast, 13km north of Hofsós. The owner, Pálína, bills it as a 'bucolic resort', and she performs magic in the kitchen, inspired by local produce and slow-cooking principles (open noon to 9.30pm; dinner mains Ikr3950 to Ikr5000). Lónkot also has boutique accommodation (including big family suites) with super sea views, and a great indoor hot-pot.

In a scenic valley halfway between Lónkot (24km) and Siglufjörður (25km) is **Bjarnagil** (☑ 467 1030; www.bjarnagil.is/en; per person without bathroom incl breakfast Ikr7500; ⊙ Jun–mid-Sep), a homey farmstay with Sibba and Trausti, a welcoming older couple with plenty of local knowledge to share. Meals and guiding in the area can be arranged with notice; sleeping-bag beds are Ikr5000.

Just north of Bjarnagil is a newly built, fully equipped three-bedroom cottage for rent (sleeps 11) at **Brúnastaðir** (☑ 467 1020; bruna@simnet.is; from Ikr22,000). The views are stupendous, and there's a flower-filled garden and loads of animals – kids will love it. Price doesn't include linen, which can be hired (as can a small boat and kayaks).

Siglufjörður

POP 1190

Sigló (as the locals call it) sits precariously at the foot of a steep slope overlooking a beautiful fjord. In its heyday it was home to 10,000 workers, and fishing boats crammed into the small harbour to unload their catch for the waiting women to gut and salt.

After the herring disappeared from Iceland's north coast in the late 1960s, Siglufjörður declined and never fully recovered.

New tunnels now link the town with Olafsfjörður and points further south, and these days Sigló is receiving warranted attention from travellers smitten by its hiking, its marina and its excellent diversions. Just reaching the town (from either direction) involves a journey that will take your breath away.

◉ Sights

★ Herring Era Museum MUSEUM

(Síldarminjasafnið; www.sild.is; Snorragata 10; adult/child Ikr1400/free; ⊙10am-6pm Jun-Aug, 1-5pm May & Sep, by appointment Oct-Apr) Lovingly created over 16 years, this award-winning museum does a stunning job of re-creating Siglufjörður's boom days between 1903 and 1968, when it was the herring-fishing capital of Iceland. Set in three buildings that were part of an old Norwegian herring station, the museum brings the work and lives of the town's inhabitants vividly to life. Start at the red building on the left, and move right.

In the first building, photographs, displays and a 1930s English film show the fishing and salting process, while upstairs the accommodation block looks as though the workers have just left. Next door is a re-created reducing plant, where herrings were separated into oil (a valuable commodity) and meal (used for fertiliser). The third building gives a sense of harbour life, with trawler boats and equipment based on life on the busy pier during the boom days.

Icelandic Folk Music Centre MUSEUM

(www.siglo.is/setur; Norðurgata 1; adult/child Ikr800/free; ⊙noon-6pm Jun-Aug) Traditional-music enthusiasts may be interested in this sweet little museum, which displays 19th-century instruments and offers recordings of Icelandic songs and chants. It's free to enter if you have a ticket to the Herring Era Museum.

🏃 Activities

Siglufjörður is a great base for hikers, with a series of interesting walks in the area. Some 19km of paths are marked along the avalanche-repelling fence above town, with numerous access points. There's a worthwhile information panel on the northern outskirts of town, beside a parking area, detailing these avalanche defences.

Another popular option is over the passes of Hólsskarð and Hestsskarð into the beautiful, uninhabited Héðinsfjörður, the next fjord to the east. This is where the tunnels connecting Siglufjörður and Olafsfjörður see the light.

In winter, ski lifts operate in the explanded, improved skifields at Skarðsdalur (✆878 3399; www.skardsdalur.is/) above the head of the fjord. A growing number of heliskiing operators work in Tröllaskagi over the winter; contact Viking Heliskiing (✆846 1674; www.vikingheliskiing.com) for info.

In summer you can opt for an ultrascenic round of golf at the newly designed nine-hole course.

✯ Festivals & Events

Folk Music Festival MUSIC

(www.siglo.is/setur) Folk-music aficionados will enjoy this relaxed five-day affair in early July.

Herring Festival CULTURAL

Siglufjörður's biggest shindig takes place on the bank-holiday weekend in early August and

---

WINTER WONDERS

You're probably aware that the number of visitors to Iceland has skyrocketed in recent years. You may well be asking: what if there was a way to experience Iceland's awesome outdoors, but with smaller crowds? There is: visit in winter. For the Northern Lights, yes, but so much more. And don't feel you need to be confined to Reykjavík and surrounds – domestic flights to Akureyri operate year-round, and there's a growing number of winter activities and operators in the country's north to help you experience the snowy-mountain magic.

Akureyri, Tröllaskagi and Mývatn are all winter wonderlands: Akureyri has winter festivals and easy access to Iceland's biggest skifield at Hlíðarfjall (p225). Tröllaskagi offers smaller skifields (at Dalvík, Ólafsfjörður and Siglufjörður), plus great heliskiing operators, and Mývatn has activities like snowshoe and cross-country ski tours, and snowmobiling on the frozen lake. A good tip is to travel from around February, when daylight hours are increasing (but don't discount Christmas-New Year as a festive time to visit).

If you're not experienced in winter driving, it's a good idea to leave that to the kitted-out professionals with their super-Jeeps and local expertise. Operators such as Saga Travel (p227), based in Akureyri, are a sure bet, but check out the websites of companies such as Bergmenn Mountain Guides (p221), Mývatn's Hike & Bike (p236) and Sel-Hótel (p241) to see what else appeals.

re-creates the gold-rush atmosphere of the town's glory days. The week leading up to it is full of events: singing, dancing, fishy feasting.

🛏 Sleeping

Siglufjörður HI Hostel HOSTEL €
(Gistihúsið Hvanneyri; ☑467 1506; www.hvanneyri.com; Aðalgata 10; dm/d without bathroom Ikr4100/11,200; 🛜) Chipped cherubs and faded gilt make up the dated decor of this quirky 1930s hotel, where stately proportions hint at wealthier times. There are 19 rooms with kitsch furnishings, a couple of TV lounges, a grand dining room and a guest kitchen. HI members get a discount of Ikr700 per person; linen hire costs Ikr1500.

Campsite CAMPGROUND €
(campsites per person Ikr800; ⊙ Jun-Aug) Oddly placed in the middle of town near the harbour, with a small bock housing showers and a laundry. There's a second patch of grass beyond the city limits – follow Suðurgata (or take Norðurtún, signed off Sorragata).

★Herring Guesthouse GUESTHOUSE €€
(☑868 4200; www.theherringhouse.com; Hávegur 5; s/d without bathroom Ikr11,900/15,900, 4-person apt Ikr39,900; 🛜) Þorir and Erla are charming, knowledgable hosts (he's a former town mayor) offering personalised service at their stylish, view-blessed guesthouse – now with two locations (the second is at Hlíðarvegur 1, behind the church). There is a guest kitchen at the main house, and a lovely (optional) breakfast spread (Ikr1750). Families will appreciate the two-bedroom apartment.

★Siglunes Guesthouse GUESTHOUSE €€
(☑467 1222; www.hotelsiglunes.is; Lækjargata 10; d with/without bathroom incl breakfast Ikr21,900/15,900; 🛜) Personality shines through in this cool guesthouse, where vintage furniture is paired with contemporary art and ultramodern bathrooms in the hotel-standard wing. There's equally appealing guesthouse rooms, a big dining hall for breakfast (included in summer rates), and a cosy bar area celebrating happy hour from 5pm to 7pm.

Hótel Sígló HOTEL €€€
(☑467 1550; www.siglohotel.is) The town's 'patron', a local man made good in the US, is behind the vibrant marina redevelopment; he is now building an upmarket, 68-room harbourside hotel (including on-site restaurant and bar). It was under construction at the time of writing, but should be open by the time you read this. Look for more details online.

🍴 Eating

The street opposite the supermarket is Aðalgata; it's home to a busy bakery and pizzeria, but come mealtime most appetites are focused on the primary-coloured marina, where old warehouses have been reborn as photogenic eateries.

★Hannes Boy ICELANDIC €€
(☑461 7730; www.raudka.is; mains Ikr3290-5990; ⊙noon-2pm & 6-10pm Jun-Aug, shorter hours Sep-May) Dressed in sunny yellow, this stylish, light-filled space is furnished with funky seats made from old herring barrels. The upmarket menu is fish-focused (naturally), with lobster soup and catch of the day fresh from the boats outside. Reservations recommended.

Kaffi Rauðka ICELANDIC €€
(www.raudka.is; mains Ikr890-2990; ⊙11am-10pm Jun-Aug, shorter hours Sep-May; 🛜) The counterpoint to neighbouring Hannes Boy, ruby-red Rauðka has a more informal air, with an all-day menu of sandwiches, salads and hearty mains such as barbecue ribs, plus good-value weekday soup/meal of the day (Ikr1190/1590). At weekends, it often stages live music.

Samkaup-Úrval SUPERMARKET
(Aðalgata; ⊙10am-7pm Mon-Fri, 11am-7pm Sat, 1-5pm Sun) Well stocked for self-caterers. ATM inside.

Vínbúðin LIQUOR STORE
(Eyrargata 25; ⊙2-6pm Mon-Thu, 1-7pm Fri, 11am-2pm Sat Jun-Aug, closed Sat Sep-May) Government-run liquor store.

ℹ Information

The town has services such as a bank, pharmacy, post office etc. The herring museum offers some tourist info, as does the **information desk** (⊙1-5pm Mon-Fri, 11am-3pm Sat & Sun Jun-Aug) inside the Ráðhús (town hall) on Gránugata.

There is a little information on the website www.fjallabyggd.is (Fjallabyggð is the municipality covering Siglufjörður and Ólafsfjörður), and plans to extend coverage at www.trollaskagi.com.

ℹ Getting There & Away

BUS

Strætó (☑540 2700; www.straeto.is) services:
➾ Bus 78 to Ólafsfjörður (Ikr700, 15min, 3 daily Mon-Fri, 1 daily Sun)

➾ Bus 78 to Akureyri (Ikr2100, 70min, 3 daily Mon-Fri, 1 daily Sun) Runs via Dalvík.

CAR

Prior to the tunnels opening in 2010, Siglufjörður and Ólafsfjörður were joined by the 62km mountain road over Lagheiði (the old Rte 82). This road was only accessible in summer; in winter the towns were 234km apart. Thanks to the new tunnels through the mountains, that connection now measures 16km.

Travelling east, there's a 4km tunnel that opens into beautiful Héðinsfjörður, before a second tunnel travels the remaining 7km to Ólafsfjörður.

Ólafsfjörður

POP 785

Beautifully locked between sheer mountain slopes and dark fjord waters, fishing town Ólafsfjörður still retains a sense of isolation, even with tunnels now linking it with Siglufjörður, its sister settlement further north.

From Akureyri, you have to pass through a thin 3km tunnel just to make your way into town, which makes for a cinematic entrance.

⊙ Sights & Activities

Ólafsfjörður receives good snow in winter, when the downhill **ski slopes** above town lurch into action. There's also an excellent **swimming pool**, and nine-hole **golf course**. Brimnes Hotel offers rental of boats and kayaks for exploration; check the hotel's website for a rundown of possible activities in the area.

Náttúrugripasafnið MUSEUM
(Aðalgata 14; adult/child Ikr600/free; ⊙10am-2pm Tue-Sun Jun-Aug) Nátúrrugripasafnið is a small bird-oriented museum; it's Ólafsfjörður's only formal sight.

🛏 Sleeping & Eating

At mealtimes, consider a jaunt up the road to Siglufjöður.

Campsite CAMPGROUND €
(per person Ikr800) Toilets, water and electricity are available; guests use the showers inside the neighbouring swimming-pool complex.

Gistihús Jóa GUESTHOUSE €€
(Joe's Guesthouse; ☑847 4331; http://joesguesthouse.is; Strandgata 2; d without bathroom incl breakfast Ikr14,000-16,000; ⊛) Joe's handsome six-room guesthouse is in a restored old post office next to the supermarket, with a lovely cafe and info centre downstairs (where breakfast is served). Compact rooms have handbasins, quirky flooring and modern chocolate-brown decor.

Brimnes Hotel & Bungalows HOTEL, COTTAGES €€
(☑466 2400; www.brimnes.is; Bylgjubyggð 2; s/d incl breakfast Ikr13,400/19,000, cottages from Ikr27,000; ⊛) The real draws at the town's primary accommodation are the fabulous lakeshore log cabins (varying sizes, sleeping up to seven), with hot tubs built into the verandah and views over the water. There are also 11 bright, freshly renovated en-suite rooms, plus a decent restaurant (mains Ikr1450–Ikr3800) serving the usual fare (soup, fish, burgers).

Kaffi Klara CAFE €
(www.kaffiklara.is; Strandgata 2; lunch Ikr900-1400; ⊙11am-7pm Jun-Aug, shorter hours Sep-May) The sweet cafe has extensive info about the area, plus a selection of soups, sandwiches and cakes. There are books and board games to help pass rainy days, plus our favourite feature: the old phone booths (this used to be the old post office).

Samkaup-Úrval SUPERMARKET
(Aðalgata; ⊙9am-7pm Mon-Fri, 11am-6pm Sat, 1-5pm Sun) For self-catering.

ⓘ Getting There & Away

Strætó (☑540 2700; www.straeto.is) services:
⇒ Bus 78 to Siglufjörður (Ikr700, 15min, 3 daily Mon-Fri, 1 daily Sun)
⇒ Bus 78 to Akureyri (Ikr1750, 55min, 3 daily Mon-Fri, 1 daily Sun) Runs via Dalvík.

Dalvík

POP 1365

Sleepy Dalvík found a snug, scenic spot between breezy Eyjafjörður and the rolling hills of Svarfaðardalur. Most tourists come here to catch the Grímsey ferry, but if you've got some time there are plenty of reasons to linger, including great activities in the area, plus interesting museums and superb accommodation.

There's a helpful **tourist information point** (☑846 4908; www.dalvikurbyggd.is; Goðabraut; ⊙10am-6pm Mon-Fri, 1-5pm Sat) at Menningarhúsið Berg, the modern cultural centre that houses the library and a cafe. Staff can help with information on the activities in the region, including horse riding, skiing, golf, canoeing, guided hiking and birdwatching.

⊙ Sights & Activities

Byggðasafnið Hvoll MUSEUM
(www.dalvik.is/byggdasafn; Karlsbraut; adult/child Ikr700/free; ⊙11am-6pm Jun-Aug) Dalvík's

quality folk museum is high on oddball factor. Skip the usual taxidermic characters (yes, another polar bear!) and find the rooms dedicated to the poignant story of local giant Jóhan Pétursson. At 2.34m (almost 7ft 7in), Jóhan was Iceland's tallest man.

Birdland Exhibition MUSEUM
(www.birdland.is; adult/child Ikr800/400; ☺noon-5pm Jun-Aug; ♠) Outside town, 5km on Rte 805, this sweet-natured, kid-friendly museum showcases quirky avian facts beside a wetland reserve beloved by birdwatchers. There is camping and a well-regarded hostel out here, plus activities – see the website www.husabakki.is.

☞ Tours

Arctic Sea Tours WHALE WATCHING
(☑771 7600; www.arcticseatours.is; 3hr tour adult/child Ikr9000/4500; ☺year-round) This professional outfit operates three-hour tours a couple of times a day in high summer (it even has tours in winter!). All tours include a short sea-angling stint, and your catch is grilled on the barbecue as soon as the boat docks.

Other options: a six-hour blue-whale safari (mid-May to June), a midnight sun cruise (departs 11pm June to mid-July), or sea-angling trips. Pick-up from Akureyri is available (Ikr2000).

Bergmenn Mountain Guides ADVENTURE TOUR
(☑698 9870; www.bergmenn.com) Based outside Dalvík is this well-regarded company, which specialises in ski touring, ski mountaineering, ice climbing, alpine climbing and other mountain-related activities. Fun fact: the name of the company's owner, Jökull Bergmann, translates as 'Glacier Mountainman' – so you know he found his calling. The company runs Arctic Heli Skiing (www.arcticheliskiing.com).

⬛ Sleeping & Eating

★Dalvík HI Hostel HOSTEL €
(Vegamót; ☑865 8391, 466 1060; www.vegamot.net; Hafnarbraut 4; dm/d without bathroom Ikr4500/11,100; ♠) This is, for our money, one of Iceland's best hostels, and certainly its prettiest – it's more like a boutique guesthouse than a budgeteer's bunkhouse. Heiða, the friendly owner, has a creative streak put to good use in quirky, vintage-inspired decor. The seven-room hostel is in the town centre, in a white building called Gimli.

The owners have more accommodation options, including three wooden cabins

(Ikr14,700) beside their home (close to the swimming pool), and Gamli Bærinn (the 'Old Farmhouse'), a gorgeously romantic self-contained cottage (Ikr21,800).

At the hostel, HI members get a discount of Ikr700 per person; prices generally exclude linen, which can be hired for Ikr1500 per person. Breakfast (Ikr1400) is a treat, served at the owners' nearby cafe, Kaffihús Bakkabræðra.

Campground CAMPGROUND €
(per campervan/tent Ikr2100/1600) Large camping area by the town pool.

★Kaffihús Bakkabræðra ICELANDIC €
(Grundargata 1; soup & salad buffet Ikr1790; ☺8am-11pm Mon-Fri, 10am-11pm Sat & Sun) Signed 'Gísli Eiríkur Helgi' and named after three brothers from a folk tale, this might just be the perfect small-town cafe: decked out in timber, full of vintage bric-a-brac and mismatched china (it's owned by the folks behind the town's retro-chic hostel), and serving delicious fish soup and waffles with homemade jams.

The locals love it (understandably), and there's a bar area and small theatre out the back.

Samkaup-Úrval SUPERMARKET
(☺10am-7pm Mon-Fri, to 6pm Sat, 1-5pm Sun) Central supermarket, by the N1.

❶ Getting There & Away
Dalvík is the jumping-off point for ferries to Grímsey (p226).

Strætó (☑540 2700; www.straeto.is) bus services:
➡ Bus 78 to Siglufjörður (Ikr1050, 30min, 3 daily Mon-Fri, 1 daily Sun)
➡ Bus 78 to Akureyri (Ikr1400, 45min, 3 daily Mon-Fri, 1 daily Sun)

Árskógsströnd
The rich agricultural region known as Árskógsströnd runs north along the western shore of Eyjafjörður, from where there are dramatic views across the water to the mountains opposite. It's the main jumping-off point for those who want to explore little Hrísey offshore.

◉ Sights & Activities

Bruggsmiðjan – Kaldi BREWERY
(Kaldi Beer; ☑466 2505; www.bruggsmidjan.is; Öldugötu 22, Árskógssandur; tour Ikr1500; ☺tours

by appointment) Árskógsströnd is the home of Bruggsmiðjan microbrewery, producing excellent, in-demand Kaldi brews using Czech techniques. The brewery is open to drop-in visitors (if the timing is good), but you're better off calling to arrange a tour (this is essential for groups). You could also consider joining a food-focused tour from Akureyri-based Saga Travel, which visits this and other local producers.

Níels Jónsson   WHALE WATCHING
(⌖867 0000; www.whales.is; 3hr tour adult/child Ikr7800/free; ⊙mid-May–mid-Sep) From Árskógsströnd, you can take short detour to Hauganes to climb aboard the former fishing boat *Níels Jónsson* for an adventure that includes fishing and whale watching (this is Iceland's oldest whale-watch operator). Hauganes is 2km off Rte 82, about 11km south of Dalvík (30km north of Akureyri).

AKUREYRI

POP 17,930

Akureyri stands strong as Iceland's second city, but a Melbourne, Manchester or Montreal it is not. And how could it be? There are only 18,000 residents! It's a wonder the city (which would be a 'town' in any other country) generates this much buzz. Expect cool cafes, quality restaurants and something of a late-night bustle – a far cry from other towns in rural Iceland.

Akureyri nestles at the head of Iceland's longest (60km) fjord, at the base of snow-capped peaks. In summer, flowerboxes, trees and well-tended gardens belie the location, just a stone's throw from the Arctic Circle. Lively winter festivals and some of Iceland's best skiing provide plenty of low-season appeal. With its relaxed and easy attitude and extensive food and accommodation choices, it's the natural base for exploring Eyjafjörður, and further afield.

History

The first permanent inhabitant of Eyjafjörður was Norse-Irish settler Helgi Magri (Helgi the Lean), who arrived in about 890. By 1602 a trading post had been established at present-day Akureyri. There were still no permanent dwellings though, as all the settlers maintained rural farms and homesteads. By the late 18th century the town had accumulated a whopping 10 residents, all Danish traders, and was granted municipal status.

The town soon began to prosper and by 1900 Akureyri's population numbered 1370.

Today Akureyri is thriving. Its fishing company and shipyard are the largest in the country, and the city's university (established in 1987) gives the town a youthful exuberance.

⊙ Sights

Akureyri has several museums, and while it's laudable that the town celebrates its artists and authors, many of these institutions are of limited interest unless you have a particular admiration for a specific artist's work. There are also museums dedicated to aviation, local industry, antique toys and motorbikes.

If you have your own vehicle, consider visiting some of greater Eyjafjörður's museums flanking the eastern and western shores.

★**Akureyrarkirkja**   CHURCH
(www.akirkja.is; Eyrarlandsvegur; ⊙generally 10am-4pm Mon-Fri) Dominating the town from high on a hill, Akureyri's landmark church was designed by Guðjón Samúelsson, the architect responsible for Reykjavík's Hallgrímskirkja. Although the basalt theme connects them, Akureyrarkirkja looks more like a stylised 1920s US skyscraper than its big-city brother.

Built in 1940, the church contains a large 3200-pipe organ and a series of rather untraditional reliefs of the life of Christ. There's also a suspended ship hanging from the ceiling, reflecting an old Nordic tradition of votive offerings for the protection of loved ones at sea. Perhaps the most striking feature is the beautiful central window in the chancel, which originally graced Coventry Cathedral in England.

The church admits visitors most days; check the board outside for opening times, as they change frequently.

Akureyri Museum   MUSEUM
(Minjasafnið á Akureyri; www.akmus.is; Aðalstræti 58; adult/child Ikr1000/free; ⊙10am-5pm Jun–mid-Sep, 2-4pm Thu-Sun mid-Sep–May) This sweet, well-curated museum houses art and historical items relating to town life, including maps, photos and re-creations of early Icelandic homes. The **museum garden** became the first place in Iceland to cultivate trees when a nursery was established here in 1899.

Nonnahús   MUSEUM
(www.nonni.is; Aðalstræti 54; adult/child Ikr1000/free; ⊙10am-5pm Jun-Aug) The most interesting

of the artists' residences, Nonnahús was the childhood home of renowned children's writer Reverend Jón Sveinsson (1857–1944), known to most as Nonni. His old-fashioned tales of derring-do have a rich local flavour. The house dates from 1850; its cramped rooms and simple furnishings provide a poignant insight into life in 19th-century Iceland.

A combined ticket for Nonnahús and the neighbouring Akureyri Museum is Ikr1400.

Centre for Visual Arts   MUSEUM
(Sjónlistamiðstöðin; www.sjonlist.is; Kaupvangs-stræti 8-12; ⊙10am-5pm Tue-Sun Jun-Aug, from noon Sep-May) FREE Stimulate your senses with a browse at this free arts centre, which combines the Akureyri Art Museum with a handful of local galleries and hosts eclectic, innovative exhibitions – from graphic design to portraiture.

★**Lystigarðurinn**   GARDENS
(www.lystigardur.akureyri.is; Eyrarlandsholt; ⊙8am-10pm Mon-Fri, 9am-10pm Sat & Sun Jun-Sep) FREE The most northerly botanical garden in the world makes a delightful picnic spot on sun-ny days. The wealth of plant life on display is truly astonishing considering the gardens' proximity to the Arctic Circle. You'll find examples of every species native to Iceland, as well as a host of high-latitude and high-altitude plants from around the world. There's also a beautifully situated cafe.

Kjarnaskógur   OUTDOORS
About 3km south of town is Iceland's most visited 'forest', the Kjarnaskógur woods. This bushland area has walking and mountain-bike trails, picnic areas and barbecues, and kids' playgrounds. In winter, the area is good for cross-country skiing. The campground at Hamrar has easy access to the woods.

🏃 Activities

In winter, snowfields draw skiers from all over the country, while independent summertime activities include hiking, biking, golf and hot-pot-hopping.

Akureryi is also the base for a multitude of tours and guided activities all over Iceland's north (see p227).

LONG WEEKEND REMIX: THE DIAMOND CIRCLE

Perfectly positioned between North America and Europe, Iceland has become the *it* destination for a cool weekend getaway. The constant stream of tourists has turned the three-day Reykjavík–Golden Circle–Blue Lagoon trip into a well-worn circuit, so why not blaze a new trail and tackle Iceland's northern triangle of stunning attractions: Mývatn, Húsavík and Akureyri. It's less legwork than you think – when you land at Keflavík International Airport, catch a connecting flight to Akureyri (you may need to travel to the capital's domestic airport). And to make things even simpler, here's a handy planner.

Day 1: Akureyri

Jump-start your visit to the north with something quintessentially Icelandic: horse riding. Trust us: these aren't your usual horses. Then, a half-day is plenty of time to bop around the streets of the city centre. Or for those who can withstand another plane ride, spend the afternoon on Grímsey, Iceland's only slice of the Arctic Circle. For dinner, a good option is Strikið or Rub23, followed by a night out on the town.

Day 2: Húsavík & Around

In the morning, head to Húsavík. First, swing by the Húsavík Whale Museum for a bit of background info, then hop aboard a whale-watching tour. Consider heading east for a walk among the canyon walls of Ásbyrgi, check out the roar of thunderous Dettifoss, then recount your whale tales over dinner back at Naustið in Húsavík.

Day 3: Mývatn

For those of you who have been drooling over the photos of Iceland's turquoise-tinted spa springs, fret not. Mývatn has its very own version of the Blue Lagoon: the Mývatn Nature Baths. After a leisurely soak, it's time to get the blood flowing again. A three-hour hike around eastern Mývatn takes in a smorgasbord of geological anomalies. A stop at stinky Hverir is a must, and, if time permits, have a wander around the steam vents at Krafla. Then make your way back to Akureyri to catch your flight, but not before visiting one last site: the heavenly waterfall Goðafoss.

Akureyri

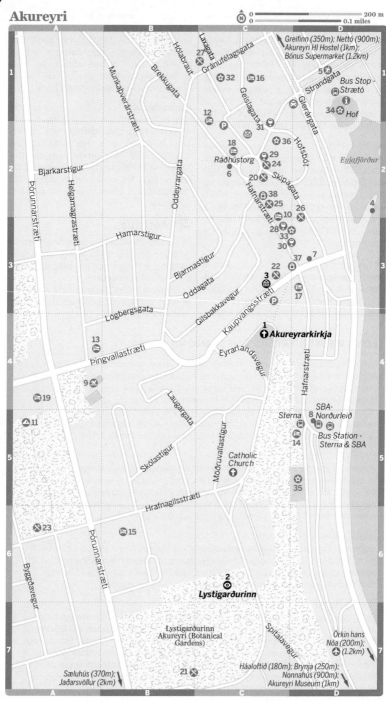

Greifinn (350m); Nettó (900m); Akureyri HI Hostel (1km); Bónus Supermarket (1.2km)

Bus Stop - Strætó

Hof

Eyjafjörður

Ráðhústorg

1 Akureyrarkirkja

Catholic Church

SBA- Norðurleið

Sterna

Bus Station - Sterna & SBA

2 Lystigarðurinn

Lystigarðurinn Akureyri (Botanical Gardens)

Örkin hans Nóa (200m); (1.2km)

Sæluhús (370m); Jaðarsvöllur (2km)

Háaloftið (180m); Brynja (250m); Nonnahús (900m); Akureyri Museum (1km)

0   200 m
0   0.1 miles

Akureyri

Sundlaug Akureyrar　　　SWIMMING POOL
(Þingvallastræti 21; adult/child Ik550/200; ◷6.45am-9pm Mon-Fri, 8am-7.30pm Sat & Sun; ⊕) The hub of local life: Akureyri's outdoor swimming pool is one of Iceland's finest. It has three heated pools, hot-pots, water-slides, saunas and steamrooms.

Ferðafélag Akureyrar　　　HIKING
(Touring Club of Akureyri; ☑462 2720; www.ffa.is; Strandgata 23; ◷3-6pm Mon-Fri Jun-Aug) For information on hiking in the area, contact Ferðafélag Akureyrar and check out its helpful website detailing (in English) the huts it operates in northern Iceland and the highlands, plus notes on the Askja Trail, and its program (in Icelandic) of hiking and skiing tours that travellers can join.

Another helpful resource is the collection of Útivist & afþreying hiking maps (there are seven in the series – #1 and #2 focus on the Eyjafjörður area); these are available at the tourist information centre.

Jaðarsvöllur　　　GOLF
(☑462 2974; www.golficeland.org; round Ikr5300-6400) Up for a game of midnight golf? At only a few degrees south of the Arctic Circle, Akureyri's par-71 Jaðarsvöllur basks in per-petual daylight from June to early August, and you can play golf here around the clock; book ahead for the midnight tee-off.

The course is home to the annual 36-hole **Arctic Open** (www.arcticopen.is), a tournament played over two nights in late June.

Hlíðarfjall Ski Centre　　　SKIING
(☑462 2280; www.hlidarfjall.is; day pass adult/child Ikr3000/1200; ⊕) Iceland's premier downhill ski slope is west of town, 5km up Glerárdalur, with 24 pistes covering all skill levels. The area has a vertical drop of 455m, with the longest trail over 2.5km. There's also 20km of cross-country ski routes.

The ski season usually runs between December and late April, with the best conditions in February and March (Easter is particularly busy). In the long hours of winter darkness, many of the downhill runs are floodlit.

There's ski and snowboard rental, two restaurants and a ski school. In season, buses usually connect the site with Akureyri; check the website for details.

Mt Súlur　　　HIKING
A pleasant but demanding day hike leads up the Glerárdalur valley to the summit of Mt

NORTH ICELAND AKUREYRI

GRÍMSEY

Best known as Iceland's only true piece of the Arctic Circle, the remote island of Grímsey (population 77), 40km from the mainland, is a lonely little place where birds outnumber people by about 10,000 to one.

Grímsey's appeal probably lies less in the destination itself, and more about what it represents. Tourists flock here to snap up their 'I visited the Arctic Circle' certificate and pose for a photo with the 'you're standing on the Arctic Circle' monument (which is actually around 20m south of the 'real' line). Afterwards, there's plenty of time to appreciate the windswept setting. Scenic coastal cliffs and dramatic basalt formations make a popular home for dozens of species of seabirds, including loads of puffins, plus the kamikaze Arctic tern. We're particularly fond of the anecdote that the airport runway has to be cleared of the terns a few minutes before aircraft are scheduled to arrive.

If sleeping inside the Arctic Circle sounds too good to pass up, two places offer accommodation. Follow the stairs up through the trapdoor at cosy **Gullsól** (☎467 3190; gullsol@visir.is; r without bathroom per person Ikr5500) to find teeny-tiny rooms perched above the island's gift shop (which opens in conjunction with ferry arrivals and sells coffee/tea and waffles). The full kitchen is handy for self-caterers; sleeping-bag beds are Ikr4000.

Things are slightly more upmarket at **Básar** (☎467 3103; www.gistiheimilidbasar.is; s/d without bathroom incl breakfast Ikr11,000/16,000), right next to the airport. Sleeping-bag accommodation here is Ikr6000. There is a guest kitchen and meals are available, and sailing and sea-angling trips can be arranged (with notice).

There's a small campground by the community centre. The only restaurant is **Krían**, open daily in summer. A general store is attached.

Getting There & Away

There are a number of options for reaching Grímsey.

Air From mid-June to mid-August, Norlandair (www.norlandair.is) operates daily flights to/from Akureyri; flights operate three times weekly the rest of the year. The bumpy 25-minute journey takes in the full length of Eyjafjörður and is an experience in itself. Ticketing is handled by **Air Iceland** (☎570 3030; www.airiceland.is); one-way fares start around Ikr10,000.

Air Excursion From mid-June to mid-August, Air Iceland offers half-day excursions from Akureyri (Ikr28,200) that include flights and a couple of hours on the island (including a guided walk). You can also do the tour from Reykjavík, taking a short domestic flight first to Akureyri.

Ferry From mid-May to August, the **Sæfari ferry** (☎458 8970; www.saefari.is) departs from Dalvík at 9am Monday, Wednesday and Friday, returning from Grímsey at 4pm (giving you four hours on the island if you're not overnighting). The journey takes three hours and costs adult/child Ikr4830/free one way.

If coming from Akureyri, unfortunately the morning bus (Strætó's bus 78) won't get you to Dalvík in good time for the boat's departure.

Dalvík-based **Arctic Sea Tours** (www.arcticseatours.is) can put together a 10-hour day tour (Ikr15,000) utilising the Sæfari ferry but filling your stopover time with guided walk, lunch, and a chance to meet locals. For a fee, it can arrange pick-up from Akureyri.

In winter, the ferry departure service remains the same; however, the ship immediately returns to Dalvík once cargo has been discharged and loaded.

Boat Excursion **North Sailing** (☎464 7272; www.northsailing.is) offers two-night sailing/ whale-watching expeditions out of Húsavík, which moor one night at Grímsey. Trips depart weekly from May to mid-July (Ikr115,000). Also out of Húsavík, **Gentle Giants** (☎464 1500; www.gentlegiants.is) has a six-hour trip to Grímsey on fast rigid inflatable boats (RIBs; they get you to the island in about an hour). Trips run twice a week in summer (Ikr63,550) but require a minimum number.

Súlur (1213m). The trail begins on Súluvegur, a left turn off Þingvallastræti just before the Glerá bridge. Give yourself at least six hours to complete the return journey.

☞ Tours

Most tours can be booked online (where up-to-date offerings and prices are found); you can also visit the information centre for assistance, or booking agents scattered around town.

Note that some operators based outside Akureyri arrange transfers to their base, for a fee (eg whale-watching tours north of Akureyri, white-water rafting in Varmahlíð).

★ Saga Travel   ADVENTURE TOUR

(☑ 558 8888; www.sagatravel.is; Kaupvangsstræti 4) Offers a rich and diverse year-round program of excursions and activities throughout the north; obvious destinations like Mývatn, Húsavík (for whale watching) and Askja in the highlands, but also innovative tours along themes such as food or art and design. Check out Saga's full program online, or drop by its office (open 7.30am to 10pm in summer).

Quirky 'midnight sun' tours depart at 10pm in June and take you to attractions like Dettifoss and Mývatn in the quiet wee hours; winter tours are varied (snowmobiling, snowshoeing, Northern Lights viewing – which is, of course, weather dependent). Private itineraries can be arranged; guides are local and well connected. Tours have a maximum of 16 participants.

SBA-Norðurleið   BUS TOURS

(☑ 550 0700; www.sba.is; Hafnarstræti 82) The bus company runs a range of sightseeing tours in north Iceland, with popular destinations including Mývatn, Dettifoss, Húsavík and Askja.

Nonni Travel   TOURS AGENCY

(☑ 461 1841; www.nonnitravel.is; Brekkugata 5) Travel agency able to hook you up with just about any tour in the area, as well as tours further afield (to Greenland and the Faroe Islands).

Ambassador   WHALE WATCHING

(www.ambassador.is; adult/child Ikr9990/4995; ⊙ mid-May–mid-Oct) A handful of places along Eyjafjörður offer whale-watching boat trips, and Akureyri now has an operator. Trips are three hours: detractors say there's a long way to travel to get to northern parts of the fjord (where whale sightings are most common), but if you treat this as a sightseeing/whale-watching combo you won't be disappointed with the glorious scenery.

The Traveling Viking   ADVENTURE TOURS

(☑ 896 3569; www.ttv.is) A company doing plenty of local tours, from the expected (Mývatn, Dettifoss, Húsavík) to the more offbeat, including a four-hour family-friendly option focusing on the 'hidden people', or winter ice-fishing. The company also gets some buzz for its *Game of Thrones*–themed tour of the Mývatn region.

Skjaldarvík   HORSE RIDING

(☑ 552 5200; www.skjaldarvik.is; 90-min ride Ikr7900) With a superb guesthouse and restaurant, 6km north of town, Skjaldarvík offers 1½-hour tours along the fjord and into the surrounding hills, departing at 10am, 2pm and 5pm daily in summer. It also offers the good-value 'Ride & Bite': 5pm horse ride followed by access to the outdoor hot-pot and a two-course dinner (Ikr11,900).

Kátur   HORSE RIDING

(☑ 695 7218; www.hestaleiga.is; Kaupangur; 1hr/2hr ride Ikr6000/8000; ⊙ Jun–mid-Sep) A few minutes southeast of Akureyri off Rte 829, Kátur is another respected outfit offering short rides.

✺ Festivals & Events

The Events & Festivals page of the www.visitakureyri.is website lists the year's big celebrations and commemorations. Winter events are getting a real boost.

Iceland Winter Games   WINTER SPORTS

(www.icelandwintergames.com) Cementing its spot as Iceland's winter-sports capital, Akureyri now hosts this international freeski and slopestyle competition in February/March. It's timed to coincide with the Éljagangur (Blizzard) festival of gloriously wintry activities (skiing, snowmobiling, dogsledding etc). Rug up!

Akureyri Town Festival   CULTURAL

Akureyri's biggest summertime fiesta, celebrated on the last weekend of August with various concerts, exhibitions and events.

🛏 Sleeping

Akureyri's accommodation scene has undergone a transformation in recent years, with a slew of new, high-quality options. That said, the town still fills up in summer – book ahead. Bear in mind, too, that there are plenty of options outside the town centre – Akureyri is surrounded by excellent rural farmstay properties (you'll need your own car for these). Consult the handy Icelandic Farm Holidays booklet or website (www.farmholidays.is).

The tourist information centre can usually help if you arrive without a booking (Ikr500 reservation fee), but your options will be limited, especially in summer.

Most accommodation is open year-round (winter weekends are especially busy with skiers). The website of the tourist office (p233) lists most options in the area. Another great source is AirBnB (www.airbnb.com), detailing private rooms, cottages, apartments and houses for rent, with strong coverage in Akureyri.

As ever, check websites for up-to-date prices and low-season rates – and shop around for discounted rates. Prices listed here are for the summer peak; most are from 2014.

Akureyri Backpackers HOSTEL €
(☏ 571 9050; www.akureyribackpackers.com; Hafnarstræti 67; dm/d without bathroom Ikr4500-5500/18,000; @ 🛜) Supremely placed in the town's heart, this backpackers has a chilled travellers vibe and includes tour-booking service and popular bar. Rooms are spread over three floors: four- to eight-bed dorms, plus private rooms with made-up beds on the top floor. Minor gripe: all showers are in the basement, as is a sauna (toilets and sinks on all levels, however).

Linen hire (in dorms) costs Ikr990; breakfast is Ikr990.

Gula Villan GUESTHOUSE €
(☏ 896 8464; www.gulavillan.is; Brekkugata 8; s/d without bathroom Ikr10,500/14,700) Owner Sigríður has a background in travel and this cheerful yellow-and-white villa shines under her care. Bright, well-maintained rooms are in a good central location. In a second building, **Gula Villan II** (Þingvallastræti 14) is run by the same folks and offers extra space in summer. Both guesthouses have guest kitchens and breakfast served on request (quite steep at Ikr2000). BYO sleeping bags to reduce the price.

Akureyri HI Hostel HOSTEL €
(Stórholt; ☏ 462 3657; www.hostel.is; Stórholt 1; dm Ikr4100, d with/without bathroom Ikr11,200/15,500; @ 🛜) Well within the city limits though slightly removed from the action, this friendly, well-run hostel is a 15-minute walk north of the city centre. There's a TV lounge and two kitchens in the main house (rooms all have TV), a barbecue deck and two self-contained cottages sleeping up to eight. The owner happily imparts local knowledge; check-in time (from 3pm) is strictly enforced.

HI members get a discount of Ikr700 per person; linen hire is Ikr1250.

City Campsite CAMPGROUND €
(Þórunnarstræti; sites per person Ikr1100, plus Ikr100 lodging tax per site; ⊙ mid-Jun–mid-Sep) This central site has a washing machine, dining area and free showers, plus a car-free policy (except for loading and unloading). Note: no kitchen. Handily, it's close to the swimming pool and a supermarket.

Hamrar Campsite CAMPGROUND €
(www.hamrar.is; sites per person Ikr1100, plus Ikr100 lodging tax per site; ⊙ mid-May–mid-Sep) This huge site, 1.5km south of town in a leafy setting in Kjarnaskógur woods, has newer facilities than the city campsite, and mountain views.

★ Skjaldarvík GUESTHOUSE €€
(☏ 552 5200; www.skjaldarvik.is; s/d without bathroom incl breafast Ikr14,900/19,900; @ 🛜) A slice of guesthouse nirvana, Skjaldarvík lies in a bucolic farm setting 6km north of town. It's owned by a young family and features quirky design details (plants sprouting from shoes, vintage typewriters as artwork on the walls). Plus: bumper breakfast buffet, horse-riding tours, hot-pot, book swap, and honesty bar in the comfy lounge.

The pretty-as-a-picture **restaurant** (mains Ikr3700–Ikr5900; open dinner June to mid-September) prepares a small but well-executed menu; it's open to nonguests, but bookings are essential. Consider the excellent 'Ride & Bite' option (p227) to combine dining and a horse ride.

★ Sæluhús APARTMENTS €€
(☏ 412 0800; www.saeluhus.is; Sunnutröð; studio/house Ikr23,700/42,500; 🛜) This awesome mini-village of modern studios and houses is perfect for a few days' R&R. Each house may be better equipped than your own back home: three bedrooms (sleeping seven), kitchen, washing machine and verandah with hot tub and barbecue. Studios are smaller, with kitchen and access to a laundry (some have hot tub, but these cost extra), and are ideal for a couple.

★ Icelandair Hotel Akureyri HOTEL €€
(☏ 518 1000; www.icelandairhotels.com; Þingvallastræti 23; d incl breakfast from Ikr28,800; @ 🛜) Icelandair added an Akureyri property to its portfolio in 2011, and did it in style. This high-class hotel showcases Icelandic designers and artists amongst its fresh, white-and-caramel-toned decor; rooms are compact but well designed. Added extras: outdoor terrace, lounge serving high tea of an afternoon and happy-hour cocktails in the early evening.

HRÍSEY

Iceland's second-largest offshore island (after Heimaey) is the peaceful, low-lying Hrísey (population 166), easily reached from the mainland. Thrust out into the middle of Ey-jafjörður, the island enjoys spectacular panoramas and is especially noted as a breeding ground and protected area for ptarmigan, as well as being home to an enormous colony of Arctic terns.

There's a small **information office** (☑ 695 0077; ⊙ 1-5pm Jun-Aug) inside Hús Hákarla-Jörundur, a small museum (admission Ikr500) on shark-fishing beside the church in the picturesque village where the boat docks. You can pick up the handy Hrísey brochure here or in Akureyri, or check out two competing websites: www.hrisey.net and www.visithrisey.is. The latter outlines some houses for rent on the island.

Incredibly tame ptarmigan frequent the village streets. From here, three marked **nature trails** loop around the southeastern part of the island and lead to some good viewpoints. Not to be missed are the tons-of-fun 40-minute **tractor trips** (☑ 695 0077; adult/child Ikr1200/free), which plough across the island, passing all the important land-marks. They leave regularly from the boat dock, generally at 10am, noon, 2pm and 4pm daily in summer.

While a leisurely half-day is enough to explore the island, consider staying overnight for a more authentic glimpse of island life. Try **Brekka** (☑ 466 1751; www.brekkahrisey.is; s/d without bathroom from Ikr9000/12,000; ⊙ mid-May–mid-Sep), Hrísey's one-stop shop for food and accommodation. It serves the usual suspects (burgers, pizzas) alongside treats like lobster soup and locally reared Galloway steak.

There's a **campground** (campsites per person Ikr1100) with its reception and amenities at the modern swimming-pool complex. The village store **Júllabúð** (⊙ 10am-5pm Mon-Thu, to 8pm Fri, noon-5pm Sat & Sun Jun-Aug, shorter hours Sep-May) sells supplies, and pizzas.

The passenger ferry **Sævar** (☑ 695 5544; ⊙ adult/child Ikr1500/750) runs between Árskógssandur and Hrísey (15 minutes) at least seven times daily year-round; see www.hrisey.net for schedules. Bus 78 from Akureyri stops at Litli Árskógur, which is about a 20-minute walk to the ferry harbour.

On Tuesday and Thursday year-round, the **Sæfari ferry** (☑ 458 8970; www.saefari.is; adult/child Ikr1230/free) runs from Dalvík to Hrísey at 1.15pm (30 minutes), returning immediately after passengers and cargo are discharged and loaded.

Hrafninn
GUESTHOUSE €€

(☑ 462 2300; www.hrafninn.is; Brekkugata 4; s/d Ikr12,900/19,900; ☎) Priced below the competition yet delivering well above, Hrafninn ('The Raven') feels like an elegant manor house without being pretentious or stuffy. All rooms have bathroom and TV; the 3rd-floor rooms have recently been renovated, and there's now a spacious 2nd-floor guest kitchen.

Hotel Natur
HOTEL €€

(☑ 467 1070; www.hotelnatur.com; Þórisstaðir; s/d incl breakfast Ikr16,800/24,000; ☎) About 15km east of Akureyri along Rte 1, this family-run property offers Nordic simplicity in its minimalist rooms, a huge dining space and breathtaking fjord views. The hotel's main accommodation is housed in the farm's old cow barn (but you'd never guess!).

Hótel Íbúðir
APARTMENTS €€

(☑ 892 9838; www.hotelibudir.is; Geislagata 10; d apt from Ikr23,900; ☎) Íbúðir has a choice of five quite luxurious apartments ranging in size (the largest sleeping eight). With a central location and balconies with town views, they make a fine choice for families and groups.

Hótel Akureyri
HOTEL €€

(☑ 462 5600; www.hotelakureyri.is; Hafnarstræti 67; s/d incl breakfast from Ikr10,600/17,100; ☎) Compact, well-equipped rooms are found at this boutique-style hotel, under friendly, service-minded new ownership and handily placed for the bus station. Front rooms have watery views, back rooms have an outlook on lush greenery (it's worth paying a little extra for fjord views).

Hótel Edda
HOTEL €€

(☑ 444 4900; www.hoteledda.is; entry on Þórunnarstræti 14; d without/with bathroom Ikr15,200/24,700; ⊙ mid-Jun–mid-Aug; P @ ☎) With 200-plus rooms, this vast summer hotel in the local boarding school is not somewhere you'll feel the personal touch. The new wing is modern with bright, well-equipped rooms (bathroom, TV); the cheaper old wing has shared bathrooms and a dated feel. Communal lounge areas are lovely. It's a short walk to the pool and botanical gardens. Breakfast costs Ikr1750.

Hótel Kea   HOTEL €€€
(☑460 2000; www.keahotels.is; Hafnarstræti 87-89; s/d incl breakfast Ikr29,200/36,500; @⊕) Akureyri's largest year-round hotel (104 rooms) and popular with groups, super-central Kea has smart business-style rooms with good facilities (including minibar and tea-/coffee-making facilities). There's little local character about it, but some rooms have balconies and fjord views. On-site is Múlaberg, a smart restaurant, plus a cosy lounge, but for our money the Icelandair hotel is a fresher (cheaper) option.

✖ Eating

Hamborgarafabrikkan   FAST FOOD €
(www.fabrikkan.is; cnr Hafnarstræti & Kaupvangsstræti; burger & fries Ikr1695-2395; ⊙11am-10pm Sun-Thu, to midnight Fri & Sat; ⊕) Iceland is one of few countries without McDonald's, but who needs them? Part of a small chain, the Hamburger Factory gives you a choice of 16 square-patty bun-fillings (primarily beef, but also lamb and chicken options). Salads, spare ribs and classic desserts (banana split!) round out the menu.

Serrano   FAST FOOD €
(www.serrano.is; Ráðhústorg 7; meals Ikr1200-1700; ⊙11am-9pm Mon-Sat, from noon Sun) Like your food fast, but fresher than you've been encountering at all those N1 grill-bars? Hit up Serrano for a bumper burrito; you can also nosh on nachos and quesadillas, or go green with salads.

Brynja   ICE CREAM €
(Aðalstræti 3; ice creams from Ikr350; ⊙9am-11pm May, 9am-11.30pm Jun-Aug, 11am-11pm Sep-Apr; ⊕) This legendary sweet shop is known across Iceland for the best ice cream in the country (it's made with milk, not cream). It's not far downhill from the botanical garden.

Blaá Kannan   CAFE €
(Hafnarstræti 96; lunchtime buffet Ikr1490; ⊙9am-11.30pm Mon-Fri, from 10am Sat & Sun) Prime

---

DIVING IN EYJAFJÖRÐUR

Thoughts of scuba diving usually involve sun-kissed beaches and tropical fish, so perhaps it's surprising that some of the world's most fascinating diving lies within Iceland's frigid waters. Most bubble-blowers flock to crystalline Silfra, but the real diving dynamo, known as **Strýtan**, lurks beneath Eyjafjörður. Strýtan, a giant cone (50m) soaring up from the ocean floor, commands a striking presence as it spews out gushing hot water. This geothermal chimney – made from deposits of magnesium-silicate – is truly an anomaly. The only other Strýtan-like structures ever discovered were found at depths of 3000m or deeper; Strýtan's peak is a mere 15m below the surface.

We had the opportunity to grab a meal with Erlendur Bogason (the man who discovered Strýtan, and now officially protects it), and he told us all about Eyjafjörður's other scuba superlatives.

In addition to majestic Strýtan, there are smaller steam cones on the other side of the fjord. Known as **Arnanesstrýtur**, these smaller formations aren't as spectacular, but the water bubbling out of the vents is estimated to be 11,000 years old. The water is completely devoid of salt, so you can put a thermos over a vent, bottle the boiling water, and use it to make hot chocolate when you get back to the surface!

Diving around the island of **Grímsey** is also memorable. The water is surprisingly clear here, but the main draw is the birdlife: bazaars of guillemots swoop down deep as they search for food. Swimming with birds is definitely a strange experience – when the visibility is particularly good it can feel like you're flying!

Interested in checking out these marvels and more? Drop Erlendur a line at his diving outfit, **Strytan Divecentre** (☑862 2949; www.strytan.is; 2-dive day trips from Ikr35,000), based at Hjalteyri, about 20km north of Akureyri.

Note that Reykjavík-based dive operators also offer multiday tours to the area; check the websites of Dive.is (www.dive.is), Diveiceland.com (www.diveiceland.com) and Scuba Iceland (www.scuba.is).

Brandon Presser

people-watching is on offer at this much-loved cafe (the 'Blue Teapot', in the dark-blue Cafe Paris building) on the main drag. The interior is timber-lined and blinged up with chandeliers; the menu offers panini and bagels, and there's a cabinet full of sweet treats.

Indian Curry Hut   INDIAN €
(Hafnarstræti 100b; dishes Ikr1795-2295; ⏱11.30am-1.30pm Tue-Fri, 5.30-9pm Tue-Sun) Add a little heat to a chilly evening with a flavourful curry from this takeaway hut.

Café Laut   CAFE €
(Eyrarlandsvegur 30; lunch buffet Ikr1490; ⏱10am-10pm) What could be better than a designer cafe in a botanical garden? This cafe has gorgeous picture windows, good coffee, a big sun terrace and a lunchtime soup-and-salad buffet, as well as bagels and panini.

Icelandair Hotel Akureyri   DESSERTS €€
(www.icelandairhotels.com; Þingvallastræti 23; high tea Ikr2300) Suffering afternoon sluggishness? Get your sugar rush on courtesy of the great-value high tea served every afternoon (2pm to 5.30pm) in the smart lounge of the Icelandair hotel. A three-tiered tray of delight: savoury, sweet, and more sweet (coffee/tea included, champagne optional). You're welcome.

Strikið   INTERNATIONAL €€
(📋462 7100; www.strikid.is; Skipagata 14; light meals Ikr2400-3500, mains Ikr3800-5000; ⏱from 11.30am Mon-Sat, 6pm Sun) Huge windows with fjord views lend a magical glitz to this 5th-floor restaurant. The menu covers all options: go for burgers if you must, or order mains showcasing prime Icelandic produce (superfresh sushi, langoustine soup, beef tenderloin, slow-cooked duck breast). Strawberry *skyr* mousse makes for a sweet end.

Örkin hans Nóa   SEAFOOD €€
(www.noa.is; Hafnarstræti 22; mains Ikr3000-5000; ⏱noon-2pm & 4-10pm) Part gallery, part furniture store, part restaurant – 'Noah's Ark' is certainly unique, and offers a simple food concept done well. The menu features a selection of fresh fish options, which are pan-fried and served with vegetables, with the pan brought to the table. Classic, effective, tasty.

Greifinn   INTERNATIONAL €€
(📋460 1600; www.greifinn.is; Glerárgata 20; mains Ikr1690-4990; ⏱11.15am-10.30pm; 🍴) Family-friendly and *always* full to bursting, Greifinn is one of the most popular spots in

town. The menu favours comfort food above all: juicy burgers, sizzling Tex-Mex, pizzas, pastas and devilish ice-cream desserts. Takeaway available.

Símstöðin   CAFE €€
(Hafnarstræti 102; meals Ikr1695-1995; ⏱9am-11.30pm; 📶🍴🥤) Cheerful, citrus-toned decor matches the fresh approach of this new, all-day cafe in the heart of town: smoothies, fresh-pressed juices and salads make it easy to feel virtuous. Don't fret, there's still plenty of cakey treats too.

Rub23   INTERNATIONAL €€€
(📋462 2223; www.rub23.is; Kaupvangsstræti 6; lunch Ikr2190-2590, dinner mains Ikr4190-6290; ⏱11.30am-2pm Mon-Fri, from 5.30pm daily) This sleek restaurant revolves around a novel idea: you choose your protein (fish or meat), then pick one of the 11 'rubs', or marinades to accompany it. Go with the chef's suggestions for cod with an Asian fusion rub, or lamb fillet with citrus-rosemary rub. There's also a separate sushi menu. Note that lunch is a more standard (rubless) affair.

Self-Catering

Akureyri has a choice of supermarkets, but none are very central.

Alaska Mini-Market   GROCERIES
(Ráðhústorg 3; ⏱8am-10pm) A convenience store with a small selection of groceries (handy if you're staying centrally), plus juices, smoothies and sandwiches.

Nettó   SUPERMARKET
(Glerárgata; ⏱10am-7pm Mon-Fri, to 6pm Sat, noon-6pm Sun) In the Glerártorg shopping mall.

Samkaup-Strax   SUPERMARKET
(Byggðavegur 98; ⏱9am-11pm Mon-Fri, 10am-11pm Sat & Sun) Near the campsite west of the centre.

Bónus   SUPERMARKET
(Langholt; ⏱11am-6.30pm Mon-Thu, 10am-7.30pm Fri, 10am-6pm Sat, noon-6pm Sun) Cut-price supermarket.

Vínbúðin   LIQUOR STORE
(Hólabraut 16; ⏱11am-6pm Mon-Thu & Sat, to 7pm Fri) Government-run alcohol shop.

🍺 Drinking & Nightlife

Akureyri Backpackers   BAR
(www.akureyribackpackers.com; Hafnarstræti 67; ⏱7.30am-11pm Sun-Thu, to 1am Fri & Sat) Always a hub of convivial main-street activity, the

AROUND AKUREYRI

If you have time and wheels, it's well worth getting off the Ring Road to explore the region around Akureyri's fjord, Eyjafjörður.

Eyjafjarðarsveit is the valley south of Akureyri, accessed by Rtes 821 and 829. The Eyjafjarðará river runs through fertile farmland – there is plenty of rural guesthouse accommodation and idyllic pastoral views with mountain backdrops. **Kaffi Kú** (www.kaffiku. is; ☺1-9pm daily mid-Jun–Aug) is a perfect pitstop – here you sit above a high-tech working dairy cowshed, dining on beef goulash soup, plus waffles and pancakes that pair perfectly with farm-fresh cream. The cafe is about 11km from Akureyri on Rte 829.

Eyjafjörður's **eastern shore** is much quieter than its western counterpart, and offers a few good places to pause among the sweeping vistas.

The eclectic **Icelandic Folk & Outsider Art Museum** (Safnasafnið; www.safnasafnid. is; adult/child Ikr1000/free; ☺10am-5pm mid-May–Aug), 12km from Akureyri on Rte 1 (look for the sculpture of a blue man), is a beautiful space filled with sunlight, plantlife and an intriguing array of art (in Icelandic, its name literally means 'the museum museum').

Further north, Rte 83 branches off the Ring Road to lead you 20km north to the tiny fishing village of **Grenivík**. En route are the photogenic turf roofs at **Laufás** (adult/child Ikr1000/free; ☺9am-5pm Jun–Aug), a preserved manor farm; and the acclaimed stables of **Pólar Hestar** (☑463 3179; www.polarhestar.is), where you can arrange short rides or saddle up for serious week-long journeys into dreamy landscapes.

Nearby are the architect-designed holiday houses **Nollur** (www.nollur.is), rented by the week in high season (minimum two nights from September to May; book online) and enjoying creature comforts and view-blessed hot-pots.

fun, timber-clad bar at Akureyri Backpackers is beloved of both travellers and locals, for its occasional live music, good-value burgers (and weekend brunches), and wide beer selection – this is a fine spot to sample the local microbrews, Kaldi and Einstök.

Götubarinn   BAR
(Hafnarstræti 95; ☺5pm-1am Thu, to 4am Fri & Sat) The locals' favourite drinking spot, fun, central Götubarinn (the Street Bar) has a surprising amount of cosiness and charm for a place that closes at 4am. There's timber, mirrors, couches, and even a downstairs piano for late-night singalongs.

Café Amour   CAFE, BAR
(Ráðhústorg 9; ☺11am-1am Sun-Thu, to 4am Fri & Sat) Café Amour lures Akureyri's bright young things with its lengthy cocktail list and New World wines. The small club upstairs is pretty garish but draws the crowds at weekends.

Kaffi Akureyri   CAFE, BAR
(Strandgata 7; ☺5pm-1am Sun-Thu, to 4am Fri & Sat) This cafe-bar gets packed on Friday and Saturday nights when bands play; it's either live music or nightclub, and it atracts a younger crowd.

☆ Entertainment

★ **Græni Hatturinn**   LIVE MUSIC
(Hafnarstræti 96) Tucked down a lane beside Blaá Kannan, this intimate venue is the best place in town to see live music – and one of the best in the country. If you get the chance, buy a ticket to anything going.

Hof   CULTURAL CENTRE
(www.menningarhus.is; Strandgata 12) Modern Hof is a cultural centre designed for music and other performing arts. Along with conference and exhibition facilities and an excellent restaurant (1862 Nordic Bistro), it's also home to Akureyri's tourist office – ask here about any scheduled performances.

Borgarbíó   CINEMA
(www.borgarbio.is; Hólabraut 12) Shows original-version mainstream films.

Nyja-Bíó   CINEMA
(www.sambio.is; Ráðhústorg) Shows original-version mainstream films.

Leikfélag Akureyrar   THEATRE
(www.leikfelag.is; Hafnarstræti 57) Akureyri's premier theatre venue hosts drama, musicals, dance and opera, with its main season running from September to May. Check the website for performances.

🛍 Shopping

Several shops on Hafnarstræti sell traditional *lopapeysur* (Icelandic woollen sweaters), books, knick-knacks and souvenirs. Remember to ask about the tax-free scheme.

★**Geysir** CLOTHING, SOUVENIRS
(www.geysir.com; Hafnarstræti 98; ⊙11am-9pm Jul, to 7pm Jun & Aug, to 6pm Mon-Fri Sep-May) We covet everything in this unique store, from the *lopapeysa*-style capes to the reindeer hides, and the old Iceland maps to the puffin-embroidered slippers.

Eymundsson BOOKS, SOUVENIRS
(www.eymundsson.is; Hafnarstræti 91-93; ⊙9am-10pm Mon-Fri, 10am-10pm Sat, noon-10pm Sun) First-rate bookshop selling maps, souvenir books and a wide selection of international magazines. There's a good cafe on-site.

Christmas Garden SOUVENIRS
(Jólagarðurinn; ⊙10am-9pm Jun-Aug, 2-9pm Sep-Dec, 2-6pm Jan-May) If you can handle the Christmas cheer out of season, this multi-level gingerbread house sells a super-festive selection of locally made decorations and traditional Icelandic Christmas foods. It's 10km south of Akureyri on Rte 821.

The Viking SOUVENIRS
(www.theviking.is; Hafnarstræti 104; ⊙8am-10pm) This hard-to-miss shop lures the masses with its oversized polar bear plunked out front (not to mention the trolls). There's a good selection of *lopapeysur* and souvenir knick-knacks.

Fold-Anna CLOTHING
(Hafnarstræti 100; ⊙9.30am-6.30pm Mon-Fri, 10am-4pm Sat & Sun) Staff can be seen knitting behind the counter as you browse this outlet loaded with *lopapeysur* and assorted crafty items.

Háaloftið ANTIQUES
(Hafnarstræti 19; ⊙1-6pm Mon-Fri, to 4pm Sat) Down near Brynja ice-cream store is this rummager's delight: 'The Attic', a store filled with antique and vintage finds. Browse the books, records, porcelain and bric-a-brac for a perfectly unique souvenir. Is there a way to get vintage snowshoes home in your suitcase?

ℹ Information

EMERGENCY

Emergency (⌧112)
Police (⌧nonemergency 464 7700; Þórunnarstræti 138)

INTERNET ACCESS

Most lodgings have free wi-fi, as do several cafes and museums. There are internet terminals at the tourist information centre and the **library** (Amtsbókasafnið á Akureyri; www.amtsbok.is; Brekkugata 17; ⊙10am-7pm Mon-Fri year-round, plus 11am-4pm Sat mid-Sep-mid-May; 🛜), for a small fee.

MEDICAL SERVICES

Akureyri Hospital (⌧463 0100; www.fsa.is; Eyrarlandsvegur) Just south of the botanical gardens.
Doctors on Duty (⌧848 2600) 24-hour number; only for urgent issues.
Apótekarinn (Hafnarstræti 95; ⊙9am-5.30pm Mon-Fri) Central pharmacy.
Heilsugæslustöðin (Primary Health Care Centre; ⌧460 4600; 3rd fl, Hafnarstræti 99; ⊙8am-4pm Mon-Fri)

MONEY

Banks (open 9am to 4pm) are clustered around Ráðhústorg. All offer foreign exchange and have 24-hour ATMs.

POST

Main Post Office (Strandgata 3; ⊙9am-6pm Mon-Fri)

TOURIST INFORMATION

Tourist Office (⌧450 1050; www.visitakureyri. is; Hof, Strandgata 12; ⊙8am-6pm mid-May-Sep, 8am-4pm Mon-Fri, noon-5pm Sat, noon-3pm Sun Oct–mid-May; 🛜) This friendly, efficient office is inside Hof. There are loads of brochures, maps, internet access and a great design store. Knowledgable staff can book tours and transport, and accommodation in the area (Ikr500).

ℹ Getting There & Away

AIR

Akureyri airport (www.akureyriairport.is) is 3km south of the city centre.

Air Iceland (⌧460 7000; www.airiceland.is) Runs flights up to eight times daily between Akureyri and Reykjavík (45 minutes), and daily in summer (three times a week in winter) from Akureyri to Grímsey (30 minutes). There's also a weekday link with Vopnafjörður and Þórshöfn in northeast Iceland. All other domestic (and international) flights are routed via Reykjavík.

Icelandair (www.icelandair.com) Has two weekly flights from June to September from Keflavík, meaning international travellers arriving into Iceland don't need to travel to Reykjavík's domestic airport to connect to Akureyri. These flights are only bookable as part of an international flight to and from Iceland with Icelandair.

BUS

Bus services are ever-changing in Iceland, so it pays to get up-to-date information on schedules and fares, from the companies themselves (websites are handy) or from tourist information centres. We list routes and fares from summer 2014.

Akureyri's **bus station** is the hub for bus travel in the north provided by SBA-Norðurleið and Sterna; Strætó operates from a stop in front of Hof. (Note: there is talk of building a central bus terminal that will serve all operators, so it pays to double-check departure points).

If you need to return to Reykjavík, consider taking an all-terrain bus route through the interior highlands, rather than along Rte 1. For more information on services along the Kjölur Route, see p312.

SBA-Norðurleið (☑ 550 0700; www.sba.is; Hafnarstræti bus terminal) services (depart from Hafnarstræti bus terminal):

➡ Bus 62 to Mývatn (Ikr3700, 2hr, 1 daily Jun–mid-Sep)

➡ Bus 62 to Egilsstaðir (Ikr9000, 4hr, 1 daily Jun–mid-Sep)

➡ Bus 62 to Höfn (Ikr17,800, 9½hr, 1 daily Jun–mid-Sep)

➡ Bus 610a to Reykjavík via the Kjölur route (Ikr15,000, 10½hr, 1 daily mid-Jun–mid-Sep)

➡ Bus 641 to Húsavík (Ikr3700, 1½hr, 2 daily mid-Jun–Aug)

➡ Bus 641 to Ásbyrgi (Ikr6200, 3hr, 1 daily mid-Jun–Aug)

➡ Bus 641 to Dettifoss (Ik8900, 4½hr, 1 daily mid-Jun–Aug)

Sterna (☑ 551 1166; www.sterna.is; Hafnarstræti 77) services (depart from Hafnarstræti bus terminal):

➡ Bus 60a to Reykjavík via Rte 1 (Ikr6900, 5½hr, 1 daily Mon-Fri mid-Jun–Aug)

➡ Bus F35a to Reykjavík via the Kjölur route (Ikr13,900, 13hr, 1 daily mid-Jun–early Sep)

Strætó (☑ 540 2700; www.straeto.is) services generally run year-round (depart from Hof building):

➡ Bus 56 to Mývatn (Ikr2100, 1½hr, 2 daily) Drops to four weekly services in winter

➡ Bus 56 to Egilsstaðir (Ikr6300, 3½hr, 1 daily) Drops to four weekly services in winter

➡ Bus 57 to Reykjavík via Rte 1 (Ikr7700, 6½hr, 2 daily)

➡ Bus 78 to Siglufjörður (Ikr2100, 70min, 3 daily Mon-Fri, 1 daily Sun) Runs via Dalvík and Ólafsfjörður.

➡ Bus 79 to Húsavík (Ikr2100, 1¼hr, 3 daily) Winter services are reduced on weekends (no services Saturday, two on Sunday).

➡ Bus 79 to Þórshöfn (Ikr5950, 4hr, 1 daily Sun-Fri summer, 3 weekly winter) This service only operates beyond Húsavík to Þórshöfn (via Ásbyrgi, Kópasker and Raufarhöfn) if prebooked. Call Strætó at least four hours before departure.

CAR

After Reykjavik, Akureyri is Iceland's second transport hub. There are several car-hire agencies – all the major firms have representation at the airport. For a fee, most companies will let you pick up a car in Akureyri and drop it off in Reykjavík or vice versa. See p369 for a list of rental agencies.

Check out www.samferda.is for information about car-pooling, or check hostel noticeboards.

⊙ Getting Around

Central Akureyri is quite compact and easy to get around on foot. Take note of the parking policies if you plan to leave your car in the town centre.

BICYCLE

A few tour agencies rent out bikes, including **Bike Akureyri** (☑ 840 9850; www.bikeakureyri. is), based out of Akureyri Backpackers. It has high-quality bikes for rent from Ikr3500/4900 for a half/full day (ask about guided tour options, too).

BUS

There's a free town bus service on four routes, running regularly 7am to 7pm weekdays (until 10pm on one route); look for the yellow buses. Not all routes run on weekends. Unfortunately, no route goes to the airport.

CAR

Akureyri has a unique parking system for Iceland (one that many northern Europeans will be familiar with). When parking in the town centre, you must set a plastic parking clock marking the time you parked, and display it on the dashboard of your car (so as to be seen through the windshield). Parking is free, but spaces are signposted with maximum parking times (from 15 minutes to two hours, enforced from 10am to 4pm). You'll be fined if your car overstays the advertised time limit. If this sounds too complicated, there is untimed parking by Hof.

ⓘ NEW TUNNEL

A new 7.5km-long road tunnel is being built on the eastern side of Eyjafjörður, which will shorten the Rte 1 journey to Húsavík by about 16km. Drivers will be able to avoid the mountain pass Víkurskarð (often blocked by winter snows), and the tunnel will ensure easier winter access to Akureyri's services for residents living east of the town. The tunnel is being built under Vaðlaheiði mountain and is expected to be completed in 2016.

BSO Taxi Stand (☑ 461 1010; www.bso.is; Strandgata) The BSO taxi stand is opposite Hof. Taxis may be booked 24 hours a day.

BSO's website (and a board at the taxi stand) outlines the cost to hire a car and driver to visit nearby sightseeing destinations.

Akureyri to Mývatn (Goðafoss)

Travellers heading from Akureyri to Mývatn (or Akureyri to Húsavík if you take a small detour) will happen across heavenly waterfall Goðafoss.

Goðafoss WATERFALL
Goðafoss (Waterfall of the Gods) rips straight through the Bárðardalur lava field along Rte 1. Although smaller and less powerful than some of Iceland's other chutes, it's definitely one of the most beautiful. Take the path behind the falls for a less-crowded viewpoint.

The falls play an important part in Icelandic history. At the Alþing (National Assembly) in the year 1000, the *lögsögumaður* (law speaker), Þorgeir, was forced to make a decision on Iceland's religion. After 24 hours' meditation, he declared the country a Christian nation. On his way home he passed the waterfall near his farm, and tossed in his pagan carvings of the Norse gods, thus bestowing the falls' present name.

Fosshóll GUESTHOUSE, CAMPGROUND €€
(☑ 464 3108; www.godafoss.is; sites per person Ikr1000, d with/without bathroom incl breakfast Ikr25,935/19,950; ⊙ mid-May–mid-Sep; 🛜) If the sound of pounding water puts you to sleep, a night in the (overpriced) rooms of sunny yellow Fosshóll, next to the falls, might be for you. There's an evening restaurant here, and orbiting the complex is a petrol station housing an information point, cafeteria and souvenir shop.

MÝVATN REGION

Undisputed gem of the northeast, Mývatn (*mee*-vaht) lake and the surrounding area are starkly beautiful, an otherworldly landscape of spluttering mudpots, weird lava formations, steaming fumaroles and volcanic craters.

The Mývatn basin sits squarely on the Mid-Atlantic Ridge and the violent geolog-

ical character of the area has produced an astonishing landscape unlike anywhere else in the country; this is the Iceland you've always imagined.

History & Geology

Ten thousand years ago the Mývatn basin was covered by an ice cap, which was destroyed by fierce volcanic eruptions that also obliterated the lake at its base. The explosions formed the symmetrical *móberg* peaks (flat-topped mountains formed by subglacial volcanic eruptions) south of today's lake, while volcanic activity to the east formed the Lúdent tephra (solid matter ejected into the air by an erupting volcano) complex.

Another cycle of violent activity more than 6000 years later created the Ketildyngja volcano, 25km southeast of Mývatn. The lava from that crater flowed northwest along the Laxárdalur valley, and created a lava dam and a new, improved lake. After another millennium or so a volcanic explosion along the same fissure spewed out Hverfell, the classic tephra crater that dominates the modern landscape. Over the next 200 years, activity escalated along the eastern shore and craters were thrown up across a wide region, providing a steady stream of molten material flowing towards Öxarfjörður. The lava dam formed during the end of this cycle created the present Mývatn shoreline.

Between 1724 and 1729 the Mývatnseldar ('Mývatn Fires') eruptions began at Leirhnjúkur, close to Krafla, northeast of the lake. This dramatic and sporadically active fissure erupted again in the 1970s (the Kröflueldar, or 'Krafla Fires'), with that episode lasting nine years.

In 1974 the area around Mývatn was set aside as the Mývatn-Laxá Nature Conservation Area, and the pseudocrater field at Skútustaðir, at the southern end of the lake, is preserved as a national natural monument.

☞ Tours

Tourism reigns supreme at Reykjahlíð and for travellers without transport there are numerous sightseeing tours in the area (some originate in Akureyri). Tours fill up fast during summer, so try to book at least a day before. The information centre can help with bookings.

A number of operators run super-Jeep tours into the highlands, to **Askja and surrounds**, from mid-June (when the route opens) until as late into September as

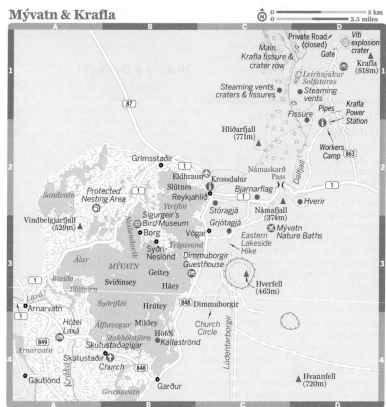

weather permits. From Akureyri it makes for a long day tour (up to 15 hours); 12-hour tours leave from Reykjahlíð.

SBA-Norðurleið   BUS TOURS

(☎ 550 0700; www.sba.is) For an abridged bus tour of Mývatn's top sights, consider linking up with the sightseeing tour operated by SBA-Norðurleið. It starts in Akureyri, but you can often hop aboard in Reykjahlíð (from Reykjahlíð in summer at 12.30pm: 3¾-hour tour, Ikr7700). There is also a winter trip.

Saga Travel   ADVENTURE TOURS

(☎ 558 888; www.sagatravel.is) Akureyri-based Saga Travel operates an array of fabulous year-round tours in the Mývatn area (see the website for full selection). Join tours from Akureyri or Reykjahlíð.

Hike & Bike   HIKING, CYCLING TOURS

(☎ 899 4845; www.hikeandbike.is; ⊙ 9am-5pm Jun-Aug) Hike & Bike has a booth by the

Gamli Bærinn tavern in Reykjahlíð, offering tour bookings and mountain-bike rental (per day Ikr4000).

There's a summer program of cycling and hiking tours, including a four-hour guided walk to Hverfell and Dimmuborgir (Ikr7900); a three-hour pedal through the backcountry (Ikr8900); or a sightseeing cycle that ends with a soak at the Nature Baths (Ikr9900, including admission).

Check the website for excellent multiday options (including five days hiking and cycling in Mývatn, or five days of mountain biking into Jökulsárgljúfur), and for winter pursuits (snowshoeing and cross-country skiing tours).

Saltvík   HORSE RIDING

(☎ 847 6515; www.saltvik.is; 1hr/2hr tour Ikr6000/8500) Just south of Reykjahlíð, Saltvík operates horseback sightseeing tours (generally daily at 10am, 1pm and 4pm June to August). It has a larger operation in Húsavík.

Safarí Hestar HORSE RIDING
(☑464 4203; www.safarihorserental.com; 1hr/2hr tour Ikr5500/9000) Scenic tours operate from Álftagerði III farm on the south side of the lake (400m west of Sel-Hótel) and take in the lakeshore and pseudocraters.

Mýflug Air SCENIC FLIGHTS
(☑464 4400; www.myflug.is; Reykjahlíð airport) Mýflug Air operates daily flight-seeing excursions (weather permitting). A 20-minute trip over Mývatn and Krafla costs Ikr13,900; a two-hour 'super tour' (Ikr45,400) also includes Dettifoss, Ásbyrgi, Kverkfjöll, Herðubreið and Askja.

❶ Getting There & Away

All buses pick up/drop off passengers at the information centre in Reykjahlíð; bus routes 62/62a, 56, 14/14a and 17/17a also stop in Skútustaðir, by the Sel-Hótel.

SBA-Norðurleið (☑550 0700; www.sba.is) services:
➠ Bus 62a to Akureyri (Ikr3700, 1¾hr, 1 daily Jun–mid-Sep)
➠ Bus 62 to Egilsstaðir (Ikr5700, 2hr, 1 daily Jun–mid-Sep)
➠ Bus 62 to Höfn (Ikr14,400, 7½hr, 1 daily Jun–mid-Sep)
➠ Bus 650 to Húsavík (Ikr3100, 40min, 2 daily mid-Jun–Aug)
➠ Bus 661 to Krafla (Ikr1700, 15min, 2 daily mid-Jun–Aug)
➠ Bus 661 to Dettifoss (Ik3700, 1hr, 1 daily mid-Jun–Aug) From Dettifoss you have the option of linking with bus 641a to Ásbyrgi, Húsavík or on to Akureyri.

Strætó (☑540 2700; www.straeto.is) services:
➠ Bus 56 to Akureryi (Ikr2100, 1½hr, 2 daily) Drops to four weekly services in winter.
➠ Bus 56 to Egilsstaðir (Ikr4550, 2hr, 1 daily) Drops to four weekly services in winter.

Reykjavík Excursions (☑580 5400; www.re.is) services:
➠ Bus 14a to Landmannalaugar along the highland Sprengisandur route (Ikr16,500, 10hr, 3 weekly Jul-Aug)
➠ Bus 17a to Reykjavík along the highland Sprengisandur route (Ikr20,500, 11½hr, 3 weekly Jul-Aug)

❶ Getting Around

There are wonderful hiking trails around Mývatn, but they're not all connected. Without wheels you may find yourself on long walks along the lakeshore road (you can always roll the dice and stick out your thumb...).

You might consider renting a car in Akureyri. During calmer weather, a good option is to hire a mountain bike from Hike & Bike. The 36km ride around the lake can be done in a day.

Reykjahlíð

POP 140

Reykjahlíð, on the northeastern shore of the lake, is the main village and Mývatn's obvious base. There's little to it beyond a collection of guesthouses and hotels, a supermarket, petrol station and information centre.

❂ Sights & Activities

Reykjahlíð Church CHURCH
During the Krafla eruption of 1727, the Leirhnjúkur crater, 11km northeast of Reykjahlíð, kicked off a two-year period of volcanic activity, sending streams of lava along old glacial moraines towards the lakeshore. On 27 August 1729 the flow ploughed through the village, destroying farms and buildings, but amazingly the wooden church was spared when the flow parted, missing the church by only metres. It was rebuilt on its original foundation in 1876, then again in 1962.

Sundlaug SWIMMING POOL
(off Hlíðavegur; adult/child Ikr600/250; ☉10am-9pm Jun-Aug, shorter hours Sep-May) If you're after a soak and don't want to cough up admission to the Nature Baths, consider Reykjahlíð's 25m outdoor swimming pool, with hot-pots and gym facilities.

⊨ Sleeping

Mývatn's popularity means that room rates have soared, and demand is far greater than supply, so don't think twice about booking ahead. Most prices are overinflated, with €220 being the norm for a run-of-the-mill hotel double in summer's peak (with guesthouse rooms not far behind). Off-season rates are considerably cheaper (by up to 50%).

Most options are located either in Reykjahlíð or at Vógar, a small cluster of buildings along the lake's eastern shore (about 2.5km south of Reykjahlíð). Additional options can be found at Dimmuborgir and along the southern shore at Skútustaðir. The website www.myvatn-hotels.com gives a rundown of many options.

See websites for up-to-date rates (and low-season rates). To save money at guesthouses, ask about sleeping-bag options (more common in the low season).

NORTH ICELAND REYKJAHLÍÐ

> **ⓘ MÝVATN ORIENTATION**
>
> Mývatn lake is encircled by a 36km sealed road (Rte 1 on the western and northern shores, and Rte 848). The main settlement is Reykjahlíð, in the northeast corner; an information centre is here, as are most sleeping and eating options.
>
> Most of the points of interest are linked by the lake's looping road, including the diverse lava formations in eastern Mývatn, the cluster of pseudocraters near southern Mývatn, and the bird-friendly marsh plains around western Mývatn.
>
> In northern Mývatn, the Ring Road (Rte 1) veers east, away from Reykjahlíð, and takes you over the Námaskarð pass to the Hverir geothermal area. Then, a turn-off to the north (Rte 863) leads to Krafla, 14km from Reykjahlíð.
>
> With your own vehicle this whole area can be explored in a day, but if you're using the bus or a bike allow two days. If you want to hike and explore more distant mountains and lava fields, allow at least three.

Bjarg
CAMPGROUND €

(☑ 464 4240; ferdabjarg@simnet.is; sites per person lkr1500, d without bathroom lkr15,900; ◷ mid-May–Sep; @ ☎) This smaller campsite has a gorgeous location on the Reykjahlíð lakeshore (almost opposite the supermarket) and features a kitchen tent, laundry service, tour-booking desk, summer rowboat rental and bike hire. Accommodation is also available in a couple of rooms in the main building.

Hlíð
CAMPGROUND, GUESTHOUSE €

(☑ 464 4103; www.myvatnaccommodation. is; Hraunbrún; campsites per person lkr1400, dm lkr4700, d incl breakfast lkr24,000, cottages lkr35,000; @ ☎) Sprawling, well-run Hlíð is 300m uphill from the church and offers a full spectrum: camping, sleeping-bag dorms and rooms with kitchen access, no-frills huts, self-contained cottages sleeping six, and en-suite guesthouse rooms. There's also laundry, playground and bike hire.

Helluhraun 13
B&B €€

(☑ 464 4132; www.helluhraun13.blogspot.com; Helluhraun 13; s/d without bathroom incl breakfast lkr13,000/18,000; ◷ Jun-Sep; ☎) Ásdis is a sunny host at this this small, homely guesthouse with lava-field views. There are just three rooms and one bathroom, but they're bright, spotless and tastefully decorated.

Eldá
GUESTHOUSE €€

(☑ 464 4220; www.elda.is; Helluhraun 15; s/d without bathroom incl breakfast lkr14,000/19,700; @ ☎) This friendly family-run operation owns three properties along Helluhraun and offers cosy, no-frills accommodation. There are guest kitchens and TV lounges, and buffet breakfast is included. All guests check in at this location.

Vógar
GUESTHOUSE, CAMPGROUND €€

(☑ 464 4399; www.vogahraun.is; Vógar; tents per person lkr1500, d with/without bathroom lkr15,400/27,700) A range of decent options here, 2.5km south of Reykjahlíð: camping, sleeping-bag accommodation in utilitarian prefab huts, and a newer block of compact guesthouse rooms, with and without bathroom. Sleeping bags reduce the price, as does staying a second night.

Vogafjós Guesthouse
GUESTHOUSE €€€

(☑ 464 3800; www.vogafjos.net; Vógar; s/d incl breakfast lkr28,600/30,000; ☎) Fresh scents of pine and cedar fill the air in these log-cabin rooms (cosy with underfloor heating), set in a lava field 2.5km south of Reykjahlíð and a few minutes' walk from the Cowshed restaurant, where breakfast is served. Most rooms sleep two, with family rooms also available.

Hótel Reynihlíð
HOTEL €€€

(☑ 464 4170; www.myvatnhotel.is; s/d incl breakfast from lkr25,400/32,300; @ ☎) The grand dame of Mývatn hotels is a smartly dressed 40-room hotel. The superior rooms aren't a noticeable upgrade; they only have slightly better views, plus a little more space. Also here is a restaurant, plus lounge-bar and sauna. We like the nine rooms at its cosier annexe, the pretty, lakeside **Hótel Reykjahlíð** (same prices).

✖ Eating & Drinking

The local food speciality is a moist, cake-like rye bread known as *hverabrauð* (often translated as 'geysir bread'). It's slow-baked underground using geothermal heat and is served in every restaurant in town.

★ **Vogafjós**   ICELANDIC €€
(www.vogafjos.net; mains Ikr2550-4700; ⊙ 7.30am-11pm; 🛜 🍴 👶) The 'Cowshed', 2.5km south of Reykjahlíð, is a memorable restaurant where you can enjoy views of the lush surrounds, or of the dairy shed of this working farm (cows are milked at 7.30am and 5.30pm). The menu is an ode to local produce: smoked lamb, house-made mozzarella, dill-cured Arctic char, geysir bread, homebaked cakes, homemade ice cream. It's all delicious.

Gamli Bærinn   ICELANDIC €€
(www.myvatnhotel.is; mains Ikr1900-4900; ⊙ 10am-11pm) The cheerfully busy 'Old Farm' tavern beside Hótel Reynihlíð serves up pub-style meals, including lunchtime soups and burgers, and dinnertime fish and steak. In the evening it becomes a local hang-out – the opening hours are often extended during weekend revelry, but the kitchen closes at 10pm.

Myllan   ICELANDIC €€
(📞 464 4170; www.myvatnhotel.is; mains Ikr2500-5850; ⊙ 6.30-9pm) Hótel Reynihlíð's in-house restaurant is the town's most upmarket and features unsurprising local faves such as smoked lamb, panfried Arctic char and grilled beef ribeye. It wouldn't be a hotel restaurant without club sandwich on the menu!

Daddi's Pizza   PIZZERIA €€
(small pizza Ikr1300-2650; ⊙ 11.30am-11pm) At Vogár campground, this small space cranks out tasty pizzas to eat in or takeaway. Try the house speciality: smoked trout, nuts and cream cheese (tastier than it sounds).

Samkaup-Strax   SUPERMARKET
(⊙ 9am-10pm mid-Jun–Aug, 10am-6pm Sep–mid-Jun) Well-stocked supermarket (with petrol pumps) next to the tourist info centre. Has a burger grill.

❶ Information

Post Office (Helluhraun; ⊙ 9am-4pm) On the street behind the supermarket. Inside is a bank and 24-hour ATM.

Tourist Information Centre (📞 464 4390; www.visitmyvatn.is; Hraunvegur 8; ⊙ 7.30am-6pm Jun-Aug, shorter hours Sep-May) The well-informed centre has good displays on the local geology, and can book accommodation, tours and transport. Pick up a copy of the hugely useful *Visit Mývatn* brochure and *Mývatn Lake* map.

Eastern Mývatn

If you're short on time, make this area your first stop. The sights along Mývatn's eastern lakeshore can be linked together on an enjoyable half-day hike (see p240).

Grjótagjá   CAVE
Game of Thrones fans may recognise it as the place where John Snow is, ahem, deflowered by Ygritte. Grjótagjá is a gaping fissure with a 45°C-water-filled cave. It's on private property – it's prohibited to bathe here, but the owners allow the public to visit and photograph. It's a beautiful spot, particularly when the sun filters through the cracks in the roof and illuminates the interior.

Hverfell   CRATER
Dominating the lava fields on the eastern edge of Mývatn is the classic tephra ring Hverfell (also called Hverfjall). This near-symmetrical crater appeared 2700 years ago in a cataclysmic eruption of the existing Lúdentarhíð complex. Rising 463m from the ground and stretching 1040m across, it is a massive and awe-inspiring landmark in Mývatn.

The crater is composed of loose gravel, but an easy track leads from the northwestern end to the summit and offers stunning views of the crater itself and the surrounding landscape. A path runs along the western rim of the crater to a lookout at the southern end before descending steeply towards Dimmuborgir.

Access to the walking track at the ring's northwestern end is via a signed gravel road – it's about 3km from the main road to the car park.

INTO THE MADDING SWARMS

Mývatn's name translates as 'lake of midges', and plaguelike swarms of these small flies are a lasting memory for many summer visitors. As infuriating as they can be, these midges are a vital food source for wildlife.

If they bother you, consider wearing a head net (which you can buy at the supermarket in Reykjahlíð, and elsewhere) – then splash on the repellent and pray for a good wind to send the little blighters diving.

Lofthellir
CAVE

The dramatic lava cave at Lofthellir is a stunning destination, with magnificent natural ice sculptures (ice trolls?) dominating the interior.

Although it's one of Mývatn's highlights, the cave is on private property and can only be accessed on a half-day tour run by Saga Travel (p236). The tour involves a 45-minute 4WD journey and a 20-minute walk across a lava field to reach the cave itself, and then special equipment (headlamps, studded boots etc) and some wriggling through tight spaces. Dress warmly.

The tour costs Ikr26,500/19,500 from Akureyri/Reykjahlíð. Note, too, that Saga Travel also offers this tour in winter, which involves snow-driving and then snowshoeing to access the cave (Ikr34,500/27,500 from Akureyri/Reykjahlíð).

Dimmuborgir
LAVA FIELD

The giant jagged lava field at Dimmuborgir (literally 'Dark Castles') is one of the most fascinating flows in the country. A series of nontaxing, colour-coded walking trails runs through the easily anthropomorphised landscape. The most popular path is the easy Church Circle (2.3km). Ask at the cafe here about free guided ranger walks in summer.

It's commonly believed that Dimmuborgir's strange pillars and crags were created about 2000 years ago when a lake of lava from the Þrengslaborgir and Lúdentarborgir crater rows formed here, over marshland or a small lake. The water of the marsh started to boil, and steam jets rose through the molten lava and cooled it, creating the pillars. As the lava continued flowing towards lower ground, the hollow pillars of solidified lava remained.

Höfði
LAVA FORMATIONS

One of the area's gentlest landscapes is on the forested lava headland at Höfði. Wildflowers, birch and spruce trees cover the bluffs, while the tiny islands and crystal-clear waters attract migratory birds.

From footpaths along the shore you'll see small caves and stunning *klasar* (lava pillars), the most famous of which rise from the water at Kálfaströnd on the southern shore of the Höfði Peninsula.

🛏 Sleeping & Eating

⭐**Dimmuborgir Guesthouse** GUESTHOUSE €€
(📞464 4210; www.dimmuborgir.is; s/d Ikr20,000/23,500, d cottages with/without bathroom Ikr33,500/24,500, all incl breakfast; 🅿) This lakeside guesthouse close to Dimmuborgir lava field has a block of en-suite rooms (with shared kitchen-dining area), plus a smattering of lovely wooden cottages. Breakfast is served in the main house behind big picture windows overlooking the lake.

Don't miss the **smokehouse** hidden in the back – check out the rows of shiny orange salmon, and stock up on the finished product for tomorrow's picnic. It's open to all.

Helgi, the owner, also operates short guided **boat tours** on the lake – a great way to get a different perspective on the region.

Kaffi Borgir ICELANDIC €€
(www.kaffiborgir.is; mains Ikr1800-4100; ⊙9am-10pm Jun-Aug, reduced hours Sep-Dec & Apr-May) Kaffi Borgir is a cafe–souvenir shop at the top of the ridge overlooking the Dimmuborgir lava field. Grab a table on the outside terrace, sample the house speciality (grilled trout), and watch the sun dance its shadows across the jagged lava bursts.

Southern Mývatn

Eastern Mývatn may be the ultimate treasure trove of geological anomalies, but the south side of the lake lures with its epic cache of pseudocraters, called **Skútustaðagígar**.

Pseudocraters were formed when molten lava flowed into the lake, triggering a series of gas explosions. These dramatic dimples then came into being when trapped subsurface water boiled and popped, forming small

---

EASTERN LAKESIDE HIKE

Although easily accessible by car, the sights along Mývatn's eastern lakeshore can also be tackled on a pleasant half-day hike. A well-marked track runs from Reykjahlíð village to Hverfell (5km), passing Grjótagjá along the way. Then it's on to Dimmuborgir (another 3km) with its collection of ruin-like lava. If you start in the late afternoon and time your hike correctly, you'll finish the day with a meal at Dimmuborgir while sunset shadows dance along the alien landscape. As an alternative, the walk from Hverfell's northwest corner to the Nature Baths is 2.3km – and the sunsets here are pretty special too.

scoria cones and craters. The most accessible pseudocrater swarm is located along a short path just across from Skútustaðir, which also takes in the nearby pond, **Stakhólstjörn**, a haven for nesting waterfowl.

The hamlet of **Skútustaðir** is the only settlement around the lake apart from Reykjahlíð. There's a cluster of tourist activity here, including a couple of hotels and a guesthouse.

🛏 Sleeping & Eating

Skútustaðir Farmhouse GUESTHOUSE €€
(☑464 4212; www.skutustadir.com; d with/without bathroom incl breakfast Ikr28,350/21,250; ⑤) Sensible prices, friendly owners and spotless facilities can be found at this recommended, expanding year-round option. Rooms in the homey farmhouse share bathroom, but there's also an annexe of five en-suite rooms, plus a two-bedroom cottage, and a new block of rooms and large guest kitchen.

★**Hótel Laxá** HOTEL €€€
(☑464 1900; www.hotellaxa.is; s/d incl breakfast Ikr31,000/37,000; ⑤) Bringing a breath of fresh air to Mývatn is this architecturally arresting, sustainably designed hotel, which opened in mid-2014 about 2km east of Skútustaðir. There are 80 modern, simple rooms – pricey but comfy, with colour schemes complementing the surrounds. The big windows and green sofas of the bar-lounge area invite contemplation; there's also a stylish on-site **restaurant** (mains mains Ikr2500–Ikr5500).

Sel-Hótel Mývatn HOTEL €€€
(☑464 4164; www.myvatn.is; s/d incl breakfast Ikr28,100/33,800; ◉⑤) Plans for expansion (the addition of 22 new rooms in time for summer 2015) should bring a welcome re-invigoration to the Sel (in the hamlet of Skútustaðir), where facilities are good but a little tired. There's a hot-pot, sauna and lounge, plus a souvenir shop-**cafeteria** (open 8am to 10pm June to August) next to the car park. The hotel's no-frills **restaurant** offers buffets favoured by tour groups (lunch/dinner buffet Ikr2700/5900).

The hotel's best feature is its packages of **winter activities**: Northern Lights, super-Jeep exploration, snowmobile tours on the frozen lake, cross-country skiing, horse riding, and some quirky choices like driving go-karts on ice. Low-season room rates are significantly cheaper.

Hótel Gígur HOTEL €€€
(☑464 4455; www.keahotels.is; s/d incl breakfast Ikr29,200/36,500; ◉⑤) The Skútustaðir lakeside location doesn't quite compensate for the overpriced, extra-compact rooms that leave little room for cat-swinging. The pretty green **restaurant** (dinner mains Ikr3990 to Ikr5600) is the hotel's best feature, offering prime lake views plus well-prepared local dishes (pan-fried trout, crème brûlée with slow-cooked rhubarb).

Western Mývatn

Laxá RIVER
The clear and turbulent Laxá (Salmon River), one of the many Icelandic rivers so named, cuts the western division of Mývatn, rolling straight across the tundra towards Skjálfandi (Húsavík's whale-filled bay). The Laxá is one of the best (and most expensive) salmon-fishing spots in the country. More affordable brown-trout fishing is also available.

Vindbelgjarfjall MOUNTAIN
The steep but relatively easy climb up 529m-high Vindbelgjarfjall, on the lake's western shore, offers one of the best views across the lake and its alien pseudocraters. The trail to the summit starts south of the peak, near the farm Vagnbrekka. Reckon on about a half-hour to reach the mount, and another half-hour to climb to the summit.

★**Sigurgeir's Bird Museum** MUSEUM
(Fuglasafn Sigurgeirs; ☑464 4477; www.fuglasafn. is; adult/child Ikr1000/500; ◉10am-6pm Jun-Aug, reduced hours Sep-May) For some birdwatching background, swing by Sigurgeir's Bird Museum, housed in a beautiful lakeside building that fuses modern design with traditional turf house. Inside you'll find an impressive collection of taxidermic avians (more than 180 types from around the world), including every species of bird that calls Iceland home (except one – the grey phalarope). Designer lighting and detailed captions further enhance the experience.

The menagerie of stuffed squawkers started as the private collection of a local named Sigurgeir Stefansson. Tragically, Sigurgeir drowned in the lake at the age of 37 – the museum was erected in his honour. The museum also houses a small cafe and lends out high-tech telescopes to ornithological enthusiasts, plus has hides for rent.

Take a look in the small water feature at the centre of the exhibition hall to see the

MARIMO BALLS

Marimo balls are bizarre little spheres of green algae that are thought to grow naturally in colonies in only a handful of places in the world (Mývatn and Lake Akan in Japan). The name *marimo* is the Japanese word for 'algae ball' – around Mývatn, the locals call 'em *kúluskítur*, which literally means 'ball of shit'. Swing by Sigurgeir's Bird Museum (p241) to check out these curious critters while you can (they live in the small pool at the centre of the exhibition space).

green surprise that lurks inside: *marimo* balls (little spheres of green algae).

Birdwatching   BIRDWATCHING
Western Mývatn offers some of the best birdwatching in Iceland, with more than 115 species present – including 28 species of ducks, 15 of them breeding nesting. Most species of Icelandic waterfowl are found here in great numbers. Three duck species – the scoter, the gadwall and the Barrow's goldeneye – breed nowhere else in Iceland.

Other species frequenting the area include harlequin and tufted ducks, mallards, scaup, whooper swans, great northern divers, Arctic terns and golden plovers. The area's bogs, marshes, ponds and wet tundra are a high-density waterfowl nesting zone. Off-trail hiking in defined nesting areas is restricted between 15 May and 20 July (when the chicks hatch), but hides near Sigurgeir's Bird Museum allow for birding.

Northern Mývatn
As the lakeshore road circles back around towards Reykjahlíð, the marshes dry up and the terrain returns to its signature stretches of crispy lava.

Eldhraun   LAVA FIELD
The lava field along Mývatn's northern lakeshore includes the flow that nearly engulfed the Reykjahlíð church. It was belched out of Leirhnjúkur during the Mývatn Fires in 1729, and flowed down the channel Eldá. With some slow scrambling, it can be explored on foot from Reykjahlíð.

Hlíðarfjall   MOUNTAIN
If you're hiking directly to Krafla from Mývatn's northern crest, you'll pass the prominent 771m-high rhyolite mountain Hlíðarfjall (also called Reykjahlíðarfjall), just before the halfway mark. Around 5km from Reykjahlíð, the mount can also be enjoyed as a pleasant day hike from the village, affording spectacular views over the lake on one side and over the Krafla lava fields on the other.

East of Reykjahlíð
Northern Mývatn's collection of geological gems lie along the Ring Road (Rte 1) as it weaves through the harsh terrain between the north end of the lake and the turn-off to Krafla. There are plenty of paths for exploring the area on foot.

Bjarnarflag   GEOTHERMAL AREA
Bjarnarflag, 3km east of Reykjahlíð, is an active geothermal area where the earth hisses and bubbles, and steaming vents line the valley. Historically, the area has been home to a number of economic ventures attempting to harness the earth's powers. (Early on, farmers tried growing potatoes here, but these often emerged from the ground already boiled.)

In the late 1960s, 25 test holes were bored at Bjarnarflag to ascertain the feasibility of a proposed geothermal power station. One is 2300m deep and the steam still roars out of the pipe at a whopping 200°C.

Later a diatomite plant was set up, but all that remains of the processing plant is the shimmering turquoise pond that the locals have dubbed the 'Blue Lagoon'. This inviting puddle is actually quite toxic and should not be confused with the Mývatn Nature Baths around the corner (sometimes called the 'Blue Lagoon of the North').

★ Mývatn Nature Baths   SPA
(Jarðböðin; www.jardbodin.is; adult/child Ikr3500/free; ⊙9am-midnight Jun-Aug, noon-10pm Sep-May) Northern Iceland's answer to the Blue Lagoon is 3km east of Reykjahlíð. Although it's smaller than its southern counterpart, it's also less hyped (probably a good thing), and it's a gorgeous place to soak in the powder-blue, mineral-rich waters and enjoy the panorama. After a relaxing soak, try one of the two natural steam baths and/or a meal at the on-site cafeteria.

Námafjall   MOUNTAIN

Vaporous vents cover the pinky-orange Námafjall ridge, which lies 3km past Bjarnarflag (on the south side of the Ring Road). Produced by a fissure eruption, the ridge sits squarely on the spreading zone of the Mid-Atlantic Ridge. As you travel the Námaskarð pass and tumble down its far side, you enter the alien world of Hverir.

Hverir   GEOTHERMAL AREA

The magical, ochre-toned world of Hverir is a lunar-like landscape of mud cauldrons, steaming vents, radiant mineral deposits and piping fumaroles. Belching mudflats and the powerful stench of sulphur may not sound enticing, but Hverir's ethereal allure grips every passer-by.

Safe pathways through the features have been roped off; to avoid risk of serious injury and damage to the natural features, avoid any lighter-coloured soil and respect the ropes.

A walking trail loops from Hverir up Námafjall ridge. This 30-minute climb provides a grand vista over the steamy surroundings.

Krafla

Steaming vents and craters await at Krafla, an active volcanic region 7km north of the Ring Road. Technically, Krafla is just an 818m-high mountain, but the name is now used for the entire area as well as a geothermal power station and the series of eruptions that created Iceland's most awesome lava field. The so-called Mývatn Fires occurred between 1724–29, when many of the fissure vents opened up. The Krafla Fires (1975–84) were very similar in nature: fissure eruptions and magma movements that occured on and off for nine years.

From Reykjahlíð, a reasonably easy **hike** of around 13km (three to four hours) leads to Hlíðarfjall and Leirhnjúkur along a marked path from near the airstrip. Another walking route (difficult; estimate three to five hours) leads from Namaskarð along the Dalfjall ridge to Leirhnjúkur.

Krafla Power Station   POWER STATION

(⊙ visitor centre 10am-5pm Jun-Aug) The idea of constructing a geothermal power station at Krafla was conceived in 1973, and preliminary work commenced with the drilling of holes to determine project feasibility. In 1975, however, after a long rest period, the Krafla fissure burst into activity. The project went ahead, however, and has been expanded since. The power plant's **visitor centre** explains how it all works.

Leirhnjúkur   LAVA FIELD

Krafla's most impressive, and potentially most dangerous, attraction is the Leirhnjúkur crater and its solfataras, which originally appeared in 1727, starting out as a lava fountain and spouting molten material for two years before subsiding.

In 1975, the Krafla Fires began with a small lava eruption by Leirhnjúkur, and after nine years of on-and-off action Leirhnjúkur became the ominous-looking, sulphur-encrusted mudhole that tourists love today. The earth's crust here is extremely thin and in places the ground is ferociously hot.

A well-defined track leads northwest to Leirhnjúkur from the Krafla parking area; with all the volcanic activity, high temperatures, bubbling mudpots and steaming vents, it's best not to stray from the marked paths.

Viti   CRATER

The dirt-brown crater of Víti reveals a secret when you reach its rim – a green pool of floodwater at its heart. The 300m-wide explosion crater was created in 1724 at the beginning of the destructive Mývatn Fires. There is a circular path around the rim of Viti to the geothermal area to its east.

Gjástykki   LAVA FIELD

This remote rift zone at the northernmost end of the Krafla fissure swarm was the source of the first eruptions in 1724, and was activated when Leirhnjúkur went off again in the 1975 eruptions. Between 1981 and 1984 the area was the main hotspot of activity in the Krafla central volcano, and the current Gjástykki lava fields date from this time.

Gjástykki is a very sensitive area and to visit you'll need to join a tour. **Saga Travel** (📞 558 888; www.sagatravel.is) tours the area (Ikr19,500 from Mývatn); you can combine Gjástykki with its tour of the Lofthellir cave.

❶ Getting There & Away

SBA-Norðurleið (📞 550 0700; www.sba.is) services:

➜ Bus 661 Reykjahlíð to Krafla (Ikr1700, 15min, 2 daily mid-Jun–Aug). Runs at 8am and 11.30am; the latter service continues on to Dettifoss. Return bus from Krafla to Reykjahlíð at 2.30pm.

NORTH ICELAND KRAFLA

MÝVATN TO EGILSSTAÐIR (RING ROAD)

Travelling between Reykjahlíð and Egilsstaðir, you'll quickly encounter the geological wonders of Námafjall and Krafla, and no doubt be lured off the Ring Road to check out mighty Dettifoss. The 4WD-only Rte F88 turn-off to Askja and Herðubreið in the highlands is about 7km past the sealed Rte 862 to Dettifoss; 3km further east, you cross bridge over the glacial river Jökulsá á Fjöllum.

Rte 864 is signposted from just east of the bridge; this is a rough gravel road that arrives at Dettifoss (eastern vantage point) after 28km, Ásbyrgi after 56km. It's best to tackle Rte 864 in a 4WD.

From here, the Ring Road takes a short-cut inland across the stark highlands of the northeast interior. If you won't be travelling into the highlands proper, you'll catch a glimpse of them here. The ostensibly barren, grey-toned landscape is dotted with low hills, small lakes caused by melting snowfields, and streams and rivers wandering aimlessly before disappearing into gravel beds.

Möðrudalur & Around

This area has always been a difficult place to eke out a living, and farms here are few and far between. Isolated Möðrudalur, an oasis in the desert, is the highest farm in Iceland at 469m (it's 8km south of the Ring Road on Rte 901, with the turnoff about 63km east of Reykjahlíð).

At Möðrudalur you'll find a popular mini-village, bustling in summer. **Fjalladýrð** (☑471 1858; www.fjalladyrd.is; sites per person Ikr1150, d without bathroom Ikr13,500, cottage excl linen Ikr19,900) is the name of the tourist service, with an array of good accommodation spread over various buildings: camping, guesthouse rooms, button-cute turf-roofed cottages, family-sized suites.

It's worth spending the night if you're interested in tackling some of Iceland's interior – Elisabet, the farm's co-owner, is a former highland ranger and Fjalladýrð runs excellent super-Jeep trips to Askja, Herðubreið and Kverkfjöll. Folks simply passing through should try the farm-fresh lamb dishes at **Fjallakaffi** (mains Ikr1690-5500). Petrol is available here (from what may be Iceland's cutest petrol station).

After visiting Möðrudalur, most travellers head 8km north to rejoin the Ring Road, but if you're looking for another diversion, consider taking gravel Rte 901 east (this is the old Rte 1, and in summer is rough but passable in a 2WD).

The remote, reconstructed turf farmhouse **Sænautasel** (☑471 1086; admission Ikr500; ☉10am-10pm Jun–mid-Sep), dating from 1843, is signposted 5km south of Rte 901, on Rte 907. It really brings the past to life...plus it sells pancakes and coffee (Ikr1200). The farmhouse is in a lovely lakeside spot, and has a basic camping area. This area was the source of inspiration for *Independent People,* the masterwork from Nobel Prize-winning writer Halldór Laxness.

HÚSAVÍK & AROUND

Húsavík

POP 2205

Húsavík, Iceland's whale-watching capital, has become a firm favourite on travellers' itineraries – and with its colourful houses, unique museums and stunning snowcapped peaks across the bay, it's easily the northeast's prettiest fishing town.

☉ Sights & Activities

Don't rush off after your whale-watching trip; Húsavík has a few surprises up its sleeve. Sadly, its quirkiest offering, the renowned Phallological Museum, has relocated to Reykjavík.

★**Húsavík Whale Museum**   MUSEUM
(Hvalasafnið; www.whalemuseum.is; Hafnarstétt; adult/child Ikr1400/500; ☉8.30am-6.30pm Jun-Aug, 9am-4pm Apr-May & Sep, 10am-3.30pm Mon-Fri Oct-Mar) This excellent museum tells you all you ever needed to know about the impressive creatures that come a-visiting Skjálfandi Bay. Housed in an old harbourside slaughterhouse, the museum interprets the ecology and habits of whales, conservation and the history of whaling in Iceland through beautifully curated displays, including several huge skeletons soaring high above (they're real!).

Exploration Museum   MUSEUM
(www.explorationmuseum.com; Héðinsbraut 3; adult/child Ikr900/500; ☉9am-5pm) Newly

Húsavík

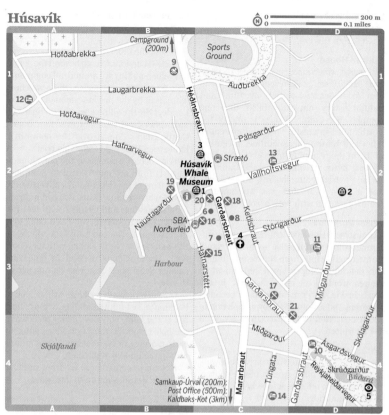

0   200 m
0   0.1 miles

Húsavík

opened in 2014, this museum salutes the history of human exploration, covering Viking voyages and polar expeditions (and has a cool 1952 snowcat parked out front). Its most unique exhibition focuses on the Apollo astronauts in Iceland in the 1960s, receiving geology training in the lunar-like landscapes near Askja. There are some great photos from this era.

Culture House   MUSEUM
(Safnahúsið; www.husmus.is; Stórigarður 17; adult/child Ikr800/free; ⊙10am-6pm Jun-Aug, 10am-4pm Mon-Fri Sep-May) A folk, maritime and natural-history museum rolled into one complex, the Culture House is one of the north's most interesting regional museums. 'Man and Nature' nicely outlines a century of life in the region, from 1850 to 1950 (lots of local flavour), while the stuffed animals include a frightening-looking hooded seal, and a polar bear that was welcomed to Grímsey in 1969 with both barrels of a gun.

Húsavíkurkirkja   CHURCH
(Garðarsbraut) Húsavík's church is quite different from anything else seen in Iceland. Constructed in 1907 from Norwegian timber, the delicately proportioned red-and-white church would look more at home in the Alps. Inside, its cruciform shape becomes apparent and is dominated by a depiction of the resurrection of Lazarus (from lava!) on the altarpiece.

Skrúðgarður   GARDENS
As scenic as the waterfront area is, a walk along the duck-filled stream of the endearing town park offers a serene break. Access is via a footbridge on Ásgarðsvegur, or beside Árból guesthouse.

Sundlaugin   SWIMMING POOL
(Laugarbrekka 2; adult/child Ikr600/300; ⊙6.45am-9pm Mon-Fri, 10am-6pm Sat & Sun Jun-Aug, shorter hours Sep-May; ⊕) The local swimming pool has hot-pots, and waterslides for kids.

🐋 Tours
Whale Watching
This is why you came to Húsavík. Although there are other Iceland locales where you can do whale-watching tours (Reykjavík and Eyjafjörður, north of Akureyri), this area has become Iceland's premier whale-watching destination, with up to 11 species coming here to feed in summer. The best time to see whales is between June and August. This is, of course, the height of tourist season, and you'll have a near-100% chance of seeing one.

Three whale-watching companies now operate from Húsavík harbour. Don't stress *too* much over picking an operator; prices are similar and services are comparable

for the standard three-hour tour (guiding, warm overalls supplied, plus hot drinks and a pastry).

Where the differences are clear, however, is in the excursions that go beyond the standard. When puffins are around, all companies offer tours that incorporate whale-watching with a sail by the puffin-festooned island of Lundey; North Sailing does this on board an atmospheric old schooner over four hours; Gentle Giants does it over 2½ hours in a high-speed RIB (rigid-inflatable boat).

Trips depart throughout the day (June to August) from around 8.30am to 8pm, and large signs at the ticket booths advertise the next departure time. Boats also run in April, May, September and October with less frequency (North Sailing even has a daily tour in November). You can't miss the offices on the waterfront: North Sailing with its yellow flags, Gentle Giants dressed in blue, and smaller Salka operating from its cafe across the road.

Questions worth asking when you're booking a last-minute standard tour: how big is the boat, and how many passengers are booked on the tour. Consider taking an early-morning or evening cruise (bus groups visit in the middle of the day).

Note: prices listed here are from summer 2014; see websites for up-to-date rates.

North Sailing   WHALE WATCHING
(📞464 7272; www.northsailing.is; Hafnarstétt 9; 3hr tour adult/child Ikr9280/4640) The original operator, with a fleet of lovingly restored traditional boats, including the oak schooners *Haukur* and *Hildur*. Its four-hour 'Whales, Puffins & Sails' tour is onboard an old schooner; when conditions are right, there may be some sailing without the engine. Overnight sailing adventures to Grímsey are available in summer.

Gentle Giants   WHALE WATCHING
(📞464 1500; www.gentlegiants.is; Hafnarstétt; 3hr tour adult/child Ikr9100/3900) Gentle Giants has a flotilla of old fishing vessels, plus recent additions of high-speed RIBs and Zodiacs, offering a way to cover more ground in the bay. Gentle Giants also runs special trips to Flatey (Flat Island) for birdwatching, and fast (and pricey) RIB trips to Grímsey. There are also sea-angling expeditions.

Salka   WHALE WATCHING
(📞464 3999; www.salkawhalewatching.is; Garðarsbraut 6; 3hr tour adult/child Ikr8640/4000)

THE WHALES OF HÚSAVÍK

Edda Elísabet Magnúsdóttir is a local marine biologist at the Húsavík Research Center (a branch of the University of Iceland), established with a focus on marine-mammal studies.

What's so special about Húsavík's geology that brings whales to the area?
Húsavík sits on a scenic bay known as Skjálfandi, which means 'the tremulous one' in Icelandic. The name is appropriate, since little earthquakes occur very frequently in the bay, usually without being noticed. These trembles are caused by the wrench fault in the earth's crust right beneath the bay. Skjálfandi's bowl-shaped topography and the infusion of fresh water from two river estuaries means that there is a great deal of nutrients collecting in the bay. The nutrient deposits accumulate during the winter months, and when early summer arrives – with its long sunlit days – the cool waters of Skjálfandi bay come alive with myriad plankton blooms. These rich deposits act like a beacon, attracting special types of mammals that are highly adapted to life in the cold subarctic waters.

What species of whale visit Húsavík?
Every summer roughly nine to 11 species of whale are sighted in the bay, ranging from the tiny harbour porpoise (*Phocoena phocoena*) to the giant blue whale (*Balaenoptera musculus*), the biggest animal known to roam the earth.

Plankton blooming kick-starts each year's feeding season; that's when the whales start appearing in greater numbers in the bay. The first creatures to arrive are the humpback whales (*Megaptera novaeangliae*) and the minke whales (*Balaenoptera acutorostrata*). The humpback whale is known for its curious nature, equanimity and spectacular surface displays, whereas the minke whale is famous for its elegant features: a streamlined and slender black body and white-striped pectoral fin.

Although the average minke whale weighs the same amount as two or three grown elephants, they are known as the 'petite cousin' of the greater rorquals. The minke whale has the tendency to leap entirely out of the water and is likely the only rorqual capable of doing so.

Several minke and humpback whales stay in the bay throughout the year, but most migrate south during the winter. The blue whale, undoubtedly the most exciting sight in Skjálfandi, is a recent summer visitor – they only started arriving around a decade ago. They usually start coming in mid-June and stay until the middle of July. Watching these highly developed hydrodynamic giants in their natural environment is just spectacular.

Other summer sightings in Skjálfandi include the orca, also known as the killer whale (*Orcinus orca;* some come to the bay to feed on fish, others come to hunt mammals), northern bottlenose whales (*Hyperoodon ampullatus;* a mysterious, deep-diving beaked whale), fin whales (*Balaenoptera physalus*), sei whales (*Balaenoptera borealis*), pilot whales (*Globicephala melas*) and sperm whales (*Physeter macrocephalus*).

Brandon Presser

A new player on the scene, taking on the long-established companies with just one 42-passenger oak boat, cheaper prices (for now) and a tighter menu of offerings. It's base is its light-filled cafe on the main street.

Other Tours

Both major whale-watching operators offer combo tours that involve cruises plus a horse ride at Saltvík. Gentle Giants offers fishing or a two-day hiking trip; North Sailing offers a unique 'Ski to the Sea' multi-day package in April, working with ski guides. See websites for details.

Saltvík Horse Farm   HORSE RIDING
(☑847 9515; www.saltvik.is; 1hr/2hr tours Ikr6000/8500; ☉mid-Apr-Oct) Short horse rides with glorious views over Skjálfandi bay are available at Saltvík horse farm, 5km south of Húsavík. It also offers week-long rides (around Mývatn, into the more-remote northeast, or along the highland Sprengisandur route), plus farmhouse accommodation.

Fjallasýn   ADVENTURE TOURS
(☑464 3941; www.fjallasyn.is) This Húsavík-based company is well established and does a variety of tours in the area: local to Húsavík or further afield to various parts of northeast

Iceland and the highlands; day or multiday tours; 4WD, hiking, birdwatching etc.

🛏 Sleeping

Húsavík Hostel
HOSTEL €

(☑ 463 3399; www.husavikhostel.com; Vallholtsvegur 9; dm Ikr5000, d without bathroom Ikr14,500; 🛜) Finishing touches were going on here when we visited. This is the only in-town budget option, so will no doubt find an eager market. It's from the same people behind the Húsavík Cape Hotel (a group of brothers); there are bunk-filled dorm rooms and a couple of private rooms (which include linen), plus kitchen.

Árbót
HOSTEL €

(☑ 464 3677; www.hostel.is; dm/d without bathroom Ikr4100/11,200; ⊙ Apr-Sep; @🛜) One of two HI hostels on tranquil, remote rural properties in the area (owned by the same family) – both about 20km south of Húsavík off Rte 85. You'll need your own transport, and to BYO all food.

To reach Árbót, take Rte 85 south from Húsavík for 14km, then look for the sign to the cattle farm (a further 4km on a good gravel road). There are high-quality facilities and comfy common areas. HI members get a discount; linen can be hired.

Campground
CAMPGROUND €

(sites per person Ikr1200; ⊙ mid-May–mid-Sep) Next to the sports ground at the north end of town, this well-maintained spot has washing machines and limited cooking facilities, but not nearly enough to cope with summertime demand. Pay at the whale museum, or to the warden who visits nightly.

★Kaldbaks-Kot
COTTAGES €€

(☑ 464 1504; www.cottages.is; 2- to 4 person cabins excl linen Ikr20,800-30,100; 2-night minimum stay; ⊙ May-Sep; @🛜) Located 3km south of Húsavík is this spectacular spread-out settlement of timber cottages that all feel like grandpa's log cabin in the woods (but with considerably more comfort). Choose your level of service: BYO linen or hire it, bring supplies or buy breakfast here (Ikr1550), served in the magnificent converted cowshed.

Minimum stay is two nights – perfect for enjoying the grounds, the hot-pots, the views, the serenity and the prolific birdlife. Options include larger houses sleeping up to 10.

Sigtún
GUESTHOUSE €€

(☑ 864 0250; www.guesthousesigtun.is; Túngata 13; s/d without bathroom incl breakfast Ikr10,500/17,500; @🛜) Free coffee machine, free laundry, a fancy kitchen and a help-yourself breakfast are draws at this small and cosy guesthouse.

Árból
GUESTHOUSE €€

(☑ 464 2220; www.arbol.is; Ásgarðsvegur 2; s/d without bathroom incl breakfast Ikr10,600/18,100) This 1903 heritage house has a pretty stream and town park as neighbours. Spacious, spotless rooms are over three levels – those on the ground and top floor are loveliest (the pine-lined attic rooms are particularly sweet). Limited guest use of the kitchen is permitted of an evening.

Fosshótel Húsavík
HOTEL €€

(☑ 464 1220; www.fosshotel.is; Ketilsbraut 22; s/d incl breakfast from Ikr23,600/28,500; @🛜) Fosshótel is a growing hotel chain, and it plans to expand and renovate this hotel in 2015. The dated standard rooms will undoubtedly benefit from a makeover, as will the restaurant area. Stay tuned: Fosshótel renovations elsewhere in Iceland have had great results (prices may increase as a result). The plan is to continue the decor's subtle whale theme.

Húsavík Cape Hotel
HOTEL €€€

(☑ 463 3399; www.husavikhotel.com; Laugarbrekka 16; s/d incl breakfast Ikr28,500/31,350; 🛜) A new boutique-y option in a former fish factory above the harbour, with plans for further expansion. Fresh, modern rooms are a good size (some with bunks, for families), but summer prices are steep.

🍴 Eating

Fish & Chips
FAST FOOD €

(Hafnarstétt 19; fish & chips Ikr1500; ⊙ 11.30am-8pm Jun-Aug) Doing exactly what it says on the label, this small window-front place on the harbour doles out good-value fish (usually cod) and chips, with a few picnic tables out front and a simple seating area upstairs. To find it, walk down the stairs opposite the church, and turn left.

Heimabakarí Konditori
BAKERY, CAFE €

(Garðarsbraut 15; ⊙ 7am-6pm Mon-Fri, to 4pm Sat & Sun) Sells fresh bread, sandwiches and sugary cakes.

★**Naustið** SEAFOOD €€
(Naustagarði 4; mains Ikr1700-3500; ☺noon-10pm) Quietly going about its business at the end of the harbour, sweetly rustic Naustið wins praise for its super-fresh fish and a fun, simple concept: skewers of fish and vegetables, grilled to order. There's also fish soup (natch), salmon and langoustine, plus home-baked pie for dessert.

Gamli Baukur ICELANDIC €€
(www.gamlibaukur.is; Hafnarstétt 9; mains Ikr3100-4990; ☺11.30am-11pm Sun-Wed, to 1am Thu, to 3am Fri & Sat Jun-Aug, shorter hours Sep-May) Among shiny nautical relics, this timber-framed restaurant-bar serves excellent food (juicy burgers, spaghetti with shellfish, organic lamb), plus the pun-tastic dessert *skyramisu*. Live music and a sweeping terrace make it one of the most happening places in northeast Iceland. Kitchen closes at 9pm.

Salka Restaurant ICELANDIC €€
(www.salkarestaurant.is; Garðarsbraut 6; mains Ikr1790-4150; ☺11.30am-10pm) Once home to Iceland's first cooperative, this historic building houses a popular restaurant serving a wildly diverse menu: everything from smoked puffin to pizza, by way of langoustine, burgers and salted cod. Also look out for its nearby summertime bistro and bar (just down the hill) – a more-casual, pub-like affair.

Hvalbakur Café CAFE €€
(Hafnarstétt 9; pizzas Ikr1950-2250; ☺8am-8pm) With a sun-trap terrace overlooking the waterfront, this cafe's new incarnation serves all-day pizzas and a big cabinet full of sandwiches, wraps, muffins and cakes.

Kasko SUPERMARKET
(Garðarsbraut 5; ☺9am-6.30pm Mon-Thu, to 7pm Fri, 10am-6pm Sat) Central supermarket.

Samkaup-Úrval SUPERMARKET
(Garðarsbraut 64; ☺10am-7pm Mon-Sat, noon-7pm Sun) South of town, by the Olís service station.

Vínbúðin LIQUOR STORE
(Garðarsbraut 21; ☺11am-6pm Mon-Thu, to 7pm Fri, to 2pm Sat Jun-Aug, shorter hours Sep-May) Government-run liquor store.

ⓘ Information

Tourist Information Centre (☑464 4300; www.visithusavik.is; Hafnarstétt; ☺8.30am-6.30pm Jun-Aug, 9am-4pm Apr-May & Sep, 10am-3.30pm Mon-Fri Oct-Mar) At the Whale Museum, with plentiful maps and brochures.

ⓘ Getting There & Away

AIR
Húsavík's airport is 12km south of town. **Eagle Air** (☑562 2640; www.eagleair.is) flies year-round between Reykjavík and Húsavík (one way Ikr27,100).

BUS
SBA-Norðurleið (☑550 0700; www.sba.is) services (depart from in front of Gamli Baukar restaurant, on the waterfront):
➡ Bus 641a to Akureyri (Ikr3700, 1½hr, 2 daily mid-Jun–Aug)
➡ Bus 641 to Ásbyrgi (Ikr2200, 50min, 1 daily mid-Jun–Aug)
➡ Bus 641 to Dettifoss (Ik5800, 2¾hr, 1 daily mid-Jun–Aug) From Dettifoss you can connect to bus 661a to Mývatn
➡ Bus 650a to Mývatn (Ikr3100, 40min, 2 daily mid-Jun–Aug)

Strætó (☑540 2700; www.straeto.is) services (depart from N1 service station):
➡ Bus 79 to Akureyri (Ikr2100, 1¼hr, 3 daily)
➡ Bus 79 to Ásbyrgi (Ikr1750, 1hr, 1 daily Sun-Fri summer, 3 weekly winter) This service only operates from Húsavík to Þórshöfn (via Ásbyrgi, Kópasker and Raufarhöfn) if prebooked. Call Strætó at least four hours before departure.
➡ Bus 79 to Þórshöfn (Ikr4200, 2¾hr, 1 daily Sun-Fri summer, 3 weekly winter) See note above.

Húsavík to Ásbyrgi

Heading north from Húsavík along Rte 85 you'll sweep along the coast of the stubby **Tjörnes Peninsula**. The area is known for its fossil-rich coastal cliffs (the oldest layers dating back about two million years).

At the tip of the peninsula is the **Mánárbakki Museum** (adult/child Ikr500/free; ☺9am-6pm Jun-Aug), home to the eclectic personal collection of friendly farmer Aðalgeir, who will give you a tour of his turf-roofed house and show you various assemblages of photos, furniture and crockery.

Giant cracks, fissures and grabens (depressions between geological faults) scar the earth at low-lying **Kelduhverfi**, where the Mid-Atlantic Ridge enters the Arctic Ocean. Like Þingvellir, the area reveals some of the most visible evidence that Iceland is being ripped apart from its core.

🛏 Sleeping & Eating

River Guesthouse GUESTHOUSE €
(☑463 3390; www.skulagardur.com; s/d without
bathroom Ikr5500/9000; 🔊) This huge blue
portacabin offers 30 simple budget rooms
with shared bathroom and kitchen. Prices
listed are for sleeping-bag beds; including
linen is Ikr6500/13,000.

Hótel Skúlagarður COUNTRY HOTEL €€
(☑465 2280; www.skulagardur.com; s/d incl breakfast Ikr16,600/23,000; 🔊) A country hotel behind an unpromising exterior (in a former
boarding school), Skúlagarður offers a warm
welcome, plus compact, modern en-suite
rooms, and a no-frills restaurant serving
good home cooking (oven-baked arctic char
or lamb fillet; mains Ikr2800 to Ikr4200).
It's 12km west of Ásbyrgi.

Keldunes GUESTHOUSE €€
(☑465 2275; www.keldunes.is; s/d without bathroom incl breakfast Ikr12,900/18,900, cottages
from Ikr18,900; 🔊) Modern guesthouse with
great kitchen-dining area, a hot-pot, and
large balconies for birdwatching; dinner is
available. There are excellent cottages with
bathroom, plus some basic cabins with
sleeping-bag beds (Ikr4000). It's 11km west
of Ásbyrgi.

JÖKULSÁRGLJÚFUR (VATNAJÖKULL NATIONAL PARK – NORTH)

In 2008 the Vatnajökull National Park – Europe's largest protected reserve – was formed
when Jökulsárgljúfur National Park merged
with Skaftafell National Park to the south.
The idea was to protect the Vatnajökull ice
cap and all of its glacial run-off under one
super-sized preserve. For more about the national park, see p292.

The Jökulsárgljúfur portion of the park protects a unique subglacial eruptive ridge and a
30km gorge carved out by the formidable
Jökulsá á Fjöllum (Iceland's second-longest
river), which starts in the Vatnajökull ice cap
and flows almost 200km to the Arctic Ocean
at Öxarfjörður. *Jökulhlaups* (flooding from
volcanic eruptions beneath the ice cap) formed
the canyon and have carved out a chasm that
averages 100m deep and 500m wide.

Vatnajökull National Park's northern section can be roughly divided into three parts.

➠ **Ásbyrgi** The northern entry. A verdant,
forested plain enclosed by vertical canyon
walls. The visitor centre is here.

➠ **Vesturdalur** The middle section,
with caves and fascinating geological
anomalies.

➠ **Dettifoss** This mighty waterfall anchors
the park's southern entrance.

A wonderful two-day hike weaves along the
canyon, taking in all of the major sights en
route. If you're not so keen on hiking, the big
attractions, such as the waterfalls at the southern end of the park and horseshoe-shaped
Ásbyrgi canyon at the northern end, are accessible by good sealed roads. The road between
Ásbyrgi and Dettifoss is due to be sealed
sometime in the next couple of years.

Better roads and increased visitor numbers will inevitably result in more facilities and changing transport schedules, so
it's worth checking the park website (or
with the visitor centre) to see what's new.
In the pipeline: rangers are developing a
mountain-biking trail through the park
(note that this will be for experienced bikers,
not daytrippers).

Note that from mid-June to mid-August,
rangers guide free daily **interpretive walks**
that depart from the visitor centre. Check
the website, or ask staff.

🚩 Tours

Summer buses to Ásbyrgi and Dettifoss
make it pretty easy to tackle the canyon on
your own. If you're after a tour, several companies can oblige, from Mývatn, Akureyri
and Húsavík.

Active North HORSE RIDING
(☑858 7080; www.activenorth.is; 2hr tour Ikr8900;
☺mid-Jun–Aug) Fancy horse-riding around a
canyon said to be formed by a mythical hoof-
print? Headquartered opposite the visitor
centre, Active North offers easy, scenic two-
hour horse-riding trips around the Ásbyrgi
canyon, departing at 10am, 2pm and 5pm. A
four-hour tour that includes a lava-cave visit
is also available on request (Ikr15,900).

🛏 Sleeping & Eating

A couple of accommodation providers are
within 15km of the park, between Húsavík
and Ásbyrgi.

The **service station** (Rte 85; ☺9am-10pm
Jun-Aug, 10am-6pm Sep-May) on Rte 85 near
the visitor centre at Ásbyrgi has a selection
of groceries, plus simple grill-bar options

(and a fuel pump). If you're hiking, it's best to purchase supplies in Akureyri or Húsavík.

National Park Campsites   CAMPGROUND €
(☑ 470 7100; www.vjp.is; sites per person Ikr1400 plus per tent Ikr100; ⊙ mid-May–Sep; 🛜) Camping inside the park boundaries is strictly limited to the official campsites at Ásbyrgi, Vesturdalur and Dettifoss.

The large, easily accessible campsite at **Ásbyrgi** has well-maintained showers (Ikr500) and laundry facilities.

Vesturdalur's campsite (open June to mid-September) is near the ranger station and has no power or hot water – toilets are the only luxury here.

The free **campsite** at Dettifoss has limited freshwater supplies, and the grounds are *strictly reserved for hikers* doing the popular two-day hike.

ℹ️ Information

The park wardens have created several excellent maps of the region. The excellent park map (Ikr350) is a useful 1:55,000 plan that ranks the local hikes by difficulty. The Útivist & afþreying maps are also handy – #3 (Ikr650) zooms in on the Ásbyrgi–Dettifoss route.

Note that there is a ranger station at Vesturdalur.

Visitor Centre (Gljúfrastofa; ☑ 470 7100; www.vjp.is; ⊙ 9am-9pm Jul–mid-Aug, to 7pm Jun & rest of Aug, 10am-4pm May & Sep; 🛜) The super-helpful office at Ásbyrgi has an information desk with brochures and maps for sale, informative displays on the area, and knowledgable staff that can help with accommodation, transport and tours in the area.

ℹ️ Getting There & Around

BUS

When Rte 862 is fully sealed between Ásbyrgi and Dettifoss (due sometime in the next couple of years), there may be changes to bus routes. Check websites, and/or with the national park visitor centre.

SBA-Norðurleið (☑ 550 0700; www.sba.is) services from Ásbyrgi:

➡ Bus 641a to Húsavík (Ikr2200, 45min, 1 daily mid-Jun–Aug)

➡ Bus 641a to Akureyri (Ikr6200, 2hr, 1 daily mid-Jun–Aug)

➡ Bus 641 to Hljóðaklettar in Vesturdalur (Ik1800, 20min, 1 daily mid-Jun–Aug)

➡ Bus 641 to Dettifoss (Ik3200, 1½hr, 1 daily mid-Jun–Aug) From Dettifoss you can connect to bus 661a to Krafla and Mývatn.

Strætó (☑ 540 2700; www.straeto.is) services from Ásbyrgi – note that bus 79 (one daily

Jökulsárgljúfur

except Saturday summer, three weekly in winter) only operates between Húsavík and Þórshöfn (via Ásbyrgi, Kópasker and Raufarhöfn) if prebooked. Call Strætó at least four hours before departure:

➡ Bus 79 to Húsavík (Ikr1750, 1hr)

➡ Bus 79 to Kópasker (Ikr1050, 30min)

➡ Bus 79 to Þórshöfn (Ikr3500, 2hr)

CAR

Rte 85 (sealed) takes you smoothly to the northern section of the park and the visitor centre at Ásbyrgi (from Húsavík it's 65km).

There are two north–south roads running parallel on each side of the canyon:

➡ **Rte 862 (west)** From the Ring Road to Dettifoss (24km), the road is sealed. North of Dettifoss, the road is gravel for the remaining 37km past Hólmatungur and Vesturdalur to Rte 85 and Ásbyrgi. There are plans to seal this route in the coming years (possibly end of 2015; enquire locally).

➡ **Rte 864 (east)** This is a poorly maintained gravel track for its 60km length; it's passable by 2WD vehicles, but its rutted and potholed surface will tire even the most patient drivers. There are no plans to improve the road's conditions.

Although the park is open all year, the gravel roads only open from late May/early June until sometime between early October and early November (weather dependent).

Make sure you stick to roads and marked trails. Off-road driving is hugely destructive to the country's fragile environment, and illegal.

Ásbyrgi

Driving off Rte 85 on to the flat, grassy plain at the northern end of the park, there's little to tell you you're standing on the edge of a massive horseshoe-shaped canyon. The lush **Ásbyrgi canyon** extends 3.5km from north to south and averages 1km in width, making it difficult to discern at its widest point.

Near the centre of the canyon is the prominent outcrop Eyjan, and towards the south the sheer, dark walls rise up to 100m. The cliffs protect a birch forest from harsh winds and hungry sheep, and the trees here grow up to 8m in height. You can climb to the summit of Eyjan from the campsite (4.5km return) or ascend the cliffs at **Tófugjá**. From there, a looping track leads around Áshöfði past the gorges.

There are two stories about the creation of Ásbyrgi. The early Norse settlers believed that Óðinn's normally airborne eight-legged horse, Slættur (known in literature as Sleipnir), accidentally touched down on earth and left one hell of a hoof-print to prove it. The other theory, though more scientific, is also incredible. Geologists believe that the canyon was created by an enormous eruption of the Grímsvötn caldera beneath distant Vatnajökull. It released an immense *jökulhlaup* (glacial flood), which ploughed northward down the Jökulsá á Fjöllum and gouged out the canyon in a matter of days. The river then flowed through Ásbyrgi for about 100 years before shifting eastward to its present course.

From the car park near the end of the road (3.5km south of the visitor centre), several easy **short tracks** lead through the forest to viewpoints of the canyon. Heading east the track leads to a spring near the canyon wall, while the western track climbs to a good view across the valley floor. The trail leading straight ahead ends at **Botnstjörn**, a small duck-filled pond at the head of Ásbyrgi.

Vesturdalur

Off the beaten track and home to diverse scenery, Vesturdalur is a favourite destination for hikers. A series of weaving trails leads from the scrub around the campsite to the cave-riddled pinnacles and rock formations of Hljóðaklettar, the Rauðhólar crater row,

NORTH ICELAND ÁSBYRGI

ÁSBYRGI TO DETTIFOSS HIKE

The most popular hike in Jökulsárgljúfur canyon is the two-day trip (around 30km) from Ásbyrgi to Dettifoss, which moves through birch forests, striking rock formations, lush valleys and commanding perpendicular cliffs while taking in all of the region's major sights. From Ásbyrgi you can follow the canyon's western rim or river's edge to Vesturdalur (12km, or three to four hours), where you'll spend the night (camping is forbidden elsewhere).

On the second day you'll continue on through to gushing Dettifoss, with two options: the considerably more difficult route involves a spectacular walk via the Hafragil lowlands (18km), the easier takes a route north of Hafragil (19.5km, six to eight hours). All up, the route is classified as challenging.

The hike can be done in both directions; however, the park rangers recommend starting in Ásbyrgi, where you can pick up the required maps and brochures. Also, the vistas reveal themselves more dramatically when travelling in a southerly direction (travelling north, you'll be walking uphill). Ever-changing bus schedules and plans for fully sealing Rte 862 mean that park staff are best placed to answer questions such as how to leave your car at Ásbyrgi and return to it by bus from Dettifoss at the end of the hike (or vice versa).

the ponds of Eyjan (not to be confused with the Eyjan at Ásbyrgi) and the canyon itself.

Hljóðaklettar   ROCK FORMATIONS

The bizarre swirls, spirals, rosettes, honeycombs and basalt columns at Hljóðaklettar (Echo Rocks) are a highlight of any hike around Vesturdalur and a puzzling place for amateur geologists. It's difficult to imagine what sort of volcanic activity produced these twisted rock forms. Weird concertina formations and repeat patterns occur throughout, and the normally vertical basalt columns (formed by rapidly cooling lava) show up on the horizontal here.

These strange forms and patterns create an acoustic effect that makes it impossible to determine the direction of the roaring river, a curiosity that gave the area its name.

A circular walking trail (3km) from the parking area takes less than an hour to explore. The best formations, which are also riddled with lava caves, are found along the river, northeast of the parking area.

Rauðhólar   CRATER ROW

The Rauðhólar (Red Hills) crater row, just north of Hljóðaklettar, displays a vivid array of colours in the cinder-like gravel on the remaining cones. The craters can be explored on foot during a 5km loop walk from the Vesturdalur parking area.

Karl og Kerling   ROCK FORMATIONS

Two rock pillars, Karl og Kerling ('Old Man' and 'Old Woman'), believed to be petrified trolls, stand on a gravel bank west of the river, a 2km return walk from the Vesturdalur car park. Across the river is Tröllahellir, the gorge's largest cave, but it's reached only on a 5km cross-country hike from Rte 864 on the eastern side.

Eyjan   ROCK FORMATIONS

From Karl og Kerling you can return to Vesturdalur by walking a 7km trail around Eyjan, a mesa-like 'island' covered with low, scrubby forests and small ponds. Follow the river south to Kallbjarg, then turn west along the track to the abandoned site of Svínadalur, where the canyon widens into a broad valley, and follow the western base of the Eyjan cliffs back to the Vesturdalur parking area.

Hólmatungur   OUTDOORS

Lush vegetation, tumbling waterfalls and an air of utter tranquillity make the Hólmatungur area one of the most beautiful in the park. Underground springs bubble up to form a series of short rivers that twist, turn and cascade their way to the canyon. The most popular walk here is the 4.5km loop from the parking area north along the Hólmá river to **Hólmáfossar**, where the harsh lines of the canyon soften and produce several pretty waterfalls.

From here you head south again on the Jökulsá to its confluence with the Melbugsá river, where the river tumbles over a ledge, forming the **Urriðafossar** waterfalls. To see the falls, you need to walk along the (challenging) trail spur to Katlar.

For the best overall view of Hólmatungur, walk to the hill **Ytra-Þórunnarfjall**, just south of the car park.

Hólmatungur is only accessible by 4WD. If you are travelling by 2WD, you can park your vehicle at Vesturdalur and do a long round-trip day hike. Camping is prohibited at Hólmatungur, but it's a great spot for a picnic lunch.

Dettifoss

The power of nature can be seen in all its glory at the mighty Dettifoss, one of Iceland's most impressive waterfalls.

Although Dettifoss is only 44m high and 100m wide, a massive 193 cu metres of water thunders over its edge every second, creating a plume of spray that can be seen 1km away. With the greatest volume of any waterfall in Europe, this truly is nature at its most spectacular. On sunny days, brilliant double rainbows form above the churning milky-grey glacial waters, and you'll have to jostle with the other visitors for the best views. Take care on the paths, made wet and slippery from the spray.

The falls can be seen from either side of the canyon. A sealed road, Rte 862, links the Ring Road with the western bank of Dettifoss, ending in a large car park and toilet facilities. From the car park, a 2.5km loop walk takes in the dramatic, canyon-edge viewpoint of Dettifoss plus views of a smaller cataract, **Selfoss**.

❶ Getting There & Away

By car, Dettifoss can be reached three ways:
➡ Rte 862 south from Ásbyrgi (37km). At the time of writing this route was still gravel, but there are plans to seal the road in coming years. Note this gravel stretch is closed in winter.

Rte 862 north from the Ring Road. The turn-off to Dettifoss is 27km east of Reykjahlíð (Mývatn); it's then an easy 24km on sealed road to reach the falls.Note that snowfall may occasionally close this road in winter.

Rte 864 on the eastern side of the river. It's gravel for its 60km length, from the Ring Road to Ásbyrgi. It's not an F road, but it is tough going in a 2WD (and impassable in winter).

Loads of tours visit the falls, and there is a summer bus service run by **SBA-Norðurleið** (☑ 550 0700; www.sba.is). Once a day from mid-June to end of August, bus 641 runs from Akureyri to Húsavík then on to Ásbyrgi, then drives south along Rte 862, stopping at Hljóðaklettar in Vesturdalur before halting at Dettifoss. The bus stops at the falls for an hour; after that, you can retrace your steps via bus 641a, or connect to bus 661a to Krafla and Mývatn.

It's well worth double-checking these bus routes and timetables, as things may change when Rte 862 is fully sealed.

NORTHEAST CIRCUIT

Bypassed by the tourist hordes who whiz around the Ring Road, this wild, sparsely populated coastal route around Iceland's remote northeast peninsula is an interesting alternative to the direct road from Mývatn to Egilsstaðir. It's an area of desolate moors and beautiful scenery, stretching to within a few kilometres of the Arctic Circle. If you're looking for unspoilt, untouristed, unhyped Iceland – well, you've found it.

🛈 Getting There & Around

AIR

Air Iceland (☑ 570 3030; www.airiceland.is) has a weekday air link connecting Akureyri with Þórshöfn and Vopnafjörður.

BUS

Strætó (☑ 540 2700; www.straeto.is) services:

Bus 79 from Akureyri to Húsavík and on to Þórshöfn along Rte 85 (and in reverse; daily except Saturday summer, three weekly winter). Note: this service only operates beyond Húsavík (calling at Ásbyrgi, Kópasker, Raufarhöfn and Þórshöfn) if prebooked. Call Strætó at least four hours before departure.

There's no bus to/from Vopnafjörður.

Kópasker

POP 120

Tiny Kópasker, on the eastern shore of Öxarfjörður 35km north of Ásbyrgi, is the first place you'll pass through before disappearing into the wilds of Iceland's far northeast.

In 1976 Kópasker suffered a severe earthquake; the small **earthquake centre** (Skjálfta Setrið; Akurgerði; ☺ 1-5pm Jun-Aug) **FREE** at the school investigates the quake and other tectonics in Iceland. South of the village, the **Byggðasafn** (☺ 1-5pm Jun-Aug) **FREE** at Snartarstaðir farm highlights local textile and handicraft traditions. Look for cute, fully dressed scarecrows in the nearby fields.

There's a free **campsite** on your way into town. Your best bet for a bed is the homely **Kópasker HI Hostel** (☑ 465 2314; www.hostel.is; Akurgerði 7; dm/d without bathroom Ikr4100/11,200; ☺ May-Oct; ☏), run by Benni. Rooms are spread across a couple of houses – everything is well maintained, and there's good birdwatching (and sometimes seal-watching) in the neighbourhood. HI members receive a discount of Ikr700 per person; linen costs Ikr1250. (Note: cash only.)

The town has a small store and fuel pump.

ROADS IN THE NORTHEAST

A sealed inland Rte 85 has recently been built to link Kópasker with the east, reaching the coast not far from Rauðanes. From the new Rte 85, Rte 874 branches north to Raufarhöfn.

The new road still carries little traffic, but it means that the unsealed but scenic old coastal route 85 (now labelled Rte 870) around the bleak and little-visited **Melrakkaslétta** (Arctic Fox Plain) is no longer maintained, so it's rough going but possible in a 2WD.

For 55km between Kópasker and Raufarhöfn, Rte 870 passes through the low-lying flatlands, ponds and marshes of this bird-rich area. There are trails and turn-offs to lonely lighthouses on remote headlands. For a long time Hraunhafnartangi was thought to be the northernmost point of the Icelandic mainland, but recent measurements have pinned that prize on its neighbour, Rifstangi, which falls just 2.5km shy of the Arctic Circle.

Raufarhöfn

POP 165

Like the setting of a Stephen King novel, distant Raufarhöfn (*roy*-ver-hup), Iceland's northernmost township, is an eerily quiet place with a prominently positioned graveyard. The port has functioned since the Saga Age, but the town's economic peak came early in the 20th century during the herring boom, when it was second to Siglufjörður in volume. Today, Raufarhöfn's rows of dull prefab housing give few clues to its illustrious past.

There are ambitious long-term plans underway to build a massive stone circle on the hill just north of town. When completed, the **Arctic Henge** (www.facebook.com/ArcticHenge) will be 50m in diameter with four gates (to represent the seasons) up to 7m in height. The plan is to use the stone henge as a finely tuned sundial to celebrate the solstices, view the midnight sun, and explain the strong local beliefs in the mythology of the Edda poem *Völuspá* (Wise Woman's Prophecy). Drop into Hótel Norðurljós to view a model of the henge.

To stay, there's a free **campsite** in the southern part of town, plus a new guesthouse, **The Nest** (☑472 9930; www.nesthouse.is; Aðalbraut 16; s/d without bathroom from Ikr9200/13,800), with bright, appealing rooms and kitchen access.

The exterior of **Hótel Norðurljós** (Northern Lights; ☑465 1233; www.hotelnordurljos.is; Aðalbraut 2; s/d Ikr12,600/21,000; ☎) seems to have been battered by one too many storms, but the interior is quite cosy. Erlingur, the owner, offers up great home cooking at the **restaurant** (three-course dinner Ikr5700).

Rauðanes

Heading south from Raufarhöfn, there's excellent hiking at Rauðanes, where marked trails lead to bizarre rock formations, natural arches, caves and secluded beaches. The turn-off to Rauðanes is about halfway between Raufarhöfn and Þórshöfn (it's a small sign), but the track is only suitable for 4WD vehicles. All cars can park 1.5km from Rte 85, from where it's a 7km loop through the strange terrain.

Þórshöfn & Around

POP 380

Þórshöfn has served as a busy port since Saga times and saw its heyday when a herring-salting station was established here in the early 20th century. Today it's a modest place but makes a good base for the remote Langanes Peninsula.

Sauðaneshús (adult/child Ikr800/free; ⊙11am-5pm Jun-Aug), the old vicarage on the church estate 7km north of town (en route to Langanes), provides insights into how locals lived 100 years ago, and houses a cafe. For tourist information in town, stop by the large swimming-pool/gym complex **Íþróttahús** (Langanesvegur 18; adult/child Ikr600/300; ⊙8am-8pm Mon-Fri, 11am-5pm Sat & Sun Jun-Aug, shorter hours Sep-May).

Þórshöfn has a **campsite** (sites per person Ikr1000) and the handsome timber **Lyngholt Guesthouse** (☑897 5064; www.lyngholt.is; Langanesvegur 12; s/d Ikr9500/13,900) near the pool, but there's also the farm property **Ytra-Aland** (☑468 1290; www.ytra-aland.is; d with/without bathroom Ikr18,000/14,000), 18km west of town. Pancakes and big smiles from hostess Bjarnveig greet guests in the morning. Sleeping-bag accommodation is possible (Ikr4500), as is dinner (and kitchen facilities), plus info on fishing and hiking in the area.

Dining options in Þórshöfn are slim. The most reliable option is the unglamorous **grill** at the N1 (burgers, lambchops etc). There's a restaurant down at the harbour (behind the N1) that changes name and incarnation frequently – it may be worth checking out. Self-cater via the **Samkaup-Strax** (⊙9.30am-6pm Mon-Fri, 10am-2pm Sat) supermarket.

Langanes

Shaped like a goose with a very large head, foggy Langanes is one of the loneliest corners of Iceland. The peninsula's flat terrain, cushioned by mossy meadows and studded with crumbling remains, is an excellent place to break in your hiking shoes.

Rte 869 ends only 17km along the 50km peninsula, and although it's possible to continue along the track to the tip at Fontur lighthouse in a 4WD vehicle, parts of the road can be difficult to navigate.

Before exploring the region, base yourself at the excellent **Ytra Lón HI Hostel** (☑846 6448; www.hostel.is/ytralon; hostel dm/d without bathroom Ikr4300/11,200, apt d from Ikr15,900), 14km northeast of Þórshöfn and just off Rte 869. It's part of a working sheep farm run by a welcoming Dutch-Icelandic family. The hostel rooms are clean and bright, and there's

HIKE OR DRIVE TO THE END OF THE EARTH

Abandoned farms, lonely lighthouses, seal colonies and craggy windswept cliffs home to prolific birdlife – there are few places in the world that feel as remote as Langanes. The highlight of the area is the new viewing platform over the bird-filled cliffs at **Skoruvíkur-bjarg**: it lies above a rock pillar that's home to thousands of northern gannets, while nearby are colonies of auks, including guillemot and puffins.

Langanes is perfect for hiking, and to help plot your route it's worth picking up the Útivist & afþreying #7 map (available at Ytra Lón and local information centres). Another excellent resource is the *Birding Trail* map, which covers birdwatching information in the northeast (from Mývatn to Langanes), with information online at www.birdingtrail.is.

If you're short on time, consider doing a 4WD tour of Langanes; Ytra Lón (p255) operates them in conjunction with Húsavík-based tour operator Fjallasýn (p247), so you can start the tour from Húsavík or from the hostel. From Ytra Lón, a 2½-hour tour to the bird cliffs of Skoruvík costs Ikr8600 (minimum two people), or you can spend five hours touring, including a visit to the abandoned village Skálar and the lighthouse at Fontur (Ikr14,400). Prebooking is required. Fjallasýn also offers a four-day guided hike through Langanes, beginning and ending at Ytra Lón; see its website for more.

a comfy common area and hot-pot. Fabulous studio apartments, each with bathroom and kitchenette, are housed in cargo containers and lined up under a greenhouse-style roof. Breakfast is available for Ikr1600; HI members get Ikr700 discount per person on hostel accommodation. Prices generally don't include linen, which can be hired (Ikr1250). (Note that at the time of writing, the future of the apartments was in doubt, so it pays to do some pretrip research.)

If you don't have your own vehicle, you can phone ahead to Ytra Lón and the owners will pick you up in Þórshöfn (for a fee).

Vopnafjörður & Around

POP 550

'Weapon fjord' was once the notorious home of a fearsome dragon that protected northeast Iceland from harm. Today, no dragons, and it's an agreeably sleepy place, well known for its superlative salmon rivers (Prince Charles has fished here).

Note that Vopnafjörður is considered to be part of east Iceland and online information is found at www.east.is. We have covered it under north Iceland for the logistics of travelling the Northeast Circuit along Rte 85.

◎ Sights & Activities

Kaupvangur   HISTORIC BUILDING
(Hafnarbyggð 4) The town's most significant building is Kaupvangur, a restored customhouse. You'll find an excellent **cafe** and **information centre** on the ground floor.

Upstairs there's a well-curated exhibit about two locals, Iceland's version of the Gershwin brothers. Also on the 2nd floor is a small display about east Iceland émigrés; down-on-their-luck locals purchased boat tickets to America from this very building.

Bustarfell   MUSEUM
(www.bustarfell.is;   adult/child   Ikr700/100;
◎10am-5pm mid-Jun–mid-Sep) This well-promoted folk museum is set in a photogenic 18th-century turf-roofed manor house southwest of town. The idyllic Cafe Croft serves homebaked cake and coffee. It's 6km off Rte 85 about 19km from Vopnafjörður (or reach it on the sealed Rte 920).

Selárdalslaug   SWIMMING POOL
(adult/child Ikr500/200;   ◎10am-8pm) This novel swimming pool lies in the middle of nowhere; it's signed 8km north of Vopnafjörður off Rte 85, just south of the river Selá. Stop for a quick soak in the geothermal waters of the hot-pot (and to admire the candlelit change rooms – there's no electricity out here).

🛏 Sleeping & Eating

There are some excellent rural guesthouses in the valleys around Vopnafjörður.

Under the Mountain/
Refsstaður II   GUESTHOUSE €
(📋 473 1562; undirfjoll@underthemountain.is; s/d without bathroom Ikr5000/8000; 🛜) Cathy, an American of Icelandic descent, has a special knack for hospitality; her farmhouse feels

homey and warm. It's about 9km south of town; first take Rte 917 past the small airstrip, then travel along Rte 919 for 4km. Sleeping-bag beds cost Ikr3500; there is kitchen access, and discounts for longer stays (call ahead in winter).

Cathy maintains the local emigration exhibit and provides an interesting perspective on life in rural Iceland.

Campsite CAMPGROUND €
(sites per person Ikr1100) Good campsite with views of the fjord and town below. Follow Miðbraut north and turn left at the school.

Hvammsgerði GUESTHOUSE €€
(☑ 588 1298; www.hvammsgerdi.is; s/d without bathroom incl breakfast Ikr10,800/16,900; ☎) Just north of the turnoff to Selárdalslaug (about 9km north of the township) is this lovely new riverside addition: a cosy, family-friendly guesthouse where there are fresh rooms, sweet pets to play with, and farm-fresh eggs at the breakfast table. Sleeping-bag beds are available (Ikr3300).

Kaupvangskaffi CAFE €
(Hafnarbyggð 4; soup buffet Ikr1250; ☉10am-10pm; ☎) It seems everyone passing through town stops here – and with good reason. Inside Kaupvangur, you'll find excellent coffee, a big lunchtime soup buffet and a pleasing array of sweet treats.

Kauptún SUPERMARKET
(Hafnarbyggð; ☉9.30am-6pm Mon-Fri, noon-4pm Sat) The supermarket shares a car park with Kaupvangur.

WORTH A TRIP

ROUTE 917

East of Vopnafjörður, the truly spectacular 73km mountain drive along mostly unpaved Rte 917 takes you over 655m Hellisheiði and down to the east coast. The road may be impassable in bad weather but in summer is generally doable in a small car. It climbs up a series of switchbacks and hairpin bends before dropping down to the striking glacial river deltas on the Héraðssandur.

Vinbúðin LIQUOR STORE
(☉4-6pm Mon-Thu, 1-6pm Fri Jun-Aug, shorter hours Sep-May) Government-run liquor store.

ℹ Information

Tourist Information Centre (☑ 473 1331; www.vopnafjordur.com; Hafnarbyggð 4; ☉11am-5pm Mon-Fri) Good information, inside Kaupvangur. Outside of opening hours you can still get brochures; look for the handy, free guides to local walking routes.

ℹ Getting There & Away

There is no bus service to Vopnafjörður.

From Vopnafjörður it's 137km to Reykjahlíð and 136km to Egilsstaðir (via Rte 85 and the Ring Road), so check fuel levels before you leave town.

It's a shorter, more scenic (and more hair-raising) route to Egilsstaðir (95km) via the gravel mountain road Rte 917.

East Iceland

Best Places to Eat

➜ Skaftfell Bistro (p273)

➜ Randulffs-sjóhus (p277)

➜ Egilsstaðir Guesthouse
(p264)

➜ Klausturkaffi (p266)

➜ Kaupfélagsbarinn (p278)

Best Places to Stay

➜ Ferðaþjónustan Mjóeyri
(p276)

➜ Skálanes (p274)

➜ Hótel Aldan (p273)

➜ Fosshotel Eastfjords (p278)

➜ Silfurberg (p280)

Why Go?

As far as you can get (some 650km) from the country's capital, Iceland's impressively varied and sparsely populated east doesn't announce itself as loudly as other parts of the country, preferring subtle charms over big-ticket attractions. The Eastfjords is the area's most wondrous destination – the scenery is particularly spectacular around the northern fjord villages, backed by sheer-sided mountains etched with waterfalls. If the weather's fine, several days spent hiking or kayaking here may be some of your most memorable in Iceland.

Away from the convoluted coast, the country's longest lake stretches southwest from Egilsstaðir, its shores lined with perfect diversions. Head further inland and you'll come to the forgotten farms, fells and reindeer-roamed heathlands of the empty east, and to Snæfell, one of Iceland's prime peaks.

Ring Road motorists often simply overnight in Egilsstaðir then speed out of the east. Lunacy! The spectacular fjords, scenic hiking trails, fascinating geology (including an abundance of stones and minerals) and friendly villages of the east are some of Iceland's unsung treasures.

Road Distances (km)

	Djúpivogur	Reykjavík	Egilsstaðir	Borgarfjörður Eystri	Seyðisfjörður	Neskaupstaður
Reykjavík	552					
Egilsstaðir	85	698				
Borgarfjörður Eystri	155	702	70			
Seyðisfjörður	111	660	27	92		
Neskaupstaður	164	703	72	140	96	
Breiðdalsvík	64	612	84	153	109	100

❶ Getting There & Away

The 'Travel Guide' pages of the East Iceland tourism website (www.east.is) outline transport to/from and within the region, including the schedule of buses in and out of the fjords.

AIR

Egilsstaðir's airport is 1km north of town. **Air Iceland** (Flugfélag Íslands; ☑ 570 3030; www.airiceland.is) flies up to five times daily year-round between Egilsstaðir and Reykjavik. Flights are popular (and in peak winter may offer the only transport connection).

BUS

To/From East Iceland Egilsstaðir is a major stop on the Ring Road.

Note that there is no winter bus connection between Egilsstaðir and Höfn.

SBA-Norðurleið (☑ 550 0720; www.sba.is) services (pick-up and drop-off at campground; note no winter services):

➡ Bus 62 to Höfn (Ikr8800, 4½ hours, one daily June to mid-September)

➡ Bus 62a to Reykjahlíð, Mývatn (Ikr5700, 2½ hours, one daily June to mid-September)

➡ Bus 62a to Akureyri (Ikr9000, four hours, one daily June to mid-September)

Strætó (☑ 540 2700; www.straeto.is) services (pick-up and drop-off opposite the N1, corner of Miðvangur):

➡ Bus 56 to Reykjahlíð, Mývatn (Ikr4550, two hours, one daily June to mid-September, four weekly rest of year)

➡ Bus 56 to Akureyri (Ikr6300, 3½ hours, one daily June to mid-September, four weekly rest of year)

❶ Getting Around

BUS

Within east Iceland It's possible to use SBA-Norðurleið's daily bus 62/62a to travel between fjords. From Egilsstaðir to Höfn, the bus stops at Reyðarfjörður, Fáskrúðsfjörður, Stöðvarfjörður, Breiðdalsvík, Berunes hostel and Djúpivogur.

Local buses run from Egilsstaðir to villages around the fjords, under the **SVAust** (☑ 471 2320; www.east.is) umbrella. Note that these buses don't carry bikes.

As well as direct services to Borgarfjörður Eystri (in summer) and Seyðisfjörður, SVAust runs the following two year-round routes, geared to service the needs of Alcoa commuters. Buses run every day (fewer services on weekends); ticket price depends on distance travelled. Check online for schedule and fare details, or ask at tourist information centres in the area.

➡ Route 1 Egilsstaðir–Reyðarfjörður–Eskifjörður–Neskaupstaður (Nordfjörður)

➡ Route 2 Reyðarfjörður–Fáskrúðsfjörður–Stöðvarfjörður–Breiðdalsvík

CAR

The Ring Road (Rte 1) steams through Egilsstaðir, but if you want to explore the Eastfjords you need to leave it here. Options:

➡ Rte 92 south to Reyðarfjörður and nearby fjords

➡ Rte 93 east to Seyðisfjörður

➡ Rte 94 north to Borgarfjörður Eystri

Car Hire If you fly into the east, or arrive by ferry from Europe without wheels, the big-name car-hire places (Avis, Budget, Hertz and Europcar) have agents in Egilsstaðir.

INLAND

Egilsstaðir

POP 2330

However much you strain to discover some underlying charm, Egilsstaðir isn't a ravishing beauty. It's the main regional transport hub, and a centre for local commerce, so its services are quite good (including quality accommodation and dining options). It's growing fast, but in a hotchpotch fashion and without a proper town centre.

Egilsstaðir's saving grace is its proximity to lovely Lagarfljót, Iceland's third-largest lake. Since Saga times, tales have been told of a monster living in its depths. If you want to do some beastie-hunting, or explore the forest on the lake's eastern bank, Egilsstaðir makes a good base.

A word of warning: if you can, avoid Egilsstaðir on Wednesday nights in summer, as the ferry to Europe sails from Seyðisfjörður (27km away) on Thursday mornings and rooms, meals and campsites in the area are in hot demand. If you are taking the ferry, book your accommodation well ahead.

❍ Sights & Activities

Recent high-profile industrial projects, such as the Kárahnjúkar hydroelectricity dam and Alcoa aluminium smelter (both opposed by environmentalist groups, but welcomed by many locals for bringing jobs to the area), have seen an influx of workers to the east.

There has been feverish house-building in Egilsstaðir and other eastern communities; in time, the hub town's entertainment facilities may grow, but at present there's not a great deal to lure visitors to Egilsstaðir itself.

Minjasafn Austurlands   MUSEUM
(East Iceland Heritage Museum; www.minjasafn.is; Laufskógar 1; adult/child Ikr800/free; ⊙1-5pm

(sidebar) EAST ICELAND EGILSSTAÐIR

East Iceland Highlights

1 Arrive in Iceland in style: sail up a lovely, long fjord to the bohemian village of **Seyðisfjörður** (p270)

2 Chat with the hidden people and snap photos of puffin posses in beautiful **Borgarfjörður Eystri** (Bakkagerði; p268)

3 Tour the forested shores of **Lagarfljót** (p265) looking for sea monsters

4 Learn the definition of 'tranquil isolation' in ruin-strewn **Mjóifjörður** (p274), verdant **Skálanes** (p274) or horse-happy **Húsey** (p264)

5 Marvel over the magnificent mineral collection in **Stöðvarfjörður** (p279)

6 Drive the hair-raising but spectacular mountain pass near **Oddsskarð** (p275) from Eskifjörður to Neskaupstaður

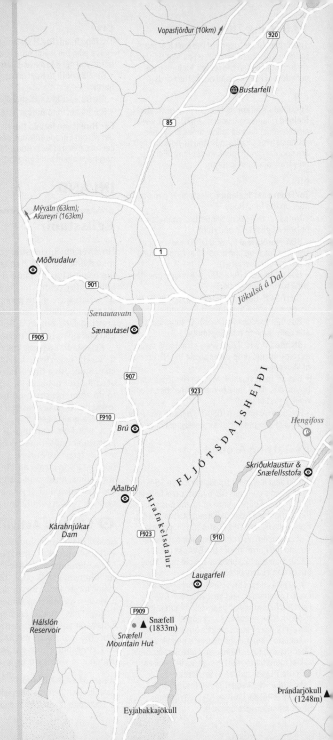

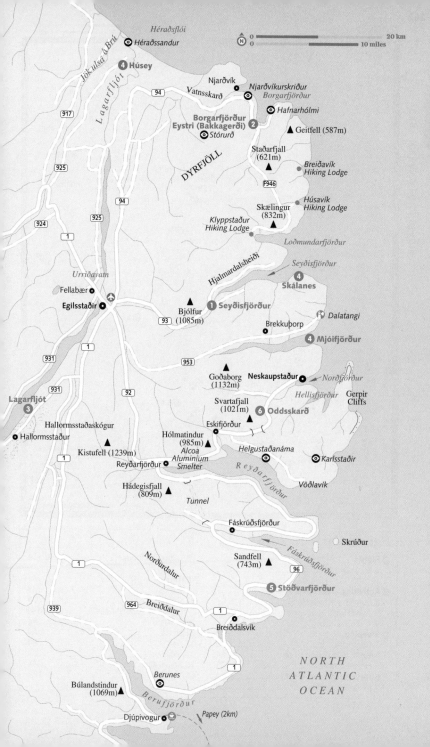

Egilsstaðir

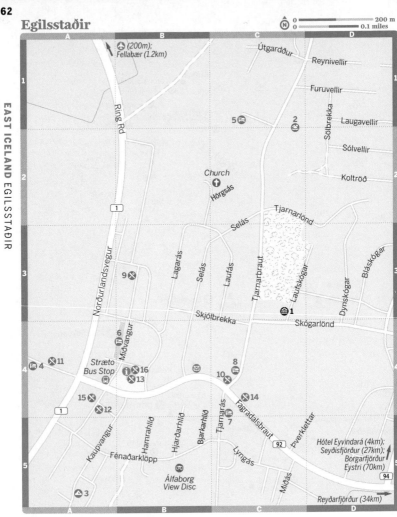

Egilsstaðir

◉ Sights
1 Minjasafn Austurlands C3

✛ Activities, Courses & Tours
2 Sundlaugin Egilsstöðum C2
Travel East .... (see 3)

🛏 Sleeping
3 Campsite A5
4 Egilsstaðir Guesthouse A4
5 Hótel Edda C1
6 Icelandair Hótel Hérað B4
7 Lyngás Guesthouse C4

8 Olga Guesthouse C4

✗ Eating
9 Bónus B3
10 Café Nielsen C4
Egilsstaðir Guesthouse .... (see 4)
11 Fjóshornið A4
12 Nettó A4
13 Salt B4
14 Skálinn C4
15 Söluskálinn A4
16 Vínbúðin B4

Jun-Aug) Egilsstaðir's cultural museum has sweet displays focusing on the region's history.

Sundlaugin Egilsstöðum
SWIMMING POOL, HOT-POT

(Tjarnarbraut 26; adult/child Ikr550/250; ⊙ 6.30am-9.30pm Mon-Fri, 10am-6pm Sat & Sun Jun-Aug, closes 1hr earlier Sep-May) The town's popular swimming pool, with saunas and hot-pots (and attached gym), is north of the centre.

⚐ Tours

Jeep Tours
JEEP TOUR

(☑898 2798; www.jeeptours.is) Knowledgable Agnar runs excellent 4WD day tours from Egilsstaðir into the highlands: to Askja and Herðubreið (Ikr38,000), to Snæfell (Ikr34,000), or on reindeer-spotting safaris. This is also one of few companies visiting Kverkfjöll as a day tour (Ikr38,000), travelling via the (sealed) Rte 910 to Kárahnjúkar dam before tackling remote 4WD tracks. Winter tours are available – check the website.

Travel East
HORSE RIDING, JEEP TOUR

(☑471 3060; www.traveleast.is; Kaupvangur 17) From its booking desk at the campground, this travel agency can hook you up with various activity tours in the region: horse riding, hiking, super-Jeep tours, skiing, sea-angling etc.

Wild Boys
HIKING TOUR

(☑864 7393, 896 4334; www.wildboys.is) A small operator that arranges guided hikes in the area, including day hikes to Snæfell, or Dyrfjöll and Stórurð near Borgarfjörður Eystri, plus multiday hikes in the eastern highland region.

★★ Festivals & Events

See 'What's On' at www.east.is for more events.

JEA Jazz Festival
MUSIC

(www.jea.is) In late June, Iceland's oldest jazz fest takes place in Egilsstaðir.

Ormsteiti
CULTURAL

(www.ormsteiti.is) The possible existence of the lake monster is a good excuse for this 10-day cultural carnival during late August.

Dagar Myrkurs
CULTURAL

Over 10 days in early November, in Egilsstaðir and Lagarfljót, the 'Days of Darkness' perversely celebrates the failing light and the onset of winter with ghost stories, Northern Lights spotting and torch-lit processions.

🛏 Sleeping

Note that throughout this chapter, prices listed are generally from 2014; refer to websites for current rates.

Lyngás Guesthouse
GUESTHOUSE €

(☑471 1310; www.lyngas.is; Lyngási 5-7; d without bathroom Ikr14,900; 🛜) Behind an uninspiring exterior is a fresh, six-room guesthouse, offering fine views, a kitchen and a couple of larger, family-friendly rooms. You can save a few krónur if you bring your own sleeping bag.

Olga Guesthouse
GUESTHOUSE €

(☑860 2999; www.gistihusolgu.com; Tjarnabraut 3; s/d without bathroom from Ikr12,400/14,700) In a good central location, dressed-in-red Olga offers five rooms that share three bathrooms and a kitchen – all rooms come with tea and coffee-making facilities, TV and fridge. Two doors down is Olga's sister, yellow Birta Guesthouse, under the same friendly ownership and with similar high-quality facilities. Breakfast can be ordered for Ikr1550.

Campsite
CAMPGROUND €

(Kaupvangur 17; sites per person Ikr1200; ⊙ Jun-Sep; @ 🛜) Camping pitches are in utilitarian rows, but it's central and facilities are reasonable – there's a laundry, and on-site cafe, but no camper kitchen. At reception you can rent bikes (Ikr3900 for 24 hours) or book tours through Travel East, which is based here.

Hótel Eyvindará
HOTEL, COTTAGES €€

(☑471 1200; www.eyvindara.is; Eyvindará II; s/d incl breakfast from Ikr18,600/23,000; ⊙ Apr-Oct; 🛜) Set 4km out of town (on Rte 94), Eyvindará is a handsome, family-run collection of new hotel rooms, plus good motel-style units and timber cottages. The cottages sit hidden among fir trees, while motel rooms enjoy verandahs and views. There's a decent restaurant too.

Hótel Edda
HOTEL €€

(☑444 4880; www.hoteledda.is; Tjarnarbraut 25; s/d Ikr19,200/21,700; ⊙ Jun–mid-Aug; @ 🛜) Based in the school opposite the swimming pool, this is a typically well-run Edda hotel. Tidy, no-frills rooms have small private bathrooms, and there's a restaurant with panoramic views.

Egilsstaðir Guesthouse
COUNTRY HOTEL €€€

(☑471 1114; www.lakehotel.is; s/d incl breakfast Ikr22,520/30,100; @ 🛜) The town was named after this farm and splendid heritage guesthouse (now big enough to warrant the 'hotel' label) on the banks of Lagarfljót, 300m west of the crossroads. In its old wing, en-suite rooms retain a sense of character.

EAST ICELAND EGILSSTAÐIR

HÚSEY

Reaching Húsey involves a long but scenic drive, 30km off the Ring Road along the rough, unsealed Rtes 925 and 926 beside the Jökulsá á Dal river (all up, about 60km from Egilsstaðir). The only reason to venture out to this isolated farm is a good one: to stay at the simple, rustic **Húsey HI Hostel** (☑ 471 3010; www.husey.de; dm/d without bathroom Ikr4030/9600).

There are horses to ride (two-hour seal-watching tours on horseback start at 10am and 5pm daily; Ikr6200), birdwatching trails to follow, and seals cavorting in the riverine backdrop. It's worth staying a few days to enjoy the homey atmosphere; longer horse treks are easily arranged. The hostel has cooking facilities, but there's nowhere to buy food, so bring supplies. Breakfast can be ordered; linen hire costs Ikr1100. Book ahead, and ask about pick-up options if you don't have your own vehicle.

In contrast, a brand-new extension houses 30 modern, slightly anonymous hotel rooms. A great restaurant is on site.

Icelandair Hótel Hérað
HOTEL €€€

(☑ 471 1500; www.icelandairhotels.is; Miðvangur 5-7; r from Ikr30,000; @ 🛜) This stylish, friendly, business-standard hotel is kitted out with the expected bells and whistles, and appealing splashes of colour. The restaurant (mains Ikr2700 to Ikr7250) here is a good place to indulge (house speciality: reindeer).

🍴 Eating

Refuelling motorists don't have to look far – quick eats can be found at the busy **Söluskálinn** (⊙ 8am-11.30pm) inside the N1 service station on the Ring Road. Those heading to the fjords can try **Skálinn** (Fagradalsbraut; ⊙ 8am-10pm Mon-Fri, 9am-10pm Sat & Sun) at the Shell station.

Bókakaffi Hlöðum
CAFE €

(www.bokakaffi.is; Helgafelli 2; soup buffets Ikr1590; ⊙ 10am-5pm Mon-Fri; 🛜) In Fellabær, at the western end of the bridge across the river from Egilsstaðir, is this sweet, low-key cafe: quality coffee, retro furniture, vinyl records, secondhand books and baked treats.

Fjóshornið
CAFE €

(⊙ 2-6pm Mon-Fri Jun-Aug) For a taste of top-quality local produce, stop by 'Cowshed Corner', beside Egilsstaðir Guesthouse, where you can buy beef and dairy products such as *skyr* (a yoghurt-like dessert), yoghurt and feta direct from the farm. Coffee and homemade cakes are available.

Salt
INTERNATIONAL €€

(www.saltbistro.is; Miðvangur 2; meals Ikr1290-3000; ⊙ 10am-11pm; 🛜📶) We totally get the appeal of this cool cafe-bistro, which offers one of the most interesting and varied menus in regional Iceland. Unfortunately, Salt can struggle with the large crowds it attracts. The food, however, is excellent: try the gourmet-topped flatbread pizza made with local barley, or opt for a burger, salad, crêpe or tandoori-baked Indian dish.

Café Nielsen
INTERNATIONAL €€

(Tjarnarbraut 1; meals Ikr1600-7100; ⊙ 11.30am-11.30pm Mon-Fri, 1-11.30pm Sat & Sun; 🛜📶) Based in Egilsstaðir's oldest house, cottagey Café Nielsen offers a wide-ranging, crowd-pleasing menu that roams from lobster soup to reindeer by way of nachos and barbecue pork sandwich. In summer there's a leafy terrace and garden. The lunch buffet (soup, salad, pasta) is Ikr1850.

★ Egilsstaðir Guesthouse
ICELANDIC €€€

(☑ 471 1114; www.lakehotel.is; lunch Ikr1290-2590, dinner mains Ikr2790-5890; ⊙ 11.30am-10pm; 🛜) Some of the east's most creative cooking happens here, and the menu is an ode to locally sourced produce (lamb, fish, game). The speciality is the beef, raised right here on the farm: try a slow-cooked fillet with Béarnaise foam, or tenderloin with goose confit. Desserts are pretty, polished affairs. Bookings advised.

Nettó
SUPERMARKET

(⊙ 9am-8pm Mon-Fri, 9am-6pm Sat, noon-6pm Sun) Behind the N1 petrol station.

Bónus
SUPERMARKET

(⊙ 11am-6.30pm Mon-Thu, 10am-7.30pm Fri, 10am-6pm Sat, noon-6pm Sun) On the Ring Road north of the N1.

Vínbúðin
LIQUOR STORE

(Miðvangi 2-4; ⊙ 11am-6pm Mon-Thu, to 7pm Fri, to 4pm Sat Jun-Aug, shorter hours Sep-May) Government-run liquor store.

ℹ Information

Tourist Information Centre (☑471 2320; www.east.is; Miðvangur 2-4; ☺8am-6pm Mon-Fri, 10am-4pm Sat & Sun Jun-Aug, 8am-4pm Mon-Fri Sep-May) Everything you need (including maps) to explore the Eastfjords and beyond.

ℹ Orientation

North past the airport and over the lake, you'll find Egilsstaðir's twin town, Fellabær. It has some accommodation options, but most services are on a large block just off the Ring Road in Egilsstaðir (note: this is a good place to position yourself if you're hitching).

ℹ Getting There & Away

Egilsstaðir is the transport hub of east Iceland. There's an airport, and all bus services (see p259) pass through.

Lagarfljót

The grey-brown waters of the river-lake Lagarfljót are reputed to harbour a fearsome monster, **Lagarfljótsormur**, which has allegedly been spotted since Viking times. The most recent 'sighting' of the serpentine beast (also called the Worm/Wyrm) caused quite a stir – in 2012 a local farmer released footage of a large creature moving in the river. The clip has attracted close to five million hits on YouTube, and garnered international news coverage. Read more at www.ormur.com.

Real or imagined, the poor beast must be pretty chilly – Lagarfljót starts its journey in the Vatnajökull ice cap and its glacial waters flow north to the Arctic Ocean, widening into a 38km-long, 50m-deep lake, often called Lögurinn, south of Egilsstaðir.

Whether you see a monster or not, it's a lovely stretch of water to circumnavigate by car. Rte 931, a mixture of sealed surfaces and gravel (gravel on the less-trafficked western shore), turns off the Ring Road about 10km south of Egilsstaðir and runs around the lake to Fellabær – a circuit of around 70km.

Hallormsstaðaskógur

Iceland's largest **forest**, Hallormsstaðaskógur is king of the woods and venerated by the arborically challenged nation. Although it's small by most countries' standards, it's a leafy reprieve after the stark, bare mountainsides to the north and south of Egilsstaðir. Common species include native dwarf birch and mountain ash, as well as 80 tree species gathered from around the world.

🛏 Sleeping & Eating

Atlavík Campsite CAMPGROUND €
(sites per person Ikr1200) In a wooded cove on the lakeshore, idyllic Atlavík is a popular campsite and is often the scene of summer weekend parties. Pedal boats, rowing boats and canoes can be hired for watery pursuits.

Höfðavík Campsite CAMPGROUND €
(sites per person Ikr1200) A second campsite on the lakeshore, Höfðavík campsite is just north of the petrol station and small and quiet.

Hótel Hallormsstaður HOTEL €€
(☑471 2400; www.hotel701.is; hotel s/d Ikr23,900/30,700, guesthouse s/d without bathroom Ikr14,250/19,400, all incl breakfast; @🖥) A veritable campus of buildings among the trees, this bucolic country retreat offers modern hotel rooms, cottages and the **Grái Hundurinn guesthouse**, plus two

ℹ ROUTE OPTIONS

Driving south from Egilsstaðir, there are a few options (for motorists heading north from Djúpivogur, read these directions in reverse!).

Route 1 From Egilsstaðir, the **Ring Road** heads south, then east through the Breiðdalur valley to Breiðdalsvík, then weaves along the coast to Djúpivogur. This Egilsstaðir–Breiðdalsvík route is 82km (note: not all of this section of the Ring Road is sealed); see p279.

Route 939 A shortcut is provided by the rough (gravel) but scenic Rte 939 via the **Öxi mountain pass** (not a great option in bad weather or fog). This pass turns off the Ring Road about 48km south of Egilsstaðir, connecting with the head of Berufjörður after 19km.

Routes 92 & 96 A third option is to travel from Egilsstaðir to Breiðdalsvík via Rtes 92 and 96, travelling via the **fjords** Reyðarfjörður, Fáskrúðsfjörður and Stöðvarfjörður. This option is only slightly longer than the Ring Road option (92km), and is sealed the entire length. This is often the only option in winter, when snow closes the Ring Road stretch at Breiðdalsheiði. It has even been mooted that the Ring Road may one day be officially rerouted to take in Rtes 92 and 96.

LOCAL KNOWLEDGE

MEET THE LOCALS

With its small population (around 11,000), distance from the capital, and with the Ring Road steaming quickly through it, east Iceland has struggled to get the traveller attention it deserves. **Tanni Travel** (☑ 476 1399; www.meetthelocals.is) hopes to change that, and is working with locals to create unique experiences. The agency is based in Eskifjörður but works all over the east, and offers a roster of guided village walks (daily from June to mid-September); it can also devise itineraries and connect you with guides and activities (particularly useful in winter). Unique in Iceland, it also offers travellers the chance to spend an evening dining in the home of locals (Ikr13,000 per person).

restaurants (a renowned dinner buffet in summer) and an inviting outdoor area.

Activities abound, including horse-riding and quad-bike tours. Bike hire is available.

Hengifoss

Hengifoss   WATERFALL
Crossing the bridge across Lagarfljót on Rte 931, you'll reach the parking area for Hengifoss, Iceland's second-highest waterfall. The falls plummet 118m into a photogenic brown-and-red-striped boulder-strewn gorge.

Getting to Hengifoss requires a return walk of one to two hours (2.5km each way). From the car park, a long staircase leads up the hillside – Hengifoss is soon visible in the distance. It's a steep climb in places but flattens out as you enter the canyon.

Halfway to Hengifoss is a smaller waterfall, **Litlanesfoss**, surrounded by vertical basalt columns in a honeycomb formation.

Skriðuklaustur

Skriðuklaustur   MUSEUM
(www.skriduklaustur.is; adult/child Ikr1000/free; ☺10am-6pm Jun-Aug, noon-5pm May & Sep) Head south from Hengifoss waterfall for 5km to reach Skriðuklaustur, the photogenic site of a 16th-century monastery and the home of an Icelandic author feted by the Third Reich. The unusual black-and-white turf-roofed building was built in 1939 by Gunnar Gunnarsson (1889–1975), and now holds a cultural centre dedicated to him. This prolific writer achieved phenomenal popularity in Denmark and Germany – at the height of his fame only Goethe outsold him.

The house also contains an exhibition about the earlier Augustinian monastery, demolished during the Reformation of 1550. Archaeological finds include bones indicating that Skriðuklaustur was used as a hospice.

★**Klausturkaffi**   CAFE **€€**
(www.skriduklaustur.is; Skriðuklaustur; lunch buffets adult/child Ikr2800/1400; ☺10am-6pm Jun-Aug, noon-5pm May & Sep) Klausturkaffi serves an impeccable lunch buffet showcasing local ingredients (seafood soup, reindeer pie, brambleberry *skyr* cake). More tantalising, however, is the brilliant all-you-can-eat cake buffet (adult/child Ikr1850/925) served between 3pm and 5.30pm.

Snæfellsstofa

National Park Visitor Centre   VISITOR CENTRE
(☑470 0840; www.vjp.is; ☺9am-6pm Mon-Fri, 10am-6pm Sat & Sun Jun-Aug, 10am-4pm Mon-Fri, 1-5pm Sat & Sun May & Sep) This centre covers the eastern territory of the behemoth Vatnajökull National Park. Excellent displays highlight the nature of the eastern highlands, and staff sell maps and offer advice to travellers wishing to hike or otherwise experience the park.

Snæfell Area

No one seems to know whether 1833m-high volcano Snæfell is extinct, or if it's just having a rest. Iceland's highest peak outside the Vatnajökull massif is relatively accessible, making it popular with hikers and mountaineers.

Snæfell looms over the southern end of Fljótsdalsheiði, an expanse of wet tundra, boulder fields, perennial snow patches and alpine lakes, stretching westwards from Lagarfljót into the highlands. It's part of the vast Vatnajökull National Park – the park website www.vjp.is has useful information, and the national park visitor centre, Snæfellsstofa, has info, maps and displays. If you want to tour the area with someone else behind the wheel, check offerings from Egilsstaðir-based Jeep Tours (p263).

Kárahnjúkar

Work on the controversial Kárahnjúkar hydroelectric plant brought improved roads around Snæfell, with the paved Rte 910 from Fljótsdalur being the best way up. The turn-off is just north of Skriðuklaustur, and the road climbs *fast* but then levels out; it's suitable for 2WDs.

A scenic 60km drive from the turn-off takes you to the dam and reservoir, where information boards and viewing areas allow you to appreciate this vast feat of engineering, as well as observe the incredible **Hafrahvammagljúfur** canyon, below the dam. Visit between 2pm and 5pm Wednesday and Saturday from June to August, when a power-company representative offers free guiding at the dam (see www.landsvirkjun.com/company/visitus).

Along Rte 910, watch for wild reindeer, and bring your swimsuit to stop at the hot springs of **Laugarfell Highland Hostel** (☑ 773 3323; www.laugarfell.is; www Ikr5500/16,000), where a comfy bed and hot dinner is available (as well as daytime snacks). The hostel is 2km off Rte 910 (OK for 2WD cars).

To travel south beyond the dam viewpoint, a large, high-clearance 4WD is required, and a GPS – this area is well off the beaten path.

Snæfell

A 4WD is required to travel Rte F909 (off Rte 910) to reach **Snæfell mountain hut** (☑ 842 4367; snaefellsstofa@vjp.is; N 64°48.250', W 15°38.600'; sites/dm per person Ikr1400/5600) at the base of the Snæfell peak. The hut sleeps 50, with a kitchen, camping area and showers.

Although climbing the mountain itself is not difficult for experienced, well-prepared hikers, the weather can be a concern and crampons are advisable. Ascending from the west is most common – it's a hike of six to nine hours, depending on ice conditions. Discuss your route with the hut warden.

One of Iceland's most challenging and rewarding hikes takes you from **Snæfell to the Lónsöræfi district** in southeast Iceland. The five-day, 45km route begins at the Snæfell hut and heads across the glacier Eyjabakkajökull (an arm of Vatnajökull) to Geldingafell, Egilssel and Múlaskáli huts before dropping down to the coast at Stafafell.

This route should not be approached lightly – it's for experienced trekkers only. You'll need a GPS and, for the glacier crossing, you must be skilled at using a rope, crampons and an ice axe. If you're unsure of your skills, you'd be wiser doing the trip commercially with the likes of Icelandic Mountain Guides (p295) – although IMG's five-day, 50km backpacking tour through Lónsöræfi (from Ikr119,000), called 'In the Shadow of Vatna-

PIT STOP!

Halfway between Egilsstaðir and Borgarfjörður sits one of east Iceland's quirkier roadside wonders: a pistachio-coloured hut surrounded by miles of nothingness. Built by a local eccentric, the structure is simply a hut to house a solar-powered refrigerated vending machine. If the power is off, flick the 'on' switch (we're not kidding) and wait two minutes (you can sign the guestbook while waiting). Then, voila: a refreshingly cold beverage or snack.

jökull', begins at Eyjabakkar wetlands east of Snæfell and avoids the glacier traverse.

Hrafnkelsdalur

Rte F923 (off Rte 910, for 4WDs only) leads you to the valley of Hrafnkelsdalur, full of sites relating to *Hrafnkell's Saga*. The remote farm **Aðalból** (☑ 471 2788; www.simnet.is/samur; sites per person Ikr1700, s/d without bathroom Ikr9900/14,800; ⊗ Jun–Aug) was the home of the saga's hero, Hrafnkell Freysgoði, and his burial mound is here. There's a marked saga trail, threading together places mentioned in the story (see boxed text, p268). There's a guesthouse and campsite; meals are available (notice required), as is petrol.

You can also access Aðalból from the Ring Road – it's 43km on unsealed Rte 923 (which becomes an F road south of the farm).

THE EASTFJORDS

The fjords are the true highlight of east Iceland. Despite (mostly) good surfaced roads and the Alcoa-related activity, the Eastfjords still seem remote – a feeling enhanced by immense, dramatic mountainsides and the tiny working fishing villages that nestle under them.

There are some superb hiking trails, you can kayak to far-off headlands, and thousands of seabirds nest along the cliffs. In a Finest Fjord competition it would be hard to pick a winner: Borgarfjörður has ethereal rhyolite cliffs and well-organised hiking, Seyðisfjörður fosters a cheery bohemian vibe, Mjóifjörður is riddled with waterfalls, and Norðfjörður has a dizzying ascent/descent. You'll just have to visit and choose your own favourite. This section is organised from north to south; note that Vopnafjörður is covered in the North Iceland chapter (p256).

HRAFNKELL'S SAGA

The saga of Hrafnkell is one of the most widely read Icelandic sagas, thanks to its succinct plot and memorable characters. The tale is particularly interesting because its premises seem to derail any modern notions of right, wrong and justice served. The only conclusions one can draw are 'it's better to be alive than dead' and 'it's better to have the support of powerful chieftains than rely on any kind of god'.

The main character, Hrafnkell, is a religious fanatic who builds a temple to Freyr on the farm Aðalból in Hrafnkelsdalur. Hrafnkell's prized stallion, Freyfaxi, is dedicated to the god, and Hrafnkell swears an oath to kill anyone who dares ride him without permission. As might be expected, someone does. Discovering the outrage, Hrafnkell takes his axe to the errant youth.

When the boy's father, Þorbjörn, demands compensation for his son's death, Hrafnkell refuses to pay up, offering instead to look after Þorbjörn in his old age. Proudly, the man refuses, and the characters are launched into a court battle that ultimately leads to Hrafnkell being declared an outlaw. He chooses to ignore the sentence and returns home.

Before long, Þorbjörn's nephew Sámur Bjarnason arrives to uphold the family honour, stringing Hrafnkell up by his Achilles tendons until he agrees to hand over his farm and possessions. Sámur then offers him a choice: to live a life of subordination and dishonour, or to die on the spot. You might think a saga hero would go for death, but Hrafnkell chooses life.

Sámur moves into Aðalból and makes a few home improvements. The pagan temple is destroyed, and the horse Freyfaxi weighted with stones, thrown over a cliff and drowned in the water below. Hrafnkell, by now convinced that his favourite god doesn't give two hoots about him, renounces his religious beliefs and sets up on a new farm, Hrafnkelsstaðir. He vows to change his vengeful nature and becomes a kind and simple farmer, becoming so well-liked in his new neighbourhood that he gains even more wealth and power than before.

One day, Sámur and his brother Eyvindur pass by en route to Aðalból. Hrafnkell's maid sees them and goads her employer into taking revenge for his earlier humiliation. Hrafnkell abandons the Mr Nice Guy routine, sets out in pursuit of the troublesome brothers, kills Eyvindur, and offers Sámur the same choice that he was offered before – give up Aðalból and live in shame, or be put to death. Sámur also decides not to die. Hrafnkell thus regains his former estates and lives happily ever after at Aðalból.

Borgarfjörður Eystri (Bakkagerði)

POP 90

This tiny village is in a stunning location, framed by a backdrop of rugged rhyolite peaks on one side and the spectacular Dyrfjöll mountains on the other; the hiking in the area is outstanding. There's very little in the village itself, although driftwood sculptures, hidden elves and crying seabirds exude a magical charm.

For local information, check out www. borgarfjordureystri.is.

◉ Sights & Activities

★ Hafnarhólmi   ISLAND
(www.puffins.is) Five kilometres past the wee church is the photogenic small-boat harbour and islet of Hafnarhólmi, home to a large **puffin colony**. The viewing platform allows you to get close to these cute, clumsy creatures (and other seabirds). The puffins arrive mid-April and are gone by mid-August, but other species (including kittiwakes and fulmars) may linger longer.

Lindarbakki   HISTORIC SITE
You can't miss the village's hairiest house: bright-red Lindarbakki (1899) is completely cocooned by whiskery green grass, with only a few windows and a giant pair of antlers sticking out. It's a private home (not open to the public); an information board outside outlines its history.

Álfaborg   NATURE RESERVE
Álfaborg (Elf Rock), the small mound and nature reserve near the campground, is the 'borg' that gave Borgarfjörður Eystri its name. Some locals believe that the queen of Icelandic elves lives here. From the 'view disc' on top there's a fabulous vista of the surrounding fields.

Bakkagerðiskirkja   CHURCH
Jóhannes Sveinsson Kjarval (1885-1972), Iceland's best-known artist, was brought

up nearby and took much of his inspiration from Borgarfjörður Eystri and surrounds. His unusual altarpiece in the small church depicts the Sermon on the Mount and is directly aimed at this village: Jesus is preaching from Álfaborg, with the mountain Dyrfjöll in the background.

Musteri Spa
SPA

(📞861 1791; www.blabjorg.is; adult/child Ikr2800/1000; ⊙2-10pm or by appointment) Underneath Blábjörg Guesthouse and enjoying supreme views, this spa features both indoor and outdoor hot tubs and saunas (the brave can take a dip in the sea).

Ævintýraland
CHILDREN'S CENTRE

(Adventure Land; admission Ikr500; ⊙1-5pm Jun-Aug; ⊕) Bring kids to sweet, petite Ævintýraland, where they can snuggle up with an iPod and listen to reinterpretations of local elf stories. There's also dress-ups, painting and magical rock collections.

★ Festivals & Events

Bræðslan
MUSIC

(www.braedslan.is) Held in an old herring plant on the third weekend of July, Bræðslan is one of Iceland's best summer concert festivals, earning itself a reputation for great music as well as its intimate atmosphere. Some big local names (and a few international ones) come to play.

Past guests include Emiliana Torrini (who used to summer in Borgarfjörður), Damien Rice, Of Monsters and Men and Mugison.

🛏 Sleeping

★ Blábjörg Guesthouse
GUESTHOUSE €

(📞861 1792; www.blabjorg.is; s/d without bathroom incl breakfast Ikr10,100/14,400; 🛜) In a cleverly converted fish factory, this well-run guesthouse features 11 pristine white rooms, plus guest kitchen and lounge. There's also an excellent apartment available. The standout feature is the downstairs spa, Musteriõ Heilsulind (guests receive discount on admission).

Campsite
CAMPGROUND €

(sites per person Ikr1000; ⊙mid-May–Sep) This well-kept site has a kitchen, a washing machine and showers. The third night is free.

Borg Guesthouse
GUESTHOUSE €

(📞472 9870, 894 4470; gistiheimilidborg.wordpress.com; s/d without bathroom Ikr8000/14,000; 🛜) Borg is a good bet for a bed (cheaper sleeping-bag options are available), since

the owner has a few options in the village. Rooms are OK if old-fashioned, with cooking and lounge facilities. Hiking, guiding and 4WD tours can be arranged.

Álfheimar Guesthouse
COUNTRY HOTEL €€

(📞471 2010; www.alfheimar.com; s/d incl breakfast Ikr20,000/23,100; ⊙May-Sep; @🛜) Easily the most upmarket option (it's the only one with private bathrooms!), Álfheimar has 30 motel-style units in long annexes. The timber-lined rooms have more atmosphere than the newer building but all are spotless and well equipped. The affable owners are a font of local knowledge; guiding and tours can be arranged.

There's a restaurant (two/three courses Ikr4900/5900) open to all (from 7pm) and offering the dish of the day from the fjord's fishermen or farmers.

🍴 Eating & Drinking

Álfacafé
ICELANDIC €€

(fish soups Ikr1900; ⊙10am-10pm Jun-Aug, to 8pm May & Sep; 🛜) The main venue for eating and drinking, with large stone-slab tables and tasty fish soup the headlining act (with decent support from the likes of flatbread with trout, plus cakes and waffles). Geological stones and souvenirs are also for sale.

Já Sæll Fjarðarborg
ICELANDIC €€

(meals Ikr1400-3500; ⊙11.30am-midnight Jun-Aug) The menu is simple and the decor uninspiring at this option inside Fjarðarborg (the community centre), but it's worth a visit for its burgers or lamb chops, and a beer among the locals. Ask about the weekly live music held here in summer.

Samkaup-Strax
SUPERMARKET

(⊙10am-6pm Mon-Fri, noon-4pm Sat & Sun Jun-Aug, 12.30-5.30pm Mon-Thu, to 6pm Fri Sep-May) The tiny Samkaup by the pier sells groceries.

ℹ Getting There & Away

BUS

The only public transport is the summer weekday bus service (one way Ikr1750) between Fjarðarborg community centre (departs 8am) and Egilsstaðir information centre (departs noon).

CAR

The village is 70km from Egilsstaðir along Rte 94, about half of which is sealed (accessible in summer in a 2WD). It winds steeply up over the Dyrfjöll mountains before dropping down to the coast. There's a petrol pump by the grocery store.

Around Borgarfjörður Eystri

There are loads of well-marked trails criss-crossing the area around Borgarfjörður – everything from easy one-hour strolls to serious mountain hiking. For a full array, get your hands on the widely available *Víknaslóðir – Trails of the Deserted Inlets* map (Ikr1000).

Dyrfjöll

One of Iceland's most dramatic ranges, the Dyrfjöll mountains rise precipitously to an altitude of 1136m between the marshy Héraðssandur plains and Borgarfjörður Eystri. The name Dyrfjöll means Door Mountain and is due to the large and conspicuous notch in the highest peak – an Icelandic counterpart to Sweden's famous Lapporten. There are walking tracks crossing the range, which allow for day hikes or longer routes from Borgarfjörður Eystri.

Stórurð, on the western flank of Dyrfjöll, is a hiker's paradise, an extraordinary place scattered with huge rocks and small glacial ponds. Along Rte 94, a number of access trails are marked. A good route is trail 9, beginning from the parking area on Vatns-skarð pass, then loop back along trail 8 (marked on the *Víknaslóðir* map). The 15km trip takes just over five hours.

Njarðvíkurskriður

A habitual site of accidents in ancient times, Njarðvíkurskriður is a dangerous scree slope on Rte 94 near Njarðvík. All the tragedies were blamed on a nuisance creature (half-man, half-beast), Naddi, who dwelt in a sea-level cave beneath the slope.

In the early 1300s, Naddi was exorcised by the proper religious authorities, and in 1306 a cross was erected on the site bearing the inscription *Effigiem Christi qui transis pronus honora, Anno MCCCVI* – 'You who are hurrying past, honour the image of Christ – AD 1306'. The idea was that travellers would repeat a prayer when passing the danger zone and therefore be protected from malevolent powers. The cross has been replaced several times since, but the current one still bears the original inscription.

Seyðisfjörður

POP 650

If you visit only one town in the Eastfjords, this should be it. Made up of multicoloured wooden houses and surrounded by snow-capped mountains and cascading water-falls, obscenely picturesque Seyðisfjörður

---

BORGARFJÖRÐUR TO SEYÐISFJÖRÐUR HIKE

Wildly wonderful and unexplored, the rugged country between Borgarfjörður and Seyðis-fjörður makes for one of the best multiday hikes in the region. To plan your journey, pick up the widely available *Víknaslóðir – Trails of the Deserted Inlets* map(Ikr1000), or contact Álfheimar (p269) or Borg (p269) accommodation in Borgarfjörður if you're looking for a guide. For hut information along this route, check www.fljotsdalsherad.is/ferdafelag (click on 'Houses').

Day 1 Start at Kolbeinsfjara, 4km outside the township of Borgarfjörður Eystri, and venture up into the mountains along the Brúnavíkurskarð pass (trail #19 on the map). Turn south (along trail #21) at the emergency hut in Brúnavík, passing beautiful Kerlingfjall further on. After your six-to-seven-hour hike (15km), settle in for the night at the outfit-ted farmhouse/campsite in Breiðavík.

Day 2 Next day features another stunning six or seven hours of hiking (13.5km along trail #30). You'll first walk through the grassy leas below Hvítafjall, then link up with the 4WD track heading south to the Húsavík lodge, where you'll spend the second night. The land between Breiðavík and Húsavík is infested with hidden people – the elf sheriff lives at Sólarfjall and the elf bishop lives at Blábjörg further south along the coast.

Day 3 Another 14km of trails are tackled in six to seven hours of hiking (along trail 37) as the path reunites with the sea at silent Loðmundarfjörður. The 4WD track ends at the Klyppstaður lodge on the Norðdalsá river delta at the uppermost point of the fjord.

Day 4 The last day links Loðmundarfjörður to Seyðisfjörður (trail 41). At the highest point of the mountain pass you'll find a logbook signed by previous hikers. As you venture down into Seyðisfjörður, you'll be treated to a watery fanfare of gushing chutes.

is the most historically and architecturally interesting town in east Iceland. It's also a friendly place with a community of artists, musicians and craftspeople.

Summer is the liveliest time to visit, particularly when the Smyril Line's ferry *Norröna* sails majestically up the 17km-long fjord to the town – a perfect way to arrive in Iceland.

If the weather's good, the scenic Rte 93 drive from Egilsstaðir is a delight, climbing to a high pass then descending along the waterfall-filled river Fjarðará.

History

Seyðisfjörður started as a trading centre in 1848, but its later wealth came from the 'silver of the sea' – herring. Its long, sheltering fjord gave it an advantage over other fishing villages, and it grew into the largest and most prosperous town in east Iceland. Most of the unique wooden buildings here were built by Norwegian merchants, attracted by the herring industry.

During WWII Seyðisfjörður was a base for British and American forces. The only attack was on an oil tanker (the *El Grillo*) that was bombed by three German warplanes. The bombs missed their target, but one exploded so near that the ship sank to the bottom, where it remains today (a good dive spot).

Seyðisfjörður's steep-sided valley has made it prone to avalanches. In 1885 an avalanche from Bjólfur killed 24 people and pushed several houses straight into the fjord. A more recent avalanche in 1996 flattened a local factory, but no lives were lost. The **avalanche monument** near the church is made from twisted girders from the factory, painted white and erected as they were found.

◎ Sights

Seyðisfjörður is stuffed with 19th-century timber buildings, brought in kit form from Norway; several of these have been transformed into cosy ateliers where local artisans work on various projects. A quick loop around town will reveal half-a-dozen places to drop some krónur, on art, handicrafts and knitwear. Also worth a look is the gallery space above the Skaftfell cultural centre.

★ Bláa Kirkjan   CHURCH
(www.blaakirkjan.is; Ránargata) The most prominent of Seyðisfjörður's timber buildings is the photogenic Blue Church. On Wednesday

evenings from July to mid-August, it's the setting for a popular series of jazz, classical- and folk-music concerts (starting at 8.30pm; tickets Ikr2000); see the website for the program. If you're leaving on the Thursday ferry, this is a lovely way to spend your final night in Iceland.

Tækniminjasafn Austurlands   MUSEUM
(www.tekmus.is; Hafnargata 44; adult/child Ikr1000/free; ⊗11am-5pm Mon-Fri Jun–mid-Sep) For insight into the town's fishing and telecommunications history, stop by this worthwhile technical museum. It's housed in two buildings on Hafnargata: the impressive 1894 home of Norwegian shipowner Otto Wathne (the old telegraph station), and a mechanical workshop from 1907.

⚡ Activities

Sundhöll Seyðisfjarðar SWIMMING POOL, HOT-POT
(Suðurgata 5; adult/child Ikr480/free; ⊗6.30-9am & 3-8pm Mon-Fri, 1-4pm Sat Jun-Aug, shorter hours Sep-May) Seyðisfjörður's indoor pool has a sauna and hot-pots.

Stafdalur Ski Area   SKIING
From about December to May, there's downhill and cross-country skiing at Stafdalur, 9km from Seyðisfjörður on the road to Egilsstaðir – contact the tourist office (p274) for details.

Hiking

Short walking trails lead from the museum area uphill to waterfalls, and to the 'sound sculpture' **Tvísöngur** – five interconnected concrete domes. Another short walk leads from the road on the north shore of the fjord (about 6km beyond the Blue Church) to the signposted **Dvergasteinn** (Dwarf Rock) – according to folklore, this is a dwarf church that followed the people's church across the fjord.

The hills above Seyðisfjörður are the perfect spot for longer hiking. **Vestdalur** is a grassy valley north of town (just before the Langahlið cottages) renowned for its glorious waterfalls. Following the Vestdalsá river, after two to three scenic hours you'll arrive at a small lake, Vestdalsvatn, which remains frozen most of the year.

Trails are marked on the widely available *Víknaslóðir – Trails of the Deserted Inlets* map (Ikr1000), and the visitseydisfjordur. com website outlines some great options, including the Seven Peaks Hike (trails climbing seven of the 1000m-plus peaks surrounding the town).

Seyðisfjörður

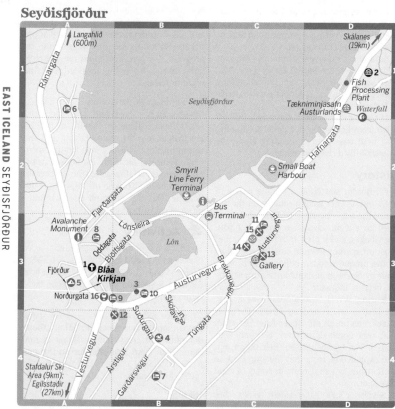

Mountain Biking

Contact kayaking guide Hlynur for rental of mountain bikes (half/one/two days Ikr2500/3000/5000). A 19km trail to Skálanes makes for a great ride.

Tours

Hlynur Oddsson KAYAKING

(☑ 865 3741; www.iceland-tour.com; ☉ Jun-Aug) For a sublime outdoor experience, contact Hlynur, a charming Robert Redford-esque character who spends his summers around town and offers tailor-made tours. With kids, you can opt for an easy half-hour paddling in the lagoon (Ikr1500); options on the fjord range from one to six hours, visiting a shipwreck or waterfalls (Ikr4000 per hour, three hours Ikr8000).

Experienced kayakers can choose longer trips, including to Skálanes (full day Ikr25,000, minimum two people). Hlynur's tours begin from outside Hótel Aldan (Snæfell).

Sleeping

Book well ahead for Wednesday nights in summer (the ferry to continental Europe leaves on Thursday mornings). Note: prices are from 2014; check websites for up-to-date rates.

★Hafaldan HI Hostel HOSTEL €

(☑ 611 4410; www.hafaldan.is; Suðurgata 8; dm Ikr4100, d with/without bathroom Ikr15,200/11,200; @ �🛜) Seyðisfjörður's first-class budget digs are housed in two locations: the **Harbour Hostel** is at Ranárgata 9, a little out of town past the Blue Church; and the **Hospital Hostel** is the more-central summertime annexe at Suðurgata 8. The annexe houses the main reception for both buildings from June to August.

The thin-walled, unremarkable private rooms at Ranárgata are compensated for by cosy, view-enriched dining and lounge areas. The annexe (the town's old hospital) includes a handful of en-suite rooms plus

Seyðisfjörður

a beautiful kitchen-dining facility. There's Ikr600 discount per person for members. Linen costs Ikr1250.

Campsite   CAMPGROUND €
(Ránargata; campsites per person Ikr1150; ☺ May-Sep; 🛜) There are two areas for camping – one sheltered, grassy site for tents opposite the church and another nearby area for vans. The service building houses kitchen, showers and laundry facilities.

★Hótel Aldan   HOTEL €€
(🖉472 1277; www.hotelaldan.com; reception at Norðurgata 2; s/d incl breakfast from Ikr17,900/23,900; 🛜) This wonderful hotel is shared across three old wooden buildings: reception and bar-restaurant (where breakfast is served) are at the Norðurgata location. The Snæfell location (in the old post office at Austurvegur 3) is a creaky, characterful three-storey place with the cheapest rooms, fresh white paintwork and Indian bedspreads; a few new ground-floor suites (sleeping four) have recently been added here. The Old Bank location (at Oddagata 6) houses a boutique guesthouse with antique furnishings and a refined air.

★Langahlíð   COTTAGES €€
(🖉897 1524; www.seydis.is; cottages per 2/6 people Ikr16,000/18,500) Book *very* early for these amazing-value three-bedroom cottages, sleeping up to six in a whole lot of comfort – including a kitchen, lounge and hot-pot on the deck with astounding views. They're about 2km north of Aldan reception.

Post Hostel   GUESTHOUSE €€
(🖉898 6242; www.posthostel.com; s/d without bathroom Ikr11,400/15,900; 🛜) The name is a little misleading – this guesthouse (in yet another old post office) has smallish rooms,

including some family-friendly ones, plus kitchen and laundry facilities. There's also a large, luxurious three-bedroom apartment for rent (Ikr45,000). In the pipeline are new en-suite rooms.

✖ Eating & Drinking

Skálinn   FAST FOOD €
(Hafnargata 2; ☺ 8am-10pm Mon-Fri, from 9am Sat, from 10am Sun) The grill bar at the petrol station does fast-food regulars, as well as inexpensive hot lunch and dinner mains.

★Skaftfell Bistro   INTERNATIONAL €€
(http://skaftfell.is/en/bistro; Austurvegur 42; meals Ikr1200-3100; ☺ from 11.30am daily, kitchen closes 10pm; 🛜🖉🍴) This fabulous bistro-bar-cultural-centre is perfect for chilling, snacking and/or meeting locals. There's a short, daily-changing menu, plus popular pizza options (including 'reindeer bliss' and 'langoustine feast'). Be sure to check out the exhibitions in the gallery space upstairs.

Hótel Aldan   ICELANDIC €€
(🖉472 1277; www.hotelaldan.is; Norðurgata 2; lunches Ikr1550-2600, dinner mains Ikr3500-9400; ☺ 7am-9pm mid-May~mid-Sep) Coffee and cakes are served all day in this country-chic spot, and lunches feature the likes of goat-cheese salad or catch of the day. In the evening, flickering candles prettify the tables, and the menu features traditional Icelandic ingredients (lamb, langoustine, reindeer, fish) with a contemporary touch. Reservations advised.

Kaffi Lára – El Grillo Bar   CAFE, BAR
(Norðurgata 3; ☺ 11.30am-1.30am Sun-Thu, to 3.30am Fri & Sat) When you can't get a table elsewhere in town, there's usually space at this friendly, two-storey cafe-bar offering

simple dishes. The must-try: El Grillo beer, brewed according to a recipe with a great backstory, and named after the bombed British tanker at the bottom of the fjord.

Samkaup-Strax SUPERMARKET
(Vesturvegur 1; ⊙9am-6pm Mon-Fri, 10am-4pm Sat, noon-4pm Sun) For self-caterers.

Vínbúðin LIQUOR STORE
(Hafnargata 4a; ⊙4-6pm Mon-Thu, 1-6pm Fri Jun-Aug, shorter hours Sep-May) Government-run liquor store.

ℹ Information

The website www.visitseydisfjordur.com is invaluable.

Landsbanki Íslands (Hafnargata 2; ⊙1.30-4pm Mon-Fri, plus 9am-noon Thu) Bank with 24-hour ATM, which can get crowded when the ferry arrives.

Tourist Office (☑472 1551; ⊙8am-4pm Mon-Fri May-Sep) In the ferry terminal building, stocking local brochures, plus info on the entire country.

ℹ Getting There & Away

BOAT

From late March to October, **Smyril Line** (www.smyrilline.com) operates a weekly car ferry, the *Norröna*, on a convoluted schedule from Hirsthals (Denmark) through Tórshavn (Faroe Islands) to Seyðisfjörður.

From mid-June to late August, the *Norröna* sails into town at 9.30am on Thursday, departing for Scandinavia two hours later. From late March to mid-June, and again from late August to October, the boat pulls in at 9am on Tuesday, leaving Wednesday at 8pm. Winter passage is also possible (departures are weather-dependent) – see the website for more.

BUS

FAS (☑893 2669, 472 1515) runs a bus service between Egilsstaðir and Seyðisfjörður (Ikr1050, around 45 minutes). Services operate year-round, one to three times daily Monday to Saturday (Sunday services operate from mid-June to mid-August). Extra services run to coincide with the ferry arrival and departure. An up-to-date schedule can be found on www.visitseydisfjordur.com.

Around Seyðisfjörður

★**Skálanes** NATURE CENTRE, GUESTHOUSE
(☑861 7008, 690 6966; www.skalanes.com; ⊙May-Sep, by arrangement Oct-Apr) You might think Seyðisfjörður is the end of the line, but further retreat is possible. The remote farm Skálanes, 19km east of Seyðisfjörður along the fjord edge, is an independent nature reserve and heritage field centre. The owner has restored the once-abandoned farmstead into a veritable Eden for amateur botanists, ecologists, archaeologists (remains from the Settlement Era have been found) and birdwatchers (more than 45 avian species).

Its isolation and experimental nature (it's plugged as a place of learning, not a regular guesthouse) will appeal to naturalists; a stay of a few days is recommended.

A variety of stay-over packages are available, incorporating guiding and meals (guests may use the kitchen). Straight-up B&B accommodation in cosily refurbished rooms goes for Ikr14,100/19,500 for a single/double; a simple two-course dinner is Ik3500.

Getting to Skálanes is an adventure in itself. You could walk all the way from Seyðisfjörður (there are footbridges across the three rivers); ride a mountain bike or paddle a kayak hired from Hlynur Oddsson. In a normal car, consider driving 13km along the rough unsealed road until you get to the river, then walking about 4km (the walk is highly recommended, but call to enquire about the state of the road before driving in a small 2WD). In a good-sized 4WD you can drive the whole way there (take care fording the rivers). A final option: have the centre pick you up from Seyðisfjörður/the river (Ikr8000/6000 return per vehicle).

Mjóifjörður

POP 35

The next fjord south of Seyðisfjörður is Mjóifjörður ('Narrow Fjord'), flanked by spectacular cliffs and rows of cascading waterfalls. The gravel road leading into the fjord (Rte 953) is slow-going for 2WDs, but once you make it in you'll be surrounded by lush hills peppered with fascinating ruins and schools of farmed fish leaping out of the frigid fjord water. A rusted herring vessel sits beached, the perfect photographic prop.

On the north side of the fjord at Brekkuþorp (often labelled Iceland's smallest village), **Sólbrekka** (☑476 0007; http://mjoifjordur.weebly.com; cottages excl linen Ikr16,000; ⊙Jun-Sep) is the one and only place to stay around here, and it's a welcome sight for hikers.

There's an old schoolhouse near the sea (open mid-June to mid-August, camping/sleeping-bag accommodation per person Ikr1000/4000), but the real treat lies up the hill – two small self-contained pine cottages sleeping six at a push (one bedroom plus sleeping loft and sofabed). There's a little afternoon cafe at the schoolhouse, and an indoor hot-pot at the cottages (open to all for a small fee). Breakfast, dinner, fishing and sightseeing boat trips can be arranged.

There's some brilliant **hiking** around Mjóifjörður. For a fee, the folks at Sólbrekka can ferry you across the fjord, from where it's a four-hour hike to Neskaupstaður, or you can climb over northern mountains to reach Seyðisfjörður on a six- to seven-hour trek. Also worth a visit: the road continues east of Brekkuþorp to the Dalatangi light, Iceland's first **lighthouse**, from 1895 (next to it is the 'modern' one, dating from 1908 and still in use).

It's 30km from Egilsstaðir to the head of Mjóifjörður, then a further 12km to Brekkuþorp. No transport runs here. The road into and out of Mjóifjörður is impassable in winter – access is by boat twice a week from Neskaupstaður.

Reyðarfjörður

POP 1135

In the Prettiest Fjord pageant, Reyðarfjörður wouldn't be in the running to take home the crown. It's a relatively new settlement, which only came into existence – as a trading port – in the 20th century.

More recently, Reyðarfjörður garnered attention when Alcoa installed a giant 2km-long aluminium smelter just beyond the town along the fjord; conservationists were up in arms. The infusion of foreign workers has added a small splash of international flavour in Reyðarfjörður and surrounding towns. Alcoa jobs (the company employs approximately 450 people) have also brought a prosperity to the region best evidenced by the new homes.

Just a note: you may see reference on maps and info boards to Fjarðabyggð – this is the municipality that centres on Reyðarfjörður and encompasses fjords from Mjóifjörður south to Stöðvarfjörður.

◎ Sights

Íslenska Stríðsárasafnið MUSEUM
(http://stridsarasafn.fjardabyggd.is; Spítalakampu; adult/child Ikr1000/free; ◎1-5pm Jun-Aug) During WWII around 3000 Allied soldiers (10 times the local population) were based in Reyðarfjörður. At the top end of Heiðarvegur you'll find the excellent Icelandic WWII Museum, which details these strange few years. The building is surrounded by mines, Jeeps and aeroplane propellers, and holds

other war relics. Photographs and tableaux provide a background to Iceland's wartime involvement.

The museum is tucked behind a rusting set of army barracks, built as part of a hospital camp in 1943 but never used for that purpose.

🛏 Sleeping & Eating

There are grill bars at the Shell and Olís petrol stations, and **Krónan supermarket** (Hafnargata 2; ◎11am-6pm Mon-Thu, to 7pm Fri, to 5pm Sat, noon-4pm Sun) for self-caterers.

Reyðarfjörður HI Hostel HOSTEL €
(Hjá Marlín; ☎474 1220, 892 0336; www.bakkagerdi.net; Vallargerði 9; dm Ikr5200, d with/without bathroom Ikr18,000/14,000, prices excl linen; @🖥🛜) Multilingual Marlín (Belgian, but resident in Iceland for over 20 years) is a warm host at this expanding spot. The primary house includes a cosy **restaurant** (◎5-8pm); a large second house down the street has simple rooms, a barbecue and a sauna. New in 2014: 12 four-bed rooms with private bathroom, in a masterfully converted furniture store (on Austurvegur)!

Linen is available for Ikr1200; HI members get a discount of Ikr500.

Tærgesen GUESTHOUSE, RESTAURANT €€
(☎470 5555; www.taergesen.com; Búðargata 4; guesthouse/motel d Ikr15,000/22,000; 🛜) Timber-lined and dressed with white window shutters, the cosy rooms above Tærgesen restaurant have loads of cottagey character (and shared bathrooms). They're inside a black corrugated-iron building from 1870; the **restaurant** (mains Ikr1120-4820; ◎10am-10pm) is known for its pizzas, and for hearty traditional fare. New to the complex: 22 spacious motel-style units with bathroom.

Next door, and under the same management, is Kaffi Kósý, a popular locals' bar open Friday and Saturday nights.

Sesam Brauðhús BAKERY, CAFE €
(Hafnargata 1; ◎7.30am-5.30pm Mon-Fri, 9am-4pm Sat) Stop by this bakery-cafe and choose from a cabinet full of sandwiches, salads and pastries.

Eskifjörður

POP 1026

This friendly, prospering little town is stretched out along a dimple in the main fjord of Reyðarfjörður. Its setting is magnificent: it looks directly onto the mighty mountain Hólmatindur (985m), rising sheer from the shining blue water.

◉ Sights

Sjóminjasafn Austurlands MUSEUM
(Strandgata 39b; adult/child Ikr1000/free; ⊙1-5pm Jun-Aug) Inside the 1816 black timber warehouse 'Gamlabuð', the East Iceland Maritime Museum illustrates two centuries of the east coast's historic herring, shark and whaling industry. For more salty-dog stories, be sure to check out Randulffs-sjóhus.

Helgustaðanáma QUARRY
The remains of the world's largest spar quarry lies east of Eskifjörður. Iceland spar (silfurberg in Icelandic) is a type of calcite crystal that is completely transparent and can split light into two parallel beams. It was a vital component in early microscopes; large quantities were exported to Europe's top scientists from the 17th century until the quarry's closure in 1924.

The largest specimen taken from Helgustaðanáma weighs 220kg and is displayed in the British Natural History Museum. Science aside, you can still see calcite sparkling in rocks around the quarry. The area is a national preserve, though, so you can't poke out pieces of crystal or take them away. Follow the gravel road past Mjóeyri, driving 8km along the coastline until you get to an information panel; the quarry is then a 500m walk uphill.

🏃 Activities

Sundlaug Eskifjarðar SWIMMING POOL, HOT-POTS
(Norðfjarðarvegur; adult/child Ikr600/200; ⊙6am-9pm Mon-Fri, 10am-6pm Sat & Sun) The swimming pool has waterslides, hot-pots and a sauna; it's on the main road into town.

Hólmanes Peninsula HIKING
The southern shore of the Hólmanes Peninsula, below the peak Hólmatindur, is a nature reserve. Hiking in the area offers superb maritime views (look out for pods of dolphins). The Hólmaborgir hike, south of the main road, is a popular loop that takes but an hour or two.

There are plenty of longer hiking routes up the nearby mountains. Multiday hikes around the peninsulas east of Eskifjörður abound; at the time of research, it was tough to obtain a hiking map locally, so ask around.

Gönguvikan (Hiking Week) is a big event on the district's annual calendar, falling the week after the summer solstice.

Oddsskarð SKIING
Given the right conditions, from mid-November to April skiing is possible on slopes near Oddsskarð, the pass leading to Neskaupstaður. See www.oddsskard.is (parts of the site are kept up to date).

🛏 Sleeping & Eating

Quick-eat options include a petrol station with a grill, and a **Samkaup-Strax** (⊙9am-6pm Mon-Fri, 10m-2pm Sat) supermarket.

Campsite CAMPGROUND €
(sites per person Ikr1000) A simple site in a pretty setting not far from the entrance to town.

Kaffihúsið GUESTHOUSE, RESTAURANT €
(☑476 1150; www.kaffihusid.is; Strandgata 10; s/d without bathroom Ikr9900/12,900; ⊙noon-10pm Sun-Thu, til 3am Fri & Sat; 🖭) You can't miss the oversized coffee cup announcing this place, primarily a **restaurant-bar** (mains Ikr2000-4700; ⊙kitchen closes at 9pm) and hang-out for locals, with regular live music. There's also a cluster of rooms in the back; they're simple affairs, all with washbasin and flatscreen TV.

⭐ Ferðaþjónustan
Mjóeyri GUESTHOUSE, COTTAGES €€
(☑477 1247, 696 0809; www.mjoeyri.is; Strandgata 120; s/d without bathroom Ikr12,500/16,500, cottages from Ikr27,300; 🖭) On the eastern edge of town, this view-blessed complex juts into the waterway at the tip of a teeny peninsula. There are guesthouse rooms in the main building, but it's the excellent, family-sized cottages spread around the property that make Mjóeyri a great choice. There are also camper amenities, and one of the funkiest hot-pots we've seen (in a converted boat).

Knowledgeable owners offer guiding and tours: hiking, skiing, hunting, fishing etc. The cottage price doesn't include linen (available for Ikr1600). Sleeping-bag accommodation in the guesthouse costs Ikr7500. Breakfast is available (Ikr1650).

Hotel Askja GUESTHOUSE €€
(☑477 1247, 696 0809; www.hotelaskja.is; s/d without bathroom Ikr11,900/15,900; 🖭) In a waterfront, corrugated-iron building with king-size views to Hólmatindur, Askja has simple rooms with kitchen access and an appealing lounge area. Use your own sleeping bag for Ikr7500; breakfast is Ikr1650.

Hótelíbúðir APARTMENT €€

(📞892 8657; www.hotelibudir.net; Strandgata 26; apt from Ikr22,500; 🛜) Four spacious, modern and fully equipped one-bedroom apartments are offered, sleeping up to four (with large kitchen and handy laundry facilities). A couple of rooms (with bathroom) are also offered here – these are roomy but randomly furnished.

★**Randulffs-sjóhus** ICELANDIC €€

(Strandgata 96; mains Ikr2590-3390; ⊙noon-9pm Jun-Aug or by appointment) This extraordinary boathouse dates from 1890, and when new owners entered it in 2008, they found it untouched for 80-odd years. The upstairs sleeping quarters of the fishermen has remained as it was found; downstairs is an atmospheric restaurant among the maritime memorabilia. Unsurprisingly, the tasty menu is heavy on fish (including local specialities: shark and dried fish).

Contact Mjóeyri to see inside the boathouse outside opening hours (Ikr1000); it also arranges rental of motorboats and fishing rods from here.

Neskaupstaður (Norðfjörður)

POP 1485

Just getting to Neskaupstaður feels like a real odyssey. You travel via the highest highway pass (632m) in Iceland, through a nerve-wracking, single-lane, 630m-long tunnel, then drop from the skies like a falcon into town; attempt to drive further east and you simply run out of road. Although it's one of the largest of the fjord towns, this dramatic end-of-the-line location makes it feel small and far far away from the rest of the world. (This may change when a new 8km tunnel from Eskifjörður opens in 2017, superseding the old route.)

As with most towns in the Eastfjords, Neskaupstaður began life as a 19th-century trading centre and prospered during the herring boom in the early 20th century. Its future was assured by the building of the biggest fish-processing and freezing plant in Iceland, Síldarvinnslan (SNV), at the head of the fjord.

◉ Sights & Activities

Safnahúsið MUSEUM

(Egilsbraut 2; adult/child Ikr1000/free; ⊙1-5pm Jun-Aug) Three collections are clustered together in one bright-red harbourfront warehouse, known as 'Museum House'. **Tryggvasafn** showcases a collection of striking paintings by prominent modern artist Tryggvi Ólafsson, born in Neskaupstaður in 1940. Upstairs, the **Maritime Museum** is one man's collection of artefacts relating to the sea, while on the top floor, the **Museum of Natural History** has a big collection of local stones (including spar from the Helgustaðanáma mine), plus an array of stuffed animals, birds, fish and pinned insects.

Fólksvangur Neskaupstaðar NATURE RESERVE

At the eastern end of town, where the road runs out, is this lovely nature reserve perfect for short strolls. Various paths run over tiny wooden bridges and past boulders, peat pits, cliffs and the sea, with a soundtrack of crying seabirds. You may see whales offshore.

Goðaborg HIKING

For serious hikers, a rewarding route takes you up Goðaborg (1148m) from the farm Kirkjuból, 8km west of town. From the summit you can descend into Mjóifjörður, the next fjord to the north; allow six hours and, due to late snows at higher altitudes, attempt it only at the height of summer.

☞ Tours

Skorrahestar HORSE RIDING

(📞477 1736; www.skorrahestar.is; Skorrastaður) Based on a farm west of town, Skorrahestar offers longer treks for experienced riders, including a three-night trek to uninhabited fjords led by Doddi, a storytelling, guitar-playing guide who is a former biologist and teacher (the perfect guide?). Short rides are also available (suggested duration: three to four hours), as is guesthouse accommodation.

✨ Festivals & Events

Eistnaflug MUSIC

(www.eistnaflug.is) A beloved metal and punk festival, Eistnaflug ('Flying Testicles') is held every summer in town on the second weekend in July. Friendly metalheads plus midnight sun.

🛏 Sleeping & Eating

Fast-food fare can be found at the grill at Olís petrol station. Picnic supplies can be picked up at the supermarkets **Samkaup-Úrval** (Hafnarbraut 13; ⊙10am-7pm Mon-Fri, noon-6pm Sat & Sun), near the petrol station, and **Nesbakki** (Bakkavegur 3; ⊙10am-7pm), closer to the campsite.

Tónspil GUESTHOUSE €
(✆477 1580; www.tonspil.is; Hafnarbraut 22; s/d without bathroom Ikr7900/13,900; 🛜) Like an extra in the film *High Fidelity*, you need to ask the dude in the music shop about the rooms above. Which are simple, but there's a handy TV-room and kitchen area with washing machine. Out of season, BYO sleeping bag for reduced prices (Ikr4900 per person).

Campsite CAMPGROUND €
(sites per person Ikr1000) High above the town, near the avalanche barriers (worth a visit for the great views). It's signposted from the hospital.

★Hildibrand Hotel HOTEL €€
(✆477 1950; www.hildibrand.com; Hafnarbraut 2; d apt from Ikr23,250) The best thing to happen to Neskaupstaður in years, this complex of 15 super-spacious, fully equipped apartments is plumb in the centre of town. Each apartment has one to three bedrooms (sleeping up to eight), full kitchen, balcony (those views!), and custom-made furniture – you may be persuaded to move in. In the pipeline: standard rooms.

Hótel Edda HOTEL €€
(✆444 4860; www.hoteledda.is; Nesgata 40; s/d Ikr19,200/21,700; ⊙early Jun–mid-Aug; @🛜) On the waterfront at the eastern end of town, this well-run summer hotel has brilliant views, neat, no-frills rooms (all with bathroom), and a reasonable dinnertime restaurant (two coures Ikr4650). Breakfast is available.

Nesbær Kaffihus CAFE €
(Egilsbraut 5; lunches Ikr800-1500; ⊙9am-6pm Mon-Wed & Fri, to 10.30pm Thu, 10am-6pm Sat, 1-6pm Sun) This cafe-bakery-craft-shop has a quintessential small-town vibe and offers cakes, sandwiches, waffles and soup.

★Kaupfélagsbarinn ICELANDIC €€
(www.hildibrand.com; Hafnarbraut 2; lunches Ikr2150-2950; dinner mains Ikr3590-5290; 🛜) Part of the new Hildibrand complex, this is easily the most upmarket restaurant in this neck of the woods. In its large, pastel-toned space, say hello to sushi, caramel-glazed cod, and *skyr* cake with lime and white chocolate. The all-day menu is similarly tempting: try the lamb burger, or lobster tagliatelle.

Fáskrúðsfjörður

POP 660

The village of Fáskrúðsfjörður (sometimes known as Búðir) was originally settled by French seamen who came to fish the Icelandic coast between the late 19th century and 1914. In a gesture to the local heritage, street signs are in both Icelandic and French.

◎ Sights & Activities

French Hospital HISTORIC BUILDING
(Hafnargata 11-14) The full story about the French seamen in Fáskrúðsfjörður can be found at Fosshotel Eastfjords, a smart new development inside the sensitively renovated former French hospital and other buildings from the era. In the hotel lobby, an excellent **museum** (adult/child Ikr1000/free) paints a detailed portrait of the French connection to the fjord (check out the recreated sailors' quarters downstairs).

Sandfell HIKING
Geologists may get a buzz from the lacolithic mountain Sandfell (743m), above the fjord's southern shore, which was formed by molten rhyolite bursting through older lava layers. It's one of the world's finest examples of this sort of igneous mountain. It's a two- or three-hour hike to the top.

🛏 Sleeping & Eating

Campsite CAMPGROUND €
(sites per person Ikr1000) Small and simple, at the west end of the village.

Guesthouse Elín Helga GUESTHOUSE €€
(✆868 2687; elinhelgak99@gmail.com; Stekkholt 20; d without bathroom Ikr14,000-17,050; 🛜) We like this guesthouse, high above town (take Skólavegur then Holtavegur), for its pine-fresh cosiness, sweet hostess and great views (note: no kitchen).

★Fosshotel Eastfjords HOTEL €€€
(✆470 4070; www.fosshotel.is; Hafnargata 11-14; r from 27,200; 🛜) This acclaimed new hotel opened in 2014 inside the former French hospital. It's all class: 26 high-quality rooms (featuring lovely decor in stylish blues and greys), plus a **restaurant** (dinner mains Ikr4600-5300) and lounge-bar with majestic views – perfect for a cake-and-coffee pit stop.

Café Sumarlina CAFE, BAR
(www.sumarlina.is; Búðavegur 59; meals Ikr1000-4350; ⊙11am-10pm; 🛜) Café Sumarlina, at

the entrance to town, is a friendly cafe-bar in a creaking wooden house, cranking out pizzas, burgers and crepes.

Samkaup-Strax SUPERMARKET
(Skólavegur 59; ⊙10am-6pm Mon-Fri, to 2pm Sat) For food supplies.

Stöðvarfjörður

POP 200

If you think geology is boring, it's worth challenging that notion in this tiny village.

◉ Sights

★ Steinasafn Petru MUSEUM
(www.steinapetra.is; Fjarðarbraut 21; adult/child Ikr1000/free; ⊙9am-6pm May-Sep) The wondrous assemblage at Petra's Stone Collection was Petra Sveinsdóttir's lifelong labour of love. Inside her house, stones and minerals are piled from floor to ceiling – 70% of them are from the local area. They include beautiful cubes of jasper, polished agate, purple amethyst, glowing creamy 'ghost stone', glittering quartz crystals...it's like opening a treasure chest.

The large garden is awash with more rocks, garden gnomes, and beachcombed flotsam and jetsam. Additional collections (including pens, matchboxes and taxidermy birds) show what an incredible hoarder Petra was.

Gallerí Snærós ART GALLERY
(www.gallerisnaeros.is; Fjarðarbraut 42; ⊙11am-5pm Jun-Aug) Long-established Gallerí Snærós showcases the works of a family of local artists who dabble in a variety of media.

Salthússmarkaður HANDICRAFTS
(Fjarðarbraut 40; ⊙11am-5pm Jun-Aug) Market offering charming handmade products.

🛏 Sleeping & Eating

Kirkjubær GUESTHOUSE €
(☑847 2966, 849 1112; www.simnet.is/birgiral; Fjarðarbraut 37a; dm Ikr4500-6000) Memorable Kirkjubær is a tiny church dating from 1925 but now in private hands. It has been renovated into a cute one-room hostel: the pulpit and altar are still there, and some of the pews are now part of the furniture. There's a kitchen and bathroom, and the beds (mostly just mattresses) are on the upper mezzanine level.

It supposedly sleeps 10, but that would be cosy! The best option would be for a family or small group to hire the whole place out (Ikr22,500, excluding linen). Birgir, the owner, lives in the yellow house below the church at Skólúbraut 1.

Campsite CAMPGROUND €
(sites per person Ikr1000) Neat campsite just east of the village.

Saxa GUESTHOUSE €€
(☑511 3055; www.saxa.is; Fjarðarbraut 41; s/d Ikr9900/18,600; 🐾) There are fresh, modern rooms at Saxa, a former supermarket (!) that also houses a pleasant cafe (snacks & meals Ikr400-3700).

Brekkan FAST FOOD €
(Fjarðarbraut 44; ⊙9.30am-10pm Mon-Fri, 10am-10pm Sat, 11am-9pm Sun) Low-key local chowhouse serving burgers and sandwiches. Also offers groceries.

THE RING ROAD: EGILSSTAÐIR TO DJÚPIVOGUR

Breiðdalur

As the Ring Road travels from Egilsstaðir to the coast it passes through Breiðdalur, Iceland's broadest valley, nestled beneath colourful rhyolite peaks.

🐾 Tours

Odin Tours Iceland HORSE RIDING
(☑849 2009; www.odintoursiceland.com) Odin Tours operates horse-riding and hiking tours in Breiðdalur, plus has a cottage for rent. It's about 24km from Breiðdalsvík.

Strengir FISHING
(☑660 6890; www.strengir.com) Strengir brings anglers to the region's salmon-rich waters and runs Eyjar Fishing Lodge, a high-end, year-round accommodation option open to all.

🛏 Sleeping & Eating

Hótel Staðarborg HOTEL €€
(☑475 6760; www.stadarborg.is; s/d incl breakfast from Ikr16,900/22,500; @🐾) Once a school, cheerful Hótel Staðarborg has neat, modern rooms, plus lake-fishing opportunities. Sleeping-bag accommodation is available

(Ikr6500), as is dinner (three courses from Ikr5200). It lies 6km west of Breiðdalsvík.

★ **Silfurberg** GUESTHOUSE €€€
(⌨475 1515; www.silfurberg.com; Þorgrímsstaðir; r incl breakfast from Ikr34,000; ☺May–mid-Sep) Silfurberg is a stunning new boutique guesthouse on a rural property 53km south of Egilsstaðir (30km from Breiðdalsvík). Style, humour and craftsmanship have been used to convert a barn into four rooms, one suite and deluxe common areas. The outdoor sauna and dome-enclosed hot-pot are icing on the cake.

Breiðdalsvík

POP 135

Fishing village Breiðdalsvík is beautifully sited at the end of Breiðdalur. It's a quiet place – more a base for walking in the nearby hills and fishing the rivers and lakes than an attraction in itself.

⌨ Tours

Tinna Adventure ADVENTURE TOUR
(⌨475 1100; www.tinna-adventure.is) New in 2014, Tinna Adventure offers sea-angling tours from Breiðdalsvík at 1pm daily in summer (Ikr10,500; reservations required); puffins and other seabirds are regularly sighted, and they guarantee you'll catch fish. Tinna also runs super-Jeep and hiking tours in the area. Enquire at Hótel Bláfell.

🛏 Sleeping & Eating

Hótel Bláfell HOTEL €€
(⌨475 6770; www.hotelblafell.is; Sólvellir 14; s/d incl breakfast Ikr17,050/23,250; 🛜) Located in the centre of 'town' (we use that term lightly), Hótel Bláfell has smart, monochrome rooms, free sauna for guests and a superb guest lounge with open fire. Don't be put off by the featureless decor of the restaurant – the evening buffet (Ikr5900) is justifiably popular.

Campers can pitch a tent at the free **campsite** out the back. The hotel's owners have recently taken over **Cafe Margret**, a cosy guesthouse and cafe outside town, on Rte 96 heading back towards Stöðvarfjörður.

Kaupfjelagið CAFE €
(Sólvellir 23; ☺10.30am-6pm Jun-Aug) Kaupfjelagið serves up coffee and light meals to passing travellers with a side order of info, souvenirs and outdoor clothing.

Berufjörður

The Ring Road meanders around Berufjörður, a long, steep-sided fjord flanked by rhyolite peaks. The southwestern shore is dominated by the obtrusive, pyramid-shaped mountain **Búlandstindur**, rising 1069m above the water.

Around Berufjörður are several historical walking routes through the rugged terrain. The best known of these climbs is from Berufjörður, the farm at the head of the fjord, and crosses the 700m Berufjarðarskarð pass into Breiðdalur.

🛏 Sleeping & Eating

★ **Berunes HI Hostel** HOSTEL €
(⌨478 8988, 869 7227; www.berunes.is; dm/d without bathroom Ikr4900/10,500, cabins from Ikr15,000; ☺Apr-Oct; @🛜) Berunes hostel is on a century-old farm run by affable Ólafur and his family. The wonderfully creaky old farmhouse has rooms and alcoves, plus kitchen and lounge; there are also rooms in the newer farmhouse, plus a campsite (Ikr1350 per person) and en-suite cabins. Breakfast includes delicious pancakes; there's also a summertime restaurant (or BYO food supplies).

HI members receive a discount; linen hire costs Ikr1350.

The hostel is 22km along the Ring Road south of Breiðdalsvík; 40km from Djúpivogur. Buses between Egilsstaðir and Höfn stop here.

Djúpivogur

POP 370

The neat historic buildings and small harbour are worth a look, but the main reason to visit this friendly fishing village at the mouth of Berufjörður is to catch the boat to Papey.

Djúpivogur (*dyoo*-pi-vor) is actually the oldest port in the Eastfjords – it's been around since the 16th century, when German merchants brought goods to trade. The last major excitement was in 1627: pirates from North Africa rowed ashore, plundering the village and nearby farms, and carrying away dozens of slaves.

◎ Sights & Activities

Langabúð Museum MUSEUM
(adult/child Ikr500/300; ☺10am-6pm Jun-Aug) Djúpivogur's oldest building is the long bright-red Langabúð, a harbourside log warehouse dating from 1790. It now houses a cafe and an unusual local museum. Downstairs

WORTH A TRIP

PAPEY

The name of offshore island Papey (Friars' Island) suggests it was once a hermitage for the Irish monks who may have briefly inhabited Iceland before fleeing upon the arrival of the Norse. This small (2 sq km) and tranquil island was once a farm, but it's now inhabited only by sunbaking seals and nesting seabirds, including a puffin posse. Other highlights include the rock Kastali (The Castle), home to the local 'hidden people'; a lighthouse built in 1922; and Iceland's oldest and smallest wooden church (from 1807).

Papeyjarferðir ([☑]862 4399; www.djupivogur.is/papey; adult/child Ikr8000/4000) runs four-hour tours to the island, spotting wildlife en route and walking the island trails. Weather permitting, tours depart Djúpivogur harbour at 1pm daily from June to August.

is a collection of works by sculptor Rikarður Jónsson (1888–1977), ranging from lifelike busts of worthy Icelanders to mermaid-decorated mirrors and reliefs depicting saga characters. Upstairs, in the tar-smelling attic, is a collection of local-history artefacts.

Eggin í Gleðivík   PUBLIC ART
Walk or drive to the waterfront behind Langabuð and follow the road west to reach this public artwork: 34 oversized eggs along the jetty, each one representing a local bird.

Bones Sitcks & Stones   GARDENS
En route to the jetty you'll pass this quirky sculpture garden full of mineral rocks, bones and assorted flotsam and jetsam.

🛏 Sleeping & Eating

Klif Hostel   HOSTEL €
([☑]478 8802; www.klifhostel.is; Kambur 1; dm Ikr5000; ⊘May-Sep; 🛜) Klif is a nice new addition to town: a small, homey, five-room hostel in the old post office. Sleeping-bag beds cost Ikr5000 per person; a double room (including linen) with shared bathroom costs a steep Ikr16,300.

Campsite   CAMPGROUND €
(sites per person Ikr1250; ⊘Apr-Oct) Behind Við Voginn, this campground is run by Hótel Framtíð (pay at the hotel's reception). There are showers, cooking and laundry facilities.

Hótel Framtíð   HOTEL €€
([☑]478 8887; www.hotelframtid.com; Vogaland 4; d with/without bathroom Ikr25,950/18,300; 🛜) This friendly hotel by the harbour is impressive for a village of this size. It's been around for a while (the original building

was brought in pieces from Copenhagen in 1906), and there's an assortment of beds (and budgets) in various buildings: sleeping-bag accommodation (Ikr10,500 per double), timber-lined hotel rooms, four cute cottages, five apartments (including two sleek, brand-new options).

Framtið's elegant **restaurant** (dinner mains Ikr4650-5960) is easily the nicest option in town. Dinner of lobster tails or lamb fillet hits the top end of the price-scale and the palate, but there are all-day pizzas too (from Ikr1800).

Langabúð Kaffihús   CAFE €
(lunches Ikr750-1700; ⊘10am-6pm Sun-Thu, to 11.30pm Fri & Sat mid-May–Sep) The in-demand cafe inside Langabúð has an old-world atmosphere and serves cakes, soup and sandwiches.

Við Voginn   FAST FOOD €
(Vogaland 2; soup of the day Ikr980; ⊘9am-9pm Mon-Fri, 11am-9pm Sat & Sun) A popular-with-locals grill, with an attached grocery store.

Samkaup-Strax   SUPERMARKET
(Búland 2; ⊘10am-6pm Mon-Fri, to 4pm Sat, noon-4pm Sun) On the main road, with a **Vínbúðin** (⊘4-6pm Mon-Thu, 1-6pm Fri Jun-Aug) attached.

ℹ Information

The town has decent facilities (bank, post office); pick up a map from the **tourist office** ([☑]478 8204; Bakki 3; ⊘9am-5pm Mon-Fri, noon-4pm Sat & Sun mid-May–mid-Sep) across from Bakkabuð craft store.

Birdlife in the area is prolific; twitchers should check out www.birds.is (good general info, despite not being up to date).

Southeast Iceland

Best Places to Eat

➡ Humarhöfnin (p304)

➡ Pakkhús (p304)

➡ Jöklasel (p304)

➡ Hólmur (p300)

Best Places to Stay

➡ Hrífunes Guesthouse (p287)

➡ Glacier View Guesthouse (p287)

➡ Guesthouse Dyngja (p302)

➡ Árnanes Country Lodge (p300)

Why Go?

The 200km stretch of Ring Road from Kirkjubæjarklaustur to Höfn is truly mind-blowing, transporting you across vast deltas of grey glacial sand, past lost-looking farms, around the toes of craggy mountains, and by glacier tongues and ice-filled lagoons. The only thing you won't pass is a town.

The mighty Vatnajökull dominates the region, its huge rivers of frozen ice pouring down steep-sided valleys towards the sea. Jökulsárlón is a photographer's paradise, a glacial lagoon where wind and water sculpt icebergs into fantastical shapes.

The bleak coastal deserts of glacial sand are remnants of calamitous collisions between fire and ice. Further inland is the epicentre of Iceland's worst volcanic event, the Lakagígar fissures. With so much desolation on display, it's not surprising that Skaftafell is so popular. This sheltered enclave between the glaciers and the sands throbs with life and colour, and the footfall of hikers.

Road Distances (km)

	Höfn	Reykjavík	Jökulsárlón	Skaftafell
Reykjavík	459			
Jökulsárlón	79	378		
Skaftafell	135	323	57	
Kirkjubæjarklaustur	200	257	122	69

Kirkjubæjarklaustur

POP 125

Many a foreign tongue has been tied in knots trying to say Kirkjubæjarklaustur. It helps to break it into bits: *Kirkju* (church), *bæjar* (farm) and *klaustur* (convent). Otherwise, do as the locals do and call it 'Klaustur' (pronounced like 'cloister').

Klaustur is tiny, even by Icelandic standards – a few houses and farms scattered across a brilliant-green backdrop. Still, it's the only real service town between Vík and Höfn, and it's a major crossroads to several dramatic spots in the interior: Landmannalaugar and Laki.

History

According to the *Landnámabók* (a comprehensive account of Norse settlement), this tranquil village situated between the cliffs and the river Skaftá was first settled by Irish monks *(papar)* before the Vikings arrived. Originally, it was known as Kirkjubær; the 'klaustur' bit was added in 1186 when a convent of Benedictine nuns was founded (near the modern-day church).

During the devastating Laki eruptions that occurred in the late 18th century, this area suffered greatly – west of Kirkjubæjarklaustur you can see ruins of farms abandoned or destroyed by the lava stream. The lava field, called Eldhraun, averages 12m thick. It contains more than 15 cu km of lava and covers an area of 565 sq km, making it the world's largest recorded lava flow from a single eruption.

◉ Sights & Activities

If you're interested in discovering the forces of nature and the history of the area, pick up the booklet *Klaustur trail* (Ikr800), which outlines a marked 20km walking trail that circles the village and takes in many of its natural features (it can be divided into shorter walks).

Kirkjugólf   ROCK FORMATION

The basalt columns of Kirkjugólf (Church Floor), smoothed down and cemented with moss, were once mistaken for an old church floor rather than a work of nature, and it's easy to see why. The honeycombed slab lies in a field about 400m northwest of the N1 petrol station: a path leads to it from beside the information board, or drive down Rte 203, where there's another gate.

Systrafoss   WATERFALL

At the western end of the village, this lovely double waterfall tumbles down the cliffs and a sign outlines three short walks in the pretty wooded area (Iceland's tallest trees grow here!). The lake Systravatn, a pleasant saunter up the cliffs above the falls, was once a bathing place for nuns. A marked 2.5km walking path leads from the lake to Kirkjugólf.

Systrastapi   ROCK FORMATION

Religious connections are particularly strong in this area. The prominent rock pillar Systrastapi (Sisters' Pillar), near the line of cliffs about 1.5km west of town, marks the spot where two nuns were reputedly executed and buried for sleeping with the devil and other such no-nos.

Steingrímsson Memorial Chapel   CHURCH

Consecrated in 1974, this triangular, distinctly atypical wood-and-stone chapel is on Klausturvegur. It commemorates Jón Steingrímsson's Eldmessa (Fire Sermon), which 'saved' the town from lava on 20 July 1783.

Landbrotshólar   GEOLOGICAL FEATURE

West of the village and south of the Ring Road is a vast, dimpled, vivid-green pseudo-crater field known as Landbrotshólar. It was formed during the Laki eruptions of 1783, when lava poured over marshland and fast-evaporating steam exploded through to make these barrow-like mounds.

⛟ Tours

Hólasport   ADVENTURE TOUR

(☑ 660 1151; www.holasport.is; ◷ May-Oct) Based at Hótel Laki just south of Klaustur, Hólasport offers super-Jeep tours, including a full-day tour to Laki for Ikr32,500, or a shorter, river-fording trip into the mountains for Ikr16,500. There are also fun, frequent quad-bike tours in the pseudo-crater-filled area of Landbrotshólar, or along black-sand beaches (from Ikr14,500).

Slóðir   HIKING TOUR

(☑ 852 2012; www.slodir.is; ◷ Jun–mid-Sep) From a base east of town, a trio of knowledgable biologist-guides offers hikes with history and nature storytelling (half-day walk Ikr5000 per person; minimum four people). Advance booking required.

🛏 Sleeping

There are plenty of high-quality, in-demand accommodation options (with on-site dining) in the beautiful landscapes around Klaustur (see also p287).

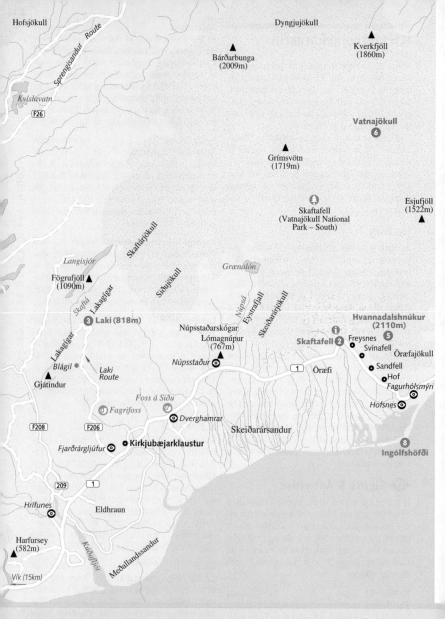

Southeast Iceland Highlights

1 Admire the ever-changing ice sculptures at the bewitching lagoon **Jökulsárlón** (p297)

2 Visit Iceland's favourite national-park pocket, **Skaftafell** (p290), an area of green and lovely life amid the vast sand deltas

3 Stride up **Laki** (p288) for views of three glaciers...

...and unbelievable volcanic devastation

4 Don crampons for an easy but exhilarating guided **glacier walk** (p293)

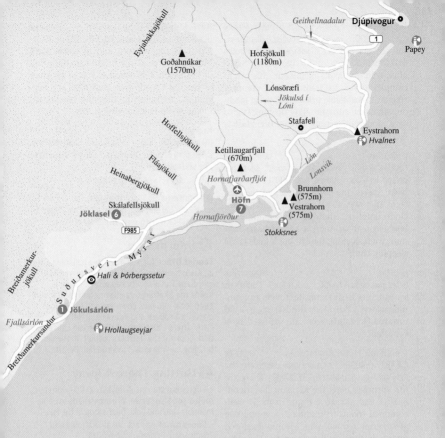

⑤ Rise above all others by scaling Iceland's highest peak, **Hvannadalshnúkur** (p295)

⑥ Try to wipe the smile off your face as you roar across the ice cap on a **snowmobile tour** (p304) from Jöklasel

⑦ Sample the delicious seafood treats netted by the local fishing fleet in the restaurants of **Höfn** (p301)

⑧ Take a tractor ride to **Ingólfshöfði** (p296) to check out puffins and dodge dive-bombing skuas

Klausturhof
GUESTHOUSE €

(☑ 567 7600; www.klausturhof.is; Klausturvegur 1-5; dm Ikr4500, d with/without bathroom Ikr17,400/14,500; ☎) With the pretty Systrafoss waterfall as its neighbour, this bright complex offers an assortment of compact rooms at reasonable prices, plus guest kitchen and an on-site cafe. BYO sleeping bag to save money on private rooms. Breakfast is Ikr1580.

Kirkjubæ II
CAMPGROUND €

(☑ 894 4495; www.kirkjubaer.com; sites per person Ikr1200, cottages Ikr18,000; ☉ Jun-Sep) Neat green site with sheltering hedges, right in town. Good service buildings include kitchen, showers and laundry. A boon in bad weather: a trio of basic new huts, each sleeping four in bunk beds (BYO sleeping bag).

Kleifar
CAMPGROUND €

(sites per person Ikr750; ☉ Jun-Aug) There's a second, very basic campsite (toilets and running water) 1.5km along Rte 203 (signposted towards Geirland), scenically situated by a waterfall.

Icelandair Hótel Klaustur
HOTEL €€

(☑ 487 4900; www.icelandairhotels.com; Klausturvegur 6; d from Ikr25,000; ☎) There are few surprises here: the Klaustur has friendly staff and attractive decor in its 57 well-equipped rooms (including a new building of superior rooms), plus a sunny enclosed dining terrace and bar-lounge. The **restaurant** (dinner mains Ikr3950-5550) features tantalising local produce (pan-fried arctic char with locally grown potatoes, blueberry-marinated lamb carpaccio, garlic-roasted langoustine).

✕ Eating

Skaftárskáli
FAST FOOD €

(Rte 1; ☉ 9am-10pm Jun-Aug, to 8pm Sep-May) For a quick bite, the usual fast-food suspects at the N1's busy all-day grill-bar may suffice. Kitchen closes 9.30pm in summer.

Systrakaffi
INTERNATIONAL €€

(www.systrakaffi.is; Klausturvegur 12; mains Ikr1000-4500; ☉ 11.30am-10pm Jun-Aug, shorter hours May & Sep) The liveliest place in town is this beloved cafe-bar (slammed in summer). Its wide-ranging menu offers soups, salads, pizzas and burgers – but understandably plays favourites with local trout and lamb.

Kaffi Munkar
CAFE €€

(Klausturvegur 1-5; mains Ikr1250-3200; ☉ 10am-10pm) At the western end of town, Kaffi Munkar serves as the bright cafe-reception of Klausturhof guesthouse. Pop in for soup of the day ('made from sunshine and vegetables', according to the cute blackboard menu), spicy chicken, or fish stew.

Kjarval
SUPERMARKET

(Klausturvegur 13; ☉ 9am-8pm Jun–mid-Sep, 10am-6pm Mon-Fri, 10am-2pm Sat mid-Sep–May) For self-caterers.

Vínbúðin
LIQUOR STORE

(Klausturvegur 15; ☉ 4-6pm Mon-Thu, 1-7pm Fri, noon-2pm Sat Jun-Aug, 5-6pm Mon-Thu, 2-6pm Fri Sep-May) Government-run alcohol store.

ℹ Information

Tourist Office (☑ 487 4620; www.visitklaustur.is; Klausturvegur 2; ☉ 8.30am-6pm mid-May–mid-Sep) The well-stocked tourist office is inside the Skaftárstofa information centre, with good local info plus coverage and exhibitions on Katla Geopark and Vatnajökull National Park. There's also a short film on the Laki eruption. Look for the 'farmers market' in the same building, selling local food and handicrafts.

ℹ Getting There & Away

Klaustur is a stop on all Reykjavík–Vík–Höfn bus routes and also serves as a crossroads to Landmannalaugar and Laki. Buses stop at the N1.

Buses travelling east call at Skaftafell and Jökulsárlón. Prices are from 2014.

Sterna (☑ 551 1166; www.sterna.is) services:

➨ Bus 12 to Höfn (Ikr4600, five hours, one daily June to mid-September) Stops for 1½ hours at Jökulsárlón.

➨ Bus 12a to Vík (Ikr1100, one hour, one daily June to mid-September)

➨ Bus 12a to Reykjavík (Ikr5800, five hours, one daily June to mid-September)

Strætó (☑ 540 2700; www.straeto.is) services:

➨ Bus 51 to Höfn (Ikr4550, 2¾ hours, two daily)

➨ Bus 51 to Vík (Ikr1050, one hour, two daily)

➨ Bus 51 to Reykjavík (Ikr5950, 4¼ hours, two daily)

Note that in winter (from mid-September to May), bus 51 drops to one service daily.

Reykjavík Excursions (☑ 580 5400; www.re.is) services:

➨ Bus 10/10a Skaftafell–Klaustur–Eldgjá–Landmannalaugar (one daily mid-June to mid-September) Can be used as a day tour, or as regular transport. Klaustur to Landmannalaugar one way is Ikr6500.

WORTH A TRIP

HRÍFUNES HOSPITALITY

Hrífunes is a tiny hamlet perfectly placed between Kirkjubæjarklaustur and Vík, in the peaceful and impossibly green surrounds of Skaftártunga. Here, you'll find two warm, hospitable guesthouses that are well worth the detour (tip: take up the memorable dinner option, there are no guest kitchen facilities).

To reach them, take Rte 209 off the Ring Road. The turnoff is 39km east of Vík, and you reach Hrífunes after 6km. Coming from Klaustur, Rte 209 is about 24km west, and you travel along it for 13km.

With a large 4WD, from Hrífunes you're well placed to tackle some of the stunning southern interior, including Landmannalaugar and the Fjallabak route.

Glacier View Guesthouse (✒770 0123; www.glacierviewguesthouse.is; s/d without bathroom incl breakfast Ikr14,000/20,000; ☺May-Oct; 🖥) Hosts Borgar and Elín are seasoned travel pros – they run a tour company for Icelanders visiting Africa, so they know how to put guests at ease in their simple, cosy home – and yes, in good weather, you can see Vatnajökull *and* Mýrdalsjökull from the roomy lounge. The multicourse dinners (Ikr5500) are superb.

Hrífunes Guesthouse (✒863 5540; www.hrifunesguesthouse.is; d with/without bathroom incl breakfast Ikr26,000/21,000; 🖥) This old community house has been revived with flair by owners Haukur and Hadda – think stylish country-farmhouse chic, plus stunning photos taken by Haukur, who runs photography tours (check out www.phototours.is). There's a cosy lounge with a fire, and gourmet dinners for Ikr6000.

➡ Bus 16/16a Skaftafell–Lakagígar via Klaustur (one daily late June to mid-September) Use as a day tour from Skaftafell or Klaustur, with 3½ hours at Laki (from Klaustur Ikr12,000).

➡ Bus 20 to Skaftafell (Ikr3000, one hour, one daily mid-June to mid-September) From Skaftafell there is a daily Reykjavík Excursions bus further east to Höfn.

➡ Bus 20a to Vík (Ikr2500, one hour, one daily mid-June mid-September)

➡ Bus 20a to Reykjavík (Ikr9500, six hours, one daily mid-June to mid-September) Stops for one hour at Vík, 25 minutes at Skógafoss.

Around Kirkjubæjarklaustur

◎ Sights & Activities

Fjarðrárgljúfur   CANYON
This darkly picturesque canyon, carved out by the river Fjarðrá, is a humbling two million years old. A walking track follows its southern edge for a couple of kilometres, with plenty of places to gaze down into its rocky, writhing depths.

The canyon is 3.5km north of the Ring Road; you can walk there across lava fields or drive along Rte 206 (take the left fork at the sign for Laki). You'll reach the canyon before it becomes an F-road.

Foss á Síðu & Dverghamrar   WATERFALL
Foss á Síðu, 11km east of Kirkjubæjarklaustur, is a head-turning waterfall that normally tumbles down from the cliffs. During especially strong sea winds, however, it actually goes straight up! Opposite the falls is the outcrop Dverghamrar ('Dwarf Rocks'), which contains classic basalt columns and is thought to be the dwelling place of some of Iceland's 'hidden people'.

🛏 Sleeping & Eating

Hörgsland   CAMPGROUND, COTTAGES €€
(✒487 6655; www.horgsland.is; sites per person Ikr1000, cottages per 2/6 people from Ikr14,100/26,650, guesthouse d with/without bathroom incl breakfast Ikr19,850/16,700; 🖥) On the Ring Road about 8km northeast of Klaustur is this mini village of spotless, spacious, self-contained cottages that can sleep six. A recent addition is a block of spic-and-span guesthouse rooms. There's also camping, plus outdoor hot-pots, and a simple shop and cafe serving breakfast and dinner.

All accommodation variations (with/without breakfast, self-service linen etc) are covered on the website. Keep your eye out for the weekly Asian buffet night here (the complex is owned by an Icelandic-Filipina couple) for some great-value, flavourful fare (Ikr3200).

Hunkubakkar GUESTHOUSE €€
(☑487 4681; www.hunkubakkar.is; s/d without bathroom incl breakfast Ikr13,400/18,100; 🛜) A photogenic option: small, red cottages are spread over a brilliant-green backdrop on this working sheep farm, 7km west of Klaustur (on Rte 206, 2km from Fjarðrárgljúfur canyon). Each of the cottages has two simple guestrooms that share a bathroom (and include kitchenette facilities). Breakfast in the new on-site restaurant is included.

Hótel Laki HOTEL €€€
(Efri-Vík; ☑487 4694; www.hotellaki.is; s/d incl breakfast from Ikr27,825/31,800; 🛜) What started as farmhouse accommodation has grown into a sprawling 64-room hotel, on scenic farmland 5km south of Klaustur on Rte 204. As well as comfortable (but overpriced) hotel rooms, there are 15 wee self-contained cottages (cheaper than the rooms), plus a nine-hole golf course, quad-bike and super-Jeep tours, large restaurant-bar and lake fishing.

The restaurant has a popular nightly buffet in summer (Ikr6900).

Lakagígar

It's almost impossible to comprehend the immensity of the Laki eruptions, one of the most catastrophic volcanic events in human history.

In the early summer of 1783, a vast set of fissures opened, forming around 135 craters; the Lakagígar (Laki craters) took in turns to fountain molten rock up to 1km into the air. These Skaftáreldar (River Skaftá Fires) lasted for eight months, spewing out an estimated volume of volcanic material over 15 cu km, with a resulting lava field (known as Eldhraun) covering an area of 565 sq km. Twenty farms in the area were wiped out by lava; another 30 were so badly damaged they had to be temporarily abandoned.

Far more devastating were the hundreds of millions of tonnes of ash and sulphuric acid that poured from the fissures. The sun was blotted out, the grass died off, and around two-thirds of Iceland's livestock died from starvation and poisoning. Some 9000 people – a fifth of the country – were killed and the remainder faced the Móðuharðindin ('the Hardship of the Mist'), a famine that followed.

The damage wasn't limited to Iceland, either. Across the northern hemisphere, clouds of ash blocked out the sun. Temperatures dropped and acid rain fell, causing devastating crop failures in Japan, Alaska and Europe (possibly even helping to spark the French Revolution). Nowadays the lava field belies the apocalypse that spawned it some 230 years ago. Its black, twisted lava formations are overgrown with soft green moss.

The Lakagígar area is contained within the boundaries of **Vatnajökull National Park** (www.vjp.is). Check the park website for excellent information for travellers.

In peak season (mid-July to mid-August), rangers are available at the Laki car parks from 11am to 3pm, and lead walks at midday Monday to Friday. An interpretive trail has been established over a gentle 500m walk – pick up the accompanying brochure (or download it) for insight into the fascinating history, geology and ecology of the area. Please stick to the marked paths in this ecologically sensitive region.

Camping is forbidden within the Laki reserve. The nearest campsite, with primitive hut facilities, a toilet and fresh water, is at Blágil, about 11km from Laki. Beds/campsites are Ikr4100/1400 per person (2014 prices); contact snorri@vjp.is.

◉ Sights

Laki MOUNTAIN
Although the peak called Laki (818m) did not erupt, it has loaned its name to the 25km-long Lakagígar crater row, which stretches northeastward and southwestward from its base. Laki can be climbed in about 40 minutes from the parking area. From the top there are boundless 360-degree views of the fissure, vast lava fields and glinting glaciers in the distance.

Lakagígar Crater Row GEOLOGICAL FEATURE
The crater row is fascinating to explore; it's riddled with black sand dunes and lava tubes, many of which contain tiny stalactites. At the foot of Laki, marked walking paths lead you in and out of the two nearest craters, including an interesting lava tunnel.

Fagrifoss WATERFALL
Fagrifoss (Beautiful Falls) is not a misnomer: this waterfall must be one of Iceland's most bewitching, with rivulets of water pouring over a massive black rock. You'll come to the turn-off on the way to Laki, about 24km along the F206. Tours to Lakagígar invariably stop here.

☞ Tours

Departures on these tours are dependent on road and weather conditions. Bring your own lunch.

Hólasport JEEP TOUR
(☑ 660 1151; www.holasport.is) Based at Hótel Laki, just south of Kirkjubæjarklaustur, Hólasport offers eight-hour super-Jeep day tours to Laki (Ikr32,500) from June until the end of October.

Reykjavík Excursions BUS TOUR
(☑ 580 5400; www.re.is) The full-day tour breaks for around 3½ hours of walking in the crater area. It is in brochures as bus route 16 and departs daily from late June to early September, at 8am from Skaftafell (Ikr15,500) and at 9am from the N1 at Kirkjubæjarklaustur (Ikr12,000).

❶ Getting There & Away

Rte F206 (just west of Kirkjubæjarklaustur) is generally passable from mid-June to mid-September (check on www.vegagerdin.is). It's a long, rugged 50km to the Lakagígar crater row. The road is absolutely unsuitable for 2WD cars, as there are several rivers to ford. Even low-clearance 4WD vehicles may not be suitable in the spring thaw or after rain, when the rivers tend to run deep. Take the bus tour if your car is unsuitable.

The Sandar

The sandar are soul-destroyingly flat and empty regions sprawling along Iceland's southeastern coast. High in the mountains, glaciers scrape up silt, sand and gravel that is then carried by glacial rivers or (more dramatically) by glacial bursts down to the coast and dumped in huge, desert-like plains. The sandar here are so impressively huge and awful that the Icelandic word (singular: sandur) is used internationally to describe the topographic phenomenon of a glacial outwash plain.

Skeiðarársandur is the most visible and dramatic, stretching some 40km between ice cap and coast from Núpsstaður to Öræfi. Here you'll encounter a flat expanse of grey-black sands, fierce scouring winds (a cyclist's nightmare) and fast-flowing grey-brown glacial rivers. A note on respect: *do not* drive off-road in these expanses. It is illegal, and hugely destructive to the fragile environment.

HOW TO AVOID BEING SKUA-ED

The great sandar on Iceland's southern coast are the world's largest breeding ground for great skuas (*Stercorarius skua* in Latin, *skúmur* in Icelandic). These large, meaty, dirty-brown birds tend to build their nests among grassy tufts in the ashy sand. You'll often see them harassing gulls into disgorging their dinner, killing and eating puffins and other little birds, or swooping down on you if you get too close to their nests.

Thankfully (unlike feather-brained Arctic terns), skuas will stop plaguing you if you run away from the area they're trying to defend. You can also avoid aerial strikes by wearing a hat or carrying a stick above your head.

Skeiðarársandur

Skeiðarársandur, the largest sandur in the world, covers a 1000-sq-km area and was formed by the mighty Skeiðarárjökull. Since the Settlement Era, Skeiðarársandur has swallowed a considerable amount of farmland and it continues to grow. The area was relatively well populated (for Iceland, anyway), but in 1362 the volcano beneath Öræfajökull (then known as Knappafellsjökull) erupted and the subsequent *jökulhlaup* (flooding caused by volcanic eruption beneath ice) laid waste the entire district. After the 1362 eruption the district became known as Öræfi (Wasteland).

The section of Ring Road that passes across Skeiðarársandur was the last bit of the national highway to be constructed – as recently as 1974 (until then, Höfnites had to drive to Reykjavík via Akureyri). Long gravel dykes have been strategically positioned to channel floodwaters away from this highly susceptible artery. They did little good, however, when in late 1996 three Ring Road bridges were washed away like matchsticks by the massive *jökulhlaup* released by the Grímsvötn (or Gjálp) eruption. There's a **memorial** of twisted bridge girders and an information board along the Ring Road just west of Skaftafell.

Núpsstaður & Núpsstaðarskógar

Adding more eye candy to an impressive road trip, precipitous palisades (known as Lómagnúpur) tower over the impossibly photogenic old turf-roofed farm at Núpsstaður. The farm buildings date back to the early 19th century, and the idyllic **chapel** is one of the last turf churches in Iceland. It was once a museum, but at the time of research the farm was closed to the public (you can't drive onto the property, but you can walk up to it). Hvoll Guesthouse is your best source for information on its status.

Inland is Núpsstaðarskógar, a beautiful woodland area on the slopes of the mountain Eystrafjall. Due to the perils of crossing the Núpsá river, this area is best explored on a tour. In July and August, **Icelandic Mountain Guides** (📱587 9999; www.mountainguide. is) runs a guided four-day (60km) backpacking hike through Núpsstaðarskógar, over to Grænalón (an ice-dammed marginal lake), across the glacier Skeiðarárjökull and then into Morsárdalur in Skaftafell. The trip costs from Ikr104,900.

🛏 Sleeping

Hvoll Guesthouse   GUESTHOUSE €€
(📱487 4785; www.road201.is; d without bathroom from Ikr15,180; ⊙mid-Mar–mid-Oct) Formerly an HI-affiliated hostel, this guesthouse (also known as Road 201) is on the edge of Skeiðarársandur (3.5km south off the Ring Road via a gravel road) and feels remote despite its large size. There's a busy atmosphere; facilities include several kitchens (bring food – the closest supermarket is 25km away in Klaustur) and a laundry.

Downside: no internet or wi-fi. Breakfast is available in summer for Ikr1600. It makes a good base for exploring Skaftafell and the surrounding sandar. Scheduled passing buses should be able to stop at the Ring Road turn-off.

Fosshótel Núpar   HOTEL €€
(📱517 3060; www.fosshotel.is; d incl breakfast from Ikr24,000; 📶) Just west of Hvoll Guesthouse, behind a portacabin-like exterior, this chain hotel offers modern, minimalist rooms, many with good views, and a somewhat soulless restaurant serving a buffet dinner (Ikr6800).

Dalshöfði Guesthouse   GUESTHOUSE €€
(📱861 4781; dalshofdi@gmail.com; s/d without bathroom incl breakfast Ikr12,300/17,600; ⊙May-Oct) A good option in this area is Dalshöfði Guesthouse, in a remote and scenic farm setting 6km north of the Ring Road. Rooms are bright and spotless, with kitchen access and

sunny outdoor deck. There's a two-bedroom apartment here too.

Skaftafell (Vatnajökull National Park – South)

Skaftafell, the jewel in the crown of Vatnajökull National Park, encompasses a breathtaking collection of peaks and glaciers. It's the country's favourite wilderness: 300,000 visitors per year come to marvel at thundering waterfalls, twisted birch woods, the tangled web of rivers threading across the sandar, and brilliant blue-white Vatnajökull with its lurching tongues of ice, dripping down mountainsides like icing on a cake.

Skaftafell deserves its reputation, and few visitors – even those who usually shun the great outdoors – can resist it. In the height of summer it may feel that every traveller in the country is here. However, if you're prepared to get out on the more-remote trails and take advantage of the fabulous hiking on the heath and beyond, you'll leave the crowds behind. Another great option: visit in winter.

There has been a significant growth in winter travel to the region, with the strong draws of Northern Lights and ice caves (which become solid and safe for visiting in the coldest months). You can still do glacier walks in winter – and the glaciers look more pristine (taking on that blue hue so beloved of photographers). In the right conditions, Svartifoss freezes in January-February (on the flipside, in winter the falls are not always accessible, due to slippery, unsafe tracks).

All flora, fauna and natural features of the park are protected, open fires are prohibited and rubbish must be carried out. In the busy area around Skaftafellsheiði, stick to the tracks to avoiding damaging delicate plant life.

There's very little accommodation close to the park, and hotels in the southeast are in incredible demand in summer – so you'll need either a tent or a firm hotel booking if you're heading this way and want to explore properly.

History

The historical Skaftafell was a large farm at the foot of the hills west of the present campsite. Shifting glacial sands slowly buried the fields and forced the farm to be moved to a more suitable site, on the heath 100m above the sandur. The district came to be known as Hérað Milli Sandur (Land Between the Sands), but after all the farms were annihilated by the 1362 eruptions, the district became the 'land under the sands' and was renamed Öræfi (Wasteland). Once the vegetation returned, however, the Skaftafell farm was rebuilt in its former location.

Skaftafell National Park was founded in 1967 by the Icelandic Government and the WWF. In June 2008 it merged with the Jökulsárgljúfur National Park in Iceland's north to form the massive wilderness area of Vatnajökull National Park.

🏃 Activities

Skaftafell is ideal for **day hikes** and also offers **longer hikes** through its wilderness regions. Most of Skaftafell's visitors keep to the popular routes on Skaftafellsheiði. Hik-ing in other accessible areas, such as the upper Morsárdalur and Kjós valleys, requires more time, motivation and planning. The park produces good maps outlining shorter hiking trails (Ikr350), and stocks larger topo maps from various publishers.

Limited wild-camping is allowed in the park – ask at the visitor centre, where you can also obtain a compulsory camping permit (free) for Kjós (note: Kjós is only accessible via a 12km hike). Also enquire about river crossings along your intended route.

Other possibilities for hikes include the long day trip beyond Bæjarstaðarskógur into the rugged Skaftafellsfjöll. A recommended destination is the 862m-high summit of the **Jökulfell ridge**, which affords a commanding view of the vast expanses of Skeiðarárjökull. Even better is an excursion into the Kjós dell.

JÖKULHLAUP!

In late 1996 the devastating Grímsvötn eruption – Iceland's fourth largest of the 20th century, after Katla in 1918, Hekla in 1947 and Surtsey in 1963 – shook southeast Iceland and caused an awesome *jökulhlaup* (glacial flood) across Skeiðarársandur. The events leading up to it are a sobering reminder of Iceland's volatile fire-and-ice combination.

On the morning of 29 September 1996, a magnitude 5.0 earthquake shook the Vatnajökull ice cap. Magma from a new volcano, in the Grímsvötn region beneath Vatnajökull, had made its way through the earth's crust and into the ice, causing the eruption of a 4km-long subsurface fissure known as Gjálp. The following day the eruption burst through the surface, ejecting a column of steam that rose 10km into the sky.

Scientists became concerned as the subglacial lake in the Grímsvötn caldera began to fill with water from ice melted by the eruption. Initial predictions on 3 October were that the ice would lift and the lake would spill out across Skeiðarársandur, threatening the Ring Road and its bridges. In the hope of diverting floodwaters away from the bridges, massive dyke-building projects were organised on Skeiðarársandur.

On 5 November, more than a month after the eruption started, the ice did lift and the Grímsvötn reservoir drained in a massive *jökulhlaup,* releasing up to 3000 billion litres of water within a few hours. The floodwaters – dragging along icebergs the size of three-storey buildings – destroyed the 375m-long Gígjukvísl Bridge and the 900m-long Skeiðará Bridge, both on the Skeiðarársandur. You can see video footage of the eruption and enormous multi-tonne blocks of ice being hurled across Skeiðarársandur at the Skaftafell and Höfn visitor centres.

Some of Grímsvötn's other creations include the Ásbyrgi canyon, gouged out by a cataclysmic flood over just a few days. In 1934 an eruption released a *jökulhlaup* of 40,000 cu metres per second, which swelled the river Skeiðará to 9km in width and laid waste to large areas of farmland.

Grímsvötn erupted again in December 1998, November 2004 and, most recently, in May 2011, when a huge ash plume was released into the atmosphere, disrupting air traffic (but with nowhere near the disruption caused by 2010's Eyjafjallajökull eruption). There was no *jökulhlaup* on any of these three occasions.

From August 2014, scientists have been monitoring seismic activity around Bárðarbunga caldera, under the northwestern part of Vatnajökull. The first fissure eruptions from this activity have been in the Holuhraun area (ie, not subglacial) but there is the possibility of an eruption occurring under ice, and a resulting *jökulhlaup*. Stay tuned.

VATNAJÖKULL NATIONAL PARK

The Park

Vatnajökull National Park was founded in 2008, joining the Vatnajökull ice cap and the former Skaftafell and Jökulsárgljúfur (p250) National Parks to form one giant megapark. With recent additions, the park now measures 13,900 sq km – nearly 14% of the entire country. Within its boundaries lies a staggering richness of landscapes, created by the combined forces of rivers, glacial ice, and volcanic and geothermal activity (yes, fire-and-ice cliche alert!).

Vatnajökull & Outlet Glaciers

Vatnajökull is the world's largest ice cap outside the poles. At 8100 sq km, it's more than three times the size of Luxembourg, with an average thickness of 400m (and a maximum of almost 1km). Under this enormous blanket of ice lie countless peaks and valleys, including a number of live volcanoes and subglacial lakes, plus Iceland's highest point – the 2110m mountain Hvannadalshnúkur.

Huge **outlet glaciers**, pleated with crevasses, flow down from the centre of Vatnajökull. There are around 30 of them, with many visible (and accessible, to varying degrees) from the Ring Road (Rte 1) in the southeast.

The best known is possibly Skaftafellsjökull, a relatively small glacier that ends within 1.5km of the campsite at Skaftafell. Another famous beauty is Breiðamerkurjökull, which crumbles into icebergs at the breathtaking Jökulsárlón lagoon.

Close to Skaftafell, companies guide glacier walks on tongues such as Svínafellsjökull and Falljökull. Between Jökulsárlón and Höfn, the national park is working with property owners to open up access to a handful of glacier tongues.

The usual common-sense rules apply: don't get too close to glaciers or walk on them without the proper equipment and guiding.

Information

The park operates four major visitor centres:

➡ Skaftafell (p294) in the south

➡ Höfn (p305) in the southeast

➡ **Jökulsárgljúfur** (Gljúfrastofa; ☑ 470 7100; www.vjp.is; ⊙ 9am-9pm mid-Jun–mid-Aug, 9am-7pm rest of Jun & Aug, 10am-4pm May & Sep) in the north

➡ Snæfellsstofa (p266) in the east

The tourist information centre at Kirkjubæjarklaustur works in conjunction with the park. The best websites for visitors planning a visit to the southern area of the park are **Vatnajökull National Park** (www.vjp.is) and **Visit Vatnajökull** (www.visitvatnajokull.is).

There is now a trail where **mountain biking** is permitted. It follows a 13km route that crosses the dry riverbed of Skeiðará and travels through Morsárdalur to the woods at Bæjarstaðarskógur. Glacier Guides (p294) offers independent mountain-bike rental (Ikr3000 for three hours) as well as five-hour guided cycling and walking tours four times a week ('Skaftafell on Wheels'; Ikr19,990, rental included).

Note that from mid-June to mid-August, rangers guide free daily **interpretive walks** that depart from the visitor centre – a great way to learn about the area. Check the website, or ask staff.

Svartifoss

Star of a hundred postcards, Svartifoss (Black Falls) is a stunning, moody-looking waterfall flanked by geometric black basalt columns. It's reached by an easy 1.8km trail leading up from the visitor centre via the campsite (about 1½ hours return).

From Svartifoss, it's worth continuing west up the track to **Sjónarsker**, where there's a view disc and an unforgettable view across Skeiðarársandur. From here you can visit the traditional turf-roofed farmhouse **Sel**; this 2½-hour, 5.3km return walk is classified easy.

Alternatively, from Svartifoss head east over the heath to the viewpoint at **Sjónarnípa**, looking across Skaftafellsjökull.

SOUTHEAST ICELAND SKAFTAFELL (VATNAJÖKULL NATIONAL PARK – SOUTH)

Skaftafell

This walk is classified as challenging; allow three hours return (7.4km).

Skaftafellsjökull

Another very popular trail is the easy one-hour return walk (3.7km) to Skaftafellsjökull. The marked trail begins at the visitor centre and leads to the **glacier face**, where you can witness the bumps and groans of the ice (although the glacier is pretty grey and gritty here). The glacier has receded greatly in recent decades, meaning land along this trail has been gradually reappearing. Pick up a brochure that describes the trail's geology.

Skaftafellsheiði Loop

On a fine day, the five- to six-hour (15.5km) walk around Skaftafellsheiði is a hiker's dream. It begins by climbing from the campsite past Svartifoss and Sjónarsker, continuing across the moor to 610m-high **Fremrihnaukur**. From there it follows the edge of the plateau to the next rise, **Nyrðrihnaukur** (706m), which affords a superb view of Morsárdalur, Morsárjökull and the iceberg-choked lagoon at its base. At this point the track turns southeast to an outlook point, **Gláma**, on the cliff above Skaftafellsjökull.

For the best view of Skaftafellsjökull, Morsárdalur and the Skeiðarársandur, it's worth scaling the summit of **Kristínartindar** (1126m). The best way follows a well-marked 2km route (classified difficult) up the prominent valley southeast of the Nyrðrihnaukur lookout, and back down near Gláma.

Morsárdalur & Bæjarstaðarskógur

The seven-hour hike (20.6km return) from the campsite to the glacial lake in Morsárdalur is ordinary but enjoyable. Alternatively, cross the Morsá at the foot of Skaftafellsheiði and make your way across the gravel riverbed to the **birch woods** at Bæjarstaðarskógur. The return walk to Bæjarstaðarskógur takes about six hours (13km return). This is also the trail to follow if you're exploring on **mountain bike**.

Tours

The highlight of a visit to Skaftafell is a **glacier hike**. It's utterly liberating to strap on crampons and crunch your way around a glacier, and there's much to see on the ice: waterfalls, ice caves, glacial mice (moss balls, not actual mice!) and different-coloured ash from ancient explosions. But – take note: as magnetic as the glaciers are, they are also riven with fissures and are potentially dangerous, so don't be tempted to stride out onto one without the right equipment and guiding.

A number of authorised guides operate in the area (and at glacier tongues further east, towards Höfn). The largest companies, Icelandic Mountain Guides and Glacier Guides, have info and booking huts in the car park at Skaftafell visitor centre, where you can talk to experts and get kitted out for glacier walks (warm clothes essential, waterproof gear and hiking boots available for hire).

Both companies go further than just easy glacier hikes, offering more-challenging options and ice climbs, right up to summiting Iceland's highest peak (Hvannadalshnúkur). Both offer combos, such as a glacier hike plus Jökulsárlón or Fjallsárlón boat trip or Ingólfshöfði visit. For many trips, they can arrange pick-up from Svínafell campsite and Hótel Skaftafell (prebooking required). See the websites for suggestions.

New and in hot demand: winter visits to **ice caves**. Local Guide is the expert for this, running tours from around mid-November to March. Winter is a super-scenic and less-crowded time to visit the national park; Icelandic Mountain Guides operates glacier walks year-round.

Prices listed below are from 2014. Websites list up-to-date rates.

Icelandic Mountain Guides   ADVENTURE TOUR

(IMG; ☑ Reykjavík office 5879999, Skaftafell 8942959; www.mountainguide.is) IMG's bestselling walk is the family-friendly 'Blue Ice Experience', with 1½ to two hours spent on the ice at Svínafellsjökull (adult/child Ikr8900/5700, minimum age eight years). These tours run from Skaftafell two to four times daily year-round (departures at 10am and 2pm, plus 11am and 3pm July and August).

There are longer, tougher walks up the same glacier (from three to 6½ hours on the ice), and ice-climbing options tailored to suit all skill levels (Ikr18,900).

See the website for IMG's impressive program of multiday cycling, hiking and super-Jeep tours, including a five-day 'Rivers and Glaciers of Vatnajökull' backpacking trip.

Glacier Guides   ADVENTURE TOUR

(☑ Reykjavík office 571 2100, Skaftafell 659 7000; www.glacierguides.is) As well as glacier walks of varying duration and difficulty, Glacier Guides also offers rock climbing, ice climbing and mountain biking from Skaftafell.

Its beginner-level walk is family-friendly 'Glacier Wonders', a 2½-hour tour with a stroll up Falljökull (adult/child Ikr8490/6500, minimum age 10 years); trips depart from Skaftafell four times daily mid-May to September. There's also a tougher five-hour walk up the same glacier (Ikr12,990), and a 6½-hour combo trip that includes glacier hiking plus ice climbing (Ikr19,990).

Local Guide   ADVENTURE TOUR

(Öræfaferðir; ☑ 894 0894; www.localguide.is) Many generations of this family have lived at the local farm Hofsnes, so their local knowledge is first-rate (they run the summertime tours to Ingólfshöfði). Their new booking agency is Local Guide HQ in Fagurhólsmýri (there's an N1 fuel pump here) – about 26km from Skaftafell.

From here, they run tailored, year-round glacier hikes and ice climbs (cost depends on the number in your group). Local Guide is also the local expert on ice caves, running tours from mid-November to March. The regular ice-cave tour costs Ikr14,900, but there's a longer tour more suited to photographers for Ikr24,900. The website outlines all options and prices.

Atlantsflug   SCENIC FLIGHT

(☑ 478 2406, 854 4105; www.flightseeing.is) Sightseeing flights offer a brilliant perspective over all this natural splendour, and leave from the tiny airfield on the Ring Road, just by the turn-off to the park visitor centre. Choose between six tour options, with views over Landmannalaugar, Lakagígar, Skaftafell peaks, Jökulsárlón and Grímsvötn. Prices start at Ikr22,000 for 30 minutes.

🍴 Sleeping & Eating

Food in the park is limited to the busy summertime cafe inside the visitor centre, which sells coffee, soup, sandwiches and a tiny selection of groceries.

The nearest hotel is at Freysnes, 5km east of the national park entrance, and there's another at Hof, a further 15km east.

Visitor Centre Campsite   CAMPGROUND €

(☑ 470 8300; www.vjp.is; sites per person Ikr1400 plus per tent Ikr100; ⊙ May-Sep; 🛜) Most visitors bring a tent to this large, gravelly, panorama-filled campsite (with laundry facilities, and hot showers for Ikr500). It gets very busy in summer (at capacity, it holds 400 pitches); reservations are only required for large groups (40-plus people). Wifi is available, as are storage lockers.

If you're looking for a less-crowded option, consider the campground at Svínafell, 8km east.

ℹ️ Information

Visitor Centre (Skaftafellsstofa; ☑ 470 8300; www.vjp.is; ⊙ 8am-9pm Jun-Aug, 9am-7pm May & Sep, 10am-5pm Mar, Apr & Oct, 11am-4pm Nov-Feb; 🛜) The helpful year-round visitor centre has an information desk with free brochures and maps for sale, informative displays on the Öræfi area, a fascinating 10-minute film about the 1996 Grímsvötn *jökulhlaup*, exhibitions, a summertime cafe and internet access. The staff here know their stuff.

❶ Getting There & Away

Skaftafell is a stop on Reykjavík–Höfn bus routes and also a departure point for wilderness areas such as Landmannalaugar and Lakagígar. There are frequent services to Jökulsárlón.

Buses depart in front of the visitor centre. Note that prices are from 2014.

Sterna (☑ 551 1166; www.sterna.is) services:
➡ Bus 12 to Höfn (Ikr3100, 3½ hours, one daily June to mid-September) Stops for 1½ hours at Jökulsárlón.
➡ Bus 12a to Reykjavík (Ikr7200, 6¾ hours, one daily June to mid-September)

Strætó (☑ 540 2700; www.straeto.is) services:
➡ Bus 51 to Höfn (Ikr2800, 1¾ hours, two daily June to mid-September, one daily rest of year)
➡ Bus 51 to Reykjavík (Ikr7700, five hours, two daily June to mid-September, one daily rest of year)

Reykjavík Excursions (☑ 580 5400; www.re.is) services:
➡ Bus 10/10a to Landmannalaugar (Ikr9000, five hours, one daily mid-June to mid-September) Runs via Eldgjá. Can be used as a day tour, or as regular transport.
➡ Bus 15 to Jökulsárlón (Ikr2500, 45 minutes, three daily mid-June to mid-September)
➡ Bus 16/16a to Lakagígar (one daily late June to mid-September) Use as a day tour, with 3½ hours at Laki (day tour Ikr15,500).
➡ Bus 19 to Höfn (Ikr5500, two hours, one daily mid-June to mid-September) Stops at Jökulsárlón.
➡ Bus 20a to Reykjavík (Ikr11,000, seven hours, one daily mid-June to mid-September) Stops for one hour at Vík, 25 minutes at Skógafoss.

Skaftafell to Jökulsárlón

Glittering glaciers and brooding mountains line the 60km stretch between Skaftafell and the iceberg-filled lagoon Jökulsárlón, and the unfolding landscape makes it difficult to keep your eyes on the road.

Freysnes, Svínafell & Svínafellsjökull

The farm **Svínafell**, 8km southeast of Skaftafell, was the home of Flosi Þórðarson, the character who burned Njál and his family to death in *Njál's Saga*. It was also the site where Flosi and Njál's family were finally reconciled, thus ending one of the bloodiest feuds in Icelandic history. There's not much to this tiny settlement now, but there is accommodation.

In the 17th century, the glacier **Svínafellsjökull** nearly engulfed the farm, but it has since retreated. On the northern side of the glacier (towards Skaftafell), a dirt road leads 2km to a car park, from where it's a short walk to the snout. Don't stride out there unaccompanied – excellent tours venture onto the glacier operated by **Icelandic Mountain Guides** (IMG; ☑ 587 9999; www.mountainguide.is). Oh, and if the landscape looks familiar, it may be because scenes from 2014's *Interstellar* were filmed here.

☞ Tours

Glacier Horses   HORSE RIDING
(☑ 847 7170; www.glacierhorses.is; tours adult/child Ikr8500/6000) Not far past Svínafell (en route to Hof), this new operator offers short (one- to 1½-hour) horse rides in view-blessed countryside, with departures at 10am, 1pm and 4pm (booking required).

⌂ Sleeping & Eating

Svínafell   CAMPGROUND €
(☑ 478 1765; www.svinafell.com; sites per person Ikr1300, cabins & rooms per person Ikr3900-4500; ☺ campground May-Sep; ☏) This well-organised place has a campsite and six basic cabins (sleeping four), and a spotless amenities block with large dining room. With your own vehicle, it's an alternative to the campsite at Skaftafell. The owner also offers sleeping-bag beds in apartments and rooms scattered about the hamlet (these are available year-round). Check current prices online.

Hótel Skaftafell   HOTEL €€
(☑ 478 1945; www.hotelskaftafell.is; Freysnes; s/d incl breakfast Ikr24,500/29,000; @☏) Formerly part of the Fosshotel chain, this is the closest hotel to Skaftafell. It's 5km east, at Freysnes, and one of very few hotels in the area, so it's in hot demand – prices reflect this. Its 63 rooms are functional rather than luxurious; staff are helpful. There's a decent **restaurant** (mains Ikr3500 to Ikr4100) plating up local produce.

Söluskálinn Freysnesi   ICELANDIC €
(☺ 9am-10pm Mon-Fri, to 8pm Sat & Sun) The petrol station opposite Hótel Skaftafell sells a well-priced hot dish of the day alongside burgers, pizzas and a decent section of groceries.

Öræfajökull & Hvannadalshnúkur

Iceland's highest mountain, **Hvannadalshnúkur** (2110m), pokes out from Öræfajökull, an offshoot of Vatnajökull. This lofty peak is actually the northwestern edge of an immense 5km-wide crater – the biggest active volcano in Europe after Mt Etna. It erupted in 1362, firing out the largest amount of tephra in Iceland's recorded history. The region was utterly devastated – hence its name, Öræfi (Wasteland).

The best access for climbing Hvannadalshnúkur is from Sandfellsheiði, about 12km southeast of Skaftafell. Most guided expeditions manage the trip in a very long and taxing day (starting around 5am), and although there are no technical skills required, the trip is both physically and mentally challenging. Total elevation gain is more than 2000m; total distance is around 23km. Independent climbers should carry enough supplies and gear for several days, and must be well versed in glacier travel.

The best time for climbing the mountain is April or May, before the ice bridges melt. Note that each year the ice bridges that make the hike possible are melting earlier and faster, so the climbing season is becoming shorter. Although trips may theoretically be possible through the summer, after June conditions may force companies to hire extra guides per group, raising the prices considerably (or the season will simply end – in 2014, the latest ascent of Hvannadalshnúkur happened in June). Check websites for more details.

Tours

Icelandic Mountain Guides, Glacier Guides and Local Guide (all based in and around Skaftafell) offer ascents of Hvannadalshnúkur; briefings are held the night before. Prices listed are from 2014.

Local Guide ADVENTURE TOUR

(Öræfaferðir; ☑ 894 0894; www.localguide.is) Einar, the company owner, holds the world record for ascents of Hvannadalshnúkur (more than 270!). He offers a ski-mountaineering ascent from March to May; price depends on the number of participants (two people costs Ikr45,000 per person).

Icelandic Mountain Guides ADVENTURE TOUR

(☑ Reykjavík office 587 9999, Skaftafell 894 2959; www.mountainguide.is) A guided 12- to 15-hour ascent costs from Ikr34,900 per person (minimum two people), including transport and equipment. Trips run three times a week April to mid-August (conditions permitting). Book in advance, and allow yourself extra days in case the weather causes a cancellation.

Glacier Guides ADVENTURE TOUR

(☑ Reykjavík office 571 2100, Skaftafell 659 7000; www.glacierguides.is) Ascent costs Ikr31,990, with a minimum two people, and run on demand from mid-May to August (conditions permitting).

Hof

At Hof there's a storybook wood-and-peat **church**, built on the foundations of a previous 14th-century building. It was reconstructed in 1884 and now sits pretty in a thicket of birch and ash with flowers growing on the grassy roof.

Sleeping & Eating

Lækjarhús COTTAGES €€

(☑ 616 1247; www.laekjarhus.is; cabins Ikr18,000; ⊙ Feb-Oct; 🌐) Lækjarhús has a trio of super-cosy self-contained cabins sleeping four people in bunks (BYO sleeping bags, or hire linen for Ikr1500 per person). There's a wee kitchenette and bathroom in each.

Hof 1 Hotel COUNTRY HOTEL €€

(☑ 478 2260; www.hof1.is; d with/without bathroom incl breakfast Ikr26,900/21,900; 🌐) Beautifully situated beneath the Öræfajökull glacier, the very civilised Hof 1 harbours an impressive collection of modern Icelandic art, a stylish lounge area, and an alluring sauna and hot-pot area. There's a variety of rooms scattered in various buildings, and a dining area serving dinner (two courses from Ikr4500).

Ingólfshöfði

While everyone's gaze naturally turns inland in this spectacular part of Iceland, there are reasons to look offshore, too – in particular to the 76m-high Ingólfshöfði promontory, rising from the flatlands like a strange dream.

In spring and summer, this beautiful, isolated **nature reserve** is overrun with nesting puffins, skuas and other seabirds, and you may see seals and whales offshore. It's also of great historical importance – it was here that Ingólfur Arnarson, Iceland's first settler, stayed the winter on his original foray to the country in AD 874.

The reserve is open to visitors. Tours begin with a fun ride across 6km of shallow tidal lagoon (in a tractor-drawn wagon), then a short but steep sandy climb, followed by a 1½-hour guided walk round the headland. The emphasis is on birdwatching, with stunning mountain backdrops to marvel over. Note that puffins usually leave around mid-August.

Tours are run by **Local Guide** (Öræfaferðir; ☑894 0894; www.localguide.is; tours adult/child Ikr6900/1000; ⊘tours 1.30pm Mon-Sat May-Aug, also 10.15am Mon-Sat Jun–mid-Aug), whose new booking agency is in Fagurhólsmýri (there's an N1 fuel pump here), about 26km from Skaftafell. The departure point for the Ingólfshöfði tour is just west of the agency (signposted), 2km off the Ring Road.

Confirm tour times via the website, where you can also book tickets (prebooking recommended).

Breiðamerkursandur

The easternmost part of the large sandar, Breiðamerkursandur is one of the main breeding grounds for Iceland's great skuas. Thanks to rising numbers of these ground-nesting birds, there's also a growing population of Arctic foxes. Historically, Breiðamerkursandur also figures in *Njál's Saga,* which ends with Kári Sölmundarson arriving in this idyllic spot to 'live happily ever after' – which has to be some kind of miracle in a saga.

The sandur is backed by a sweeping panorama of glacier-capped mountains, some of which are fronted by deep lagoons. **Kvíárjökull glacier** snakes down to the Kvíá river and is easily accessible from the Ring Road – look for the sign for Kvíármýrarkambur just west of the bridge over the river. Leave your car in the small car park and follow the path into the scenic valley.

The 742m-high **Breiðamerkurfjall** was once a nunatak enclosed by Breiðamerkurjökull and Fjallsjökull, but the glaciers have since retreated and freed it.

A small sign off the Ring Road indicates Fjallsárlón, and gives access to two glacial lagoons with a diminutive river flowing between them. Take the left fork for **Fjallsárlón**, where icebergs calve from Fjallsjökull, or right for a lengthier track to **Breiðárlón**, another outlet of Breiðamerkurjökull (also the source of Jökulsárlón). The road to Breiðárlón is very rough going.

Fjallsárlón
Glacial Lagoon Boat Tours BOAT TOUR
(☑666 8006; www.fjallsarlon.is; adult/child Ikr5500/3000; ⊘10am-5pm mid-May–mid-Sep) It's a bumpy kilometre from the Ring Road to the parking area for Fjallsárlón – and it's

here that a new company has set up, offering 45-minute zodiac boat trips among these lagoon icebergs (as an alternative to the cruises at busy Jökulsárlón, 10km further east and directly on the Ring Road).

Fjallsárlón is not as large or as dramatic as Jökulsárlón, but it is more isolated and therefore considerably less crowded, which has its own appeal. The walking trail to the boat's departure point at the lagoon shore is more intrepid. And there is also an intimacy to a tour on this lagoon – you don't have to travel as far to reach the glacier snout, for example.

Jökulsárlón

A host of spectacular, luminous-blue icebergs drift through Jökulsárlón **glacier lagoon**, right beside the Ring Road between Höfn and Skaftafell. Even when you're driving along, expecting this surreal scene, it's still a surprise. It's worth spending a couple of hours here, admiring the wondrous ice sculptures (some of them striped with ash layers from volcanic eruptions), scouting for seals or taking a boat trip.

The icebergs calve from Breiðamerkurjökull, an offshoot of Vatnajökull, crashing down into the water and drifting inexorably towards the Atlantic Ocean. They can spend up to five years floating in the 25-sq-km-plus, 260m-deep lagoon, melting, refreezing and occasionally toppling over with a mighty splash, startling the birds. They then move on via Jökulsá, Iceland's shortest river, out to sea.

Although it looks as though it's been here since the last ice age, the lagoon is only about 80 years old. Until the mid-1930s Breiðamerkurjökull reached the Ring Road; it's now retreating rapidly (up to a staggering 500m per year), and the lagoon is consequently growing.

The lagoon boat trips are excellent, but you can get almost as close to those cool-blue masterpieces by walking along the shore, and you can taste ancient ice by hauling it out of the water. On the Ring Road west of the car park, there are designated parking areas where you can walk over the mounds to visit the lake at less-touristed stretches of shoreline.

It's also highly recommended that you visit the rivermouth (there are car parks on the ocean side of the Ring Road), where you'll see ice boulders resting photogenically

JÖKULSÁRLÓN FILM CREDITS

Jökulsárlón is a natural film set, and a popular backdrop for commercials. It starred briefly in *Lara Croft: Tomb Raider* (2001), pretending to be Siberia – the amphibious tourist-carrying boats were even painted grey and used as Russian ships. You might also have seen it in *Batman Begins* (2005), or the James Bond film *Die Another Day* (2002), for which the lagoon was specially frozen and six Aston Martins were destroyed on the ice.

on the black-sand beach as part of their final journey out to sea.

If you're in the area in late August, don't miss the annual **fireworks display** held here as a fundraiser for the local search and rescue team. Entry is usually around Ikr1000, with buses running from Höfn for the event. See www.visitvatnajokull.is for details.

A new **walking trail** has been marked from the western car park, leading to Breiðárlón (10km one way) and Fjallsárlón (15.3km).

🕝 Tours

Glacier Lagoon

Amphibious Boat Tours BOAT TOUR
(☑478 2222; www.icelagoon.is; adult/child Ikr4000/1000; ⊙9am-7pm Jun-Aug, 10am-5pm Apr-May & Sep-Oct) Take a memorable 40-minute trip in an amphibious boat, which trundles along the shore like a bus before driving into the water. Onboard guides regale you with factoids about the lagoon, and you can taste 1000-year-old ice. There is no set schedule; trips run from the eastern car park (by the cafe) regularly – at least half-hourly in summer.

Note that the last boat tour departs about one hour before closing time. Tours may be available from November to March, depending on demand and weather conditions – contact the operators.

The same company also offers hour-long lagoon tours on zodiacs (adult/child Ikr6500/3250; not recommended for kids under 10), but demand for the amphibious boats often sees the zodiacs here being under-utilised.

Ice Lagoon Zodiac Boat Tours BOAT TOUR
(☑860 9996; www.icelagoon.com; adult/child Ikr6500/4900; ⊙9am-5.30pm mid-May–mid-Sep)

A second, smaller operator deals exclusively with zodiac tours of the lagoon. It's a one-hour experience, with a maximum 20 passengers per boat, and it travels at speed up to the glacier edge (not done by the amphibious boats) before cruising back at a leisurely pace. It pays to book these tours in advance, online; minimum age six years.

The company was operating from the eastern car park in 2014, but may switch to the west in 2015 – check the website.

Ice Walk GLACIER HIKE
(☑866 3490; www.icewalk.is; ⊙tour Ikr12,500) Local guide Thor offers glacier hikes on Breiðamerkurjökull, with daily departures from the Jökulsárlón car park at 10am and 2.30pm (booking advised). You spend two to three hours on the ice.

🛏 Sleeping & Eating

If you have a campervan with toilet, it's OK to stay in the car park. Otherwise camping by the lagoon isn't condoned (particularly not on the eastern side, where there are lots of nesting birds). The closest hotel is Hali, 12km east.

Cafe CAFE €
(⊙9am-7pm Jun-Aug, 10am-5pm Sep-May) The year-round cafe beside the lagoon is a good pitstop for information and a snack, but its small, dated space is totally overwhelmed in summer.

❶ Getting There & Away

Countless tours take in Jökulsárlón.

Sterna (☑551 1166; www.sterna.is) bus 12/12a between Reykjavík and Höfn runs daily from June to mid-September. Travelling in either direction, it stops for 1½ hours at Jökulsárlón (enough time for a boat ride).

Strætó (☑540 2700; www.straeto.is) bus 51 between Reykjavík and Höfn runs twice daily from June to mid-September (once daily the rest of the year) and stops here. It simply drops off or picks up passengers, it doesn't linger.

Reykjavík Excursions (☑580 5400; www.re.is) has two summer services of note:

➡ Bus 15 runs a loop between Skaftafell visitor centre and Jökulsárlón (Ikr2500, 45 minutes, two to three daily mid-June to mid-September)

➡ Bus 19 runs from Höfn to Skaftafell and back again each day, stopping for a lengthy spell at the lagoon in either direction (to Höfn Ikr3500, one hour, one daily mid-June to mid-September).

Jökulsárlón to Höfn

The heavenly stretch of Ring Road from Jökulsárlón to Höfn is lined with around 20 rural properties (many with glaciers in their backyards) offering accommodation. Many of them have expanded in the past couple of years – even still, in summer, demand for rooms far exceeds supply (and prices are high). Book well ahead.

Sights & Activities

Gentle, family-friendly lures include a petting zoo, ice-cream producer, quality museum, bird-filled wetlands and outdoor hot-pots. Those looking for a little more exertion will find walks to (or on) glacier tongues, horse riding, quad-bike rides and snowmobile safaris.

Þórbergssetur   MUSEUM
(www.thorbergur.is; adult/child Ikr1000/free; ⊙9am-8pm) This cleverly crafted museum (its inspired exterior looks like a shelf of books) pays tribute to the most famous son of this sparsely populated region – writer Þórbergur Þórðarson (1888–1974), who was born at Hali in Suðursveit. Þórbergur was a real maverick (with interests spanning yoga, Esperanto and astronomy), and his first book *Bréf til Láru* (Letter to Laura) caused huge controversy because of its radical socialist content.

Þórbergssetur also functions as a kind of cultural centre, with changing art exhibitions, and a quality **cafe-restaurant** (dinner mains Ikr2900-5500) where the speciality is Arctic char. There's a cluster of accommodation surrounding it.

Tours

Glacier Jeeps   ADVENTURE TOUR
(✐478 1000, 894 3133; www.glacierjeeps.is) If you want to get up onto Vatnajökull, the daddy of all local glaciers, for a snowmobile or super-Jeep tour (p304), then this area is where you branch vertically off into the mountains. Rte F985, which leads up to Jöklasel, is about 35km east of Jökulsárlón; Glacier Jeeps can transport you there from the small Ring Road car park.

Sleeping & Eating

The majority of places along this stretch have in-house restaurants. Self-caterers should stock up on groceries in Kirkjubæjarklaustur or Höfn.

We list these options from west to east. Note that most prices are from 2014.

Skyrhúsid   GUESTHOUSE €€
(✐899 8384; d from Ikr14,000; 🛜) This cute, petite guesthouse is in Hali, just past Þórbergssetur. It's a cosy place with just nine fresh rooms (no guest kitchen), and a tiny, colourful breakfast area.

Vagnsstaðir HI Hostel   HOSTEL €
(✐478 1048; www.hostel.is; dm/d without bathroom Ikr4300/11,400; ⊙Apr–mid-Oct; 🛜) Snowmobiles litter this Ring Road property, HQ of Glacier Jeeps. It's a small, bunk-heavy hostel with sunny enclosed dining area, plus there are additional six-bed cottages (each with toilet, but not shower) next to the main building. The common complaint is that the limited bathroom facilities and small kitchen are now inadequate for the number of beds.

Hótel Smyrlabjörg COUNTRY HOTEL, RESTAURANT €€
(✐478 1074; www.smyrlabjorg.is; s/d incl breakfast Ikr20,300/30,000; 🛜) A good choice if you're after mod-cons but still want sheep roaming the car park, mountain views, and peace and quiet. This large, welcoming hotel (recently doubled in size) has a restaurant renowned for country hospitality and a bountiful evening buffet (Ikr6200).

Skálafell   GUESTHOUSE €€
(✐478 1041; www.skalafell.net; d with/without bathroom incl breakfast Ikr23,000/19,000; 🛜) At the foot of Skálafellsjökull, this friendly working farm has a handful of rooms in the family farmhouse, and also in motel-style units. There are no cooking facilities, but dinner is available.

In cooperation with the national park, the knowledgeable owners here offer information and have set up marked **walking trails** (open to all) in the surrounding glaciated landscapes.

The **Hjallanes loop** is about 7km and takes two to three hours to walk – see the guesthouse website (go to Walking Paths under 'The Area') for information on it and other trails.

Hali Country Hotel   HOTEL, RESTAURANT €€
(✐478 1073; www.hali.is; d with/without bathroom incl breakfast from Ikr32,200/20,800; 🛜) The Þórbergssetur museum acts as reception and restaurant for this smart option, the closest hotel to Jökulsárlón (and one of a cluster of places at Hali settlement). There

VATNAJÖKULL BEER

We're a sucker for a good sales pitch, and this beer has it in spades: 'frozen in time' beer brewed from 1000-year-old water (ie Jökulsárlón icebergs), flavoured with locally grown arctic thyme. It's brewed by Ölvisholt Brugghús near Selfoss, and sold in restaurants around the southeast. Give it a try for its fruity, malty flavour.

are a few high-standard choices in various buildings: en-suite hotel rooms (no kitchen facilities), guesthouse rooms (shared bathrooms and kitchen), plus a couple of two-bedroom self-contained apartments.

Glacier Adventure (🗷 699 1003; www.glacieradventures.is) is a local operator based out of Hali. Haukur guides glacier walks in the area, of varying lengths and degrees of difficulty, starting from Ikr11,500.

Heinaberg Guesthouse   GUESTHOUSE €
(🗷 4781497; www.heinaberg.is; s/d Ikr9900/14,900; 🛜) Friendly Birgir runs this good-value new option, with small, chalet-style rooms in a homey lodge on a working dairy farm. It's spic-and-span, with kitchen access and great views; breakfast is Ikr1500.

★Hólmur   GUESTHOUSE, RESTAURANT €
(🗷 478 2063; www.eldhorn.is/mg/gisting; s/d without bathroom Ikr10,000/13,200; 🛜) A perfect pitstop for families, Hólmur offers well-priced farmhouse accommodation (ask about sleeping-bag rates for extra savings) and a sweet, smile-inducing **farm zoo** (⊙10am-5pm, adult/child Ikr700/500) with an abundance of feathered and furry friends – even reindeer.

The family works in cooperation with the national park to provide information services, and is very well placed for exploration of **Fláajökull**. Also on site is a **cafe-restaurant** (with plans for relocation in 2015 to a larger building on the farm), and something of a surprise: beautifully presented, restaurant-quality dishes – grilled langoustine, slow-roasted pork belly, crème brûlée made from farm-laid duck eggs (dinner mains Ikr3400 to Ikr5900). The cafe is open for light food during the day, and meals in the evening.

Lambhús   COTTAGES €€
(🗷 662 1029; www.lambhus.is; cottages excl linen Ikr15,000-19,000; ⊙Jun-Aug; 🛜) Ducks and horses, plus nine cute, compact self-catering cottages (sleeping four to six and ideal for families), are scattered about this vista-blessed property, owned by an affable, multilingual family with years of guiding experience. Linen can be hired (Ikr2000 per person).

Brunnhóll   COUNTRY HOTEL, RESTAURANT €€
(🗷 478 1029; www.brunnholl.is; s/d incl breakfast from Ikr18,700/24,000; ⊙Apr-Oct; 🛜) The hotel at this friendly dairy farm has simple, decent-sized rooms with big views. Outside the June-to-August peak, sleeping-bag accommodation is available from Ikr4800. The good folk at Brunnhóll are also the makers of delicious Jöklaís (this name means 'Glacier Icecream'), which you can sample at the summertime **dinner buffet** (Ikr5800) open to all. Or stop in anytime to buy a scoop or tub.

Hoffell   COUNTRY HOTEL, GUESTHOUSE €€
(Glacier World; 🗷 478 1514; www.glacierworld.is; d with/without bathroom Ikr29,600/16,900) The guesthouse at Hoffell has bright, fresh rooms with shared bathroom and guest kitchen. In mid-2014, a new building opened, housing hotel-style en-suite rooms (in a converted cowshed!).

As well as friendly owners, what really acts as a drawcard are the activities here (also accessible to nonguests): **quad-bike tours** (from Ikr12,500) to the glacier, and a collection of **outdoor hot-pots** (Ikr500; open 7am to 11pm).

In cooperation with the national park, Hoffell's owners offer information on their incredible surrounds, including the 4km road to **Hoffellsjökull**.

Hótel Glacier   COUNTRY HOTEL €€
(🗷 478 1400; www.hoteljokull.is; Nesjaskóli; d with/without bathroom Ikr21,700/13,700; ⊙May-Sep; @🛜) Found 8km north of Höfn in a former school is this well-run, well-priced option (also known as Hótel Jökull) – it's another place that has added 40 new en-suite rooms to its repertoire (this time in a converted sports stadium!). There's a restaurant serving up a nightly fish buffet (Ikr5900).

★Árnanes
Country Lodge   COUNTRY HOTEL, RESTAURANT €€
(🗷 478 1550; www.arnanes.is; d with/without bathroom incl breakfast Ikr28,200/22,100; 🛜) This polished rural 21-room locale is 6km

GET YOUR GLACIER ON

Vatnajökull National Park authorities are working with a handful of landowners in this region to open up public access to some areas of raw natural beauty. These areas are signed off the Ring Road – for now, they are not especially well known, so you stand a good chance of finding yourself a tranquil pocket of glaciated wonder.

The guesthouses mentioned here act as information points (maps are available), or you can stop by the information centre in Höfn to ask about road conditions, and to find out if any other areas have become newly accessible. Info is also under 'Destinations' on the national park website, www.vjp.is.

➡ Walking paths in the **Hjallanes** and **Heinaberg** area, accessible from Skálafell (p299) guesthouse (or Heinabergjökull can be reached by a rough, 8km road that is unsuited to small 2WDs).

➡ A great walking trail (including new suspension bridge) leads to the **Fláajökull** glacial tongue. The access road is signposted off the Ring Road right by Hólmur guesthouse and travels 8km (gravel but manageable in a 2WD) to a small car park with pit toilet.

➡ From the Hoffell guesthouse, a 4km drive leads to **Hoffellsjökull** glacier tongue, calving into a small lake. The road is rough and at the time of research it wasn't suitable for 2WDs, but there are plans to improve this.

from Höfn and has motel units and guesthouse rooms. Árnanes also has a large family home available in a nearby residential area (with five en-suite bedrooms). There's an agreeable summertime **restaurant** (mains Ikr2500-5500) showcasing the outstanding local produce, and horse-riding tours for all skill levels (open to nonguests).

Fosshótel Vatnajökull HOTEL €€€
(📞478 2555; www.fosshotel.is; r incl breakfast from Ikr33,100; 🌐) In the past year this upmarket chain hotel, 14km northwest of Höfn, has grown from 26 to 66 rooms. The modern timber-and-concrete extension has been smartly done, with blue and grey hues that represent the impressive natural world you can see from the windows. By 2015, the older rooms will have received a makeover too. There's a **restaurant** (dinner mains Ikr4000–6500) on site.

Höfn

POP 1700

Although it's no bigger than many European villages, the southeast's main town feels like a sprawling metropolis after driving through the emptiness on either side. Its setting is stunning; on a clear day, wander down to the waterside, find a quiet bench and just gaze at Vatnajökull and its brotherhood of glaciers.

'Höfn' simply means 'harbour', and is pronounced like an unexpected hiccup (just say 'hup' while inhaling). It's an apt name – this modern town still relies heavily on fishing and fish processing, and is famous for its *humar* (often translated as lobster, but technically it's langoustine).

Bus travellers use Höfn as a transit point, and most travellers stop to use the town's services, so prebook accommodation in summer.

◎ Sights & Activities

Gamlabúð VISITOR CENTRE, MUSEUM
(www.vjp.is; ⊙8am-8pm Jun-Aug, 10am-6pm May & Sep, 10am-noon & 4-6pm Oct-Apr) The 1864 warehouse that once served as the regional folk museum has been moved from the outskirts of town to a prime position on the Höfn harbourfront. It's been refurbished to serve as the town's visitor centre, with good exhibits explaining the marvels of the region's flagship national park (including flora and fauna), plus documentaries being screened.

If you're interested, there are various museum-style exhibitions around town, including a rock collection and an old stockfish shed with displays on fishing and seafaring.

Waterfront
WATERFRONT

There are a couple of short **waterside paths** where you can amble and gape at the views – one by Hótel Höfn, and another round the marshes and lagoons at the end of the promontory Ósland (about 1km beyond the harbour – head for the seamen's monument on the rise). The latter path is great for watching seabirds, though watch out for dive-bombing Arctic terns.

From the seamen's monument, you can follow a **nature trail** that has been set up to model the solar system – it's been 'scaled down 2.1 billion fold', and has its sizes and distances in correct proportion.

Sundlaug Hafnar
SWIMMING POOL, HOT-POT

(Víkurbraut 9; adult/child Ikr600/200; ⊘6.45am-9pm Mon-Fri, 10am-7pm Sat & Sun) The town's popular outdoor swimming pool has waterslides, hot-pots and steam bath.

Silfurnesvöllur
GOLF

(Dalbraut; 9 holes 1/2 people Ikr3500/5000) There's a nine-hole golf course and small clubhouse at the end of Dalbraut at the northern end of town. How often do you get to play under the midnight sun with a view of glaciers? Club hire is Ikr2000.

⚡ Festivals & Events

Humarhátíð
FOOD

Every year in late June or early July, Höfn's annual langoustine festival honours this tasty crustacean, hauled to shore in abundance by the local fishing fleet. There's usually a fun fair, flea markets, dancing, music, ice-sculpture competitions, lots of alcohol and even a few langoustines.

🛏 Sleeping

Here we list accommodation in the town itself, but there are numerous good options (most with in-house dining) along the Ring Road west of town (see p299). Summer rates in this in-demand town are high.

There are also a number of apartments rented out around town – the best place to see what's available is via booking.com.

Höfn Camping & Cottages
CAMPGROUND €

(☑478 1606; www.campsite.is; Hafnarbraut 52; campsites per person Ikr1200, cabins Ikr17,000-22,000; ⊘May–mid-Oct; @⊛) Lots of travellers stay at the campsite on the main road into town, where super-helpful owners and extensive local info are among the draws. There are 11 good-value cabins, sleeping up

to six – some have private toilet, but all use the amenities block for showers. There's also a playground, laundry, and a store selling camping gear.

HI Hostel
HOSTEL €

(☑478 1736; www.hostel.is; Hvannabraut; dm/d without bathroom Ikr4500/11,200; ⊛) Follow the signs from the N1 to find Höfn's sole budget option, hidden away in a residential area and with some primo views. It's a sprawling space (a former aged-care home) that's usually bustling with travellers in summer, with the requisite facilities including laundry and kitchen (but no lounge areas). There's an Ikr700 discount for members; linen is Ikr1650.

★ Guesthouse Dyngja
GUESTHOUSE €€

(☑846 0161; www.dyngja.com; Hafnarbraut 1; d without bathroom incl breakfast from Ikr18,500; @⊛) A lovely young couple have opened this petite five-room guesthouse in a prime harbourfront locale, and filled it with charm and good cheer: rich colours, record player and vinyl selection, self-service breakfast, outdoor deck and good local knowledge. There's a good new addition: a downstairs suite with private bathroom.

Hótel Edda
HOTEL €€

(☑444 4850; www.hoteledda.is; Ránarslóð 3; s/d Ikr24,700/27,200; ⊘mid-May–Sep; @⊛) Under new ownership and with a superb lobby lounge and terrace, the well-located harbourside Edda makes a decent choice. All neat, no-frills rooms have bathroom, some have great glacier views.

Nýibær Guesthouse
GUESTHOUSE €€

(☑478 2670; http://nyibaerguesthouse.wordpress.com; Hafnarbraut 8; d with/without bathroom incl breakfast Ikr26,500/21,500; ⊛) This pretty, cosily decorated guesthouse has no kitchen facilities but puts on a fine breakfast spread. There are eight pricey rooms, including two with private bathroom, and a family room sleeping four. The hand-knitted socks and mittens on sale here are beautiful!

Höfn Inn
HOTEL €€

(☑478 1544; www.hofninn.is; Vesterbraut 3; s/d incl breakfast from Ikr15,000/21,000; ⊛) This modern, offbeat place offers a dozen spacious rooms next door to the N1 on the road into town. There are some quirky touches (pebble floors, quasi-kitsch artworks, bizarre 'hand' chairs) but overall facilities are decent, with bathroom, TV and kettle in each room.

Höfn

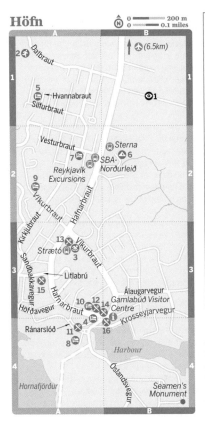

N
0 — 200 m
0 — 0.1 miles

↑ (6.5km)

SOUTHEAST ICELAND HÖFN

Hótel Höfn
HOTEL €€€

(☑478 1240; www.hotelhofn.is; Víkurbraut; d incl breakfast from Ikr28,000; ⚹) Höfn's business-class hotel is often busy with tour groups in summer. Nicely renovated rooms feature safe neutral tones, and views are a knockout – you'll want one with a glacier view (but bear in mind that so does everyone else!). There's also a fresh-faced on-site restaurant, Ósinn (dinner mains Ikr3940-6490), open year-round.

✖ Eating & Drinking

Humar (langoustine, or 'Icelandic lobster') is the speciality on Höfn menus – tails or served whole, grilled with garlic butter is the norm, and prices for main dishes are Ikr6000-plus. If that stretches your budget, you'll find cheaper crustacean-centric options too: bisque, sandwiches, or langoustine-studded pizza or pasta. Mmmm.

Hafnarbúðin
FAST FOOD €

(Ránarslóð; snacks & meals Ikr320-1550; ☺9am-10pm) A fabulous relic, this old-school diner has a cheap-and-cheerful vibe, a menu of grill-bar favourites (burgers, toasted sandwiches, and what may be the cheapest langoustine baguette in town, at Ikr1200). There's even a drive-up window!

Kaffi Nýhöfn
CAFE €€

(www.nyhofn.is; sandwiches Ikr800-2500; ☺10.30am-6.30pm Jun-Aug) This sweet 'Nordic bistro' offers lovely service and an interesting menu of Danish open sandwiches and homebaked cakes. It's in the home that Höfn's first settler built in 1897, and still retains its refined, old-world atmosphere.

Kaffi Hornið
ICELANDIC €€

(☑478 2600; www.kaffihorn.is; Hafnarbraut 42; lunch buffet Ikr2100, mains Ikr1590-7390; ☺11.30am-11pm) This log-cabin affair is an unpretentious bar and restaurant – although the atmosphere is more polished at Humarhöfnin and Pakkhús, the langoustine dishes here are similarly priced. There's a good lunchtime soup-and-salad buffet, and a menu stretching from reindeer burgers to lamb chops. Excellent craft-beer selection.

RIDING ON THE VATNAJÖKULL ICE CAP

Although Vatnajökull ice cap and its attendant glaciers look spectacular from the Ring Road, most travellers will be seized by a wild desire to get closer. However, access to Vatnajökull is limited to commercial tours...unless you happen to be set up for a serious polar-style expedition. The ice cap is riven with deep crevasses, which are made invisible by coverings of fresh snow, and there are often sudden, violent blizzards. But don't be disheartened! You can travel way up into the whiteness on organised snowmobile and super-Jeep tours.

The easiest route up to Vatnajökull is the F985 4WD track (about 35km east of Jökulsárlón, 45km west of Höfn) to the broad glacial spur Skálafellsjökull. The 16km-long road is practically vertical in places, with iced-over sections in winter. Please don't even think of attempting it in a 2WD car – you'll end up with a huge rescue bill.

At the top, 840m above sea level, is Jöklasel, the base for Glacier Jeeps (p299). The **restaurant** (lunch buffets Ikr2900; ⊙ lunch 11.15am-2pm Jun–mid-Sep) at Jöklasel must have the most epic views in Iceland – it's like being on top of the world. (Note: there is no accommodation at Jöklasel.)

From here, the most popular tour option is the awesome one-hour **snowmobile ride**. You get kitted out with overalls, helmets, boots and gloves, then play follow-the-leader along a fixed trail. It's great fun, and although it only gives you the briefest introduction to glacier travel, an hour of noisy bouncing about with the stink of petrol in your nostrils is probably enough for most people! If the skidoo isn't your thing, you can also take a more-sedate super-Jeep ride onto the ice. The company also offers longer skidoo excursions, or glacier hiking.

If you have your own 4WD transport, the snowmobile or super-Jeep options cost Ikr19,500. For Ikr21,000, you get transport to Jöklasel from the Ring Road. Prices are per person, with two people to a skidoo – there's Ikr8500 extra to pay if you want a skidoo to yourself. At 9.30am and 2pm daily from May to October, Glacier Jeeps collects people in a super-Jeep from the parking area at the start of the F985. It's essential to call ahead to reserve a space – a day in advance is usually enough for small parties.

Glacier Jeeps runs its snowmobile and super-Jeep tours in the winter months too – times vary, and tours depart from the company's base at Vagnsstaðir hostel.

There are no scheduled buses that work in with the Glacier Jeeps schedule to drop you at a suitable time at the F985 car park. If you're without your own wheels, consider using the services of Höfn-based **Vatnajökull Travel** (🕿 894 1616; www.vatnajokull.is), which can take you up to Jöklasel and then drive you to Jökulsárlón for a lagoon boat trip. Prices vary according to what you select; contact the company for a quote.

★ **Humarhöfnin** ICELANDIC €€€
(🕿 478 1200; www.humarhofnin.is; Hafnarbraut 4; mains Ikr3900-7900; ⊙ noon-10pm Jun-Aug, 6-10pm Apr, May & Sep) Humarhöfnin offers 'Gastronomy Langoustine' in a cute, cheerfully Frenchified space with superb attention to detail: herb pots on the window sills, roses on every table. Mains centred on pincer-waving little critters cost upwards of Ikr6500, but there are also more budget-friendly dishes including a fine langoustine baguette (Ikr3900).

★ **Pakkhús** ICELANDIC €€€
(🕿 478 2280; www.pakkhus.is; harbourfront; mains Ikr3190-6000; ⊙ noon-10pm May-Sep) Hats off to a menu that tells you the name of the boat that delivers its star produce. In a stylish harbourside warehouse, Pakkhús delivers a level of kitchen creativity you don't often find in rural Iceland. First-class local langoustine, lamb and duck tempt tastebuds, while clever desserts end the meal in style – who can resist a dish called 'skyr volcano'?

Nettó SUPERMARKET
(Miðbær; ⊙ 9am-8pm Mon-Fri, 9am-6pm Sat, noon-6pm Sun Jun-Aug, shorter hours Sep-May) Supermarket with (bakery) in the central Miðbær shopping centre. Stock up – in either direction, it's miles to the next grocery selection!

Vínbúðin LIQUOR STORE
(Miðbær; ⊙ 2-6pm Mon-Thu, 11am-7pm Fri, shorter hours Sep-May) Government-run liquor store.

ⓘ Information

Gamlabúð Visitor Centre (☑ 470 8330; www.
visitvatnajokull.is; ☺ 8am-8pm Jun-Aug, 10am-
6pm May & Sep, 10am-noon & 4-6pm Oct-Apr)
Harbourfront Gamlabúð houses a national park
visitor centre with excellent exhibits, plus local
tourist information. Ask about activities and
hiking trails in the area.

ⓘ Getting There & Away

AIR

Höfn's airport is 6.5km northwest of town. **Eagle
Air** (☑ 562 2640; www.eagleair.is) flies year-round
between Reykjavík and Höfn (one way Ikr28,100).

BUS

Bus companies travelling through Höfn have
different stops (crazy!) so make sure you know
which operator you're travelling with and confirm where they pick up from.

Buses heading from Höfn to Reykjavík stop
at all major towns and landmarks: Jökulsárlón,
Skaftafell, Kirkjubæjarklaustur, Vík, Skógar,
Hvolsvöllur, Hella and Selfoss.

Note that there is no winter bus connection between Egilsstaðir and Höfn (ie bus 62a doesn't
run). These prices are from 2014.

SBA-Norðurleið (☑ 550 0720; www.sba.is)
services (stop at N1 petrol station):
➡ Bus 62a to Egilsstaðir (Ikr8800, five hours,
one daily June to mid-September) Stops at
Djúpivogur, Breiðdalsvík and fjords along Rtes
92 and 96.
➡ Bus 62a to Mývatn (Ikr14,400, 7½ hours, one
daily June to mid-September)
➡ Bus 62a to Akureyri (Ikr17,800, 9¼ hours,
one daily June to mid-September)

Sterna (☑ 551 1166; www.sterna.is) services
(pick up/drop off at campground and hostel):
➡ Bus 12a to Reykjavík (Ikr9900, 10¾ hours,
one daily June to mid-September)

Strætó (☑ 540 2700; www.straeto.is) services
(pick up/drop off out front of the swimming pool):
➡ Bus 51 to Reykjavík (Ikr10,150, seven hours,
two daily June to mid-September, one daily rest
of year)

Reykjavík Excursions (☑ 580 5400; www.
re.is) services (from N1):
➡ Bus 19 to Skaftafell (Ikr5500, 4¼ hours, one daily
mid-June to mid-September) Stops at Jökulsárlón
for 2½ hours. Can be used as a day tour returning to
Höfn (with five hours at Skaftafell, return kr9500).

Höfn to Djúpivogur

The 105km stretch around Iceland's southeast corner, from from Höfn to Djúpivogur,
is another impossibly scenic stretch, the
road curving past only a handful of farms
backed by precipitous peaks.

There are no towns, and aside from the
detour to Viking Cafe (p306), no places for
a coffee (or toilet) break.

Lón

The name Lón (Lagoon; pronounced 'lone')
sums up the nature of this shallow bay enclosed by two long spits between the slightly
spooky mountains Eystrahorn and Vestrahorn (marked on some maps as Austurhorn
and Vesturhorn). To the northwest is the
delta of Jökulsá í Lóni river, where an enormous colony of swans nests in spring and
autumn.

As with other peaks in the region, the
batholithic **Eystrahorn** at the eastern end
of Lón was formed as a subsurface igneous
intrusion, gradually revealed through erosion. This is the best access for strolls on
the sandspit enclosing the eastern portion
of Lón.

At the western end of Lón, the commanding **Vestrahorn** and its companion **Brun-
nhorn** form a cape between Skarðsfjörður
and Papafjörður. Travel down the signposted road to Stokksnes to explore this striking area, known as Horn – the Viking Cafe
(p306) is here, as is a farm-owner charging
for land access.

Stafafell

In the middle of nowhere, Stafafell is a
lonely farm, lost under the mountains. It's
a good hiking base for exploring Lónsöræfi.
The website www.stafafell.is is rich in local
information.

A trio of brothers own the farm: one operates a guesthouse and has a few simple cottages for rent; another runs a basic campsite
in summer. No food is on offer – you need
to bring supplies from Höfn (35km away) or
Djúpivogur (70km).

There are a number of day hikes in the
hills and valleys north of Stafafell. Perhaps
the best day hike is a well-marked, 14.3km
(four- or five-hour) return walk from Stafafell to **Hvannagil**, a colourful rhyolite canyon on the eastern bank of the river Jökulsá
í Lóni. Pick up a route description from the
farmhouse.

Buses between Höfn and Egilsstaðir pass
Stafafell and will stop on request.

WORTH A TRIP

VIKING CAFE

About 7km east of the Höfn turn-off, just before the Ring Road enters a tunnel through the Almannaskarð pass, take the signposted road heading south to Stokksnes radar station. After 4.5km, in a wild setting under moodily gothic Litla Horn mountain, you'll find a cool little outpost: the **Viking Cafe** (www.vikingcafe-iceland.com; ⊘ 9am-7pm Jun–mid-Sep), where coffee, waffles and cake are served.

The farm-owner runs the cafe and charges visitors Ikr600 to explore his incredible property, including a photogenic Viking village filmset and miles of black-sand beaches.

Note that the filmset (built in 2009 by Icelandic film director Baltasar Kormakúr) may finally see action soon, when Baltasar directs *Vikings*, a long-gestating film project he started writing more than a decade ago. The set will hopefully remain in place after its film duties are done.

You can camp in the area (with permission from the farm-owner; per person Ikr1000).

🛏 Sleeping

Stafafell Guesthouse   GUESTHOUSE, COTTAGES €
(☑ 478 1717; www.stafafell.is; r without bathroom per person Ikr3750, cottages Ikr15,000) In a rustic farmhouse by the tiny church, there's a basic guesthouse with kitchen facilities. There are also a couple of self-contained cottages, sleeping four. Prices here exclude linen (available for hire, for Ikr1750 per person).

Lónsöræfi

If you're in Iceland to get in touch with your inner hermit, the remote, rugged nature reserve Lónsöræfi could be on your hit-list. This protected wilderness, inland from Staftafell, contains some colourful rhyolite mountains, and at 320 sq km is one of Iceland's largest conservation areas.

Hiking in this area is challenging and only for experienced hikers (some trails require substantial river crossings). Longer hikes range towards the eastern part of Vatnajökull, and northwest to Snæfell (see p267). You can camp at sites in the reserve, and there are mountain huts along the Snæfell–Lónsöræfi hike, which ends (or begins) at the Illikambur parking area.

The only road into the reserve is the F980, a rough track off the Ring Road that ends after 25km at Illikambur. It's only suitable for super-Jeeps and experienced drivers – there

is a deep, fast-flowing river to cross (small 4WDs will simply not cut it here). Contact **Fallastakkur** (☑ 478 1517; www.fallastakkur.is) if you want hiker transport to/from Lónsöræfi (Ikr10,000 one way, minimum two people).

Although Lónsöræfi isn't part of Vatnajökull National Park, the park's website (www.vjp.is) has details of hiking trails, and the visitor centres at Skaftafell, Höfn and Skríðuklaustur (in the east, covering the Snæfell region of the national park) can advise on options and sell topo maps, which you will certainly require. There is good info (especially on access to the area) on the Stafafell Guesthouse website (www.stafafell.is).

🖒 Tours

Iceguide   ADVENTURE TOUR
(☑ 661 0900; www.iceguide.is) As well as glacier hikes and ice-cave tours, Höfn-based Óskar operates super-Jeep day trips into Lónsöræfi that include a couple of hours' hiking. The price is Ikr21,900 per person (minimum of two people). This is a great option for non-hardcore hikers.

Icelandic Mountain Guides   HIKING TOUR
(IMG; ☑ 587 9999; www.mountainguide.is) IMG offers a five-day, 50km backpacking tour through Lónsöræfi (from Ikr119,000), staying in mountain huts (travelling north to south). It's in its program under the name 'In the Shadow of Vatnajökull'.

The Highlands

Best Natural Wonders

➡ Askja (p316)

➡ Herðubreið (p316)

➡ Hveravellir (p311)

➡ Kverkfjöll (p318)

➡ Drekagil (p316)

➡ Kerlingarfjöll (p311)

Best Places to Take a Dip

➡ Víti (p316)

➡ Hveravellir (p311)

➡ Laugafell (p313)

➡ Kerlingarfjöll (p311)

Why Go?

You may have travelled the Ring Road thinking that Iceland is light on towns; that sheep seem to outnumber people; that you haven't encountered an N1 service station for many a kilometre. Well, you ain't seen nothing yet. In the interior highlands, there are practically no services, accommodation, bridges – or guarantees if something goes wrong.

Gazing across the desolate expanses, you could imagine yourself in the Australian outback, or, as many have noted, on the moon. And those aren't overactive imaginations at work – *Apollo* astronauts trained here before their lunar landing.

This isolation, in essence, is the reason that people visit. Although some travellers are disappointed by the interior's ultra-bleakness, others are humbled by the sight of nature in its rawest form. The solitude is exhilarating, the views are vast, the access is limited (these 4WD-only roads are generally only open in summer's peak, but are served by all-terrain buses), and it's immensely tough but equally rewarding to hike or bike these cross-country routes.

Good to Know

Kjölur route (Rte 35) North–south route across the country. Served by summer buses. No rivers to ford.

Sprengisandur route (Rte F26) North–south route across the country. Served by summer buses.

Öskjuleið (Askja route; Rte F88 or F905/910) Access from Iceland's north to Askja caldera and Herðubreið mountain. Served by numerous tour operators – especially from Mývatn.

Kverkfjöll route (Rte F905, F910, then F902) Access from Iceland's north (or east, via Rte 910) to Kverkfjöll ice caves. Served by a few tour operators.

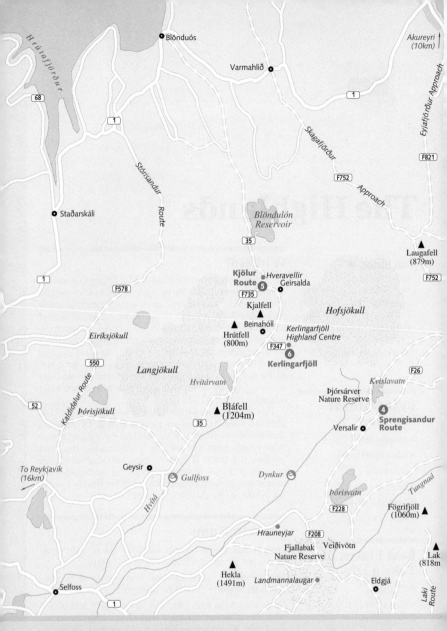

The Highlands Highlights

1 Hike across the lava field at blustery **Askja** (p316), then soak in the tepid waters of Víti crater

2 Marvel at icy sculptures hidden in the geothermal caves at **Kverkfjöll** (p318)

3 Pay homage to the Queen of the Mountains, **Herðubreið** (p316)

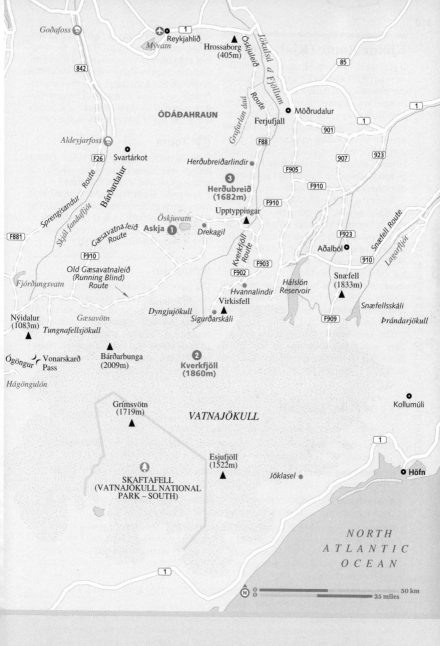

Godafoss
Reykjahlíð
Mývatn
Hrossaborg
(405m)
Öskjuleið
842
Jökulsá á Fjöllum
85
1
ÓDÁÐAHRAUN
Möðrudalur
Grafarlandaá Route
Ferjufjall
901
Aldeyjarfoss
F88
923
F26
Svartárkot
Herðubreiðarlindir
907
F905
Sprengisandur Route
Bárðardalur
Herðubreið
(1682m)
F910
F910
Skjálfandafljót
Öskjuvatn
Upptyppingar
F881
Gæsavatnaleið Route
Askja
Drekagil
Kverkfjöll Route
F923
Aðalból
Snæfell Route
F910
Old Gæsavatnaleið
(Running Blind)
Route
F903
F902
Hálslón
Reservoir
Snæfell
(1833m)
910
Lagarfljót
Fjórðungsvatn
Hvannalindir
Virkisfell
Snæfellsskáli
Nýidalur
(1083m)
Gæsavötn
Dyngjujökull
Sigurðarskáli
F909
Þrándarjökull
Tungnafellsjökull
Ögöngur
Vonarskarð
Pass
Bárðarbunga
(2009m)
Kverkfjöll
(1860m)
Hágöngulón
Grímsvötn
(1719m)
VATNAJÖKULL
Kollumúli
SKAFTAFELL
(VATNAJÖKULL NATIONAL
PARK – SOUTH)
Esjufjöll
(1522m)
Jöklasel
Höfn
1
1
NORTH
ATLANTIC
OCEAN
0   50 km
0   25 miles

4 Pity the melancholy ghosts and outlaws on Iceland's longest, loneliest north–south track, the **Sprengisandur route** (p312)

5 Spice up the endless vistas of desolation with stops at hot springs and climbable crags along the notorious **Kjölur route** (p310)

6 Don hiking boots to investigate the new, improved trails around the majestic massif **Kerlingarfjöll** (p311)

Kjölur Route (Kjalvegur)

If you want to sample Iceland's central deserts but don't like the idea of ford crossings, the 200km Kjölur route has had all its rivers bridged. In summer there are even scheduled daily buses that use it as a 'shortcut' between Reykjavík and Akureyri. The bus may be an appealing option at first; however, while the first hour of outback desolation is riveting, the other nine hours can be snooze-inducing if you aren't planning to disembark anywhere along the way.

From the south, Rte 35 starts just past Gullfoss, passing between two large glaciers before emerging near Blönduós on the northwest coast. It reaches its highest point (around 700m) between the Langjökull and Hofsjökull ice caps, near the mountain Kjalfell (1000m). Its northern section cruises scenically past Blöndulón, a large reservoir used by the Blanda hydroelectric power station. Road conditions in the north are better than those in the south.

The Kjölur route usually opens in mid-June, and closes sometime in September, depending on weather conditions. Note that the route is labelled Rte 35 (not F35); it is still a mountain road, and while it is technically possible to drive a 2WD along the route, it is absolutely not recommended (there are potholes/puddles that could near-swallow a small car, you'll do damage to the car's underside, and your journey will be slow and very bumpy). Car-hire companies expressly forbid the use of 2WD rentals on the route.

☞ Tours

A bit of online digging will reveal hiking, biking and horse-riding tours along the Kjölur route (also search 'Kjalvegur').

Icelandic Mountain Guides (☑ 587 9999; www.mountainguides.is) has excellent highland hiking trips, including a four-day 45km trekking tour along the Kjölur, from Hveravellir to Hvítárvatn (from Ikr130,000).

Hvítárvatn

The pale-blue lake Hvítárvatn, 35km northeast of Gullfoss, is the source of the glacial river Hvítá – a popular destination for Reykjavík-based white-water rafting operators. A glacier tongue of Iceland's second-largest ice cap, Langjökull, calves into the lake and creates icebergs, adding to the beauty of this spot.

ⓘ GETTING AROUND

Before you embark on your highlands journey, take note:

Weather conditions Can be fickle and snow isn't uncommon, even in midsummer. Check www.vedur.is for forecasts.

Road-opening dates Depend on weather conditions, and usually occur any time from early June to early July. Check www.vegagerdin.is.

4WD vehicles Highlands routes are strictly for robust, high-clearance 4WD vehicles, as jagged terrain and treacherous river crossings are not uncommon.

Convoy It's recommended that vehicles travel in pairs, so if one gets bogged or breaks down, the other can drag it out, fetch help or transport passengers to shelter. There is increased traffic in July and August on the most popular routes, so this is not an absolutely necessary precaution during summer, but is recommended if you are heading onto less-travelled tracks.

Fill up before setting out There are no petrol stations in the highlands, except at Hrauneyjar, south of the Sprengisandur route.

Buses and/or tours These make a good alternative to driving yourself. You can use the 4WD summer buses on the Kjölur and Sprengisandur routes as a day tour (travelling between, say, Reykjavík and Akureyri in one burst), or as a regular bus, hopping on and off along the route. Tour operators offer comfortable super-Jeep vehicles and experienced drivers/guides.

No off-road driving In the highlands, as with everywhere in Iceland, stick to roads and marked trails. Off-road driving is hugely destructive to the country's fragile environment, and illegal.

KJÖLUR HIKING

Looking for an independent multiday hike in the area?

Old Kjalvegur route (www.fi.is/en/hiking-trails) An easy and scenic three-day hike (39km) from Hvítárvatn to Hveravellir. The trail follows the original horseback Kjölur route (west of the present road), via the Hvítárnes, Þverbrekknamúli and Þjófadalir mountain huts.

Hringbrautin (www.kerlingarfjoll.is/routes) A challenging three-day circuit (47km) around Kerlingarfjöll, starting and ending at Kerlingarfjöll Highland Centre, with huts at Klakkur and Kisubotnar.

In the marshy grasslands northeast of Hvítárvatn is Ferðafélag Íslands' oldest hut, Hvítárnes, built in 1930. From the Kjölur road, where the bus will drop you, it's an 8km walk along the 4WD track to the hut.

Kerlingarfjöll

Until the 1850s Icelanders believed that this mountain range (10km off Rte 35 on Rte F347) harboured the worst outlaws. It was thought they lived deep in the heart of the 150-sq-km range in an isolated Shangri-la-type valley. So strong was this belief that it was only in the mid-19th century that anyone ventured into Kerlingarfjöll, and it was only in 1941 that the range was properly explored by Ferðafélag Íslands (Iceland Touring Association).

It's certainly dramatic. The colourful landscape is broken up into jagged peaks and ridges, the highest of which is Snækollur (1477m), and it's scattered with hot springs. A stunningly colourful 5km (90-minute) walk leads from the Highland Centre to the geothermal area of Hveradalir. Alternatively, you can drive 15 minutes to a parking area at Mt Keis, from where Hveradalir is a short walk.

At **Kerlingarfjöll Highland Centre** (summer 664 7878, year-round 664 7000; www.kerlingarfjoll.is; sites per person Ikr1550, d with bathroom incl breakfast Ikr29,300; mid-Jun–mid-Sep;) there is a handful of huts and houses, with various bathroom configurations and linen options (sleeping-bag accommodation Ikr4950 to Ikr6500). There's also a campsite, guest kitchen, simple restaurant and natural hot-pots. Check the website for details of local trails. Note: petrol is not available here (despite its symbol still appearing on some maps and signs).

Hveravellir

Hveravellir is a popular geothermal area of fumaroles and hot springs, signposted 30km north of the Kerlingarfjöll turn-off (approximately 90km north of Gullfoss). Among its warm pools are the brilliant-blue Bláhver; Öskurhólshver, which emits a constant stream of hissing steam; and a luscious human-made bathing pool. Another hot spring, Eyvindurhver, is named after the outlaw Fjalla-Eyvindur. Hveravellir is reputedly one of the many highland hideouts of this renegade.

At **Hveravellir** (summer 452 4200, year-round 894 1293; www.hveravellir.is; site/dm per person Ikr1200/4500; mid-Jun–mid-Sep) there are two hikers huts with about 50 beds (linen available for Ikr1400; private room from Ikr8000 per person). There's also a campsite, cooking facilities (only available for hut guests, not campers) and a basic cafe. Staff can help with information on local hiking trails, and activities.

Petrol is no longer available at Hveravellir.

Sleeping

As well as the popular options at Kerlingarfjöll and Hveravellir, two organisations operate huts along the route (BYO sleeping bag). It's necessary to prebook.

Ferðafélag Íslands HUT €
(568 2533; www.fi.is; dm Ikr4500-5000) The following huts have toilets and a kitchen (no utensils though). Huts are listed from south to north: **Hvítárnes** (N 64°37.007', W 19°45.394'; sleeps 30), northeast of Hvítárvatn lake, with a volunteer warden for most of July and August; **Þverbrekknamúli** (N 64°43.100', W 19°36.860'; sleeps 20), about 4km southeast of the mini ice cap Hrútfell; and **Þjófadalir** (N 64°48.900', W 19°42.510'; sleeps 12), at the foot of the mountain Rauðkollur, about 12km southwest of Hveravellir.

Gljásteinn HUT €
(486 8757; www.gljasteinn.is; sites/dm per person Ikr1000/4500; mid-Jun–Aug) Has three

THE HIGHLANDS KJÖLUR ROUTE (KJALVEGUR)

THE BADLANDS

Historically in Iceland, once a person had been convicted of outlawry they were beyond society's protection and aggrieved enemies could kill them at will. Many *útilegumenn* (outlaws), such as the renowned Eiríkur Rauðe (Erik the Red), voluntarily took exile abroad. Others escaped revenge-killing by fleeing into the mountains, valleys and broad expanses of the harsh Icelandic interior, where few dared pursue them.

Undoubtedly, anyone who could live year-round in these bitter, barren deserts must have been extraordinary. Icelandic outlaws were naturally credited with all sorts of fearsome feats, and the general populace came to fear the vast badlands, which they considered to be the haunt of superhuman evil. The *útilegumenn* thereby joined the ranks of giants and trolls, and provided the themes for popular tales such as the fantastic *Grettir's Saga*.

One particular outlaw has become the subject of countless Icelandic folk tales. Fjalla-Eyvindur ('Eyvindur of the Mountains'), a charming but incurable 18th-century kleptomaniac, fled into the highlands with his wife, and continued to make enemies by rustling sheep to stay alive. Throughout the highlands you'll see shelters and hideouts attributed to him and hear tales of his ability to survive in impossible conditions while always staying one jump ahead of his pursuers.

very well-appointed huts on or just off the route. From south to north: **Fremstaver** (N 64°45.207; W 19°93.699'; sleeps 25), on the south slopes of the mountain Bláfell; **Árbúðir** (N 64°609.036; W 19°702.947'; sleeps 30), on the banks of the Svartá river, right on Rte 35 about 42km north of Gullfoss (the Sterna bus service stops here); and **Gíslaskáli** (N 64°744.187; W 19°432.508'; sleeps up to 50), 4km north of the turn-off to Kerlingarfjöll, and 1km off Rte 35.

ℹ Getting There & Away

BICYCLE

Of all the interior routes, Kjölur is probably the best for cycling. For a humorous account, read Tim Moore's *Frost on My Moustache*.

BUS

In summer, scheduled buses travel along the Kjölur route between Reykjavík and Akureyri (in both directions). These services are included in a number of bus passports.

SBA-Norðurleið (☑ 550 0770, 550 0700; www.sba.is) services:
➥ Bus 610 Reykjavík–Akureyri, 610a Akureyri–Reykjavík (1 daily mid-Jun–early Sep) SBA's service takes 10½ hours for the complete journey, with half-hour stops at Geysir and Gullfoss. There's a 15-minute stop at Kerlingarfjöll, and an hour at Hveravellir (time for a dip). The entire journey costs Ikr15,000.

Sterna (☑ 551 1166; www.sterna.is) services:
➥ Bus F35 Reykjavík–Akureyri, F35a Akureyri–Reykjavík (1 daily mid-Jun–early Sep) It's 13 hours to do the full journey – treat it as a day

tour if you like, as it takes in stops along the Golden Circle (including Gullfoss and Geysir) and pauses for 2½ hours at Kerlingarfjöll, 30 minutes at Hveravellir. A ticket for the full journey is Ikr13,900.

CAR

Drivers with 4WD vehicles will have no problems on the Kjölur route. You won't find a car-rental agency that provides insurance to those with plans of taking a 2WD.

Note that if you're in a 2WD and curious for a taste of the highlands, the first 14km of the route (north of Gullfoss) are sealed.

Sprengisandur Route

To Icelanders, the name Sprengisandur conjures up images of outlaws, ghosts and long sheep drives across the barren wastes. The Sprengisandur route (F26) is the longest north–south trail, and crosses bleak desert moors that can induce a shudder even today in a 4WD.

Sprengisandur offers some wonderful views of Vatnajökull, Tungnafellsjökull and Hofsjökull, as well as Askja and Herðubreið from the western perspective. An older route, now abandoned, lies a few kilometres west of the current one.

The Sprengisandur route proper begins at Rte 842 near Goðafoss in northwest Iceland. Some 41km later, you'll pass through a red metal gate as the road turns into F26. There's a poster explaining the sights and finer points of the route, and 3km later you'll happen upon one of Iceland's most photogenic waterfalls, **Aldeyjarfoss**. Churning water bursts over the cliff's edge as it splashes through a narrow canyon lined with the signature honeycomb columns of basalt.

After the falls, the Sprengisandur route continues southwest through 240km of inhospitable territory all the way to Þjórsárdalur. There are two other ways to approach Sprengisandur (see p314), both of which link up to the main road about halfway through.

The route generally opens around the start of July.

Laugafell

The main site of interest on the Skagafjörður approach is Laugafell, an 879m-high mountain with some hot springs bubbling on its northwestern slopes. You can stay nearby at the Ferðafélag Akureyrar **huts** ([✍] Jul-Aug 822 5192; www.ffa.is; N 65°01.614', W 18°19.923'; sites/dm Ikr1200/6000), with 35 beds, a kitchen and a magnificent, geothermally heated, natural swimming pool. There's a warden on-site in July and August. Outside of July and August, contact FFA via its website.

A few tour companies out of Akureryi, including The Traveling Viking (p227), offer 4WD day tours to this area.

Nýidalur

Nýidalur (also known as Jökuldalur), the range just south of the Tungnafellsjökull ice cap, was discovered by a local traveller in 1845. With a campsite, two Ferðafélag Íslands **huts** ([✍] Jul-Aug 860 3334; www.fi.is; N 64°44.130', W 18°04.350'; sites/dm Ikr1200/6500), sleeping up to 120 people, and lots of hiking possibilities, it makes a great break in a Sprengisandur journey. The huts have kitchen facilities (no utensils), showers and a summer warden (July and August).

There are two rivers – the one 500m from the hut may be difficult to cross (even for a 4WD). Ask the warden for advice on conditions.

Þórisvatn

Before water was diverted from Kaldakvísl into Þórisvatn from the Tungnaá hydroelectric scheme in southwest Iceland, it had a surface area of 70 sq km. Now it's one of the country's largest lakes at 85 sq km. It's 11km northeast of the junction between Rte F26 and the Fjallabak route.

Hrauneyjar

Somewhat unexpectedly, in the bleakest position imaginable (west of Þórisvatn in the Hrauneyjar region), you'll find a year-round guesthouse and hotel! They lie at the crossroads of the Sprengisandur route (F26) and the F208 to Landmannalaugar, so are handy for highland attractions and have marked walking trails in the area.

Hrauneyjar Guesthouse ([✍] 487 7782; www. hrauneyjar.is; d with/without bathroom incl breakfast Ikr25,100/18,950; [@][✆]) offers small, basic guesthouse rooms, and an overpriced sleeping-bag option (single/double Ikr10,350/12,800). From mid-June to mid-September there is access to a guest kitchen in the sleeping-bag annexe; there's also a basic restaurant serving lunch and dinner.

If you want luxuries – comfier rooms, bar and smart restaurant, hot-pot and sauna – head for **Hotel Highland** ([✍] 487 7782; www.hotelhighland.is; s/d incl breakfast Ikr35,800/39,500; [@][✆]), under the same owners and 1.4km from the guesthouse. These extra comforts come at a premium.

Petrol and diesel are available at Hrauneyjar Guesthouse. There is sealed road to Hrauneyjar from the west on Rte 32. The guesthouse also cleverly offers 4WDs for rent (a pricey Ikr29,500 for 12 hours), so you can consider some highland exploring from here even if you're touring in a 2WD.

Veiðivötn

This beautiful area just northeast of Landmannalaugar is an entanglement of small desert lakes in a volcanic basin, a continuation of the same fissure that produced Laugahraun in the Fjallabak Nature Reserve. This is a wonderful place for wandering, following 4WD tracks that wind across the tephra sands between the numerous lakes (popular for trout fishing). Access is via Rte F228, east of Hrauneyjar.

❶ Getting There & Away

BUS

In July and August, **Reykjavík Excursions** ([✍] 580 5400; www.re.is) operates two scheduled services along the Sprengisandur route. These services are included in a number of bus passports.

Reykjavík Excursions services:
➜ Bus 14 Landmannalaugar–Mývatn, 14a Mývatn-Landmannalaugar (3 weekly Jul-Aug)

Total journey 10 hours. Although it's a scheduled bus, it's used as a tour of sorts, with extended pauses at Nýidalur, Aldeyjarfoss and Goðafoss. Fare for the entire route is Ikr16,500.

➡ Bus 17 Reykjavík–Mývatn, 17a Mývatn–Reykjavík (3 weekly Jul-Aug) Total journey 11½ hours. Again, although it's a scheduled bus, it's also used as a tour, with breaks at Nýidalur, Aldeyjarfoss and Goðafoss. Fare for the entire route is Ikr20,500.

CAR

There's no fuel along the route. Goðafoss to Hrauneyjar is 240km, so plan accordingly.

The nearest petrol stations are at Akureyri (from the Eyjafjörður approach); Varmahlíð (from the Skagafjörður approach) or Fosshóll, near Goðafoss (if you're coming from the north along the main route through Bárðardalur). There is petrol at Hrauneyjar if you're driving from the south.

Eyjafjörður approach From the north, the F821 from southern Eyjafjörður (south of Akureyri) connects to the Skagafjörður approach at Laugafell.

Skagafjörður approach From the northwest the 81km-long F752 connects southern Skagafjörður (the nearest town is Varmahlíð on the Ring Road) to the Sprengisandur route. The roads join near the lake Fjórðungsvatn, 20km east of Hofsjökull.

Öskjuleið (Askja Route)

The Öskjuleið runs across the highlands to Herðubreið (1682m), the Icelanders' beloved 'Queen of the Mountains', and to the desert's most popular marvel, the immense Askja caldera.

The usual access road is Rte F88, which leaves the Ring Road 32km east of Mývatn at **Hrossaborg**, a 10,000-year-old crater shaped like an amphitheatre, used as a filmset for the Tom Cruise sci-fi film *Oblivion* (2013). Askja is also accessible further east via Rtes F905 and F910 (close to Möðrudalur).

For much of the way the F88 is a flat journey, following the western bank of the Jökulsá á Fjöllum glacier river, meandering across tephra wasteland and winding circuitously through rough, tyre-abusing sections of the 4400-sq-km **Óðáðahraun** (Evil Deeds Lava Field).

After a long journey through the lava- and flood-battered plains, things perk up at the lovely oasis of Herðubreiðarlindir, at the foot of Herðubreið. The route then wanders westwards through dunes and lava flows

past the Dreki huts and up the hill towards Askja, where you leave your car to walk the remaining 2.4km to the caldera.

Askja is part of the vast Vatnajökull National Park, so the park website (www.vjp.is) has excellent information.

✦ Activities

For independent hikers, the website of **Ferðafélag Akureyrar** (FFA, Touring Club of Akureyri; www.ffa.is) outlines details of the **Askja Trail**. This is the organisation's walking trail with huts across the Óðáðahraun, starting from Herðubreiðarlindir and ending at Svartárkot farm in upper Bárðardalur valley (Rte 843). Hut beds must be booked well in advance with FFA; see the website.

Also see the national-park website (www.vjp.is) for hiking information.

For hiker transport in the area, your best best is Mývatn Tours. It can drop you at a hut and arrange to pick you up a few days later.

☞ Tours

Hiking Tours

Ferðafélag Akureyrar   HIKING
(FFA; ☑ 462 2720; www.ffa.is; Strandgata 23, Akureyri) A couple of times a year (usually in July), Ferðafélag Akureyrar organises five-day hut-to-hut hiking tours (Ikr59,600 per person) along the Askja Trail. See 'Touring Program' on its website for details; the program is in Icelandic, so look for 'Öskjuvegur' in July to see specific dates.

Icelandic Mountain Guides   HIKING
(IMG; ☑ 587 9999; www.mountainguides.is) IMG runs guided multiday backpacking hikes in the area, including a five-day, 95km traverse from Mývatn to Askja (from Ikr115,900), or a six-day, 95km trek from Askja to Nýidalur (from Ikr134,000).

Super-Jeep Tours

A number of operators run super-Jeep tours to Askja, from mid-June (when the route opens) until as late into September as weather permits.

From Akureyri it makes for a long day (up to 15 hours); a better base is Reykjahlíð at Mývatn (even then, tour time is around 11 to 12 hours). If you want a more relaxed pace (and a chance to experience highland evening stillness), consider a two-day tour.

For all tours, you are expected to bring/order a packed lunch; some operators (Geo, Saga) stop for a late-afternoon coffee at Möðrudalur en route home. Bring your swimsuit and towel too, should you fancy a dip in Víti crater at Askja.

If you're short on time, scenic flights from Mývatn over Askja are possible via Mývatn Tours.

It's worth noting that with the growth of tourism in recent years, many of these companies are offering more highland exploration, including multiday tours, guided hikes, and 4WD treks to lesser-known natural features. There is also a notable growth in winter tours (in huge, weather-defying super-Jeep vehicles). These guys will all be at the ready when tourism opens up to the Bárðarbunga volcanic area after the 2014 eruptions. See websites for latest prices and offerings.

Fjalladýrð
JEEP TOUR

(✆471 1858; www.fjalladyrd.is) Based at Möðrudalur farm on Rte 901 – perfectly placed for Askja access via F905 and F910. Has excellent accommodation and eating options right at its departure point. Tours to Askja cost Ikr29,800. Also offers day trips climbing Herðubreið (Ikr31,000) or visiting Kverkfjöll ice caves (Ikr31,000), and two-day trips taking in Askja, Kverkfjöll and Vatnajökull (Ikr65,800).

Fjallasýn
JEEP TOUR

(✆464 3941; www.fjallasyn.is) Scheduled daily bus tours from Reykjahlíð (from Ikr19,000), but also offers super-Jeep tours (from Ikr29,000); check the website for the difference in these offerings. Also offers plenty of interior explorations (including a two-day tour to Kverkfjöll upon request) and guided hiking options. Can depart from the company's base in Húsavík.

Geo Travel
JEEP TOUR

(✆864 7080; www.geotravel.is) Small-group tours from Reykjahlíð (Ikr27,500). Works with Fjallasýn to offer a two-day tour to Askja and Kverkfjöll (Ikr78,000).

Jeep Tours
JEEP TOUR

(✆898 2798; www.jeeptours.is) While the rest of these companies approach Askja from the north, Jeep Tours runs unique tours out of Egilsstaðir in east Iceland. Visit Askja (Ikr39,000), or Kverkfjöll as a day tour (Ikr39,000). Tours travel via the (sealed) Rte 910 to Kárahnjúkar dam before tackling lesser-known 4WD tracks. Lunch packs available.

LUNAR LANDSCAPES

If the endless grey-sand desert and jagged lava formations of Ódáðahraun appear otherworldly, you'll understand why NASA astronauts of the *Apollo* mission twice visited the area around Askja (more specifically, the area south of the F910 east of Askja) for astrogeological field trips in the 1960s.

Mývatn Tours
BUS TOUR

(✆464 1920; www.askjatours.is) Tours in a large 4WD bus daily July to August (Ikr21,000), and three or four times a week the rest of the summer (while roads are open). This is the best option if you want hikers' transport to the area, and to be picked up another day.

Saga Travel
JEEP TOUR

(✆558 888; www.sagatravel.is) Very reliable option from Akureyri; also picks up in Mývatn (Ikr45,000/38,000 from Akureyri/Mývatn). Saga also offers a slower-paced two-day trip, overnighting in either a mountain hut or campsite (price is variable).

SBA-Norðurleið
BUS TOUR

(✆550 0700; www.sba.is) Runs a popular three-day Askja–Kverkfjöll–Vatnajökull tour, weekly from July to mid-/late August. It departs from Akureyri and picks up in Mývatn. Cost is Ikr42,900, which includes transport and guide (but not food or accommodation).

Herðubreiðarlindir

The oasis Herðubreiðarlindir, a nature reserve thick with green moss, angelica and the pinky-purple flower of the Arctic river beauty (*Epilobium latifolium*), was created by springs flowing from beneath the Ódáðahraun lava. You get a superb close-up view of Herðubreið from here (unless, of course, you're greeted by dense fog and/or a wall of blowing sand).

The mini tourist complex has an information office staffed by summer wardens, a campsite and the 30-bed Þorsteinsskáli hut (✆822 5191; www.ffa.is; N 65°11.544', W 16°13.360'; sites/dm Ikr1200/6000), a comfy lodge with showers and kitchen.

Behind the hut is another Fjalla-Eyvindur 'convict hole': Eyvindur is believed to have occupied it during the winter of 1774–75, when he subsisted on angelica root and raw horsemeat stored on top of the hideout to retain heat inside.

Herðubreið

Iceland's most distinctive mountain (1682m) has been described as a birthday cake and a lampshade, but Icelanders call it (more respectfully) the 'Queen of the Mountains'. It crops up time and again in the work of local poets and painters, entranced by its beauty.

If Herðubreið (meaning 'broad shoulders') appears to have been made in a jelly mould, that's not far off base. It's a *móberg* mountain, formed by subglacial volcanic eruptions. In fact, if Vatnajökull was to suddenly be stripped of ice, Grímsvötn and Kverkfjöll would probably emerge looking more or less like Herðubreið.

If you wish to climb Herðubreið, beware that a topographic sheet won't do you any good here. As serenely beautiful as the queen may be, the hike can be unrelenting and frustrating if you are not properly prepared. In the spring, as the weather warms slightly, there are a lot of falling rocks, which can alter paths and topography. Clouds often shroud the mountain, which makes it difficult to find your way. A GPS is a must, as is a helmet, plus crampons and an ice axe (and experience in using them).

From the Þorsteinsskáli hut, a marked trail runs to Herðubreið and you can then hike all the way around it in a day. Herðubreið was once thought to be unclimbable, but it was eventually scaled in 1908. Under optimum conditions you can climb the mountain in summer over one long day. The route to the top ascends the western slope. We don't want you to get the wrong idea, however; this climb is demanding, and the threat of snow, rockfall, landslide or bad weather makes it impossible to tackle without the proper mountaineering gear. Don't go alone, prepare for foul weather, and it is imperative you discuss your intentions with the wardens at Herðubreiðarlindir. Consider joining a tour – Fjalladýrð (p315) and Fjallasýn (p315) can arrange this.

Drekagil

The name of the gorge Drekagil, 35km southwest of Herðubreið, means 'Dragon Canyon', after the form of a dragon in the craggy rock formations that tower over it. The canyon (behind the Ferðafélag Akureyrar Dreki huts) resembles something out of Arizona or the Sinai; bitter winds and freezing temperatures just don't suit this desert landscape!

The **Dreki huts** (Askja Camp; ☑ 822 5190; www.ffa.is; N 65°02.503', W 16°35.690'; sites/dm per person Ikr1200/6500; ☺ mid-/late Jun–early Sep) are an ideal base for a day or two of exploring the area. Not only does the dramatic Drekagil ravine offer an easy stroll up to an impressive waterfall, but you can also walk 8km up the marked trail to Askja. There is also a marked 20km trail to the Bræðrafell hut. The Dreki huts sleep a total of 60, and there are showers, a kitchen, an information centre and a summertime warden. Camping is also permitted, but the wind and cold may become oppressive.

Free, ranger-led, one-hour hikes leave from the Askja car park at 1pm daily mid-July to mid-August.

At Dreki the Gæsavatnaleið route (F910) turns off the Öskjuleið to cross some intimidating expanses and connect with the Sprengisandur route at Nýidalur, some 125km away. This involves a number of river crossings and is only for large vehicles.

Askja

The utterly desolate Askja caldera is the main destination for all tours in this part of the highlands. This immense 50-sq-km caldera shouldn't be missed – and it's an easy 2.4km walk from the car-park area. As you approach, you'll find it difficult to imagine the sorts of forces that created it.

The cataclysm that formed the lake in the Askja caldera (and the Víti crater) happened relatively recently (in 1875) when 2 cu km of tephra was ejected from the Askja volcano. The force was so strong that bits of debris actually landed in Continental Europe. Ash from the eruption poisoned large numbers of cattle in northern Iceland, sparking a wave of emigration to America. It's quite daunting to realise that such cataclysmic events could be replayed at any time.

After the initial eruption, a magma chamber collapsed and created a craterous 11-sq-km hole, 300m below the rim of the original explosion crater. This new depression subsequently filled with water and became the sapphire blue lake **Öskjuvatn**, the second-deepest in Iceland at 220m.

In 1907 German researchers Max Rudloff and Walther von Knebel were rowing on the lake when they completely vanished; their bodies were never found. It was suggested that the lake may have hazardous quirks, possibly odd currents or whirlpools; but a rickety canvas boat and icy water could easi-

BÁRÐARBUNGA VOLCANO

On 16 August 2014, sensors began picking up increased seismic activity in and around Bárðarbunga, one of many volcanoes that lie underneath Vatnajökull ice cap. This immense volcano system is under the northwest part of the ice cap.

The magma in the Bárðarbunga caldera formed an 'intrusive dike' (tunnel of magma) through the ground under an outlet glacier named Dyngjujökull. On 29 August, a fissure eruption, complete with spectacular lava fountains, began in Holuhraun, a 200-year-old lava field about 5km away from the Dyngjujökull glacial edge.

Scientists have been monitoring developments, preparing for various scenarios. They've observed that the Bárðarbunga caldera is sinking, with a depression forming in the ice above it. This indicates that an eruption may occur under Vatnajökull.

Scientists believe there are a few options for how the Bárðarbunga activity will play out. The subsidence of the caldera may stop and the Holuhraun eruption decline gradually. Or, the Holuhraun eruption may be prolonged or strengthened, and lengthen southwards under Dyngjujökull. Bárðarbunga itself may erupt, or other eruptive fissures (like the one at Holuhraun) could open up.

Any eruptions that occur under ice present danger of glacier melt (causing destructive *jökulhlaup*, or meltwater floods), and a likelihood of ashcloud – potentially along the lines of the Eyjafjallajökull eruption of 2010, which grounded air traffic in Europe for six days (and tripped up newsreaders around the world).

There is no way of knowing what developments may occur, or when this activity will subside. And can you visit? At the time of writing, the only option was to see the eruption from the air. The Holuhraun fissure eruption is occurring in a remote, uninhabited region (south of Askja), with the only immediate dangers as a result of the sulphuric gases being released and causing some nasty pollution in varying parts of the country (depending on prevailing winds). But, the possibility of further eruptions and flooding mean that certain parts of the highlands are off-limits to all. Roads are closed (these are remote, 4WD-access roads).

If and when the area is deemed safe for visitors, there will no doubt be tour operators ready to take tourists to (and charge them handsomely!).

The tour operators that service Askja and Kverkfjöll from Mývatn, Möðrudalur and Egilsstaðir (listed on p314) will be best placed to offer such tours, but be aware that this is a remote area, with tough access, so be prepared to cough up!

In the meantime, keep up to date on Bárðarbunga (and any other volcanic activity that may arise) via various websites: the Icelandic Meteorological Office (www.vedur.is) and the Icelandic National Broadcasting Service (www.ruv.is) are good places to start.

THE HIGHLANDS ÖSKJULEIÐ (ASKJA ROUTE)

ly explain their deaths. There's a stone cairn and memorial to the men on the rim of the caldera.

In the 1875 eruption a vent near the northeastern corner of the lake exploded and formed the tephra crater Víti, which contains geothermal water. This is one of two well-known craters called Víti, the other being at Krafla near Mývatn. (FYI: Víti means 'hell' in Icelandic.)

Although a bit on the chilly side if you're expecting a soothing swim (temperatures range between 22°C and 30°C), a dip in Víti's milky blue pool is one of the highlights of an Askja adventure (and is sometimes done sans swimsuit). The route down is slippery but not as steep as it looks; it may be closed for safety reasons by park officials.

❶ Getting There & Away

There's no public transport along the Öskjuleið, but there are plentiful tours (see p314). Alternatively, hire a large 4WD and prepare for a rocky ride (seek advice on fording rivers; see p370). The route usually opens in mid- to late June.

If you take F88 into Askja, it's a good idea to leave along F910 so you don't have to retrace all of your steps. Other options from Askja include heading east towards Egilsstaðir, or west on the Gæsavatnaleið route (F910) to Sprengisandur (ask locally for advice on conditions). To reach Kverkfjöll ice caves, head east on F910, then south on F902.

There are no petrol stations anywhere on the route. The nearest ones are at Möðrudalur (90km from Askja) and Mývatn (130km north of Askja).

Kverkfjöll Route

As its name suggests, this 108km-long route creeps southwards to the Kverkfjöll ice caves. It connects Möðrudalur (70km east of Mývatn, off the Ring Road) with the Sigurðarskáli hut, 3km from the lower caves, via the F905, F910 and F902. After visiting Askja, you can follow up with a trip to Kverkfjöll by driving south along the F902.

Along the way are several sites of interest, including the twin pyramid-shaped **Upptyppingar hills** near the Jökulsá á Fjöllum bridge, and the **Hvannalindir** oasis where there is yet another of good ol' Fjalla-Eyvindur's winter hideouts. Hvannalindir lies about 20km north of the Sigurðarskáli hut.

Kverkfjöll is actually a mountain spur capped by the ice of Kverkjökull, a northern tongue of Vatnajökull. Over time, it's also come to refer to the hot-spring-filled ice caves that often form beneath the eastern margin of the Dyngjujökull ice.

Besides being the source of the roiling Jökulsá á Fjöllum, central Iceland's greatest river, Kverkfjöll is also one of the world's largest geothermal areas. The lower **Kverkfjöll ice caves** lie 3km from the Sigurðarskáli hut; they're about a 15-minute walk from the 4WD track's end.

Here the hot river flows beneath the cold glacier ice, clouds of steam swirl over the river and melt shimmering patterns on the ice walls, and there you have it – a spectacular tourist attraction. Perhaps this was the source of the overworked fire-and-ice cliché that pervades almost everything ever written about Iceland.

Large blocks of ice frequently crash down from the roof – don't enter the ice caves or you risk being caught in their heated combat. Also, the giant blocks of ice can alter the entrance to the cave – it's best to ask where the safest access point is currently located (there's only one point of entry, and it's not an issue if you are on a tour). There can be a danger of sulphur inhalation further inside the cave. From the lower ice caves, ranger-led tours continue up onto the glacier itself.

The large **Sigurðarskáli hut** (Kverkfjöll Hut; ☑ summer 863 9236, year-round 863 5813; www.fljotsdalsherad.is/ferdafelag; N 64°44.850',

W 16°37.890'; sites/dm per person Ikr1300/6000; ☉ mid-Jun–early Sep) has comfortable accommodation and a well-maintained campsite. A 2km-return marked hike from behind the hut takes you up **Virkisfell** (1109m) for a spectacular view over Kverkfjöll and the headwaters of the Jökulsá á Fjöllum.

The road to Kverkfjöll usually opens around mid- to late June. It's good to get to Kverkfjöll early in the season because there's a higher chance of accessing the caves (warmer weather = tumbling ice blocks and bouts of glacial melting). Ask the ranger first about cave conditions and for recommendations for a successful exploration of the area; consider joining a tour to take advantage of ranger expertise.

Kverkfjöll is part of the vast Vatnajökull National Park, so the park website (www.vjp. is) has information.

☞ Tours

Without a robust 4WD vehicle, the only way to visit Kverkfjöll is on a tour. If you do have your own vehicle you can park and walk up to the ice caves – anywhere further is strictly ill-advised.

As well as short walks in the area, the park rangers offer guided hikes in good weather: four hours onto the glacier (Ikr7500), or nine hours to the geothermal area (Ikr13,500); prices include equipment. Call ☑ 863 9236 (in summer) for tour details.

Besides the ranger-led tours, there are tour packages involving transport and guiding. Note that Fjallasýn (p315) has hiking tours in the area, Jeep Tours (p315) offers a day trip here from Egilsstaðir, and Fjalladyrð (p315) has two-day tours from Möðrudalur.

Another option to consider is the popular three-day Askja–Kverkfjöll–Vatnajökull tour run by bus company **SBA-Norðurleið** (☑ 550 0700; www.sba.is). It leaves on Mondays from July to mid-/late August from Akureyri (8.15am) and Mývatn (10am). The cost is Ikr42,900, which includes transport and guide. You must bring your own food and organise your own accommodation (either book Sigurðarskáli hut or bring a tent).

❶ Getting There & Away

Drivers note: the petrol station at Möðrudalur is the last place to fill up.

Understand Iceland

Iceland Today

A decade or two back, Iceland began to carve itself a niche in the collective global conscience thanks to quirky musicians achieving unexpected international success. Then it really hit the headlines, with a collapsed banking system in 2008 and an unpronounceable, plane-grounding volcanic eruption in 2010. But these events have proved that there's no such thing as bad publicity: all that free exposure put Iceland's charms under the spotlight, and tourism has boomed.

Best on Film

101 Reykjavík (2000) Dark comedy exploring sex, drugs and the life of a loafer in downtown Reykjavík.
Jar City (2006) Carefully crafted detective thriller based on the novel by Arnaldur Indriðason.
Heima (2007) Follow Sigur Rós as they perform throughout Iceland.
The Secret Life of Walter Mitty (2013) Iceland's landscapes take centre stage (as Iceland, Greenland and the Himalaya).
Of Horses and Men (2013) A surreal portrait of the intertwining lives of men and horses.

Best in Print

The Draining Lake (Arnaldur Indriðason; 2004) One of many engrossing tales from a master of Nordic Noir.
Independent People (Halldór Laxness; 1934–35) Bleak tragi-comedy from the Nobel Laureate.
The Sagas of Islanders (Jane Smiley et al; 2001) Excellent, readable translations of Iceland's epic, often brutal tales.
Devil's Island (Einar Kárason; 1983) American culture clashes with rural tradition in postwar Reykjavík.
Burial Rites (Hannah Kent; 2012) Haunting novel based on the true story of the last public execution in Iceland.

Tourism: the 'New Klondike'?

Earth-rending eruptions are par for the course in Iceland, so the international attention garnered by Eyjafjallajökull's ash-filled outburst was truly unusual to the local population. The Iceland tourism board quickly capitalised on the event by launching its 'Inspired By Iceland' campaign, and the push for more tourists became a smash hit – frustrations from the continent transformed into curiosity, and travellers started arriving. Word quickly spread: Iceland's natural beauty is astounding and its people welcoming (the world's *most* welcoming, according to the World Economic Forum ranking in 2013, in a report that examined 140 countries based on travel and tourism competitiveness).

And so began the 'new Klondike', as some locals have described it: the boom in businesses catering to the boom in tourists. Iceland has been registering record-breaking tourist numbers: it hosted around 1 million international visitors in 2014 (up from 489,000 in 2010), with no signs of a slow-down – especially if the country's volcanoes continue to provide spectacles that capture media and traveller attention (case in point: 2014's Bárðarbunga eruption). Winter visitor numbers are also spiking, with every traveller's bucket list now seemingly topped by 'see Northern Lights'.

The Good with the Bad

There's little escape from the tourist rush in the peak of summer, especially in Reykjavík and the south (where most visitors spend time). Locals are generally welcoming – to a point. When polled, Icelanders acknowledge the economic recovery tourism has stimulated, and the job opportunities created. They appreciate many of the services that have grown to cater to the increased traffic (more great music festivals, for example, and more restaurants and nightlife). Many locals admit that foreign traveller curiosity has piqued their own interest in Icelandic nature and culture.

But Icelanders are also voicing valid concerns: that the population of 325,000 (and its existing infrastructure) is ill-equipped to handle the demands of one-million-plus visitors. Stories are rife of Reykjavík landlords evicting tenants so they can turn their properties into guesthouses or list their apartments on Airbnb. The media hones in on instances of tourists deliberately disrespecting nature (off-road driving is the perfect way to madden Icelanders, as is not following swimming-pool etiquette) or taking dangerous risks out of ignorance (such as hiking in poor weather without proper equipment or getting vehicles stuck in rivers).

Protecting the Goose that Lays the Golden Egg

An important debate is taking place about whether Iceland's fragile environment can withstand the pressure it's now under. The country's unspoilt natural landscape is cited by 80% of tourists as a factor influencing their decision to visit. But how much tourism can Iceland's waterfalls, hiking trails and lava fields sustain, and how can they be adequately protected while still giving travellers the experience they expect?

This extends to bigger questions about the future of the tourism industry. If figures continue to grow at the current rate, Iceland could be hosting 2 million visitors in 2020. While it's near-impossible to be disappointed by the country's magnificent landscapes, how can invested locals ensure that traveller satisfaction extends to other areas? What about the new experience of heavy crowds at some sites, or the lack of public toilets in some tourist areas? What about the road network, accommodation quality, or overall value for money (a common gripe, especially with prices rising each season)? How can travellers be educated to minimise their impact? And, perhaps most importantly, how can Icelanders avoid becoming marginalised in their own country?

An Energetic Future

Tourism now exceeds fishing as Iceland's dominant industry, and has helped Iceland bounce back from its banking crisis. But to ensure that prosperity continues, even if the tourism boom comes to a crashing halt, Iceland is shoring up its position as a green-energy superpower, looking to export its know-how (and quite possibly its actual energy, transmitted via undersea cables) to foreign shores. It's wooing more big-business energy users, to try to convince them to set up shop (large aluminium smelters are already here for the cheap, abundant power). Public and private enterprises are exploring the options for producing 'green fuels' such as biomethane and biodiesel. Iceland as a 'green Saudi Arabia'? Anything is possible.

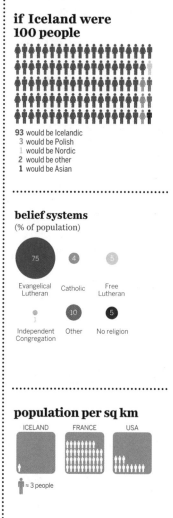

POPULATION: **325,671**

AREA: **103,000 SQ KM**

TOURISTS: **807,300 (2013)**

ELECTRICITY PRODUCTION FROM RENEWABLES: **100%**

GDP GROWTH: **3.5%**

SHEEP: **476,000**

if Iceland were 100 people

93 would be Icelandic
3 would be Polish
1 would be Nordic
2 would be other
1 would be Asian

belief systems
(% of population)

75 Evangelical Lutheran
4 Catholic
5 Free Lutheran
1 Independent Congregation
10 Other
5 No religion

population per sq km

ICELAND   FRANCE   USA

≈ 3 people

History

Geologically young, staunchly independent and frequently rocked by natural (and more recently financial) disaster, Iceland has a turbulent and absorbing history of Norse settlement, literary genius, bitter feuding and foreign oppression. Life in this harsh and unforgiving landscape was never going to be easy, but the everyday challenges and hardships have cultivated a modern Icelandic spirit that's highly aware of its stormy past, yet remarkably resilient, fiercely individualistic, quietly innovative and justifiably proud.

Early Travellers & Irish Monks

History of Iceland, by Jon R Hjalmarsson, is an absorbing account of the nation, from time of settlement to the book's publication in the 1990s.

A veritable baby in geological terms, Iceland was created around 20 million years ago. It was only around 330 BC, when the Greek explorer Pytheas wrote about the island of Ultima Thule, six days north of Britain by ship, that Europe became aware of a landmass beyond the confines of their maps, lurking in a 'congealed sea'.

For many years rumour, myth and fantastic tales of fierce storms, howling winds and barbaric dog-headed people kept explorers away from the great northern ocean, *oceanus innavigabilis*. Irish monks were the next to stumble upon Iceland: they regularly sailed to the Faroe Islands looking for solitude and seclusion. It's thought that Irish *papar* (fathers) settled in Iceland around the year 700. The Irish monk Dicuil wrote in AD 825 of a land where there was no daylight in winter, but on summer nights 'whatever task a man wishes to perform, even picking lice from his shirt, he can manage as well as in clear daylight'. This almost certainly describes Iceland and its long summer nights. The *paper* fled when the Norsemen began to arrive in the early 9th century.

The Vikings Are Coming!

After the Irish monks, Iceland's first permanent settlers came from Norway. The Age of Settlement is traditionally defined as the period between 870 and 930, when political strife on the Scandinavian mainland caused many to flee. Most North Atlantic Norse settlers were ordinary Scandinavian citizens: farmers, herders and merchants who settled right across Western Europe, marrying Britons, Westmen (Irish) and Scots.

TIMELINE	AD 600–700	850–930	871
	Irish monks voyage to uninhabited Iceland, becoming the first (temporary) settlers. There is little archaeological evidence, although the element 'papar' (fathers) crops up in certain place names.	Norse settlers from Norway and Sweden arrive, call the island Snæland (Snow Land), then Garðarshólmi (Garðar's Island), and finally Ísland (Iceland). Scattered farmsteads rapidly cover the country.	Norwegian Viking Ingólfur Arnarson, credited as the country's first permanent inhabitant, sails to the southwest coast; in time he makes his home in a promising-looking bay that he names Reykjavík.

It's likely that the Norse accidentally discovered Iceland after being blown off course en route to the Faroe Islands. The first arrival, Naddoddr, sailed from Norway and landed on the east coast around 850. He named the place Snæland (Snow Land) before backtracking to his original destination.

Iceland's second visitor, Garðar Svavarsson, circumnavigated the island and then settled in for the winter at Húsavík on the north coast. When he left in the spring some of his crew remained, or were left behind, thereby becoming the island's first residents.

Around 860 the Norwegian Flóki Vilgerðarson uprooted his farm and family and headed for Snæland. He navigated with ravens, which, after some trial and error, led him to his destination and provided his nickname, Hrafna-Flóki (Raven-Flóki). Hrafna-Flóki sailed to Vatnsfjörður on the west coast but became disenchanted after seeing icebergs floating in the fjord. He renamed the country Ísland (Iceland), and returned to Norway; although he did eventually come back to Iceland, settling in the Skagafjörður district on the north coast.

Credit for the first intentional settlement, according to the 12th-century *Íslendingabók,* goes to Ingólfur Arnarson, who fled Norway with his blood brother Hjörleifur. He landed at Ingólfshöfði (southeast Iceland) in 871, then continued around the coast and set up house at a place he called Reykjavík (Smoky Bay), named after the steam from thermal springs there. Hjörleifur settled near the present town of Vík, but was murdered by his slaves shortly after.

As for Ingólfur, he was led to Reykjavík by a fascinating pagan ritual. It was traditional for Viking settlers to toss their high-seat pillars (a symbol of authority and part of a chieftain's paraphernalia) into the sea as they approached land. The settler's new home was established wherever the gods brought the pillars ashore – a practice imitated by waves of settlers who followed from the Norwegian mainland.

Assembling the Alþing

By the time Ingólfur's son Þorsteinn reached adulthood, the whole island was scattered with farms, and people began to feel the need for some sort of government. Iceland's landowners gathered first at regional assemblies to trade and settle disputes, but it became apparent that a national assembly was needed. This was a completely novel idea at the time, but Icelanders reasoned that it must be an improvement on the oppressive system they had experienced under the Nordic monarchy.

In the early 10th century Þorsteinn Ingólfsson held Iceland's first large-scale district assembly near Reykjavík, and in the 920s the self-styled lawyer Úlfljótur was sent to study Norway's law codes and prepare something similar that would be suitable for Iceland.

Where to Find Viking Vibes

National Museum, Reykjavík

Reykjavík 871 +/-2 museum, Reykjavík

Þingvellir National Park, near Selfoss

Víkingaheimar, Njarðvík

Eiríksstaðir (reconstruction), Dalir

Stöng farmstead, Þjórsárdalur

Njál's Saga sites, Hvolsvöllur

HISTORY ASSEMBLING THE ALÞING

The word Viking is derived from *vík*, which means bay or cove in Old Norse and probably referred to Viking anchorages during raids.

930	986	1000	1100–1200
The world's oldest existing parliament, the Alþing, is founded at Þingvellir. The Icelanders' law code is memorised by an elected law speaker, who helps to settle legal matters at annual parliamentary gatherings.	Erik the Red founds the first permanent European colony in Greenland, building the settlements of Eystribyggð and Vestribyggð in the southwest of the country.	Iceland officially converts to Christianity under pressure from the Norwegian king, though pagan beliefs and rituals remain. Leif the Lucky lands in Newfoundland, becoming the first European to reach America.	Iceland's literary Golden Age, during which the Old Norse sagas are written. Several are attributed to Snorri Sturluson – historian, poet and the sharpest political operator of this era.

At the same time Grímur Geitskör was commissioned to find a location for the Alþing (National Assembly). Bláskógar, near the eastern boundary of Ingólfur's estate, with its beautiful lake and wooded plain, seemed ideal. Along one side of the plain was a long cliff with an elevated base (the Mid-Atlantic Ridge), from where speakers and representatives could preside over people gathered below.

In 930 Bláskógar was renamed Þingvellir (Assembly Plains). Þorsteinn Ingólfsson was given the honorary title *allsherjargoði* (supreme chieftain) and Úlfljótur was designated the first *lögsögumaður* (law speaker), who was required to memorise and annually recite the entire law of the land. It was he, along with the 48 *goðar* (chieftains), who held the actual legislative power.

THE VIKINGS

Scandinavia's greatest impact on world history probably occurred during the Viking Age. In the 8th century, an increase in the numbers of restless, landless young men in western Norway coincided with advances in technology, as Nordic shipbuilders developed fast, manoeuvrable boats sturdy enough for ocean crossings.

Norwegian farmers had settled peacefully in Orkney and the Shetlands as early as the 780s, but the Viking Age officially began in bloodshed in 793, when Norsemen plundered St Cuthbert's monastery on Lindisfarne, an island off Britain's Northumberland coast.

The Vikings took to monasteries with delight, realising that speedy raids could bring handsome rewards. They destroyed Christian communities and slaughtered the monks of Britain and Ireland, who could only wonder what sin they had committed to invite the heathen hordes. However, the Vikings' barbarism was probably no greater than the standard of the day – the suddenness and extent of the raids led to their fearsome reputation.

In the following years Viking raiders returned with great fleets, terrorising, murdering, enslaving and displacing local populations, and capturing whole regions across Britain, Ireland, France and Russia. They travelled to Moorish Spain and the Middle East, attacking Constantinople six times, and even served as mercenaries for the Holy Roman Empire.

Icelandic tradition credits the Norse settlement of Iceland to tyrannical Harald Hårfagre (Harald Fairhair), king of Vestfold in southeastern Norway. Filled with expansionist aspirations, Harald won a significant naval victory at Hafrsfjord (Stavanger) in 890. The deposed chieftains chose to flee rather than surrender, and many wound up in Iceland.

While Viking raids continued in Europe, Eiríkur Rauðe (Erik the Red) headed west with around 500 others to found the first permanent European colony in Greenland in 986. Eiríkur's son, Leif the Lucky, went on to explore the coastline of northeast America in the year 1000, naming the new country Vínland (Wineland). Permanent settlement was thwarted by the *skrælings* (Native Americans), who were anything but welcoming.

Viking raids gradually petered out, and the Viking Age ended with the death of King Harald Harðráði, last of the great Viking kings, who died in battle at Stamford Bridge, England, in 1066.

1104	1200	1241	1397
Hekla's first eruption in historical times. The volcano covers Þjórsárdalur valley and its prosperous medieval farms with a thick layer of ash, rock and cinders.	Iceland descends into anarchy during the Sturlung Age. The government dissolves and, in 1281, Iceland is absorbed by Norway.	Seventy armed men arrive at Snorri Sturluson's home in Reykholt, ordered to bring him to Norway to face treason charges. Snorri never leaves – he is stabbed to death in his cellar.	On 17 June the Kalmar Union is signed in Sweden, uniting the countries of Norway, Sweden and Denmark under one king. As part of this treaty, Iceland comes under Danish control.

Although squabbles arose over the choice of leaders and allegiances were continually questioned, the new parliamentary system was a success. At the annual convention of the year 1000, the assembled crowd was bitterly divided between pagans and Christians, and civil war looked likely. Luckily, Þorgeir, the incumbent law speaker, was a master of tact. The *Íslendingabók* relates that he retired to his booth, refusing to speak to anyone for a day and a night while he pondered the matter. When he emerged, he decreed that Iceland should accept the new religion and convert to Christianity, although pagans (such as himself) were to be allowed to practise their religion in private. This decision gave the formerly divided groups a semblance of national unity, and soon the first bishoprics were set up at Skálholt in the southwest and Hólar in the north.

Over the following years, the two-week national assembly at Þingvellir became the social event of the year. All free men could attend. Single people came looking for partners, marriages were contracted and solemnised, business deals were finalised, duels and executions were held, and the Appeals Court handed down judgements on matters that couldn't be resolved in lower courts.

Iceland's 1100 Years: The History of a Marginal Society, by Gunnar Karlsson, provides an insightful, contemporary history of Iceland from settlement onwards.

Anarchy & the Sturlung Age

The late 12th century kicked off the Saga Age, when epic tales of early settlement, family struggles, romance and tragic characters were recorded by historians and writers. Much of our knowledge of this time comes from two weighty tomes, the *Íslendingabók,* a historical narrative from the Settlement Era written by 12th-century scholar Ari Þorgilsson (Ari the Learned), and the detailed *Landnámabók,* a comprehensive account of the settlement.

Despite the advances in such cultural pursuits, Icelandic society was beginning to deteriorate. By the early 13th century the enlightened period of peace that had lasted 200 years was waning. Constant power struggles between rival chieftains led to violent feuds and a flourishing of Viking-like private armies, which raided farms across the country. This dark hour in Iceland's history was known as the Sturlung Age, named for the Sturlungs, the most powerful family clan in Iceland at the time. The tragic events and brutal history of this 40-year era is graphically recounted in the three-volume *Sturlunga Saga.*

As Iceland descended into chaos, the Norwegian king Hákon Hákonarson pressured chieftains, priests and the new breed of wealthy aristocrats to accept his authority. The Icelanders, who saw no alternative, dissolved all but a superficial shell of their government and swore their allegiance to the king. An agreement of confederacy was made in 1262. In 1281 a new code of law, the Jónsbók, was introduced by the king, and Iceland was absorbed into Norwegian rule.

The Althing at Thingvellir, by Helmut Lugmayr, explains the role and history of the oldest parliament in the world and includes a section on Þingvellir's unique geology.

1402–04	1550	1590	1602
The Black Death sweeps across Iceland, 50 years after its devastating journey across mainland Europe, and kills around half of the population.	King Christian III's attempts to impose Lutheranism finally succeeds after the Catholic bishop Jón Arason is captured in battle and beheaded at Skálholt, along with two of his sons.	Bishop Guðbrandur Þorláksson's lovely – and quite accurate – map of Iceland is published. The sea is sprinkled with whale-like monsters, and it notes that Hekla 'vomits stones with a terrible noise'.	Denmark imposes a trade monopoly, giving Danish and Swedish firms exclusive trading rights in Iceland. This leads to unrestrained profiteering by Danish merchants and Iceland's slow impoverishment.

Norway immediately set about appointing Norwegian bishops to Hólar and Skálholt and imposed excessive taxes. Contention flared as former chieftains quibbled over high offices, particularly that of *járl* (earl), an honour that fell to the ruthless Gissur Þorvaldsson, who in 1241 murdered Snorri Sturluson, Iceland's best-known historian and writer.

Meanwhile, the volcano Hekla erupted three times, covering a third of the country in ash; a mini–ice age followed, and severe winters wiped out livestock and crops. The Black Death arrived, killing half the population, and the once indomitable spirit of the people seemed broken.

Enter the Danes

Iceland's fate was now in the hands of the highest Norwegian bidder, who could lease the governorship of the country on a three-year basis. In 1397 the Kalmar Union of Norway, Sweden and Denmark brought Iceland under Danish rule. After disputes between church and state, the Danish government seized church property and imposed Lutheranism in the Reformation of 1550. When the stubborn Catholic bishop of Hólar, Jón Arason, resisted and gained a following, he and his two sons were taken to Skálholt and beheaded.

The Complete Sagas of Icelanders, edited by Viðar Hreinsson, is a must for saga fiends. It's a summary translation of saga tales, featuring all the main yarns, along with a few shorter fantasy tales.

In 1602 the Danish king imposed a crippling trade monopoly whereby Swedish and Danish firms were given exclusive trading rights in Iceland for 12-year periods. This resulted in large-scale extortion, importation of spoilt or inferior goods, and yet more suffering that would last another 250 years. However, one positive eventually came from the monopoly. In an attempt to bypass the embargo and boost local industry, powerful town magistrate Skúli Magnússon built weaving, tanning and wool-dyeing factories – the foundations of the modern city of Reykjavík.

Even More Misery

Talk about getting kicked while you're down! As if impoverishment at the hands of Danish overlords was not enough, Barbary pirates got in on the action, raiding the Eastfjords and the Reykjanes Peninsula before descending on the Vestmannaeyjar in 1627. The defenceless population attempted to hide in Heimaey's cliffs and caves, but the pirates ransacked the island, killing indiscriminately and loading 242 people onto their ships. The unfortunate Icelanders were taken to Algiers, where most were sold into slavery. Back home, money was scrimped and saved as ransom, and eventually 13 of the captives were freed. The most famous was Guðríður Símonardóttir, who returned to Iceland and married Hallgrímur Pétursson, one of Iceland's most famous poets – the three bells in Hallgrímskirkja are named after the couple and their daughter.

During the same period, Europe's witch-hunting craze reached Icelandic shores. Icelandic witches turned out mostly to be men – of the 130

1625–85	1627	1703	1783–84
Period of the notorious Westfjords witch-hunts: 21 Icelanders are executed, beginning with Jón Rögnvaldsson, burned at the stake for 'raising a ghost' and possessing sinister-looking runic writing.	The 'Turkish Abductions' take place: Barbary pirates raid the east of Iceland and the Vestmannaeyjar, taking hundreds of people prisoner and killing anyone who resists them.	Iceland's first census reveals that the country's population is a tiny 50,358; 55% are female. Men – physical labourers – are more affected by malnutrition and famine.	The Laki crater row erupts, pouring out poisonous gas clouds that kill 25% of the population and more than 50% of livestock. The haze covers Europe, causing freak weather conditions, flooding and famine.

cases that appear in the court annals, only 10% involve women. The luckiest defendants were brutally flogged; 21 of the unluckiest were burned at the stake, mostly for making their neighbours sick or for possessing magical writing or suspicious-looking amulets.

It may have been the Age of Enlightenment in Europe, but it's a wonder any Icelanders survived the 18th century. In this remote outpost in the North Atlantic, the population (all of 50,000) was holding on for dear life, in the face of a powerful smallpox epidemic (which arrived in 1707 and killed an estimated 18,000 people) and a series of volcanic eruptions: Katla in 1660, 1721 and again in 1755; Hekla in 1693 and 1766; and Öræfajökull in 1727.

And then things got really bad. In 1783 the Laki crater row erupted, spewing out billions of tonnes of lava and poisonous gas clouds for a full eight months. Fifty farms in the immediate area were wiped out, and the noxious dust and vapours and consequent Haze Famine went on to kill around 9000 Icelanders – first the plants died, then the livestock, then the people. The ash clouds affected the whole of Europe, causing freak weather conditions, including acid rain and floods. Authorities in Denmark seriously contemplated relocating the remaining Icelandic population (which numbered only 47,000 in 1801) to Denmark.

Island on Fire, by Alexandra Witze and Jeff Kanipe, examines the Laki eruptions – the cataclysmic event by which Icelanders measure all other volcanic eruptions.

Return to Independence

After five centuries of oppressive foreign rule and conscious of a growing sense of liberalisation across Europe, Icelandic nationalism flourished in the 19th century. By 1855 Jón Sigurðsson, an Icelandic scholar, had successfully lobbied for restoration of free trade, and by 1874 Iceland had drafted a constitution and regained control of its domestic affairs.

Iceland's first political parties were formed during this period, and urban development began in this most rural of countries. Still, it wasn't enough to stave off the wave of emigration that had started: between 1870 and 1914, some 16,000 Icelanders left seeking a better life in North America. They emigrated for a number of reasons – in part because the growing fishing industry could not employ all the workers who wished to escape the hard labour of rural life and move to the new urban centres. Oh, and because of yet another volcanic eruption spewing livestock-poisoning ash (Askja, 1875).

By 1918 Iceland had signed the Act of Union, which effectively released the country from Danish rule, making it an independent state within the Kingdom of Denmark.

Iceland prospered during WWI as wool, meat and fish exports gained high prices. When WWII loomed, however, Iceland declared neutrality in the hope of maintaining its important trade links with both Britain and Germany.

Wasteland With Words: A Social History of Iceland, by Sigurður Gylfi Magnússon, draws on the detailed diaries and letters of Icelanders in past centuries, with a particular focus on on the years from 1850 to 1940.

1786	1855–90	1917–18	1918
The official founding of Reykjavík (currently inhabited by fewer than 200 souls). The settlement is granted a trade charter, and merchants are enticed to settle here with tax breaks.	Iceland moves towards independence, with the restoration of free trade and a draft constitution. Not everyone sticks around to see it: many Icelanders emigrate to start life afresh in North America.	Iceland is struck by the 'Winter of the Great Frosts'. Temperatures plummet to a record low of -38°C (-36.4°F), and icebergs block all ports.	Denmark's grip on Iceland gradually loosens. Following Home Rule in 1904, the Act of Union is signed on 1 December 1918, making Iceland an independent state within the Kingdom of Denmark.

On 9 April 1940 Denmark was occupied by Germany, prompting the Alþing to take control of Iceland's foreign affairs once more. A year later, on 17 May 1941, the Icelanders requested complete independence. The formal establishment of the Republic of Iceland finally took place at Þingvellir on 17 June 1944 – now celebrated as Independence Day.

Burial Rites, by Hannah Kent, is a novel based on the true story of the last public execution in Iceland. It's set in 1829 and is meticulously researched, beautifully evoking the hardships of rural Icelandic life.

WWII & the USA Moves In

As a result of Germany's occupation of Denmark in 1940, Iceland was in charge of its wartime foreign affairs (and on the path to full independence, which was officially established before the war's end). Wartime Iceland's complete lack of military force worried the Allied powers and so in May 1940 Britain, most vulnerable to a German-controlled Iceland, sent in forces to occupy the island. Iceland had little choice but to accept the situation, but ultimately the country's economy profited from British construction projects and spending.

When the British troops withdrew in 1941 the government allowed American troops to move in, on the understanding that they would move out at the end of the war. Although the US military left in 1946, it retained the right to re-establish a base at Keflavík should war threaten. After the war, and back under their own control, Icelanders were reluctant to submit to any foreign power. When the government was pressured into becoming a founding member of NATO in 1949, riots broke out in Reykjavík. The government agreed to the proposition on the conditions that Iceland would never take part in offensive action and that no foreign military troops would be based in the country during peacetime.

These conditions were soon broken. War with Korea erupted in 1950, and in 1951 at NATO's request the US, jumpy about the Soviet threat, once again took responsibility for the island's defence. US military personnel and technology at the Keflavík base continued to increase over the next four decades, as Iceland served as an important Cold War monitoring station. The controversial US military presence in Iceland only ended in September 2006, when the base at Keflavík finally closed.

Iceland Saga, by Magnús Magnússon, offers an entertaining introduction to Icelandic history and literature, and explains numerous saga events and settings.

Modern Iceland

In the 20th century, Iceland transformed itself from one the poorest countries in Europe to one of the most developed.

Following the Cold War, Iceland went through a period of growth, rebuilding and modernisation. The Ring Road was completed in 1974 – opening up transport links to the remote southeast – and projects such as the Krafla power station in the northeast and the Svartsengi power plant near Reykjavík were developed. A boom in the fishing industry saw Iceland extend its fishing limit in the 1970s to 200 miles (322km). This, however, precipitated the worst of the 'cod wars', as the UK refused to recognise the

1940–41	1944	1974	1975
After the Nazis occupy Denmark, the UK sends British troops to invade and occupy neutral Iceland, concerned Germany might acquire a military presence there. A US base is later established at Keflavík.	A majority of Icelanders vote for independence from Denmark, and the Republic of Iceland is formally established on 17 June. King Christian X telegrams his congratulations.	The Ring Road around the island is completed when the Skeiðarárbrú bridge opens on 14 July. Until now, Höfn has been one of the most isolated towns in Iceland.	The third in a series of 'cod wars' takes place between Iceland and the UK. These disputes over fishing rights in the North Atlantic flare up in the 1950s and 1970s, as Iceland expands its territorial waters.

new zone. During the seven-month conflict, Icelandic ships cut the nets of British trawlers, shots were fired, and ships on both sides were rammed.

The fishing industry has always been vital to Iceland, although it's had its ups and downs – quotas were reduced in the 1990s so stocks could regenerate after overfishing. The industry went into recession, leading to an unemployment rate of 3% and a sharp drop in the króna. The country slowly began a period of economic regeneration as the fishing industry stabilised. Today the industry still provides 40% of export earnings, more than 12% of GDP, and employs nearly 5% of the workforce. It remains sensitive to declining fish stocks.

In 2003 Iceland resumed whaling as part of a scientific research program, despite a global moratorium on hunts. In 2006 Iceland resumed

ICELAND'S ECONOMIC MELTDOWN

Everything was looking so rosy. Between 2003 and early 2008, Iceland was full of confidence and riding high. But much of the country's wealth was built over a black hole of debt – its banks' liabilities were more than 10 times the country's annual GDP. The ripples of the worldwide financial crisis became a tidal wave by the time they reached Icelandic shores, washing away the country's entire economy.

By October 2008 the Icelandic stock market had crashed; the króna plummeted, losing almost half its value overnight; all three national banks went into receivership; and the country teetered on the brink of bankruptcy.

Help came for Iceland in November 2008 with a US$2.1 billion International Monetary Fund (IMF) loan and a US$3 billion bailout from Scandinavian neighbours. Nevertheless, spiralling inflation, wage cuts and redundancies meant that Icelanders' incomes fell by a quarter in real terms. Protestors rioted in Reykjavík, furious with a government they felt had betrayed them by not downsizing the bloated banking system.

The crash was a terrible blow to Icelanders – its legacy included high household debt, high inflation, record unemployment (peaking at 9.4% in early 2009, but sitting around 4% to 5% in 2014) and emigration for work (some 5000 Icelanders moved to Norway in the four years following the crash).

But, incredibly, the economic situation has begun to right itself. Where other countries in financial straits chose to bail out their financial institutions, the Icelandic government refused to use taxpayers' money to prop up the failing banks. Instead, it made the Icelandic social welfare system its priority, choosing to help those citizens who were worst affected by the crash and let the private banks' creditors take the hit. Though bank creditors (many of them hedge funds) are still trying to recoup their money, Iceland's approach has won praise from the International Monetary Fund and from numerous economists.

This unique decision appears to be paying off – other nations are still floundering in the financial mire and dealing with record unemployment rates, Iceland appears to be on the rise again.

1986	2006	2008	2009
The beginning of the end of the Cold War? General Secretary Mikhail Gorbachev and President Ronald Reagan agree to meet at a summit in Höfði House, Reykjavík.	The controversial US military base at Keflavík closes down after 45 years in service; the government also approves the resumption of commercial whaling.	The worldwide financial downturn hits Iceland particularly hard, precipitating the worst national banking crisis ever when all three of the country's major banks collapse.	Iceland formally applies for EU membership – a contentious issue among the population. Formal accession talks begin in 2010 but are suspended in 2013, and the application is withdrawn by a new government in 2014.

commercial whaling, in spite of condemnation from around the world. Hunting of minke whales and endangered fin whales continues, drawing further international rebukes.

Financial Crash & Beyond

One of the most famous essays on Iceland's financial crash of 2008 is Michael Lewis' 'Wall Street on the Tundra', written for *Vanity Fair* in 2009. Search for it online – it's a cracking read (and not very complimentary towards Iceland). Follow it with 'Lost', from *The New Yorker* (March 2009).

Iceland's huge dependence on its fishing industry and on imported goods means that the country has always had relatively high prices and a currency prone to fluctuation. Its exact vulnerability was brought into focus in September 2008, when the global economic crisis hit the country with a sledgehammer blow. Reykjavík was rocked by months of fierce protest, as the then-government's popularity evaporated along with the country's wealth.

Prime Minister Geir Haarde resigned in January 2009. His replacement, Jóhanna Sigurðardóttir, hit international headlines as the world's first openly gay prime minister. Her first major act was to apply for EU membership, with the eventual aim of adopting the euro as the country's new currency, in an effort to stabilise the economy. EU membership was then (and continues to be now) a contentious issue.

Iceland again hit global headlines in April 2010, when the ash cloud from the eruption under Eyjafjallajökull ice cap shut down European air traffic for six days, causing travel chaos across much of the continent. In comparison to the Eyjafjallajökull eruptions, the Grímsvötn volcano, which erupted the following year, was a mere trifle – its ash cloud only managed to cause three days of air-traffic disruption. In 2014, Bárðarbunga's rumblings have again shone a spotlight onto Iceland's volatility – and served as a reminder of its ability to potentially close airspace.

But events in Iceland have proven that there's no such thing as bad publicity: triggered by the 2010 eruption, and all the free exposure it generated for Iceland, tourism has boomed. The country has become the fastest-growing travel destination in Europe, with all the benefits (economic growth, employment) and headaches (infrastructure issues, environmental impact) that entails.

Icelanders went to the polls in April 2013 with the national economy on the path to recovery, but with the population smarting from the government's tough austerity measures (higher taxes, spending cuts). The results showed a backlash against the ruling Social Democrats; the centre-right camp (comprising the Progressive Party and the Independence Party) successfully campaigned on promises of debt relief and a cut in taxes, as well as opposition to Iceland's application to join the EU.

The two parties formed a coalition government. In early 2014 the government halted all negotiations with the EU – despite promising a referendum on whether or not to proceed with membership negotiations. Although polls show a majority of Icelanders still oppose joining the EU, making such a move without the promised referendum was deeply unpopular.

2010	2013	2013	2014
The volcano under Eyjafjallajökull glacier begins erupting in March. In April its 9km-high ash plume brings European flights to a standstill for six days. The eruption is declared over in October.	In parliamentary elections, voters deliver a backlash against the Social Democrats' austerity measures in the wake of the financial crisis. A new coalition of centre-right parties forms government.	The number of international visitors to Iceland numbers 807,000 (up from 320,000 in 2003). A year later, that number hovers around 1 million.	In mid-August, sensors begin picking up increased seismic activity around Bárðarbunga, a large volcano system under the Vatnajökull ice cap. A small eruption begins at Holuhraun, with more activity expected.

Natural Wonders

It's difficult to remain unmoved by the amazing diversity of the Icelandic landscape. Contrary to popular opinion, it's not completely covered in ice, nor is it a treeless, lunar landscape of congealed lava flows and windswept tundra. Both of these habitats exist, but so too do steep-sided fjords, rolling emerald-green hills, glacier-carved valleys, bubbling mudpots and vast, desert-like wasteland. It is this rich mix of scenery and the possibility of experiencing such extremes, so close together, that attract, and then dazzle, most visitors.

Volatile Iceland

Plonked firmly on the Mid-Atlantic Ridge, a massive 18,000km-long rift between two of the earth's major tectonic plates, Iceland is a shifting, steaming lesson in schoolroom geology. Suddenly you'll be racking your brains to remember long-forgotten homework on how volcanoes work, what a solfatara is, and why lava and magma aren't quite the same thing.

Iceland is one of the youngest landmasses on the planet, formed by underwater volcanic eruptions along the joint of the North American and Eurasian plates around 20 million years ago. The earth's crust in Iceland is only a third of its normal thickness, and magma (molten rock) continues to rise from deep within, forcing the two plates apart. The result is clearly visible at Þingvellir, where the great rift Almannagjá broadens by between 1mm and 18mm per year, and at Námafjall (near Mývatn), where a series of steaming vents mark the ridge.

At 103,000 sq km, Iceland is roughly the size of Portugal, or the US state of Kentucky. Within its borders are some 30 active volcanoes. Its landscape is comprised of 3% lakes, 11% ice caps and glaciers, 23% vegetation, and 63% wasteland.

Volcanoes

Thin crust and grating plates are responsible for a whole host of exciting volcanic activities in Iceland. The country's volcanoes are many and varied – some are active, some extinct, and some are dormant and dreaming, no doubt, of future destruction. Fissure eruptions and their associated craters are probably the most common type of eruption in Iceland. The still-volatile Lakagígar crater row around Mt Laki is the country's most unearthly example. It produced the largest lava flow in human history in the 18th century, covering an area of 565 sq km to a depth of 12m.

Several of Iceland's liveliest volcanoes are found beneath glaciers, which makes for dramatic eruptions as molten lava and ice interact. The main 2010 Eyjafjallajökull eruption was of this type: it caused a *jökulhlaup* (flooding caused by volcanic eruption beneath an ice cap) that damaged part of the Ring Road, before throwing up the famous ash plume that grounded Europe's aeroplanes. Iceland's most active volcano, Grímsvötn, which lies beneath the Vatnajökull ice cap, behaved in a similar fashion in 2011.

Iceland not only has subglacial eruptions, but also submarine ones. In 1963 the island of Surtsey exploded from the sea, giving scientists the opportunity to study how smouldering chunks of newly created land are colonised by plants and animals. Surtsey is off-limits to visitors, but you can climb many classical-looking cones such as Hekla, once thought to be the gateway to Hell; Eldfell, which did its best to bury the town of Heimaey in 1974; and Snæfellsjökull on the Snæfellsnes Peninsula.

Recent eruptions in Iceland have tended to be fairly harmless – they're often called 'tourist eruptions' because their fountains of magma, electric storms and dramatic ash clouds make perfect photos but cause relatively little damage. This is partly due to the sparsely populated land, and partly because devastating features such as fast-flowing lava, lahars (mudslides) and pyroclastic surges (like the ones that obliterated Pompeii and Herculaneum) are usually absent in this part of the world.

The main danger lies in the gases that are released: suffocating carbon dioxide, highly acidic sulphur-based gases, and the deadly fluorine that poisoned people and livestock during the Laki eruptions. The Icelandic Met Office (Veðurstofa Íslands; www.vedur.is) keeps track of eruptions and the earthquakes that tend to proceed them, plus the emissions that follow; its work during 2014's Bárðarbunga seismic events and volcanic activity includes daily factsheets.

Geysers, Springs & Fumaroles

Iceland's Great Geysir gave its name to the world's spouting hot springs (it comes from the Icelandic for 'to gush'). It was once very active, frequently blowing water to a height of 80m, but earthquakes have altered the pressures inside its plumbing system and today it is far quieter. Strokkur now demonstrates the effect admirably, blasting a steaming column into the air every five to 10 minutes.

Geysers are reasonably rare phenomena, with only around 1000 existing on earth. However, in Iceland water that has percolated down through the rock and been superheated by magma can emerge on the surface in various other exciting ways. Some of it boils into hot springs, pools and rivers – you'll find natural hot water sources all around Iceland, including the springs at Landmannalaugar, the river at Hveragerði and the warm blue-white pool in the bottom of the Víti Crater. Icelanders have long harnessed these soothing gifts of nature, turning them into geothermal swimming pools and spas, the smartest of which are Mývatn Nature Baths and the Blue Lagoon. These latter two are not, however, natural hot springs – they are manmade lagoons fed by the water output of the nearby geothermal power plants!

Fumaroles are places where superheated water reaches the surface as steam – the weirdest Icelandic examples are at Hverir, where gases literally scream their way from sulphurous vents in the earth. Lazier, messier bloops and bubblings take place at mudpots, for example at Krýsuvík on the Reykjanes Peninsula, where heated water mixes with mud and clay. The colourful splatterings around some of the mudpots are caused

For background information about the country's diverse geology, check out the revised 2nd edition (published mid-2014) of *Iceland – Classic Geology in Europe*, by Þór Þórdarson and Armann Hoskuldsson.

GEOLOGICALLY SPEAKING

Everywhere you go in Iceland you'll be bombarded with geological jargon to describe the landscape. The following terms will let you one-up the other geological neophytes.

Basalt The most common type of solidified lava. This hard, dark, dense volcanic rock often solidifies into hexagonal columns.

Igneous A rock formed by solidifying magma or lava.

Moraine A ridge of boulders, clay and sand carried and deposited by a glacier.

Obsidian Black, glassy rock formed by the rapid solidification of lava without crystallisation.

Rhyolite Light-coloured, fine-grained volcanic rock similar to granite in composition.

Scoria Porous volcanic gravel that has cooled rapidly while moving, creating a glassy surface with iron-rich crystals that give it a glittery appearance.

Tephra Solid matter ejected into the air by an erupting volcano.

by various minerals (sulphurous yellow, iron-red), and also by the extremophile bacteria and algae that somehow thrive in this boiling-acid environment.

Ice & Snow

Glaciers and ice caps cover around 11% of Iceland; many are remnants of a cool period that began 2500 years ago. Ice caps are formed as snow piles up over millennia in an area where it's never warm enough to melt. The weight of the snow causes it to slowly compress into ice, eventually crushing the land beneath the ice cap.

Iceland's largest ice cap, Vatnajökull in the southeast, covers about 8% of the country and is the largest in the world outside the poles. This immense glittering weight of ice may seem immovable, but around its edges, slow-moving rivers of ice – glaciers – flow imperceptibly down the mountainsides. Like rivers, they carry pieces of stony sediment with them, which they dump in cindery-looking moraines at the foot of the mountain, or on vast gravelly outwash plains such as the Skeiðarársandur in southeast Iceland. This can occur very quickly, if volcanoes under the ice erupt and cause a *jökulhlaup* (glacial flood): the *jökulhlaup* from the 1996 Grímsvötn eruption destroyed Iceland's longest bridge and swept Jeep-sized boulders down onto the plain.

Several of Iceland's glaciers have lakes at their tips. Jökulsárlón is a stunning place to admire icebergs that have calved from Breiðamerkurjökull. Luminous-blue pieces tend to indicate a greater age of ice, as centuries of compression squeeze out the air bubbles that give ice its usual silvery-white appearance (icebergs may also appear blue due to light refraction).

Glaciers have carved out much of the Icelandic landscape since its creation, forming the glacial valleys and fjords that make those picture-postcard photos today. The ice advances and retreats with the millennia, and also with the seasons, but there are worrying signs that Iceland's major ice caps – Vatnajökull, Mýrdalsjökull in the southwest, and Langjökull and Hofsjökull in the highlands – have been melting at an unprecedented rate since 2000. Glaciologists believe the ice cap Snæfellsjökull in the west (with an average ice thickness of only 30m), as well as some of the outlet glaciers of the larger ice caps, could disappear completely within a few decades.

Wildlife

Mammals & Marine Life

Apart from birds, sheep and horses, you'll be lucky to have any casual sightings of animals in Iceland. The only indigenous land mammal is the elusive Arctic fox, best spotted in remote Hornstrandir, in the Westfjords – wildlife enthusiasts can push pause on their holiday and monitor these creatures while volunteering at the Arctic Fox Center (www.arcticfoxcenter.com; p199). In east Iceland, herds of reindeer can sometimes be spotted on the road. The reindeer were introduced from Norway in the 18th century and now roam the mountains in the east. Polar bears very occasionally drift across from Greenland on ice floes, but armed farmers make sure they don't last long.

In contrast, Iceland has a rich marine life, particularly whales. On whale-watching tours from Húsavík in northern Iceland (among other places), you'll have an excellent chance of seeing cetaceans, particularly dolphins, porpoises, minke whales and humpback whales. Sperm, fin, sei, pilot, killer and blue whales also swim in Icelandic waters and have been seen by visitors. Seals can be seen in the Eastfjords, on the Vatnsnes Peninsula in northwest Iceland, in the Mýrar region on the southeast coast (including at Jökulsárlón), in Breiðafjörður in the west, and in the Westfjords.

Iceland isn't truly an Arctic country – the mainland falls short of the Arctic Circle by a few kilometres. To cross that imaginary boundary, you'll need to travel to the island of Grímsey, Iceland's only real piece of Arctic territory.

NATURAL WONDERS WILDLIFE

In 2002 scientists discovered the world's second-smallest creature, *Nanoarchaeum equitans*, living in near-boiling water in a hydrothermal vent off the north coast of Iceland. The name means 'riding the fire sphere'.

LITTLE NORTHERN BROTHERS

Cute, clumsy and endearingly comic, the puffin (*Fratercula arctica,* or *lundi* as they're called in Icelandic) is one of Iceland's best-loved birds. Although known for its frantic fluttering and crash landings, the bird is surprisingly graceful underwater and was once thought to be a bird-fish hybrid.

The puffin is a member of the auk family and spends most of its year at sea. For four or five months it comes to land to breed, generally keeping the same mate and burrow (a multiroom apartment!) from year to year. Until very recently, 60% of the world's puffins bred in Iceland, and you would see them in huge numbers around the island from late May to August. However, over the last decade, the puffin stock has gone into a sudden, sharp decline in the south of Iceland. They still visit the south, but in smaller numbers and with considerably less breeding success. The reason is uncertain, but it's thought that warming ocean temperatures have caused their main food, sand eels, to decline. It's also possible that hunting and egg collection have had an unanticipated effect.

For twitchers, the good news is that puffins in the north seem unaffected (for now). The photogenic birds continue to flitter around the cliffs of Grímsey and Drangey, as well as in Borgarfjörður Eystri and the Westfjords.

Birds

Birdlife is prolific, at least from May to August. On coastal cliffs and islands around the country you can see a mind-boggling array of seabirds, often in massive colonies. Most impressive for their sheer numbers are gannets, guillemots, gulls, razorbills, kittiwakes, fulmars and puffins. Less numerous birds include wood sandpipers, Arctic terns, skuas, Manx shearwaters, golden plovers, storm petrels and Leach's petrels. In addition, there are many species of ducks, ptarmigans, whooping swans, redwings, divers and gyrfalcons, and two species of owl. For information on where to see birds in Iceland, see p40.

Imported by the Vikings, the pure-bred Icelandic horse *(Equus scandinavicus)* is a small, tough breed perfectly suited to the country's rough conditions. Icelandic horses have five gaits, including the unusual *tölt* – a running walk so smooth that riders can drink a glass of beer without spilling a drop.

Flowers & Fungi

Although ostensibly barren in places, the vegetation in Iceland is surprisingly varied – you just need to get close to see it. Most vegetation is low growing, staying close to the ground and spreading as much as possible to get a better grip on the easily eroded soil. Even the trees, where there are any, are stunted. As the old joke goes, if you're lost in an Icelandic forest, just stand up.

If you're visiting in summer, you'll be treated to incredible displays of wildflowers blooming right across the country. Most of Iceland's 450 flowering plants are introduced species – especially the ubiquitous purple lupin, once an environmental help, now a hindrance. A nationwide poll was held in 2004 to choose a national flower. The mountain avens *(Dryas octopetala),* known as *holtasóley* (heath buttercup) in Icelandic, was the worthy winner. Look out for it on gravel stretches and rocky outcrops – its flowers are about 3cm in diameter, with eight delicate white petals and an exploding yellow-sun centre.

Coastal areas are generally characterised by low grasses, bogs and marshlands, while at higher elevations hard or soft tundra covers the ground.

Another common sight when walking just about anywhere in Iceland is the profusion of fungi. There are about 2000 types growing here, and you'll see everything from pale white mushrooms to bright orange flat caps as you walk along trails, by roadsides or through fields.

A Guide to the Flowering Plants and Ferns of Iceland, by Hörður Kristinsson, is the best all-round field guide to Icelandic flowers.

In southern and eastern Iceland new lava flows are first colonised by mosses, which create a velvety green cloak across the rough rocks. Older lava flows in the east and those at higher elevations are generally first colonised by lichens. Confusingly, Icelandic moss *(Cetraria islandica),* the grey-green or pale brown frilly growth that you'll see absolutely everywhere, is actually lichen.

National Parks & Reserves

Iceland has three national parks and more than 100 nature reserves, natural monuments and country parks, with a protected area of 18,806 sq km (about 18% of the entire country).

Umhverfisstofnun (Environment Agency of Iceland; www.ust.is) is responsible for protecting many of these sites. Its website contains information on its work to promote the protection as well as sustainable use of Iceland's natural resources, including on how travellers can tread lightly. The agency also recruits summer volunteers each year, to work in conservation projects within the parks. For information on volunteering, see p364.

Þingvellir National Park (p106; www.thingvellir.is), Iceland's oldest national park, protects a scenic 84-sq-km lake, the geologically significant Almannagjá rift, and is the site of the original Alþing (National Assembly). The park is a Unesco World Heritage Site.

Snæfellsjökull National Park (p178; www.ust.is/snaefellsjokull-national-park) in west Iceland was established in June 2001. The park protects the Snæfellsjökull glacier (made famous by Jules Verne), the surrounding lava fields and coast.

Vatnajökull National Park (p250 & p290) is the largest national park in all of Europe and covers roughly 13% of Iceland. It was founded in 2008 by uniting two previously established national parks: Skaftafell in southeast Iceland, and Jökulsárgljúfur further north. The park protects the entirety of the Vatnajökull ice cap, the mighty Dettifoss waterfall, and a great variety of geological anomalies.

Energy Dilemmas

Iceland's small population, pristine wilderness, lack of heavy industry and high use of geothermal and hydroelectric power give it an enviable environmental reputation. Its use of geothermal power is one of the most creative in the world, and the country's energy experts are now advising Asian and African industries on possible ways to harness geothermal sources.

However, power supplies provided free by bountiful nature are not just of interest to Icelanders. Foreign industrialists in search of cheap energy also have their eye on the country's glacial rivers and geothermal hotspots. Alcoa, an American aluminium-smelting company, was responsible for one of Iceland's most controversial schemes: the Kárahnjúkar hydroelectric station in east Iceland, completed in 2009, was the biggest construction project in Iceland's history. It created a network of dams and tunnels, a vast reservoir, a power station and miles of power lines to supply electricity to a fjord-side smelter 80km away in Reyðarfjörður.

Alcoa makes much PR out of its efforts to reduce its carbon footprint – and it's true, the aluminium it manufactures in Iceland uses cheap, green energy from renewable sources (that was the whole point of closing two US smelters and setting up here). What can't be denied is that the mega-dam that was built specifically to power the Alcoa plant has devastated the landscape. Environmentalists raised serious objections to the project, on a number of grounds, but the locals were less vocal – many were grateful for the work opportunities coming to the area. Bear in mind that east Iceland has a population of only 12,500 – then imagine how hard it might be to fight government decisions and multinational corporations.

The Power of Power

The Kárahnjúkar dam and aluminium smelter are a dramatic illustration of the dilemma Iceland faces.

To ensure economic prosperity, Iceland is seeking to shore up its position as a green-energy superpower. Thanks to its endless geothermal and hydroelectric energy sources (and now new wind turbines), Iceland generates more electricity per capita than any other country in the world

Garden angelica *(Angelica archangelica)* grows wild in many parts of Iceland. It's been valued as a medicinal herb since Viking times, and these days is appearing in more and more recipes. Kaldi beer even has a brew (known as Stinnings Kaldi) with angelica as an ingredient.

(double as much as second-place Norway) – 80% of that electricity is sold to a handful of international companies in Iceland (such as aluminium smelters), but exporting electricity would bring in new revenue.

Iceland and the UK are exploring the feasibility of exporting clean hydroelectric energy via a 1000km subsea power cable running from Iceland to the UK (a project known as IceLink in the UK – read more at askjaenergy.org). Iceland is also hoping to expand its power-intensive industries – including a vision to become a global datacentre hub, home to the servers housing all our digitised information.

WHALING IN ICELAND

In the late 19th century, whale hunting became a lucrative commercial prospect with the arrival of steam-powered ships and explosive harpoons. Norwegian hunters built 13 large-scale whaling stations in Iceland, and hunted until stocks practically disappeared in 1913. Icelanders established their own whaling industry between 1935 and 1986, when whale numbers again became dangerously low and commercial hunting was banned by the International Whaling Commission (IWC). Iceland resumed commercial whaling in 2006, to the consternation of environmentalists worldwide. When asked 'why is Iceland whaling today?', the answer is not a simple one.

Iceland's authorities stress that the country's position has always been that whale stocks should be utilised in a sustainable manner like any other living marine resource. Its catch limits for common minke whales and fin whales follow the advice given by the Marine Research Institute of Iceland regarding sustainability – the advice for the 2014 and 2015 seasons is for an annual maximum catch of 229 minke whales and 154 fin whales, respectively.

Those numbers stir passions, especially given that fin whales are classified as endangered on the International Union for Conservation of Nature (IUCN) Red List. Members of Iceland's tourism board are strong objectors, stating that Iceland's whaling industry has a detrimental effect on whale watching (although this is disputed by the Ministry of Industries and Innovation). It has to be said that while there may be plenty of anti-whaling commentators on social media, Iceland's tourism numbers are hardly suffering.

The industry has attracted international condemnation – in September 2014, a formal diplomatic protest (known as a démarche) against whaling was delivered to the Icelandic government from 35 nations, including the US, Australia and members of the EU. But arguments against whaling hold little sway in Iceland, and past protests seem to have fallen on deaf ears. What may make authorities pay attention, however, is a new US-based campaign: 'Don't Buy From Icelandic Whalers' encourages the public not to buy fish from whalers, and puts pressure on fish suppliers and retailers to ensure they do not source from Icelandic companies linked to whaling. This may start to hit Iceland's fishing industry where it hurts.

Still, it's interesting to note that a mid-2013 survey of Icelanders found close to 60% were in favour of the hunting of fin whales, 9% were against and 24% were neutral (even considering that 75% of Icelanders never buy whale meat, and much of the catch is exported to Japan). The fishing industry is of paramount importance to the country, and many Icelanders put forward the argument that culling whales preserves fish stock (this is a simplified argument, refuted by many studies – the WWF, for example, publishes a few on its website that conclude the greatest threat to fish stock is posed by mismanagement of fisheries).

The fishing industry is of paramount importance to the country, and many believe that culling whales preserves fish stocks (although this is refuted by studies). Most of all, whaling has become intrinsically linked to national pride. Icelanders have a long tradition of not letting others dictate their actions, and in the face of worldwide criticism, asking Icelanders whether they support whaling is tantamount to asking whether they support Iceland.

Ironically, 35% to 40% of Icelandic whale meat consumption is by curious tourists. In 2012 the International Fund for Animal Welfare (IFAW) and IceWhale (Icelandic Whale Watching Association) launched a high-profile 'Meet Us Don't Eat Us' campaign to encourage visitors to go whale watching rather than whale tasting.

But if such initiatives go ahead, the power must still be harnessed, and power plants and power lines must be built for such a purpose. Where will these be located? What other tracts of Iceland's highland wilderness may be threatened by industrial megaprojects? Landvernd, the Icelandic Environment Association (an environmental NGO; www.landvernd. is), has proposed that the central highlands be protected with the establishment of a national park. Economic profit versus the preservation of nature – it's an age-old battle. Watch this space.

The Impact of Tourism on Nature

A million visitors per year are now clamouring for their dream holiday in Iceland's vast natural playground. And guess what? This boom in visitor numbers is threatening the very thing everyone is travelling to see: Iceland's unspoilt nature.

Plans for a Nature Pass

There is a nascent government proposal to introduce a one-off fee (perhaps an arrival tax payable at the airport, or a nature pass you purchase depending on the length of your stay), ensuring travellers contribute to the protection and maintenance of natural sites. It doesn't seem like an unreasonable request – especially when one looks at it in the context of Iceland's tiny population, now hosting hordes of trekkers and buses full of holidaymakers needing a car park, a toilet block, picnic tables, rubbish bins, improved signage, not to mention rangers providing information and safety advice etc.

Stay tuned for developments – and don't be surprised to learn of a nature tax or pass in some form, implemented for summer 2015. The pressure is on the authorities to find a solution soon – in summer 2014 landowners controversially began charging visitors for access to natural attractions on their property (formerly freely accessed sites such as Geysir and Hverir), before courts ruled this unlawful.

Travel Safely, Tread Lightly

Here are a few tips on staying safe and eco-aware (and on the good side of locals):

Heed local warnings and advice No-one is trying to spoil your holiday – when a local tells you that the your car isn't suitable for a particular road, or an area is off-limits because of a sulphur-emitting eruption or fear of a glacial outburst flood, it's because they know this country and what it's capable of.

Plan properly Check weather-forecast and road-condition websites. Pack a good map, the appropriate gear, and common sense. No hiking in jeans, no attempting to cross rivers in small cars, no striding out onto glaciers without proper guiding and equipment.

Respect nature Your country probably doesn't have subglacial volcanoes, geothermal areas and vast lava fields. That's why you're visiting Iceland, no? So take care not to damage it. If you've hired a 4WD, whatever you do, stick to marked trails; off-roading is illegal and causes irreparable damage to the fragile landscape.

Travel green Check out the website Nature.is – it's chock-full of amazing tips on travelling green in Iceland, and has an associated *Green Map* and app, with a goal of making ecofriendly choices easier for everyone.

Dreamland: A Self-Help Manual for a Frightened Nation, by Andri Snær Magnason, critically examines the government's decisions over Kárahnjúkar. The powerful documentary based on the book, *Dreamland* (2009), won critical acclaim.

The Forlagið (Mál og Menning) series of maps now includes some fun themed ones – if it's your cup of tea, pick up their *Fuglakort* (Birdwatcher's Map), *Höggunarkort* (Tectonic Map), *Jarðfræðikort* (Geological Map) or *Plöntukortið* (Botanical Map). The text is in Icelandic, English and German.

NATURAL WONDERS THE IMPACT OF TOURISM ON NATURE

Icelandic Culture: Sagas to Sigur Rós

Iceland blows away petty concerns such as isolation, never-ending winter nights and a small population with a glowing passion for all things cultural. The country's unique literary heritage begins with its high-action medieval sagas, and stretches to today's Nordic Noir bestsellers. Every Icelander seems to play in a band, and the country produces a disproportionate number of world-class musicians. The way of life and grand landscapes inspire visual artists who use film, art and design to capture their unique Icelandic perspectives.

Literature

Bloody, mystical and nuanced, the late 12th- and 13th-century sagas are some of Iceland's greatest cultural achievements. Reverend Hallgrímur Pétursson's 1659 *Passíusálmar* (Passion Hymns) were an Icelandic staple, sung or read at Lent. Nobel Prize–winning author Halldór Laxness put Iceland on the 20th-century literary map. But Icelanders aren't resting on their laurels: today the country produces the most writers and literary translations per capita of any country in the world.

The Sagas

An old Icelandic saying is *Betra er berfættum en bókarlausum að vera* ('It's better to be barefoot than bookless'). Icelanders are still passionate about the written word, so it's fitting that Reykjavík is a Unesco City of Literature, with tours and programs to match.

Iceland's medieval prose sagas are some of the most imaginative and enduring works of early literature – epic, brutal tales that flower repeatedly with wisdom, magic, elegiac poetry and love.

Written down during the 12th to early 14th centuries, these prose sagas look back on the disputes, families, doomed romances and larger-than-life characters (from warrior and poet to outlaw) who lived during the Settlement Era. Most were written anonymously, though *Egil's Saga* has been attributed to Snorri Sturluson. Some are sources for historical understanding, such as *The Saga of the Greenlanders* and *Saga of Erik the Red,* which describe the travels of Erik and his family, including his son Leif (a settler in North America).

The sagas, written over the long, desperate centuries of Norwegian and Danish subjugation, provided a strong sense of cultural heritage at a time when Icelanders had little else. On winter nights, people would gather for the *kvöldvaka* (evening vigil). While the men twisted horsehair ropes and women spun wool or knitted, a family member would read the sagas and recite *rímur* (verse reworkings of the sagas).

The sagas are very much alive today. Icelanders of all ages can (and do) read the sagas in Old Norse, the language in which they were written 800 years ago. Most people can quote chunks from them, know the farms where the characters lived and died, and flock to cinemas to see the latest film versions of these eternal tales. Check out the Icelandic Saga Database (www.sagadb.org) for more on sagas.

Eddic & Skaldic Poetry

The first settlers brought their oral poetic tradition with them from other parts of Scandinavia, and the poems were committed to parchment in the 12th century.

Eddic poems were composed in free, variable meters with a structure very similar to that of early Germanic poetry. Probably the most well known is the gnomic *Hávamál,* which extols the virtues of the common life – its wise proverbs on how to be a good guest are still quoted today.

Skaldic poems were composed by *skalds* (Norwegian court poets) and are mainly praise-poems of Scandinavian kings, with lots of description packed into tightly structured lines. As well as having fiercely rigid alliteration, syllable counts and stresses, skaldic poetry is made more complex by *kennings,* a kind of compact word-riddle. Blood, for instance, is 'wound dew', while an arm might be described as a 'hawk's perch'.

The most renowned *skald* was saga anti-hero Egil Skallagrímsson. In 948, after being captured and sentenced to death, Egil composed the ode *Höfuðlausn* (Head Ransom) for his captor Eirík Blood-Axe. Flattered, the monarch released Egil unharmed.

Modern Literature

Nobel Prize–winner Halldór Laxness is Iceland's modern literary genius. Another author you may come across is the early-20th-century children's writer Reverend Jón Sveinsson (nicknamed Nonni), whose old-fashioned tales of derring-do have a rich Icelandic flavour and were once translated into 40 languages; *At Skipalón* is the only one readily available in English. Sveinsson's house in Akureyri is now an interesting museum. Two other masters of Icelandic literature are Gunnar Gunnarsson (1889–1975) and Þórbergur Þórðarson (1888–1974). You'll have to look out for their work in secondhand bookshops.

Iceland publishes the greatest number of books per capita in the world, and the literacy rate is a perfect 100%.

For more up-to-date and easily available fare, try Einar Kárason's outstanding *Devil's Island,* about Reykjavík life in the 1950s; it's the first of a trilogy, but unfortunately the other two parts haven't yet been translated into English. Hallgrímur Helgason's *101 Reykjavík* is the book on which the cult film was based. It's a dark comedy following the torpid life and fertile imagination of out-of-work Hlynur, who lives in downtown Reykjavík with his mother. Even blacker is *Angels of the Universe,* by Einar Már Gudmundsson, which is about a schizophrenic man's spells in a psychiatric hospital. Svava Jakobsdóttir's *Gunnlöth's Tale* blends contemporary life with Nordic mythology.

Currently surfing the Nordic Noir tidal wave is Arnaldur Indriðason, whose Reykjavík-based crime fiction permanently tops the bestseller

TOP ICELANDIC SAGAS

Egil's Saga Revolves around the complex, devious but sensitive Egil Skallagrímsson, and much of it is set near modern-day Borgarnes. A renowned poet or *skald,* triumphant warrior and skilled negotiator, Egil is also the grandson of a werewolf/shapeshifter, and unlike most Saga protagonists, lived to a ripe old age.

Laxdæla Saga A tragic saga set in northwest Iceland around Breiðafjörður and the Dalir: bitter marriages, thwarted love and murder abound.

Njál's Saga Two of Iceland's greatest heroes, Njál and Gunnar, are drawn into a fatal, 50-year family feud.

Gisli Sursson's Saga The quintessential outlaw story, Gisli's tale involves revenge, fratricide and banishment.

Völsungasaga (Saga of the Völsungs) Parts of this saga may seem familiar – Richard Wagner *(Der Ring des Nibelungen)* and JRR Tolkien *(Lord of the Rings)* both swiped episodes.

Eyrbyggja Saga A minor saga set around the Snæfellsnes Peninsula, worth reading for its offbeat, supernatural tone; definitely the only medieval Icelandic work where ghosts are taken to court over their hauntings.

HALLDÓR LAXNESS

Over his long lifetime, Nobel Prize–winner Halldór Laxness (1902–98) succeeded in reshaping the world of Icelandic literature, and reviving the saga-scale story. Today he is Iceland's most celebrated 20th-century author.

Laxness was born as Halldór Guðjónsson, but he took the name of his family's farm Laxnes (with an extra 's') as his nom de plume. Ambitious and inquisitive, Laxness had his first work published at the age of 14, and began his restless wanderings at 17. He wrote his first novel, *Undir Helgahnúk* (Under the Holy Mountain), from a monastery during a period of fervent Catholicism. Laxness then left for Italy, where his disaffection with the church and increasingly leftist leanings led to the writing of *Vefarinn Mikli frá Kasmír* (The Great Weaver from Kashmir). In the 1930s he moved to the US to try his luck in the fledgling Hollywood film industry, before becoming enthralled with communism and travelling widely in the Soviet Bloc. In 1962 the author settled at Laxnes, near Þingvellir, for good (his home is now a museum). It was here that he wrote *Skáldatími* (Poets' Time), a poignant recantation of everything he'd ever written in praise of the Communist Party.

In 1955, Laxness won the Nobel Prize for Literature and became – in true Icelandic style – a hero of the people. His works are masterpieces of irony, and his characters, however misguided, are drawn with sympathy. Unfortunately only a portion of his 51 novels and countless short stories, articles, plays and poems are currently available in translation, the most famous of which is *Independent People* (1934–35). This bleak tragi-comedy is told in lush, evocative language and deals with the harsh conditions of early-20th-century Icelandic life. It focuses on the bloody-minded farmer Bjartur of Summerhouses and his toiling family, and creates a detailed depiction of traditional farmstead life. Also fascinating is *Iceland's Bell*, a saga-like portrait of extreme poverty and skewed justice, set in an Iceland subjugated by Danish rule. Other translated works are *World Light, The Fish Can Sing, Paradise Reclaimed, The Atom Station* and *Under the Glacier*.

lists. Many of his novels are available in English, including *Voices,* the award-winning *Silence of the Grave, The Draining Lake,* and our favourite, *Tainted Blood* (also published as *Jar City,* and the inspiration for a film of the same name). Yrsa Sigurðardóttir's thrillers have also been widely translated – her latest are *I Remember You* and *Someone to Watch Over Me.* Or look for Guðrún Eva Mínervudóttir's *The Creator,* a dark psychological novel; or former Sugarcube band-member Sjón's *The Blue Fox,* a fantasy-adventure tale set in the 19th century.

Music

Pop

Iceland punches above its weight in the pop music world. Internationally famous Icelandic musicians include (of course) Björk and her former band, The Sugarcubes. When you're in Reykjavík, look out for the best-selling *Gling Gló,* a collection of Björk-sung jazz standards and traditional Icelandic songs; a recording that's quite difficult to find outside the country.

Sigur Rós have followed Björk to stardom. Their biggest-selling album *Takk* (2005) garnered rave reviews around the world. It was followed by the poppier *Með suð í eyrum við spilum endalaust* (2007); the band's concert movie *Heima* (2007) is a must-see. After a long hiatus they released their sixth and seventh studio albums: *Valtari* (2012) and *Kveikur* (2013). Lead singer Jónsi had success with his joyful solo album *Go* (2010).

Indie-folk Of Monsters and Men stormed the US charts in 2011 with their debut album, *My Head is an Animal.* The track 'Little Talks' from that album reached number one on the Billboard US Alternative Songs chart in 2012. Their song 'Silhouettes' was on the soundtrack for *The Hunger Games: Catching Fire.*

Most lately Ásgeir Trausti, who records simply as Ásgeir, had a break-out hit with *In the Silence* (2014), an English-language album, and has been selling out concerts internationally.

You may also be familiar with Emiliana Torrini, the Icelandic-Italian singer who sang the spooky 'Gollum's Song' in the Lord of the Rings film *The Two Towers* (2002).

Back home, Reykjavík has a flourishing music scene with a constant-ly changing line-up of new bands and sounds – see www.icelandmusic. is for an idea of the variety. Seabear, an indie-folk band, have spawned several top music-makers such as Sin Fang (try *Flowers* from 2013) and Sóley (*We Sink* from 2012). Árstíðir record minimalist indie-folk, and had a 2013 YouTube viral hit when they sang a 13th-century Icelandic hymn a cappella in a train station in Germany. GusGus, a local pop-electronica act, have nine studio albums to their credit and opened for Justin Tim-berlake at his sold-out 2014 concert in Reykjavík.

Other local acts include FM Belfast (an electronica band who set up their own recording label to release their first album, *How to Make Friends*, 2008); their latest is *Brighter Days*, 2014); múm (experimen-tal electronica mixed with traditional instruments; their latest is *Smile-wound*, 2013); Mínus (whose thrashy guitars have supported Foo Fight-ers and Metallica; but now may be on hiatus); Hafdís Huld (spiky female popstress); and ebullient garage-rockers Benny Crespo's Gang. HAM was a relatively early hard-rock band which released its first album in 1988 but have lately seen a resurgence after a 16-year break and the release of *Svik, harmur, og dauði* (Betrayal, Tragedy and Death; 2011). Retro Ste-fsson is a newer alt-pop act, and Hermigervill makes electro-pop and shows up on concert circuits.

Similarly, Reykjavík's live-music venues are ever-changing – the best thing to do is to check the free website/paper *Reykjavík Grapevine* (www.grapevine.is) for current news and listings. And if your trip co-incides with one of the country's many music festivals, go! The fabu-lous Iceland Airwaves music festival (held in Reykjavík in November) showcases Iceland's talent along with international acts, as does Secret Solstice (June) and ATP Festival (July). Þjóðhátíð (National Festival) in Vestmannaeyjar, attracts over 16,000 people for four days of music and debauchery in late July or early August.

Traditional Music

Until rock and roll arrived in the 20th century, Iceland was a land prac-tically devoid of musical instruments. The Vikings brought the *fiðla* and the *langspil* with them from Scandinavia – both a kind of two-stringed box rested on the player's knee and played with a bow. They were never solo instruments but merely served to accompany singers.

Instruments were generally an unheard-of luxury and singing was the sole form of music. The most famous song styles are *rímur* (poetry or stories from the sagas performed in a low, eerie chant; Sigur Rós have dabbled with the form), and *fimmundasöngur* (sung by two people in harmony). Cut off from other influences, the Icelandic singing style bare-ly changed from the 14th century to the 20th century; it also managed to retain harmonies that were banned by the church across the rest of Europe on the basis of being the work of the devil!

You'll find choirs around Iceland performing traditional music, and there are compilation albums, such as *Inspired by Harpa – The Tra-ditional Songs of Iceland* (2013), that give a sampling of Icelandic folk songs or *rímur*.

Reykjavík's cutting-edge Harpa concert hall with its fa-cade of glimmer-ing hexagons has four state-of-the art stages and amazing acous-tics. It's a great place to catch a show.

ICELANDIC CULTURE: SAGAS TO SIGUR RÓS MUSIC

Reykjavík Arts Festival (late May to early June) is an interesting chance to see the intersection of Icelandic visual, literary, musical and performing arts.

Cinema

Iceland's film industry is young – regular production started around the early 1980s – but it's created some distinctive work to date. Icelandic short films have received all kinds of international awards. Full-length features are rarer, but they often contain the same quirky, dark subject matter and superb cinematography, using Iceland's powerful landscape as a backdrop.

For a list of the latest on Icelandic feature films, documentaries and animation, visit the website www.icelandic filmcenter.is.

In 1992 the film world first took notice of Iceland when *Children of Nature* was nominated for an Academy Award for Best Foreign Film. In it, an elderly couple forced into a retirement home in Reykjavík make a break for the countryside. The director, Friðrik Þór Friðriksson, is something of a legend in Icelandic cinema circles. *Cold Fever* (1994), *Angels of the Universe* (2000) and *The Sunshine Boy* (2009) are well worth watching.

Another film that put Reykjavík on the cinematic map is *101 Reykjavík* (2000), directed by Baltasar Kormákur and based on the novel by Hallgrímur Helgason. This dark comedy explores sex, drugs and the life of a loafer in downtown Reykjavík. Kormákur's *Jar City* (2006) stars the ever-watchable Ingvar E Sigurðsson as Iceland's favourite detective, Inspector Erlendur, from the novels by Arnaldur Indriðason. Kormákur's 2012 film, *The Deep*, was a hit, and in 2013 he launched into Hollywood life with *2 Guns,* starring Denzel Washington and Mark Wahlberg, and *Everest* (2015) starring Keira Knightley, Robin Wright and Jake Gyllenhaal.

Dagur Kári is another Icelandic director who has achieved international success. His films include *Nói Albinói* (2003), about a restless adolescent in a snowed-in northern fjord town, and the English-language *The Good Heart* (2009), which received a standing ovation at its premiere at the 2009 Toronto International Film Festival. Also look out for Hilmar Oddsson's *Kaldaljós* (Cold Light; 2004), a slow-moving, poignant film about life in an isolated fjord town, with a stunning performance from the little boy on whom it centres.

Hafsteinn Gunnar Sigurðsson's first feature film *Either Way* (2011), about two road workers painting stripes on the highway, was remade in the US by David Gordon Green as *Prince Avalanche* (2013). His *Paris of the North* (2014) is a father-son comedy-drama set in remote east Iceland and was a hit at film festivals.

Benedikt Erlingsson's 2013 *Of Horses and Men* was an indie sensation for its surreal portrait of the intertwining lives of men and horses, from the horses' perspective. It was nominated as Iceland's entry to the Academy Awards. Erlingsson is also an actor, and had a role in Rúnar Rúnarsson's 2011 *Volcano* (Eldfjall), about an aging couple who evacuated from the Vestmannaeyjar (Westman Islands) during the eruption of Eldfjall, and how they reconcile illness with family. The quirky 2012 documentary *The Final Member* details the bizarre quest for a *homo sapiens* penis for the Icelandic Phallological Museum in Reykjavík.

READY FOR ITS CLOSE-UP

Iceland has become a Hollywood darling for location shooting. Its immense alien beauty and the government's 20% production rebate for film-makers have encouraged Hollywood directors to make movies here. Try to spot the Icelandic scenery in blockbusters such as *Tomb Raider* (2001), *Die Another Day* (2002), *Batman Begins* (2005), *Flags of Our Fathers* (2006), *Stardust* (2007), *Journey to the Centre of the Earth* (2008), *Prometheus* (2012), *Oblivion* (2013), *Star Trek: Into Darkness* (2013), *The Secret Life of Walter Mitty* (2013), *Noah* (2014) and the HBO series *Game of Thrones*. *Star Wars Episode VII* was shot here too.

Film and TV directors aren't the only ones who ditch the CGI when they can get the real thing in Iceland. Musicians shoot videos here too, from Björk and Of Monsters and Men, to Sigur Rós. Don't miss Sigur Rós' inspiring concert film *Heima* (2007), starring the Icelandic people and their roaring falls and towering mountains. Bon Iver's 2011 video *Holocene* is six minutes that the Icelandic Tourist Board should co-opt for their ad campaigns.

Painting & Sculpture

Many of Iceland's most successful artists have studied abroad before returning home to wrestle with Iceland's enigmatic soul. The result is a European-influenced style, but with Icelandic landscapes and saga-related scenes as key subjects. Refreshingly, you'll find museums stocked with wonderful works by men and women alike.

The first great Icelandic landscape painter was the prolific Ásgrímur Jónsson (1876–1958), who produced a startling number of Impressionistic oils and watercolours depicting Icelandic landscapes and folk tales. You can see his work at the National Gallery in Reykjavík.

One of Ásgrímur's students was Johannes Kjarval (1885–1972), Iceland's most enduringly popular artist, who grew up in the remote east Iceland village of Borgarfjörður Eystri. His first commissioned works were, rather poignantly, drawings of farms for people who were emigrating, but he's most famous for his early charcoal sketches of people from the village and for his surreal landscapes. A whole beautiful building of the Reykjavík Museum of Art (Kjarvalsstadir) is named for him.

Sculpture is also very well represented in Iceland, with works dotting parks, gardens and galleries across the country. The most famous Icelandic sculptors all have museums dedicated to them in Reykjavík. Notable exponents include Einar Jónsson (1874–1954), whose mystical works dwell on death and resurrection, and Ásmundur Sveinsson (1893–1982) whose wide-ranging captivating kinetic work celebrate Iceland, its stories and its people. Don't miss Reykjavík Art Museum's Asmundarsafn, the artist's peaceful former studio filled with inspiring sculptures. Sigurjón Ólafsson (1908–92) specialised in busts but also dabbled in abstract forms. Gerður Helgadóttir (1928–75) made beautiful stained glass and sculpture, and has a museum dedicated to her in Kópavogur. You'll also find her work in Reykjavík's Hljómskálagarður Park, along with pieces by Gunnfríður Jónsdóttir (1889–1968), Nína Sæmundson (1892–1962), Þorbjörg Pálsdóttir (1919–2009) and Ólöf Pálsdóttir (1920–).

Iceland's most famous contemporary painter is probably pop-art icon Erró (Guðmundur Guðmundsson), who has donated his entire collection to Reykjavík Art Museum's Hafnarhús. Danish-Icelandic artist Olafur Eliasson (1967–) creates powerful installations and designed the facade of Reykjavík's dazzling concert hall, Harpa.

Architecture & Design

Iceland's Viking longhouses have succumbed to the ravages of time, but traditional turf-and-wood techniques were used right up until the 19th century. There is a good example at Glaumbær (north Iceland).

Guðjón Samúelsson (1887–1950), perhaps one of Iceland's most famous 20th-century architects, worked to create a distinctive Icelandic style, and you will find his minimalist buildings all over the country, from Hallgrímskirkja and the nearby swimming pool, Sundhöllin, in Reykjavík, to Þingvallabær (the farmhouse at Þingvellir) and Héraðsskólinn, formerly a school in Laugarvatn. *A Guide to Icelandic Architecture* (Association of Icelandic Architects) looks at 250 Icelandic buildings and designs.

Iceland's coterie of unique designers, artists and architects tend to be Reykjavík based. Many form collectives and open shops and galleries, full of handmade, beautiful work. Reykjavík's Iceland Design Centre (www.icelanddesign.is) has loads more information, and their DesignMarch annual event (www.designmarch.is) opens hundreds of exhibitions and workshops to the public.

Check out the Designers and Farmers Project (www.designersandfarmers.com/en), which united Iceland's locally sourced produce with the country's penchant for all things streamlined and thoughtfully made.

ICELANDIC CULTURE: SAGAS TO SIGUR RÓS PAINTING & SCULPTURE

Many Icelandic painters and musicians are serious creative artists in multiple disciplines. Some are making a splash overseas, like Ragnar Kjartansson, who represents this newest breed of Icelandic artist: part painter, part actor, director or musician. Reykjavík Art Museum's Hafnarhús and Reykjavík galleries do a great job showcasing them.

The Museum of Design and Applied Art (www.honnunarsafn.is) in Garðabær, 7.5km south of Reykjavík, showcases the local design scene from the early 20th century to today.

Icelandic Attitudes

Centuries of isolation and hardship have instilled particular character traits in the small, homogenous Icelandic population. Their connection to their homeland, history and countrymen is deeply felt, even if the land reciprocates that love with some sharp edges. The nation's 325,000 souls tend to respond to life's challenges with a compelling mix of courage, candour and creativity, edged with a dark, dry humour.

Iceland is the world's most peaceful country according to the Global Peace Index, which has ranked the country top of the pops every year since 2008. The GPI bases its findings on factors such as levels of violent crime, political instability and what percentage of a country's population is in prison.

The Little Book of the Icelanders, by Alda Sigmundsdóttir, is a wonderful collection of 50 miniature essays on the 'quirks and foibles' of the Icelandic people, written by an insightful Icelander who returned to live in the country after 22 years abroad.

'Þetta reddast' & the National Psyche

Icelanders have a reputation as tough, hardy, elemental types, and rural communities are still deeply involved in the fishing and/or farming industries. Geographically speaking, 'rural' could be said to define most of the country outside the capital region – and it's home to only 36% of Iceland's total population.

Naturally enough for people living on a remote island in a harsh environment, Icelanders are self-reliant individualists who don't like being told what to do. The current whaling debate is a prime example. Although most Icelanders wouldn't dream of eating whale meat, a majority are in support of hunting – a silent sticking-up of two fingers at the disapproving outside world.

But these steadfast exteriors often hide a more dreamy interior world. Iceland has always had a rich cultural heritage and an incredibly high literacy rate, and its people have a passion for all things artistic. This enthusiasm is true of the whole country, but it's particularly noticeable in downtown Reykjavík, where seemingly everyone plays in a band, dabbles in art or design, makes films or writes poetry or prose – they're positively bursting with creative impulses.

This buoyant, have-a-go attitude was hit hard during the financial meltdown. Soup kitchens sprang up in the city and thousands of younger people left Iceland to try their luck in Norway. But Icelanders have resilience built into their DNA. In just a few short years, emigration rates fell, and confidence started springing up around the country, mushrooming along with new businesses catering to the tourist boom. The country has regained its belief in the old saying '*Þetta reddast*' (roughly translated, 'it will all work out okay'). The phrase is so frequently used it has been described as the country's motto.

Although their pride may have taken a temporary kicking, Icelanders are calmly, rightfully patriotic. Icelandair wishes a heartfelt 'Welcome home!' to its Icelandic passengers when the plane touches down at Keflavík. Citizens who achieve international success are quietly feted: celebrities such as Björk and Sigur Rós reflect prestige onto their entire homeland.

Town layouts, the former US military base, and the prevalence of hot dogs and Coca-Cola point to a heavy US influence, but Icelanders consider their relationship with the rest of Scandinavia to be more important. Although they seem to conform to the cool-and-quiet Nordic stereotype, Icelanders are curious about visitors and eager to know what outsiders think of them: 'How do you like Iceland?' is invariably an early question. And an incredible transformation takes place on Friday and Saturday nights, when inhibitions fall away and conversations flow as fast as the alcohol.

Work Hard, Play Hard

In the last century the Icelandic lifestyle has shifted from isolated family communities living on scattered farms and in coastal villages to a more urban-based society, with the majority of people living in the southwestern corner around Reykjavík. Despite this more outward-looking change, family connections are still very strong, although young people growing up in rural Iceland are more likely to move to Reykjavík to study and work.

Icelanders work hard (the retirement age is 70) and often at a number of jobs, especially in summer's peak when there is money to be made feeding, accommodating, driving and guiding thousands of tourists. The locals have enjoyed a very high standard of living in the late 20th and early 21st centuries – but keeping up with the Jónssons and Jónsdóttirs came at a price. For decades, Icelanders straight out of university borrowed money to buy houses or 4WDs and spent the rest of their days living on credit and paying off loans. Then, in 2008, the crash occurred, and that huge national debt suddenly had to be paid back. People wondered how Iceland would ever work itself out of its economic black hole. And yet, with characteristic grit, resilience, adaptability and imagination, Icelanders are hauling their country back from disaster.

The Icelandic addiction to grafting is counterbalanced by recreational indulgences. The bingeing in Reykjavík on Friday and Saturday nights is an example of relaxation gone mad. So too are the hundreds of summer houses you'll see when you're driving around the Golden Circle, and the exceptional number of swimming pools, which form the social hub of Icelandic life.

Women in Iceland

In 2013, Iceland held the top spot (for the fifth consecutive year) in the World Economic Forum's Global Gender Gap Index. The index measured and ranked 136 countries on one important aspect of gender equality — the relative gaps between women and men across four key areas: health, education, economics and politics. Iceland continues to be the country with the narrowest gender gap in the world – this means Icelandic women have greater access to health and education, and are more politically and economically empowered than women in other countries.

The Viking settlement of Iceland clearly demanded toughness of character, and the sagas are full of feisty women (for example, Hallgerður

Iceland has one of the world's highest life expectancies – 81 years for men and 84 years for women.

WHAT'S IN A NAME?

Icelanders' names are constructed from a combination of their first name and their father's (or, more rarely, mother's) first name. Girls add the suffix *dóttir* (daughter) to the patronymic and boys add *son*. Therefore, Jón, the son of Einar, would be Jón Einarsson. Guðrun, the daughter of Einar, would be Guðrun Einarsdóttir.

Because Icelandic surnames only usually tell people what your dad's called, Icelanders use first names, even when addressing strangers. It makes for a wonderfully democratic society when you're expected to address your president or top police commissioner by their first name. And yes, trivia buffs, the telephone directory is alphabetised by first name.

About 10% of Icelanders have family names (most dating back to early settlement times), but they're rarely used. In an attempt to homogenise the system, government legislation forbids anyone to take on a new family name or adopt the family name of their spouse.

There's also an official list of names that Icelanders are permitted to call their children, and any additions to this list have to be approved by the Icelandic Naming Committee. For the 5000 or so children born in Iceland each year, the committee reportedly receives about 100 applications and rejects about half. Among its requirements are that given names must be 'capable of having Icelandic grammatical endings', and may not 'conflict with the linguistic structure of Iceland'.

Höskuldsdóttir, who declines to save her husband's life due to a slap that he gave her years earlier). For centuries, Icelandic women had to take care of farms and families while their male partners headed off to sea. Women and men struggled equally through Iceland's long, dark history; modern gender equality is a pretty recent phenomenon.

Women gained full voting rights in 1920, but it wasn't until the 1970s that protest movements reached Iceland and attitudes began to change. Particularly powerful was the 'women's day off' on 24 October 1975: the country ceased to function when 90% of Icelandic women stayed away from work and stay-at-home mums left children with their menfolk for the day.

In 1980 Iceland became the first democracy to elect a female president, the much-loved Vigdís Finnbogadóttir. In 2009, the world's first openly gay prime minister, Jóhanna Sigurðardóttir, came into power. Iceland has among the highest rate of women's participation in the labour market among OECD countries, at 78.5%.

The social care system is so good that women have few worries about the financial implications of raising a child alone: maternity leave provisions are excellent, childcare is affordable, there is no sense that motherhood precludes work or study, and there's no stigma attached to unmarried mothers. The country isn't perfect – sexual violence and unequal pay are still issues – but Icelandic women are well educated and independent, with the same opportunities as Icelandic men.

Iceland only had one TV channel until 1988 – which went off air on Thursdays so that citizens could do something more productive instead. It's said that most children born before 1988 were conceived on a Thursday...

Icelandic Ancestry & Genetic Research

Biotech research is big in Iceland – thanks, in part, to the 12th-century historian Ari the Learned. Ari's Landnámabók and Íslendingabók mean that Icelanders can trace their family trees right back to the 9th century.

In 1996, neuroscience expert Dr Kári Stefánsson recognised that this genealogical material could be combined with Iceland's unusually homogenous population to produce something unique – a country-sized genetic laboratory. In 1998 the Icelandic government controversially voted to allow the creation of a single database, by presumed consent, containing all Icelanders' genealogical, genetic and medical records. Even more controversially, the government allowed Kári's biotech startup company deCODE Genetics to create this database, and access it for its biomedical research, using the database to trace inheritable diseases and pinpoint the genes that cause them. The decision sparked public outrage in Iceland and arguments across the globe about its implications for human rights and medical ethics. Should a government be able to sell off its citizens' medical records? And is it acceptable for a private corporation to use such records for profit?

While the arguments raged (and investors flocked), the company set to work. The database was declared unconstitutional in 2003, deCODE was declared bankrupt in 2010, and sold to US biotech giant Amgen in 2012. By that time, deCODE had built a research database using DNA and clinical data from more than 100,000 volunteers (one-third of the population), and had done work in isolating gene mutations linked to heart attacks, strokes and Alzheimer's disease. deCODE continues to unravel the mysteries of the human genome, and in 2014 began a controversial new drive to encourage more Icelanders to voluntarily donate their genetic material to its database.

Even though Icelanders speak the nearest thing to Viking in existence, Iceland is the least purely Scandinavian of all the Nordic countries. DNA studies have shown that much of Icelanders' genetic make-up is Celtic, suggesting that many Viking settlers had children by their British and Irish slaves.

Religious Beliefs

Norse

At the time of the Settlement Era, Iceland's religion was Ásatrú, which means 'faith in the Aesir' (the old Norse gods). Óðinn, Þór (Thor) and Freyr were the major trinity worshipped across Scandinavia. Óðinn, their chief, is the god of war and poetry, a brooding and intimidating presence.

In Iceland most people were devoted to Þór (Icelandic names such as Þórir, Þórdís and Þóra are still very popular). This burly, red-haired god of the common people controlled thunder, wind, storm and natural disaster, and was a vital deity for farmers and fishermen to have on their side. Freyr and his twin sister Freyja represent fertility and sexuality. Freyr brought springtime, with its romantic implications, to both the human and the animal world, and was in charge of the perpetuation of all species.

Icelanders peacefully converted to Christianity more than a thousand years ago, but the old gods linger on. The Ásatrú religion evolved in the 1970s, almost simultaneously in Iceland, the US and the UK. Whereas membership of other religions in Iceland has remained fairly constant, Ásatrúarfélagið (Ásatrú Association; www.asatru.is) is growing. It is now Iceland's largest non-Christian religious organisation, with approximately 2400 members in 2014.

Christianity

Traditionally, the date of the decree that officially converted Iceland to Christianity has been given as 1000, but research has determined that it probably occurred in 999. What is known is that the changeover of religions was a political decision. In the Icelandic Alþing (National Assembly), Christians and pagans had been polarising into two radically opposite factions, threatening to divide the country. Þorgeir, the *lögsögumaður* (law speaker), appealed for moderation on both sides, and eventually it was agreed that Christianity would officially become the new religion, although pagans were still allowed to practise in private. Today, as in mainland Scandinavia, most Icelanders (around 80%) belong to the Protestant Lutheran Church – but many are nonpractising. Church attendance is very low.

In his book *The Almost Nearly Perfect People*, author Michael Booth seeks to explore 'the truth about the Nordic miracle'. He presents some great stats and entertaining insights on Icelanders, from crash culprits to *huldufólk* superstitions.

ICELANDIC ATTITUDES RELIGIOUS BELIEFS

SUPERNATURAL ICELAND: GHOSTS, TROLLS & HIDDEN PEOPLE

Once you've seen some of the lava fields, eerie natural formations and isolated farms that characterise much of the Icelandic landscape, it will come as no surprise that many Icelanders believe their country is populated by *huldufólk* (hidden people) and ghosts.

In the lava are *jarðvergar* (gnomes), *álfar* (elves), *ljósálfar* (fairies), *dvergar* (dwarves), *ljúflingar* (lovelings), *tívar* (mountain spirits) and *englar* (angels). Stories about them have been handed down through generations, and many modern Icelanders claim to have seen them...or at least to know someone who has.

As in Ireland, there are stories about projects going wrong when workers try to build roads through *huldufólk* homes: the weather turns bad, machinery breaks down, labourers fall ill. In mid 2014 Iceland's 'whimsy factor' again made international news when a road project to link the Álftanes peninsula to the Reykjavík suburb of Garðabær was halted after campaigners warned it would disturb elf habitat.

As for Icelandic ghosts, they're substantial beings – not the wafting shadows found elsewhere in Europe. Írafell-Móri (*móri* and *skotta* are used for male and female ghosts, respectively) needed to eat supper every night, and one of the country's most famous spooks, Sel-Móri, got seasick when he stowed away in a boat. Stranger still, two ghosts haunting the same area often join forces to double their trouble. Rock stacks and weird lava formations around the country are often said to be trolls, caught out at sunrise and turned forever to stone. But living trolls are seldom seen today – they're more the stuff of children's stories.

Surveys suggest that more than half of Icelanders believe in (or at least entertain the possibility of) the existence of, *huldufólk*. But a word of warning: many Icelanders get sick of visitors asking them whether they believe in supernatural beings. Their pride bristles at the 'Those cute Icelanders! They all believe in pixies!' attitude...and even if they don't entirely disbelieve, they're unlikely to admit it to a stranger. If you want to know more, and ask all the questions you can, join a tour in Hafnarfjörður (see p92), or sign up for a course at the **Icelandic Elf School** (Álfaskólinn; www.elfmuseum.com) in Reykjavík. Yes, there really is such a place, and it runs four-hour introductory classes most Fridays.

Icelandic Cuisine

If people know anything about Icelandic food, it's usually boundary-pushing dishes such as fermented shark or sheep's head. It's a pity the spotlight doesn't shine as brightly on Iceland's delicious, fresh-from-the-farm ingredients, the seafood bounty hauled from surrounding waters, the innovative dairy products or the clever historic food-preserving techniques that are finding new favour with today's much-feted New Nordic chefs.

North: The New Nordic Cuisine of Iceland, by chefs Gunnar Karl Gíslason and Jody Eddy, is a beautiful new book that profiles traditional Icelandic food producers, many of them suppliers to Gunnar's first-class Dill restaurant.

Food Heritage

For much of its history, Iceland was a poverty-stricken hinterland. Sparse soil and cursed weather produced limited crops, and Icelandic farmer-fishermen relied heavily on sheep, fish and seabirds to keep from starving. Every part of every creature was eaten – fresh or dried, salted, smoked, pickled in whey or even buried underground (in the case of shark meat), with preserving techniques honed to ensure food lasted through lean times.

Fish, seafood, lamb, bread and simple vegetables still form the typical Icelandic diet. Local food producers and chefs are rediscovering old recipes and techniques with a renewed sense of pride in the country's culinary heritage, and the results can be quite special. The strong Slow Food movement prioritises locally grown food over imports, with restaurants proudly flagging up regional treats.

Staples & Specialities

Fish & Seafood

'Half of our country is the sea', runs an old Icelandic saying. Fish is still the mainstay of the Icelandic diet: you'll find it fresh-caught at market stalls and in restaurant kitchens, from where it emerges boiled, pan-fried, baked or grilled.

In the past, Icelanders merely kept the cheeks and tongues of *þorskur* (cod) – something of a delicacy – and exported the rest; but today you'll commonly find cod fillets on the menu, along with *ýsa* (haddock), *bleikja* (Arctic char) and meaty-textured *skötuselur* (monkfish). Other fish include *lúða* (halibut), *steinbítur* (catfish), *sandhverfa* (turbot; not an indigenous fish), *síld* (herring), *skarkoli* (plaice) and *skata* (skate). During the summer you can try *silungur* (freshwater trout) and *villtur lax* (wild salmon). Farmed salmon is *eldislax*; it's available year-round, and appears on countless menus in smoked form.

Harðfiskur, a popular snack eaten with butter, is found in supermarkets and at market stalls. To make it, haddock is cleaned and dried in the open air until it has become dehydrated and brittle, then it's torn into strips.

Shrimp *(rækja)*, scallops *(hörpudiskur)* and blue mussels *(kræklingur)* are harvested in Icelandic waters – mussels are at their prime during the very beginning and the end of summer. *Humar* (or *leturhumar)* are a real treat: these are what Icelanders call 'lobster', although the rest of us know them as langoustine. Höfn, in southeast Iceland, is particularly well known for them and even has an annual lobster festival.

Where to Find Fresh...

Langoustines: Höfn

Tomatoes: Flúðir

Reindeer: Egilsstaðir & Eastfjords

Hverabrauð ('hot springs bread'): Mývatn

Mussels: Stykkishólmur

Foal: Skagafjörður

Meat

Icelandic lamb is hard to beat. During summer, sheep roam free to munch on chemical-free grasses and herbs in the highlands and valleys, before the September *réttir* (sheep roundup), after which they are corralled for the winter. The result of this life of relative luxury is very tender lamb with a slightly gamey flavour. You'll find lamb fillets, pan-fried lamb or smoked lamb on most restaurant menus.

Beef steaks are also excellent but not as widely available, and are consequently more expensive. Horse is still eaten in Iceland, although it's regarded as something of a delicacy – so if you see 'foal fillets' on the menu, you're not imagining things.

In eastern Iceland wild reindeer roam the highlands, and reindeer steaks are a feature of local menus. Hunting is highly regulated; reindeer season starts in late July and runs well into September.

Birds have always been part of the Icelandic diet. *Lundi* (puffin) used to appear smoked or broiled in liver-like lumps on dinner plates, although it's a rarer sight these days following a worrying crash in puffin numbers. Another seabird is *svartfugl;* it's commonly translated as 'blackbird' on English-language menus, but what you'll actually get is guillemot. High-class restaurants favouring seasonal ingredients may have roasted *heiðagæs* (pink-footed goose) in autumn.

Sweets & Desserts

Don't miss *skyr,* a delicious yoghurt-like concoction made from pasteurised skimmed milk. Despite its rich and decadent flavour, it's actually low in fat and is often mixed with sugar, fruit flavours (such as blueberry) and cream to give it an extra-special taste and texture. *Skyr* can be found in any supermarket and as a dessert in restaurants.

Icelandic *pönnukökur* (pancakes) are thin, sweet and cinnamon flavoured. Icelandic *kleinur* (twisted doughnuts) are a chewy treat, along with their offspring *ástarpungar* (love balls), deep-fried, spiced balls of dough. You'll find these desserts in bakeries, along with an amazing array of fantastic pastries and cakes – one of the few sweet legacies of the Danish occupation.

Food lovers may be tempted by the 'Local Food and Gourmet' tour run by Saga Travel (www.sagatravel.is), which allows travellers to sample fish, beef, lamb, beer and ice cream from food producers in the fertile farmland around Akureyri.

ICELANDIC CUISINE STAPLES & SPECIALITIES

TASTEBUD TOURING

We think that the incredible local fish and lamb should be high on your hit-list in Iceland. You may be considering the 'novelty value' of sampling the likes of whale, puffin and even *hákarl* (rotted Greenland shark), but please do consider your actions (see p79). Try these delicious blasts of local flavour instead.

Skyr Rich and creamy yoghurt-like staple, sometimes sweetened with sugar and berries. You can consume it in yoghurt-style drinks or local desserts, playing a starring role in cheesecake and crème brulée (or even 'skyramisu') concoctions.

Hangikjöt Literally 'hung meat', usually smoked lamb, served in thin slices (it's traditionally a Christmas dish).

Harðfiskur Brittle pieces of wind-dried haddock ('fish jerky'?), usually eaten with butter.

Pýlsur Icelandic hot dogs, made with a combination of lamb, beef and pork, and topped with raw and deep-fried onion, ketchup, mustard and tangy remoulade (ask for *'eina með öllu'* – one with everything).

Liquorice Salt liquorice and chocolate-covered varieties fill the supermarket sweets aisles.

Rúgbrauð Dark, dense rye bread. Look for *hverabrauð* in Mývatn – it's baked underground using geothermal heat.

A BANQUET OF BODY PARTS

Eyeball a plate of old-fashioned Icelandic food, and chances are it will eyeball you back. In the past nothing was wasted, and some traditional specialities look more like horror-film props than food. You won't be faced with these dishes on many menus, though – they're generally only eaten at þorramatur (literally, 'food of Þorri') buffets during the Þorrablót midwinter feast (named for the month of Þorri in the Old Norse calendar, and corresponding to mid-January to mid-February). Plentiful brennivín (schnapps) is the expected accompaniment.

Svið Singed sheep's head (complete with eyes) sawn in two, boiled and eaten fresh or pickled.

Sviðasulta (head cheese) Made from bits of svið pressed into gelatinous loaves and pickled in whey.

Slátur (the word means 'slaughter') Comes in two forms: lifrarpylsa is liver sausage, made from a mishmash of sheep intestines, liver and lard tied up in a sheep's stomach and cooked (kind of like Scottish haggis). Blóðmör has added sheep's blood (and equates to blood pudding).

Súrsaðir hrútspungar Rams' testicles pickled in whey and pressed into a cake.

Hákarl Iceland's most famous stomach churner, hákarl is Greenland shark, an animal so inedible it has to rot away underground for six months before humans can even digest it. Most foreigners find the stench (a cross between ammonia and week-old roadkill) too much to bear, but it tastes better than it smells... It's the aftertaste that really hurts. A shot of brennivín is traditionally administered as an antidote.

Local dairy farms churn out scrumptious scoops of homemade ice cream – they're often featured on the menus of nearby restaurants. Alongside boring old vanilla sit novel flavours such as beer, liquorice and béarnaise sauce.

Salt Eldhús (www. salteldhus.is) is a small cooking school in Reykjavík that offers a 'Local in Focal' cooking course for visitors, using local ingredients to create a three-course meal.

Drinks

Nonalcoholic

Life without kaffi (coffee) is unthinkable. Cafes and petrol stations will usually have an urn of filter coffee by the counter, and some shops offer complimentary cups to customers. Snug European-style cafes selling espresso, latte, cappuccino and mocha are ever-more popular, popping up even in the most isolated one-horse hamlets (the coffee isn't always good, though). Tea is available, but ranks a very poor second choice – the brand sitting on most supermarket shelves makes a feeble brew.

Besides all that coffee, Icelanders drink more Coca-Cola per capita than any other country. Another very popular soft drink is Egils Appelsín (orange soda) and the home-grown Egils Malt Extrakt, which tastes like sugar-saturated beer.

It isn't a crime to buy bottled water in Iceland, but it should be. Icelandic tap water generally comes from the nearest glacier, and is some of the purest you'll ever drink.

Alcoholic

For some Icelanders, drinking alcohol is not about the taste – getting trollied is the aim of the game. Particularly in Reykjavík, it's the done thing to go out at the weekend and drink till you drop.

You must be at least 20 years old to buy beer, wine or spirits, and alcohol is only available from licensed bars, restaurants and the government-run Vínbúðin liquor stores (www.vinbudin.is). There are roughly 50 shops around the country; most towns have one, and the greater Reykjavík area has about a dozen. In larger places, they usually open from 11am to 6pm Monday to Thursday and on Saturdays, and 11am to 7pm on Fridays (closed Sundays). In small communities, the Vínbúðin store may only open for an hour or two in the late afternoon/evening. Expect queues around 5pm on a Friday. The cheapest bottles of imported wine cost from Ikr1300. Beer costs about a third of what you'll pay in a bar.

Petrol stations and supermarkets sell the weak and watery 2.2% brew known as pilsner, but most Icelanders would sooner not drink it at all. The main brands of Icelandic beer – Egils, Gull, Thule and Viking – are all fairly standard lager or pils brews; you can also get imported beers. In recent years a slew of good local distilleries and breweries have sprung up all over Iceland, concocting whiskey, vodka and dozens of high-calibre craft beers – check our cheat sheet (p85) for your next bar-room order. Look out, too, for seasonal beers – the ones brewed for the Christmas period are especially popular.

Reports of astronomical prices for boozing in Iceland are not altogether true – a pint of beer in a bar costs around Ikr800 to Ikr1200. In Reykjavík, many venues have early-evening happy hours that cut costs to between Ikr500 and Ikr700 per beer. Download the smartphone Reykjavík Appy Hour app to gladden your drinking budget.

The traditional Icelandic alcoholic brew is *brennivín* (literally 'burnt wine'), a potent schnapps made from fermented potatoes and flavoured with caraway seeds. It has the foreboding nickname *svarti dauði* (black death) and it's essential drinking if you're trying any tasty tidbits with a *þorramatur* flavour.

> Beer Day (1 March) dates back to the glorious day in 1989 when beer was legalised in Iceland (it was illegal for most of the 20th century). As you'd expect, Reykjavík's clubs and bars get particularly wild.

Where to Eat & Drink

Restaurants

Iceland's best restaurants are in Reykjavík, but some magnificent finds are mushrooming up beyond the capital, catering to travellers looking for authentic local flavours. These restaurants are tapping into the network of unsung local producers: barley farmers, mussel harvesters, veggie growers, the neighbouring sheep farmer and local fisherman. At many places, your meal's food miles will be *low*. You want local and seasonal? You've come to the right place.

Bear in mind that the price difference between an exceptional restaurant and an average one is often small, so it can be well worth going upmarket. Often, though, in rural Iceland you may not have a huge choice – the town's only eating place may be the restaurant in the local hotel, supplemented by the grill in the petrol station. And in peak summer, you may struggle to get a table without a reservation, and/or face long waits.

À la carte menus usually offer at least one fish dish, one veggie choice (invariably pasta) and a handful of meat mains (lamb stars, of course). Many restaurants also have a menu of cheaper meals such as hamburgers and pizzas. Soup will invariably appear – as a lunchtime option (perhaps in the form of a soup-and-salad buffet), or as a dinnertime starter. *Fiskisúpa* (fish soup) comes courtesy of various family recipes, while *kjötsúpa* (meat soup) will usually feature veggies and small chunks of lamb.

> Chef Anthony Bourdain described *hákarl* as 'probably the single worst thing I have ever put in my mouth'.

EATING PRICES

The eating reviews in this book are divided into the following price categories based on the cost of an average main course.

€ less than Ikr2000 (€13)

€€ Ikr2000–5000 (€13–32)

€€€ more than Ikr5000 (€32)

In Reykjavík, and to a lesser extent Akureyri, there are some ethnic restaurants, including Thai, Japanese, Italian, Mexican, Indian and Chinese.

Opening hours for restaurants are usually 11.30am to 2.30pm and 6pm to 10pm daily. Note that even in summer, restaurants may stop serving meals around 9pm.

Cafes & Pubs

Downtown Reykjavík has a great range of bohemian cafe-bars where you can happily while away the hours sipping coffee, people-watching, scribbling postcards or tinkering on your laptop. Menus range from simple soups and sandwiches to fish dishes and designer burgers. Recent years have seen cafe menus morph into more restaurant-like menus (with an attendant hike in prices). The cafe scene is spreading, too, with some cool new spots scattered around the country.

Many of Reykjavík's cafes morph into wild drinking dens in the evenings (mostly Fridays and Saturdays). Suddenly DJs appear, coffee orders turn to beer, and people get progressively louder and less inhibited as the evening goes on, usually until sometime between 4am and 5am. Outside the capital, things are considerably more subdued, although Friday and Saturday nights do see action in Akureyri.

Hot-Dog Stands & Petrol Stations

Icelanders do enjoy fast food! If you see a queue in Reykjavík, it probably ends at a *pýlsur* (hot dog) stand. Large petrol stations often have good, cheap, well-patronised grills and cafeterias attached. They generally serve sandwiches and fast food from around 11am to 9pm or 10pm. Some also offer hearty set meals at lunchtime, such as meat soup, fish of the day or plates of lamb. Cafeterias at N1 service stations anywhere along the Ring Road are invariably busy.

Supermarkets & Bakeries

Every town and village has at least one small supermarket. The most expensive is 10-11, but it's generally open late. Bónus (easily recognised by its yellow-and-pink piggy sign) is the country's budget supermarket chain. Others include Hagkaup, Kjarval, Krónan, Nettó, Nóatún, Samkaup-Strax and Samkaup-Úrval. Opening times vary greatly; in Reykjavík most are open from 9am to 11pm daily, but outside the capital hours are almost always shorter. Sunday hours may be limited or nonexistent.

We can't praise the old-school Icelandic *bakarí* (bakeries) enough. Most towns have one (it may be part of a supermarket), generally open from 7am or 8am until 4pm on weekdays (sometimes also Saturdays). They sell all sorts of inexpensive fresh bread, buns, cakes, sandwiches and coffee, and usually provide chairs and tables.

Iceland has to import most of its groceries, so prices are steep – roughly two or three times what you'd pay in North America or Europe. Fish (tinned or smoked) and dairy products represent the best value and are surprisingly cheap. Some fruit and vegetables are grown locally, and these tend to be fresh and tasty, but imported vegetables sometimes look pretty sad by the time they hit the supermarket shelves.

Vegetarians & Vegans

You'll have no problem in Reykjavík – there are some excellent meat-free cafe-restaurants in the city, and many more eateries offer vegetarian choices (you'll probably want to eat every meal at Gló). Outside the capital most restaurants have at least one veggie item on the menu – although as this is routinely cheese-and-tomato pasta or pizza, you could get very bored. Vegans will usually have to self-cater.

Sweet, peppery caraway is used to flavour Icelandic cheese, coffee, bread and *brennivín*. In late August, after the plant has flowered, some Reykjavíkers make a trip to Viðey island to gather caraway seeds.

Check out *50 Crazy Things to Taste in Iceland*, by Snæfríður Ingadóttir (great photos by Þorvaldur Örn Kristmundsson), for a few fun pictorials of Iceland's traditional eats.

Survival Guide

Directory A–Z

Accommodation

Iceland has a full spectrum of accommodation options, from hikers' huts to business-standard hotels, hostels, working farms, guesthouses, apartments and school-based summer rooms. Luxury and boutique hotels are predominantly found in Reykjavík and tourism hotspots in the southwest, with a select few in regional pockets.

There's been a boom of new hotels and guesthouses, and many existing ones have expanded and upgraded to cater to the rapid increase in tourist numbers. Even still, demand often outstrips supply in tourist hotspots (eg. the capital, the south, Mývatn). Summer prices are *high*, and getting higher with increasing demand.

For the prices charged, accommodation is often of a lower standard than you might expect from a developed European destination. Although rooms are generally spotless, they are usually small, with thin walls and limited facilities.

Please note the following:

➡ We recommend that between June and August travellers book all accommodation in advance (note there is rarely any need to prebook campsites).

➡ Tourist information centres will generally have details of all the accommodation in their town/region. Larger centres have a booking service, where they will book accommodation for a small fee (usually around Ikr500). Note that this service is for walk-in visitors, not for prebooking via email. And don't rely on this – areas can and do book out quickly.

➡ Most accommodation providers in Iceland list their offerings on the website Booking.com – this is a useful tool as it can list all the available accommodation in a town/region on a specified date. You *may* get a better rate contacting the property direct.

➡ Prices for summer 2014 are generally listed in our reviews (or for summer 2015, when these were readily available). Travellers must expect that prices will rise from year to year. Websites will invariably list up-to-date prices.

➡ From September to May, most guesthouses and hotels offer discounts of 20% to 50% on their summer prices. Again, check websites for up-to-date prices.

➡ Many hotels and guesthouses close during winter; where this is the case, opening times are shown in the review. Many hotels and guesthouses close over the Christmas–New Year period. If no opening times are shown, accommodation is open year-round.

➡ Some accommodation lists its prices in euro. This is to ward against currency fluctuations; payment is made in Icelandic krónur.

➡ Many guesthouses and farmstays offer numerous options: camping; rooms with/without bathrooms, with made-up beds or sleeping-bags; cottages with/without kitchen and/ or bathroom. We try our best to explain what's available, but listing prices for all permutations is close to impossible. Check websites for full coverage.

➡ Our reviews indicate whether a private bathroom is offered; whether linen is included or there is a sleeping-bag option; and if breakfast is included in the price.

Camping

➡ *Tjaldsvæði* (organised campsites) are found in almost every town, at some rural farmhouses and along

SLEEPING WITH THE LOCALS

Two recommended websites can help you find a bed with a local host:

Airbnb (www.airbnb.com) Has private rooms, cottages, apartments and houses for rent throughout Iceland, with a large concentration in the capital.

Couchsurfing (www.couchsurfing.com) Access a great network of travellers hosting travellers.

major hiking trails. The best sites have washing machines, cooking facilities and hot showers, but others just have a cold-water tap and a toilet block. Some are attached to the local *sundlaug* (swimming pool), with shower facilities provided by the pool for a small fee.

➡ Icelandic weather is notoriously fickle, and if you intend to camp it's wise to invest in a good-quality tent. There are a few outfits in Reykjavík that offer rental of camping equipment, and some car-hire companies can also supply you with gear such as tents, sleeping mats and cooking equipment.

➡ With the increase in tourist numbers, campgrounds are getting busier, and the amenities block housing one or two shower cubicles is hardly enough to cope with the demand of dozens of campers.

➡ It is rarely necessary to book a camping place in advance. Many small-town campsites are unstaffed – there is a contact number for a caretaker posted on the amenities block, or an instruction to head to the tourist information centre/ swimming pool to pay; alternatively, a caretaker may visit the campsite in the evening to collect fees.

➡ Wild camping is possible in some areas but in practice it is often discouraged. In national parks and nature reserves you *must* camp in marked campsites, and you need to get permission

before camping on fenced land in all other places.

➡ When camping in parks and reserves the usual rules apply: leave sites as you find them, use biodegradable soaps, carry out your rubbish.

➡ Campfires are not allowed, so bring a stove. Butane cartridges and petroleum fuels are available in petrol stations. Blue Campingaz cartridges are not always readily available; the grey Coleman cartridges are more common.

➡ Camping with a tent or campervan/caravan usually costs Ikr1000 to Ikr1400 per person. Electricity is often an additional Ikr800. Many campsites charge for showers.

➡ A new 'lodging tax' of Ikr107 *per site* per night was introduced a few years ago; some places absorb this cost in the per-person rate, others make you pay it in addition to the per-person rate.

➡ Consider purchasing the Camping Card (www.campingcard.is), which costs €105 (in 2015) and covers 28 nights of camping at 44 campsites throughout the country for two adults and up to four children (but doesn't

include the lodging tax, or any charges for electricity or showers). Full details online.

➡ Most campsites open from mid-May to mid-September. Large campsites that also offer huts or cottages may be open year-round.

➡ The free accommodation directory *Áning* (available from tourist information centres) lists many of Iceland's campsites, but is not exhaustive.

Emergency Huts

➡ There are bright-orange survival huts on high mountain passes and along remote coastlines (usually marked on country maps in some way). The huts are stocked with emergency rations, fuel and blankets (and a radio to contact help). Note that it is illegal to use them in a non-emergency.

Farmhouse Accommodation

➡ Many rural farmhouses offer campsites, sleeping-bag spaces, made-up guestrooms and cabins and cottages. Over time, some 'farmhouses' have evolved into large country hotels.

➡ Facilities vary: some farms provide meals or have a guest kitchen, some have outdoor hot-pots (hot tubs), and many provide horse riding or can organise activities such as fishing. Roadside signs signal which farmhouses provide accommodation and what facilities they offer.

➡ Rates are similar to guesthouses in towns, with sleeping-bag accommodation around

SLEEPING PRICE RANGES

The following price categories are based on the high-season price of a double room:

€ less than Ikr15,000 (€100)

€€ Ikr15,000–30,000 (€100–200)

€€€ more than Ikr30,000 (€200)

Ikr6000 and made-up beds from Ikr9000 to Ikr14,000 per person. Breakfast (if not included in the room price) costs around Ikr1500 to Ikr2000, while an evening meal (usually served at a set time) costs around Ikr7000.

➡ Some 180 farm properties are members of Icelandic Farm Holidays (www. farmholidays.is), which publishes an annual listings guide called *Discover Rural Iceland;* free from most tourist information centres.

Guesthouses

➡ The term *gistiheimilið* (guesthouse) covers a variety of properties, from family homes renting out a few rooms to custom-built motels.

➡ Guesthouses vary enormously in character from stylish, contemporary options to plain, chintzy or dated decor. A surprisingly high number of them offer rooms only with shared bathroom.

➡ Most are comfortable and homey, with guest kitchens, TV lounges and buffet-style breakfast (either included in the price or for Ikr1500 to Ikr2000 extra).

➡ Some guesthouses offer sleeping-bag accommodation at a price significantly reduced from that of a made-up bed. Some places don't advertise a sleeping-bag option, so it pays to ask.

➡ As a general guide, sleeping-bag

accommodation costs Ikr6000, double rooms Ikr14,000 to Ikr20,000, and self-contained units from Ikr15,000 per night.

Hostels

➡ Iceland has 32 well-maintained hostels administered by **Hostelling International Iceland** (www. hostel.is). In Reykjavík and Akureyri, there are also independent backpacker hostels. Bookings are recommended at all of them, especially from June to August.

➡ About half the Hostelling International hostels open year-round. Check online for opening-date info.

➡ All hostels offer hot showers, cooking facilities and sleeping-bag accommodation, and most offer private rooms. If you don't have a sleeping bag, you can hire linen (varies, but around Ikr1500 per stay).

➡ Breakfast (where available) costs Ikr1500 to Ikr2000.

➡ Join **Hostelling International** (www.hihostels. com) in your home country to benefit from HI member discounts of Ikr700 per person. Nonmembers pay around Ikr4100 for a dorm bed; single/double rooms cost Ikr6900/11,200 (more for private bathrooms). Children aged five to 12 get a discount of Ikr1500.

Hotels

➡ Every major town has at least one business-style hotel, usually featuring comfortable but innocuous rooms with private bathroom, phone, TV and sometimes minibar. Invariably the hotels also have decent restaurants.

➡ Summer prices for singles/doubles start at around Ikr16,000/22,000 and include a buffet breakfast. Rates for a double room at a nice but non-luxurious hotel in a popular tourist area in peak summer can easily top Ikr30,000.

➡ Prices drop substantially outside high season (June to August), and cheaper rates may be found via online booking engines.

➡ The largest local chains are **Icelandair Hotels** (www. icelandairhotels.is) and the expanding **Fosshótel** (www. fosshotel.is) and **Keahotels** (www.keahotels.is) chains. New ones are cropping up – **Stracta Hótels** (www. stractahotels.is) is a new chain with plans to expand beyond its first base in Hella.

SUMMER HOTELS

➡ Once the school holidays begin, many schools, colleges and conference centres become summer hotels offering simple accommodation. Most open from early June to late August (some are open longer), and 12 are part of a chain called Hótel Edda, overseen by the Icelandair Hotels chain.

➡ Accommodation tends to be simple: rooms are plain but functional, usually with twin beds, a washbasin and shared bathrooms, although a number of the hotels have rooms with bathroom, and a handful offer 'Edda Plus' rooms, with private bathroom, TV and phone.

➡ A few Edda hotels have dormitory sleeping-bag spaces; most Edda hotels have a restaurant.

SLEEPING-BAG ACCOMMODATION

Iceland's best-kept secret is the sleeping-bag option offered by hostels, numerous guesthouses and some hotels. For a fraction of the normal cost you'll get a bed without a duvet; you supply your own sleeping bag.

Taking the sleeping-bag option doesn't mean sleeping in a dorm – generally you book the same private room, just minus the linen. The sleeping-bag option usually means BYO towel, too (a pillowcase is also worth packing).

Sleeping-bag prices will never include breakfast, but you'll often have the option of purchasing it.

Note that the option to use your own sleeping bag is more prevalent *outside* the peak summer period.

→ Expect to pay around Ikr5000 for sleeping-bag accommodation (where available); Ikr25,000/15,000 for a double room with/without private bathroom.

Mountain Huts

→ Private walking clubs and touring organisations maintain *skálar* (mountain huts; singular *skáli*) on many of the popular hiking tracks. The huts are open to anyone and offer sleeping-bag space in basic dormitories. Some also have cooking facilities, campsites and a summertime warden.

→ The huts at Landmannalaugar, Þórsmörk and around Askja are accessible by 4WD, and you reach huts in Hornstrandir by boat. Many mountain huts are on hiking trails and accessible only by hiking to them.

→ GPS coordinates for huts are included in destination chapters.

→ The main organisation providing mountain huts is **Ferðafélag Íslands** (Iceland Touring Association; Map p56; ☏568 2533; www.fi.is; Mörkin 6, Reykjavík) which maintains 38 huts around Iceland (some in conjunction with local walking clubs). The best huts have showers, kitchens, wardens and potable water; simpler huts usually just have bed space, toilet and a basic cooking area. Beds cost Ikr4500 to Ikr6500 for nonmembers. Camping is available at some huts for Ikr1200 per person.

→ Other organisations include **Ferðafélag Akureyrar** (Touring Club of Akureyri; ☏462 2720; www.ffa.is; Strandgata 23, Akureyri), operating huts in the northeast (including along the Askja Trail), and **Útivist** (☏562 1000; www.utivist.is; Laugavegur 178, Reykjavík), which has huts at Básar and Fimmvörðuháls Pass in Þórsmörk.

→ It's essential to book with the relevant organisation as places fill up quickly.

Activities

Iceland's dramatic scenery, vast tracts of wilderness and otherworldly atmosphere make it a superb playground for outdoor enthusiasts see p38 for more information.

Children

Iceland is a fairly easy place to travel with children, and although there aren't many activities especially aimed at youngsters, the dramatic scenery, abundance of swimming pools and friendliness of the locals help to keep the kids happy. If your children like science projects, they will probably love the bird colonies, waterfalls, volcanic areas and glaciers. A number of activities can keep them busy, such as short hikes, super-Jeep tours, horse riding, whale watching, boat rides and easy glacier walks (for the latter, the minimum age is around eight to 10 years).

Once you've decided on a family holiday in Iceland, one of the biggest considerations will be what to see and where to go. It may be a good idea to limit yourselves to one part of the island to avoid boredom-induced tantrums and bouts of carsickness. Reykjavík is the most child-friendly place simply because it has the greatest variety of attractions and facilities.

Check out the *Íslandskort barnanna* (Children's Map of Iceland), aimed at kids and published by Forlagið (Mál og Menning) with text in Icelandic and English.

Practicalities

→ For kids, admission to museums and swimming pools varies from 50% off to free. The age at which children must pay adult fees varies from place to place (anywhere from 12 to 18 years).

→ On internal flights and tours with Air Iceland, children aged two to 11 years

pay half-fare and infants under two fly free.

→ Most bus and tour companies offer a 50% reduction for children aged four to 11 years; Reykjavík Excursion tours are free for under 11s, and half-price for those aged 12 to 15.

→ International car-hire companies offer child seats for an extra cost (book in advance).

→ The changeable weather and frequent cold and rain may put you off camping as a family, but children aged two to 12 are usually charged half-price for camping, hostel, farmhouse and other accommodation. Under-twos can usually stay for free.

→ Many places offer rooms accommodating families, including hostels, guesthouses and farmstays. Larger hotels often have cots (cribs), but you may not find these elsewhere.

→ Many restaurants in Reykjavík and larger towns offer discounted children's meals, most have high chairs.

→ Toilets at museums and other public institutions may have dedicated baby-changing facilities; elsewhere, you'll have to improvise.

→ Attitudes to breastfeeding in public are generally relaxed.

→ Formula, nappies (diapers) and other essentials are available everywhere.

Customs Regulations

Iceland has quite strict import restrictions. For a full list of regulations, see www.customs.is.

Alcohol duty-free allowances for travellers over 20 years of age:

→ 1L spirits and 1L wine and 6L beer, OR

→ 3L wine and 6L beer, OR

→ 1L spirits and 9L beer, OR

→ 1.5L wine and 9L beer, OR

➡ 12L beer

➡ Visitors over 18 years can bring in 200 cigarettes or 250g of tobacco products.

➡ You can import up to 3kg of food (except raw eggs, some meat and dairy products), provided it's not worth more than Ikr25,000.

➡ To prevent contamination, recreational fishing and horse-riding clothes require a veterinarian's certificate stating that they have been disinfected. Otherwise officials will charge you for disinfecting clothing when you arrive. It is prohibited to bring used horse-riding equipment (saddles, bridles etc). See www.mast.is.

➡ Many people bring their cars on the ferry from Europe (see p368). Special duty-waiver conditions apply for stays of up to one year.

Electricity

230V/50Hz

230V/50Hz

Embassies & Consulates

A handful of countries have formal embassies in Reykjavík. Up-to-date details of embassies and consulates within Iceland can be found on the Icelandic Ministry of Foreign Affairs website (www.mfa.is; click on Diplomatic Missions, then Foreign Missions).

Food

You'll find information on food and special dishes, as well as price categories used for eating reviews in this book, in the Icelandic Cuisine chapter, p348.

Gay & Lesbian Travellers

Icelanders have a very open, accepting attitude towards homosexuality, though the gay scene is quite low-key, even in Reykjavík (see p84).

Health

Travel in Iceland presents very few health problems.

Climate

Akureyri

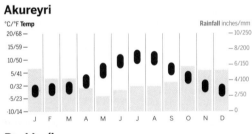

Reykjavík

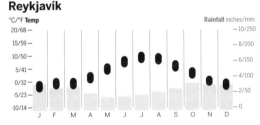

Vík

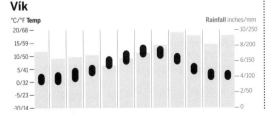

Tap water is safe to drink, the level of hygiene is high and there are no endemic nasties. Specific travel vaccinations are not required.

Healthcare

The standard of healthcare is extremely high and English is widely spoken by doctors and medical clinic staff. Note, however, that there are limited services outside of large urban areas.

For minor ailments, pharmacists can dispense valuable advice and over-the-counter medication (for pharmacies, look for signs for *apótek*). They can advise as to when more specialised help is required. Medical care can be obtained by visiting a healthcare centre, called *heilsugæslustöð* in Iceland. Centres in greater Reykjavík can be found at www.heilsu-gaeslan.is; in regional areas, ask at a tourist office or your accommodation for advice on the closest healthcare centre.

Citizens of other Nordic countries need only present their passport to access healthcare. Citizens of the European Economic Area (EEA) are covered for emergency medical treatment on presentation of a European Health Insurance Card (EHIC). Apply online via your government health department's website.

Citizens from other countries can obtain medical assistance but must pay in full (and later be reimbursed by their insurance provider, if they have one). Purchasing travel insurance is strongly advised. For more detailed information on healthcare for visitors, see www.sjukra.is/english/tourists/.

Hypothermia & Frostbite

The main health risks are caused by exposure to extreme climates; proper preparation will reduce the risks. Even on a warm day in the mountains, the weather can change rapidly – carry waterproof garments and warm layers, and inform others of your route.

➡ Acute hypothermia follows a sudden drop of temperature over a short time. Chronic hypothermia is caused by a gradual loss of temperature over hours. Hypothermia starts with shivering, loss of judgement and clumsiness. Unless rewarming occurs, the sufferer deteriorates into apathy, confusion and coma. Prevent further heat loss by seeking shelter, wearing warm, dry clothing, drinking hot, sweet drinks and sharing body warmth.

➡ Frostbite is caused by freezing and the subsequent damage to bodily extremities. It is dependent on wind chill, temperature and the length of exposure. Frostbite starts as frostnip (white, numb areas of skin), from which complete recovery is expected with rewarming. As frostbite develops, however, the skin blisters and becomes black. Loss of damaged tissue eventually occurs. Your should wear adequate clothing, stay dry, keep well hydrated and ensure you have adequate kilojoule intake to prevent frostbite. Treatment involves rapid rewarming.

Insurance

➡ Although Iceland is a very safe place to travel, theft does occasionally happen, and illness and accidents are always a possibility. A travel insurance policy to cover theft, loss and medical problems is strongly recommended.

➡ Always check the policy's small print to see if it covers any potentially dangerous sporting activities, such as hiking, rock climbing, horse riding, skiing or snowmobiling.

Internet Access

➡ We use the (📶) symbol to indicate where wi-fi is available to guests/customers. The (@) symbol indicates where there is a computer for guest use.

➡ Wi-fi is common in Iceland: you can get online in most sleeping and eating venues across the country. Often it's free for guests/customers, but occasionally there may be a small charge. In many places you'll need to ask staff for an access code. Most of the N1 service stations have free wi-fi.

➡ There are computer terminals for public internet access in most Icelandic libraries, even in small towns (often with a small fee). Many tourist information centres also have a public internet terminal, often free for brief usage.

Legal Matters

Icelandic police are generally low-key and there's very little reason for you to end up in their hands. Worth knowing:

➡ Drink-driving laws are strict. Even two drinks can put you over the legal limit of 0.05% blood-alcohol content; the penalty is loss of your driving licence plus a large fine.

➡ If you are involved in any other traffic offences – speeding, driving without due care and attention etc – you may be asked to go to the station to pay the fine immediately.

➡ Drunk and disorderly behaviour may land you in a police cell for a night, but you will usually be released the following morning.

➡ Penalties for possession, use or trafficking of illegal drugs are strict (long prison sentences and heavy fines).

Maps

➡ In recent years Iceland has been busy building new roads and tunnels, and sealing gravel stretches. We recommend you purchase a recently updated country map.

➤ Tourist information centres have useful free maps of their town and region. They also stock the free tourist booklet *Around Iceland,* with information and town plans. Tourist info centres, petrol stations and bookshops all sell road atlases and maps.

➤ The map publisher **Ferðakort** (www.ferdakort.is) sells its maps online and has a dedicated map department at **Iðnú bookshop** (Map p56; www.ferdakort.is; Brautarholt 8; ☺10am-5pm Mon-Thu, to 4pm Fri). Forlagið (Mál og Menning) is another reputable map publisher with a wide range – browse them at the Mál og Menning **store** (Map p60; ☎580 5000; Laugavegur 18; ☺9am-10pm Mon Fri, 10am 10pm Sat) in the capital.

➤ Both companies have a good touring map of Iceland (1:500,000 or 1:600,000; approximately Ikr2000), useful for general driving. Ferðakort's more in-depth 1:200,000 Road Atlas (Ikr5000) includes details of accommodation, museums and swimming pools. Both companies also produce plenty of regional maps – Forlagið (Mál og Menning) has a series of eight regional maps at 1:200,000 (Ikr1700 each). There are also 31 highly detailed topographic maps at a scale of 1:100,000, covering the entire country and ideal for hikers, plus

ESSENTIAL: CREDIT CARD PIN

Note: a four-digit PIN is required to make credit- or debit-card purchases, and is essential for operating unmanned petrol pumps, so ensure you have a PIN-enabled card before you leave home.

themed maps (for example on sagas, geology or birdwatching).

➤ Serious hikers can ask for maps at local tourist information centres or at national park visitor centres, both of which often stock inexpensive maps detailing regional walks and hikes.

Money

Iceland is an almost cashless society where credit is king. Locals use plastic for even small purchases.

As long as you're carrying a valid card, you'll have no need for travellers cheques and will need to withdraw only a limited amount of cash from ATMs. Contact your financial institution to make sure that your card is ap-proved for overseas use.

If you prefer more tradi-tional methods of carrying money, travellers cheques and banknotes can be ex-changed for Icelandic curren-cy at all major banks.

ATMs

➤ Almost every town in Iceland has a bank with an ATM, where you can withdraw cash using MasterCard, Visa, Maestro or Cirrus cards.

➤ Diners Club and JCB cards connected to the Cirrus network have access to all ATMs.

➤ You'll also find ATMs at larger petrol stations and in shopping centres.

Credit & Debit Cards

➤ Visa and MasterCard (and to a lesser extent Amex, Diners Club and JCB) are accepted in most shops, restaurants and hotels.

➤ You can pay for the Flybus from Keflavík International Airport to Reykjavík using plastic – handy if you've just arrived in the country.

➤ If you intend to stay in rural farmhouse accommodation or visit isolated villages, it's

a good idea to carry enough cash to tide you over.

Currency

➤ The Icelandic unit of currency is the króna (plural krónur), written as Ikr here, and often written elsewhere as ISK.

➤ Coins come in denominations of Ikr1, Ikr5, Ikr10, Ikr50 and Ikr100.

➤ Notes come in denominations of Ikr500, Ikr1000, Ikr2000, Ikr5000 and Ikr10,000.

➤ Some accommodation providers and tour operators quote their prices in euro, but these must be paid in Icelandic currency.

➤ For current exchange rates, see www.xe.com.

Tipping

As service and VAT are al-ways included in prices, tip-ping isn't required in Iceland.

Opening Hours

➤ Many attractions and tourist-oriented businesses in Iceland are only open for a short summer season, typically June to August.

➤ As tourism increases at a rapid pace, some businesses are vague about their opening and closing dates (increasingly, seasonal restaurants or guesthouses may open sometime in May, or even April, or stay open until the end of September or into October, if demand warrants it).

➤ With the growth of winter tourism, a number of businesses are feeling their way towards year-round trading. Note that many Icelandic hotels and guesthouses close from Christmas Eve to New Year's Day.

➤ The best advice is to check websites, and ask around. In such a small country, someone will know someone who can help you out with a

TAX-FREE SHOPPING

Anyone who has a permanent address outside Iceland can claim up to a 15% refund on purchases when they spend over Ikr4000 (at a single point of sale). Look for stores with a 'tax-free shopping' sign in the window, and ask for a form at the register.

If the refund amount on a single form exceeds Ikr5000, you have to show the goods to customs when leaving the country and receive a customs stamp (note: this doesn't apply to woollen goods).

To obtain your refund, you can mail the completed forms for a credit card refund (ensure you've written your credit card number on the form/s). Or you can present the paperwork for a cash refund at an international refund point (Keflavík airport or Seyðisfjörður ferry port). A third alternative is to obtain a cash refund from a 'city refund point' – these include the main tourist information offices in Reykjavík and Akureyri, but also the service desks at the Kringlan and Smáralind shopping centres in the capital. Full details are outlined at www.taxfreeworldwide.com/Iceland.

tour or transport or a meal – you just need to ask!

➡ Note that most museums (especially outside the capital) only have regular, listed opening hours during summer (June to August). From September to May they may advertise restricted opening hours (eg, a couple of hours once a week), but many places are happy to open on request, with a little forewarning – you don't need to be a large group, just get in touch via the museum website or the local tourist office.

➡ Opening hours in general tend to be far longer from June to August, and shorter from September to May. Standard opening hours:

Banks 9am–4pm Monday to Friday

Cafe-bars 10am–1am Sunday to Thursday, 10am to between 3am and 6am Friday and Saturday

Cafes 10am–6pm

Offices 9am–5pm Monday to Friday

Petrol stations 8am–10pm or 11pm

Post offices 9am–4pm or 4.30pm Monday to Friday (to 6pm in larger towns)

Restaurants 11.30am–2.30pm and 6-9pm or 10pm

Shops 10am–6pm Monday to Friday, 10am–4pm Saturday; some Sunday opening in Rey-

kjavík shopping centres and major shopping strips

Supermarkets 9am–8pm (later in Reykjavík)

Vínbúðin (government-run alcohol stores) Variable; many outside Reykjavík only open for a couple of hours per day

Post

➡ The Icelandic postal service (www.postur.is) is reliable and efficient, and rates are comparable to those in other Western European countries.

➡ A postcard/letter to Europe costs Ikr180/310; to places outside Europe it costs Ikr240/490. A full list of rates is online.

Public Holidays

Icelandic public holidays are usually an excuse for a family gathering or, when they occur on weekends, a reason to rush to the countryside and go camping. If you're planning to travel during holiday periods, particularly the Commerce Day long weekend, you should book mountain huts and transport well in advance.

National public holidays in Iceland:

New Year's Day 1 January

Easter March or April Maundy Thursday and Good Friday to

Easter Monday (changes annually)

First Day of Summer First Thursday after 18 April

Labour Day 1 May

Ascension Day May or June (changes annually)

Whit Sunday and Whit Monday May or June (changes annually)

National Day 17 June

Commerce Day First Monday in August

Christmas 24 to 26 December

New Year's Eve 31 December

School Holidays

➡ The main school holiday runs from the first week of June to the third week of August; this is when most of the Edda and summer hotels open.

➡ The winter school holiday is a two-week break over the Christmas period (around 20 December to 6 January). There is also a spring break of about a week, over the Easter period.

Safe Travel

Iceland has a very low crime rate and in general any risks you'll face while travelling here are related to road safety, the unpredictable weather and the unique geological conditions.

PRACTICALITIES

Discount Cards Students and seniors qualify for discounts on internal flights, some ferry and bus fares, tours and museum entry fees, but you'll need to show proof of student status or age.

DVDs & Videos Iceland uses the PAL video system, and falls within DVD zone 2.

Laundry Public facilities are tough to find. Campgrounds, hostels and guesthouses may have a washing machine for guest use (for a fee). Business hotels may offer a pricey service. Some apartments include a washing machine.

Newspapers & Magazines The daily paper *Morgunblaðið* (www.mbl.is) is in Icelandic; its website has local news in English. For excellent tourist-oriented and daily-life articles about Iceland in English, check out the freebie newspapers *Iceland Review* (www.iceland review.com) and *Reykjavík Grapevine* (www.grapevine.is).

Radio RÚV (Icelandic National Broadcasting Service; www.ruv.is) has two radio stations: Rás 1 (news, weather, cultural programs) and Rás 2 (pop music, current affairs). BBC World Service is available at FM 103.5.

Smoking Illegal in enclosed public spaces, including in cafes, bars, clubs, restaurants and on public transport. Most accommodation is nonsmoking.

Weights & Measures Metric

A good place to learn about minimising your risks while travelling in Iceland is **Safetravel** (www.safetravel. is). The website is an initiative of the Icelandic Association for Search and Rescue (ICE-SAR); it also provides information on ICE-SAR's 112 Iceland app for smartphones and explains procedures for leaving a travel plan with ICE-SAR or a friend/contact.

Road Safety

➡ There are unique hazards for drivers, such as livestock on the roads, single-lane bridges, blind rises and rough gravel roads.

➡ For road conditions, see www.vegagerdin.is or call ☎1777.

➡ For more information on driving in Iceland, see p368.

Weather Conditions

➡ Never underestimate the weather. Proper clothing and equipment is essential.

➡ Visitors need to be prepared for inclement conditions year-round. The weather can change without warning, and it's essential for hikers to get a reliable forecast before setting off – call ☎902 0600 (press 1 after the introduction) or visit www.vedur.is/english for a forecast in English.

➡ Emergency huts are provided in places where travellers run the risk of getting caught in severe weather.

➡ If you're driving in winter, carry food, water and blankets in your car.

➡ Hire cars in winter generally have snow tyres fitted.

Geological Risks

➡ When hiking, river crossings can be dangerous, with glacial run-off transforming trickling streams into raging torrents on warm summer days. See p370 for more information on how to cross rivers safely.

➡ High winds can create vicious sandstorms where there is loose volcanic sand.

➡ Hiking paths in coastal areas are often only accessible at low tide, so seek local advice and obtain the relevant tide tables.

➡ In geothermal areas, stick to boardwalks or obviously solid ground. Avoid thin crusts of lighter-coloured soil around steaming fissures and mudpots.

➡ Be careful of the water in hot springs and mudpots – it often emerges out of the ground at 100°C.

➡ In glacial areas beware of dangerous quicksand at the ends of glaciers, and never venture out onto the ice without crampons and ice axes (even then, watch out for crevasses).

➡ Snowfields may overlie fissures, sharp lava chunks or slippery slopes of scoria (volcanic slag).

➡ Always get local advice before hiking around live volcanoes.

➡ Only attempt isolated hiking and glacier ascents if you know what you're doing. Talk to locals and/or employ a guide.

➡ It's rare to find much by way of warning signs or fences in areas where accidents can occur (large waterfalls, glacier fronts, cliff edges). Use common sense, and supervise children well.

Telephone

➡ Public phones are elusive in mobile-crazy Iceland. There may be a payphone outside the post office or bus station, and at the local petrol station. Many payphones accept credit cards as well as coins. Local calls are charged at around Ikr20 per minute.

➡ To make international calls while in Iceland, first dial the international access code ☑00, then the country code, the area or city code, and the telephone number.

➡ To phone Iceland from abroad, dial your country's international access code, Iceland's country code (☑354) and then the seven-digit phone number (note: Iceland has no area codes).

➡ Toll-free numbers in Iceland begin with ☑800; mobile phone numbers start with ☑6, ☑7 or ☑8.

➡ There's an online version of the phone book at http://en.ja.is/.

➡ Useful numbers: directory enquiries ☑118 (local), ☑1811 (international).

Mobile Phones

➡ The cheapest and most practical way to make calls at local rates is to purchase an Icelandic SIM card and pop it into your own mobile phone (tip: bring an old phone from home for that purpose). Before leaving home, make sure that your phone isn't blocked from doing this by your home network. If you're coming from outside Europe, also check that your phone will work in Europe's GSM 900/1800 network (US phones work on a different frequency).

➡ You can buy a prepaid SIM card at bookstores, grocery stores and petrol stations throughout the country.

Top-up credit is available from the same outlets. When purchasing a SIM card, there are two main players: Iceland telecom **Síminn** (www.siminn.is/prepaid) provides the greatest network coverage; **Vodafone** (www.vodafone.is/en/prepaid) is not far behind. Both companies have voice-and-data starter packs including local SIM cards; Síminn's costs Ikr2000 (and includes Ikr2000 in call credit).

Phonecards

➡ The smallest denomination phonecard (for use in public telephones) costs Ikr500, and can be bought from grocery stores, petrol stations and Síminn telephone offices.

➡ Low-cost international phonecards are also available in many shops and kiosks.

Time

➡ Iceland's time zone is the same as GMT/UTC (London), but there is no daylight-savings time.

➡ From late October to late March Iceland is on the same time as London, five hours ahead of New York and 11 hours behind Sydney.

➡ In the northern hemisphere summer, Iceland is one hour behind London, four hours ahead of New York and 10 hours behind Sydney.

➡ Iceland uses the 24-hour clock system and all transport timetables and business hours are posted accordingly.

Tourist Information

Tourist information centres are helpful, friendly and well informed, and can be invaluable in helping you find accommodation, book tours or see the best an area has to offer.

Note that if you arrive in a town after the tourist information centre has closed, the local petrol station is often a good bet for maps and information.

Websites

The official tourism site for the country is **Visit Iceland** (www.visiticeland.com), which has comprehensive information. Visit its 'Inspired by Iceland' site (www.inspiredbyiceland.com) to be, well, inspired.

Each region also has its own useful site/s:

Reykjavík (www.visitreykjavik.is)

Southwest Iceland (www.visitreykjanes.is, www.south.is)

West Iceland (www.west.is)

The Westfjords (www.westfjords.is)

North Iceland (www.northiceland.is, www.visitakureyri.is)

East Iceland (www.east.is)

Southeast Iceland (www.south.is, www.visitvatnajokull.is)

Travellers with Disabilities

Iceland can be trickier than many places in northern Europe when it comes to access for travellers with disabilities.

➡ For details on accessible facilities, get in touch with the information centre for people with disabilities, **Þekkingarmiðstöð Sjálfsbjargar** (☑550 0118; www.thekkingarmidstod.is). Its website is only in Icelandic.

SMARTPHONE APPS

There's an incredible range of smartphone apps. Useful, practical ones include the vital 112 Iceland app for safe travel, Veður (weather), and apps for bus companies such as Strætó and Reykjavík Excursions. Offline maps come in handy.

A good general app is Be Iceland. There are plenty more that cover all sorts of interests, from history and language to aurora-spotting, or walking tours of the capital. The Reykjavík Appy Hour app gets special mention for listing happy hours and their prices!

➡ A good resource is the website **God Adgang** (www. godadgang.dk), a Danish initiative adopted in Iceland. Follow the instructions to find Icelandic service providers that have been assessed for the accessibility label.

➡ These two companies are particularly good for tailor-made accessible trips around the country: **All Iceland Tours** (www.alliicelandtours.is) and **Iceland Unlimited** (www. icelandunlimited.is).

➡ Most museums and other attractions offer reduced admission prices for travellers with disabilities. For travel, Air Iceland offers reduced rates, as does the Smyril Line ferry.

➡ Reykjavík's city buses have a 'kneeling' function so that wheelchairs can be lifted onto the bus; elsewhere, however, public buses don't have ramps or lifts.

Visas

Iceland is one of 26 member countries of the Schengen Convention, under which the EU countries (all but Bulgaria, Croatia, Romania, Cyprus, Ireland and the UK) plus Iceland, Norway, Liechtenstein and Switzerland have abolished checks at common borders.

The visa situation for Iceland is as follows.

➡ Citizens of EU and Schengen countries – no visa required for stays of up to three months.

➡ Citizens or residents of Australia, Canada, Japan, New Zealand and the USA – no visa required for tourist visits of up to three months. Note that the total stay within the Schengen area must not exceed three months in any six-month period.

➡ Other countries – check online at www.utl.is.

➡ To work or study in Iceland a permit is usually required – check with an Icelandic embassy or consulate in person or online.

➡ For questions on visa extensions or visas and permits in general, contact the **Icelandic Directorate of Immigration, Útlendingastofnun** (www. utl.is).

Volunteering

A volunteering holiday is a worthwhile (and relatively inexpensive) way to get intimately involved with Iceland's people and landscapes. As well as the following options, consider a stint at the **Arctic Fox Center** (Melrakkasetur; ☎456 4922; www.arcticfoxcenter.com; adult/child Ikr900/free; ☉9am-8pm Jun-Aug, 10am-5pm May & Sep, reduced hours Oct-Apr) in the wilds of the Westfjords.

Iceland Conservation Volunteers (ICV; www.ust.is/ the-environment-agency-of-iceland/volunteers/) Iceland's environment agency, known as Umhverfisstofnun (UST), recruits more than 200 volunteers each summer for work on practical conservation projects around the country, mainly creating or maintaining trails in Vatnajökull National Park. Places on its short-term programs (under four weeks) are usually arranged through its partner volunteer organisations, including UK-based The Conservation Volunteers (www.tcv.org.uk) and Working Abroad (www.working-abroad.com), or Iceland-based SEEDS and Worldwide Friends. Longer-term placements are also possible on Trail Teams that work together for 11 weeks over the summer; see the UST website for details.

SEEDS (www.seeds.is) Iceland-based SEEDS organises work camps and volunteering holidays, primarily focused on nature and the environment (building trails, ecological research), but also construction or renovation of community buildings, or assistance at festivals and events.

Volunteer Abroad (www. volunteerabroad.com) Offers an overview of possible projects in Iceland. Note that many of the projects listed are under the remit of Iceland's Environment Agency (Umhverfisstofnun), but arranged through various international volunteering organisations.

Worldwide Friends (Veraldarvinir; www.wf.is) Iceland-based Worldwide Friends runs work camps that largely support nature and the environment, but there are also options for involvement in community projects, and art and cultural events.

WWOOF (www.wwoof independents.org) World Wide Opportunities On Organic Farms (also known as Willing Workers On Organic Farms) has a handful of farm properties in Iceland that accept wwoofers, although there is no national WWOOF organisation. In return for volunteer help, WWOOF hosts offer food, accommodation and opportunities to learn about organic lifestyles.

Transport

GETTING THERE & AWAY

Iceland has become far more accessible in recent years, with more flights from more destinations. Ferry transport makes a good alternative for Europeans wishing to take their own car.

Flights, tours and rail tickets can be booked online at www.lonelyplanet.com/bookings.

Entering the Country

➡ Iceland is part of the Schengen agreement, which eliminates border passport control between Schengen countries in Europe.

➡ There is passport control when entering Iceland from a country outside the Schengen area. Some nationalities need a visa to enter Iceland, see p364.

➡ For entry into the Schengen area, you must have a passport valid for three months beyond your proposed departure date.

➡ As long as you are in possession of the right documentation, immigration control should be a quick formality.

Air

Airports & Airlines

AIRPORTS

➡ Iceland's main international airport is **Keflavík International Airport** (www.kefairport.is), 48km southwest of Reykjavík.

➡ Internal flights and those to Greenland and the Faroe Islands use the small **Reykjavík Domestic Airport** (Reykjavíkurflugvöllur; www.reykjavikairport.is) in central Reykjavík.

AIRLINES

A growing number of airlines fly to Iceland (including budget carriers) from destinations in Europe and North America. Some airlines have services only from June to August. Find a list of airlines serving the country at www.kefairport.is/English/Service/Airlines/.

Icelandair (www.icelandair.com) is the national carrier, with an excellent safety record. **Air Iceland** (Flugfélag Íslands; www.airiceland.is) is the main domestic airline, but also flies to destinations in Greenland and the Faroe Islands. **WOW Air** (www.wowair.com) is an Icelandic low-cost carrier, serving a growing number of European and North American destinations.

Sea

➡ **Smyril Line** (www.smyrilline.com) operates a pricey but well-patronised weekly car ferry, the *Norröna*, from Hirsthals (Denmark) through Tórshavn (Faroe Islands) to Seyðisfjörður in east Iceland.

➡ Boats run year-round between Denmark and the

CLIMATE CHANGE & TRAVEL

Every form of transport that relies on carbon-based fuel generates CO_2, the main cause of human-induced climate change. Modern travel is dependent on aeroplanes, which might use less fuel per kilometre per person than most cars but travel much greater distances. The altitude at which aircraft emit gases (including CO_2) and particles also contributes to their climate change impact. Many websites offer 'carbon calculators' that allow people to estimate the carbon emissions generated by their journey and, for those who wish to do so, to offset the impact of the greenhouse gases emitted with contributions to portfolios of climate-friendly initiatives throughout the world. Lonely Planet offsets the carbon footprint of all staff and author travel.

Faroe Islands; Iceland is part of the set itinerary from late March until October. Limited winter passage is possible (departures are weather-dependent) – see the website.

➡ Fares vary widely, depending on dates of travel, what sort of vehicle (if any) you are travelling with, and cabin selection.

➡ Sample one-way fares from Hirtshals to Seyðisfjörður (journey time 47 hours) for two passengers and a small car in high season (mid-June to mid-August) is €559 per person, including berths in the cheapest cabin. For a solo traveller (without vehicle), the one-way high-season fare begins at €261 for a dorm-style 'couchette'.

➡ It's possible to make a stopover in the Faroe Islands. Contact Smyril Line or see the website for trip packages.

GETTING AROUND

There's no train network in Iceland. The most common way for visitors to get around the island is to drive a rental car.

There's a decent bus network operating from approximately mid-May to mid-September between major destinations, but don't discount internal flights to help you maximise your time.

Air

➡ Iceland has an extensive network of domestic flights, which locals use almost like buses. In winter a flight can be the only way to get between destinations, but weather at this time of year can play havoc with schedules.

➡ Almost all domestic flights depart from the small domestic airport in Reykjavík (ie. *not* the major international airport at Keflavík).

➡ A handful of airstrips offer regular sightseeing flights,

eg Mývatn, Skaftafell and Reykjavík domestic airport.

Airlines in Iceland

Air Iceland (Flugfélag Íslands; www.airiceland.is) Not to be confused with international carrier Icelandair. Destinations covered: Reykjavík, Akureyri, Grimsey, Ísafjörður, Egilsstaðir and Þórshöfn. Offers some fly-in day tours. Online deals for one-way flights start at around Ikr9500.

Eagle Air (www.eagleair.is) Operates scheduled flights to five smaller airstrips from Reykjavík: Vestmannaeyjar, Húsavík, Höfn, Bíldudalur and Gjögur. One-way flights cost Ikr19,200 to Ikr28,300. There are also a number of day tours.

Bicycle

➡ Cycling is a fantastic (and increasingly popular) way to see the country's landscapes, but you should be prepared for harsh conditions. Gale-force winds, driving rain, sandstorms, sleet and sudden flurries of snow are possible at any time of year.

➡ Worth knowing: the large bus lines carry bikes, so if the weather turns bad or that highlands bike trip isn't working out as planned, consider the bus. The number of bikes that can be carried on a bus can't be guaranteed, but bikes are usually allowed when there is space. It's free to take a bike on Strætó services; other companies (Sterna, SBA-Norðurleið) charge around Ikr3500.

➡ A brilliant resource: the English pages of the website of the **Icelandic Mountain Bike Club** (http://fjallahjolaklubburinn.is). It links to the annually updated *Cycling Iceland* map – an invaluable source of info (we encountered it infrequently in tourist offices, so it may pay to access it online before you travel).

➡ Puncture-repair kits and spares are hard to come by outside Reykjavík, so bring your own or stock up in the

capital. On the road, it's essential to know how to do your own basic repairs.

➡ If you want to tackle the interior, the Kjölur route has bridges over all major rivers, making it fairly accessible to cyclists. A less-challenging route is the F249 to Þórsmörk. The Westfjords also offer some wonderful, challenging cycling terrain.

➡ Keep an eye out for a new series of cycling books by Ómar Smári Kristinsson. The first is *The Biking Book of Iceland – Day Trip Cycle Circuits – Part 1: The Westfjords*. More books are in the works, but with a lengthy timeframe.

Transporting Bicycles to Iceland

➡ Most airlines will carry your bike in the hold if you pack it correctly in a bike box.

➡ Reykjavík City Hostel offers facilities to assemble and disassemble bikes and will store bike boxes (it's adjacent to the city campground); at Keflavík airport, **Bílahótel** (www.bilahotel.is) offers luggage storage (including bike boxes).

➡ The Smyril Line ferry from Denmark transports bikes for €15 each way.

Hire

➡ Various places rent out mountain bikes, but in general these are intended for local use only, and often aren't up to long-haul travel.

➡ If you intend to go touring, it's wise to bring your bike from home or purchase one when you arrive; alternatively, **Reykjavík Bike Tours** (www.icelandbike.com) has touring bikes for rent.

Boat

Several year-round ferries operate in Iceland. See the relevant regional sections for more information. Major routes:

➡ Landeyjahöfn–Vestmannaeyjar (www.herjolfur.is)

- ➡ Stykkishólmur–Brjánslækur (www.seatours.is)
- ➡ Dalvík–Hrísey/Grímsey (www.saefari.is)
- ➡ Arskógssandur–Hrísey (www.hrisey.net)

From June to August, Bolungarvík and Ísafjörður have regular boat services to points in Hornstrandir (Westfjords).

Bus

➡ Iceland has an extensive network of long-distance bus routes, with services provided by a number of companies. The free *Public Transport in Iceland* map has an overview of routes – look for it in tourist offices and bus terminals, especially in Reykjavík.

➡ From roughly mid-May to mid-September there are regular scheduled buses to most places on the Ring Road, into the popular hiking areas of the southwest, and to larger towns in the Westfjords and Eastfjords and on the Reykjanes and Snæfellsnes Peninsulas. The rest of the year, services range from daily to nonexistent.

➡ In summer, there are 4WD buses along a few F roads (mountain roads), including the highland Kjölur and Sprengisandur routes (inaccessible to 2WD cars).

➡ Worth knowing: many bus services can be used as day tours (the bus spends a few hours at the final destination before returning to the departure point, and may stop for a half-hour at various tourist destinations en route), or as regular transport (you can get off at a certain point and travel further a day or two later).

➡ Bus companies may operate from different terminals or pick-up points. In Reykjavík, there are a few bus terminals; in small towns, buses usually stop at the main petrol station, but it pays to double check.

Companies

Main bus companies:

Reykjavík Excursions (☏580 5400; www.re.is)

SBA-Norðurleið (☏550 0700; www.sba.is)

Sterna (☏551 1166; www.sterna.is)

Strætó (☏540 2700; www.straeto.is)

Bus Passes

Bus operators offer 'bus passports' every summer (valid from mid-June to the first week of September), with the aim of making public transport around the island as easy as possible. At the time of research, none of the passports cover the Westfjords, but services along the highland Sprengisandur and Kjölur routes can be included.

If you're considering touring Iceland by bus, do your homework before buying a bus pass. It's still significantly more convenient (and may be cheaper, if you are two or more) to hire your own vehicle.

Passes lock you into using the services of one company, and no Icelandic bus company offers the perfect network – each has significant geographic gaps in service, and most routes only run once per day. Strætó has the biggest network but is not a part of any pass. You may be better off buying separate tickets for each leg of your journey, using the bus service that offers you the best route at the time.

'Iceland On Your Own' Passports Reykjavík Excursions and SBA-Norðurleið work together to offer 'Iceland On Your Own' passports; full details are found at www.ioyo.is. The strengths of these passports: services along both the highland Kjölur and the Sprengisandur routes; good services in the south (using the strong Reykjavík Excursions network), and coverage in the north that includes Akureyri to Húsavík, Ásbyrgi and Dettifoss (using SBA-Norðurleið's network). Disadvantages: They're not cheap! There's a gap in Ring Road coverage on the west coast, with circular passes heading north via the highland Kjölur route, then taking the Ring Road.

Circle Passport Reykjavík to Varmahlíð via the Kjölur route, then follows the Ring Road around the country (Ikr42,000).

Beautiful South Passport Travel along the full south coast (Reykjavík to Höfn); includes routes to Gullfoss,

---

ESSENTIAL WEB RESOURCES

Four websites every traveller should know about:

Safetravel (www.safetravel.is) Learn about minimising risks while travelling in Iceland.

Icelandic Met Office (Veðurstofa Íslands; www.vedur.is) Never underestimate the weather in Iceland, or its impact on your travels. Get a reliable forecast from this site (or call ☏902 0600, and press 1 after the introduction).

Vegagerðin (www.vegagerdin.is) Iceland's road administration site details road openings and closings around the country. Vital if you plan to explore Iceland's little-visited corners and remote interior.

Carpooling in Iceland (www.samferda.is) Handy site that helps drivers and passengers link up. Passengers often foot some of the petrol bill. It's a savvy alternative to hitching (for passengers), or a way to help pay for car rental and fuel (for drivers).

Þórsmörk, Landmannalaugar and Lakagígar (5/9/11 days Ikr36,000/53,000/60,500).

Beautiful South Circle Passport South coast (Reykjavík to Skaftafell), plus Landmannalaugar (Ikr22,000).

Highlights Passport Kjölur and the Sprengisandur routes, plus south coast and northern area around Akureyri/Húsavík – but no coverage in the east, from Mývatn to Höfn (7/11/15 days Ikr46,500/66,000/80,000).

Highland Circle Passport Valid for one circular route taking in the Sprengisandur and Kjölur routes; also covers Reykjavík to Skaftafell (Ikr44,000).

Combo Passport Combines the Ring Road (except for the western part) and the two highland routes, plus a few additional south-coast routes (7/11/15 days Ikr58,000/77,000/91,500).

Hiking on Your Own This is the best-seller, and with good reason. If you're hiking Laugavegur, it lets you get dropped at Landmannalaugar and picked up at the route's end in Þórsmörk (or vice versa). If you're hiking Fimmvörðuháls, you can transfer between Skógar and Þórsmörk (Ikr12,500).

Sterna Passports Sterna has two passports utilising its network. Pros: cheaper than the opposition. Services the entire Ring Road (including the west coast), and has a highland route too (Kjölur, but not Sprengisandur). Cons: limited routes off the Ring Road.

East Circle Passport Reykjavík to Varmahlíð via the Kjölur route, then follows the Ring Road around the country (Ikr39,500).

Full Circle Passport Travels the Ring Road, pure and simple (Ikr37,500).

Car & Motorcycle

➡ Driving in Iceland gives you unparalleled freedom to discover the country and, thanks to good roads and light traffic, it's all fairly straightforward.

➡ The Ring Road (Rte 1) circles the country and, except for a couple of small stretches in east Iceland, is paved. Beyond the Ring Road, fingers of sealed road or gravel stretch out to most communities.

➡ In coastal areas driving can be spectacularly scenic, and incredibly slow as you weave up and down over mountain passes and in and out of long fjords. Even so, a 2WD vehicle will get you almost everywhere in summer (note: *not* into the highlands, or on F roads).

➡ In winter heavy snow can cause many roads to close; mountain roads generally only open in June and may start closing as early as September. For up-to-date information on

road conditions, visit www.vegagerdin.is.

Bring Your Own Vehicle

➡ Car hire in Iceland is expensive, so bringing your own vehicle may not be as crazy as it sounds. The Smyril Line ferry from Denmark is busy in summer bringing vehicles to Iceland from all over Europe (book passage well ahead).

➡ For temporary duty-free importation, drivers must carry the vehicle's registration documents, proof of valid insurance (a 'green card' if your car isn't registered in a Nordic or EU-member country) and a driving licence.

➡ Permission for temporary duty-free importation of a vehicle is granted at the point of arrival for up to 12 months, and is contingent upon agreeing to not lend or sell your vehicle. For more information, contact the **Directorate of Customs** (www.customs.is).

➡ If you're staying for a long period, you might consider shipping your own vehicle via **Eimskip** (www.eimskip. is) shipping services. Be aware that this is *not* a cheap option, and involves heavy paperwork, but it may be useful for long-stayers who have lots of gear or a well

---

F ROADS

We can think of a few choice F words for these bumpy, at times almost-nonexistent tracts of land, but in reality the 'F' stands for *fjall* (mountain). Do not confuse F roads with gravel stretches of road (regular gravel roads are normally fine for 2WDs, although some of them are bumpy rides for small, low-clearance cars).

F roads are indicated on maps and roadsigns with an 'F' preceding the road number (eg, F26, F88 etc).

F roads only support 4WDs. If you travel on F roads in a hired 2WD you'll invalidate your insurance. F roads are unsafe for small cars: do yourself a favour and steer clear, or hire a 4WD (or take a bus or super-Jeep tour).

Before tackling any F road you should educate yourself about what lies ahead (for example, river crossings) and whether or not the entire route is open. See www.vegagerdin.is for road closure details.

While some F roads may almost blend into the surrounding nature, driving off marked tracks is *strictly prohibited* everywhere in Iceland, as it damages fragile ecosystems.

BUYING FUEL

Most smaller petrol stations are unstaffed, and all pumps are automated – though there is the time-consuming option of going inside the service station to ask staff to manually switch on the pump, enabling you to fill up and pay for your fuel afterwards.

To fill up using the automated service, put your credit card into the machine's slot (you'll need a card with a four-digit PIN) and follow the instructions. Enter your PIN, then the maximum amount you wish to spend, then wait while the pump authorises your purchase. Entering a maximum amount pre-approves your card for that capped amount, but you are only charged for the cost of the fuel put into your vehicle (this can be any amount you wish, up to the pre-approved capped amount). If you require a receipt, re-enter your card into the slot. The first time you fill up, visit a staffed station while it's open, in case you have any problems.

Note that you need a PIN for your card – for petrol and for most other card purchases in Iceland. Arrange one with your bank before you leave home. If you don't have a PIN, buy prepaid cards from an N1 station that you can then use at the automated pumps.

set-up camper/4WD. Eimskip has six shipping lines in the North Atlantic.

Driving Licences

You can drive in Iceland with a driving licence from the US, Canada, Australia, New Zealand and most European countries. If your licence is not in Roman script, you need an International Driving Permit (normally issued by your home country's automobile association).

Fuel & Spare Parts

➡ There are regularly spaced petrol stations around Iceland, but in the highlands you should check fuel levels and the distance to the next station before setting off.

➡ At the time of research, unleaded petrol and diesel cost about Ikr245 (€1.60) per litre.

➡ Some Icelandic roads can be pretty lonely, so carry a jack, a spare tyre and jump leads just in case.

➡ In the case of a breakdown or accident, your first port of call should be your car-hire agency.

➡ Although the Icelandic motoring association **Félag Íslenskra Bifreiðaeigenda** (FÍB; www.fib.is) is only open to locals, if you have breakdown cover with an automobile association affiliated with ARC Europe you may be

covered by the FÍB – check with your home association.

➡ FÍB's 24-hour breakdown number is ☎511 2112. Even if you're not a member, it can provide information and phone numbers for towing and breakdown services.

Car Hire

➡ Travelling by car is often the only way to get to parts of Iceland. Although car-hire rates are expensive by international standards, they compare favourably to bus or internal air travel, especially if there are a few of you to split the costs.

➡ To rent a car you must be 20 years old (23 to 25 years for a 4WD) and hold a valid licence.

➡ The cheapest cars on offer, usually a small hatchback or similar, cost from around Ikr12,000 per day in high season (June to August). Figure on paying from around Ikr24,000 for the smallest 4WD that may offer higher clearance than a regular car but isn't advised for most river crossings. Rates include unlimited mileage and VAT, and usually collision damage waiver (CDW). Weekly rates offer some discount. From September to May you should be able to find considerably better daily rates and deals.

➡ Check the small print, as additional costs such as extra insurance, airport pick-up charges and one-way rental fees can add up.

➡ In the height of summer many companies run out of rentals. Book ahead.

➡ Many travel organisations (eg Hostelling International Iceland, Icelandic Farm Holidays) offer package deals that include car hire.

➡ Most companies are based in the Reykjavík and Keflavík areas, with city and airport offices. Larger companies have extra locations around the country (usually in Akureyri and Egilsstaðir).

➡ For ferry passengers arriving via Seyðisfjörður, contact car-hire agencies in nearby Egilsstaðir. Car hire companies include:

Átak (www.atak.is)

Avis (www.avis.is)

Budget (www.budget.is)

Cheap Jeep (www.cheapjeep.is)

Europcar (www.europcar.is) The biggest hire company in Iceland.

Geysir (www.geysir.is) Lists its daily/weekly summer and winter prices for each of its vehicles on its website.

Go Iceland (www.goiceland. com) Also rents out camping equipment (tents, mattresses, stoves).

Hertz (www.hertz.is)

SADcars (www.sadcars.com) Older fleet, therefore (theoretically) cheaper prices.

Saga (www.sagacarrental.is)

CAMPERVAN HIRE

Combining accommodation and transport costs into campervan rental is a popular option – and has extra appeal in summer, as it allows for some spontaneity (unlike every other form of accommodation, campsites don't need to be prebooked).

The large car-hire companies usually have campervans for rent, but there are some more offbeat choices, from backpacker-centric to family-sized, or real 4WD setups.

Camper Iceland (www.camper iceland.is)

Happy Campers (www.happy campers.is)

JS Camper Rental (www.js.is) Truck campers on 4WD pickups.

Kúkú Campers (www.kuku-campers.is) Artwork-adorned campers, plus gear rental (tent, barbecue, guitar, surfboard etc).

MOTORCYCLE HIRE

Biking Viking (www.bikingviking. is) Motorcycle rental, tours and service.

Insurance

➡ A vehicle registered in Nordic or EU-member countries is considered to have valid automobile insurance in Iceland. If your vehicle is registered in a non-Nordic or non-EU country, you'll need a 'green card', which proves that you are insured to drive while in Iceland. Green cards are issued by insurance companies in your home country; contact your existing insurer.

➡ When hiring a car, check the small print; most vehicles

CROSSING RIVERS

While trekking or driving in Iceland's highlands you're likely to face unbridged rivers that must be crossed. There are a few rules to follow.

➡ Melting snow causes water levels to rise, so the best time to cross is early in the morning before the day warms up, and preferably no sooner than 24 hours after a rainstorm.

➡ Avoid narrow stretches, which are likely to be deep – the widest ford is likely to be shallowest. The swiftest, strongest current is found near the centre of straight stretches and at the outside of bends. Choose a spot with as much slack water as possible.

➡ Never try to cross just above a waterfall and avoid crossing streams in flood (identifiable by dirty, smooth-running water carrying lots of debris and vegetation).

For hikers

➡ A smooth surface suggests that the river is too deep to be crossed on foot. Anything more than thigh-deep isn't crossable without experience and extra equipment.

➡ Before attempting to cross deep or swift-running streams, be sure that you can jettison your pack in midstream if necessary.

➡ Lone hikers should use a hiking staff to probe the river bottom for the best route and to steady themselves in the current.

➡ Never try to cross a stream barefoot. Bringing wetsuit boots or sandals if you want to keep your hiking boots dry.

➡ While crossing, face upstream and avoid looking down or you risk getting dizzy and losing balance. Two hikers can steady each other by resting their arms on each other's shoulders.

➡ If you do fall while crossing, don't try to stand up. Remove your pack (but don't let go of it), roll onto your back and point your feet downstream, then try to work your way to a shallow eddy or to the shore.

For drivers

➡ If you're not travelling in convoy, consider waiting for other traffic. Watch where and how experienced drivers cross. You may need to check the depth and speed of the river by wading into it (using techniques described for hikers, including a hiking staff). A good rule of thumb: if you would not want to wade through a river you should not drive through it.

➡ Work with the water – drive diagonally across in the direction of the current, making sure you're in a low gear. Drive steadily, without stopping or changing gear, just slightly faster than the water is flowing (too slow and you risk getting stuck, or letting water up the exhaust).

come with third-party insurance and collision damage waiver (CDW) to cover you for damage to the car. Also check the excess (the initial amount you will be liable to pay in the event of an accident) as this can be surprisingly high.

➡ Hire vehicles are not covered for damage to the tyres, headlights and windscreen, or damage caused to the car's underside by driving on dirt roads, through water or in ash- or sandstorms. Many companies will try to sell you additional insurance to cover these possibilities. You need to consider whether this is appropriate for you and your plans, and how prepared you are to cough up in the event of such occurrences (and the cost of the insurance versus factors such as the length of your rental and what regions you plan to visit). There is no way of predicting what climatic conditions you might meet on your trip.

Road Conditions & Hazards

Good main-road surfaces and light traffic make driving in Iceland relatively easy, but there are some specific hazards. Watch the 'Drive Safely on Icelandic Roads' video on www.drive.is for more.

Livestock Sheep graze in the countryside over the summer, and often wander onto roads. Slow down when you see livestock on or near roadsides.

Unsurfaced roads The transition from sealed to gravel roads is marked with the warning sign 'Malbik Endar' – slow right down to avoid skidding when you hit the gravel. Most accidents involving foreign drivers in Iceland are caused by the use of excessive speed on unsurfaced roads. If your car does begin to skid, take your foot off the accelerator and gently turn the car in the direction you want the front wheels to go. Do not brake.

Blind rises In most cases roads have two lanes with steeply cambered sides and no hard shoulder; be prepared for oncoming traffic in the centre of the road, and slow down and stay to the right when approaching a blind rise, marked as 'Blindhæð' on road signs.

Single-lane bridges Slow down and be prepared to give way when approaching single-lane bridges (marked as 'Einbreið Brú'). Right of way is with the car closest to the bridge.

Sun glare With the sun often sitting so low to the horizon, sunglasses are recommended.

Winter conditions In winter make sure your car is fitted with snow tyres or chains, and carry a shovel, blankets, food and water.

Ash & sandstorms Volcanic ash and severe sandstorms can strip paint off cars; strong winds can even topple your vehicle. At-risk areas are marked with orange warning signs.

F roads Roads suitable for 4WD vehicles only are F-numbered.

River crossings Few interior roads have bridges over rivers. Fords are marked on maps with a 'V'.

Road Rules

➡ Drive on the right

➡ Front and rear seat belts are compulsory

➡ Dipped headlights must be on at all times

➡ Blood alcohol limit is 0.05%

➡ Mobile phone use is prohibited except with a hands-free kit

➡ Children under six years must use a car seat

➡ Do not drive off-road (ie. off marked roads and 4WD trails)

SPEED LIMITS

➡ Built-up areas: 50km/h

➡ Unsealed roads: 80km/h

➡ Sealed roads: 90km/h

Hitching

➡ Hitching is never entirely safe, and we don't recommend it. Travellers who hitch should understand that they are taking a small but potentially serious risk. Nevertheless, we met scores of tourists who were hitching their way around Iceland and most had positive reports. Single female travellers and couples tend to get a lift the quickest.

➡ Patience is a prerequisite of hitching, and logic is important too – be savvy about where you position yourself. Try standing at junctions, near petrol stations or even by Bónus supermarkets.

➡ When you arrive at your accommodation it can't hurt to let people know where you're aiming for the next day. There may be another traveller going that way who can give you a ride.

Local Transport

Bus

➡ Reykjavík has an extensive network of local buses connecting all the suburbs, and running to Akranes, Borgarnes, Hveragerði, Selfoss and Hvalfjarðarsveit. See www.straeto.is for information on routes, fares and timetables.

➡ Local bus networks operate in Akureyri, Ísafjörður, and the Reykjanesbær area.

Taxi

➡ Most taxis in Iceland operate in the Reykjavík area, but many of the larger towns also offer services. Outside of Reykjavík, it's usually wise to prebook.

➡ Taxis are metered and can be pricey. Tipping is not expected.

Tours

See the planning section, p44, for information about organised tours within Iceland.

Language

Icelandic belongs to the Germanic language family, which includes German, English, Dutch and all the Scandinavian languages except Finnish. It's related to Old Norse, and retains the letters 'eth' (ð) and 'thorn' (þ), which also existed in Old English. Be aware, especially when you're trying to read bus timetables or road signs, that place names can be spelled in several different ways due to Icelandic grammar rules.

Most Icelanders speak English, so you'll have no problems if you don't know any Icelandic. However, any attempts to speak the local language will be much appreciated.

If you read our coloured pronunciation guides as if they were English, you'll be understood. Keep in mind that double consonants are given a long pronunciation. Note also that öy in our pronunciation guides is like the '-er y-' in 'her year' (without the 'r') and that kh is like the 'ch' in the Scottish *loch*. Stress generally falls on the first syllable in a word.

BASICS

Hello.	*Halló.*	ha·loh
Good morning.	*Góðan daginn.*	gohth-ahn dai·in
Goodbye.	*Bless.*	bles
Good evening.	*Gott kvöld.*	khot kverld
Good evening.	*Goða nótt.*	khoh-th-ah noht
Thank you	*Takk./ Takk fyrir.*	tak/ tak fi·rir
Excuse me.	*Afsakið.*	af·sa·kidh
Sorry.	*Fyrirgefðu.*	fi·rir·gev·dhu

WANT MORE?

For in-depth language information and handy phrases, check out Lonely Planet's phrasebooks range. You'll find them at **shop.lonelyplanet.com**.

READING ICELANDIC

Letter	Pronunciation
Á á	ow (as in 'how')
Ð ð	dh (as the 'th' in 'that')
É é	ye (as in 'yet')
Í í	ee (as in 'see')
Ó ó	oh (as the 'o' in 'note')
Ú ú	oo (as in 'too')
Ý ý	ee (as in 'see')
Þ þ	th (as in 'think')
Æ æ	ai (as in 'aisle')
Ö ö	eu (as the 'u' in 'nurse')

Yes.	*Já.*	yow
No.	*Nei.*	nay

How are you?
Hvað segir þú gott? — kvadh se·yir thoo got

Fine. And you?
Allt fínt. En þú? — alt feent en thoo

What's your name?
Hvað heitir þú? — kvadh hay·tir thoo

My name is ...
Ég heiti ... — yekh hay·ti ...

Do you speak English?
Talar þú ensku? — ta·lar thoo ens·ku

I don't understand.
Ég skil ekki. — yekh skil e·ki

It will be OK.
Þetta reddast. — thah·tah rah·dohst

DIRECTIONS

Where's the (hotel)?
Hvar er (hótelið)? — kvar er (hoh·te·lidh)

Can you show me (on the map)?
Geturðu sýnt mér (á kortinu)? — ge·tur·dhu seent myer (ow kor·ti·nu)

What's your address?
Hvert er heimilisfangið þitt? — kvert er hay·mi·lis·fan·gidh thit

EATING & DRINKING

What would you recommend?
Hverju mælir þú með?   kver·yu mai·lir thoo medh

Do you have vegetarian food?
Hafið þið   ha·vidh thidh
grænmetisrétti?   grain·me·tis·rye·ti

I'll have a ...
Ég ætla að fá ...   yekh ait·la adh fow ...

Cheers!
Skál!   skowl

I'd like a/the ..., please.	Get ég fengið ..., takk.	get yekh fen·gidh ... tak
table for (four)	borð fyrir (fjóra)	bordh fi·rir (fyoh·ra)
bill	reikninginn	rayk·nin·gin
drink list	vínseðillinn	veen·se·dhit·lin
menu	matseðillinn	mat·se·dhit·lin
that dish	þennan rétt	the·nan ryet

bottle of (beer)	(bjór)flösku	(byohr)·fleus·ku
(cup of) coffee/tea	kaffi/te (bolla)	ka·fi/te (bot·la)
glass of (wine)	(vín)glas	(veen)·glas
water	vatn	vat
breakfast	morgunmat	mor·gun·mat
lunch	hádegismat	how·de·yis·mat
dinner	kvöldmat	kveuld·mat

EMERGENCIES

Help!   Hjálp!   hyowlp
Go away!   Farðu!   far·dhu

Call ...!   Hringdu á ...!   hring·du ow ...
  a doctor   lækni   laik·ni
  the police   lögregluna   leu·rekh·lu·na
I'm lost.
Ég er villtur/villt. (m/f)   yekh er vil·tur/vilt

Where are the toilets?
Hvar er snyrtingin?   kvar er snir·tin·gin

Numbers

1	einn	aydn
2	tveir	tvayr
3	þrír	threer
4	fjórir	fyoh·rir
5	fimm	fim
6	sex	seks
7	sjö	syeu
8	átta	ow·ta
9	níu	nee·u
10	tíu	tee·u
20	tuttugu	tu·tu·gu
30	þrjátíu	throw·tee·u
40	fjörutíu	fyeur·tee·u
50	fimmtíu	fim·tee·u
60	sextíu	seks·tee·u
70	sjötíu	syeu·tee·u
80	áttatíu	ow·ta·tee·u
90	níutíu	nee·tee·u
100	hundrað	hun·dradh

SHOPPING & SERVICES

I'm looking for ...
Ég leita að ...   yekh lay·ta adh ...

How much is it?
Hvað kostar þetta?   kvadh kos·tar the·ta

That's too expensive.
Þetta er of dýrt.   the·ta er of deert

It's faulty.
Það er gallað.   thadh er gat·ladh

Where's the ...?   Hvar er ...?   kvar er ...
  bank   bankinn   bown·kin
  market   markaðurinn   mar·ka·dhu·rin
  post office   pósthúsið   pohst·hoo·sidh

TRANSPORT

Can we get there by public transport?
Er hægt að taka   er haikht adh ta·ka
rútu þangað?   roo·tu thown·gadh

Where can I buy a ticket?
Hvar kaupi ég miða?   kvar köy·pi yekh mi·dha

Is this the ... to (Akureyri)?	Er þetta ... til (Akureyrar)?	er the·ta ... til (a·ku·ray·rar)
boat	ferjan	fer·yan
bus	rútan	roo·tan
plane	flugvélin	flukh·vye·lin

What time's the ... bus?	Hvenær fer ... strætisvagninn?	kve·nair fer ... strai·tis·vag·nin
first	fyrsti	firs·ti
last	síðasti	see·dhas·ti
One ... ticket (to Reykjavík), please.	Einn miða ... (til Reykjavíkur), takk.	aitn mi·dha ... (til rayk·ya·vee·kur) tak
one-way	aðra leiðina	adh·ra lay·dhi·na
return	fram og til baka	fram okh til ba·ka

I'd like a taxi ...	Get ég fengið leigubíl ...	get yekh fen·gidh lay·gu·beel ...
at (9am)	klukkan (níu fyrir hádegi)	klu·kan (nee·u fi·rir how·de·yi)
tomorrow	á morgun	ow mor·gun

How much is it to ...?
Hvað kostar til ... ?   kvadh kos·tar til ...

Please stop here.
Stoppaðu hér, takk.   sto·pa·dhu hyer tak

Please take me to (this address).
Viltu aka mér til (þessa staðar)?   vil·tu a·ka myer til (the·sa sta·dhar)

GLOSSARY

See the Icelandic Cuisine chapter (p348) for useful words and phrases dealing with food and dining, and the Transport chapter (p365) for road safety terms and signs.

á – river (as in Laxá, or Salmon River)
álfar – elves
austur – east

basalt – hard volcanic rock that often solidifies into hexagonal columns
bíó – cinema
brennivín – local schnapps
bær – farm

caldera – crater created by the collapse of a volcanic cone

dalur – valley

eddas – ancient Norse books
ey – island

fell – see fjall
fjall – mountain
fjörður – fjord
foss – waterfall
fumarole – vents in the earth releasing volcanic gas

gata – street
geyser – spouting hot spring
gistiheimilið – guesthouse
gjá – fissure, rift

goðar – political and religious leaders of certain districts in the times before Christianity (singular goði)

hákarl – putrid shark meat
hestur – horse
hot-pot – outdoor hot tub or spa pool, found at swimming baths and some accommodation; in Icelandic, hot-pot is heitur pottur
hraun – lava field
huldufólk – hidden people
hver – hot spring
höfn – harbour

ice cap – permanently frozen glacier or mountain top
Íslands – Iceland

jökull – glacier, ice cap

kirkja – church
kort – map

Landnámabók – comprehensive historical text recording the Norse settlement of Iceland
laug – pool; one that is suitable for swimming
lava tube – underground tunnel created by liquid lava flowing under a solid crust
lón – lagoon
lopapeysa/lopapeysur (sg/pl) – Icelandic woollen sweater
lundi – puffin
mudpot – bubbling pool of superheated mud

mörk – woods or forest; colloquially mörk also refers to the goals in football, and the earmarks of sheep
nes – headland
norður – north

puffling – baby puffin

reykur – smoke, as in Reykjavík (literally 'Smoky Bay')

safn – museum
sagas – Icelandic legends
sandur – sand; can also reference a glacial sand plain
scoria – glassy volcanic lava
shield volcano – gently sloped volcano built up by fluid lava flows
sími – telephone
skáli – hut, snack bar
stræti – street
suður – south
sumar – summer
sundlaug – heated swimming pool

tephra – rock/material blasted out from a volcano
tjörn – pond, lake
torg – town square

vatn – lake, water
vegur – road
vestur – west
vetur – winter
vík – bay
vogur – cove, bay

Behind the Scenes

SEND US YOUR FEEDBACK

We love to hear from travellers – your comments keep us on our toes and help make our books better. Our well-travelled team reads every word on what you loved or loathed about this book. Although we cannot reply individually to your submissions, we always guarantee that your feedback goes straight to the appropriate authors, in time for the next edition. Each person who sends us information is thanked in the next edition – the most useful submissions are rewarded with a selection of digital PDF chapters.

Visit **lonelyplanet.com/contact** to submit your updates and suggestions or to ask for help. Our award-winning website also features inspirational travel stories, news and discussions.

Note: We may edit, reproduce and incorporate your comments in Lonely Planet products such as guidebooks, websites and digital products, so let us know if you don't want your comments reproduced or your name acknowledged. For a copy of our privacy policy visit lonelyplanet.com/privacy.

OUR READERS

Many thanks to the travellers who used the last edition and wrote to us with helpful hints, useful advice and interesting anecdotes:
Ilianna Anagnostakou, Mary Attick, Greta Björnsdóttir, Sébastien Blond, Rod Dawson, Joaquín Diaz, Benjamin Doyle, William Driscoll, Barbara Gaffin, Maria Garcia, Josh Guenther, Roger Hart, Friederike Hammer, Martin Hellwagner, Justin Iettinga, Grace Heusner, Mildred Howard, Hartmut Kaiser, Sophie Kendall, Tim Kendrick, Britta Lambertz, Mark Lautzker, Erica Lazarow, Anna Leivers, Michelle Lester-Smith, Samira Lindner, Elisa Maccagnoni, Diane Moody, Lita Nelsen, Anthony Newgrosh, William Norman, Carmen Parada, Fika Perié, Lorna Pimperton, Christa Rieser, Francesco Rosa, Markus Rudolf, Michal Rudziecki, Jane Senior, Berglind Sigmarsdóttir, Elke Sims, Ron Sims, Barney Smith, Frank Techel, Isabel Vadis, Trudy van der Velde, Ondra Veltrusky, Callie Wallace

AUTHOR THANKS

Carolyn Bain

Thanks to James for commissioning me for my all-time favourite job, and big bouquets to my outstanding co-author Alexis, for project passion and polished prose. Once again, I could list half the Icelandic phonebook given the amount of people who helped, informed and/or entertained me on this trip, from Kyle Clunies Ross, Ragnheiður Sylvia Kjartansdóttir and Kristjana Rós Guðjohnsen in Reykjavík to Elín Þorgeirsdóttir in Hrífunes. Along the way, I enjoyed the company of Sigrun Kalyan Sigurðardóttir, Þórhildur Gísladóttir and Jón Thor Hannesson; guiding and ace 4WDing from Anton Freyr Birgisson, Mirjam Blekkenhorst, and highland men Óðinn and Agnar; and local wisdom from Sævar Freyr Sigurðsson, Guðmundur Ögmundsson and Helga Árnadóttir. Locals who so sweetly welcomed me back included Knútur, Vicki, Pálína, Sibba, Þórir and Erla, Örn, Bjarni and Heiða, Valla, Hlynur, Berglind, Cathy, Ásmundur and so many more. Villi Vernharðsson at Möðrudalur was super-kind, as was Áskell Heiðar Ásgeirsson at Bræðslan, and Bergþór Karlsson. This list could run to a page or more – so many wonderful people, so many acts of warmth and kindness. A heartfelt *takk fyrir.*

Alexis Averbuck

My work on Iceland was a labour of love supported by many helping hands. Big thanks to Heimir Hansson for all things Westfjords. Jónas Gunnlaugsson welcomed me at the Arctic Fox Centre. At Reykjavik 871±2, anthropologist Eva Dal's enthusiasm was infectious, her explanations superlative. Helga Garðarsdóttir at Ferðafélag Íslands shared insider tips about the

Laugavegurinn. Thanks to Jón Magnússon and Hallgrímur Stefans for double-checking my Icelandic, from *rúntur* to *djammið*. Carolyn was an unstintingly generous and insightful collaborator and project leader. Respect to James for the astute attention and care he brought to the book. Kristinn Viggósson rose above being a host, making Iceland feel like home. Yva & John became inspiring family. Ryan was, as always, a peachy partner in crime.

ACKNOWLEDGMENTS

Climate map data adapted from Peel MC, Finlayson BL & McMahon TA (2007) 'Updated World Map of the Köppen-Geiger Climate Classification', *Hydrology and Earth System Sciences*, 11, 163344.

Cover photograph: Skógafoss, Skógar, South Iceland, Guido Cozzi / 4Corners ©.

THIS BOOK

This 9th edition of Lonely Planet's *Iceland* guidebook was researched and written by Carolyn Bain and Alexis Averbuck. The 8th edition was written by Brandon Presser, Carolyn Bain and Fran Parnell, and the 7th was written by Fran and Brandon. This guidebook was produced by the following:

Destination Editor
James Smart
Product Editor
Elizabeth Jones
Senior Cartographer
Valentina Kremenchutskaya
Book Designer
Clara Monitto
Assisting Editors Imogen Bannister, Penny Cordner, Justin Flynn, Victoria Harrison, Bella Li, Rosie Nicholson, Charlotte Orr, Saralinda Turner, Jeanette Wall
Cover Researcher
Naomi Parker

Thanks to Sasha Baskett, Ryan Evans, Samantha Forge, Larissa Frost, James Hardy, Kate James, Andi Jones, Claire Naylor, Karyn Noble, Jessica Rose, Diana Saengkham, Angela Tinson, Anna Tyler, Tony Wheeler, Amanda Williamson

Index

Map Legend

Sights
- Beach
- Bird Sanctuary
- Buddhist
- Castle/Palace
- Christian
- Confucian
- Hindu
- Islamic
- Jain
- Jewish
- Monument
- Museum/Gallery/Historic Building
- Ruin
- Shinto
- Sikh
- Taoist
- Winery/Vineyard
- Zoo/Wildlife Sanctuary
- Other Sight

Activities, Courses & Tours
- Bodysurfing
- Diving
- Canoeing/Kayaking
- Course/Tour
- Sento Hot Baths/Onsen
- Skiing
- Snorkelling
- Surfing
- Swimming/Pool
- Walking
- Windsurfing
- Other Activity

Sleeping
- Sleeping
- Camping

Eating
- Eating

Drinking & Nightlife
- Drinking & Nightlife
- Cafe

Entertainment
- Entertainment

Shopping
- Shopping

Information
- Bank
- Embassy/Consulate
- Hospital/Medical
- Internet
- Police
- Post Office
- Telephone
- Toilet
- Tourist Information
- Other Information

Geographic
- Beach
- Hut/Shelter
- Lighthouse
- Lookout
- Mountain/Volcano
- Oasis
- Park
- Pass
- Picnic Area
- Waterfall

Population
- Capital (National)
- Capital (State/Province)
- City/Large Town
- Town/Village

Transport
- Airport
- Border crossing
- Bus
- Cable car/Funicular
- Cycling
- Ferry
- Metro station
- Monorail
- Parking
- Petrol station
- S-Bahn/S-train/Subway station
- Taxi
- T-bane/Tunnelbana station
- Train station/Railway
- Tram
- Tube station
- U-Bahn/Underground station
- Other Transport

Note: Not all symbols displayed above appear on the maps in this book

Routes
- Tollway
- Freeway
- Primary
- Secondary
- Tertiary
- Lane
- Unsealed road
- Road under construction
- Plaza/Mall
- Steps
- Tunnel
- Pedestrian overpass
- Walking Tour
- Walking Tour detour
- Path/Walking Trail

Boundaries
- International
- State/Province
- Disputed
- Regional/Suburb
- Marine Park
- Cliff
- Wall

Hydrography
- River, Creek
- Intermittent River
- Canal
- Water
- Dry/Salt/Intermittent Lake
- Reef

Areas
- Airport/Runway
- Beach/Desert
- Cemetery (Christian)
- Cemetery (Other)
- Glacier
- Mudflat
- Park/Forest
- Sight (Building)
- Sportsground
- Swamp/Mangrove

OUR STORY

A beat-up old car, a few dollars in the pocket and a sense of adventure. In 1972 that's all Tony and Maureen Wheeler needed for the trip of a lifetime – across Europe and Asia overland to Australia. It took several months, and at the end – broke but inspired – they sat at their kitchen table writing and stapling together their first travel guide, *Across Asia on the Cheap*. Within a week they'd sold 1500 copies. Lonely Planet was born.

Today, Lonely Planet has offices in Franklin, London, Melbourne, Oakland, Beijing and Delhi, with more than 600 staff and writers. We share Tony's belief that 'a great guidebook should do three things: inform, educate and amuse'.

OUR WRITERS

Carolyn Bain

Coordinating Author, North Iceland, East Iceland, Southeast Iceland, The Highlands Melbourne-born Carolyn has had an ongoing love affair with the Nordic region, ignited as a teenager living in Denmark and regularly rekindled over 14 years of writing guidebooks to glorious northern destinations such as Iceland, Denmark, Sweden and Nordic-wannabe Estonia (see more at carolynbain.com. au). This is her second time working on the *Iceland* guidebook, feeding her addiction to *skyr*, fjords, secret hot-pots and glacier trails, puffins, *lopapeysur* and the music of Ásgeir. There were some outstanding moments on this research trip – just a sample: hot-pot soaks in midnight sun, Askja on a 20-degree day (really!), a ticket to Bræðslan, and spelunking in an ice cave. Carolyn also wrote the Plan Your Trip, Understand and Survival Guide sections of this book.

Read more about Carolyn at:
lonelyplanet.com/members/carolynbain

Alexis Averbuck

Itineraries, Reykjavík, Southwest Iceland & the Golden Circle, West Iceland, The Westfjords, Icelandic Culture Alexis' love of remote, icy landscapes and untouched mountain ranges started with her year spent living in Antarctica, but now it's been fully co-opted by Iceland. A self-proclaimed glacier geek, Alexis loves exploring Iceland's more remote byways: from surreal lava fields and sparkling fjords to ice-blue glacier tongues. She also thrives on Icelandic culture, pouring over the sagas and following the super music scene. A travel writer for two decades, Alexis also covers Antarctica, France and Greece for Lonely Planet, has crossed the Pacific by sailboat and is a painter – see her work at www.alexisaverbuck.com.

Read more about Alexis at:
lonelyplanet.com/members/alexisaverbuck

Published by Lonely Planet Publications Pty Ltd
ABN 36 005 607 983
9th edition – May 2015
ISBN 978 1 74321 475 6
© Lonely Planet 2015   Photographs © as indicated 2015
10 9 8 7 6 5 4 3 2
Printed in China